Juvenile Justice

This book is dedicated to the memory of John Karns,
JD, PhD. An Associate Professor appointed to the faculty of
the Graduate School of Public and International Affairs at the
University of Pittsburgh, Dr. Karns was the architect of the Administration
of Justice program at the University. He was a good man and a good friend.

Juvenile Justice

Process

and

Systems

Gus Martin

California State University, Dominguez Hills

SAGE Publications
Thousand Oaks ▪ London ▪ New Delhi

For information:

Sage Publications, Inc.
2455 Teller Road
Thousand Oaks, California 91320
E-mail: order@sagepub.com

Sage Publications Ltd.
1 Oliver's Yard
55 City Road
London EC1Y 1SP
United Kingdom

Sage Publications India Pvt. Ltd.
B-42, Panchsheel Enclave
Post Box 4109
New Delhi 110 017 India

Printed in the United States of America

Library of Congress Cataloging-in-Publication Data

Martin, Gus.
Juvenile justice : process and systems / Gus Martin.
        p. cm.
Includes bibliographical references and index.
ISBN 0-7619-3082-5 (cloth)
    1. Juvenile justice, Administration of—-United States. 2. Juvenile justice, Administration of—Cross-cultural studies. I. Title.
HV9104.M2657 2005
364.36'0973—dc22   2004022905

This book is printed on acid-free paper.

05   06   07   08   10   9   8   7   6   5   4   3   2   1

Acquisitions Editor:	Jerry Westby
Editorial Assistant:	Vonessa Vondera
Production Editor:	Denise Santoyo
Copy Editor:	Kathryn Geddie
Typesetter:	C&M Digitals (P) Ltd.
Indexer:	Kathy Paparchontis
Cover Designer:	Michelle Lee Kenny

Contents

Acknowledgments

I am indebted for the support and encouragement of many people in bringing this venture to completion. Without their patient professionalism and constructive criticism, this project would not have incorporated the comprehensiveness and completeness that was its underlying objective from the beginning.

Thanks are extended to colleagues who shared their expert advice and suggestions for crafting this volume. In particular, I thank my good colleagues in the Department of Public Administration and Public Policy at California State University, Dominguez Hills, and Dean Jim Strong in the College of Business Administration and Public Policy for their support and understanding about the demands of the writing process. I also wish to acknowledge the contribution of my former colleagues of the Graduate School of Public and International Affairs at the University of Pittsburgh, who first mentored my desire to teach and write about juvenile justice process. These colleagues include professors Lee Weinberg and the late Jack Karns, as well as Dean Kerry Ban.

I am grateful for the contributions of the juvenile justice professionals who shared their professional insight for the Professional Profiles features: Dave Farley, Dr. James "Buddy" Howell, Captain Sharyn Buck, Chief Robert McNeilly, the Honorable Timothy K. Lewis, and our former student Carol Chudy.

Deep appreciation is especially extended to the panel of peer reviewers assembled by the very able editors and staff of Sage Publications during several rounds of review. Their insightful, constructive comments and critical analysis was truly invaluable. Special appreciation is also extended to the very professional and expert attention given to this project by the editorial group at Sage, and in particular to Jerry Westby, Denise Simon, Vonessa Vondera, and Denise Santoyo; they are indeed an exceptional shop.

And of course, I thank my wife and children for their constant support, encouragement, and humor during the course of this project.

Introduction
and Rationale

Welcome to *Juvenile Justice: Process and Systems*. This is a textbook for those who wish to explore the theory and practice of providing justice to juveniles. Students and instructors who fully engage themselves in the recommended course of instruction offered in the pages that follow will acquire a solid foundation for understanding the history, philosophy, and components of the juvenile justice system. Readers will also discover that their facility for critically assessing juvenile justice policies—and the effectiveness of branches of the system—will be greatly improved.

At the outset it is important to understand that the study of juvenile justice process and systems is an investigation of a truly unique network that is predicated on a distinctive body of theory. This field of study is roughly comparable to the study of the criminal justice system because both require the acquisition of knowledge about institutions, their history, and their purpose. The juvenile justice and criminal justice systems are designed to regulate behavior and protect society. However, the manner in which they accomplish these goals is often quite divergent. For example, juvenile justice is concerned with the welfare of those who are processed through the system, and it uses a long-standing philosophy of rehabilitation (rather than punishment) to do so. Juvenile justice is also intended to remedy cases of both juvenile deviance and juvenile victimization, so that lawbreakers and children in need pass through the system. And, significantly, juvenile justice can be rendered either formally or informally, depending on the facts of each case.

This textbook is designed to be a primary textbook for students enrolled in a single-semester course. The content of *Juvenile Justice: Process and Systems* is directed to courses of instruction whose subject areas include justice process, crime and deviance, justice institutions and systems, and law-enforcement policy. It can be incorporated into classes covering the administration of justice, juvenile justice process, juvenile delinquency, criminology, sociology, political science, public administration, and other disciplines in the social sciences. The intended level of instruction is undergraduate students, and the writing style is directed to, and at the level of, these students.

No prerequisites are specifically recommended, but an introductory grounding within one of the following disciplines would be helpful: administration of justice, criminal justice, political science, or sociology.

Course Overview and Pedagogy

Juvenile Justice: Process and Systems introduces readers to juvenile justice in the contemporary era, with contextual grounding in the historical origins of modern process and systems. It is a review of institutions, procedures, and theories that are specifically directed toward addressing the problems of juvenile deviance and victimization. An investigation will be made of the theoretical and historical foundations of each component of the juvenile justice system. The rationales underpinning juvenile justice processes and programs will also be investigated.

The pedagogical approach of *Juvenile Justice: Process and Systems* is designed to stimulate critical thinking by students. Students and instructors will find that each chapter follows a sequence of instruction that builds upon previous chapters, and thus incrementally enhances the reader's knowledge of each topic. Chapters incorporate the following features:

- *Chapter Opening Vignettes.* Each chapter is introduced by an overview of the subject under investigation. The chapter introduction provides perspective for the incorporation of each chapter's topic into the broader themes of the textbook.
- *Chapter Perspectives.* Chapters incorporate focused presentations of perspectives that explore people, events, and organizations that are relevant to the subject matter of each chapter.
- *Chapter Summary.* A concluding discussion recapitulates the main themes of each chapter and introduces the subject matter of the following chapter.
- *Discussion Boxes.* Following the chapter summary, Discussion Boxes present provocative information and pose challenging questions to stimulate critical thinking and further debate.
- *Key Terms and Concepts.* Important terms and ideas introduced in each chapter are listed for review and discussion. These Key Terms and Concepts are further explored in the book's Glossary.
- *Recommended Web Sites and Web Exercises.* Recommended Web sites and Internet exercises at the ends of chapters have been designed for students and instructors to explore and discuss information found on the Internet.
- *Recommended Readings.* Suggested readings are listed at the end of each chapter for further information or research on each topic.

Chapter Guide

This volume is organized into four thematic units, each consisting of several chapters. A Glossary is included after the substantive chapters.

Part I ("Understanding Juvenile Justice Process and Systems") investigates fundamental considerations that are essential for developing a contextual understanding of juvenile justice process. Within Part I, *Chapter 1* ("Juvenile Justice: An Introduction") presents an overview of basic concepts that are developed in later chapters. The discussion explores the concepts of juvenile justice and juvenile justice process. It also provides introductory discussions of the juvenile justice system, procedures, and policy challenges. *Chapter 2* ("Historical Perspectives") investigates the historical roots of juvenile justice. A timeline is developed that extends from early history, through English beginnings, and into the modern era in the United States. Important movements and philosophies are examined in detail. *Chapter 3* ("Juvenile Delinquency: Theories of Causation") discusses theories of juvenile deviance. Classical, biological, psychological, and sociological theories are examined, as are the critical theories. Attention is given to explaining juvenile deviance vis-à-vis adult criminal deviance. *Chapter 4* ("The Delinquency Picture: Measuring Juvenile Deviance") introduces readers to common methodologies used to report delinquency and crime. Several reporting systems are introduced and discussed, including a review of the types of data that are derived from these systems. Practical applications of these measurements are presented. *Chapter 5* ("Children in Trouble and Children in Need") explains the special mission of the juvenile justice system to serve a broader population in comparison to the criminal justice system. Typologies of youths served by the system are discussed in detail. The underlying philosophies of rehabilitation and treatment are examined.

Part II ("Process and Systems: Official Components") examines the roles of the police, juvenile court, and corrections systems. Within Part II, *Chapter 6* ("The Role of the Police") discusses the mission of the police to enforce the law, maintain order, and serve the community. It also discusses the special mission of the police toward juvenile offenders and victims, with an explanation of police discretion. *Chapter 7* ("The Role of the Court") discusses the duty of the juvenile judicial system to process cases involving the interests of youths. It also discusses the central role of the court in the system. Judicial discretion is explained. *Chapter 8* ("Institutional Corrections for Juveniles") investigates the historical and modern purpose of juvenile corrections. Correctional philosophies and goals are critically assessed. Models for confinement and release into the community are also assessed.

Part III ("Process and Systems: Community-Based Components") reviews the unique community-based innovations found in the juvenile justice system. Within Part III, *Chapter 9* ("Juvenile Probation, Parole, and Aftercare") investigates the conditions of release that are commonly imposed on juveniles who have been processed through the juvenile justice system. The concepts of noninstitutional and postinstitutional corrections will be discussed. Critical assessment is made of the viability and effectiveness of probation, parole, and aftercare. *Chapter 10* ("Community-Based Juvenile Programs") assesses the unique links that have been made between the juvenile justice system and the community. The role of the community as a component of the system is investigated, as are the diversity of programs that have been developed. Readers are introduced to placement alternatives and types of institutions found in the community.

Part IV ("Final Perspectives and Projections") concludes our examination of juvenile justice. Within Part IV, *Chapter 11* ("Antisocial Youth Cultures and the Case of Youth Gangs") is a case study of the national gang problem. The history and causes of street gangs are presented, as are the demographic characteristics of gangs. Policies aimed at suppressing gang behavior are assessed. *Chapter 12* ("Global Perspectives: Juvenile Justice in an International Context") is an assessment of several juvenile justice systems that are presented as case studies. International approaches are compared with the American approach. The role of culture and history is explained. *Chapter 13* ("What Is to be Done? Projections and Conclusion") discusses likely future challenges for the juvenile justice system. It also discusses the likely configuration of the juvenile justice system in the near future. Policies designed to manage juvenile justice are summarized.

A glossary and several appendixes follow the substantive chapters. The glossary and Appendix A (containing important cases, laws, and legislation) briefly summarize each of the key terms, concepts, and laws explored in the book. Appendix B references organizations that are central components of the juvenile justice system, and Appendix C summarizes Web-based exercises. All appendixes are intended to be reference sections for students as they progress through their course of instruction; they are also useful pedagogical tools for instructors.

PART I

Understanding Juvenile Justice Process and Systems

1

Juvenile Justice

An Introduction

In comparison to the adult criminal justice system, the juvenile justice system applies different standards and procedures to those who are processed through the system. Offenses that would otherwise be dealt with quite severely in the criminal justice system are addressed in a very different manner by the juvenile justice system. For example, on the night of July 7, 2002, juvenile Patrick V. and 19-year-old adult Christopher Conley committed an act of arson that resulted in extensive damage to a boating company in Maine.[1] Patrick V. and Conley illegally entered a Southern Maine Marine Services building, intending to steal a marine radio. When they noticed surveillance cameras (which were inoperable), they tried to locate videotapes with the intention to destroy them. Having failed to locate the nonexistent tapes, the two set fire to the building by spreading gasoline around an oil tank, emplacing propane tanks nearby, and detonating all of them with a flare. The fire destroyed the building. Two boats, three boat trailers, motors, tools, manuals, and other equipment were also lost.

Arson is a serious crime, and Conley was tried and convicted as an adult; his sentence was approximately five years in prison. In contrast, Patrick V. was charged with juvenile delinquency, for which (and based upon his age until adulthood) he could receive a maximum term of detention of no more than 57 months. The court ordered Patrick V. to be detained for 30 months in a juvenile facility, with supervised release into the community for 27 months.

Juvenile delinquency and the victimization of children are issues that have a direct impact on the welfare of society. In communities across the country—in every region and every city—juveniles who break the law and children who suffer from abuse and neglect are the concerns of society as a whole. Although many people wish to presume that juvenile delinquency and child victimization happen outside of their communities, the fact is that these problems persist everywhere. They occur in out-of-the-way rural areas, cosmopolitan cities, wealthy suburbs, and provincial small towns. They also occur in the South, the Northeast, the West, the Midwest, and U.S. territories. It is for this reason, and as a matter of national necessity, that the concept of **juvenile justice** permeates American society at every level.

Juvenile justice is perhaps best defined as the fair handling and treatment of youths under the law. It is a philosophy that recognizes the right of young people to due process protections when they are in trouble, and personal protections when they are in need. **Juvenile justice process** refers to distinct procedures established to assure the fair *administration* of youths under the law. These procedures are carried out in accordance with institutions designed for the administration of justice in general, and juvenile justice in particular. The **juvenile justice system** is composed of institutions that have been organized to manage established procedures as a way to achieve justice for all juveniles. These institutions include the police, juvenile courts, juvenile corrections, and community-based agencies and programs.

In the modern era, it is usually taken for granted that juveniles who break the law or who are victimized deserve special attention. However, true juvenile justice is a concept that originated in the relatively recent past. It was only during the nineteenth century that reformers and members of the Child-Saving Movement (discussed in Chapter 2) developed a sense of obligation toward the welfare of all children. They took it upon themselves to correct the behavior of juvenile offenders and to rescue children who suffer from poverty, abuse, and "idleness." During the course of the next century, juvenile justice frequently came to the forefront of social and political affairs. This occurred because of a deep cultural discernment that society has three fundamental obligations toward young people:

- First, protect the general public from juvenile offenders.
- Second, protect individual juveniles from victimization.
- Third, provide treatment for both offenders and victims.

Historically, these obligations were undertaken within the context of rehabilitation. However, during the late twentieth century this approach was complemented by a new philosophy of punishment directed toward violent and otherwise criminal juveniles. In this regard, the modern era's crackdown on adult crime is also a crackdown on serious juvenile delinquency, so much so that many juvenile offenders have been tried and punished as adults. Nevertheless, those who enter into the juvenile justice system (as opposed to the adult criminal system) are theoretically eligible to receive rehabilitative intervention.

In order to prepare for our full investigation of juvenile justice process, which will come in subsequent chapters, the following themes are discussed in this chapter:

- Conceptual Introduction: Finding Justice for Juveniles
- Systemic Introduction: The Juvenile Justice System in Brief
- Procedural Introduction: Dispensing Juvenile Justice
- Policy Introduction: Challenges for Juvenile Justice

CHAPTER PERSPECTIVE 1.1

Teen Violence in Schools[2]

How prevalent is the problem of violence in the nation's schools? The good news is that research published in 2001 showed that the incidence of violence declined during the decade of the 1990s.[3] Between 1992 and 1998, student victimization by all nonfatal crimes fell from 144 per 1,000 to 101 per 1,000, a decline from 3.4 million crimes to 2.7 million. Victimization by nonfatal violent crimes such as rape and aggravated assault likewise declined between 1992 and 1998, from 48 per 1,000 to 43 per 1,000. Significantly, the rate of violent deaths in schools (murder and other homicides) showed a steady decline, especially in comparison to violent deaths outside of school: Fewer than 1% of murdered children were killed in a school venue during the first half of the 1998 to 1999 school year. And, despite the visibility and coverage of multiple deaths related to tragic school shootings, the number of multiple homicides also declined.

The relative declines in violent crimes are positive trends, but what are the consequences of teen violence in schools?

When violence occurs, it has an impact that extends beyond the perpetrator and his or her victim. Because this type of event occurs in an institution dedicated to learning, violent incidents often disrupt educational routines and distract students and teachers from the fundamental goal of promoting education. Violence can create a climate of fear, so that students may literally be afraid to use restrooms or walk around the campus. If violence should occur with some frequency, it also indicates that adults and school administrators have lost control of the campus, and have little ability to maintain order.

Intervention is critically necessary when violence occurs. In most cases, the first responders to violent incidents are teachers and other administrators. Many incidents, such as relatively minor fights or assaults, can be resolved by the school district by imposing administrative sanctions. Sanctions may include warnings, suspensions, or expulsions in serious cases. When major incidents occur, school administrators will seek police intervention. Many school districts now employ school police, so that officers may already be on campus, or at least within close proximity. If police are asked to intervene, offenders face the possibility of referral into the juvenile justice system.

Conceptual Introduction: Finding Justice for Juveniles

How can justice be fairly dispensed to young people? Which institutions best serve the needs of youths and the community? Can the needs of juveniles and society ever be balanced, and at the same time preserve justice for the nation's children?

In reply to these questions, state and local governments have established official and nonofficial institutions as part of an extensive network that was designed to promote juvenile justice. For example, during the nineteenth century the first juvenile courts were organized under the assumption that children have specialized needs that cannot be adequately addressed in adult court.[4] Since then, completely separate juvenile justice systems have arisen that in many ways parallel the adult criminal justice system, but which nevertheless represent society's answers to the questions of providing special justice to young people. The police,[5] courts, corrections,[6] and community[7] all form a partnership for the implementation of contemporary philosophies of juvenile justice.

Definitional Concept: Juveniles

Use of the word *juvenile* should be clearly understood to refer to a legal classification that is established within the parameters of culture and social custom. When considering this classification, one should appreciate that it fundamentally refers to those who are below the age of another classification—known as the class of *adults*. This cultural approach toward defining childhood and adulthood has existed since the dawn of organized society. For example, in ancient and medieval cultures, children as young as seven years of age were classified as adults. In the modern era, laws determine when a person is an adult, and juveniles have become a defined class of nonadult persons who receive special treatment under the law. Thus, although certain fundamental constitutional protections are extended to both adult and nonadult classifications alike, there also exist different rules, laws, and penalties that set nonadults apart in how society deals with them.

Concept: Legal Fictions. In the United States, state legal codes define juvenile status in accordance with specified age thresholds. Although these thresholds are usually designated in the upper teen years (for example, 16, 17, or 18 years of age), there are special circumstances in which juveniles may be redesignated as fictional adults for the purpose of determining how to process them. These are **legal fictions**, which in general refer to exceptions to an accepted rule, and within the context of juveniles refer to the extraordinary handling of young people outside of usual laws and procedures. The

Photo 1.1   Youthful gun play. Teenagers show off a handgun.

following examples illustrate these exceptions as they pertain to defining adulthood:

- *Juvenile criminals.*[8] The modern crackdown on crime has led to the passage of many provisions in state crime codes that permit the full prosecution of some juveniles in the adult criminal justice system. These youths officially cease to be juvenile delinquents and become defined as criminals.

- *Emancipated youths.* State systems permit juveniles to become "emancipated" from the control of their parents or the state under certain circumstances (such as marriage). This is predicated on a threshold age. They become *de jure* (legal) adults, thus allowing them to enter into contracts, own real estate, and accept responsibilities that would normally not be legally binding.

Thus, youths are defined as juveniles until they either cross a state-mandated age threshold, commit a serious criminal violation of the law, or are legally emancipated prior to crossing an established age threshold. Unless they are designated as legal adults, they will be subject to juvenile-focused laws and procedures.

Broad Concepts: Official and Nonofficial Juvenile Justice Institutions

Conceptually, there are differences in the missions and purposes of the components of the juvenile justice system. In comparison to the criminal justice system, there are more organizations and programs, and even agencies, that serve both the criminal and juvenile systems and that must comply with juvenile-system-specific guidelines. Perhaps the best way to envision these differences is to understand the following broad classifications within the juvenile justice system:

- *Official juvenile justice institutions*. These institutions are composed of the traditional *triumvirate* of the police, courts, and corrections. These are the same central components of the adult criminal justice system. Depending on the circumstances of each case, procedures can be quite formal and onerous, just as they are in the criminal system. Serious juvenile offenders, and even those who have committed lesser offenses, are frequently processed through official institutions. When juveniles are processed through these institutions, they are under the custody and guardianship of the state, and the state is responsible for correcting, rehabilitating, or otherwise saving, such youths.

- *Nonofficial juvenile justice institutions*. Unlike the adult system, the juvenile justice system also marshals the resources of community and local government service agencies. Nonofficial institutions are ideally regulated and inspected by the state, and many are private institutions that operate either for-profit or not-for-profit agencies. Community-based private organizations (including nonprofits) and government service agencies are given primary responsibility for rehabilitating and rescuing eligible young people. Youths who have committed lesser offenses, or are victims, are preferably processed through these nonofficial institutions, because they are in need of treatment rather than strict corrections or punishment. Depending on the circumstances of each case, community-based procedures are designed to be as informal and as welcoming as possible.

Each component of these broad classifications will be discussed in detail in subsequent chapters. For now, it is worth noting that the adoption of a philosophy of juvenile justice—that is, one specifically designed to protect and regulate youths—has necessitated the implementation of an important policy objective: the redirection of the scope of youth-focused intervention away from adult-based models. Official and nonofficial institutions are integral parts of the juvenile justice system, and formal and informal proceedings are accepted alternatives. Thus, the juvenile justice system has come to encompass a much broader array of programs and agencies in comparison to the criminal justice system.

Focused Concepts: Foundational Considerations for Providing Justice to Juveniles

Youths who are served by official and nonofficial juvenile justice institutions are subject to several foundational considerations, of which they almost certainly are completely unaware. These foundational considerations are conceptual presumptions that have come to represent the guiding principles for dispensing justice to juveniles in the United States.[9] Although these considerations are not uniformly applied across all states and all juvenile justice systems—in essence, not every jurisdiction is the same—they generally reflect the following concepts:

Juvenile Justice Extends to All Youths. There is an expanded conceptualization of justice in the juvenile system. Unlike the adult criminal justice system, which has a law enforcement mission, the juvenile system is designed to serve both offenders and victims. Cases of juvenile delinquency and minor offenses (such as truancy) are corrected by the system. So too are cases of abuse, neglect, homelessness, and other problems that pose a danger to the welfare of young people. Constitutional considerations such as due process extend to juveniles who are brought before juvenile authorities.

Juveniles Must Be Subject to Adult Control. Within the Anglo-American approach toward juvenile justice, laws require that youths be under the protection and control of an adult authority, such as parents, guardians, or the state. In many ways, juvenile *rights* are actually *privileges* that are regulated by an adult authority. Ideally, justice will be served by maintaining the bonds between children and their parents or guardians. This is a priority objective, even if family intervention is required. Should the family unit be dysfunctional or unable to control the behavior of a youth, the state will step in to provide adult control and guidance, often by removing the child from his or her household.

The Juvenile Justice System Alleviates Stigma. One long accepted theory of juvenile rehabilitation is that youths who are brought into judicial and correctional systems are in jeopardy of becoming negatively stigmatized. **Stigma** refers to the imprinting of disgrace or shame on a person, so that they are thereafter judged by adults and peers in accordance with this impression. An important purpose of creating a separate justice system for juveniles is to reduce the possibility of stigmatization. This is accomplished by promoting rehabilitation and treatment, and by changing the legal language that is used when youths are processed through the system. For example, serious lawbreakers are labeled as *delinquents* rather than *criminals*.

Serious Juvenile Offenders Can Be Waived Into the Adult System. Although rehabilitation forms the underpinning for dispensing justice in the juvenile justice system, states and the federal government have enacted laws that leave open the possibility for punishing serious juvenile offenders as criminals. Violent offenses by juveniles that would normally be classified as felonies if committed by adults are regularly waived (transferred) into the adult criminal justice system. There, juveniles are subject to the full range of penalties normally reserved for adults.

Systemic Introduction: The Juvenile Justice System in Brief

As discussed previously, our examination of the juvenile justice system involves the following components:

- Official institutions, consisting of the police, the juvenile court, and juvenile corrections
- Nonofficial institutions, consisting of community-based agencies and organizations, many of which are private and/or nonprofit groups

Each component is composed of extensive layers of bureaucracy, so that it is perhaps more correct to refer to them as *subsystems* within the juvenile justice system. When juveniles are processed through the juvenile justice system, each subsystem works in combination with the others. They each serve a unique function, and, depending on the manner in which a person is processed through every phase, there are a large number of possible outcomes. Figure 1.1 summarizes the range of possible outcomes for those who move through the system and each subsystem.[10]

There are literally tens of thousands of agencies and millions of employees that operate within these subsystems.[12] Because of the sheer size of the juvenile justice system, it is impossible to argue that there exists a single model for all agencies in every jurisdiction. In fact, jurisdictions often differ significantly from each other. Nevertheless, the following profiles summarize the several subsystems within the juvenile justice system.[13] All will be discussed in detail in subsequent chapters.

The Police Subsystem

The role of the police is to enforce the law and maintain order in the community. This subsystem is quite extensive. In 2000, there were approximately 18,000 police agencies employing more than one million full-time sworn and nonsworn personnel.[14] They are intimately involved in juvenile justice issues. As indicated in Table 1.1, they mostly operate locally, and are thus in close proximity to towns and neighborhoods.

For juvenile offenders and victims, local police are often their first contact with juvenile justice authorities. The reason for this is simply stated: Juvenile offenders who break the law are frequently taken to the police as a first

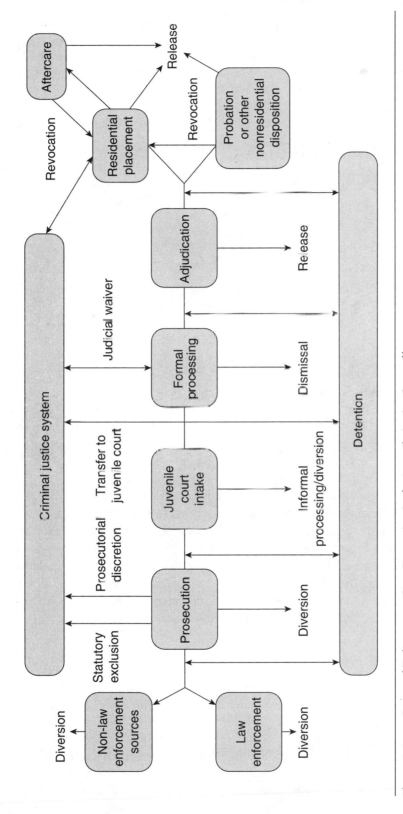

Figure 1.1 Stages of Delinquency Case Processing in the Juvenile Justice System[11]

TABLE 1.1   STATE AND LOCAL LAW ENFORCEMENT AGENCIES[a]

Problems with juveniles are addressed at the local level, and the police are frequently the first responders to allegations of delinquency or victimization. A snapshot of the extent of the police subsystem for the year 2000 indicates how large it is. The number of law enforcement agencies and personnel are indicated in this table.

Type of Agency	Number of Agencies	Total Full-Time Personnel
Local police	12,666	565,915
County sheriff	3,070	293,823
Primary state	49	87,028
Special jurisdiction	1,376	69,650
Texas constable	623	3,080
Total	17,784	1,019,496

a. Adapted from Bureau of Justice Statistics. *Sourcebook of criminal justice statistics—2002*. Washington, DC: U.S. Department of Justice.

option, or the police may apprehend them while observing them commit an offense. Youths who have been victimized or whose welfare is at risk are likewise referred to police custody—for their own protection. Regardless of whether a youth is a lawbreaker or a victim, the police are empowered to decide what the next step will be for their young charges. The police may exercise discretion to release them, administer stern admonishments, return them to parental custody, or process them into another component of the juvenile justice system. All of these options are conducted within the parameters of the police mission to maintain order.

It should be noted that there is virtually no contact between federal law enforcement agencies and juvenile offenders or victims. Federal agencies are highly specialized in comparison to state and local agencies. They include the Drug Enforcement Administration (DEA), the Federal Bureau of Investigation (FBI), and the Bureau of Alcohol, Tobacco, Firearms and Explosives (ATF&E). Thus, there is little chance for intervention by federal law enforcement agencies in juvenile affairs unless youths are involved in significant (and very serious) criminal activity.

The Judicial Subsystem

The judicial component of the juvenile justice system is composed of many of the same personnel as found in the adult system. These include judges, administrators, prosecutors, and defense counsel. It is a civil (rather than criminal) system, so there is also a significant amount of participation by social workers, probation officers, case managers, and other professionals whose primary duty is to inform and advise the court on the status of each juvenile. Depending on the severity of charges brought against a suspect, juveniles may be waived outside of the juvenile judicial system and sent to the adult criminal judicial system.[15]

The juvenile court is arguably the center of the juvenile justice system. Juvenile courts have the authority to function in much the same manner as courts in the criminal justice system. However, one must bear in mind that they are civil courts, and thus also have a duty to redress a number of social issues that lie outside of the authority of their counterparts in the adult criminal system. In the juvenile system, judges not only must render decisions on the fate of lawbreakers but also must weigh what would be in the best interest of children and their families. For this reason, juvenile courts often operate quite formally to resolve some cases (such as delinquency cases) but may opt to act informally in other cases (such as abuse cases). Depending on the local operating rules of specific jurisdictions, juvenile courts can exercise varying degrees of discretion to proceed formally or informally.

Figure 1.2 illustrates the number of juveniles processed at each phase of the juvenile court subsystem.

The Corrections Subsystem

Juvenile correctional institutions are regulated under state law and must comply with state and federal mandates for the humane treatment of youths who have been consigned to locked or other residential facilities. Many correctional subsystems are extensively bureaucratic—largely because they must provide every need for their residents, such as food, shelter, clothing, medical care, and sanitation. The underlying mission of juvenile corrections is to treat and rehabilitate youths. Although many facilities are highly restrictive, and confinement conditions can approximate those found in some adult facilities, it is the duty of this subsystem to "correct" the behavior of offenders.[17]

Unlike adult correctional systems, which are essentially networks of large penal (punishment) facilities, juvenile correctional systems can be very innovative. For example, states frequently use community-based correctional facilities to house young offenders. These facilities may be homes, dormitories, or camps in rural areas. Thus, although there exists a very real possibility of confinement in large and unpleasant facilities, there also exists a chance to serve *good time* in homelike or campuslike environments located in neighborhoods or the countryside. It must also be understood that abused, neglected, and abandoned children are placed in facilities that specialize in care for this class of youths. Modern correctional systems try to separate juvenile offenders from child victims as a matter of policy.

The Community-Based Subsystem

Unlike the adult criminal justice system, local communities are an integral part of the youth-serving system. This subsystem can be especially innovative

Delinquency cases can be resolved in many different ways. Depending on the facts of the case, they may be handled either formally or informally. The following figure indicates the numbers and percentages of delinquents at each phase of juvenile court proceedings at the time these data were reported.

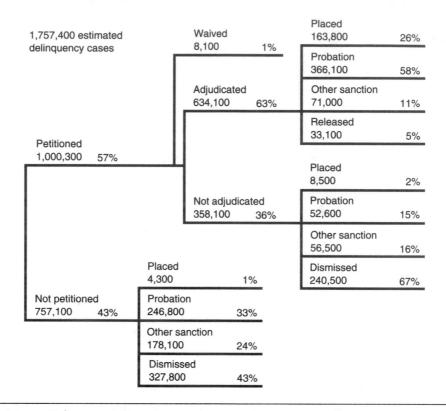

Figure 1.2   Delinquency Cases Processed in Juvenile Court—1998[16]

because it is comprised of many different types of agencies. These include for-profit private agencies, nonprofit private organizations, and neighborhood-based public government programs. They receive referrals of youths from two sources: first, those who have been transferred out of the official juvenile justice system (e.g., probationers and parolees); and second, those who have been diverted directly into community-based programs and agencies. Regardless of the manner in which youths are placed in community venues, they are likely to receive more individualized treatment than they would otherwise receive in formal correctional institutions.

Procedural Introduction:
Dispensing Juvenile Justice

Although the procedures of the juvenile justice system are similar to those of the adult system, the language it uses is very different. In order to soften the impact of being processed into the juvenile system, and in deference to its underlying rehabilitative mission, unique procedural labels have been affixed to each phase of dispensing juvenile justice. The following discussion summarizes several of these phases, with the caveat that every jurisdiction has designed its own approach to juvenile justice process. Each phase will be discussed in detail in subsequent chapters.

Custody

Police officers are trained (or at least should be trained) to be well-versed in procedures for rendering control over youths, in comparison to dealing with adults. Under specified circumstances, the police may detain juveniles, but these youths are technically said to have been *taken into custody* rather than *arrested*. An arrest refers to the detention of a criminal suspect, which in practice denotes either adults or juveniles who have been waived into the criminal justice system. In comparison, custody suggests a broader concept of detention than does an arrest. For example, custody does not refer exclusively to the detaining of lawbreakers, and an officer may take youths into custody for a number of reasons:

- Suspicion of delinquency
- Suspicion of violations of youth-centered prohibitions, such as alcohol or tobacco use, truancy, or curfews
- Suspected victimization, such as abuse, neglect, or abandonment
- Children in need of care, such as homeless or injured youths

Youths who are taken into custody may be sent to juvenile facilities pending resolution of their case. If the police or other significant parties believe that a case warrants the attention of the juvenile court, a formal *petition* may be made to the court asking for its intervention. Petitions describe the juvenile's problems that should be resolved by the court. They are issued for allegations of delinquency as well as for cases of alleged victimization. Aside from the police, the other members of the community who may make petitions to juvenile court typically include teachers, parents, and neighbors. Petitions are the formal beginning of juvenile court proceedings.

Intake

Intake is a process that is used to determine whether a juvenile should be released or processed through the juvenile justice system. It is roughly comparable to an initial appearance or preliminary hearing in the adult system. *Intake officers* are officials of the court who are usually probation officers or a court-employed social worker. Officers review an individual's case and preside over *intake hearings*. During these hearings, the testimony of interested parties is solicited, and may include parents, neighbors, teachers, the police, and victims. The juvenile's entire profile is considered, including prior offenses or victimization, social conditions, psychological or physical conditions, feelings and opinions, and general deportment.

Intake hearings may result in dismissal, release into custody of parents or other guardian, referral to community-based care, or referral to the court for full prosecution or other procedures. If a youth is to be detained in an institution pending final resolution of his or her case, a *detention hearing* may be held to determine the mode of detention. Detention may be very restrictive or minimally restrictive.

Adjudication

Juveniles never stand before a juvenile court for a *trial*. Rather, they go through an *adjudicatory hearing,* which is the juvenile justice system's counterpart to trials in the adult criminal justice system. Although adjudicatory hearings can be somewhat informal, they have increasingly become more akin to criminal court proceedings when cases of serious delinquency are heard. In many delinquency hearings, procedures can be quite formal and adversarial, with opposing prosecution and defense counsels, strict rules of evidence, and sworn witnesses. The vast majority of adjudicatory hearings are bench proceedings, meaning that no jury will be convened, and the judge alone is empowered to make findings of fact and rendering final judgment.

In the juvenile justice system, judges do not render *verdicts* on the facts of the case. They instead make an *adjudication,* which either supports the facts of the petition (the equivalent of a *conviction* in a criminal trial) or rejects them (the equivalent of a criminal *acquittal*). If the facts of the petition are supported, the court will conduct a hearing to consider arguments on how to dispose of the case. At this phase, the consequences of delinquency can be quite serious.

Dispositions

When an adult is convicted of a crime, he or she will often appear before the court at a later date to be sentenced. This is known as a *sentencing hearing,* and the juvenile justice system's counterpart is referred to as a *dispositional hearing*. Its purpose is philosophically distinguishable from a sentencing hearing, because a *disposition* is rendered in the best interest of the child, whereas an adult sentence is usually imposed to punish an offender. Thus, regardless of the terms of each disposition, they represent a theoretical attempt by the juvenile justice system to design the most effective means to treat and rehabilitate young people. Dispositional terms may range in severity and intensity from nonintrusive or largely symbolic conditions to highly intrusive confinement in locked facilities.

Policy Introduction:
Challenges for Juvenile Justice

Juvenile justice systems have historically undergone periodic changes in philosophy. They have also experienced significant organizational reconfigurations. It is a truism that one of the only consistencies in juvenile justice process has been its adaptation to the prevailing cultural and political trends of the time.

In actuality, how cooperative is the juvenile justice system? Do the various components form an integrated network, or do they sometimes operate at cross-purposes? Which philosophies are most effective? What are the ongoing challenges for juvenile justice in the United States?

In the modern era, two fundamental challenges are likely to continue to have an impact on juvenile justice process:

- Designing an effective organizational configuration for the system
- Periodic reexaminations of existing philosophies and models for dealing with juveniles

Widening the Net:
Configuring the Juvenile Justice System

The juvenile justice system is a uniquely configured network consisting of many levels of government and the community. It is at once quite bureaucratic, and yet maintains strong connections to local neighborhoods. It has also come to marshal the resources of many sectors of society—sectors that may not otherwise be predisposed to become partners under a common policy umbrella. These disparate organizations and sectors have become part of an extensive policy agenda, which has had important consequences for the welfare of society as a whole.

The most essential challenges to maintaining some semblance of cohesion within the juvenile justice system are, first, coordinating effective communication between subsystems, and second, creating a desire for cooperation. These two factors—communication and cooperation—are important considerations for designing an effective organizational configuration for the system.

The Necessity of Communication. Regarding the need for communication, many governmental and private agencies and programs are unfortunately disconnected from each other. Separations along lines of communication can be the result of many factors, such as:

- *Internal bureaucracy.* Bureaucratic separation at the same level of government, wherein agencies sometimes duplicate tasks or overlook issues and cases, can be the result of poor organization (or *turf* competition).

- *External bureaucracy.* Poor lines of communication between separate governments are not uncommon; municipal agencies may have inefficient links with county agencies, or local agencies may not comply effectively with state rules and regulations.

- *Community–government isolation.* Disconnect often exists between community-based and government agencies, with neighborhood organizations pursuing agendas that may conflict with government plans.

The Necessity of Cooperation. Regarding the desire for cooperation, official and unofficial organizations often have conflicting agendas. For example, the police may be more interested in order maintenance than long-term treatment plans, whereas community-based nonprofits may have the reverse priorities. In addition, there may be an underlying sense of competition rather than cooperation between agencies or programs. For example, depending on the economic climate, there may be limitations on available financial resources, so that agencies may engage in *one-upmanship* to demonstrate that they merit funding more than their counterparts.

Consequences. In reality, there are often missteps in communication, as well as cases of intentional noncooperation. Because of the extensive and diverse configurations of juvenile justice systems, this means that there is frequent division between actors. They do not always live up to the ideal of a cooperative network, and the consequences can be dire.

Unfortunately, there are many stories describing incompetence, mistreatment, corruption, and cover-ups within dysfunctional juvenile justice systems. Investigations occasionally reveal criminal behavior within subsystems, such as troubling reports of beatings, neglect, or other inhumane treatment in correctional institutions. Poor implementation of programs by community-based organizations is not uncommon, and it is often the result of poor and incompetent oversight by government agencies—in other words, some problems are so blatant that even a cursory inspection would have revealed their deficiencies. Such problems and consequences pose ongoing challenges for the proper implementation of justice for juveniles.

Dealing With Juveniles: Competing Philosophies and Models

There has never been a universally accepted philosophy on how to best conceptualize justice for juveniles. Nor has there existed a single model for how to administer juvenile justice. This challenge is not exclusive to the juvenile system, but has also been a challenge for the provision of adult-centered criminal justice.

For the most part, both the juvenile and criminal justice systems have passed through historical eras wherein philosophies and models have

Photo 1.2   Young members of a Los Angeles girl's gang flash gang signs. Many youths grow up
in the presence of routine criminal activity.

reflected the norms of society at particular points in history. Subsystems—
that is, the police, courts, corrections, and community-based programs—
have also adapted to the philosophies of different historical eras. The
historical progression of juvenile justice is discussed in Chapter 2, and each
subsystem's unique history is discussed in its respective chapter. However, it
is useful at this point to understand several philosophies and models.

Rehabilitation Model. This is the original approach toward juvenile justice,
and still a fundamental concept. Rehabilitation refers to using institutions
and programs to reclaim troubled youths. Under this model, methods and
agencies are established to mold delinquents into productive adults, and
victims into healthy adults.

Treatment Model. Also referred to as the *medical model,* this approach
applies a therapeutic standard for evaluating the effectiveness of intervention. Psychological counseling, physical (health) regimens, and behavior
modification are stressed as foundations for full rehabilitation. Punishment
and detention are rejected as being counterproductive to successful treatment and rehabilitation. This approach is applicable for juvenile offenders
and victims.

Punishment Model. Also referred to as the *crime control model*, it emphasizes the authority of the state in responding to deviant behavior. Punishment is an end in itself, and the removal of offenders from society is desirable. Under this model, hard confinement, discipline, regimentation, and fear are considered to be effective correctional methods. It parallels the modern crackdown on adult criminality. Obviously, the punishment model is directed toward juvenile offenders rather than victims.

Just Deserts Model. A consequence of the crackdown on crime, this model applies the old adage of "an eye for an eye" when determining the fate of an offender. Conceptually, it advocates the imposition of punishments that fit the crime. As a corresponding approach to the punishment model, juvenile offenders will receive the punishments they deserve from juvenile court judges. Again, this is obviously appropriate only for offenders rather than victims.

PROFESSIONAL PROFILE CHAPTER 1

Project Director for Operation Weed & Seed and Grants and Development Officer—City Mayor's Office

Juvenile justice process is essentially a function of policies and programs that are designed by public servants who are members of government agencies. Government service is quite literally service on behalf of the greater community. Although some government workers are rarely in direct contact with members of the community, many public servants have a great deal of contact with community-based groups and agencies. It is important to understand not only the mission of public service but also the motivations and dedication of those who are "in the trenches" and directly responsible for community-focused programs.

I.   Personal Profile

    A.   Name:
        Dave Farley

    B.   Agency:
        Office of the Mayor, City of Pittsburgh

    C.   Rank and/or Title:
        Grants and Development Officer
        Project Director for Operation Weed & Seed

    D.   Education (Schools and Degrees):
        Johns Hopkins University
        BA (Subject unknown)
        University of Pittsburgh
        MS, ABD, Social Psychology

E.   Professional Organizations/Community Group Memberships:
Children's Home of Pittsburgh Board of Directors
Democratic Committeeman, Fourteenth Ward, City of Pittsburgh
President of the Board of Directors, Fourteenth Ward Democratic Club
Pennsylvania (PA) Psychological Association
U.S. Department of Justice Project Safe Neighborhoods Task Force
Pittsburgh YMCA Collegiate Board of Management
Vice Chair of the Board of Directors, Friends of the Riverfront

II. Professional Profile

A.   What personal or other background experiences led to your decision to *choose* this profession?

I'm a product of the 1960s and its emphasis on direct citizen action to effect changes in government. Being part of the government allows a person to blend activism, concern for people, knowledge of how to make effective change, and a certain degree of wisdom in ways that can really make desirable change happen. I had served in the U.S. Navy, gone to graduate school, and worked for the Mental Health Association as Director of Evaluation and Research. I'd been the Chair of the Government Affairs Committee of the PA Psychological Association, and I knew my way around public policy and politics.

Now, I have been a public employee for many years, and have served three different mayoral administrations in various positions, including

- Senior Planner in the Personnel Department. I advised the Director of Personnel about employment and training policies and wrote federal grant documents and reports.
- Assistant Director of Personnel and Manager of the Pittsburgh Partnership. I was in charge of all aspects of the City of Pittsburgh's employment and training system and programs, with a staff of 60 people.
- Government Affairs Officer. I was the City of Pittsburgh's chief lobbyist and represented the Mayor in state and national organizations.
- Grants and Development Officer. In the Mayor's office I am the coordinator for the City of Pittsburgh's external funding activities of its departments and public authorities (i.e., federal and state grants and other funds that are received in addition to the usual tax revenue of the city). I also serve as Project Director for Operation Weed & Seed, a joint federal–local law enforcement and community reinvestment initiative that has been under way in Pittsburgh in one form or another since 1992.

B.   Please state a few of your personal reasons/motivations for your decision to *continue* in this profession.

Public service is often hard work, but it is honorable work when done well. I have worked hard to make a difference in my community, and I've been fortunate to have had an opportunity to make real changes in Pittsburgh through my work in government. Over many years a successful government employee gains a sophisticated understanding of how to actually make some of the changes that can improve our civic life in very direct ways. The "community activist" in me finds it satisfying to help citizens and to teach them how to relate effectively to their local government structures. Of course, being part of the government also means you can't escape responsibility for some of the actions that are taken (even when some of them are not your fault or are the result of processes in which you had no significant role). But that is the nature of politics and public service, and you accept that as part of the "deal" or you're very unhappy and not long for this profession. On balance I've been able to make some important structural, legislative, and policy decisions that really have improved the lives of Pittsburghers to the extent that local government and its partners can do that appropriately.

C. **Which job experiences have had an important impact on you?**

The following accomplishments have, I think, had the most impact on me and the community:

- Creating capacity in communities, such as when I have invented neighborhood groups where ones didn't exist before
- Pioneering the development of Pittsburgh's network of neighborhood employment centers in 1987
- Successfully drafting legislation and lobbying the federal Congress to change the Housing and Community Development Act in 1993, specifically to benefit Pittsburgh
- Working with groups of residents to improve public safety and to bring new programs to communities
- Making the federal Weed & Seed effort so successful in reducing crime in Pittsburgh that local funds were subsequently appropriated by Pittsburgh City Council to continue and expand the project
- Helping Pittsburgh employment programs and public safety efforts to win national awards

D. **What has been a particularly *satisfying* job experience?**

See C above.

E. **What has been a particularly *challenging* job experience?**

Having to argue with uncreative administrators about the value of particular approaches to problems. Because it is often very costly for the public sector if it makes mistakes (unlike in the private sector, where mistakes can be more or less written off), public administrators tend to be cautious about taking risk or about doing things in different ways (even when it's apparent to most reasonable people that different ways would be better!). Some caution should be part of any decision in the public sector, of course, but too much of that makes the whole system bog down and suffer from inertia and possibly fall victim to problems that get out of hand because no one's taken any aggressive actions to address them when that could have had a desirable effect. When you're fortunate enough to be able to take some of your own risks within the government—as I have been for much of my career—and you do take those risks, and they succeed, you may also find some degree of resentment from the unduly cautious people. If some of those people happen to be in positions that you need to interact with or who control government resources you need to accomplish your assignments, it can be difficult from time to time, but you work through it eventually. Those kinds of challenges may be in the environment regardless of where you work, however. The difference is that in the public sector it is often harder to get around or to remove unduly cautious people who resent the success of others.

F.   What do you think the future holds for your profession?

Government will always be around in some form. It is likely that people working in government will need greater ranges of skills and experience. It's also likely that there will probably be somewhat fewer people employed, and those who are will be working with many other agencies, consultants, and contractors to get the work of government accomplished efficiently and effectively. There is a certain degree of "ebb and flow" to government and the esteem in which it's held by many people. When times are good, many citizens don't need a lot from their governments, but when times are bad, many of those same individuals howl about why there isn't more government activity. Of course, activity costs money, even in government, and citizens must deal with the fact that services aren't free—they will eventually pay for them with tax dollars. There is also a trend toward consolidation in local government (probably long overdue in some instances). That means there may not be as many of the "supernumerary" kinds of jobs or outsourceable positions that have come to characterize some local governments for many observers. The successful local governments, however, will hire creative, broadly knowledgeable, experienced people who have some understanding and acceptance of the political environment of accountability in which public sector activities must take place, yet who are willing to work hard and to function to bring services to the people.

G.   What kind of advice/guidance would you give to interested students?

There is no doubt that public sector activities and government can affect the lives of people in positive (and, unfortunately, sometimes negative) ways. If you believe strongly in a vision of how the lives of people ought to be affected, then you should consider a career in government. If you're only looking for a job, then go to work in a bank.

Chapter Summary

Juvenile justice is a ubiquitous concept in the United States. It is a unique and separate system that encompasses juvenile justice processes (procedures) and a juvenile justice system (juvenile-focused institutions). Conceptually, the term *juvenile* is a classification defined by law that refers to nonadults who are subject to different rules, laws, and penalties. However, laws also create legal fictions that permit juveniles to be prosecuted as criminals, or emancipated from adult controls.

Juvenile justice institutions include official institutions, such as the police, courts, and corrections, and nonofficial institutions, such as community-based agencies and programs. It is proper to consider these components as subsystems within the greater juvenile justice system. Procedurally, dispensing justice to juveniles involves procedures that are similar to those found in the adult system, but which have been designated under different terms. These terms include custody, intake, adjudication, and disposition; counterparts in the adult system are arrest, first appearance/preliminary hearing, trial, and sentencing.

There exist ongoing policy challenges for providing justice to juveniles. These include the issue of developing adequate communications between members of the juvenile justice system and assuring cooperation between them. The consequences of noncommunication and noncooperation can be dire for society. There also exist several competing philosophies and models for dealing with juveniles. These include traditional rehabilitation models, medical-inspired treatment models, punishment models, and just deserts. It should be expected that these concepts will continue to shape juvenile justice process in the future.

Chapter 2 begins our detailed investigation of juvenile justice process and systems. It provides a historical perspective for understanding the scope of juvenile justice, and it presents instructive discussion of the many cultural approaches for resolving problems involving juveniles.

Questions for Review

1. What types of approaches have been considered and developed for dealing with juvenile offenders and victimized youths?

2. Why have these approaches evolved and changed over the years?

3. What are the principal components of the juvenile justice system?

4. What are the primary duties of the components of the system?

5. How are juvenile offenders processed through the juvenile justice system?

6. How do the principal components of the system interact as juveniles are processed by them?

7. Which critical issues must be addressed by juvenile justice professionals and policy makers?

8. How do juvenile justice professionals try to resolve these critical issues?

Key Terms and Concepts

The following topics were discussed in this chapter and are found in the Glossary:

Emancipated Youths

Just Deserts Model

Juvenile

Juvenile Criminals

Juvenile Justice

Juvenile Justice Process

Juvenile Justice System

Legal Fictions

Nonofficial Juvenile Justice Institutions

Official Juvenile Justice Institutions

Punishment Model

Rehabilitation Model

Stigma

Treatment Model

DISCUSSION BOX

Curfews as a Juvenile Crime-Fighting Strategy

This chapter's Discussion Box is intended to stimulate critical discussion about the purpose and effectiveness of curfew laws.

Curfews have long been used in the United States to control the behavior of specified groups of people. They have been used to keep drifters and the homeless off streets, confine African American slaves to their quarters, maintain law and order during civil unrest, and regulate Japanese Americans during the Second World War. Criminals who have been released on probation or parole are often subject to strict curfews.

Curfews have also long been used to regulate the activities of juveniles. Juvenile-focused curfew laws apply to juvenile probationers and parolees in the same manner as they do to similarly situated adults. However, unlike adult curfews (which are rare and exceptional), juvenile-focused laws can mandate that all young persons be away from an area after a designated time, regardless of their status as probationers or parolees. Laws that affect all juveniles typically stipulate an age of regulation, often for persons under the age of 18 years. Curfews can apply to entire cities or to specified streets or locations, and they frequently target shopping malls, neighborhoods, or parks. Designated times are usually an appointed time at night, such as 10:00 P.M. until dawn. Juveniles who violate curfews may be taken into custody and will usually be returned to their homes.

The purpose of juvenile curfew laws is to prevent juvenile crime and victimization. Their underlying goal is to protect youths from harm after hours in certain locations and to maintain order by preempting potential violations of the law. In order to do this, curfews regulate the times when youths will be potentially unsupervised by an adult. So, for example, juveniles will be supervised during school and curfew hours and unsupervised for only a narrow period of time. This rationale has made juvenile curfew laws a regular feature of order maintenance in American communities.

Discussion Questions

1. Are juvenile curfew laws necessary? If so, why?

2. Should juvenile curfews be imposed over wide geographic areas, or for limited purposes in specified areas?

3. Are juvenile curfews effective? Do they reduce juvenile deviance?

4. Who should bear the ultimate responsibility for complying with curfew restrictions?

5. Do curfew laws tie up police and other resources that can be better used elsewhere?

Recommended Readings

The following publications provide general and issue-specific discussions on juvenile justice process and the juvenile justice system.

Cox, S. M., Conrad, J. J., & Allen, J. M. (2003). *Juvenile justice: A guide to theory and practice.* Boston: McGraw-Hill.

McShane, M. D., & Williams, F. P., III. (2003). *Encyclopedia of juvenile justice.* Thousand Oaks, CA: Sage.

Miller, W. B. (2001). *The growth of youth gang problems in the United States: 1970–98.* Washington, DC: U.S. Department of Justice.

Puzzanchera, C., Stahl, A. L., Finnegan, T. A., Tierney, N., & Snyder, H. N. (2003). *Juvenile court statistics.* Washington, DC: U.S. Department of Justice.

Snyder, H. N., & Sickmund, M. (1999). *Juvenile offenders and victims: 1999 National report.* Washington, DC: U.S. Department of Justice.

Notes

1. See United States of America v. Patrick V., 359 F.3d 3 (1st Cir. 2004).

2. For a discussion of policy considerations, see Jones, T. L. (2001). *Effective response to school violence: A guide for educators and law enforcement personnel.* Springfield, IL: Charles C Thomas.

3. Data are derived from Small, M., & Dressler Tetrick, K. (1999). School violence: An overview. In Office of Juvenile Justice and Delinquency (2001, June). *Juvenile Justice, 8,* 3–12. See also Griffin, P. Violence in schools. In *In Summary.* Pittsburgh, PA: National Center for Juvenile Justice.

4. Chapter 7 discusses the juvenile court in detail.

5. Chapter 6 discusses the role of the police in detail.

6. Chapter 8 discusses juvenile corrections in detail, and Chapter 9 discusses juvenile probation and parole.

7. Chapter 10 discusses the role of the community as a component of the juvenile justice system.

8. For a discussion of issues associated with dealing with juvenile criminals, see Crews, G. A., & Montgomery, R. H. (2001). *Chasing shadows: Confronting juvenile violence in America.* Upper Saddle River, NJ: Prentice Hall.

9. See Feld, B. C. (2000). *Cases and materials on juvenile justice administration.* St. Paul, MN: West Group.

10. Snyder, H. N., & Sickmund, M. (1999). *Juvenile offenders and victims: 1999 National report.* Washington, DC: U.S. Department of Justice.

11. Ibid.

12. See Bureau of Justice Statistics. (n.d.). *Sourcebook of criminal justice statistics—2002.* Washington, DC: U.S. Department of Justice.

13. See McCord, J., Spatz Widom, C., & Crowell, N. A. (Eds.). (2001). *Juvenile crime, juvenile justice.* Washington, DC: National Academy Press.

14. Ibid. (p. 39).

15. See Fagan, J., & Zimring, F. E. (Eds.). (2000). *The changing borders of juvenile justice: Transfers of adolescents to the criminal court.* Chicago. The University of Chicago Press.

16. Puzzanchera, C., Stahl, A. L., Finnegan, T. A., Tierney, N., & Snyder, H. N. (2003). *Juvenile court statistics.* Washington, DC: U.S. Department of Justice.

17. See American Correctional Association. (2002). *Juvenile justice today: Essays on programs and policies.* Laurel, MD: American Correctional Association.

2 Historical Perspectives

Within the context of government-imposed law and order, the concept of "juvenile rights" is a very new historical concept. In the modern United States, juveniles are protected under the Constitution in much the same manner as are adults. This is true even when juveniles are confronted with serious allegations. For example, in 1993 an 83-year-old woman was killed in her own home after being severely beaten and stabbed.[1] The murder occurred in Cook County, Illinois. An 11-year-old boy, known in court documents as A.M. to protect his identity, was tried as a juvenile delinquent and found to be responsible by a juvenile court judge on a charge of first-degree murder. Because he was processed as a juvenile, A.M. received a sentence of only 5 years probation.

Despite the seeming leniency of this sentence for such a heinous crime, A.M. was granted release after a petition of habeas corpus[2] was filed on his behalf. The rationale for this decision was that the police had failed to protect A.M.'s right against self-incrimination because they did not read him his Miranda[3] rights until after he had confessed to the killing. On appeal, the court held that A.M. had been "in custody" when he confessed and therefore eligible for Miranda protections.

This chapter surveys the history of juvenile justice process across several eras and cultures. At the outset, it is important for readers to understand that although modern societies typically disconnect juvenile justice process from criminal justice administration, this was not the custom for much of human history. In fact, quite the reverse is true. For millennia, juvenile justice was merely subsumed under the broader concept of criminal justice, and harsh punishments were imposed on juveniles to protect the prevailing social order. No distinction was made between delinquency and criminality, so that juvenile offenders were deemed to be nothing more than young criminals and were treated accordingly. While there are a few distant historical examples of rudimentary juvenile-focused standards of justice, most societies simply treated juvenile offenders in the same manner as deviant adults. Even in societies that took into account the special status of young people, identical punishments were meted out to juveniles and adults alike.

It was only after centuries of human civilization that what we now term *juvenile justice* began to develop outside of an adult criminal justice context. Thus, the concept of promoting a distinct form of justice for children and teenagers is a relatively new development in the history of civilization and the administration of justice. Figure 2.1 depicts a historical view of juvenile justice process.

	Millennium	Crackdown on juvenile deviance.
Modern Era	1984	*Schall v. Martin* allows preventive detention of juveniles.
• **Just Deserts**		
20th-Century America	1975	*Breed v. Jones* protects juveniles against double jeopardy.
• **1970s**	1974	Juvenile Justice and Delinquency Prevention Act was passed.
• **Great Society**		
• **Great Depression**	1974	Office of Juvenile Justice and Delinquency Prevention established.
• **Progressive Era**		
• **Juvenile Courts**	1971	*McKeiver v. Pennsylvania*. Denied trial by jury in juvenile proceedings.
	1970	*In re Winship* entitled juveniles to standard of proof beyond a reasonable doubt.
	1968	Juvenile Delinquency Prevention and Control Act was passed.
	1968	Youth Service Bureaus founded.
	1967	*In re Gault* mandated due process for juvenile court proceedings.
	1966	*Kent v. United States* mandated due process in juvenile courts prior to transfer to criminal court.
	1960s	The Great Society and social activism reform juvenile justice.
	1951	Federal Youth Corrections Act was passed.
	1938	Juvenile Court Act was passed.
	1937	National Council of Juvenile and Family Court Judges formed.
	1925	*A Standard Juvenile Court Act* was proposed.
	1899	The Illinois Juvenile Court Act created the first juvenile court.
	1874	Children's tribunals established in Massachusetts.
	Early 1900s	Progressive Era began a long period of juvenile justice reform.
Colonial to 19th Century	Late 1800s	Reform schools began home-like and trade treatment.
	Mid-1800s	Child-Saving Movement "rescued" at-risk juveniles.
• **Child Savers**	1838	*Ex parte Crouse* reaffirmed the state's *parens patriae* power.
• **Colonial Era**	1825	The first House of Refuge opened in New York City.
	1646	The Stubborn Child Law was passed in Puritan Massachusetts.
	1600s	Puritanical correction of at-risk children influences juvenile doctrine in early America.

Figure 2.1   Historical Perspectives on Juvenile Justice

(Continued)

Old England	1817	The London Philanthropic Society was formed.
	1704	The Hospital of St. Michael was founded in Rome, later influencing English juvenile justice doctrine.
• Reform Movement		
• Renaissance	1601	Workhouses were constructed to provide work for at-risk juveniles.
• Feudal Period		
	1555	Bridewell Workhouse established.
	Feudal Era	*Parens patriae* became part of English tradition and law.
	6th–7th Century	Æthelbert created the first code written in English.
Early History	Rome	*Patria potestas* governed the role of children in Roman society.
• Rome	About	The Code of Hammurabi applied *lex talionis* to the treatment
• Babylon	1750 B.C.	of juveniles.

Figure 2.1 (Continued)

The discussion in this chapter reviews:

- Beginnings: Juveniles in Early History
- Roots of Anglo-American Law: Juvenile Justice in Old England
- Juvenile Justice in America: The Colonial Period Through the Nineteenth Century
- Juvenile Justice in America: The Twentieth Century
- Juvenile Justice in America: The Modern Era

CHAPTER PERSPECTIVE 2.1

Historical Perspectives on the Juvenile Court

Until the establishment of the first family and juvenile court in 1899 by the Illinois Juvenile Court Act, juvenile-focused policies and procedures in the United States were fragmentary. Reformers certainly developed and advocated a philosophy of benevolent societal intervention, but juvenile proceedings were not managed in states by centralized juvenile-focused judicial systems. Instead, private philanthropic agencies managed juvenile homes and institutions, while the state processed juvenile offenders through adult court systems and confined youthful offenders in the same facilities as adults.

Separate juvenile court systems were the culmination of decades-long social evolution during the nineteenth century. This evolution began during the 1820s when philanthropic groups such as the Society for the Prevention of Juvenile Delinquency advocated the separation of juvenile and adult transgressors. This reflected the then-enlightened notion that juveniles who were tried and convicted in adult criminal courts would become more inclined toward a life of crime if housed with adult criminals.

Institutionalization in Houses of Refuge and reform schools seemed to reformers to be the answer to juvenile reform and rehabilitation. However, conditions were frequently deplorable in both institutions, the Houses were prison-like, and the reform schools were hard and exploitative environments. The general plight of children at that time was cause for great concern: Many labored in factories and mines, roamed unsupervised or abandoned in cities, and had poor safety nets if orphaned. It seemed to the child savers and other activists that the time had come to redefine the state's role for at-risk children. To them, juvenile courts would be the logical venue for the treatment of juvenile offenders and victims.

The first court adopted several concepts that have endured in juvenile justice systems to the present day: *Parens patriae*, treatment, rehabilitation, uniquely juvenile-focused proceedings, delinquency, and diversion to social service agencies.

Beginnings: Juveniles in Early History

Prehistorical societies were tribal and tradition-bound, with rudimentary norms of control that were used to maintain group cohesion, promote order, and punish wrongdoers. These norms of control were not "laws" per se in the same sense as modern legal codes, but they did create codes of conduct for members of the group. When ruling hierarchies were established, the concept of *retaliation* became the central feature of justice, along with other forms of punishment such as confinement and banishment. Under this concept, victims were permitted to exact revenge against assailants and other transgressors. Retaliation is still routinely practiced in a number of modern societies; for example, the United States has adopted retaliation as the underlying principle for "retribution" and "just deserts" models of criminal punishment.[4]

Ancient Babylon

Approximately 4,000 years ago, sometime around 1750 B.C.E., King Hammurabi of Babylon in Sumeria presided over the first state known to be governed by a written legal code.[5] The **Code of Hammurabi** supplanted tribal custom and uniformly applied laws governing everyday social interactions such as trade, inheritance, marriage, and contracts. Very severe penalties were exacted for deviant behavior, and corporal punishment, banishment, and execution were commonly imposed for criminal and moral offenses. These penalties reflected the state's application of *lex talionis,* or the "law of retaliation." *Lex talionis* mandated the infliction of the same injury that was caused to another—quite literally a limb for a limb, an eye for an eye, and a tooth for a tooth. The purpose of Hammurabi's Code, and other legal systems that adopted *lex talionis,* was to impose these punishments equally to all members within social hierarchies. This meant that the powerful within each class would suffer the same penalties as the weak within the class.

Babylonian Patriarchy and the Treatment of Children. The Code of Hammurabi also incorporated complex provisions for marriage, fidelity, and family solidarity. It did so by designating the husband as the unquestioned head of the household. Children—that is, the offspring from a freeman's wife, concubine, and/or slave—were under the father's control until emancipated by marriage. Children were an extension of their father, so that the father could hire out a child's labor, children could be indentured to others for their father's debts, or he could sell them. Girls could be given by fathers to serve the gods in temples, or given away as concubines, with no choice in the matter. Boys were required to be obedient and respectful to the father, on pain of extreme physical punishment such as amputation. For example, the Code stated: "If a son strike his father, one shall cut off his hands."[6]

Thus, laws that we would now term juvenile justice provisions were enacted entirely for the preservation of Babylonian patriarchy. Juvenile delinquency was viewed as rebellion against the father, and the law brutally enforced youths' respect for, and fear of, paternal authority. Children and teenagers could be treated as little more than property.

The Roman Empire

Roman law has had a direct influence on modern European legal codes, with most continental legal systems having roots in ancient Roman codes. Roman jurisprudence was derived from the following two sources:

- *The Twelve Tables.* Developed circa 450 B.C.E., this is the earliest codification of Roman law and the source for later Roman laws.
- *Code of Justinian.* A code of laws written during the reign of Justinian, Emperor of the Eastern Empire. It was originally promulgated in 529 C.E., and comprised twelve books. It became one of four compilations of Roman law known collectively as the *Corpus Juris Civilis.*

Roman Patriarchy. In ancient Rome, a doctrine known as *patria potestas* established the roles of children within society and the family unit.[7] Under *patria potestas,* the father had absolute control over his household, which included his wife, children, and slaves. In the Roman household, children were at the bottom of the household's hierarchy and had fewer rights than slaves (who were considered to be vital to an orderly estate). Fathers literally had the power of life and death over members of the household, as illustrated in the following passage from the Twelve Tables of Rome:

> A father shall have the right of life and death over his son born in lawful marriage, and shall also have the power to render him independent, after he has been sold three times.[8]

Children were required by law and custom to give absolute obedience to the father, and disobedience by children could lead to the father's imposition of corporal punishment or the child's sale into slavery. There could be no intervention by the state in matters of paternal discipline of children, so that children essentially had no rights other than the good will of their father. Nevertheless, although the father's authority was unquestioned, he was expected to act responsibly. Children could be emancipated by the father, and frequently were.

As time progressed, and the Empire gradually developed a sophisticated legal system, *patria potestas*'s harshness was softened, and it eventually came to refer to the father's right to own any property possessed by members of his household. Roman law also came to forbid practices such as the fatal exposure of unwanted infants (usually girls) to the elements. Christian philosophers such as Augustine advocated the spread of a concept known as *paterna pietas*, or "fatherly love," as a moral alternative to *patria potestas*. Nonetheless, *patria potestas* was the predominant doctrine governing the treatment of children, and the system had a significant impact on later English doctrines of juvenile justice.

Roots of Anglo-American Law: Juvenile Justice in Old England

In early England, Roman Catholic canon (sacred) law and English secular (nonchurch) law were completely separate systems of justice. Each developed its own traditions with regard to crime, morality, and (in the case of canon law) salvation of the soul. Separate traditions were also developed on the question of controlling children.

In sacred legal tradition, which was derived from ancient Hebrew rabbinical law,[9] the church held that children under the age of seven years could not be convicted of spiritual offenses because they were incapable of reason. Children of this age were considered to be too innocent to commit a sin. This was an early application of what is now referred to as individual *capacity* in the administration of criminal justice.

From the sacred legal tradition, English secular laws likewise held that children under the age of 7 years could not be convicted for criminal offenses, and youths between the ages of 7 and 14 years could be tried as adult criminals only if they could be shown to have an adult's capacity to appreciate the nature of their offense. Secular authorities considered people to be adults at the age of 14 years, and these youths were subjected to full criminal trial and punishment.

Feudal England: Life as "Nasty, Brutish, and Short"[10]

The feudal era in England was one of frequent internecine warfare, invasions, disease, and strict class and social divisions.[11] There were high mortality rates for children, abandonment of infants was a common practice, and poor or homeless children were made into servants. There were few rights for juveniles. Strict corporal punishment was meted out to children for minor offenses such as disobedience, crying, or whining. Adolescent males were considered to be the most useful children, and other young people were simply declared to be "undesirable." Undesirables included mentally or physically handicapped children, young (and hence unproductive) children, and frequently girls.

The treatment of juvenile criminal offenders reflected feudal attitudes toward child desirability and deviant behavior. When tried before a criminal court, juvenile transgressors could expect to be punished as harshly as adult criminals. Anglo-Saxon laws typically focused on the nature of the offense rather than one's age. For example, Æthelbert I, King of Kent (560 to 616 C.E.), who is credited with writing the first code of crimes and punishment in the English language, made no provision for young offenders. None of Æthelbert's laws differentiated deviant behavior by adults and juveniles, and none of the mandated punishments took age into account. This meant in practice that young criminals were tortured, burned, hung, and confined in dank dungeons for long periods of time. Juveniles were regularly imprisoned in the same cells as adults, and received no special accommodations.[12]

The Role of the State Under Common Law. English tradition and law—which came to be known as the **common law**[13]—was strongly paternal, with familial authority centered on the father. Families were quite dependent on the father, and wives and children had virtually no rights vis-à-vis those of the head of the household; a father's word was always binding on his spouse and offspring. However, a father was also responsible for the behavior of his dependents, meaning that the English crown could hold him accountable for his children, and the king or queen would not hesitate to restore order should children exhibit deviant behavior. In the eyes of the crown, such behavior indicated that the father had lost control over his children, and the king or queen was obligated to intervene as a surrogate father. This authority became known as *parens patriae*, whereby the monarch became "father of the country" and was authorized to remove children from paternal authority for the greater good of all.[14] Children thus became **wards of the state**, and were theoretically protected by the monarch in his or her capacity as guardian.

The practice of removal under *parens patriae* was usually not as benign or magnanimous as one might assume. Children were often kept in asylums or jails, and removal by the crown could occur if the child exhibited conditions that we would now diagnose as epilepsy, mental illness, or mental retardation. This situation led some parents to confine children with disabilities to their rooms or in cellars and attics—literally bound up and locked in, sometimes through adulthood. Nevertheless, *parens patriae* is still deeply fixed in modern Anglo-American juvenile justice doctrine, and the doctrine continues to empower the state to claim legally mandated parental rights over children under certain circumstances.

The Renaissance Period in England

The European Renaissance dates from the late fourteenth century. During this period, newly emergent perceptions of family and childhood began to develop in England. The father was still deemed to be head of the household, but practices of abandonment and designations of undesirability began to erode. Children could be "bound out" by the father for working arrangements lasting for days or years. This practice eventually led to the development of systems of apprenticeship, whereby children worked for years to learn a trade under the tutelage of a master tradesman. Thus, the treatment of juveniles in England began to reflect the general spread of humanism in Europe.

In London, the **Bridewell Workhouse** was established in 1555 as both a workhouse and poorhouse for disorderly, indebted, or otherwise indolent offenders. Bridewell reflected the predominant rehabilitation philosophy of the time—adult and child offenders should be put to work under severe discipline to teach them good habits. In debtor's prisons and facilities like Bridewell, debtors were imprisoned until they could pay their debts. Under this philosophy, convict labor (both adults and children) was regularly leased out to merchants for profit. Juveniles caught begging or loitering in the streets were also sent to Bridewell to correct their wayward behavior and profit from their labor. The English Parliament approved of the Bridewell concept so much that legislation was passed to build a workhouse/poor-house in every county.

As the Bridewell system grew, Parliament enacted legislation known at the **Poor Laws.** Under these laws, Queen Elizabeth I oversaw the creation of a system whereby indebted adults and poor children were indentured as servants for a period of years as a means to account for their debts. Elizabeth also created a system of overseers who supervised the indenturing of idle and impoverished children for fixed terms of apprenticeship and servitude. These youthful indentured servants worked for well-to-do families until they were 21 years of age or older, with the understanding that their masters would treat them humanely and train them as apprentices. The English state's acceptance of responsibility for juveniles continued to grow over time, so that new laws were passed in 1601 to construct large workhouses with the goal of providing meaningful work for incorrigible and idle juveniles. It should be understood that this system only emphasized the provision of work and trade skills for these children, and not the provision of education.

Toward the Modern Era in England: The Reform Movement

English approaches to juvenile reform during the Enlightenment (the eighteenth to nineteenth centuries) were significantly influenced by the Hospital of Saint Michael in Rome.[15] The Hospital was a correctional institution rather than a venue for medical care. It was built in 1704 by Pope Clement XI, and was among the first correctional institutions dedicated exclusively to reforming incorrigible and otherwise criminal juveniles. The Hospital operated under a congregate silence system, meaning that juvenile inmates labored and dined together in a central hall, but were required to be silent when doing so. Hard work and biblical study in silence were considered to be the keys to reforming juvenile transgressors.

The nineteenth century was a reformist era for juvenile justice in England. Behaviors that we would now define as juvenile delinquency began to be recognized as a separate category of deviant behavior exclusive to juveniles. Youth homes and juvenile courts were established during this era. The London Philanthropic Society, founded in 1817, adopted the philosophy of the Hospital of Saint Michael. The Society was at the forefront of the Reform Movement, which had an important impact on juvenile justice in the United States. It opened the first treatment-focused juvenile facilities in England, known as the **Houses of Refuge**. The House of Refuge model was also incorporated by reformers in nineteenth-century America, who likewise experimented with providing treatment for juveniles as a method of rehabilitation.

Juvenile Justice in America: The Colonial Period Through the Nineteenth Century

Juvenile justice advanced dramatically from early America to the twentieth century. From the beginning, English traditions and laws were adapted to the American context, initially with a strongly religious interpretation of child behavior and correction. Because of intensely disruptive demographic and social restructuring during the Industrial Revolution, reformers of the Enlightenment adopted new treatment-focused precepts about how to deal with wayward youths. It was during the nineteenth century that juvenile justice institutions and philosophies became recognizable as modern responses to the needs of young people.

English Roots During the Colonial Period

English colonists in North America adopted many of the home country's philosophies on criminal justice, corrections, juvenile justice, and familial authority.[16] For example, the concept of *parens patriae* was readily transferred to the colonies. Remedies for the problems of delinquency, incorrigibility, and idleness were quite similar to English remedies of the period. For example, juvenile offenders were often housed in jails and prisons with adults. Colonial communities also adopted the indentured apprenticeship system for idle and impoverished children, as well as England's system of age-based criminal culpability. Thus, colonial children under the age of

7 years could not be convicted of a felony, those between the ages of 7 and 14 years were presumed to not have adult capacity unless proven otherwise, and those older than 14 years of age were tried as adults.

The Puritan Movement. During the colonial period, the Puritan Movement had an important early influence on the development of American juvenile justice. Puritans were followers of a religious reform movement who sought to "purify" the Church of England by promoting strict adherence to the Bible. Members of the movement came to North America in the seventeenth century to establish communities governed by their interpretations of faith. Although these settlements were centered in Tidewater, Virginia, and the Massachusetts Bay Colony, the Puritans had a pronounced effect throughout the English colonies.

Puritans advocated strict obedience to God's authority, and believed that the failure to correct spiritual transgressions in human society would invite the wrath of God against all. In their view, corporal and capital punishments were necessary to assure spiritual salvation. Adult and child transgressors were therefore subjected to severe spiritual "correction." The Puritans gave children special attention, an event that was arguably a significant progression in the history of juvenile justice, despite severe penalties for young transgressors. If anything, the Puritans concluded that parental and community intervention was necessary for the spiritual salvation of young people, albeit through the application of duress.

Puritanical Juvenile Justice. Laws governing colonial family life were firmly paternalistic, with the father given unquestioned authority over the household. Deference was given to the father's authority and wisdom in dealing with matters within his house. The Puritans in particular referenced the Ten Commandments and other biblical authority in their legal codes. Puritanical laws permitted fathers to mete out harsh physical punishments to disobedient wives and children, and early colonial laws imposed the death penalty on disobedient children.[17] A typical Massachusetts law of the time stated:

> If a man have a stubborn or rebellious son of sufficient years of understanding, viz. sixteen, which will not obey the voice of his father or the voice of his mother, and that when they have chastened him will not harken to them, then shall his father and mother, being his natural parents, lay hold on him and bring him to the magistrate assembled in Court, and testify to them by sufficient evidence that this their son is stubborn and rebellious and will not obey their voice and chastisement, but lives in sundry notorious crime. Such a son shall be put to death.[18]

Another law from Puritan Massachusetts explains the consideration of age-based capacity, the typically harsh Puritanical practice of spiritual correction, and attendant circumstances:

If any child, or children, above sixteen years of age, and of sufficient understanding shall CURSE or SMITE their natural FATHER or MOTHER, he or they shall be put to death, unless it can be sufficiently testified that the Parents have been very unchristianly negligent in the education of such children: so provoked them by extreme and cruel correction, that they have been forced thereunto, to reserve themselves from death or maiming.[19]

Massachusetts's **Stubborn Child Law** (1646) was the first official recognition of status offenses in the colonies. An underlying rationale for this law was the presumption that children required stern discipline as a form of spiritual correction. Interestingly, the Stubborn Child Law remained codified and unchanged in Massachusetts for more than three centuries.

Toward the Modern Era in America: The Refuge and Child Savers Period

Background. The colonial period of American juvenile justice lasted from the time of the Puritans' settlements—arguably dating from the Stubborn Child Law—until the philosophies of the Enlightenment and the Reform Movement were accepted during the third decade of the nineteenth century. Several social catalysts were behind the demise of the colonial-influenced system. These included massive European immigration, the Industrial Revolution, and the social restructuring that accompanied these events.[20]

During the later years of the eighteenth century, new industrial working populations began to concentrate in communities around new textile factories. This new mode of production required entire families to move from rural areas to growing urban centers, as the growth of a wage-earning working class began to include the labor of all members of the family—fathers, mothers, and children. Families migrated to large urban areas such as Philadelphia, New York, Boston, and Chicago in search of work. Migrants and new immigrant populations who settled in these urban areas often lived in terrible conditions, so that poverty and disease became endemic. Inevitably, the traditional Anglo-American practice of voluntary and indentured apprenticeship died out as child labor was used extensively in the new factories and mines. The transition from child apprenticeships to a child labor force was a logical (albeit inhumane) progression—children were replaceable, inexpensive, and physically ideal for many jobs on weaving looms and other machinery. Child labor became so pervasive that approximately half of the textile workers were children, working for long hours away from their parents. Children who did not work roamed the streets, often forming gangs, committing crimes, or sometimes simply living idly as vagrants.

Industrialization and migration had a dramatic impact on old family customs and laws governing juveniles. Industrial management's authority supplanted paternal authority over working children, and pervasive poverty

Photo 2.1 Children sit in juvenile court while their cases are reviewed by three female judges, 1945.

among idle children in congested urban settings served to increase the numbers of poor children who took to the streets, beyond parental authority. All of these disruptions created a potential powder keg that had to be addressed by government and the legal system.

Houses of Refuge. Religious and philanthropic reformers concluded that institutions would have to be established to house and correct deviant juveniles. Middle- and upper-class reformers turned private homes into communities of needy children, where education, food, and shelter were provided. Many of these children had been removed from lower-class migrant and immigrant homes that had been deemed "unfit" according to middle- and upper-class standards of the time. These efforts were a precursor to a much broader movement to rescue needy children.

In 1823, New York's Society for the Prevention of Pauperism advocated the creation of "Houses of Refuge" to institutionalize vagrant and criminal juveniles. In the same year, the New York Society for the Reformation of Juvenile Delinquents was founded, and by 1825 the first American House of Refuge opened in New York City.[21] It was intended to house only juveniles who could, in the estimation of the authorities, be saved and reintegrated into society. Typical residents were idle street youths, thieves, and vandals. Youths who committed more serious offenses were incarcerated in jails and prisons. The underlying purposes of the Houses of Refuge were rehabilitation and reform—not punishment. This philosophy continues into the modern era, and so juvenile delinquents and other youthful offenders are never "punished" per se; they are, instead, reformed and rehabilitated as a matter of policy. This idea caught on among reformers in other cities, and Houses of Refuge were established in at least 20 cities by the 1860s.

By modern standards, the Houses of Refuge were hard and authoritarian institutions. Methods of reform and rehabilitation in the nineteenth century included beatings, physical discomfort, verbal abuse, and contracting out child labor to the private sector. Children were punished with solitary confinement, and some Houses were prisonlike. It was considered important to strictly regulate every minute of the residents' days, and typical regimens included mandatory work, education, and prayer. These methods were akin to behavior modification, because reformers at that time considered regimentation, corporal punishment, and other practices to be rehabilitative. For example, contracted child laborers would theoretically learn a trade, and in this sense these Houses stand out as historical precursors to modern trade schools. In retrospect, it is highly questionable whether such stern conditions delivered much if any therapy or rehabilitation. And yet, they reflected the standard of benevolence for that time period.

Houses of Refuge were managed by philanthropic organizations, many with a religious or ethnocentric mission. Accepted methods of reform—as harsh as they were—were considered to be the duty of the state under *parens patriae*. Those who administered the Houses took on the attitude that they would reform children and remedy the failures of their parents. The power to involuntarily commit children to Houses of Refuge under court order was decided in the Pennsylvania case of *Ex parte Crouse* in 1838.[22] In this case, an incorrigible girl's mother had the girl committed to a House of Refuge in Philadelphia. The father sued for her release, but an appeals court decided in favor of the state's power to commit the girl. The court ruled that under *parens patriae,* the state had a duty and an interest to help and reform deviant children. The court summed up the fundamental philosophy of juvenile justice during this era:

> The object of charity is reformation, by training its inmates to industry; by imbuing their minds with principles of morality and religion; by furnishing them with means to earn a living; and above all, by separating them from the corrupting influence of improper associates. To this end, may not the natural parents, when unequal to the task of education, or unworthy of it, be superseded by *parens patriae,* or common guardianship of the community?[23]

The Child-Saving Movement. Another reform movement arose in the United States during the middle of the nineteenth century, known as the **child savers.**[24] It promoted a more experimental and progressive approach to juvenile justice than the Houses of Refuge model.[25] The fundamental philosophy of the child savers was that environmental conditions can have a deleterious effect on children—bad environments produce bad children.[26] In order to rescue these children, it was deemed absolutely necessary to remove them from these bad environments. Child savers also believed that criminal prosecution and incarceration of juveniles were morally repugnant and socially disgraceful. Rather than being jailed, juveniles should be sent to institutions dedicated to reforming and rehabilitating wayward youths. This approach mandated that the state and society reconsider how juvenile delinquents should be treated, and accept the responsibility of "saving" at-risk young people. Thus, the Child-Saving Movement promoted several concepts:

- Children should not be treated the same as adult offenders.
- Each individual child should be treated as a unique individual with unique needs.
- Juvenile justice process should be less onerous than adult criminal process.

One example of the child savers' philosophy put into practice was the creation of reformatories—better known as **reform schools**—which were conceptually different from the Houses of Refuge. Reform schools softened the severity of the Houses and sought to create a homelike environment for residents with an emphasis on education. A conceptual shift moved juvenile justice doctrine toward nurturing and protecting predelinquent juveniles. Hard work and strict discipline were coupled with education and security to reorient at-risk youths. Chicago was a center for the Child-Saving Movement, led by the Chicago Children's Aid Society. The Chicago Reform School was a prototypical model for these institutions, and was instrumental in promoting a national shift away from corrections and toward homelike rehabilitation. During the later decades of the nineteenth century, many Houses of Refuge were replaced by reform schools, and reform schools became established in all states by the end of the nineteenth century. They were located in both urban and rural areas, and some began to label themselves "training" and "industrial" schools.

Juvenile Justice in America: The Twentieth Century

The reforms of the nineteenth century culminated in what can be best described as the *juvenile court period* of juvenile justice. Juvenile courts were a manifestation of a broader reformist period known as the Progressive Era, which existed from the late nineteenth century through the first two decades of the twentieth century.[27] The transition to a separate judicial system was

Photo 2.2   Convicts attending classes at a prison for juveniles in the United Kingdom during the 1920s.

gradual, beginning during the later years of the nineteenth century. At the conclusion of this transition, the philosophy and institutions that were created radically transformed juvenile justice process. Government, the courts, and private institutions all became integral participants in an ever-expanding juvenile justice system. As a result, the reforms of the late nineteenth and early twentieth centuries established standards and institutions that continued well into the modern era.

A New Philosophy: The Progressive Era

The Progressives were government reformers and private philanthropists who were active around the early twentieth century. They were members of educated elites and privileged classes who sought to alleviate the hardships of poverty and industrial exploitation. Examples of Progressive Era reforms include:

- Social work systems
- Conservation
- Federal government activism and regulation in the private sector
- Establishment of the first juvenile courts
- Diversion of children out of formal criminal proceedings

Progressives believed that children are not inherently evil or antisocial. Instead, delinquent children are the product of their environments—meaning that poverty, dysfunctional families, and abnormal cultural values are responsible for youthful transgressions. Because of these factors, juveniles should receive treatment for their behavior, and children suffering from toxic environmental inputs should be considered *dysfunctional* rather than *criminal*. Youth-focused social service agencies were created and professional social workers were trained to reform troubled youths. Many Progressive reforms have had a long-term impact on juvenile justice administration.

It must be noted that the Progressive Movement's sense of *noblesse oblige* was not entirely selfless. Progressives certainly volunteered the good services of their social standing and wealth, but they also understood that failure to alleviate hardship among the poor and working classes could lead to social upheaval and outright rebellion. Thus, reforms were advocated in part to preserve the power base of the elites, protect their privileges, and maintain racial segregation.[28]

A New System: Juvenile Courts

Progress toward separation of juvenile and criminal court proceedings began in the final decades of the nineteenth century. In 1874, Massachusetts passed legislation requiring separate court hearings for juveniles, known as **children's tribunals**. In 1877, New York passed similar legislation, and mandated the separation of adult and juvenile offenders. In 1898, Rhode Island passed a juvenile court law. In 1899, Colorado passed the first legislation in the nation to establish guidelines for trying truant "juvenile disorderly persons," known as the Compulsory School Act. Although none of these efforts created true juvenile court systems, as we know them today, the laws were certainly forerunners of modern juvenile court systems.

The First Juvenile Court. In July 1899, the **Illinois Juvenile Court Act** was passed. The bill, officially entitled the Act to Regulate the Treatment and Control of Dependent, Neglected and Delinquent Children, was the first comprehensive and modern juvenile justice statute. The act codified several then-radical doctrines, namely the following:

- Youths under the age of 16 who engaged in certain deviant behaviors should be classified as "juvenile delinquents."
- Special rules of procedure should govern the adjudication of cases heard before juvenile courts.

- Child and adult offenders should be separated.
- Children are victims of their environments and should be reformed and rehabilitated.

The first juvenile court system was established to make these doctrines operational.[29] It was a new model and a new system, completely disconnected from the adult criminal justice system. Cases falling under its jurisdiction included all delinquency, dependency, and child-neglect cases. The formality of proceedings was minimized, and separate facilities were established for youths and adults in the justice system. Significantly, the final shift toward juvenile reform and rehabilitation, begun in the nineteenth century, was completed. Youths who were processed through the juvenile court were to be treated rather than punished, with the objective of disengaging the effects of their previously toxic environments. Henceforth, courts would act as advocates on behalf of juvenile offenders and would base their decisions on a determination of what serves the "best interests of the child." Separate procedures, records, personnel, and institutions became the norm. A fundamental tenet of the juvenile court period was to eliminate stigma from the administration of juvenile justice. Rather than label juveniles as criminal offenders being processed through criminal justice systems, a new terminology was written for juvenile proceedings.

The Progressive Era waned during the 1920s and ended by the time of the Great Depression. Nevertheless, Progressive theories about juvenile treatment and the institutionalization of juvenile courts had received national acceptance on the eve of the Great Depression. By 1925, 46 states had established juvenile court systems.

Juvenile Justice From the Great Depression to the Great Society

As state-level reform culminated in nationwide acceptance of juvenile courts, the federal government actively encouraged the formulation of a national juvenile justice agenda. In 1925, the federal Children's Bureau and the National Probation Association proposed the adoption of *A Standard Juvenile Court Act*. During the Great Depression (dating from the 1929 Black Thursday Stock Market Crash),[30] President Franklin D. Roosevelt reformed national government policy to alleviate the massive civil and economic dislocation brought on by the collapse of the stock market. Known as the New Deal, Roosevelt's programs were distinguished by massive federal government intervention and coordination at the state and local levels. The New Deal influenced national policy through the postwar era.

During the New Deal, jurists and the federal government embarked on a national effort to address the problem of at-risk juveniles. For example, in 1936 the Children's Bureau oversaw the first national disbursement of child welfare grants to the states for at-risk juveniles. In 1937, a body of juvenile court judges organized the National Council of Juvenile and Family Court Judges. In 1938, Congress passed the Juvenile Court Act, which essentially promoted national adoption of many concepts of juvenile justice administration that had been originally enacted under the Illinois Juvenile Court Act of 1899. Rehabilitation and treatment of juveniles had become pervasive as a matter of policy. There also developed a generalized and final acceptance of several classes of at-risk children, each requiring different modalities of treatment:

- *Juvenile delinquents.* Persons under the age of majority who commit offenses that would be classified as crimes in the adult criminal justice system. As delinquents, these offenders are processed through the juvenile justice system.
- *Status offenders.* Offenders who violate laws that regulate the behavior of persons under the age of majority. These laws do not apply to adults.
- *Abused children.* Child victims of emotional, sexual, or physical mistreatment. These are victims of proactive assaults or exploitation by an abuser.
- *Neglected children.* Child victims who do not receive proper care from parents or other guardians. Neglected children include those who are unfed, poorly sheltered, left alone, not cleaned, or otherwise maltreated.
- *Dependent children.* Children who are abandoned by parents or guardians, or otherwise uncared for.
- *Incorrigibles.* Youths whose behavior is not controlled, or cannot be controlled, by an authority figure. These are children who are in chronic conflict with authority.

The commitment for developing a national consensus on juvenile treatment continued after the end of the Great Depression through the years of the Second World War and the postwar era. During the 1940s, state and national conferences were held on juvenile issues. Legislation during the 1950s institutionalized the youth treatment model at the federal level. For example, the Federal Youth Corrections Act of 1951 established the Juvenile Delinquency Bureau in the Department of Health, Education, and Welfare. The Youth Counsel Bureau in New York City was typical of a growing consensus during the 1950s that the juvenile justice system should allow some at-risk youths to be diverted out of the court system. The Youth Counsel Bureau formally diverted noncritical offenders into a counseling system after referral from parents, schools, courts, or the police.

The New Era of Juvenile Rights: Juvenile Justice During the Great Society

The decade of the 1960s was a period of great social and cultural transition in the United States.[31] Culturally, the end of officially sanctioned racial segregation and discrimination, constitutional protection for civil rights, new liberty for women, the Cold War, and political and social strife defined the times. Politically, federal policy mandated the national coordination of sweeping domestic and foreign agendas. During the presidency of Lyndon B. Johnson, from 1963 to 1968, the federal government provided massive expenditures for domestic social reform programs while at the same time waging an ever-escalating war in Vietnam. This dual policy of domestic restructuring and international interventionism by the Johnson administration was called the Great Society.[32]

During this period, the American family changed as mothers entered the workforce, the divorce rate increased, and greater numbers of children were raised in single-parent households. The previous profile of delinquents as urban youths from the lower and working classes was revised during the 1960s, as increasing numbers of suburban and rural youths from the middle and upper classes became delinquent offenders. The Great Society responded with national family and youth initiatives, as well as a vast "War on Poverty." Federal funds were directed to programs that sought to disconnect the deleterious linkage between poverty, crime, and delinquency, particularly in the urban core. With urban racial tensions at an unprecedented high— approximately 125 race riots occurred in 1968 alone after the assassination of Dr. Martin Luther King, Jr.—federal initiatives also sought answers to the special problems of nonwhite urban youths.

The concept of *juvenile rights* became a central tenet of juvenile justice initiatives during the 1960s, so that the Great Society can be considered a time of unprecedented protection of juvenile constitutional rights. Several seminal court cases, laws, and agencies redefined the purpose of the juvenile justice system. At the heart of these initiatives was the recognition that juveniles are entitled to constitutional due-process protections.

Kent v. United States. In 1966, the United States Supreme Court began an era of national judicial involvement in juvenile justice from the highest level of the court system. In *Kent v. United States*,[33] the Supreme Court rendered a decision that inaugurated a line of decisions on juvenile due process, *parens patriae,* and constitutional requirements for court processes involving juveniles.

Morris Kent, Jr., was a teenager arrested for a September 1961 break-in, burglary, and rape in Washington, DC. Kent, who was 16 at the time, had a police record because of suspicion in 1959 that he was responsible for a series of burglaries and an attempted purse snatching. Under Washington, DC, law, Kent's case fell under the exclusive jurisdiction of the juvenile court. During interrogation, he confessed to the charges and discussed other similar incidents. After his admission, his mother retained legal counsel, and a psychiatric examination found him to suffer from severe psychopathology. The juvenile court judge held that Kent's case should be transferred to the jurisdiction of an adult criminal court. The juvenile judge made this decision without a hearing, and without consulting with Kent, his attorney, or his parents. The U.S. District Court for the District of Columbia found him guilty of six counts of burglary and robbery, and sentenced him to 5 to 15 years in prison for each count. In their appeal, which eventually reached the Supreme Court, Kent's attorneys argued that a sufficient hearing should have been held before the juvenile court, and that absent such a hearing, it was unfair to transfer Kent's case to an adult criminal court.

The Supreme Court reversed the district court's decision, holding that in cases such as Kent's an adequate hearing must be convened at the juvenile court level prior to transfer to criminal court. In addition to a hearing, juveniles have a right to counsel, and their lawyers must have access to social records, probation records, or other reports that may be considered by the court. The Supreme Court also held that juveniles and their counsel are entitled to statements of reasons for the juvenile court's decision. The Supreme Court mandated in an appendix that states consider the following factors prior to transferring juveniles to adult criminal court:

- Whether the offense was committed against persons or property, with greater weight given to offenses against persons, especially if a victim was injured
- Whether the offense was perpetrated aggressively, violently, with premeditation, or willfully
- Whether transfer is required in light of the egregiousness of the offense and the need to protect the community
- Consideration of the juvenile's maturity and sophistication, as determined by his or her home, environment, and emotional development
- Consideration of the juvenile's history and prior record
- Consideration of whether an offense should be tried and disposed in a single court, when the juvenile's co-suspects are adults who will be brought to trial in an adult criminal court
- Consideration of the merit of the complaint

Kent firmly required states to provide at least minimal due-process protections in their juvenile court proceedings. However, the impact of *Kent* was limited to its specific context. The following year, these protections were significantly reinforced and broadened by the Supreme Court.

In re Gault. In 1967, the Supreme Court rendered a decision that mandated sweeping due-process requirements for state juvenile court proceedings. This decision, in *In re Gault*,[34] guaranteed many of the same procedural rights for juveniles as held by adults.

Gerald Gault, 15, was taken into custody with a friend in Arizona when a neighbor complained that the boys had made an obscene phone call. Gault was on probation at the time. The authorities made no attempt to notify Gault's parents about his detention, and it was not until that evening that his mother arrived at the detention center and was informed about his charges and that a preliminary hearing would occur the next day in the judge's chambers. At this first hearing, no specific charges were made (other than a general charge of "delinquency"), the parents were not given details about the nature of the charges, Gault was unrepresented by counsel, and the complainant was neither present nor identified. In his statement, Gault admitted dialing the number, but said that his friend had made the remarks. After being held for two days, Gault was released and returned for a second hearing four days later. During the second hearing, there was no sworn testimony, no representation by counsel, no transcript, and the complainant was not present. Gault's mother requested that the complainant should be present to make out the voice of the obscene caller. The juvenile judge rejected her request, Gault was adjudicated delinquent, and he was ordered to the State Industrial School until the age of 21. Had he been an adult, he would have received a fine or two months in jail rather than six years' incarceration. Gault's attorney argued on appeal that the teenager's constitutional rights had been violated because he had been deprived of due process.

The Supreme Court reversed the juvenile court's decision, holding that juveniles have certain constitutional due-process rights that must be protected by state juvenile justice systems. Henceforth, states must protect the following due-process rights for juveniles:

- Right to representation by counsel
- Right to confront and cross-examine complainants and witnesses
- Right to protection against self-incrimination
- Right to notice of charges brought by the authorities

In re Gault had an unprecedented and incomparable impact on the juvenile justice system. Its mandate is unequivocal: States are required to protect the constitutional rights of juveniles brought before juvenile courts. In this regard, the case is arguably the most important decision on juvenile rights ever rendered by the U.S. Supreme Court.

Great Society Legislation. In 1968, Congress passed the Juvenile Delinquency Prevention and Control Act to create an ongoing, nationally coordinated effort to reduce the incidence of juvenile delinquency. The act, which was in effect until passage of the 1974 Juvenile Justice and Delinquency Prevention Act, required the U.S. Department of Health, Education, and Welfare (HEW) to develop and coordinate a comprehensive strategy for reducing juvenile delinquency. Under this law, states were to receive federal funds for the implementation of state delinquency prevention, juvenile rehabilitation, research, and training programs. HEW's Delinquency Prevention Administration eventually coordinated a broad effort to create national standards for delinquency prevention.

Also in 1968, Congress enacted the Omnibus Crime Control and Safe Streets Act to earmark federal monies and technical assistance for state and local programs to modernize their justice systems. This program, along with HEW's program, and the Model Cities program of the Department of Housing and Urban Development, led to the creation of **Youth Service Bureaus**. The Youth Service Bureaus had been recommended in 1967 by a presidential commission report entitled *The Challenge of Crime in a Free Society,* and were intended to be a primary center for dealing with juvenile delinquents and status offenders. Youth Service Bureaus were to coordinate their activities with juvenile courts, the police, and probation agencies. Most bureaus were eventually closed during budget cuts under presidents Jimmy Carter and Ronald Reagan.

These laws and programs, coupled with Supreme Court support for juvenile justice reform, signified the fundamental restructuring of juvenile justice process during this period in the United States.

Strengthening Juvenile Rights: Juvenile Justice During the 1970s

The 1960s ended with unabated momentum for the expansion of juvenile rights. Federal initiatives and the Supreme Court continued to press for greater national standards and coordination of juvenile justice process. This effort led to increased research on the effectiveness of contemporary theories and institutions used for juvenile treatment and rehabilitation. The 1970s were a time of greater due-process protections for juveniles, coupled with greater emphasis on "net widening," or expansion of alternatives to the institutionalization of juveniles.

The Juvenile Justice and Delinquency Prevention Act (JJDP). The JJDP, passed by Congress in 1974, replaced the Juvenile Delinquency Prevention and Control Act of 1968. The bill, which received overwhelming support in the House and Senate, tied federal funding to state restrictions on the detention and institutionalization of juvenile delinquents. Discretionary block grants were released to assist in alternative dispositions of juvenile offenders. This legislation also created the Office of Juvenile Justice and Delinquency Prevention (OJJDP) within the U.S. Department of Justice. The ultimate goal was to implement the concept that incarceration would be done only as means of last resort. Thus, the JJDP has become a key catalyst for the deinstitutionalization of juvenile offenders and the separation of juvenile offenders from adult offenders.

The policy impacts of the JJDP were that the number of incarcerated juveniles declined markedly, and community-based programs were greatly expanded. Significantly, juveniles were removed or separated from facilities where adults were housed. Although the JJDP was amended during the 1990s to permit highly restrictive detentions of juvenile offenders, its underlying impact has been to widen the net of the juvenile justice system.

The "Four Ds." The juvenile rights era can be summarized by classifying its principal features as deinstitutionalization, diversion, due process, and decriminalization—termed the *Four Ds*.[35] Although the Four Ds were scaled back during the general crackdown on crime during the 1980s and 1990s, these features continue to be important reference markers for juvenile justice policy. These concepts are summarized as follows, and are explored further in Chapter 10:

- Deinstitutionalization: A preference for using community-based programs to treat juvenile offenders
- Diversion: The process of moving juveniles out of the juvenile court and detention systems and into community-based alternatives
- Due Process: Recognition and protection of juvenile constitutional rights when brought before the juvenile justice system
- Decriminalization: The process of creating standards to recategorize some juvenile offenses as a way to deemphasize the criminalization of juvenile transgressions

In re Winship. In 1970, the Supreme Court held that juveniles accused of delinquent offenses are entitled to a strict standard of proof before they can be adjudicated delinquent. The case was *In re Winship*.[36] Samuel Winship was a 12-year-old boy who was adjudicated delinquent in New York Family Court for stealing $112 from a purse in a locker. The standard of proof used in the adjudication was "preponderance of the evidence," which is the same standard used in civil cases. The court acknowledged that the burden was not met for the much stricter standard of proof "beyond a reasonable doubt," but this standard was not required under New York law. Winship was remanded to a training school for 18 months, with possible extensions until he was 18 years old. This potential 6-year sentence was challenged on appeal, under the argument that the preponderance of the evidence standard was unconstitutional.

The Supreme Court's holding was that juveniles accused of crimes should be accorded the same standard of proof as adults, that is, proof beyond a reasonable doubt. The policy outcome has been that juvenile delinquents are adjudicated under the standard of proof beyond a reasonable doubt, and status offenders can be adjudicated using the lesser standard of proof. In practice, many jurisdictions use the stricter standard for all juvenile proceedings.

McKeiver v. Pennsylvania. Although juveniles received many of the same due-process rights enjoyed by adults during the juvenile rights period, not all of these rights were mandated for juvenile proceedings. For example, there is no right to trial by jury, an issue that was decided in 1971 by the Supreme Court in *McKeiver v. Pennsylvania*.[37]

Joseph McKeiver, 16, was charged with the felony offenses of larceny, receiving stolen goods, and robbery. His case was heard before a juvenile court judge; he was adjudicated delinquent and remanded to a juvenile development center. McKeiver's attorney had requested a jury trial, which was denied. On appeal, the Supreme Court held that trial by jury is not constitutionally mandated in juvenile adjudications. The significance of this case is that juvenile courts may proceed without giving recognition to every due-process consideration. In essence, juvenile delinquency proceedings are not constitutionally akin to adult criminal proceedings.

Breed v. Jones. After *McKeiver*, the Supreme Court considered whether double jeopardy attaches for juvenile adjudications. Double jeopardy refers to the prohibition against a second prosecution for the same offense—to be twice put in jeopardy.[38] This issue as it pertains to juveniles was decided in 1975 in *Breed v. Jones*.[39]

Jones, 17, was adjudicated delinquent in a California juvenile court for robbery with a deadly weapon. At his dispositional hearing (comparable to a sentencing hearing in adult criminal court), the court determined that Jones could not be treated by facilities in the juvenile justice system; his case was transferred to criminal court, where he was prosecuted and found guilty. Jones's counsel argued on appeal that he had been twice put in jeopardy for the same offense in violation of the U.S. Constitution. The Supreme Court agreed, holding that his adjudication in juvenile court and subsequent prosecution was indeed double jeopardy.

One policy outcome of *Breed v. Jones* was that states began to enact legislation making it easier to transfer juveniles to criminal court after minimal process before a juvenile court. This policy became a common feature for the administration of justice during the 1980s, when the juvenile and criminal justice systems shifted toward stricter treatment of both juvenile and adult offenders.

Table 2.1 summarizes important juvenile rights cases decided from the reform era to the modern era.

_____ Juvenile Justice in America: The Modern Era

During the late 1970s, a cultural and political reexamination of the administration of justice occurred. Crime rates had increased, recidivism was widespread, and juvenile violence seemed to be increasing in frequency and ferocity. The public perception was that the criminals were "winning," and that they had been granted too many rights. As the 1980s began, and the conservative administration of President Ronald Reagan came to power, a major crackdown on crime began that has lasted into the new millennium. Law and order, and the welfare of victims and society, supplanted public concern for the welfare of offenders. The modern era of juvenile justice came to reflect this growing cultural and political intolerance for criminal behavior.

TABLE 2.1 IMPORTANT JUVENILE RIGHTS CASES

Juvenile rights was an unknown concept for most of human history. With the advent of the Reform Movement, the Progressives, and the Great Society, juvenile rights became deeply ingrained in juvenile justice doctrine. In the United States, court decisions have played a prominent role in the promotion of juvenile rights.

This table summarizes the historical importance of several juvenile rights cases.

Case	Year	Holding	Policy Outcome
Ex parte Crouse	1838	Enforcement of *parens patriae* is constitutionally recognized.	State intervention as guardian became common practice.
Kent v. United States	1966	Adequate hearings are required in juvenile court prior to transference to adult court.	Due process applied to narrow legal question.
In re Gault	1967	Juveniles have broad due-process rights.	Sweeping protections created for juvenile offenders.
In re Winship	1970	High burden of proof is required for juvenile offenders.	Proof beyond a reasonable doubt adopted in states.
McKeiver v. Pennsylvania	1971	Juveniles have no right to jury in juvenile court.	Placed restrictions on juvenile due-process protections.
Breed v. Jones	1975	Jeopardy attaches in juvenile court.	Juveniles have protection from double jeopardy.
Shall v. Martin	1984	Preventive detention can be used for juveniles.	Constitutional detention standards are established.

Juvenile court proceedings became more formal and adversarial during this period. As adult criminal courts adopted the punitive sentencing philosophies of just deserts, retribution, and deterrence, juvenile courts likewise dealt more harshly with violent, unrepentant, and chronically deviant juveniles. Juvenile correctional institutions became more restrictive, emulating adult institutions by categorizing facilities according to their level of security, such as *maximum*, *medium*, and *strict*. Some secure juvenile training facilities were moved into the countryside away from community-based reform programs, thus returning in many cases to the philosophy of removing juvenile offenders from society.

Transfers of juveniles to adult criminal court increased, as did the ease of these transfers. Juveniles considered to be a threat to society became subject to preventive detentions pending adjudication, just as adults could be detained pending trial. In *Schall v. Martin*,[40] decided in 1984, the Supreme Court upheld the constitutionality of preventive detention by juvenile authorities. It held that juveniles can be detained without violating their due-process rights if they pose a high risk of further delinquency. *Schall* additionally set due-process standards for detention hearings, requiring that notice, opportunity to be heard, and a factual statement be given to offenders prior to preventive detention. Also during this period, standards for juvenile court jurisdiction were modeled differently among the states but were categorized as follows:

- Exclusive jurisdiction: The juvenile court is the only venue that can hear juvenile cases for certain offenses.
- Original jurisdiction: Certain juvenile offenses must originate in the juvenile system, but they can be waived to the criminal justice system.
- Concurrent jurisdiction: Several courts have authority to hear certain offenses.
- No jurisdiction: State law mandates that juvenile offenders of a certain age will automatically be transferred to adult criminal court for trial on certain offenses, such as first-degree murder.

In the modern era, the juvenile justice system exists in all states, as mandated under state statutes. National initiatives and agencies (such as Justice's OJJDP) coordinate juvenile justice policy. The police, courts, and correctional systems have all become partners with a wider net of private, non-profit, and public juvenile service agencies. Thus, the modern juvenile justice system has become an integral part of the broader justice system, and its administration has become the responsibility of an ever-widening net of governments, agencies, and programs.

Chapter Summary

From the time of ancient civilizations, the question of how to deal with children in trouble and children in need has been addressed in accordance with the cultural norms of the time. Definitions of acceptable childhood behavior have varied widely throughout history: From the days when amputation was prescribed for disobedient sons in Babylon; to harsh *parens patriae* in medieval England; to capital punishment for incorrigible children in the Puritan settlements; to the codification of juvenile rights in the modern United States.

Table 2.2 summarizes the historical perspectives on juvenile justice developed in this chapter.

During the first half of the twentieth century, the United States began to systematically address youth problems and juvenile delinquency. Modern social sciences developed new theories about the causes of juvenile delinquency, and government intervention expanded at the state and federal levels. This intervention reflected the cultural values of the times. Juvenile courts were established, and reformers' ideologies became part of the juvenile justice system. At the federal level, Progressive Era reformers and New Deal bureaucrats established social welfare programs that influenced policy for the remainder of the century.

TABLE 2.2   HISTORICAL PERSPECTIVES ON JUVENILE JUSTICE

Every period in recorded human history has applied its own laws and customs for the control of children and correcting deviant juvenile behavior. Interpretations of deviance have reflected the idiosyncrasies of each society. It must be remembered that opinions on control and correction must take into account the cultural contexts of these societies.

This table summarizes the juvenile justice environments, types of juvenile justice institutions, and underlying philosophies of several time periods.

Time Period	Juvenile Justice Environment	Important Events	Juvenile Justice Institutions	Underlying Philosophy
Early history	Absolutist paternalism	1. Code of Hammurabi 2. Twelve Tables; Code of Justinian	Paternalistic family authority	*Lex talionis*, obedience to the father
Old England	*Parens patriae*	1. Monarchist intervention 2. Reform Movement	State intervention, homes, agencies	Reform and rehabilitation
Colonial America	Puritanical paternalism	Stubborn Child Law	Paternalistic family, societal sanctions	Obedience to the parents, spiritual correction
19th-century America	Reformist activism	1. Child-Saving Movement 2. Illinois Juvenile Court Act	Homes, agencies, courts	Reform and rehabilitation
20th-century America	Reformist activism, legislation, cases	1. Progressive legislation 2. Juvenile rights cases	Homes, agencies, courts	Reform and rehabilitation
Modern America	Net widening, just deserts	1. Broad interventionist system 2. Crackdown on juvenile crime	Homes, agencies, courts	Reform, rehabilitation, and just deserts

During the second half of the twentieth century, Great Society reforms mandated uniform standards of juvenile justice coordination. Seminal Supreme Court cases forever changed the nature of juvenile justice process in the United States. The general emphasis on delinquency prevention was a hallmark of the era, and it reflected the recognition that delinquency spanned all classes and regions. Deinstitutionalization, diversion, due process, and decriminalization became the underlying philosophies of the era. This emphasis on the Four Ds abated somewhat in the modern era, as American society struggled to cope with rising criminality, recidivism, and juvenile delinquency. The entire justice system reacted to growing cultural intolerance for criminality by treating youthful and adult offenders more severely. Juvenile courts gradually became more formal and adversarial.

Chapter 3 reviews theories of causation. These theories seek to explain why individuals engage in delinquent and criminal deviance.

Questions for Review

1. What are the principal historical periods for what we now call juvenile justice?

2. What were the different approaches to the status of youths during different eras?

3. How were juveniles treated during the various historical periods?

4. What was the role of government during the eras?

5. What were the role and status of parents during past eras?

6. In what ways were the various approaches justified by different societies?

7. Why did the concept of juvenile justice arise in the relatively recent past?

Key Terms and Concepts

The following topics were discussed in this chapter and are found in the Glossary:

Abused Children	Common Law
Breed v. Jones	Dependent Children
Bridewell Workhouse	*Ex parte Crouse*
Children's Tribunals	Four Ds, The
Child-Saving Movement	Houses of Refuge
Code of Hammurabi	Illinois Juvenile Court Act
Code of Justinian	Incorrigibles

In re Gault

In re Winship

Juvenile Delinquency
Prevention and Control
Act of 1968

Juvenile Delinquents

Juvenile Justice and Delinquency
Prevention Act of 1974

Kent v. United States

Lex Talionis

McKeiver v. Pennsylvania

Neglected Children

Paterna Pietas

Patria Potestas

Poor Laws

Reform Schools

Schall v. Martin

Status Offenders

Stubborn Child Law

Twelve Tables, The

Ward of the State

Youth Service Bureaus

DISCUSSION BOX

Idealism and the Child-Saving Movement

This chapter's Discussion Box is intended to stimulate critical discussion about the Child-Saving Movement and its impact on juvenile justice philosophy and process.

Anglo-American philosophy toward juvenile justice developed a distinctly innovative approach toward juvenile reform and rehabilitation. This unique approach began in ancient and medieval England, progressed through doctrines developed under *parens patriae* (in England) and the Puritans (in America), and culminated in reform movements on both sides of the Atlantic.

In the United States, reformers in the 1800s accepted the societal responsibility for controlling and "rescuing" urban youths. As industrial workers and immigrants settled in urban areas, the child savers believed that only benevolent intervention could save poor and working-class juveniles. Organizations were formed to supervise at-risk children, direct them to trade and labor programs, and promote moral and physical health. Child savers were mostly idealistic philanthropists and activists drawn from the privileged classes who committed their resources out of a sense of *noblesse oblige*. Public and private facilities were dedicated to rescuing at-risk youths, eventually leading to the establishment of Houses of Refuge and reform schools during the nineteenth century. Child labor was regularly bound out to the private sector, and conditions in these facilities were often harsh by modern standards.

Philosophies and programs introduced by the Child-Saving Movement in the United States, England, and Scotland influenced the course of juvenile justice into the new millennium.

Discussion Questions

1. In retrospect, nineteenth-century philosophies of juvenile reform were inconsistent with modern sociological and psychological theory. What effect do you think the child savers had on children processed through their facilities?

2. Does the child-saving philosophy make sense? Was it a wise approach to treating at-risk children? Or were the child savers naïve?

3. Were the child savers truly benevolent and selfless? What other societal factors may have motivated them?

4. Assume the reform movement did not occur in England and the United States. What do you think would have happened if the child-saving philosophy had been rejected?

5. Should a modern version of the Child-Saving Movement be advocated? How should it be updated in theory and programs?

Recommended Web Sites

The following Web sites provide general discussions and contextual/historical overviews of juvenile justice.

American Bar Association Juvenile Justice Center: http://www.abanet.org/crimjust/juvjus/
Building Blocks for Youth: http://www.buildingblocksforyouth.org/
Children's Advocacy Institute: http://www.caichildlaw.org
Juvenile Justice FYI: http://www.juvenilejusticefyi.com/

Note: The Web site URLs and exercises below are also from the book's study site: http://www.sagepub.com/martin

Web Exercise

Using this chapter's recommended Internet sites, conduct an online investigation of contextual/historical discussions of juvenile justice.

- What commonalities and differences in perspective do these groups advocate?
- Is there anything that strikes you as being particularly similar to historical approaches to juvenile justice process?
- Are any of the policies advocated by these groups pioneering in their approaches?

For an online search of the history and context of juvenile justice process, students should use a search engine and enter the following keywords:

"History of Juvenile Justice"

"Juvenile Justice Organizations"

Recommended Readings

The following publications provide discussions on the history of juvenile justice process and criminal justice administration.

Binder, A., Geis, G., & Dickson, D. B. (1988). *Juvenile delinquency: Historical, cultural, legal perspectives.* New York: MacMillan.

Friedman, L. M. (1973). *A history of American law.* New York: Simon and Schuster.

Platt, A. M. (1991). *The child savers: The invention of delinquency* (2nd ed.). Chicago: University of Chicago Press.

Sanders, W. B. (Ed.). (1970). *Juvenile offenders for a thousand years.* Chapel Hill, NC: University of North Carolina Press.

Shelden, R. G. (2001). *Controlling the dangerous classes: A critical introduction to the history of criminal justice.* Boston: Allyn & Bacon.

Notes

1. See A.M. v. Jerry Butler, 360 F.3d 787 (7th Cir. 2004).

2. A command by the court to the state to produce a prisoner and show cause why he or she should be detained.

3. See Miranda v. Arizona, 384 U.S. 436, 16 L. Ed. 2d 694, 86 S. Ct. 1602 (1966).

4. See Garland, D. (1990). *Punishment and modern society: A study in social theory.* Chicago: University of Chicago Press.

5. See King, L. W. (1910–1911). The Code of Hammurabi. With commentary from Charles F. Horne, Ph.D. (1915) and Rev. Claude Hermann Walter Johns, M.A., Litt.D. Encyclopaedia Britannica (11th ed). Chicago: Encyclopaedia Britannica.

6. Mays, L. G., &. Winfree, T., Jr. (2000). *Juvenile justice* (p. 32). Boston: McGraw-Hill.

7. See Watson, A. (1970). *The laws of ancient Romans.* Dallas, TX: Southern Methodist University Press.

8. Law I (The *Patria Potestas*), Table IV, Concerning the rights of a father, and of marriage, Roman codes, Twelve Tables, 5th century B.C.E. In L. G. Mays & T. Winfree, Jr. (2000). *Juvenile justice.* Boston: McGraw-Hill.

9. For a layperson's introduction to the Talmud, see Cohen, A., & Neusner, J. (1995). *Everyman's Talmud: The major teachings of the Rabbinic sages.* New York: Schocken Books.

10. Hobbes, T., & Macpherson, C. B. (Eds.). (1982). *Leviathan.* New York: Penguin Classics. Commenting on the state of nature, Hobbes described life as

follows: "No arts; no letters; no society; and which is worst of all, continual fear, and danger of violent death; and the life of man, solitary, poor, nasty, brutish, and short."

11. A history of England during the height of its feudal period is found in Barlow, F. (1999). *The feudal kingdom of England, 1042–1216*. New York: Longman.

12. A good historical account of juvenile justice is found in Sanders, W. B. (Ed.). (1970). *Juvenile offenders for a thousand years*. Chapel Hill, NC: University of North Carolina Press.

13. Common law was judge-made law, and based on case precedent. It still represents a significant body of law in Anglo-American legal systems.

14. See Rendleman, D. R. (1979). *Parens patriae*: From chancery to the juvenile court. In F. L. Faust & P. J. Branington (Eds.). *Juvenile justice philosophy*. St Paul, MN: West Publishing.

15. Also known as the Hospice of San Michele.

16. Friedman, L. M. (1973). *A history of American law* (pp. 27–90). New York: Simon and Schuster.

17. Biblical authority was cited for this practice, for example at Deuteronomy 21:18–21.

18. Springer, C. E. (1987). *Justice for juveniles* (2nd ed., p. 50). Washington, DC: Office of Juvenile Justice and Delinquency Prevention.

19. From *The book of general lawes and libertyes concerning the inhabitants of Massachusetts*. In L. G. Mays & T. Winfree, Jr. (2000). *Juvenile justice*. Boston: McGraw-Hill.

20. A good discussion of the socioeconomic impact of the industrial revolution may be found in Hobsbawm, E. (1996). *The age of revolution: 1789–1848*. New York: Random House.

21. For a period account of the New York House of Refuge, first published in 1869, see Peirce, B. K. (1969). *Half century with juvenile delinquents: Or the New York House of Refuge and its times*. Glen Ridge, NJ: Patterson Smith.

22. Ex parte Crouse, 4 Whart. 9 (Pa. 1838).

23. Ibid.

24. The Child-Saving Movement also arose in England and Scotland during the mid-nineteenth century.

25. For a history of the Child-Saving Movement, see Platt, A. M. (1991). *The child savers: The invention of delinquency* (2nd ed.). Chicago: The University of Chicago Press.

26. See Platt, A. (2003). The rise of the Child-Saving Movement: A study in social policy and correctional reform. In T. C. Calhoun & C. L. Chapple (Eds.). *Readings in juvenile delinquency and juvenile justice*. Upper Saddle River, NJ: Prentice Hall.

27. For more information about the Progressive Era, see Gould, L. L. (2000). *America in the Progressive Era: 1890–1914*. Boston: Allyn and Bacon.

28. For a discussion of social tension during this era, see Fink, L. (Ed.). (2001). *Major problems in the Gilded Age and the Progressive Era: Documents and essays* (2nd ed.). Boston: Houghton Mifflin.

29. For a discussion of the first juvenile court legislation, see Tuthill, Hon. R. S. (2003). The juvenile court law in Cook County, Illinois, 1899. In T. C. Calhoun & C. L. Chapple. *Readings in juvenile delinquency and juvenile justice.* Upper Saddle River, NJ: Prentice Hall.

30. For a history of the factors leading to the Great Depression and its aftermath, see Galbraith, J. K. (1997). *The great crash 1929.* Boston: Houghton Mifflin.

31. For a history of the 1960s, see Gitlin, T. (1993). *The sixties: Years of hope, days of rage.* New York: Bantam Books.

32. A history of the Johnson administration and the Great Society may be found at Goodwin, D. K. (1991). *Lyndon Johnson and the American dream.* New York: St. Martin's.

33. Kent v. United States, 383 U.S. 541, 86 S. Ct. 1045, 16 L. Ed. 2d 84 (1966).

34. In re Gault, 387 U.S. 1, 19–21, 26–28, 87 S. Ct. 1428, 1439–1440, 1442–1444, 18 L. Ed. 2d 527 (1967).

35. Empey, L. (1978). *American delinquency: Its meaning and construction.* Homewood, IL: Dorsey. See also Empey, L., Stafford, M. C., & May, C. H. (1999). *American delinquency: Its meaning and construction* (4th ed.). Belmont, CA: Wadsworth.

36. In re Winship, 397 U.S. 358, 90 S. Ct. 1068, 25 L. Ed. 2d 368 (1970).

37. McKeiver v. Pennsylvania, 403 U.S. 528, 547, 91 S. Ct. 1976, 1987, 29 L. Ed. 2d 647 (1971).

38. The Fifth Amendment to the U.S. Constitution reads, in part, ". . . nor shall any person be subject for the same offence to be twice be put in jeopardy of life or limb. . . ."

39. Breed v. Jones, 421 U.S. 519, 533, 95 S. Ct. 1779, 1787, 44 L. Ed. 2d 346 (1975).

40. Schall v. Martin, 467 U.S. 253, 104 S. Ct. 2403, 81 L. Ed. 2d 207 (1984).

3

Juvenile Delinquency

Theories of Causation

Many theories have been advanced to explain the cause of juvenile delinquency. Some are quite sophisticated, whereas others are predicated on rather basic "instinctive" conclusions that may or may not have a basis in fact. Many juvenile curfews are based on an instinctive conclusion that youths are likely to be victimized or get into trouble after certain hours. For example, in August 1994 the Town of Vernon, Connecticut, enacted its first juvenile curfew law.[1] It forbade persons under 18 to be in any public place or business. The rationale was that town leaders had noticed groups of juveniles loitering in town, and prior to the law a teenager had been murdered. Surveys also indicated that youths were fearful about gangs, weapons, and victimization. According to leaders, the curfew was passed for the protection of young people and to reduce the incidence of delinquency.

From Sunday through Thursday, the prohibited hours were from 11:00 P.M. until 5:00 A.M., and on Friday and Saturday the prohibited hours were from 12:01 A.M. until 5:00 A.M. Unfortunately for the town leaders, the curfew law was held to be unconstitutional because it unfairly restricted the right of free movement, and hence the equal protection rights of juveniles.

From the time of the first civil communities, every society has declared certain modes of behavior to be unacceptable or criminal in nature. Early customs and laws mandated compliance and punishment for the greater good of the group, city, or nation. In the modern era, the codification of norms of behavior is universal, and within contemporary societies the designation of some behaviors as criminal is fairly uncomplicated by definition: Most people have an instinctive understanding that criminal deviance involves egregiously (outrageously bad) illegal acts for which perpetrators can be punished. A less instinctive—and more technical—definition requires that these acts involve:

A positive or negative act in violation of penal law; an offense against the State. . . . An act committed or omitted in violation of a public law. . . . Crimes are those wrongs which the government notices as injurious to the public, and punishes in what is called a "criminal proceeding," in its own name. . . . A crime may be defined to be any act done in violation of those duties which an individual owes to the community, and for the breach of which the law has provided that the offender shall make satisfaction to the public.[2]

It is important to remember that the concept of juvenile delinquency is a relatively modern development, as is the notion of juvenile justice. As discussed in Chapter 2, premodern societies simply punished juvenile offenders as if they were nothing more than young criminals. Very often, this approach was rooted in the presumption that the causes of delinquency are inseparable from criminal causation, and that all such behavior should be similarly punished.

Practitioners and researchers have sought for generations to explain why juveniles engage in criminal deviance. Is such behavior a matter of individual choice? Can our understanding of biology and psychology explain delinquency? To what extent do environmental factors influence juvenile deviance? Are juvenile delinquents likely to become adult criminals? Historically, professionals have proposed a number of factors that theoretically explain delinquent behavior. Each theory represents the height of scientific understanding in each era. This is important, because policies derived from these theories have not only sought to isolate juvenile offenders but have also tried to manage the root causes of their behavior. Thus, punishments, rehabilitative techniques, detentions, and other controls have been designed to target the accepted explanatory factors.

This chapter investigates the causes of delinquency. Several historical theoretical models—from ancient explanations through the modern era—are discussed. Models developed during ancient and medieval eras will seem quite ridiculous from our modern vantage point, largely because many of them were based on little more than superstition and quasi-science (nearly scientific, but not quite). Similarly, many models developed during the modern era have reflected scientific and ideological biases of the time—all of which were accepted as "rational" explanations by contemporary experts. Nevertheless, if we are to understand present theory we must investigate contemporary contexts and the past. This is necessary not only because we consistently build new insight upon previous constructs, but also because it is likely that experts in the not too distant future will question some commonly accepted explanations from the present era.

Table 3.1 summarizes the types of theories of criminal causation explored in this chapter's discussion and their basic hypotheses.

The discussion in this chapter will review the following themes:

- Foreword to Theories of Juvenile Deviance
- Superstition and Myth: Early Theories of Delinquency and Crime
- Choice and Responsibility: Theories of the Classical School

TABLE 3.1   THEORIES OF CRIMINAL CAUSATION

Human society has developed innumerable explanations for criminal causation. Theoretical traditions have been developed throughout the ages as representing each society's understanding of themselves and their environment. In prescientific societies, superstition represented an amalgam of spiritual and natural understanding. After the European Enlightenment, theoretical traditions represented an attempt to find the true root causes of deviance.

This table summarizes the theoretical traditions that were developed to explain why some members of society violate the norms and customs of the group.

Theoretical Traditions	Sources of Deviance	Quality of Influence	Critiques of Theoretical Traditions
Early theories	Forces of nature Spirits/demons/devils	Deterministic	Unscientific superstition
Classical School	Rational personal choice	Free will	Politically motivated Heavy emphasis on punishment Little regard for rehabilitation
Biological theories	Evil, shown through facial features Brain development or underdevelopment Evolutionary primitiveness Heredity Body types	Deterministic	Rooted in quasi-science Overly deterministic
Psychological theories	Personality & childhood dysfunction Stimulus-response/reward-punishment Psychopathic personality	Modified deterministic	Not explanatory for all people/groups
Sociological theories	Normlessness Strain between means & goals Social structures/social ecology Learning from social interactions	Modified deterministic	Too much emphasis on poor classes Minimal emphasis on other factors Difficult to operationalize
Critical theory	Societal inequities Dominant & subordinate group conflict Capitalism, racism, & repression	Modified deterministic	Overly ideological Impractical for policy making

- Physical Qualities and Causation: Biological Theories
- The Mind and Causation: Psychological Theories
- Society and Causation: Sociological Theories
- The Impact of Injustice: Critical Theory

CHAPTER PERSPECTIVE 3.1

Teenage Drug Use and Delinquency

Many theories of causation have been developed to account for deviant behavior among adults and juveniles. It is safe to conclude that none of these explanations fully account for all cases of crime and juvenile delinquency. However, experts agree that a correlation exists between drug use and deviance.[3]

Alcohol and tobacco are the drugs of choice for many juveniles. Many adults tacitly condone smoking and drinking because cigarette and alcohol consumption are socially acceptable among adults. Even adults who do not condone teenage drinking often remark that "at least it's not drugs." Illicit drugs, such as cocaine, marijuana, and LSD, are not culturally acceptable among most segments of the adult population, and their use by juveniles is roundly condemned.

Among juveniles, abuse of illicit drugs is linked to a range of problems. Illicit drug use among juveniles has been a national problem since the late 1960s, with annual data reporting that sizable percentages of high school students have used drugs. During the decades following the 1960s, larger numbers of juveniles began using drugs at younger ages, and drugs have been associated with delinquency.[4] One point must be clearly understood when considering these data: Drug use is *itself* a form of juvenile delinquency.

What is the association between drug use and other types of delinquency? Part of the answer lies in the sort of behavior often associated with youthful drug users: truancy, poor academic performance, run-ins with adult authorities, participation in the juvenile justice system, and counter-cultural or "underground" lifestyles. These behaviors are common among many drug users, and juveniles are often prone to experimentation when exposed to these lifestyles.

Juveniles who traffic in drugs are by definition delinquents or criminals (if prosecuted in the criminal justice system). A good deal of juvenile drug dealing is conducted by street gangs. Some gangs have become known as so-called drug gangs because of their heavy involvement in the drug trade. Drug gangs are loose associations of youths whose primary activity is to reap a profit—often substantial earnings—from drug sales. The drug trade can be exceptionally dangerous, so that this type of illicit enterprise is also associated with guns, violence, intimidation, and extortion.

Foreword to Theories of Juvenile Deviance _____

Although many theories have been propounded (put forward for consideration) to explain juvenile deviance—a number of which are discussed in this chapter—no single theory has been universally accepted by experts. Many theories have been designed to explain particular aspects of deviance (and have reasonably done so) but were not designed to explain *all* aspects of deviance (and have not done so). Also, every theory has adherents who focus on the strengths of the theory and critics who point out its weaknesses.

Theories claiming to have found "the" explanation for juvenile deviance are readily criticized because they cannot easily account for significant and unique distinctions based on gender, race, class, and culture. Causes of juvenile deviance span socioeconomic, racial, regional, and gender categories. Factors commonly accounting for deviant behavior include family dysfunction, substance abuse, low self-esteem, disadvantaged communities, and peer pressure.[5]

As a foreword to discussing these theories, we shall consider a general background to causes of juvenile delinquency, first by summarizing common factors influencing juvenile behavior and then by presenting a profile of juvenile deviance.

Fundamentals: Common Factors Influencing Juvenile Behavior

Juveniles who live in unstable homes and social environments are deemed to be *at-risk* children because of their vulnerability to detrimental influences. Depending on the type and degree of these influences, unstable environments can induce antisocial behavior in children, often resulting in criminally deviant behavior later in life. Juvenile deviance is influenced by a number of factors. Among these are family, socioeconomic class, and educational experiences.

Family. Family background is one of the most potent influences on juvenile development. Norms, values, models of behavior, and other imprints emanate from the family unit, and these factors create an internalized "blueprint" for the child's personality, beliefs, and attitudes.[6] It is within the family unit that children receive most of their information about how to interact with other people and society. Healthy and nurturing families instruct members on how to interact using functional norms of behavior, whereas unhealthy family environments instruct members on how to interact using dysfunctional norms. Thus, dysfunctional families transfer dysfunctional norms to their children.

When antisocial and criminal norms exist within families, laypersons and experts agree that this can lead to one readily observable outcome: Criminal dysfunctional and deviant behaviors run in some families. For example, an association exists between marital instability and delinquency, so that the manifestations of a discordant marital environment—such as stress, estrangement, coldness, and unhealthy boundaries—produce a disproportionately high incidence of delinquent behavior in children who grow up in these environments.[7] Families that disintegrate into divorce can also exhibit a higher incidence of delinquency if the resulting arrangement continues to promote intra-family dysfunction. This certainly does not mean that all single-parent homes are likely to produce dysfunctional children; the key is whether the family unit is healthy. Discord and divorce in two-parent households are much more disruptive than stable, loving one-parent households.[8]

Photo 3.1   Growing up in the city. Two youths display a tough attitude.

Socioeconomic Class. Past conventional wisdom held that children from poor and working-class backgrounds—that is, youths born into the "dangerous classes"[9]—are much more likely to engage in delinquent behavior. The historical analysis presented in Chapter 2 illustrates how juvenile reform efforts such as the Child-Saving Movement focused their attentions on urban poor and working-class youths, many of whom were children of immigrants. Even as late as the 1950s and early 1960s, experts argued that class background was a significant explanatory variable for delinquent propensities.[10] This presumption has since been vigorously challenged, as statistical data began to indicate during the 1960s that delinquency is also quite common among middle-class youths.

Reasons for middle-class delinquency include parental pressure, peer pressure, uncertainty for the future, experimentation with intoxicating substances, experimenting with alternative lifestyles, and strong youth subcultures. Having considered (and accepted) the observation that middle-class delinquency is a significant problem, one must also keep in mind that theorists continue to identify certain dysfunctional norms among very poor urban subcultures. Research on the inner-city **underclass** has found that large numbers of the urban poor are caught in a chronic generational cycle of poverty, low educational achievement, teenage parenthood, unemployment, and welfare dependence.[11] Underclass theorists argue that antisocial behaviors have become entrenched norms within chronically impoverished inner-city environments, so that delinquency and criminality are now endemic facts of life.[12]

Educational Experiences. Educational experiences are, in many ways, a coequal influence on juvenile development, along with family and socioeconomic factors, because school environments can shape many youths' sense of opportunity and self-worth. For example, school dropouts and poor academic performers exhibit a higher incidence of delinquency and crime than graduates and academic achievers.

Academic achievement is considered to be one of the principal stepping-stones toward success in American society. In an ideal environment, opportunities for education, mentoring, and encouragement to excel should be equally available for all children. Unfortunately, educational opportunities are not equally available to all youths for a number of reasons. Socioeconomic and demographic factors can also have an impact on educational opportunities and performance,[13] so that poor children often experience a very different educational environment in comparison to middle-class children. This is particularly apparent in inner-city, underclass environments, where educational achievement is frequently not a strong norm of behavior.[14] For example, norms of behavior on school grounds can be problematic depending on whether socially accepted values are instilled for academic competition, deportment, and study habits. Underachievement in school can also be exacerbated by teachers' perceptions and expectations based on appearance, gender, race, and socioeconomic class.

A Profile of Juvenile Deviance: Inception, Progression, and Outcome

Readers should think of *deviance* as encompassing the following concepts:

- *Deviance.* "Behavior that is contrary to the standards of conduct or social expectations of a given group or society."[15]
- *Criminal deviance.* Antisocial behavior by persons who violate laws prohibiting acts defined as criminal by city, county, and state lawmakers or the U.S. Congress. Both adults and juveniles (those waived into criminal courts) can be convicted of crimes.
- *Juvenile deviance.* Antisocial behavior by youths, which includes status offenses (violations of laws exclusively governing juvenile behavior) and delinquent acts (behavior that would be criminal if juveniles were tried as adults).

Several features of youthful antisocial behavior can be identified to outline the theoretical progression from juvenile delinquency to adult criminality. This outline should not be taken as a definitive description of this process, or as advocating its inevitability. Rather, it is a summary delineation of central factors that can explain the relationship between delinquency and criminality.

Inception of Juvenile Deviance: A Life of Crime? Do child offenders become adult criminals? If so, what effect does one's age at the *inception* of deviant behavior have on the progression of this behavior toward criminality? Research on these questions has identified a relationship between the early inception of delinquency and later adult criminality.[16] These studies indicate that the likelihood of a person's chronic wrongdoing decreases as one's age of inception increases. In other words, the older one is when one commences breaking the law, the less likely he or she is to continue committing offenses. Long-term delinquency tends to be found among those who begin their careers earliest in life.

Progression of Juvenile Deviance: Habitual Behavior. Habitual (chronic) juvenile delinquency is characteristically associated with age of inception, and yet it is not necessarily associated with increased incidence or with expertise (specialization) in certain offenses. In other words, although an early inception of juvenile deviance is associated with chronic wrongdoing, this does not necessarily mean that the number of offenses increases with early inception. Some studies have found that arrests increase after 13 years of age and crest at age 17, while other studies hold that this may be true for some types of offenses, but not all.[17] Juvenile delinquents also tend to be *generalist* offenders, in that they typically commit a variety of offenses rather than develop an area of expertise.[18]

Thus, it appears that age of inception can be a factor for habitual *continuation* of deviant behavior as youths mature, but not necessarily for acceleration in numbers of all offenses, nor for the development of expertise.

Outcome of Juvenile Deviance: Criminality. Many adult criminals were juvenile delinquents, so that for many criminals the progression toward criminality does indeed begin at a young age. Delinquents who become criminals tend to be people who never overcame the environmental and idiosyncratic (uniquely personal) factors that led them to engage in chronically deviant behavior. These individuals are career criminals who have essentially accepted deviant lifestyles that last well into adulthood, often ending with long periods of incarceration. However, this is not always the case. Some delinquents quit engaging in antisocial behavior and never progress into adult criminality. In essence, they "outgrow" delinquency in the same manner that most functional juveniles mature into behaviors that result in responsible adulthood. Reasons for individuals halting their delinquent behavior include maturing into responsibility, fear of punishment (being "scared straight"), and an acceptance of mainstream values and lifestyles.

Superstition and Myth: Early
Theories of Delinquency and Crime

Early human communities thought it necessary to devise culturally acceptable explanations for why adults and juveniles violate the rules and laws of

Photo 3.2   At-risk youths? Young boys pose in front of a graffiti-covered wall. The age of inception for delinquent behavior is an important factor for future criminal behavior.

the group. The purpose of these explanations was to formulate systematic parameters for identifying the sources of social order, reasons for disorder, and sanctions against those responsible for breaking norms of behavior. Keeping in mind that ancient and medieval society conflated what we now term *delinquency* with criminality, it is instructive to explore several premodern explanations for criminal deviance.

Many early attempts to explain deviance were grounded in spiritualism and naturalism.[19] That is, social stability came from a harmonious relationship with forces beyond the corporeal world, and human criminality was a consequence of a wrongdoer's inappropriate connection with supernatural powers or nature-based influences. Offenses were essentially spiritual "sins" or crimes against the natural order, and punishments were considered to be in accordance with nature or divinely sanctioned. This presumption of linkage between order, disorder, and nonhuman influences became part of the body of laws and traditions in many early societies, albeit with a number of cultural adaptations.

In this section, two early theories of delinquency and criminality will be examined. These include **naturalism** and **demonology**.

Naturalism

Naturalism refers to the ancient practice of linking human affairs to the natural world and inferring that human behavior is derived from the forces of nature. Just as the tides are affected by the sun and the moon, so too are human passions and fortunes. All that is necessary is for humans to become adept at understanding how the forces of nature work, and develop the ability to interpret these forces. Naturalism is therefore a **deterministic theory** of criminal causation, because it eliminates individual responsibility for one's lack of responsible self-control.

Ancient civilizations around the Mediterranean region often concluded that human behavior is driven by nature. Natural "signs" were observed to divine the course of human events, and offerings were given to appeal for favors, or to appease perceived signs of punishment. For example, the Romans had a propensity for studying flights of birds and reading the entrails of sacrificial beasts to divine their fortunes. Romans also believed that the moon, or *Luna,* influenced human behavior. Our word *lunatic* comes from the ancient belief that criminal or otherwise bizarre behavior is caused by phases of the moon. The Greeks consulted oracles, such as the famous one at Delphi, who sometimes divined fortunes by inhaling sacred vapors, hallucinating, and babbling fortunes that required interpretation by holy guides. Burnt offerings were also made to discern the will of the gods and appease them. Greeks believed a great deal in living one's life as virtuously as possible, and that a virtuous person was a good person. One method for determining one's virtue was to observe the contours of one's body, because virtue was manifest in human appearance. Thus, good people were pleasing to the eye, and people literally stood naked before the court while officials debated their virtue.

Demonology

For many centuries, humans believed that evil creatures—demons or devils—wielded great influence over humans, sometimes possessing them and making them commit offenses against the greater good. Criminal behavior and delinquency were not considered to be a consequence of free will; instead, these offenses were manifestations of conflict between creatures of evil and chaos against deities of goodness and order. Demonology is also a deterministic theory of criminal causation.

When people committed crimes against society, they were also committing offenses against the deified order, and remedies and punishments were meted out accordingly. Painful ordeals (i.e., torture) were devised to elicit confessions or drive out the demonic spirits. Driving out evil demons, known as *exorcism,* was frequently quite excruciating. For example, a number of ancient cultures engaged in the practice of drilling holes in the skull (known as *trephining*), which supposedly allowed evil spirits to depart from their human "host." Medieval and Renaissance-era Christians considered crimes to be offenses against God and the Roman Catholic Church, and used burning, maiming, breaking, and beating to drive out supernatural invaders. These were also effective techniques for producing confessions of possession, although suspects who refused to confess were often considered to be so under the influence of the devil that they were unsalvageable. Basically, confession was evidence of possession, and *failure* to confess was evidence of possession.

Should the spirits or demons refuse to leave their human host (either with or without confessions), the possessed person was executed. Clearly, these tests and remedies were torturous ordeals *ab initio,* so that the suspected human host was quite an unlucky person at every phase of the inquiry. As a sidebar, it should be noted that mental illness was also explained as evidence of spirit possession, with similar methods used for salvaging the unfortunate human host.

Choice and Responsibility: Theories of the Classical School

During the late eighteenth and early nineteenth centuries, new theorists investigating criminal and delinquent causation began to apply scientific methods to explain deviant behavior. These theorists—the first true criminologists—focused on the personal responsibility of individuals for their behavior. The new theories they developed roundly rejected naturalism and demonology as explanations for delinquency and criminality, an approach that was typical of the rationalism of the European Enlightenment. Rationality and humanitarianism were at the heart of Enlightenment philosophy, and this was reflected in the new approaches for explaining and responding to deviant behavior.

Crime and Free Will

The **Classical School** is typical of **free will theories of criminal causation,** which regard deviant behavior as a product of individual rational choice. Such rational choice is grounded in the human desire for pleasure and aversion to pain. Because of this emphasis on human-centered rationality, classical theorists argued that perpetrators should be held personally accountable for criminal and delinquent acts, and punished accordingly. Since the criminal's calculus for making this choice is the acquisition of a benefit from criminal behavior (pleasure), society must develop policies to increase the costs for this benefit (pain). Thus, punishment would become increasingly harsher as one's deviance becomes more egregious; the costs of crime must always outweigh the benefits. Having made this observation, it should be noted that the Classical School was actually quite progressive in the history of theories of causation. Its basic assumptions are the following:

- Humans are fundamentally rational and enjoy free will. Crime is an outcome of rationality and free will. People choose to engage in criminal rather than conformist behavior.
- Criminality is morally wrong and is an affront against social order and the collective good of society.
- Civil society must necessarily punish criminals to deter individual wrongdoers and other would-be criminals.
- Punishment should be proportional to the nature of the criminal offense, and never be excessive. It must also be a guaranteed response to criminality, and meted out quickly.

The Classical School originated with the writings of Cesare Beccaria in Italy, who published *An Essay on Crimes and Punishment* in 1764.[20] His discussion of why crime occurs and how society should respond to it was groundbreaking, and it resulted in widespread debate. Beccaria advocated the then-radical proposition that punishment should be swift, certain, and proportional. He also argued that both corporal and capital punishments should be abolished, and that most (if not all) criminal laws should be revised accordingly. The philosopher Jeremy Bentham in England promoted Beccaria's thesis in the late eighteenth and early nineteenth centuries, primarily in his book *An Introduction to the Principles of Morals and Legislation*.[21] Bentham believed that humans rationally seek pleasure and avoid pain, so that rational people can be deterred from criminal deviance. Nevertheless, criminals conclude that the pleasure derived from crime counterbalances the pain of punishment. Bentham further argued that deterrence would be accomplished by the *certainty* of punishment, and by making the severity of each punishment surpass any benefit derived from the crime.

Because free will and rational choice are at the center of Classical criminology, it naturally represents a rejection of deterministic theories of deviance. However, as debate was joined during the nineteenth century on the question of what constitutes free will and choice, the Classical School modified its philosophy by acknowledging that juveniles and mentally ill adults do not have the same capacity to make rational choices as do mature, sane adults. Therefore, special consideration was gradually developed for these classes of offenders. This modification is sometimes referred to as the **neoclassical** approach to deviance.

The American Context

The Classical School had a significant resurgence in the United States during the latter quarter of the twentieth century. Central values of

Classical School philosophy were adapted to the American cultural context as part of the nation's crackdown on juvenile delinquents and criminals. As a consequence, the underlying philosophy of American criminal justice has shifted away from attempting to rehabilitate offenders and moved toward punishment, incapacitation, and deterrence. In many states, there is a fundamental Classical School presumption that juvenile and adult offenders have exercised free will and made a rational choice, so that any mitigating circumstances involving an individual's social history or family background are deemed secondary to his or her calculation to break the law.

As applied within the American context, offenders commonly receive mandatory sentences for specified offenses, and most states have passed legislation to punish offenders in proportion to their crimes. For example, aggravating circumstances such as the use of firearms are punished more severely. Many juvenile delinquents are now waived into the adult system, and individual criminals receive longer and more severe sentences. Nationally, more prisons have been built and more offenders have been imprisoned.

On a final note, it is interesting to consider that what was once a ground-breaking and radical philosophy during its time has come to be labeled as a conservative policy in the modern era. An ongoing criticism of the modern approach to the Classical School is that it does not take into account a criminal's idiosyncratic circumstances. It is also criticized by civil libertarians as weighing too heavily in favor of punishment, without incorporating philosophies of rehabilitation.

Physical Qualities and Causation: Biological Theories

Biological theories refer to the effect of congenital (inherited physical) traits on human behavior. They present strongly deterministic explanations of delinquency and criminality, and hold that some people are "naturally born criminals" with physical qualities that govern their deviant tendencies. These qualities include genetic, biological, and biochemical profiles that theoretically cause, or have a strong effect upon, one's propensity for deviant behavior. This thesis has existed for many centuries, and it began to receive scientific—or what we would now consider to be *quasi*-scientific—credence during the late eighteenth century.[22]

The central implication of biological determinants is that free will is at best a secondary cause of delinquency. Rather, the blame for deviant behavior shifts to internal physical qualities, which explain one's predisposition for criminal conduct. In this section, several biological theories of delinquency and criminality are examined. These include:

- An Honest Appearance: Physiognomy
- Bumps on the Head: Phrenology
- Evolutionary Primitiveness: Atavism
- The Bad Seed: Heredity
- Body Types: Somatotyping

An Honest Appearance: Physiognomy

The concept of an "honest face" or an "evil face" has been deeply ingrained in human culture, probably since prehistory. Medieval-era Europeans ascribed moral and behavioral traits to physical appearance. In particular, facial characteristics were deemed to be indicators of moral character, so that facially pleasing people were more likely to be given the benefit of the doubt than facially "displeasing" people. This practice, known as **physiognomy**, is arguably similar to the naturalistic approach to physical virtue adopted by the ancient Greeks. Many researchers from the Enlightenment through the late nineteenth century supported these observations as scientifically valid findings. Physiognomists dutifully reported the soundness of a variety of physiognomic traits and measured their prominence among criminals and other undesirables in comparison to the general population.

In the modern era, which is supposedly guided by scientific principles, many laypersons continue to adopt physiognomic attitudes toward others. Protruding eyebrows, receding foreheads, sinister noses, jutting jawbones, and certain *looks* on faces are popularly considered to be indicators of deviance. These attitudes hearken back to eras of quasi-scientific research.

Bumps on the Head: Phrenology

A variation (or progression) on the theme of physiognomy was the proposition that human behavior is determined by bodily functions emanating from the organs. Premodern theorists had long posited that secretions from the stomach, kidneys, heart, spleen, and other organs affect moods, emotions, and conduct. During the late eighteenth and early nineteenth centuries, Franz Gall systematically promoted his theory that the brain is the source of all personality, including deviant personality. His theories, eventually systematized as **phrenology**, caught on among many members of the scientific community, who focused their research on head shapes.

Lumps, bumps, indentations, protuberances, and other cranial features were considered by phrenologists to be indicators of brain development. Scientists devised brain "maps" that sketched out the specific locations of certain feelings, emotions, and behavioral attributes. An underdeveloped location on the skull suggested underdevelopment of that portion of the brain, and overdeveloped skull locations suggested overdevelopment of portions of the brain. Using brain maps as guides, experts believed that they could postulate criminal/delinquent skull shapes, as well as creative, intelligent, insane, and unintelligent skull shapes. The skulls and brains of deceased criminals were studied by phrenologists in laboratories to support their position. Phrenology was a viable theory throughout the nineteenth century, and lingered to the beginning of the twentieth century. It arguably still exists at the level of popular culture, in films and carnivals.

Evolutionary Primitiveness: Atavism

Cesare Lombroso, an Italian prison physician, departed from Gall's phrenological movement by examining a variety of physical anomalies in humans. In his influential book *The Criminal Man* in 1876,[23] Lombroso argued that criminals could be identified by primitive physical anomalies present at birth. To him, these anomalies do not *determine* criminality, but they are indicators of criminal *predisposition*. Although his theory was less deterministic than that of the phrenologists, who relied on the shape of one's skull as a determinant for criminality, his approach was certainly deterministic in the sense that for Lombroso some people are literally born as criminals.

Lombroso made postmortem observations of criminals and concluded that they are anthropologically less developed humans—evolutionary throwbacks who are intellectually undeveloped compared with modern humans. Criminals are therefore *atavistic* creatures with uncivilized criminal dispositions, and the characteristic of these people was called **atavism**. Lombroso's approach used the growing fascination of nineteenth-century scientists with the theories of Charles Darwin, author of *The Origin of Species* and founder of modern evolutionary science.[24] It was therefore quite natural for Lombroso to suggest that criminality and evolution are linked. Because physical abnormalities are indicators of evolutionary primitiveness, Lombroso identified the following traits as evidence of atavism:

- Bent noses
- High cheekbones
- Lack of earlobes
- Prominent lips
- Elongated arms
- Jutting jaws

Since Lombroso's conclusions were observational, he recognized that not all criminals exhibited these physical features. He theorized that passions such as avarice and opportunism could be caused by societal and other environmental inputs. Thus, biology and life experiences can combine to "trigger" criminality in some people.

Although modern criminologists reject Lombroso's theory of evolutionary primitiveness, he is recognized as being one of the founders of the

Positivist School of criminology. His theory of congenital predisposition toward delinquency and criminality greatly influenced later positivist inquiry into deviant behavior. Positivists began to theorize that biology, society, and environment can affect human behavior, and that these influences can lead to criminality among those who are predisposed toward deviant behavior. Lombroso's contribution was to suggest that biology and culture in combination are central causes of delinquency and crime.

The Bad Seed: Heredity

Delinquency and crime often run in families. The question of why this occurs has been a subject of criminological inquiry for some time. Hereditary explanations of causation hold that criminality in some families is hereditary, and that deviance is genetically encoded in those born into the family group. Thus, a *bad seed* is theoretically inherited and passed from generation to generation. Richard Dugdale's research on the Juke family, published in 1877, was among the first scientific studies that systematically argued in favor of a genetic basis for immorality, crime, and delinquency.[25]

The validity of hereditary explanations can logically be tested by studying the behavior of siblings, twins, and children raised away from their criminally inclined biological parents. Studies of adopted children indicate that a greater incidence of deviance occurs among those whose biological father has been a criminal in comparison to when the adoptive father has engaged in criminal behavior. Other research on twins has indicated that identical twins have a higher likelihood for delinquency and criminality than fraternal twins. However, there is an important caveat that must be kept in mind when considering research on heredity: Research has not identified a 100% correlation between heredity and crime, and studies have not identified an explanatory variable for hereditary deviance. Other explanatory factors must also be considered, such as personal experiences and environmental influences. In other words, the genetic "bad seed" argument does not explain correlations between heredity, family dysfunction, underclass cultural norms, and antisocial group dynamics.[26]

Chromosome theory represents an example of the modern approach to heredity theory. Chromosomes, which are composed of DNA, contain the genetic code for human gender differences. Gender is determined from chromosomal arrangements, so that women typically have an "XX" pattern and men have an "XY" pattern. Some people have anomalous patterns, which include "XXX" for some women and "XYY" for some men. During the 1960s, scientists investigated the theoretical implications of the "XYY" pattern. Research was reported in 1965 suggesting that "XYY" males are more prevalent in prison populations than in society.[27] These "super males" were reported to be more aggressive than typical "XY" males, and therefore more prone to criminal deviance than "XY" males. Subsequent research challenged these findings and the methodology used, in particular the fact that less than 5% of males exhibit this pattern, and therefore the theory has little predictive value.[28] However, chromosome theory represents an important example of how modern scientific knowledge can be used to update older theories. Research continues on possible connections between chromosomes and criminality.

Body Types: Somatotyping

Another revision of older theories consigned human body types to three categories, percentages of which theoretically exist in different individuals. This practice, known as **somatotyping**, sought to identify certain body types that are more likely to be found among offenders. William Sheldon and other researchers promoted somatotype research during the mid-twentieth century. In his book *Varieties of Delinquent Youth*,[29] Sheldon identified three somatotypes that he argued are prevalent in male juveniles, classified as follows:

- Mesomorphs: People who are muscular, sinewy, narrow in waist and hips, and broad-shouldered
- Ectomorphs: People who are fragile, thin, narrow, and delicate
- Endomorphs: People who are pudgy, round, soft, short-limbed, and smooth-skinned

Sheldon assigned a scale of 0 to 7 for the prevalence of each somatotype in individuals, with 0 being a complete absence of the type, and 7 indicating a strong prevalence. He concluded that a high degree of mesomorphy and a low degree of ectomorphy were found in juvenile delinquents and other aggressive, violent individuals. Although many experts criticized his theory, other researchers concurred with Sheldon's conclusion that delinquents and other offenders are more likely to be muscular mesomorphs than thin ectomorphs or pudgy endomorphs.[30] Critics responded that somatotyping is inherently inaccurate and subjective and does not adequately explain the role of environmental factors on the predisposition of some to engage in deviant behavior.[31]

Table 3.2 summarizes the attributes of several biological theories of criminal and delinquent causation.

_____ The Mind and Causation: Psychological Theories

The relatively new science of psychology has significantly influenced criminology, so much so that psychological theories of delinquency and criminality figure prominently among many explanations of deviance given by practitioners and researchers. Psychological theories have also become

TABLE 3.2   BIOLOGICAL THEORIES OF DELINQUENT CAUSATION

Biological theories were developed as deterministic explanations of delinquency and criminal behavior. They have historically sought to discover physiological bases for deviance and have generally applied the scientific knowledge of their time to this endeavor. New discoveries and theories have continually supplanted older approaches.

This table summarizes several biological theories developed to explain delinquency and criminality.

Theory	Indicators of Deviance	Effect on Behavior	Critique of Theory
Physiognomy	Facial features Physical features	Goodness or evil Honesty or dishonesty Crime and delinquency	Quasi-scientific Not supported empirically
Phrenology	Brain development Contour of the skull	Feelings, emotions, attitudes Crime and delinquency	Quasi-scientific Not supported empirically
Atavism	Primitive physical anomalies Anthropological traits	Intellectual regression Congenitally deviant predisposition	Quasi-scientific Not supported empirically
Heredity	Criminality in family Extra "Y" chromosome in males	Congenital deviance	Not 100% correlation Other intervening factors exist
Somatotyping	Body features Relative percentage of mesomorphy	Predisposition for deviance Aggression, violence	Inherent inaccuracy and subjectivity

well-known to the general public, as evidenced by the extent to which they are prominently featured in popular culture productions such as novels, films, and television shows. Most of these theories have stimulated a great deal of debate among experts and laypersons, largely because they are fundamentally subjective in nature and their explanatory value is disputable.

Psychological theories ascribe deviant behaviors to cognitive and personality disorders brought on by one's environment, brain chemistry, or some other condition. Such theories are not as rigorously deterministic as other approaches to causation, because they allow for some degree of free will—albeit a disordered free will. In this sense, they are a modified (or less complete) form of determinism. Several elements are commonly present in psychological explanations of delinquency and crime:

- Criminals and delinquents do not (or cannot) differentiate right from wrong.
- Psychological abnormalities are caused by a number of factors, including detrimental behavioral conditioning, diseased minds, and learning from toxic environments.
- Offenders have disordered or abnormal personalities.
- Some offenders cannot control themselves.
- Personality develops during childhood, which affects behavior during adulthood.

Several psychological theories of delinquency and criminality are examined in this section, including:

- Psychoanalytic Theory
- Conditioning Theory
- Psychopathology Theory

Personality, Behavior, and Childhood: Psychoanalytic Theory

Early theorists of psychoanalysis, such as Carl Jung[32] and Sigmund Freud,[33] attempted to construct systematic models to explain human personality. The personality systems they designed created classifications to explain interlinkages between one's personality and behavior. Sigmund Freud was the founder of psychoanalysis, and his research is the foundation for psychoanalytic theory.

During the late nineteenth and early twentieth centuries, Freud wrote that individual personalities have three fundamental components, which strongly affect one's behavior:

- *Id*. Primal, selfish drives and desires. All persons are born with the basic desire for self-gratification, with no regard for others. Infants were considered by Freud to be perfect examples of the predominance of the id.

- *Ego*. The rational mind. As children mature, the ego places checks on the id's desires and channels them into behavioral choices. Selfishness is suppressed, and consideration is given by youths to the welfare of others.

- *Superego*. The guiding moral conscience, which weighs the ego's choices and labels them according to the personality's definitions of right and wrong. Guilt, shame, and other emotions reflect the influence of the superego. As humans mature, the libido, or sex drive, emerges. The libido is checked by the interplay between an individual's id, ego, and superego.

Healthy development of the id, ego, and superego occurs early in life, so that early experiences are critical for future adult behavior. Troubling or traumatizing events during childhood can become catalysts for delinquency and criminality. Juvenile delinquents and adult criminals are, according to psychoanalytic theory, persons without sufficiently developed egos and superegos. If the moralistic superego is weak, a person can easily act out on his or her primal urges without remorse (an unchecked id), and mislabel deviance as acceptable behavior. When people without superegos act out on these urges, their behavior is socially unacceptable. Such behavior, if illegal, forces society to define the individuals as delinquents or criminals, and to deal with them accordingly. Thus, people who have poorly developed super-egos and egos are incapable of acting outside of their own interests and are roughly analogous to *psychopaths* in the modern era. Psychopaths, also termed *sociopaths,* are deemed to be unable to empathize with other people's feelings or well-being.

Freud also argued that human personalities are formed during several phases of childhood development. Abnormal personalities and other psychological imbalances begin to form during these phases, and can reflect the phase in which the problem developed. For example, according to Freudian theory, if a person regresses to or becomes fixated in their phallic phase of development (ages three to five years), they may become sexually deviant and engage in illicit sex practices such as prostitution or rape.

Learning by Experiencing: Conditioning Theory

It is a truism that every person's future behavior is conditioned by past experiences. In other words, we learn from lifetime events and base our decisions, perceptions, and conduct on these events. According to conditioning theorists, these experiences—or environmental stimuli—underlie socially acceptable behavior, as well as delinquency and criminality.

The pioneer behind conditioning theory is Ivan Pavlov, a Russian physiologist who conducted behavioral experiments on dogs during the late nineteenth and early twentieth centuries.[34] The basic attributes of his experiments were stimulus–response and reward–punishment. His laboratory dogs were stimulated to respond with certain behaviors. Pavlov's methods were remarkably simple: The dogs were rewarded when they responded correctly, and punished when the responded incorrectly. Pavlov's most famous experiment involved conditioning dogs to salivate at the ring of a bell. He initially rang a bell each time the dogs were fed (which stimulated them to salivate), and eventually simply rang the bell without food. The result was that the dogs were stimulated to salivate even though no food was given. Extrapolating these observations to human behavior, Pavlov's experiments theoretically demonstrate that behavior is predicated on lifetime stimuli.

During the latter half of the twentieth century, B. F. Skinner and other researchers promoted behavioral psychology.[35] Their underlying theory of stimulus–response added to the progression of conditioning theory. Many behaviorists concluded that human criminals and delinquents could be conditioned to continue their behavior in a manner similar to Pavlov's dogs.

According to this school, environmental stimuli operate either as punishers or reinforcers. Criminals and delinquents are stimulated (reinforced) by their environment to continue acting out deviantly until they are punished in some manner. Therefore, when offenders are repeatedly rewarded for their deviance and receive no punishment for breaking the law, they are likely to continue until the authorities catch them.

Psychopathology Theory

The concept of the psychopathic personality was developed during the 1950s to describe criminals who behaved cruelly and seemingly with no empathy for their victims. The observation that some criminals are apparently unable—that is, they have no capacity—to appreciate the feelings of their victims led to a great deal of research on this behavior. In essence, free will is a secondary motivation for this type of delinquent or criminal. The condition was wholly developed and described by 1964 in the book *The Mask of Sanity*, written by Hervey Cleckley.[36]

Psychopaths (sociopaths) are considered to be people who have no conscience—in Freudian terms, no superego. They are severely dysfunctional in their relationships with other people, and are fundamentally selfish, unpredictable, untruthful, and unstable. The term is sometimes used to describe very aggressive delinquents and criminals who act out spontaneously without an observable motive. This aggressiveness and impulsiveness are typical manifestations of the psychopathic personality, which is why many become lawbreakers.

Table 3.3 summarizes the attributes of several psychological theories of criminal and delinquent causation.

Society and Causation: Sociological Theories

The foregoing theories of causation have focused on the personal idiosyncrasies of individuals to explain delinquency and crime. These personal attributes—such as an individual's physical or psychological makeup—have been used by researchers and practitioners to formulate theories of deviance and to design policies to deal with lawbreakers. However, one commonality is that all of these theories look at the personal (internal) attributes of people. In the alternative, and using an *external* approach, sociologists have examined the role of societal factors to explain human behavior.

Sociologists study interrelationships between individuals, socioeconomic groups, social processes, and societal structures. They have long examined the association between societal factors and criminal causation, focusing on the effects of society on individual and collective behavior. Sociological theories are not strongly deterministic, in that they tend to explain *predispositions* toward criminal deviance, and they therefore allow for some degree of free will.

TABLE 3.3   PSYCHOLOGICAL THEORIES OF CAUSATION

Psychological theories of causation apply research and theory of psychology to criminology. As new understandings of the human psyche are proposed, psychologists have had an important explanatory impact on theories of causation. Although psychological theories are not strongly deterministic, they do provide insight on predispositions for deviant behavior.

This table summarizes several psychological theories developed to explain delinquency and criminality.

Theory	Indicators of Deviance	Effect on Behavior	Critique of Theory
Psychoanalysis	Weak superego Incomplete personality development	Psychopathology Regressed or fixated personality	Not explanatory for all people/groups
Conditioning	Responses to environmental stimuli	Crime and delinquency	Not all people respond to these stimuli Not explanatory for all people/groups
Psychopathology	Dysfunctional personality Lack of conscience	Unpredictability, instability Aggressiveness Crime and delinquency	Difficult to diagnose linkage to crime Need further research

Beginning in the 1920s, the Chicago School of Sociology (centered at the University of Chicago) pioneered modern sociological research. A great deal of research and a number of theories since that time have been developed, and continue to be developed, to improve our understanding of the relationship between society and human deviance. Several elements are commonly present in sociological explanations of delinquency and crime:

- Socioeconomic conditions and pressures shape individual and collective behavior.
- Inequality and deprivation are associated with delinquency and criminality.
- Subcultural norms are often at odds with accepted norms of society, creating tensions that can result in subcultural conflict with the greater society.
- Delinquency and crime are associated with underclass conditions such as poverty, neighborhood degeneration, low educational achievement, inadequate housing, and family dysfunction.

Several sociological theories of delinquency and criminality are examined in this section, including:

- Anomie and Strain Theories
- Social Ecology (Structural) Theory
- Differential Association Theory

Norms, Means, and Ends: Anomie and Strain Theories

Durkheim and Anomie Theory. The great sociologist Emile Durkheim first studied anomie during the late nineteenth century.[37] The concept generally refers to a state of "normlessness" vis-à-vis the accepted norms of the greater society. *Norms* are rules, and a consensus, about the way people should behave in society. Durkheim concluded that after social upheavals such as wars, traditional norms of behavior no longer work, thus causing societal normlessness. Suicide, crime, and other crises exist in societies that do not develop effective norms. Anomie refers to a broad breakdown of norms in society, or a disconnection between an individual from the norms of his or her society's contemporary values. Durkheim's theories have had great influence on sociology, continuing well into the modern era.

Merton's Strain Theory. Anomie was applied to criminology during the 1930s by Robert Merton and others, who studied the tension between socially acceptable goals and the means one is permitted by society to use for achieving those goals.[38] Merton's theory focused on the *availability* of goals and means. He posited that the greater society encourages its members to use acceptable means to achieve acceptable goals. In the United States, "acceptable means" include hard work, prudent savings, and higher education. Acceptable goals include comfort, leisure time, social status, and wealth. However, not all members of society have an equal availability of resources to achieve society's recognized goals, thus creating *strain* for these less empowered members. Strain is manifested as a desire to achieve these goals, and one's inability to acquire the legitimate means to attain them. In theory, those who do not have access to acceptable means may resort to illegitimate and illicit avenues to achieve their goals. In other words, those without resources and access may become delinquents or criminals to achieve comfort, leisure, status, and wealth.

The implications of Merton's and his fellow researchers' findings are clear: Lack of opportunity and inequality are central causal factors for delinquency and crime. However, anomie and strain theory have been criticized for placing too much emphasis on deviance emanating from the poorer classes, and for failing to adequately explain why so many youths and adults who suffer from strain do not turn to delinquency or crime.

Concentric Urban Zones:
Social Ecology (Structural) Theory

Another contribution from the University of Chicago in the 1920s was research on the *structural* sources of criminal deviance.[39] Urban researchers conducted longitudinal studies (studies over time) on Chicago communities, which were mapped and classified into concentric urban zones.[40] They observed that some urban zones had a higher incidence of crime over time, regardless of which ethnic group moved into the zone. Researchers concluded that the social structures of these areas affected the quality of life for inhabitants. By definition, urban "structural conditions" include overcrowding, poor sanitation, inadequate transportation, unemployment, poverty, poor schools, transience, births out of wedlock, and low employment. These factors contribute to high delinquency and crime rates because of resulting widespread social instability.[41]

Social ecology research generally describes prevalent physical and social structures that affect the quality of life in American cities. These studies commonly report the following urban "ecological" factors:[42]

- Explanations for deviance must take social structures into account.
- Delinquency and crime rates in urban areas vary markedly in identified neighborhoods and other designated concentric zones.
- Rates of delinquency and crime are highest in urban core zones—the inner city—and lowest outside of these cores.
- Other problems common to the underclass also exist in inner-city neighborhoods and other designated zones.

Social ecology theory has been criticized for overreliance on social structures to explain delinquency and crime. According to critics, other factors such as anomie or in-migration of criminally inclined people (who drive out law-abiding residents) can also explain deviance. Nevertheless, research on social ecology is likely to continue to be conducted and refined.

Differential Association Theory

Edwin Sutherland described the theory of differential association in his 1939 book, *Principles of Criminology*.[43] Differential association is a process of social learning, in which criminals and law-abiding people learn their behavior from associations with others. People imitate or otherwise internalize the quality of these associations. Delinquency (and criminality) are learned behaviors that are acquired from interacting with others who participate in criminal lifestyles, so that the difference between offenders and nonoffenders lies in individual choices. In other words, offenders and nonoffenders strive for similar goals, but they choose different avenues to achieve those goals. These choices are based on the lessons they take from exposure to certain kinds of life experiences. In particular, those with strong attachments to delinquents are more likely to become delinquents, and people who grow up in criminal milieus will adopt deviant values that can result in delinquency and crime.

Although differential association theory has been criticized for relying on variables that are difficult to operationalize, it remains a potent and influential approach to explaining delinquency and crime. Its appeal is perhaps grounded in its proposition that all persons possess the same learning processes, which are developed through communicating and interacting with groups of people. The difference between criminals and noncriminals

TABLE 3.4   SOCIOLOGICAL THEORIES OF CAUSATION

Sociologists have historically studied the role of people and groups in society, and the effect society has had on its members. For sociological theorists, the broader society has certain inherent features and structures that cause some members to engage in delinquent and criminal behavior. These theories sometimes reflect the political ideology of the times in which they were designed.

This table summarizes several sociological theories developed to explain delinquency and criminality.

Theory	Indicators of Deviance	Effect on Behavior	Critique of Theory
Anomie and strain	Normlessness Strain between means and goals	Illicit attainment of goals	Too much emphasis on poorer classes Not explanatory for all people/groups
Social ecology	Quality of life Surrounding and social structures	High crime and delinquency rates	Failure to consider other factors
Differential association	Dysfunctional environment Dysfunctional associations	Illicit achievement of goals Achievement of illicit goals	Difficult to operationalize variables

is that they base their choices on different lessons learned from their different experiences. Norms and values are similarly learned, but some people internalize deviant norms and values.

Table 3.4 summarizes the attributes of several sociological theories of criminal and delinquent causation.

The Impact of Injustice: Critical Theory

Critical theories of causation challenge the "orthodoxy" of criminology by arguing that deviance is a product of inequities created in all societies. These inequities are endemic to socioeconomically hierarchical societies, which allow many members of society to prosper, but which also prevent many members from participating in this prosperity. Two critical theories of delinquency and criminality are examined in this section:

- Conflict theory
- Radical criminology

Conflict Theory

Conflict theories of causation hypothesize that social tensions and conflicts are indelible features of society. Conflicts arise between dominant groups and "subordinate" classes, races, genders, political groups, ethnic groups, and other defined outsiders in society.[44] The fundamental characteristic of these tensions is that they often pit the *haves* against the *have-nots*, with the latter being labeled as criminals or insurgents during these conflicts. Because such tensions are indelible, they can at best be controlled by social institutions rather than completely eradicated. In practice, this means that the have-nots must be coerced to obey the laws and rules of those in power.

From this perspective, laws and rules are simply instruments of control used by ruling elites to maintain control of key institutions, and thereby shut out others who might challenge the authority of the elites. The focus of conflict theories is on the entire economic and political system, and the socioeconomic tensions theoretically created by this system.

Radical Criminology

During the 1960s and 1970s, a good deal of theory and research on delinquency and criminality reflected the political and social discord of the period. Critical theorists challenged previous conventions of criminal causation, arguing that delinquency and criminality were caused by society's inequitable ideological, political, and socioeconomic makeup.[45] Proponents of the emergent radical approach argued that because power and wealth have been unequally distributed, those who have been politically and economically shut out understandably resort to criminal antagonism against the prevailing order. According to radical criminologists, these classes will continue to engage in behavior labeled as criminal until society remedies the plight of the powerless and disenfranchised.

Critical theories similar to radical criminology frequently use Marxist theory to critique the role of capitalist economics in creating socioeconomic inequities.[46] Marxist perspectives on criminology argue that the ruling capitalist classes exploit the labor of the lower classes and co-opt them by convincing them that capitalism is actually beneficial for them.[47] Marxist-oriented radical criminologists hold that ruling elites have used their own interpretations of justice to maintain their status. Hence, the criminal justice system is inherently exploitative and unfair toward criminals who originate from the lower classes. The fact that African Americans, Latinos, and the poor are overrepresented in prisons is explained as a manifestation of the inherent unfairness at the core of the existing capitalist "establishment."

One readily apparent criticism of critical theories is that they rely exclusively on political and economic ideologies to explain delinquency and criminality. Other factors are given cursory attention. Few empirical findings support the ideology-based premises of critical theories, and few workable policy recommendations have been made. For example, policies based on the precepts of Marxist radical criminology would require a fundamental reordering of the political and economic system in the United States. This is impractical, unpopular, and highly unlikely to occur.

Chapter Summary

A large number of theories have been developed to identify and explain the causes of juvenile and criminal deviance. Early attempts to explain deviance applied the then-accepted notion that natural and supernatural forces affect human fortunes and behavior. Some of these early deterministic theories held that the natural world is reflected in human appearance and behavior; others held that possession by demons and devils is responsible for criminality and mental illness. Superstition was supplanted by rationalism during the European Enlightenment. Classical School theorists were protocriminologists who focused on individual responsibility for delinquency and criminality. The Classical School's approach is grounded in free will theories of causation, which apply rationalism to explain each criminal's decision to break the law.

The propagation of modern scientific methods of inquiry included the application of empirical reason to the new field of criminology. Biological explanations of causation are deterministic theories that study the effects of congenital traits on human behavior. Although many early biological theories—physiognomy, phrenology, and atavism—are quasi-scientific by modern standards, they represent a serious effort to bring scientific rigor to the study of criminal causation. Biological inquiry continues unabated, with new fields of inquiry such as DNA research providing new bases for exploring the causes of delinquency and criminality. Social sciences such as psychology and sociology have also been the source of a rich diversity in theories of causation. Psychological explanations are grounded in several research traditions, such as psychoanalysis, conditioning, and psychopathology. These explanations are not as deterministic as biological theories, for they leave open the possibility of deviant free will. Sociological approaches examine the effects of social structures and processes on the behavior of individuals and groups of people. Societal conditions theoretically affect people's collective perceptions of the availability of opportunities and the intensity of deprivations, so that delinquency and crime are reactions to certain types of environments. Critical theory is counterconventional in the sense that it challenges orthodox theories of criminal causation. In essence, they lay the blame for delinquency and crime on socioeconomic and political inequalities. Conflict theory and radical criminology represent typical critical approaches, arguing that fundamental changes must be made in society to remedy criminal deviance.

Chapter 4 presents an overview of approaches and techniques used to measure the incidence of delinquency, crime, and victimization. This is an important field of inquiry because policies are frequently based on the interpretation of statistical data.

Questions for Review

1. In general, what are the underlying theories for explaining juvenile deviance?

2. What were the primary theories of causation in the premodern era?

3. What are the main presumptions of the Classical School?

4. What are the roles of choice and responsibility in the Classical School?

5. What are the main presumptions of biological theories?

6. How have biological traits been used to explain deviant behavior?

7. What are the main presumptions of psychological theories?

8. How have psychological traits been used to explain deviant behavior?

9. What are the main presumptions of sociological theories?

10. How have sociological factors been used to explain deviant behavior?

11. What are the main presumptions of critical theories?

Key Terms and Concepts

The following topics were discussed in this chapter and are found in the Glossary:

Anomie and Strain Theories

Atavism

Chromosome Theory

Classical School of Causation

Conditioning Theory

Conflict Theories of Causation

Criminal Deviance

Critical Theory

Demonology

Deterministic Theories of Criminal Causation

Deviance

Differential Association Theory

Free Will Theories of Criminal Causation

Juvenile Deviance

Naturalism

Neoclassical Approach to Deviance

Physiognomy

Positivist School of Criminology

Psychoanalytic Theory

Psychopathology Theory

Radical Criminology

Social Ecology (Structural) Theory

Somatotyping

Underclass, The

DISCUSSION BOX

Pop Culture and Delinquency

This chapter's Discussion Box is intended to stimulate critical discussion about the alleged association between popular culture and teen behavior.

Conventional wisdom in the United States holds that a causal relationship exists between popular culture and juvenile misbehavior. Many laypersons and experts blame television, films, and music for a perceived decline in values and norms among young people. The argument is that popular entertainment offers a glamorous interpretation of harmful lifestyles that include drug use, sexual irresponsibility, and irreverence toward parental authority. When seen on the big screen or heard on CDs, these lifestyles are theoretically attractive to teenagers. This analysis concludes that teenagers do imitate these lifestyles, and that by glorifying these behaviors the film and music industries bear responsibility for the supposed decline in healthy values and norms among juveniles.

A logical extension of this analysis is that popular culture is also associated with juvenile delinquency. It is a fact that films marketed to juveniles are often violent; it is also a fact that many rock and rap songs contain violent lyrics. If these forms of entertainment promote deviance, and if some teenagers are inclined to act out on glamorized popular themes, is it not logical to conclude that popular culture contributes to juvenile delinquency?

Discussion Questions

1. Does popular culture contribute to delinquency?

2. If an association exists, what are the policy implications? What would you do?

3. Is the presumption that inner-city music causes violent delinquency a racist presumption?

4. What analysis would a conditioning theorist give? A conflict theorist?

5. Who should be responsible for monitoring or regulating popular culture directed to teenagers?

Recommended Web Sites

The following Web sites investigate and discuss theoretical causes of juvenile delinquency and violence.

Birth Psychology and Violence (APPPAH):[48] http://www.birthpsychology.com/violence/index.html

Center for Substance Abuse Research: http://www.cesar.umd.edu/

Juvenile Justice Bulletin, October 1998: http://ojjdp.ncjrs.org/jjbulletin/9810_2/contents.html

Partnerships Against Violence Network: http://www.pavnet.org/

Youth Crime Watch of America: http://www.ycwa.org/

Note: The Web site URLs and exercises below are also from the book's study site: http://www.sagepub.com/martin

Web Exercise

Using this chapter's recommended Internet sites, conduct an online investigation of the causes of juvenile delinquency.

- What are common sources of juvenile deviance and violence?
- What are some of the common approaches used by agencies to explain and address the causes of juvenile delinquency?
- How effective do you think these organizations are?

For an online search of the causes of delinquency, students should use a search engine and enter the following keywords:

"Juvenile Deviance"

"Youth Crime"

Recommended Readings

The following publications provide discussions on the causes of delinquency and criminal deviance.

Belknap, J. (1996). *The invisible woman: Gender, crime, and justice.* Belmont, CA: Wadsworth.

Bohm, R. M. (2001). *A Primer on delinquency and crime theory* (2nd ed.). Belmont, CA: Wadsworth.

Lynch, M. J., & Groves, W. B. (1989). *A primer in radical criminology* (2nd ed.). Albany, NY: Harrow and Heston.

Milovanovic, D. (1997). *Postmodern criminology.* Hamden, CT: Garland.

Walker, S., Spohn, C., & DeLone, M. (1996). *The color of justice: Race, ethnicity, and crime in America.* Belmont, CA: Wadsworth.

Notes

1. See Janet Ramos, Angel Ramos, and Richard Ramos v. Town of Vernon and Rudolph Rossmy, 353 F.3d 171 (2d Cir. 2003).

2. Black, H. C. (1968). *Black's law dictionary: Definitions of the terms and phrases of American and English jurisprudence, ancient and modern* (rev. 4th ed., pp. 444–445). St. Paul, MN: West Publishing.

3. For a discussion of research findings on drug use and delinquency, see Calhoun, T. C., & Chapple, C. L. (Eds.). (2003). *Readings in juvenile delinquency and juvenile justice* (p. 236, et seq.). Upper Saddle River, NJ: Prentice Hall.

4. See Crowe, A. H. (1998, May). *Drug identification and testing in the juvenile justice system*. Washington, DC: Office of Juvenile Justice and Delinquency Prevention.

5. See DuRant, R. H., & Cadenhead, C. (1994, April). Factors associated with the use of violence among urban black adolescents. *Journal of Public Health, 84,* 4.

6. For a critical review of research on the intricate relationship between family background and teen delinquency, see Smith, C. A., and Stern, S. B. (1997, September). Delinquency and antisocial behavior: A review of family processes and intervention research. *Social Service Review, 71,* 3.

7. See Gorman-Smith, D., Tolan, P. H., Loweber, R., & Henry, D. B. (1998, October). Relation of family problems to patterns of delinquent involvement among urban youth. *Journal of Abnormal Child Psychology, 26,* 5.

8. For a groundbreaking study of the effects of divorce on children and parents, see Wallerstein, J. S., & Kelly, J. B. (1996). *Surviving the breakup: How children and parents cope with divorce*. New York: Basic Books.

9. For a discussion of criminal justice and the "dangerous classes," see Shelden, R. G. (2001). *Controlling the dangerous classes: A critical introduction to the history of criminal justice*. Boston: Allyn & Bacon.

10. See Cloward, R. A., & Ohlin, L. E. (1966). *Delinquency and opportunity: A theory of delinquent gangs*. New York: Free Press.

11. For an excellent discussion of the underclass, see Wilson, W. J. (1987). *The truly disadvantaged: The inner city, the underclass, and public policy*. Chicago: The University of Chicago Press.

12. For a discussion of the underclass and gang behavior, see Bursik, R. J., & Grasmick, H. G. (2000). The effect of neighborhood dynamics on gang behavior. In J. Miller, C. L. Maxson, & M. W. Klein (Eds.). *The modern gang reader* (2nd ed.). Los Angeles: Roxbury Publishing.

13. See Alwin, D. F., & Thornton, A. (1984, December). Family origins and the schooling process: Early versus late influence of parental characteristics. *American Sociological Review, 49,* 6.

14. See Blair, S. L., & Legazpi Blair, M. C. (1999, Summer). Racial/ethnic differences in high school students' academic performance: Understanding the interweave of social class and ethnicity in family context. *Journal of Comparative Family Studies, 30,* 3.

15. Rush, G. E. (2000). *The dictionary of criminal justice* (5th ed., p. 106). New York: Dushkin/McGraw-Hill.

16. See Blumstein, A., Farrington, D. P., & Moitra, S. (1985). Delinquency careers: Innocents, amateurs, and persisters. In M. Tonry & M. Norval. *Crime and justice: An annual review* (6th ed.). Chicago: University of Chicago Press; see also

Wolfgang, M. E., Thornberry, T. P., & Figlio, R. M. (Eds.). (1987). *From boy to man, from delinquency to crime*. Chicago: University of Chicago Press.

17. See Ageton, S. S., & Elliott, D. S. (1978). *The incidence of delinquent behavior in a national probability sample of adolescents*. Boulder, CO: Behavioral Research Institute.

18. See Hamparian, D. M. (1980). *The violent few: A study of dangerous juvenile offenders*. Lexington, MA: Lexington Books.

19. For a history of criminal justice, see Johnson, H. A., & Travis Wolfe, N. (1996). *History of criminal justice* (2nd ed.). Cincinnati, OH: Anderson.

20. The book was a best seller in America. For an edited translation of Beccaria's essay, see Becarria, C. (1992). *An essay on crimes and punishment*. Wellesley, MA: Branden Publishing.

21. Burns, J. H., & Hart, H. L. A. (Eds.). (1996). *The collected works of Jeremy Bentham: An introduction to the principles of morals and legislation*. New York: Oxford University Press.

22. For a discussion of biological and other theories of causation, see Curran, D. J., & Renzetti, C. M. (1994). *Theories of crime*. Boston: Allyn & Bacon.

23. For an examination of Lombroso's work, see Gibson, M. (2002). *Born to crime: Cesare Lombroso and the origins of biological crime*. New York: Praeger.

24. Darwin's pathbreaking work is presented in Darwin, C. (1964). *On the origin of species: A facsimile of the first edition*. Cambridge, MA: Harvard University Press.

25. See Dugdale, R. L. (1985). *The Jukes: A study in crime, pauperism, disease, and heredity* (3rd ed.). New York: G. P. Putnam's Sons.

26. See Bohm, R. M. (2001). *A primer on delinquency and crime theory* (2nd ed.). Belmont, CA: Wadsworth Publishing.

27. See Jacobs, P., Brunton, M., Meville, M. M., et al. (1965, December). Aggressive behavior, mental subnormality, and the XYY male. *Nature, 208,* 1351-1352.

28. See Marsh, F. H., & Katz, J. (Eds.). (1985). *Biology, crime, and ethics: A study of biological explanations for criminal behavior*. Cincinnati, OH: Anderson.

29. See Sheldon, W. (1949).*Varieties of Delinquent Youth*. New York: Harper and Row.

30. See Glueck, S., & Glueck, E. (1949). *Physique and criminality*. Cambridge, MA: Harvard University Press; see also Glueck, S., & Glueck, E. (1950). *Unraveling juvenile delinquency*. Cambridge, MA: Harvard University Press.

31. See, e.g., Laub, J. H. (1987). *Reanalyzing the Glueck Data: A New Look at Unraveling Juvenile Delinquency*. Paper presented at the meeting of the American Society of Criminology. Montreal, Canada.

32. For a good introduction to the work of Jung, see Campbell, J. (Ed.). (1976). *The portable Jung*. New York: Penguin Books.

33. For a good introduction to the work of Freud, see Gay, P. (Ed.). (1989). *The Freud reader*. New York: W. W. Norton.

34. For a selection of the writings of Pavlov, see Pavlov, I. P. (2001). *I.P. Pavlov: Selected works*. Honolulu, HI: University Press of the Pacific.

35. See Skinner, B. F. (1953). *Science and human behavior*. New York: Macmillan.

36. For a later discussion of Cleckley's original work, see Cleckley, H. M. (1976). *The mask of sanity: An attempt to clarify some issues about the so-called psychopathic personality* (5th ed.). St. Louis, MO: Mosby.

37. See Durkheim, E. (1951). *Suicide* (J. A. Spaulding & G. Simpson, Trans.). New York: Free Press; see also Durkheim, E. (1994). *The division of labor in society* (W. D. Halls, Trans.). New York: Free Press.

38. See Merton, R. K. (1938). Social structure and anomie. In *American Sociological Review*, 3; see also Merton, R. K. (1968). *Social theory and social structure* (enlarged ed.). New York: Free Press.

39. For discussions of seminal research on social ecology, see Park, R. E., & Burgess, E. (1924). *Introduction to the science of sociology* (2nd ed.). Chicago: University of Chicago Press; see also Park, R. E. (Ed.). (1925). *The city*. Chicago: University of Chicago Press.

40. See Shaw, C. R. (1942). *Juvenile delinquency in urban areas*. Chicago: University of Chicago Press; see also Burgess, E. W. (1952). The economic factor in juvenile delinquency. *Journal of Criminal Law*, 43.

41. For pioneering work on delinquency patterns in transitional urban zones in Chicago, see Shaw, C. R., & McKay, H. D. (1972). *Juvenile delinquency and urban areas* (Rev. ed.). Chicago: University of Chicago Press.

42. For a discussion of associations between social ecology and deviance, see Wilks, J. A. (Ed.). Ecological correlates of delinquency and crime. In *Task force report: Crime and its impact—An assessment*. (1967). President's Commission on Law Enforcement and the Administration of Justice. Washington, DC: U.S. Government Printing Office.

43. Sutherland, E. H. (1939). *Principles of criminology* (3rd ed.). Philadelphia: J. B. Lippincott.

44. For a discussion of labeling theory, see Becker, H. S. (1963). *Outsiders: Studies in the sociology of deviance* (Rev. ed.). New York: Free Press.

45. See Krisberg, B. (1975). *Crime and privilege: Toward a new criminology*. Englewood Cliffs, NJ: Prentice-Hall.

46. See Chambliss, W. J., & Seidman, R. B. (1982). *Law, order and power*. Reading, MA: Addison-Wesley.

47. See Chambliss, W. J., & Seidman, R. B. (1982). *Law, order and power*. Reading, MA: Addison-Wesley; see also Quinney, R. (1970). *The social reality of crime*. Boston: Little, Brown.

48. Association for Pre- & Perinatal Psychology and Health.

4 The Delinquency Picture

Measuring Juvenile Deviance

Although researchers try to provide accurate data as basic components for the crafting of sound policies many policies are based not on the reality of delinquency rates but on perceptions. These perceptions of juvenile deviance often drive law and policy. For example, on April 20, 1999, 14 students and one teacher were killed during a shooting rampage at Columbine High School in Littleton, Colorado. A climate of concern and fear arose as communities introspectively sought to understand how this could have happened. Three days after the Columbine shootings, two students at Cambridge Junior High School in Cambridge, Ohio, were investigated for allegedly planning a similar attack.[1] Rhys Williams and Zach Durbin became the subjects of emergency measures when three of their classmates reported that the two had intimated that they were planning a Columbine-like attack.

School and juvenile authorities removed them from the school and their parents, placed them in a juvenile detention facility, imposed house arrest on them, and suspended them from school. Durbin was eventually prosecuted on an aggravated menacing charge but was acquitted. Williams did not have charges filed against him. Lawsuits filed on behalf of the boys failed, with the courts holding that juvenile officials did have probable cause to arrest them, and that the school suspensions satisfied due-process protections.

Policy makers cannot craft workable solutions to juvenile delinquency without accurate information. The allocation of resources to *hot spots* and critical problems cannot be done in a vacuum; it requires the creation of a delinquency picture as a matter of necessity. Measuring juvenile deviance is, without question, of paramount importance for building and maintaining a viable juvenile justice system.

The task of measuring the incidence of delinquency, crime, and victimization involves a diversified group of people using a variety of research tools. Statisticians, social scientists, practitioners, the media, and knowledgeable laypersons all contribute to some degree in the measuring and reporting of deviance and victimization. A number of research and reporting methods are used, ranging from detailed annual reports by federal and state law enforcement agencies to the findings of grassroots organizations. When considering the utility of research findings, it is important to remember that well-designed research methodologies ideally address three questions: How accurate are the research data? How reliable is the research methodology? Is the research generalizable? These qualities—accuracy, reliability, and generalizability—reflect the soundness of research findings, and are summarized as follows:[2]

- *Research accuracy*. Data with few errors. Research methodologies are designed to reduce error and increase the likelihood of accurate findings.
- *Research reliability*. The ability of the research method to produce the same results each time it is used. In other words, the method is a reliable research tool.
- *Research generalizability*. The ability of research findings to be applied to another set of circumstances or questions. Most research has limited generalizability.

We focus in this chapter on several renowned and accepted reporting methodologies. These include the Uniform Crime Reports (UCR), the National Crime Victimization Survey (NCVS), *Juvenile Court Statistics*, and self-reported data. We also explore the policy implications of data derived from these studies. It will be interesting to look at whether different reporting methodologies present distinct perspectives on delinquency and crime to policy makers. In other words, what can policy makers learn from the patterns of delinquency and crime reported by these studies? Do different methodologies suggest different policy options? If so, what is the utility of these studies?

Foreword: Statistics and Perceptions

Before delving into reporting methodologies, a preliminary word must be offered about quantitative (statistical) data that measure and report delinquency and crime. A brief discussion must also be made about the role of the media in the public's perception of delinquency and crime rates.

The Utility of Statistics

For many people—experts and laypersons alike—the mere mention of the word *statistics* is likely to elicit a mixture of anxiety and confusion. Of the innumerable students who have had to study statistics to meet their undergraduate or graduate course requirements, the experience was certainly a memorable one, but not necessarily a pleasant one. Nevertheless, statistics are a critical cornerstone of policy analysis. Quantitative facts and data provide necessary information to analysts and policy makers on a large number of questions. The interpretation of these facts and data often drives social policy, as well as the *criticism* of social policy. Crime statistics include data on the age of offenders, thus providing resources for measuring juvenile delinquency. Statistics also include regional data, which are useful for evaluating the allocation of law enforcement and social service resources locally and nationally. Other policy-relevant crime statistics include the following:

- Arrests
- Probation and parole
- Rates of offenses
- Numbers of complaints
- Types of offenses
- Incarceration rates
- Lengths of sentences
- Demographic data on offenders and victims (e.g., race, gender, age)

Experts interpret and manipulate these data to analyze the significance of statistical means, modes, medians, and percentages.

The Media and Public Perception of Crime

The *media* refers to a network of private communications agencies that report information on current events to the general public. This information, or news, is derived from human and documentary sources that are theoretically (and ideally) reliable. Broadcast news agencies include private radio, television, and cable networks. Print media include private newspapers and news magazines, and alternative news outlets include Internet-based magazines, journals, and Web sites. In the modern era, news agencies develop their own styles and perspectives, which affect the manner in which they report information. These styles and perspectives also affect what kind of information they choose to report. Delinquency and crime are often at the forefront of media coverage and are frequently the featured report for primetime broadcasts or newspaper headlines. Arguably, the entertainment industry (films and television) is also responsible for providing the public with information about delinquency and crime—albeit in a rather sensational and inaccurate manner.

The media do affect the public's *perception* of delinquency and crime. For example, reporting on so-called "crime waves," "gang wars," and celebrity cases regularly grips the attention of the public. Thematic series of reports devote a significant amount of coverage and time to school shootings, teenage binge drinking, drug use, or child kidnappings. Intensive coverage of

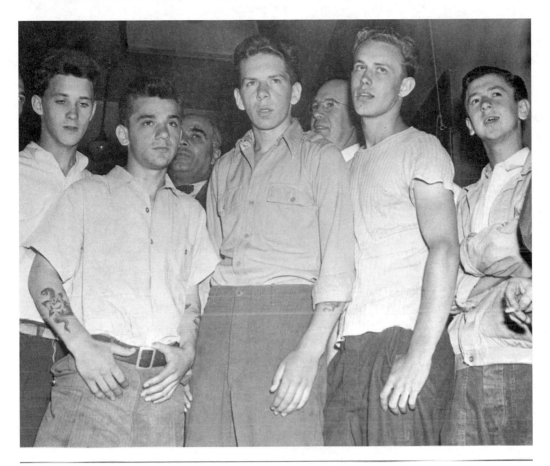

Photo 4.1   Juvenile delinquents pose after confessing to committing a crime in 1948. Fear of delinquency and crime often does not reflect the rate of offenses.

specific crimes is often unrelenting and lurid, and sensationalist media outlets intentionally and routinely try to arouse the public's passions. Thus, the media can create a popular (rather than empirical) measurement of crime that many people readily believe. Rumors, conventional wisdom, and culture are important factors for formulating the public's understanding of their environment. In effect, popular perceptions of delinquency and crime are frequently affected by the content and style of news reporting, with the result being that popular opinions do not always reflect their particular community's statistical reality. Popular television "reality shows" add to this perception by broadcasting dramatic police chases and apprehensions from cities around the country.

The discussion in this chapter reviews

- Tools of the Trade: Estimating and Reporting Delinquency and Crime
- Applying the Data: Identifying Patterns of Delinquency and Crime
- Postscript: Juvenile Victimization

CHAPTER PERSPECTIVE 4.1

Why Conduct Research on Delinquency and Crime?

Scientific research on delinquency and crime is a critical element of the policy-making process, and is used by experts to identify and interpret behavioral trends. Modern research agendas use a number of methodologies to acquire and report data on delinquency crime. The type of data sought by researchers are typically drawn from arrest data (the number of cases cleared by police agencies); victimization surveys (household surveys of victims of crimes); *Juvenile Court Statistics* (cases processed by juvenile courts); and self-reported data (surveys asking respondents about their own criminal behavior). These data can either be quantitative data, which give a numerical designation to data, or qualitative data, which delve into the reasons underlying certain trends in behavior. Researchers are ideally objective and unbiased in their investigation of deviance.

Research methods collect data and facts to identify and describe a particular environment. However, one must understand that criminal justice research is not limited to any single discipline. It is an interdisciplinary field of inquiry that can involve researchers from a variety of social sciences, including anthropologists, sociologists, political scientists, and psychologists. All researchers propose theories to explain the reality of delinquency and crime, and use accepted methods to test their theories and conduct their research.

Data analysis refers to the interpretation and manipulation of data. It is from data analysis that research has its greatest impact on society. Depending on how data are interpreted, policy makers recommend policies that can broadly affect how offenders are treated, which institutions receive political or financial support, and whether new paradigms are adopted.

Tools of the Trade: Estimating and Reporting Delinquency and Crime

How prevalent is the problem of juvenile delinquency? What resources are needed to remedy youthful deviance? How should these resources be allocated? Policy makers and other experts understand that the answers to these questions require hard data, for the benefit of both young offenders and society. For this reason, measuring the frequency of delinquency and crime is a central component of criminology and criminal justice policy making. Researchers and practitioners generally acquire data on juvenile and criminal deviance from several sources using a variety of methodologies.

These sources and methodologies, which represent the predominant models for reporting and evaluating deviance, are classified as follows:

- *Arrest data.* These are data that report the number of cases that were *cleared* by police agencies. **Clearances** are arrests that have been made for reported crimes. Arrest data refer only to people taken into custody on suspicion of delinquency and criminal behavior, not to *convictions* for this behavior. Local law enforcement agencies report cleared cases to the Federal Bureau of Investigation (FBI), which publishes this information in its annual *Uniform Crime Reports: Crime in the United States.*[3]

- *Victimization surveys.* These data are derived from surveys of victims of crimes. Most victimization surveys compile **household data**, which involves questioning respondents about whether members of their households have been victims of delinquency or crime. Perhaps the best known victimization survey is the National Crime Victimization Survey, which is an annual household survey conducted by the U.S. Department of Justice's Bureau of Justice Statistics.

- *Juvenile court statistics.* These provide data on cases processed by juvenile courts. Reports by organizations such as the Office of Juvenile Justice and Delinquency Prevention and the National Center for Juvenile Justice contain statistics on juvenile court proceedings. These data include case statistics at the local jurisdiction level.

- *Self-reported data.* These are surveys of juveniles and adults, asking respondents about their personal criminal behavior within a specified time period. Originally designed to measure delinquent behavior, and later extended to adult criminality, these studies are usually conducted by researchers on local and regional levels.

Arrest data, juvenile court data, and victimization data are reported as **official data** (or official statistics). Official data are compiled by law enforcement agencies, courts, and correctional systems at national, regional, and local levels. Federal research offices such as the Office of Juvenile Justice and Delinquency Prevention,[4] Bureau of Justice Statistics,[5] and National Institute of Justice[6] also publish official data. Self-reported data are generally compiled by academic researchers, and are usually not considered to be official data.

Police Data: The Uniform Crime Reports

The FBI publishes an annual statistical document that is arguably the most influential compilation of official data. Known as the **Uniform Crime Reports** (UCR), the publication evaluates arrest data for juveniles and adults. All law enforcement agencies are asked to voluntarily participate in the UCR. Participating agencies regularly submit information on clearances (arrest data) for 29 offenses to the FBI, which then constructs a statistical profile of crime in the United States based on these arrest data. One feature of the UCR—time comparisons of crime rates—has a significant impact on policy. These timelines serve as indicators for whether crime is increasing or decreasing within specified demographic and geographic data sets.

The concept for a UCR dates from 1929, when the FBI began to publish the findings of a voluntary reporting system, and 1930, when Congress passed legislation tasking the FBI with assembling crime data and reporting trends in crime. From this beginning, it took decades for the modern UCR to be produced, as most publications from that time reported an incomplete national crime profile. However, during the 1960s a more complete national reporting system took shape when the National Sheriffs' Association formed the Committee on Uniform Crime Reporting to promote participation by sheriffs' departments. The UCR is now a massive undertaking, and is:

> [A] nationwide, cooperative statistical effort of nearly 17,000 city, county, and state law enforcement agencies voluntarily reporting data on crimes brought to their attention. During 2000, law enforcement agencies active in the UCR program represented nearly 254 million United States inhabitants or 94 percent of the total population as established by the Bureau of the Census.[7]

The UCR reports crime and victimization in several ways and over different time periods. For example, data are compiled annually or quarterly according to race, gender, age, and jurisdiction size. Perhaps its most powerful information is found in the classification of criminal offenses as **Part I offenses** (also known as Index Crimes) and **Part II offenses**. These classifications are designed to differentiate serious offenses from lesser crimes for the purpose of assessing the national crime rate.

Part I offenses are eight serious crimes that either occur frequently (such as motor vehicle theft) or are considered to be inherently unacceptable behavior (such as forcible rape and arson). These offenses are felonies, which are technically defined as criminal violations that are punishable by imprisonment for a minimum of one year. In point of fact, Part I offenses are often punished by long-term incarceration or capital punishment (should death result while committing a Part I felony). This classification includes four violent crimes (criminal homicide, forcible rape, robbery, and aggravated assault) and four property crimes (burglary, larceny-theft, motor vehicle theft, and arson). Part I offenses are also known as Index Crimes because they form a mathematical index, or composite picture, of crime in the United States. This composite picture is drawn at the city, county, and state levels over time. Chapter Perspective 4.2 summarizes Part I offenses.

CHAPTER PERSPECTIVE 4.2

Uniform Crime Reports: Defining Part I Offenses

The Federal Bureau of Investigation classifies eight serious felonies as Index (Part I) Offenses. These crimes are defined as follows:[8]

- *Criminal homicide*. Murder, nonnegligent manslaughter: the willful killing of one human being by another. . . . Manslaughter by negligence: the killing of another person through gross negligence.
- *Forcible rape*. The carnal knowledge of a female forcibly and against her will.
- *Robbery*. The taking or attempting to take anything of value from the care, custody, or control of a person . . . by force or threat of force or violence and/or by putting the victim in fear.
- *Aggravated assault*. An unlawful attack by one person upon another for the purpose of inflicting severe or aggravated bodily injury. This type of assault usually is accompanied by the use of a weapon or by means likely to produce death or great bodily harm.
- *Burglary*. The unlawful entry of a structure to commit a felony or a theft. Attempted forcible entry is included.
- *Larceny-theft*. The unlawful taking, carrying, leading, or riding away of property from the possession or constructive possession of another.
- *Motor vehicle theft*. The theft or attempted theft of a motor vehicle.
- *Arson*. Any willful or malicious burning or attempt to burn, with or without intent to defraud, a dwelling house, public building, motor vehicle or aircraft, personal property of another, and so forth.

Part II offenses are offenses that either occur relatively infrequently, are considered to be less serious than Part I crimes, or are "victimless" social order crimes. These are essentially offenses that are not listed in Part I. As indicated in Chapter Perspective 4.3, several Part II offenses have been legalized in some states (such as gambling and prostitution), and the final listed offenses really are not criminal offenses at all (suspicion, curfew and loitering, runaways). The latter two classifications pertain only to juveniles.

CHAPTER PERSPECTIVE 4.3

Uniform Crime Reports: Defining Part II Offenses

The Federal Bureau of Investigation classifies 21 lesser offenses as Part II offenses, including the final two that specifically address juvenile status offenses. These offenses are defined as follows:[9]

- *Other assaults*. Assaults and attempted assaults where no weapons are used and which do not result in serious or aggravated injury to the victim.
- *Forgery and counterfeiting*. Making, altering, uttering, or possessing, with intent to defraud, anything false in the semblance of that which is true.
- *Fraud*. Fraudulent conversion and obtaining money or property by false pretenses.

- *Embezzlement.* Misappropriation or misapplication of money or property entrusted to one's care, custody, or control.
- *Stolen property—buying, receiving, possessing.* Buying, receiving, and possessing stolen property.
- *Vandalism.* Willful or malicious destruction, injury, disfigurement, or defacement of any public or private property . . . without consent of the owner or persons having custody or control.
- *Weapons—carrying, possessing.* All violations of regulations or statutes controlling the carrying, using, possessing, furnishing, and manufacturing of deadly weapons or silencers.
- *Prostitution and commercialized vice.* Sex offenses of a commercialized nature, such as prostitution, keeping a bawdy house, procuring, or transporting women for immoral purposes.
- *Sex offenses.* Statutory rape and offenses against chastity, common decency, morals, and the like.
- *Drug abuse violations.* Offenses relating to the unlawful possession, sale, use, growing, and manufacturing of narcotic drugs.
- *Gambling.* Promoting, permitting, or engaging in illegal gambling.
- *Offenses against the family and children.* Nonsupport, neglect, desertion, or abuse of family and children.
- *Driving under the influence.* Driving or operating any vehicle or common carrier while drunk or under the influence of liquor or narcotics.
- *Liquor laws.* State and/or local liquor law violations except drunkenness and driving under the influence.
- *Disorderly conduct.* Breach of the peace.
- *Vagrancy.* Begging, loitering, and so forth.
- *All other offenses.* All violations of state and/or local laws except those listed above and traffic offenses.
- *Suspicion.* No specific offense; suspect released without formal charges being placed.
- *Curfew and loitering laws (persons under age 18).* Offenses relating to violations of local curfew or loitering ordinances where such laws exist.
- *Runaways (persons under age 18).* Limited to juveniles taken into protective custody under provisions of local statutes.

The FBI also publishes an annual **Crime Clock** in the UCR, which depicts the frequency of the commission of major crimes. It is an interesting representation of the seriousness of crime in the United States. Figure 4.1 reproduces the Crime Clock for 2000.

Although UCR data create a useful picture of the extent of crime and delinquency, it is important to caution against interpreting these measurements beyond the limitations imposed by the type of data used. The UCR reports *arrests*—not convictions, unreported offenses, or unsolved crimes—which means that there are no data for the commission of crimes in which no suspect was caught. There are also unmeasured problems such

The Crime Clock is published annually by the FBI. It is a good snapshot of the frequency of serious crime in the United States. The following example is typical of how it is presented.

Every 2.7 seconds
One Crime Index Offense

Every 22.1 seconds One Violent Crime

Every 35.3 seconds One Aggravated Assault

Every 1.2 minutes One Robbery

Every 5.5 minutes One Forcible Rape

Every 32.4 minutes One Murder

Every 3.0 seconds One Property Crime

Every 4.5 seconds One Larceny-theft

Every 14.7 seconds One Burglary

Every 25.3 seconds One Motor Vehicle Theft

Figure 4.1   The Crime Clock[10]

Source: Federal Bureau of Investigation. (2003). *Uniform crime reports, 2002: Crime in the United States*. Washington, DC: Department of Justice.

as whether police discretion was biased in some manner when arrests were made. Nor is there a deeper qualitative (nonstatistical) analysis or profile of perpetrators and victims—this is best accomplished by survey and interview data. As a consequence, it is reasonable to conclude that the UCR does not include other important data, and may in fact underreport the true extent of delinquency and crime. It also does not measure possible socioeconomic associations with the extent and type of delinquency and crime. Nevertheless, the UCR is a very useful tool for policy makers despite its limitations.

Surveying the Public: National Crime Victimization Survey

Victimization surveys have been performed since 1966. Researchers and practitioners designed them as an alternative resource to the UCR, which was considered to provide an incomplete assessment of crime in the United States. By 1975, this effort resulted in an ongoing survey, which became the **National Crime Victimization Survey** (NCVS). The NCVS is a self-report survey that reports information derived from household surveys conducted each year by the U.S. Department of Justice's Bureau of Justice Statistics. The NCVS, which is usually made twice annually, asks approximately 48,000 households (80,000 to 101,000 persons) whether members of their household ages 12 years and older have been victims of crimes. Prepared in collaboration with the U.S. Census Bureau, these surveys make available important information that cannot be provided by arrest data derived from studies such as the UCR. This information includes

- Unreported crimes
- Extent and type of teenage victimization
- Extent and type of young adult victimization
- Racial characteristics of victims
- Victimization comparisons across age, race, gender, and geographic regions

The NCVS reports the incidence of victimization from selected violent crimes and property crimes. This selection is not as comprehensive as the UCR or *Juvenile Court Statistics* (discussed below), and it differs from these data resources in several ways. For example, the NCVS defines the crimes of rape and assault more broadly than the UCR. Also, homicide is excluded—for the simple reason that homicide victims cannot be interviewed. Nevertheless, for the purposes of researching victimization, the NCVS crimes do represent prevalent types of crimes likely to be encountered by victims. The NCVS reports victimization from the following crimes:

- Rape/sexual assault
- Robbery
- Aggravated assault
- Simple assault
- Burglary
- Motor vehicle theft
- Property theft

An important advantage of NCVS methodology over the UCR is that people who are interviewed answer whether they or a member of their household have been victims of crime during the previous 6 or 12 months, regardless of whether the incident was reported to the authorities or cleared by the police. Hence, statistically sound data are collected for unreported and unsolved crimes, whereas UCR data are compiled from arrest records on reported crimes. This is particularly important because interviewers can probe the reasons for why people do not report victimization. For example, rape victims may fear stigma or shame, and property crime victims may simply believe that the police cannot solve the crime. Because of this distinction, many researchers and practitioners consider the NCVS to be a more accurate estimate of the national crime rate than the UCR. An important (and somewhat disturbing) difference in findings between the two reports is that the NCVS regularly reports a much higher crime rate than does the UCR—this difference is sometimes doubled, tripled, or quadrupled. In other words, many experts believe that official data from the UCR severely *underestimate* the true level of crime in the United States.

Youths in the Judicial System: *Juvenile Court Statistics*

The federal government has been collecting juvenile court data since 1929, when researchers reported and described cases handled in 1927. Since 1975, the U.S. Department of Justice's Office of Juvenile Justice and Delinquency Prevention (OJJDP) has managed an extensive archive of automated records of juvenile court cases. This archive, known as the **National Juvenile Court Data Archive**,[11] was established to promote research on juvenile justice. The Archive works in close collaboration with the National Center for Juvenile Justice, a private nonprofit research organization founded in 1973.[12] The National Center for Juvenile Justice has published many reports (often under the auspices of the OJJDP), including data on juvenile justice processes and an annual report of *Juvenile Court Statistics*. The latter document, the *Juvenile Court Statistics* series, has become an important resource for researchers and practitioners.[13]

The *Juvenile Court Statistics* series regularly reports offenses using classifications that are similar to the Part I and Part II classifications found in the FBI's Uniform Crime Reports. Delinquency (the Part I equivalent) is reported separately from status offenses (the Part II equivalent). Delinquency offenses are classified as follows:

- *Person offense*. Criminal homicide, forcible rape, robbery, aggravated assault, simple assault, other violent sex offenses, and other person offenses
- *Property offense*. Burglary, larceny-theft, motor vehicle theft, arson, vandalism, trespassing, stolen property, and other property offenses
- *Drug law violation*. Drug abuse offenses, generally referring to using illicit substances as well as licit substances, such as inhalants
- *Public order offense*. Obstruction of justice, disorderly conduct, weapons offenses, liquor law violation, nonviolent sex offenses, and other public order offenses

TABLE 4.1 EXAMPLE OF TYPICAL DELINQUENCY DATA REPORTED BY RACE IN JUVENILE COURT STATISTICS[a]

Juvenile court statistics are reported in a similar manner as crime data in the FBI's Uniform Crime Reports. This table, from the OJJDP's 2003 edition of *Juvenile Court Statistics*, is an example of how the incidence of delinquency is reported by race.

Most Serious Offense	1989[b]	1994[b]	1998[b]	Percent Change[b] 1989–1998 (%)	1994–1998 (%)
White	827,800	1,093,100	1,185,400	43	8
Person	121,000	209,700	250,200	107	19
Property	515,700	605,300	558,100	8	−8
Drugs	45,100	79,600	131,500	192	65
Public order	146,000	198,500	245,600	68	24
African American	352,200	512,100	508,200	44	−1
Person	86,800	139,400	141,600	63	2
Property	177,600	226,600	205,400	16	−9
Drugs	31,100	49,000	56,000	80	14
Public order	56,700	97,100	105,200	86	8
Other Races	41,300	61,500	63,800	54	4
Person	6,500	11,700	12,000	84	3
Property	26,400	36,100	34,100	29	−6
Drugs	1,500	2,600	5,000	228	91
Public order	6,900	11,100	12,700	83	15

a. Adapted from Puzzanchera, C., Stahl, A. L., Finnegan, T. A., Tierney, N., & Snyder, H. N. (2003). *Juvenile court statistics 1998* (p. 15). Washington, DC: Office of Juvenile Justice and Delinquency Prevention.

b. Detail may not add to totals because of rounding. Percent change calculations are based on unrounded numbers.

Status offenses are classified as follows:

- *Runaway*. Departing from the custody of a parent or guardian without permission
- *Truancy*. Failure to attend school without authorization
- *Ungovernable*. Disobedience and incorrigibility
- *Liquor*. Underage purchase, possession, or ingestion of alcohol
- *Miscellaneous*. Curfews, tobacco prohibitions

Delinquency offenses are evaluated in several ways, including by age, gender, race, region, and over time. Table 4.1 illustrates the kind of delinquency data typically reported by race in official *Juvenile Court Statistics*.

TABLE 4.2   EXAMPLE OF TYPICAL STATUS OFFENSE DATA REPORTED BY RACE IN
JUVENILE COURT STATISTICS[a]

Juvenile court statistics are reported in a manner similar to crime data in the FBI's Uniform Crime Reports. This table, from the OJJDP's 2000 edition of *Juvenile Court Statistics*, is an example of how the national incidence of status offenses is reported by race.

Most Serious Offense	1988[b]	1993[b]	1997[b]	Percent Change[b] 1988–1997 (%)	Percent Change[b] 1993–1997 (%)
White	57,600	72,400	99,500	96	48
Runaway	9,600	14,500	17,500	82	21
Truancy	14,600	23,300	29,600	102	27
Ungovernable	9,000	10,400	15,600	73	50
Liquor	24,400	24,200	36,800	51	52
African American	11,700	18,500	22,700	122	26
Runaway	2,400	4,400	5,600	130	28
Truancy	5,000	8,600	9,600	91	11
Ungovernable	3,500	3,900	5,200	51	32
Liquor	800	1,600	2,300	185	47
Other Races	2,800	7,300	4,200	104	0
Runaway	400	1,000	900	130	−10
Truancy	1,000	1,800	1,300	35	−29
Ungovernable	400	2500	400	5	−20
Liquor	1,000	2,000	1,600	57	−19

a. Puzzanchera, C., Stahl, A. L., Finnegan, T. A., Snyder, H. N., Poole, R. S., & Tierney, N. (2000). *Juvenile court statistics 1997* (p. 51). Washington, DC: Office of Juvenile Justice and Delinquency Prevention.

b. Detail may not add to totals because of rounding. Percent change calculations are based on unrounded numbers.

Status offenses can pose serious social order challenges for the juvenile justice system; however, they are not as severely disruptive to society as are index offenses. Status offenses are also evaluated according to age, gender, race, region, and over time. Table 4.2 illustrates the kind of status offense data typically reported by race in official *Juvenile Court Statistics*.

Surveying Delinquents and Criminals: Self-Reported Data

Self-report studies attempt to estimate the incidence of delinquency or crime by investigating the individual profiles of juvenile and adult offenders. Researchers ask respondents about the nature of their own delinquency and criminality, so that, unlike statistical or victimization studies, self-report data provide insights into the motives, personalities, and conduct of offenders. Such data also report crimes for which no clearances have been made and where no one has admitted victimization. In this way, data for crimes known only to the perpetrators can be compiled.

Another advantage of self-report studies is that a composite of deviant behavior can emerge, which provides a much richer profile of the nature of delinquency and crime—all from the point of view of the perpetrator. For example, theoretical associations can be identified between violent deviance and an individual's home environment, substance abuse, poverty, or gang affiliations, or information about reasons for delinquency in high schools can be investigated. These data provide excellent insight into the lives of juvenile delinquents and adult offenders that cannot be elicited from quantitative data such as the UCR and *Juvenile Court Statistics* or victimization surveys such as the NCVS.

The **National Youth Survey** (NYS) is an example of self-report data. It is a longitudinal study of a national sample of 1,725 juveniles, and involves the distribution of several series of questionnaires to the juveniles. During the course of the NYS, it became clear that the incidence of violent delinquency among youths is significantly higher than reported by official data such as the UCR and NCVS. It also reported that the onset of violent delinquency begins at an early age, and that escalation from lesser offenses to serious offenses is more prevalent than found in other studies. One significant data set indicated that a small number of violent juveniles commit the majority of violent offenses. Having made this observation, it is important to note that juvenile delinquency has increased and declined repeatedly over time.

The reliability of self-report studies has been criticized and debated for some time.[14] An obvious intuitive criticism asks why a respondent would be truthful about his or her delinquency or criminal behavior. Who would confess their criminal activities to a perfect stranger? Another problem is whether some young respondents simply brag about, or make up, what they report. Despite the seeming logic to these criticisms, experts generally agree that most research using this methodology is sound, and that the findings are valid. This is because researchers have successfully gained the trust of respondents by guaranteeing the anonymity or confidentiality of their subjects.

Applying the Data: Identifying Patterns of Delinquency and Crime

Official data—Uniform Crime Reports, the National Crime Victimization Survey, and *Juvenile Court Statistics*—are used by policy makers to determine how to respond to delinquency and criminal behavior. Because of the distinctions in methodology discussed previously, each source of official data provides different insights into how to combat illicit deviance. Table 4.3 is a comparison summary of official data derived from the UCR, NCVS, and *Juvenile Court Statistics*.

TABLE 4.3   COMPARISON OF INFORMATION DERIVED FROM OFFICIAL DATA

Official data are elicited from law enforcement agencies, courts, and correctional systems at national, regional, and local levels. Federal agencies coordinate the compilation and reporting of these data.

This table summarizes the features of official data sources.

Features	Official Report		
	Uniform Crime Reports	**National Crime Victimization Survey**	**Juvenile Court Statistics**
Crimes measured	Criminal homicide Forcible rape Robbery Aggravated assault Burglary Larceny-theft Motor vehicle theft Arson 21 Part II offenses	Rape/sexual assault Robbery Aggravated assault Simple assault Burglary Motor vehicle theft Property theft	*Person Offense:* Criminal homicide, forcible rape, robbery, aggravated assault, simple assault, other violent sex offense, other person offense *Property Offense:* Burglary, larceny-theft, motor vehicle theft, arson, vandalism, trespassing, stolen property offense, other property offense *Drug Law Violation* *Public Order Offense:* Obstruction of justice, disorderly conduct, weapons offense, liquor law violation, nonviolent sex offenses, other public order offense
Coverage	Clearances by police departments	Crimes reported by victims	Juvenile cases processed through juvenile courts
Methodology	FBI collection and publication of data on cleared cases from police departments	Periodic household surveys	Collection and publication of data from juvenile courts
Coordinating body	Federal Bureau of Investigation, U.S. Department of Justice	Bureau of Justice Statistics, U.S. Department of Justice	National Center for Juvenile Justice and Office of Juvenile Justice and Delinquency Prevention

What patterns of delinquency and criminal activity emerge from these studies? How do practitioners and everyday citizens interpret crime data? Crime rates (average incidence per segment of population) are used by experts, the media, and average laypersons to frame their own opinions about the juvenile/criminal justice environment. Criminal justice and delinquency data are the primary source of reliable information about the extent of crime in society. Before exploring these data, let us first discuss important social and cultural perspectives on the impact of crime on society.

Preliminary Perspectives and Contexts

Individuals and communities form their own opinions of crime and are affected by criminal behavior in ways that are not readily apparent. For this reason, it is helpful to frame a preliminary context for understanding patterns of crime from the perspective of the American public. We shall look at the public's fear of crime, the costs of delinquency and crime, and the problem of violent juveniles. These issues are important reference points for analyzing patterns of deviance.

Fear of Delinquency and Crime. An interesting theoretical model was popularized during the early 1990s, when researchers and other experts coined the term "**superpredator**" to refer to a fresh wave of violent young offenders who were expected to arise in the new century. This new wave of violence would emanate from a new generation of youths. These youths would theoretically be prone to extreme violence, and the increase in arrests of juveniles for violent offenses during the 1980s seemed to confirm the likelihood of this new typology. Projections for the superpredator phenomenon were influenced by the growing problem of juvenile violence that continued into the beginning of the 1990s.[15] This new predatory typology never really emerged, and in fact juvenile violence declined during the latter years of the decade. Nevertheless, the theory reflected more than hypothetical projections by experts; it also reflected general cultural concern that a fearsome criminal subculture had arisen among a young, primarily urban, population.

From a cultural perspective, it is not an exaggeration to state that the fear of delinquency and crime is high in many urban and suburban communities. In fact, it has become endemic in recent years. This fear is not necessarily based on the general public's examination of official statistics, but rather is rooted in community *perceptions* of delinquency and crime. In other words, community perceptions of high crime rates are often disconnected from the statistical reality of a relatively lower rate of crime.[16] These perceptions can be exacerbated by impassioned discussions about superpredators or cycles of crime by experts and in the media.

What is to account for this generalized anxiety? Influences from life experiences, community norms, and popular information are likely sources of public perception and misperception. Several factors may be cited:

- Personal experiences with victimization, or knowing someone who has been victimized
- Media sensationalizing of high-profile crimes, especially fear-inducing cases involving child kidnappings, school shootings, or serial slayings
- Nationwide policy adaptations to certain kinds of crime, such as the adoption of Megan's Laws to track sexual predators and Amber Alerts to locate abducted children
- Entertainment industry story lines in films and television, usually hyping incredible feats of criminality and crime suppression

Thus, high-profile cases and policies, sensational reporting, and popular culture can create a climate of fear and anxiety that has little to do with findings from data or official reports. Popular sentiment is often moved by events of the day rather than explanations of longitudinal trends within demographic groups and regions. In effect, although official statistics have periodically shown declines in certain crimes, there is usually no concomitant (simultaneously associated) reduction in public worry about possible victimization.

Costs of Delinquency and Crime. A report published by the Bureau of Justice Statistics (BJS) stated that crime victims lost an estimated $15.6 billion in direct costs in 2002.[17] This estimate, based on data findings from the National Crime Victimization Survey, reflects the magnitude of economic losses suffered by individual victims. The BJS study also reported individuals' direct losses from specific crimes, as indicated in Table 4.4.

In another study, the National Institute of Justice (NIJ) estimated that total direct and indirect losses attributable to delinquency and crime total $105 billion each year.[18] These losses include medical costs, property losses, and workplace losses. The NIJ study assigned values to seemingly intangible losses such as chronic emotional distress, pain and suffering, and disability. These factors increased the estimated amount of annual losses to a staggering $450 billion.

Studies such as the BJS and NIJ reports are, of course, only estimates of the costs of delinquency and crime. However, assuming that they create a relatively sound projection of annual losses, the economic consequences of criminal behavior on society are quite profound. Individuals, communities, and governments bear the burden of absorbing these losses, as well as the responsibility for allocating resources to the investigation, prosecution, and incarceration of perpetrators. One can readily see from this perspective that the "war on crime" is one of the most expensive social problems in history.

Violent Juveniles. A violent juvenile is one who commits a violent offense rather than a property offense. Recalling the findings of the National Youth Survey, which concluded that a relatively small number of violent juveniles commit the majority of violent offenses, it should also be noted that more

TABLE 4.4   INDIVIDUAL LOSSES FROM DELINQUENCY AND CRIME

Direct economic losses from delinquency and crime have been high. Direct losses refer to individual costs such as medical care, lost work time, and property losses.

This table, from a report published by the U.S. Department of Justice's Bureau of Justice Statistics, summarizes typical annual losses to victims of crime.[a]

Total Economic Loss to Victims of Crime, 2002	
Type of Crime	**Amount ($)**
All crimes	16,906,000,000
Personal crimes	1,370,000,000
Crimes of violence	1,338,000,000
Rape	15,000,000
Robbery	496,000,000
Assault	827,000,000
Property Crimes	14,198,000,000
Theft	4,643,000,000
Motor vehicle theft	6,214,000,000
Household burglary	3,341,000,000

a. Adapted from Bureau of Justice Statistics. (2002). Total economic loss to victims of crime. In *Criminal victimization in the United States*. Washington, DC: U.S. Department of Justice. Web site at http://www.ojp.usdoj.gov/bjs/abstract/cvus/economic973.htm

teenagers today are violent in comparison to youths in previous generations.[19] This is despite the fact that juvenile arrests for violent crimes decreased steadily during the decade of the 1990s and into the new millennium.[20] Juvenile violence has become a widespread problem in American society, so much so that the criminal justice system has responded with routine criminal prosecutions of juvenile offenders as adults. In fact, violent juvenile behavior tends to be more common in the United States than in other democratic societies.[21] Although the rate of juvenile arrests for some violent offenses declines periodically (arrests for murder and nonnegligent manslaughter fell 62% between 1992 and 2001),[22] juvenile violence is still high. A number of socioeconomic reasons have been offered to explain the frequency of violent juvenile behavior, including the following:

- Drug and alcohol abuse
- Organized associations of youths (gangs)
- Cultures of violence in some neighborhoods
- "Underclass" socioeconomic norms and conditions
- Easier access to firearms and willingness to use them
- Onset of delinquency at younger age

TABLE 4.5   ARRESTS OF VIOLENT JUVENILE OFFENDERS[a]

Arrests of juveniles for violent behavior generally declined through the 1990s and into the new millennium. Arrests for Part I Index Crimes decreased, while non-Index Crime assaults increased. These are certainly favorable data. However, the numbers continue to indicate a relatively high incidence of teenage violence.

This table shows the number of juvenile arrests for juveniles under the age of 15 years, under the age of 18 years, and the percentage decline for those under the age of 18 years from 1992 to 2001.

Most Serious Offense	Number of Juvenile Arrests Under Age 15	Number of Juvenile Arrests Under Age 18	Percent Change Under Age 18 1992–2001 (%)
Crime Index (Part I) total[b]	150,223	407,106	−30.7
Violent Crime Index (Part I)	22,146	67,002	−21
Murder and nonnegligent manslaughter	114	957	−62
Forcible rape	1,180	3,119	−24.5
Robbery	4,354	18,111	−23.5
Aggravated assault	16,498	44,815	−2.8
Other assaults (non-Index Crime)	70,642	183,142	16.2

a. Adapted from Bureau of Justice Statistics. (2003). *Sourcebook of criminal justice statistics, 2002*. Washington, DC: U.S. Department of Justice.

b. Not every Part I Index Crime is presented, so the total number of arrests do not reflect the totals for the listed offenses.

It is likely that no single factor explains the increase in teenage violence during the last generation. However, when factors are combined (as is often the case), they can create the necessary elements for an increased likelihood of violent delinquency. Because these socioeconomic problems are entrenched and unlikely to be resolved in the near future, violent teenage behavior is likely to continue at an unacceptably high rate. Table 4.5 summarizes arrests for violent juvenile behavior in 2000.

Delinquency and the Crime Picture

Compared with other nations that also do not suffer from domestic political turmoil, the United States is a violent country. It has a much higher incidence of lethal and nonlethal criminal violence than other Western democracies, and the American homicide rate is quite high among industrialized countries. The criminal use of firearms is also very high, so that "handguns were used to murder 2 people in New Zealand, 15 in Japan, 30 in Great Britain, 106 in Canada, and 9,390 in the United States."[23] An

Photo 4.2 Juveniles await processing after being taken into custody in 1954.

example of the implications of these data is found in research published by the American Medical Association, which noted that a quarter-century of high gang-related homicides in Los Angeles County had made homicide "a major public health problem" in the region.[24]

As discussed previously, public perceptions of juvenile and adult deviance are often out of alignment with actual crime rates. An example of how official data can aggravate this problem is found in arrest data for juvenile offenders: One popular perception is that youth violence is exceptionally high, and, indeed, juvenile offenders are *more likely* to be caught and arrested than are adult offenders.[25] Thus, in terms of arrest numbers, it would seem that juveniles, compared with adults, commit a larger number of crimes. However, these findings simply mean that more juvenile cases are *cleared* than are adult cases. Recent data also show that while the number of juvenile clearances is relatively high, "the proportion of crimes law enforcement attributed to juveniles has declined in recent years."[26] Nevertheless, these declines in delinquency and crime rates do not readily translate into adjustments in popular thinking or public perceptions.

Profiling Juvenile Deviance. Juvenile violence was rather high during the decade of the 1980s through the early 1990s, when Part I violent crimes increased by 200%.[27] However, as a proportion of the overall juvenile population, juvenile criminality has been consistently fairly low. Only a relatively small percentage of juveniles are arrested for criminal offenses and only a small percentage of these arrestees are arrested for violent Part I index offenses. As a proportion of serious offenses, those committed by juveniles are also relatively low. In 2000, "Juveniles were involved in 9% of murder arrests, 14% of aggravated assault arrests, 33% of burglary arrests, 25% of robbery arrests, and 24% of weapons arrests."[28]

Popular perceptions aside, research data show that many more Part I violent crimes, such as murder, are committed by adults on a substantially larger scale than by juveniles. "Arrests of juveniles accounted for 12% of all violent crimes cleared in 2000—specifically, 5% of murders, 12% of forcible rapes, 16% of robberies, and 12% of aggravated assaults."[29] And unlike adults, juveniles tend to be arrested in groups at a proportionately higher rate. Therefore, several individuals might be arrested for one assault or theft, which would be reflected as a higher number of arrested perpetrators in official statistics. Having made this observation, it should be remembered that the number of juveniles that have been arrested for violent offenses is still high—98,900 for violent Part I index crimes in 2000 and 236,800 for non-Index Crime assaults in the same year. By any estimation, these were significant numbers of youthful suspects who were accused of serious offenses.

Most juvenile cases are not index offenses but rather noncriminal status offenses, which are not included in many official reports. Typical cases reported in *Juvenile Court Statistics* involve runaways, truants, ungovernable behavior, and liquor law violations. Unlike the rate of index offenses, which declined for juveniles during the 1990s and early millennium, there has been a steady increase in the number of status cases brought before juvenile courts. Overall, the most common status offenses are violations of underage drinking laws and truancy. Table 4.6 summarizes the increasing incidence of status offense cases.

One Caveat on Delinquency and Crime Data. Clearly, data on delinquency and crime have a significant effect on policy decisions and public perceptions. For example, the foregoing discussion outlined the good news that arrest data and *Juvenile Court Statistics* indicated an impressive decline in juvenile responsibility for serious offenses during the latter years of the 1990s and first years of the millennium. However, it should be remembered that quantitative statistical data count only those cases that were cleared by arrests or processed through juvenile courts. On the other hand, *qualitative data* (surveys and interviews) often provide a richer understanding of offenders and illegal behavior that cannot be elicited from quantitative research.

Self-report studies have been conducted since the 1940s to investigate undetected (hidden) teenage delinquency. The purpose of these studies has been to reveal data on delinquency and criminal behavior that cannot be

TABLE 4.6   EXAMPLES OF THE INCREASING INCIDENCE OF STATUS OFFENSES[a]

Status offenses are behaviors prohibited by law, but only when committed by a juvenile. Juveniles suspected of committing status offenses can only be brought before juvenile courts. Unlike the rate of Index Crime offenses committed by juveniles, the incidence of status offenses has increased steadily over time.

This table shows the consistent rise in numbers of status offenses.

Most Serious Offense	1988[b]	1993[b]	1997[b]	Percent Change[b] 1988–1997 (%)	1993–1997 (%)
Status offenses	79,000	112,300	158,600	101	41
Runaway	12,400	19,900	24,000	93	21
Truancy	20,600	33,700	40,500	96	20
Ungovernable	12,900	14,900	21,300	65	43
Liquor	26,200	27,800	40,700	56	46
Miscellaneous	6,900	16,000	32,100	367	100

a. Adapted from Puzzanchera, C., Stahl, A. L., Finnegan, T. A., Snyder, H. N., Poole, R. S., & Tierney, N. (2000). *Juvenile court statistics 1997* (p. 37). Washington, DC: Office of Juvenile Justice and Delinquency Prevention.

b. Detail may not add to totals because of rounding. Percent change calculations are based on unrounded numbers.

discovered by the Uniform Crime Reports. Interestingly, self-reported data have consistently indicated that juvenile delinquency occurs at a higher rate than reported by the UCR or *Juvenile Court Statistics*.[30] Other findings typically made by self-report studies in comparison to official statistics include the following:

- A much larger number of teenage participants admit to committing delinquent and status offenses than are reported by official statistical data.
- Juvenile delinquency is not as predominant among the poor, but rather occurs in all socioeconomic classes. Lower class youths commit more offenses per individual, but large numbers of members of other classes also engage in delinquent behavior.[31]
- Gender profiles for delinquent behavior are marked by a higher incidence of female delinquency than indicated in the UCR and *Juvenile Court Statistics*. Although girls are less likely to commit serious offenses, self-reported data nevertheless suggest that official data severely undercount female offenders.[32]
- Racial differences in delinquent behavior are not as pronounced as suggested in the UCR and other official data. Comparisons of African American and white offenders suggest that African Americans are more likely to commit serious offenses, but that the rate of offenses is more similar in both communities than reported by official statistics.[33]

These findings suggest that deeper qualitative analyses (surveys, interviews, focus groups, etc.) are needed to explain delinquency and criminality than can be made by exclusively using official statistics.

Postscript: Juvenile Victimization

Juvenile victimization refers to the mistreatment of young people. It can occur at home, in schools, or on the street. Types of victimization include criminal victimization, abuse (physical, sexual, and emotional), parental neglect, and child dependency. It is often the *flip side* of juvenile delinquency, as delinquents victimize other youths. Or, it may involve familial mistreatment by parents and other family members. Reported data on victimization show that different types of ill treatment occur at different rates. For example, juveniles who were victimized by parents were abused at the following rates:[34]

- 60% of victimized children were neglected.
- 25% suffered physical abuse.
- 13% were sexually abused.
- 6% were abused emotionally.
- 12% of victimized children suffered from "other" abuses such as abandonment, drug-addicted births, and medical neglect.

Other findings are interesting and disturbing. Within families, girls are twice as likely to be killed or hurt by family members as are boys, and younger children are more likely to be murdered than older children. Within racial groups, juveniles are more likely to be killed or hurt by members of their own race; however, more African Americans die by criminal violence than do white youths despite the fact that African Americans represent roughly 13% of the population.

Children who are victimized can suffer emotional damage that may cause them to act out, often developing behavioral disorders. Victimized children may be unable to interact normally with adults, teachers, or other children. They can also become antisocial, eventually becoming juvenile delinquents or adult criminals.

The Victimization Picture

Just as a delinquency and crime picture emerges from information gathered from official data, a victimization picture can also be drawn from statistical and survey research investigating the mistreatment of juveniles. Experts frequently debate the extent of juvenile victimization, and whether data accurately measure mistreatment, because there is evidence that "hidden" victimization is quite prevalent. **Hidden victimization** refers to unreported incidents of child abuse, neglect, dependency, exploitation, or other victimization.

During the 1980s to the early 1990s, the rate of juvenile victimization increased dramatically—by 155% between 1980 and 1993.[35] This rate subsequently declined markedly during the 1990s and into the millennium, in line with the overall decline in both delinquency and crime. For example, the National Crime Victimization Survey reported that the rate of juvenile crime victimization declined during the years 1999 and 2000. The number of violent crimes per 1,000 persons 12 to 15 years of age fell from 74.4 in 1999 to 60.1 in 2000, for a decline of 19.2%.[36] Among persons 16 to 19 years of age, the rate fell from 77.4 per 1,000 persons in 1999 to 64.3 in 2000, for a decline of 16.9%.[37] These were significant decreases in victimization over a short period of time. Recent data also show that juvenile victimization from violent crimes declined during the decade of the 1990s and into the millennium in several important categories. For example:

> Ninety percent of murder victims in 2000 . . . were 18 years of age or older. The other nearly 1,600 murder victims were under the age of 18. This figure is substantially less than that of the peak year of 1993, when almost 2,900 juveniles were murdered. The last year in which fewer than 1,600 juveniles were murdered was 1985.[38]

Although these data reported decreases in crime victimization (certainly good news), juveniles are still victimized at a higher average rate than older age groups. In fact, juveniles are greatly overrepresented as victims of crimes in comparison to other age categories. Deaths by homicide have occurred in significant numbers. For example, the UCR reported that 1,357 of 14,054 murder victims were under the age of 18 years in 2002. The following statistics are typical of victimization from previous years:

- 36% of juvenile murder victims were killed by people they knew.
- 25% were killed by unknown murderers.
- 22% of victims were killed by their parents.
- 11% of juvenile victims were murdered by strangers.
- 5% were killed by other family members.[39]

Table 4.7 summarizes the disproportionate rate of crime victimization experienced by teenagers.

Hidden Victimization

There are limitations to the utility of data used to draw the victimization picture, because official and unofficial research provides data on *detectable* juvenile victimization. Unfortunately, much juvenile victimization is not detected by researchers or juvenile justice authorities, and hence is never counted.

Crime and delinquency statistics reported by the UCR and *Juvenile Court Statistics* certainly provide useful information about the extent of deviant behavior committed against, and suffered by, juveniles. However, victimization

TABLE 4.7   COMPARISON OF CRIME VICTIMIZATION BY AGE CATEGORY[a]

Although teenage crime victimization declined in recent years, a larger proportion teenagers were victimized at rates much higher than other age categories. This table compares victimization by age group per 1,000 persons.

Age of Victim	Number of Violent Criminal Victimization Per 1,000 Persons		
	1999	2000	Percent Change (%)
12–15 years	74.4	60.1	−19.2
16–19 years	77.4	64.3	−16.9
20–24 years	68.5	49.4	−27.9
25–34 years	36.3	34.8	−4.1
35–49 years	25.2	21.8	−13.5
50–64 years	14.4	13.7	−4.9
65+ years	3.8	3.7	−2.6

a. Adapted from Rennison, C. M. (2000, June). Crime victimization 2000: Changes 1999–2000 with trends 1993–2000. *National Crime Victimization Survey* (p. 4). Washington, DC: U.S. Department of Justice.

by adults against children is frequently not reported, primarily because it occurs in the home or is otherwise outside the purview of information collection by researchers. For example, the NCVS has historically solicited information about victimization only from interviewees who are 12 years of age and older. This means that younger children who might be victimized by adults or other youths were not counted by the NCVS. One study estimated that the NCVS failed to count as many as 51% of sexual assaults, 26% of aggravated assaults, 22% of simple assaults, and 9% of robberies committed against persons under the age of 18 years.[40]

These findings are compounded by the fact that most victimizations are not reported to the authorities—which means that relatively few victimizing parents or victimized children are brought before juvenile or criminal authorities, or counted in criminal/juvenile justice studies.

PROFESSIONAL PROFILE CHAPTER 4

Juvenile Justice Researcher—United States Department of Justice

Juvenile justice policy is ideally designed to address specific problems existing in the community. The question of how to target limited monetary and organizational resources is one that constantly challenges policy makers. Researchers play a critical role in identifying the nature and extent of juvenile-related problems. Researchers also provide information to policy makers that can demonstrate the effectiveness of programs and whether the allocation of resources has indeed paid off in the short and long term.

I. Personal Profile

A. Name:
James C. Howell

B. Agency:
U.S. Department of Justice, Office of Juvenile Justice and Delinquency Prevention, U.S. Department of Justice (Retired)

Adjunct Researcher, National Youth Gang Center, Institute for Intergovernmental Research, Tallahassee, FL

Adjunct Professor, Department of Criminology and Criminal Justice, University of South Carolina, Columbia, SC

C. Rank and/or Title:
Director of Research and Program Development, Office of Juvenile Justice and Delinquency Prevention, U.S. Department of Justice

D. Education (Schools and Degrees):
East Texas Baptist College—Marshall, Texas
BA, Sociology, 1965
Stephen F. Austin State University—Nacogdoches, Texas
MA, Sociology, 1966
University of Colorado—Boulder, Colorado
PhD, Sociology (Concentration: Criminology), 1973

E. Professional Training:
Management training received at the U.S. Department of Justice

F. Professional Organizations/Community Group Memberships:
American Society of Criminology

II. Professional Profile

A. What personal or other background experiences led to your decision to *choose* this profession?

I never intended to become a "fed," as federal workers are sometimes called. It happened as a result of happenstance, quite frankly. I cultivated an interest in juvenile justice while working on the doctoral degree in sociology at the University of Colorado. I had planned a university-based teaching and research career. A fellow graduate student who had planned a similar career convinced me that we should spend a year in Washington, DC, exploring the federal side of things, to be better prepared for teaching and research. We chose the U.S. Department of Justice because of our shared interest in juvenile justice. That anticipated year in the nation's capital turned out to be 23 years. I am eternally grateful that my friend talked me into going to Washington, DC, because it turned out to be a unique experience in administering juvenile justice.

B. Please state a few of your personal reasons/motivations for your decision to *continue* in this profession.

Shortly after I had taken a research position in the U.S. Department of Justice, the first major federal juvenile justice office, the Office of Juvenile Justice and Delinquency Prevention (OJJDP) was established. I had the unusual experience of helping to establish the OJJDP and of working toward implementing the progressive legislation that authorized it, the Juvenile Justice and Delinquency Prevention Act of 1974 (P.L. 93-415). It was a thrill to be in a position to help shape the priorities of the new OJJDP, and to determine what kinds of programs, research, and data collection would be funded nationwide. I could not force myself to leave this situation and pursue the career I originally intended at the university level. My job was too much fun to abandon.

C. Which job experiences have had an important impact on you?

Associating regularly with renowned people in the juvenile delinquency field in my position at OJJDP was a thrilling experience. After getting to know many of them, I came to see that they did not possess extremely unique capabilities. In other words, I saw that I could become one of them, that perhaps I *could* make a worthwhile contribution to the field. It was not the impossible dream that I imagined when I arrived in Washington, DC.

D. What has been a particularly *satisfying* job experience?

A colleague and I at the OJJDP recognized that our office had an obligation to take stock of what was known about delinquency and about ways to prevent and reduce it, and to attempt to package this information in a user-friendly format. We thought such a product might assist practitioners and policy makers in the juvenile justice field in taking a more balanced approach to dealing with juvenile delinquency. We undertook a review of research, programs, and management tools for dealing with serious, violent, and chronic juvenile offenders and organized this information in a way that practitioners could put it into everyday practice. We called the product a "Comprehensive Strategy for Serious, Violent, and Chronic Juvenile Offenders." It empowers communities to solve their own delinquency problem, and it has been implemented to one degree or another in 20 states that we know of.

E. What has been a particularly *challenging* job experience?

The most challenging part of my federal experience was dealing with the politics that go along with working in Washington, DC. It was a hard lesson for me to accept that "might," instead of "right," rules in the nation's capitol. However, I survived by learning that when you're armed with sound research and other reliable information, one can prevail in most political circumstances.

F. What do you think the future holds for your profession?

I daresay no human service field is more intriguing than juvenile justice—which I define broadly, to include prevention, early intervention, treatment, and control. It's a grand, uniquely American component of the criminal justice apparatus. Exciting developments are occurring on a number of fronts, the most exciting—to me at least—are the business of diffusing research into practice, and integrating the juvenile justice system with other child and adolescent service systems (i.e., mental health, health, child welfare, social services, and education). These are the current frontiers. The next frontier is likely to be recognition of the critical role of the juvenile justice system in preventing and reducing adult criminality, and the integration of the two systems. You can easily make important contributions in these areas.

G. What kind of advice/guidance would you give to interested students?

Get a graduate degree—at least the master's—before you take a job. Go to Washington, DC, or your state capital to work for a few years before you choose your professional niche. The graduate degree will qualify you for a meaningful position in federal or state government. Either experience will broaden your perspective and prepare you for making a more worthwhile contribution. In addition, you'll make valuable contacts that will serve you well in your personal growth and career opportunities.

Chapter Summary

A large amount of research has been conducted since the early twentieth century that has measured the characteristics and frequency of delinquency, crime, and victimization. Extensive data have been assembled to create detailed profiles of delinquency and crime within geographic regions, demographic groups (e.g., race, gender, and age), and type of offense. Researchers and practitioners use these findings to recommend policy agendas for addressing the problems of juvenile and adult deviance and victimization. Although often outside of the attention or interest of the general public, both quantitative (statistical) and qualitative (survey and interview) research have had a great deal of influence on the configuration of the juvenile and criminal justice systems.

Estimating and reporting delinquency and crime involves the acquisition of data from several sources using a variety of methodologies. Arrest data report local-level clearances in quantitative terms (arrests of suspects). Statistics on clearances are collected by the FBI and published in its annual *Uniform Crime Reports: Crime in the United States*. This influential publication is widely publicized by the media and private agencies. Victimization surveys are qualitative studies that usually collect household interview data to assess the degree of victimization in the United States. The National Crime Victimization Survey is the best known and most widely reported victimization survey. These studies are important because they frequently observe higher crime rates than are observed in arrest data research such as the UCR. *Juvenile Court Statistics* specifically focuses on juvenile cases processed by juvenile courts. The collection and evaluation of these statistics are coordinated by the federal Office of Juvenile Justice and Delinquency Prevention and the private National Center for Juvenile Justice. Juvenile court data are important because information is collected at the local jurisdictional level, thus providing experts with useful data for policy options. Self-reported data are surveys of juveniles and adults about their own deviant behavior. These surveys are usually local or regional level studies conducted by private or academic researchers.

Patterns of delinquency, crime, and victimization suggest that the United States has a much higher level of criminal violence than other Western democracies. Public perceptions of juvenile and adult deviance generally hold that the crime rate is high, even during periods of statistical declines. Delinquency and crime rates rose and fell similarly during recent decades. Both were high during the 1980s through the early 1990s and then declined during the mid-1990s through the early years of the new millennium. Juvenile delinquents and criminals make up a small percentage of the over all juvenile population. As a proportion of all crimes, regardless of age-group, juveniles commit a significantly smaller percentage of serious offenses than do adults. The fact is that most juvenile offenders are status offenders rather than delinquents, so that most cases handled by juvenile courts involve relatively minor transgressions.

The rate of juvenile victimization was high during the 1980s and into the early 1990s before declining during the late 1990s and into the new millennium, roughly matching the cycle of delinquency and crime during the same period. Despite reported declines in victimization, juveniles suffer as victims of delinquency and crime at a rate disproportionate to other age-groups. In addition, the disturbing fact is that hidden victimization probably accounts for a much higher rate of victimization than will never be known.

Chapter 5 investigates children in trouble (juveniles who break the law) and children in need (juveniles who must be rescued from their circumstances). The discussion addresses modern problems of young people, profiles of troubled and needy children, and ways to help these youths.

Questions for Review

1. What is the utility of statistics?

2. How are public perceptions of delinquency and crime affected by statistics?

3. Explain the rationale and methodology of the Uniform Crime Reports.

4. Explain the rationale and methodology of the National Crime Victimization Survey.

5. Explain the rationale and methodology of self-reported data.

6. Explain the rationale and methodology of juvenile court data.

7. What do data indicate about patterns of delinquency and crime?

8. How are juvenile victimization rates measured?

Key Terms and Concepts

The following topics were discussed in this chapter and are found in the Glossary:

Arrest Data

Clearances

Crime Clock

"Hidden" Victimization

Household Data

Juvenile Court Statistics

Juvenile Victimization

National Crime Victimization Survey

National Juvenile Court Data Archive

National Youth Survey

Official Data

Part I Offenses

Part II Offenses

Research Accuracy

Research Generalizability

Research Reliability

Self-Reported Data

Superpredator

Uniform Crime Reports

Victimization Surveys

DISCUSSION BOX

Girls as Delinquents and Status Offenders

This chapter's Discussion Box is intended to stimulate critical discussion about delinquency, status offenses, and gender.

Gender differences are readily apparent in the commission of some delinquent and status offenses. On an annual basis, girls represent approximately 14% of juveniles in community corrections programs and 8% of juveniles held in secure institutions.[41] For delinquent offenses, girls made up 25% of juvenile arrests and only 16% of juvenile arrests for violent crimes in 1997.[42] The rate of status offenses committed by girls has increased markedly, by 105% between the years 1988 and 1997—with nearly as many truant females as males.

Gender-based data on status offenses are of particular interest, because some behavior is disproportionately found among boys or girls. For example, while most liquor violations are committed by boys, most runaways are girls. The following table is a comparison of status offenses, indicated by gender, from 1988 to 1997:[43]

Most Serious Offense (Gender)	1988	1993	1997	Percent Change	
				1988–1997 (% Change)	1993–1997 (% Change)
Status offenses (males)	47,000	64,100	92,800	98	45
Runaway	4,700	7,300	9,700	105	33
Truancy	11,100	18,100	21,600	95	19
Ungovernable	6,600	8,000	11,700	78	47
Liquor	19,900	19,800	27,700	39	40
Miscellaneous	4,700	10,900	22,100	370	103
Status offenses (females)	32,100	48,200	65,800	105	36
Runaway	7,700	12,600	14,300	86	14
Truancy	9,600	15,600	18,900	98	21
Ungovernable	6,300	6,900	9,500	51	39
Liquor	6,300	8,000	13,100	108	63
Miscellaneous	2,200	5,100	10,000	358	94

Reasons cited for female participation in delinquency include interpersonal problems and stresses, influences from peer group members, home dysfunction, substance abuse, and dysfunctional neighborhoods.

Discussion Questions

1. What do you think are the deeper reasons behind the greater number of female than male runaways?

2. What accounts for the fact that many fewer girls are confined in juvenile corrections and secure institutions?

3. Are male juveniles more prone to delinquent behavior than female juveniles? If so, why?

4. What explains the high number of status offenses committed by girls?

5. To what extent do you think female delinquents grow up to become female criminals? What about girls who are status offenders?

Recommended Web Sites

The following Web sites report research and data on juvenile delinquency and crime:

Center on Juvenile & Criminal Justice: http://www.cjcj.org/
National Center for Juvenile Justice: http://ncjj.org
National Council on Crime and Delinquency: http://www.nccd-crc.org/
National Juvenile Court Data Archive: http://ojjdp.ncjrs.org/ojstatbb/njcda/
Office of Juvenile Justice and Delinquency Prevention: http://ojjdp.ncjrs.org/

Note: The Web site URLs and exercises below are also from the book's study site:
   http://www.sagepub.com/martin

Web Exercise

Using this chapter's recommended Internet sites, conduct an online investigation of research and data on juvenile delinquency and crime.

- In your opinion, which research methodology makes the most sense to you? Why?
- In what ways are the databases similar? How do they differ?
- In your opinion, which database on juvenile delinquency is the most useful for policy makers?

For an online search of delinquency statistics and methodologies, students should use a search engine and enter the following keywords:

"Delinquency Research"

"Delinquency Statistics"

Recommended Readings

The following publications provide information on research methods for delinquency, criminal justice, and criminology.

Bureau of Justice Statistics. (n.d.). *Sourcebook of criminal justice statistics.* Washington, DC: U.S. Department of Justice.

Champion, D. J. (1993). *Research methods for criminal justice and criminology.* Englewood Cliffs, NJ: Regents/Prentice Hall.

Fitzterald, J. D., & Cox, S. M. (1994). *Research methods in criminal justice* (2nd ed.). Chicago: Nelson-Hall.

Hagan, F. E. (2000). *Research methods in criminal justice and criminology* (5th ed.). Boston: Allyn & Bacon.

Maxfield, M. G., & Babbie, E. (1995). *Research methods for criminal justice and criminology.* Belmont, CA: Wadsworth.

Notes

1. See Rhys Williams, Gail Allen, and David Allen, et al. and Zachary Durbin, and Bobbi LaCross v. Cambridge Board of Education, et al., Fed. App. 0169P (6th Cir. 2004).

2. For a good discussion of research methods for criminal justice, see Hagan, F. E. (2000). Research methods in criminal justice and criminology (5th ed.). Boston: Allyn & Bacon.

3. Federal Bureau of Investigation. (2001). *Uniform crime reports, 2000: Crime in the United States.* Washington, DC: Department of Justice.

4. Office of Juvenile Justice and Delinquency Prevention. (n.d.). Available online at http://ojjdp.ncjrs.org/

5. Bureau of Justice Statistics. (n.d.). Available online at http://www.ojp.usdoj.gov/bjs/

6. National Institute of Justice. (n.d.). Available online at http://www.ojp.usdoj.gov/nij/

7. Federal Bureau of Investigation. (2001). *Uniform crime reports, 2000: Crime in the United States* (p. 1). Washington, DC: Department of Justice.

8. Federal Bureau of Investigation. (2003). *Uniform crime reports, 2002: Crime in the United States* (Appendix II). Washington, DC: Department of Justice.

9. Ibid.

10. Ibid.

11. The National Juvenile Court Data Archive. (n.d.). Available online at http://ojjdp.ncjrs.org/ojstatbb/njcda/

12. The National Center for Juvenile Justice is the research branch of the National Council of Juvenile and Family Court Judges. The National Council's Web site can be accessed at http://www.ncjfcj.org/

13. See Puzzanchera, C., Stahl, A. L., Finnegan, T. A., Tierney, N., & Snyder, H. N. (2003). *Juvenile court statistics 1998.* Washington, DC: Office of Juvenile Justice and Delinquency Prevention.

14. See Nettler, G. (1978). *Explaining crime.* New York: McGraw-Hill.

15. For an excellent discussion of the challenge of projecting juvenile deviance and the superpredator phenomenon, see Office of Juvenile Justice and Delinquency Prevention. (2000, February). *Challenging the myths. Juvenile Justice Bulletin, 1999 National Report Series.* Washington, DC: U.S. Department of Justice.

16. See Bennett, G. (1987). *Crimewarps: The future of crime in America* (p. xiv). Garden City, NY: Anchor/Doubleday.

17. Adapted from Bureau of Justice Statistics. (2002). Total economic loss to victims of crime. In *Criminal victimization in the United States.* Washington, DC: U.S. Department of Justice. Web site at http://www.ojp.usdoj.gov/bjs/abstract/cvus/economic973.htm

18. Miller, T. R., Cohen, M. A., & Wiersema, B. (1996, February). *Victim costs and consequences: A new look.* Washington, DC: U.S. Department of Justice.

19. Sickmund, M., Snyder, H. N., & Poe-Yamagata, E. (1997, August). *Juvenile offenders and victims: 1997 Update on violence* (p. 24). Washington, DC: Office of Juvenile Justice and Delinquency Prevention.

20. Adapted from Bureau of Justice Statistics. (2003). *Sourcebook of criminal justice statistics, 2002.* Washington, DC: U.S. Department of Justice.

21. See Kelley, B. T., Huizinga, D., Thornberry, T. P., & Loeber, R. (1997, June). Epidemiology of serious violence. *OJJDP Juvenile Justice Bulletin* (p. 1). Washington, DC: U.S. Department of Justice.

22. Adapted from Bureau of Justice Statistics. (2003). *Sourcebook of criminal justice statistics, 2002.* Washington, DC: U.S. Department of Justice.

23. Handgun Control. (n.d.). Available online at http://www.bradycampaign.org/facts/research/firefacts.asp

24. Hutson, H. R., Anglin, D., Kyriacou, D. N., Hart, J., & Spears, K. (1995). The epidemic of gang-related homicides in Los Angeles County from 1979 through 1994. *The Journal of the American Medical Association, 274,* 1031–1036.

25. Ibid.

26. Ibid. (p. 10).

27. See Chesney-Lind, M. (1998). *Trends in delinquency and gang membership*. Honolulu, HI: Center for Youth Research, University of Hawaii at Manoa.

28. Snyder, H. N. (2002). *Juvenile arrests 2000* (p. 1). Washington, DC: U.S. Department of Justice.

29. Ibid.

30. For early research on higher rates discovered by self-report studies, see Erickson, M. L., & Empey, L. T. (1963, December). Court records, undetected delinquency, and decision making. *Journal of Criminal Law, Criminology, and Police Science*, *54*. See also Short, J. F., Jr., & Nye, F. I. (1958, November-December). Extent of unrecorded juvenile delinquency: Tentative conclusions. *Journal of Criminal Law, Criminology, and Police Science*, *49*.

31. See Johnson, R. E. (1980, May). Social class and delinquent behavior: A new test. *Criminology*, *18*, 86.

32. For an analysis of gender statistics in delinquency, see Poe-Yamagata, E., & Butts, J. A. (1996). *Female offenders in the juvenile justice system: Statistics summary*. Washington, DC: U.S. Department of Justice. See also Cernkovich, S., & Giordano, P. (1979). A comparative analysis of male and female delinquency. *Sociological Quarterly*, *20*, 131.

33. Huizinga, D., & Elliott, D. S. (1987, April). Juvenile offenders: Prevalence, offender incidence, and arrest rates by race. *Crime and Delinquency*, *33*, 206. See also Elliott, D. S., & Ageton, S. S. (1980, February). Reconciling race and class differences in self-reported and official estimates of delinquency. *American Sociological Review*, *45*, 95.

34. From National Center on Child Abuse and Neglect. (1999). *Child maltreatment 1997: Reports from the states to the National Child Abuse and Neglect Data System*. Washington, DC: U.S. Department of Health and Human Services.

35. Ibid.

36. Rennison, C. M. (2000, June). Crime victimization 2000: Changes 1999–2000 with trends 1993–2000. *National Crime Victimization Survey* (p. 4). Washington, DC: U.S. Department of Justice.

37. Ibid.

38. Snyder, H. N. (2002). *Juvenile arrests 2000* (p. 3). Washington, DC: U.S. Department of Justice.

39. Data from Snyder, H. N. (1999). *Juvenile offenders and victims: 1999 National report* (p. 18). Washington, DC: National Center for Juvenile Justice.

40. Snyder, H. N. (1994). *The criminal victimization of young children*. Pittsburgh, PA: National Center for Juvenile Justice.

41. American Correctional Association. (1999). *1998 Directory*. College Park, MD: American Correctional Association.

42. Snyder, H. N. (1988). *Court careers of juvenile offenders*. Pittsburgh, PA: National Center for Juvenile Justice.

43. Adapted from Puzzanchera, C., Stahl, A. L., Finnegan, T. A., Snyder, H. N., Poole, R. S., & Tierney, N. (2000). *Juvenile court statistics 1997* (p. 46). Washington, DC: Office of Juvenile Justice and Delinquency Prevention.

5 Children in Trouble and Children in Need

The juvenile justice system serves not only youths who break the law but also youths who are victimized by others. In fact, it is the legal duty of many youth-serving institutions to protect children from harm. Unfortunately, the system sometimes fails to successfully protect these children. For example, on January 22, 1999, Ammy Dovangsibountham ran away from home after approximately three years of sexual abuse by her stepfather, Sounthaly Keosay.[1] The police found Ammy and took her to a juvenile detention center in Sioux City, Iowa, where intake workers interviewed her about why she had run away. She explained the years of abuse, and said that her mother did not believe her when Ammy confided in her. Ammy remained in protective custody as a Child in Need of Assistance for more than a month, and eventually began alleging that her stepfather had threatened to harm her if she told anyone about the abuse. In February, Keosay was arrested and charged with sexual abuse. Ammy was reunited with her mother after Keosay's arrest.

Unfortunately, Keosay's bond was set at only $13,000, which he easily posted, and he was released. Officials believed that the low bail was justified because his threats were only a ploy to control his stepdaughter. Ammy found out about the release and was fearful for her safety. The police patrolled around her mother's home as a safety precaution. However, on March 17, 1999, the police found the bodies of Ammy and her mother. They also found the body of Keosay, who had murdered them before committing suicide.

The juvenile justice system is best described as a network. This network consists of agencies, institutions, and people who are dedicated to providing rehabilitation and remediation (corrective or salvaging) services to troubled and needy adolescents. The population of juveniles served by this network includes both juvenile offenders and juvenile victims. Unlike the criminal justice system, which is primarily concerned with securing society from criminal victimization and punishing offenders, the juvenile justice system must address a broader spectrum of issues affecting adolescents. These issues certainly include securing society from chronically deviant youths, but they also involve rehabilitating young offenders, removing young victims from toxic environments, and generally rescuing juveniles from living as victims or in conflict with authority. Thus, the criminal justice system's emphasis on controlling and punishing adult deviance represents a much narrower focus in comparison to the juvenile justice system's expansive emphasis on the provision of security, rehabilitation, and remediation services.

Two types of youths are served by the juvenile justice system, illustrating the scope of this network:

- *Children in trouble.* Youths who violate the law, either as juvenile delinquents or as status offenders. Some delinquent offenders are waived into criminal court and tried as adults.
- *Children in need.* Youths who are not properly cared for by an adult, for example, abused, neglected, or abandoned children.

Children in trouble are young people who engage in problem behaviors, generally defined as behavior that is legally or culturally unacceptable. Youths who live in environments that are conducive to encouraging these activities, or who exhibit antisocial behaviors that can lead to early deviance, are termed **at-risk juveniles**. In some states, *all* juveniles within defined age ranges are defined as at-risk, but for our purposes, we shall discuss youths who fit the profile for possible deviance. In accordance with this definition, at-risk juveniles tend to have difficulty in school, have conflicted relationships with parents and peers, and have repeated problems with authority figures and institutions. Rebelliousness, associations with antisocial peer groups, and incorrigibility are common behaviors among at-risk juveniles. Unacceptable behaviors do, of course, include severe deviance such as property destruction, theft, burglary, violence, and other criminal conduct. However, children in trouble also engage in other forms of behavioral deviance such as dropping out of school, alcohol and drug abuse, early sexual activity and pregnancy, gang associations, and generally antisocial behavior.

Children in need are youths who require official intervention to remove them from harmful environments and to remediate the effects of these environments. They are victims of abuse, neglect, abandonment, or other evidence of adult failure to properly care for them. Unlike the adult criminal justice system, which has minimal jurisdiction and resources to remediate adult victimization (other than punitive sanctions against criminal perpetrators), the juvenile justice system is designed to rescue children in need. Official intervention includes the proactive removal of children in need from toxic environments, their placement in designated "safe places" such as group homes, and managing their progress until they reach the age of majority. Not every official intervention requires removal, and instead may involve the supervision of home environments by social workers or other officials to assure the health and safety of children within the household.

This chapter investigates the background to problems encountered by children in trouble and children in need, including risk environments and their participation in socially unacceptable behaviors. Problems unique to these populations are also addressed, as well as the many challenges posed to the juvenile justice system for helping juvenile offenders and victims. The discussion in this chapter reviews

- Modern Problems: Young People and Risk Factors
- Youths in Conflict With Authority: Children in Trouble
- Youths Requiring Intervention: Children in Need
- Rescuing Youths: Helping Children in Trouble and Children in Need

CHAPTER PERSPECTIVE 5.1

Sexual Exploitation of Juveniles

It is important to understand that sexual exploitation of children by adults is a criminal offense across the county. Every state has enacted statutes prohibiting adults from procuring juveniles for sexual purposes. Included in this prohibition are incest (sex with family members), statutory rape (sex with persons under the age of majority), and fondling (sexual touching of a child's body). Sexual exploitation and abuse refers to the:

> ". . . involvement of the child in sexual activity to provide sexual gratification or finan-
> cial benefit to the perpetrator, including contacts for sexual purposes, prostitution,
> pornography, or other sexually exploitative activities. . . ."[2]

Although most child victims are exploited by someone they know, most of these victims are exploited by a parent or guardian, usually involving a male parent assaulting girl children. Girls are exploited much more than boys—up to three times as often.[3] Approximately one third of victims are under the age of 12 years, and many victims are very young children— including cases of infants being assaulted. All of these examples represent criminal behavior by adults.

Indicators of sexual exploitation include behavioral signs, such as depression, anger, fear, sexual sophistication, shyness around physicians, status offenses, or delinquency. Unfortunately, cases of exploitation are often reported in homes, day care centers, religious institutions, and other environments. Approximately 100,000 cases are reported annually, although experts estimate that up to 90% of cases are never reported—the "hidden" victimization of children.

Modern Problems: Young People and Risk Factors

The historically foundational movements promoting the concept of juvenile justice—the Child-Savers Movement, Houses of Refuge, and Chicago juvenile court—addressed very basic problems of young people, such as delinquency, incorrigibility, and idleness. These problems unfortunately still exist, but they persist in quite different forms than in the past, because they are present in conjunction with new challenges unique to juveniles in the modern era. Newer problems such as modern juvenile violence, substance abuse, poverty and homelessness, the needs of special populations, and risk factors place greater numbers of juveniles at risk of committing serious offenses that can lead to serious confrontations with authority.

Juveniles and Violence in the Modern Era

Young people are both victims and perpetrators of violence. As victims, the facts of many cases have received extensive scrutiny and have led to reexaminations of public policy. As perpetrators, the facts of several high-profile cases have boosted the public's perception that juvenile violence is epidemic, and have consequently led to popular support for stronger measures against young violent offenders.

Juveniles as Victims of Violence. Juvenile victimization is regularly at the forefront of public and media attention, and high-profile cases receive particular scrutiny. Some of these cases eventually have an impact on public policy, such as when children are kidnapped, assaulted, or murdered. Examples of widely covered cases of victimization include the following incidents from around the country:

- In California, Polly Klaas was kidnapped from her bedroom during a slumber party and murdered. Her killer, Richard Allen Davis, was a lifelong criminal. Cases like this have led to policies such as "three-strikes" laws to keep recidivists permanently behind bars.
- In New Jersey, Megan Kanka was kidnapped, raped, and murdered by Jesse Tammendequas, a twice-convicted sex offender who lived several doors away from her family. Every state has since passed Megan's Laws, which require formerly convicted sex offenders to register when they move into neighborhoods.
- In South Carolina, Susan Smith drowned her two sons by shutting them inside her vehicle and submerging it in a lake. She concocted a ruse accusing an unidentified African American male of kidnapping her boys, adding a racial dimension to the case.
- In Colorado, JonBenét Ramsey was murdered in the basement of her family home. The police never solved the case.

Although the foregoing examples are certainly horrific, and were publicly reported, they represent only a few examples of a much larger problem: the fact that teenagers are victimized by violent crime at higher rates than adults:

> Persons between ages 12 and 15 years and 16 and 19 years had higher rates of violent crime victimization than those 25 years or older. Persons 12 to 19 years of age were twice as likely as those 25 to 34 years of age and 3 times as likely as those 35 to 49 years of age to be victims of violent crimes. . . . For the crime of aggravated assault, individuals between ages 16 and 19 years had a significantly higher rate of victimization than any other age group.[4]

There has been a high toll in juvenile victimization over time. This is not a new phenomenon—during a 10-year period between 1985 and 1995, approximately 25,000 youths were murdered.[5] It must be remembered that these data represent reported and known incidents, and that most incidents of physical and sexual victimization remain unreported and undiscovered—the so-called hidden victimization that is discussed in Chapter 4. These incidents occur secretly within insular households or institutions and are never reported to outsiders or the authorities. Thus, unreported victimization occurs inside dysfunctional families, schools, day care centers, religious institutions, and youth organizations. Individual victimizers are typically authority figures such as older relatives, teachers, care providers, clergy, and youth organization leaders.

Juveniles as Perpetrators of Violence. Juvenile perpetration of violence also receives extensive coverage, particularly when the cases seem to have implications for society as a whole. It is not an exaggeration to conclude that some of these cases have shocked the conscience of the nation, as indicated in the following incidents:

- In New York City, teenagers on a "wilding" spree in Central Park raped, beat, and nearly killed an investment banker who became known as the "Central Park jogger." She suffered a fractured skull and nearly bled to death. Popular sentiment called for increased placement of juveniles into the adult criminal justice system.
- In West Paducah, Kentucky, a student fired on a prayer group at Heath High School, killing 3 and wounding 5 people.
- In Jonesboro, Arkansas, two students lying in ambush outside Westside Middle School opened fire on students and teachers who exited the school after a fire alarm had been pulled. They killed 5 people and wounded 10 others.
- In Littleton, Colorado, two students embarked on a killing spree at Columbine High School. The pair murdered 12 students and one teacher before committing suicide.

During the mid-1980s, arrests of juveniles for violent offenses increased, a trend that continued into the mid-1990s before declining into the years of the new millennium. Prior to this welcome decline (which was unanticipated), the decade-long spike in violent activity led many analysts and practitioners to predict a continued upsurge in juvenile violence well into the early twenty-first century. As discussed in Chapter 4, many theorists argued that a new type of violent juvenile offender—the superpredator—would characterize the new generation of delinquents. Theorists writing on the superpredator profile described them as "kids that have absolutely no respect for human life and no sense of the future."[6] As the delinquency rate declined during the latter years of the 1990s and into the new millennium, the superpredator phenomenon did not occur. Chapter Perspective 5.2 discusses the superpredator scare.

CHAPTER PERSPECTIVE 5.2

The Superpredator Scare

During the spike in crime and delinquency from the early 1980s to the 1990s, dire predictions were made about the near future. Some experts argued that trends in juvenile violence, gang behavior, and underclass values would become so deeply entrenched that a new breed of violent juvenile criminal would emerge. Vast numbers of these young criminals, termed "superpredators," would (according to these experts) terrorize the American urban core well into the new millennium.

This concept, first introduced in Chapter 4, presented a fearsome profile that described this new breed of delinquent as "fatherless, Godless, and jobless . . . radically impulsive, brutally remorseless youngsters, including ever more teenage boys, who murder, assault, rob, burglarize, deal deadly drugs, join gun-toting gangs, and create serious communal disorders."[7] Superpredators theoretically arise from dysfunctional homes, inadequate schools, and morally bankrupt communities. According to proponents of this theory, the most effective countermeasures against the expected superpredator epidemic are strict enforcement of the law and a return to basic moral values.

Fortunately for American society, the superpredator phenomenon never arose in urban communities. During the 1990s (and into the new millennium), juvenile "arrests for serious violent offenses and property offenses declined" steadily both nationally and in most states.[8] In retrospect, the superpredator scare was in part a political analysis that recommended polemical remedies for a complex social problem.

Risky Behaviors: Youths and Substance Abuse

"Substance abuse" refers to experimentation with illicit (illegal) drugs—including those that are specifically prohibited for use by juveniles. Many adolescents have used alcohol, drugs, and tobacco. Researchers have long

Photo 5.1 A teenager drinks alcohol from a bottle. Substance abuse is often associated with juvenile delinquency and status offenses.

associated substance abuse with juvenile delinquency.[9] This does not mean that substance abuse or other problems are universally present, or *directly* cause delinquency. However, this association has been noted as being persistent among many youths who engage in serious acts of delinquency. Alcohol and drugs in particular have been associated with violent teen deviance and are considered to be among the most serious problems of youths in the modern era.

Alcohol and Tobacco. Although juveniles ingest the same illegal drugs that are abused by adults—such as marijuana, cocaine, and heroin—some legal substances are specifically banned from use by minors. For example, adults legally and commonly use tobacco and alcohol, but their purchase and use by juveniles are prohibited, and violators are classified as status offenders. There is a dichotomy (two or more opinions) in these policies, as evidenced by the fact that the purchase and use of tobacco products by minors is regulated by many, but not all, states. The national movement to ban underage smoking and chewing is part of a larger American cultural movement to become a smokeless society. Hence, many states prohibit underage tobacco purchases as a means to end early addiction to nicotine. A similar motive is given for regulating underage access to alcoholic beverages, which in every state can be legally purchased and consumed only by persons 21 years of age and older. For those under the age of 21, nearly every use of alcohol is a status offense. This means that although the age of majority is often set at 18 years of age, persons between 18 and 21 can be charged as status offenders for liquor law violations.

Intoxicating Drugs. Illicit drug use (including alcohol) by juveniles peaked during the early 1980s, declined during the mid-1980s to the early 1990s, and then showed a slow increase. As reported by the Office of Juvenile Justice and Delinquency Prevention in 1998,

> After years of continuous decline, reported drug use by high school seniors grew in several categories after 1992. Eighth and 10th graders reported similar increases in drug use, although their levels of use were below those of 12th graders.[10]

Although drug abuse during the 1990s and the new millennium was well below the incidence of use during the 1970s and 1980s, a slow increase in usage occurred for marijuana, cocaine, alcohol, and other illicit drugs. Many studies confirmed this trend. One study noted the following percentages of 12th graders admitting to using illicit substances in the previous year:[11]

- 74% used alcohol.
- 38% used marijuana.
- 9% used hallucinogens.
- 6% used cocaine.
- 6% used inhalants.
- 1% used heroin.

Table 5.1 compares the incidence of drug use among teenagers for the years 1979 and 2001.

The annual number of juvenile arrests for drug abuse and liquor-law violations has been significant during the past 30 years. In a typical annual example, 220,700 juveniles were arrested for drug-abuse violations, and 158,500 were arrested for liquor-law violations. Another 19,600 were arrested for driving under the influence.[12]

Risky Environments: Poverty and Homelessness

Poor Children. The proportion of children living in poverty is significantly higher in the United States than in other Western democracies, possibly two to three times higher.[13] The National Center for Children in Poverty published the following findings on child poverty:[14]

- 16% of American children—almost 12 million—lived in poverty in 2001, meaning their parents' income was at or below the federal poverty level. This is about the same number of children who lived in poverty in 1980.

TABLE 5.1   PREVIOUS MONTH USE OF MARIJUANA AND COCAINE BY TEENAGERS

Substance abuse by middle- and high-school students declined markedly after the early 1980s, but remained steady during the 1990s and into the new millennium. This trend was true for all drugs, particularly marijuana, cocaine, and alcohol. This table is a representative example of the extent of usage for all drugs, marijuana, and cocaine.[a]

Substance	1979	2001
Any drug	16.3%	9%
Marijuana	14.2%	8%
Cocaine	1.5%	0.4%

a. Office of National Drug Control Policy. (n.d.). Available online at http://www.whitehouse drugpolicy.gov/drugfact/index.html

- 7% of American children—5 million—lived in extreme poverty. This was a 17% increase from 2000. The parents of these children made half the federal poverty level.
- 57% of African American children were from low-income families (down 3% from 2000); 64% of Latino (up 7%) and 34% of white children (up 3%) were from low-income families.

The child poverty rate during the latter quarter of the twentieth century was consistently high, peaking during the years 1983 and 1993. Figure 5.1 illustrates the long-term incidence of child poverty during the period 1975 to 2001.

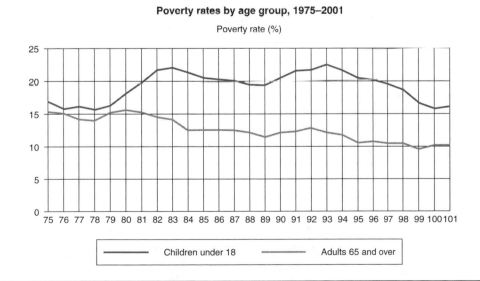

Poverty rates by age group, 1975–2001

Poverty rate (%)

Children under 18   Adults 65 and over

Figure 5.1   Child Poverty in the United States[a]

a. Reprinted from Lu, Hsien-Hen. *Low income children in the United States.* New York: National Center for Children in Poverty, 2003.

Poverty alone does not cause delinquency or unacceptable behaviors in young people. However, poverty makes families more vulnerable to the vagaries of precarious economic conditions, and increases the likelihood of hardships for juveniles. For example, extreme poverty exposes children to malnutrition, unhealthy environments, poor medical care, and squalor. Underclass behaviors (such as teenage pregnancy, low educational achievement, and chronic unemployment) are common in some poor communities, so that youths are reared among dysfunctional norms and behaviors. When poor children are culturally isolated in the underclass subculture, the likelihood of delinquency increases, as does the probability of multigenerational poverty.

Homeless Children. Homelessness among young people is manifested in several ways: As members of homeless families, as **runaways,** or as **thrownaways.**[15] The first category represents children who are homeless, but have adult guardians, while the latter two categories represent youths who are independently homeless and unaccompanied by adults. Runaways and thrownaways are subcategories of missing children, and are discussed below.

The number of homeless families increased during the turn of the millennium, as did the overall rate of homelessness among children. Families with children have recently represented a steadily increasing proportion of homeless people. In fact, the National Coalition for the Homeless has reported that "families with children are among the fastest growing segments of the homeless population."[16] The Coalition also reported the following data on age and family demographics of homelessness:[17]

- In 2001, the U.S. Conference of Mayors' survey of 27 urban areas indicated that children under the age of 18 years accounted for 25.3% of the urban homeless population.
- Nationally in the year 2000, approximately 39% of the homeless population were children.
- In 2001, unaccompanied minors comprised 4% of the urban homeless population.
- Also in 2001, the U.S. Conference of Mayors' survey of 27 urban areas indicated that families comprised 40% of the homeless population, an increase from previous years.
- Nationally in the year 2000, approximately 39% of the homeless population were children.
- Single mothers and children make up the largest group of people who are homeless in rural areas.

Homeless lifestyles are exceptionally stressful for families and children. Homeless young people often change schools, move from place to place, have little privacy, and have difficulty obtaining basic necessities of life (such as clothing and food). Consequently, emotional, behavioral, and learning problems are common among homeless children. They are frequently restless, frustrated, aggressive, or introverted, and have poor social skills.

Missing Children

Missing children are young persons who are unaccounted for. They are "missing" in the sense that they are not resident with an adult or institution that has been designated as their legitimate place of residence. The circumstances under which children go missing are categorized as follows:[18]

- *Parental or family abductions.* A family member either takes a child or fails to return a child after a legal visit.
- *Stranger or nonfamily abductions.* A forced unauthorized taking, detention, or luring of a child.
- *Runaways.* Children who leave home and stay away at least overnight without permission.
- *Thrownaways.* Children who are forced to leave home, or who are not permitted to return home.
- *Otherwise missing.* Miscellaneous reasons for absence, such as injury, disability, or age (wandering away).

It is striking that of the hundreds of thousands of children who are reported missing annually,[19] the largest proportion are runaways and thrownaways. Interestingly, most runaways are teenage girls (approximately 58%), most are gone for three days or more (about 52%), and most are recidivist runaways.[20] Table 5.2 summarizes the annual incidence of missing children.

TABLE 5.2   THE INCIDENCE OF "MISSING" CHILDREN

Hundreds of thousands of children go missing each year. This table lists *average* and *serious* annual incidence of missing children, by category.[a] The serious column signifies extreme circumstances surrounding the abduction or voluntary absence.

Extreme circumstances include family members moving a child out of state, ransom or murder by strangers, and runaways and thrownaways without secure places to stay.

Missing Child Category	Average Annual Incidence	Average Annual Serious Incidence
Parental/family abduction	354,100	163,200
Stranger/nonfamily abduction	3,200–4,600	200–300
Runaways	450,700	133,500
Thrownaways	127,100	59,200
Otherwise missing	438,200	139,100

a. See Snyder, H. N., & Sickmund, M. (1999). *Juvenile offenders and victims: 1999 National report* (p. 38). Washington, DC: U.S. Department of Justice.

The AMBER Plan. In the Fall of 2001, the National Center for Missing & Exploited Children promulgated the America's Missing: Broadcast Emergency Response Plan, commonly known as the AMBER Plan. The plan was first developed in 1996 as a memorial to Amber Hagerman, a nine-year-old girl who was kidnapped and murdered in Arlington, Texas. The concept of the plan is described as follows:[21]

> The AMBER Plan is a voluntary partnership between law enforcement agencies and broadcasters to activate an urgent bulletin in the most serious child-abduction cases. Broadcasters use the Emergency Alert System (EAS), formerly called the Emergency Broadcast System, to air a description of the abducted child and suspected abductor.

The AMBER Plan is coordinated by state and local governments, which ideally cooperate under a nationwide emergency alert umbrella when children are missing. When authorities suspect that a child has been abducted, **Amber Alerts** are promulgated that describe the victim, provide a profile of the abductor, and describe any special circumstances of the case. Amber Alert bulletins are broadcast on freeway alert signals, giving descriptions of suspected vehicles including license plate numbers. Since its inception, scores of missing children have been rescued under the system.

Unique Needs: Special Populations of Adolescents

Many youths who enter the juvenile justice system have special needs that necessitate professional intervention. These adolescents represent populations who sometimes require prolonged treatment or remediation for their needs. This is because they are often behaviorally or mentally impaired, causing them to act out unacceptably. When this happens, society is certain to respond—either through treatment or remediation, or simply by dealing with the perpetrator as a deviant offender. The following conditions exemplify special populations of young people:

- *Attention deficit disorder.* A behavioral disorder typified by deficient attention ability, chronically active physical movements (such as fidgeting), and poor self-control.
- *Prenatal exposure to diseases and drugs.* Children born of mothers who either had a venereal disease or actively abused substances such as alcohol or drugs during pregnancy. Babies can contract the mother's venereal disease or suffer mental retardation or addiction from the mother's prenatal alcohol or drug abuse.
- *Learning disabilities.* Deficits in learning processes, such as poor reading ability, lack of ability to memorize or follow directions, and incapability to distinguish or otherwise manage letters or numerals.

- *Emotional disturbance.* Emotionally disturbed youths exhibit extremes in emotions. These can include impulsiveness, aggression, or polar (extreme) mood swings.

All special juvenile populations require programs and facilities that can treat their conditions and control potential exhibitions of unacceptable behavior. The purpose of specialized programs and facilities is to intervene early in the lives of special populations to help them manage their conditions and to make them as productive as possible. They protect juveniles from eventual conflicts with authority.

Risk Factors

Many policy makers and researchers have attempted to identify specific environments, or domains, that promote an increased probability of delinquent behavior. These experts reason that if key features of these environments can be isolated, then specific policies can be crafted to reduce the possibility of delinquency. Researchers have generally concluded that juvenile delinquency occurs at higher rates for adolescents who are exposed to, or grow up in, identifiably unwholesome environments. Within these environments, certain factors—known as **risk factors**—can make youths more prone to engage in illegal or otherwise unacceptable behaviors. Risk factors are defined as:

> . . . indicators of the pathways children and adolescents take to serious, violent, and chronic juvenile delinquency . . . the major risk factor domains [are] families, schools, peer groups, communities, and individual characteristics . . . Risk factors predict increased risk for developing a problem or disorder.[22]

The five domains for risk factors—families, schools, peers, communities, and individuals—each have certain chronic subenvironments that can produce a high incidence of unacceptable behaviors.[23] For example, risk factors within the family domain can include divorce, poverty, adoption, welfare dependency, and underclass values. As indicated in Table 5.3, these subenvironments can be incorporated into the risk factor domains.[24]

Youths in Conflict With Authority: Children in Trouble

Many children in trouble are from broken homes or dysfunctional families, have been abused or neglected, or grow up in other toxic environments such as severe poverty. These young people were defined previously as juveniles

TABLE 5.3   RISK FACTOR DOMAINS AND CHRONIC SUBENVIRONMENTS[a]

Five risk factor domains have been identified by researchers and experts. These unacceptable behaviors include substance abuse, delinquency, teen pregnancy, dropping out of school, and violence. Several chronic subenvironments have been observed that are conducive to producing unacceptable behaviors among youths, and are summarized in this table.

Community	Family	School	Peers/Individuals
Availability of drugs	Family history of problem behaviors	Academic failure in elementary school	Early and persistent antisocial behavior
Availability of firearms	Family management problems	Poor commitment to school	Rebelliousness and aggressiveness
Laws and norms favoring drugs, firearms & crime	Chronic family conflict	Truancy	Friends engaging in problem behavior
Media portrayals of violence	Parental approval of problem behavior	Moving frequently to new schools	Early commencement of problem behavior
Transitions and mobility	Parental criminal behavior	Dropping out	Constitutional & congenital factors
Community disorganization			
Extreme economic deprivation			

a. Adapted from Howell, J. C. (2003). *Preventing & reducing juvenile delinquency: A comprehensive framework* (p. 105). Thousand Oaks, CA: Sage.

who violate the law, either as juvenile delinquents or as status offenders. Both categories of offenders are technically noncriminal youths because neither are processed through the criminal justice system. This holds true even for juvenile delinquents who commit acts that are defined as serious felonies; as long as they remain in the juvenile justice system, they are treated as delinquents and not criminals. However, it is important to remember that although all status offenders retain their designation as juveniles, not all delinquents remain in the juvenile justice system.

Most states have established criteria under which some delinquent offenders can be waived into criminal court, tried in the same manner as adults, and punished accordingly. Many states also bypass the juvenile-to-criminal court waiver process altogether and automatically try serious offenders in criminal court as adults. These issues are discussed more fully in Chapter 7, but it is interesting at this point to note that waivers out of juvenile court began to decline during the mid-1990s. What explained this new trend? The answer is interesting and uncomplicated: States began to send greater numbers of offenders *directly* to criminal courts, thus circumventing the juvenile justice system *ab initio* (from the beginning).[25]

Age of Majority

Every state and the federal government have adopted statutory designations that officially define one's status as a juvenile or an adult. These designations are based on age, and the legal age of transition from juvenile status to adulthood is termed the **age of majority**. Jurisdictions of juvenile courts are delimited by each state's age-based criteria, so that when offenders reach the designated age of majority, they automatically become subject to criminal court jurisdiction. Technically, both status offenders and juvenile delinquents are lawbreakers who have not yet passed a state's legally defined age of majority.

There is some consensus, but no unanimity, on the question of establishing ages of majority. Although most states place the age of majority at 18 years old, seven states place the age at 17 years old, and three states designate the age of majority at 16 years old. Under federal law, juveniles are defined as persons under the age of 18.[26] Table 5.4 summarizes the ages of majority adopted under state and federal laws.[27]

Status Offenders

Status offenses are defined by one's age, pertaining solely to persons under the age of majority. These offenses are deemed by society to be unacceptable

TABLE 5.4   AGE OF MAJORITY

Each state and the federal government officially define the age of majority for persons within their jurisdiction. Prior to reaching the age of majority, offenders are subject to juvenile court jurisdiction. After an offender's age of majority is passed, criminal court jurisdiction is invoked.

This table lists the ages of majority under state and federal jurisdiction.[a]

Age When Subject to Criminal Court Jurisdiction	States
16	Connecticut, New York, North Carolina
17	Georgia, Illinois, Louisiana, Massachusetts, Michigan, Missouri, South Carolina, Texas
18	Federal, Alabama, Alaska, Arizona, Arkansas, California, Colorado, Delaware, District of Columbia, Florida, Hawaii, Idaho, Indiana, Iowa, Kansas, Kentucky, Maine, Maryland, Minnesota, Mississippi, Nebraska, Nevada, New Hampshire, New Jersey, New Mexico, North Dakota, Ohio, Oregon, Pennsylvania, Rhode Island, South Dakota, Tennessee, Utah, Vermont, Virginia, Washington, West Virginia, Wyoming

a. From Puzzanchera, C., Stahl, A. L., Finnegan, T. A., Tierney, N., & Snyder, H. N. (2003). *Juvenile court statistics 1998*. Washington, DC: Office of Juvenile Justice and Delinquency Prevention.

TABLE 5.5 LONGITUDINAL DATA: STEADY INCREASES IN PETITIONED STATUS OFFENSE CASES

Longitudinal data (long-term over time) are useful to explain trends in juvenile deviance. For example, these data show that the number of status offenses has increased annually in the United States. This table is an example of how longitudinal data can be used to summarize the number of petitioned status cases brought before juvenile courts nationally over a 10-year period.[1]

Most Serious Offense	1988	1993	1997
Status offenses	79,000	112,300	158,600
Liquor law violations	26,200	27,800	40,700
Truancy	20,600	33,700	40,500
Runaway behavior	12,400	19,900	24,000
Ungovernableness	12,900	14,900	21,300
Miscellaneous[1]	6,900	16,000	32,100

1. Curfew, tobacco, etc.

behaviors, and include: runaway behavior, truancy, ungovernableness, under-age use of alcohol or tobacco products, and curfew violations. Absent concomitant (occurring together or accompanying) criminality, persons above the age of majority may engage in these behaviors without violating the law.

When considering behavior patterns for specific status offenses, truancy is the most common offense for youths under age 15 years, and liquor law violations are most frequent for youths 16 years of age and older. Curfew violations also occur at fairly high rates in these age groups. Experts have debated whether chronic (repeated or extreme) behavior for particular types of status offenses are more or less likely to lead to **career escalation**. Career escalation refers to the progression from relatively minor offenses toward more serious delinquent or criminal offenses. One aspect of this debate asks whether truants and liquor-law violators tend to be chronic offenders to a greater degree than runaways. Some experts conclude that truants and liquor-law violators are more likely to escalate toward more serious delinquent or criminal activities, while others have found no significant escalation toward delinquency and crime.[28] Regardless of linkage with career escalation, the fact is that status offenses have been steadily increasing over time. In comparison, delinquency rates increased and then declined during the last two decades.

It is useful to make a longitudinal (long-term over time) comparison of juvenile deviance. Table 5.5 is a longitudinal *snapshot* of status offending, and compares rate of increases in status offenses over a 10-year period.[29] It is interesting to note that in 10 years there was no decline or leveling off in any category for any year.

States try to act in the "best interest" of the child when dealing with status offenders, and therefore apply creative approaches and standards for labeling and processing these offenders. For example, a number of states have officially decriminalized status offenses, meaning that offenders are not deemed to be lawbreakers. Other states have reclassified status offenders as *dependent children*, so that youths are diverted to child and youth service agencies rather than juvenile courts. Many of these approaches and standards are specifically designed to soften potential trauma for young status offenders entering into the juvenile justice system for the first time. Thus, a principal reason for diversion outside of the juvenile courts is society's concern about stigmatizing nondelinquent offenders. The fear is that stigma in court might stimulate chronic behavior in status offenders, leading to more youths engaging in recidivist and delinquent behavior. This is a legitimate concern, because chronic status offenders are nearly always referred to juvenile court.

Juvenile Delinquents

A juvenile delinquent is a person who commits an offense that would be considered a crime had the offender been over the age of majority. Thus, delinquent offenses are not synonymous with status offenses. Juvenile delinquents

Photo 5.2   A group of juveniles vandalizing an abandoned building. Some acts of juvenile delinquency are a result of destructive "fun."

have committed the same offenses as adult criminals, including serious felonies, but because they have been designated as delinquents, they are processed through the juvenile justice system. Hence, even though an adolescent may have committed a particularly egregious offense, the word *delinquent* is used in lieu of *criminal,* in part to reduce the likelihood of stigmatizing young serious offenders.

Readers will recall from Chapter 4 that self-reported data are surveys of youths asking them to report their juvenile acts. As discussed previously, one of the most influential self-report studies was the National Youth Survey (NYS), which examined a national cohort (sample) of 1,725 youths ages 11 to 17 years from 1976 to 1980. The NYS reported that delinquency increased by nearly 50% during this period, showing that the delinquency rate was high and escalating during these years. Another influential self-report study is the **Monitoring the Future Study** (MTF), which has measured delinquency and drug abuse among a national sample of high school seniors since 1982, with 8th and 10th graders added in 1991. Analyses of NYS and MTF data indicate that drug use and delinquency were highest during the 1980s and early 1990s before declining.

Data from another interesting study—the FBI's **Supplementary Homicide Report**—carefully compiled data on juvenile homicide offenders. The Supplementary Homicide Report did not report self-reported data. Data collected during the period 1984 to 1994 provide an interesting historical snapshot of patterns of juvenile homicide.[30] According to these data, juvenile homicides increased markedly during the mid-1980s and early 1990s, with most offenders 15 to 17 years of age. Males committed the vast majority of homicides, and 61% of homicide offenders were African American juveniles. Also, more than 80% of homicides were committed using a firearm, with males and older adolescents more likely to use a gun. Significantly, most victims were of the same race as their assailants.

Significant numbers of youths are arrested annually for serious offenses, mostly for property crimes. Table 5.6 summarizes the number of juvenile arrests for serious delinquent offenses.[31]

It is important to understand that although the 2001 data for arrests are significant, and the proportion of offenses perpetrated by juveniles is reportedly high, these data represent an overall decline in comparison to data reported during the 1980s and early 1990s. For example, the 1990s saw substantial declines for burglary and motor vehicle theft and a moderate decline for arson.

As is the case with some status offenders, many juvenile delinquents are chronic offenders. They engage in repeated and serious delinquency, sometimes committing acts of serious property vandalism or physical violence. Chronic offenders are in a sense "career delinquents" because they intend to continue in their behavior without pause, perhaps envisioning themselves as someday becoming career adult criminals. They represent classic cases of career escalation. Many, but certainly not all, career delinquents are from poor urban backgrounds, often growing up with underclass values. For

TABLE 5.6   JUVENILE ARRESTS FOR INDEX CRIMES, 2001

Index Crimes are the most serious felonies reported by the FBI in its annual Uniform Crime Report. Juveniles account for many of these crimes, although the greatest proportion of juvenile offenses are property crimes.

This table reports the number of arrests of juveniles for serious (index) felonies.[a]

Offense Charged	Total All Ages	Ages Under 15	Ages Under 18	Ages Over 18
Crime Index total	11,554,737	150,223	407,106	1,147,631
Percent distribution Crime Index	100	9.7	26.2	73.8
Violent crime	434,391	22,146	67,002	367,389
Percent distribution violent crime	100	5.1	15.4	84.6
Property crime	1,120,346	128,077	340,104	700,242
Percent distribution property crime	100	11.4	30.4	69.6
Murder & nonnegligent manslaughter	9,426	114	957	8,469
Forcible rape	18,576	1,180	3,119	15,457
Robbery	76,667	4,354	18,111	58,566
Aggravated assault	329,722	16,498	44,815	284,907
Burglary	198,883	23,287	61,623	137,260
Larceny-theft	806,093	92,317	238,605	567,488
Motor vehicle theft	102,607	8,425	33,563	69,044
Arson	12,763	4,048	6,313	6,450

a. Adapted from Federal Bureau of Investigation. (2002). *Crime in the United States 2001* (p. 244). Washington, DC: U.S. Department of Justice.

recidivist delinquents, acquiring an education, developing interpersonal skills, and investigating quality employment are all secondary to their anti-social behaviors and lifestyles. By the time they reach the age of majority, chronic delinquent offenders typically have few skills, poor education, and a great deal of experience with the justice system.

_____ Youths Requiring Intervention: Children in Need

Children in need were defined previously as juveniles who are not properly cared for by an adult, and who may be taken into the juvenile justice system for their own protection under the doctrine of *parens patriae*. Many of these youths are placed in foster and group homes and are monitored by child welfare agencies. It has been noted that experts generally describe several categories of children in need:

- *Dependent children.* Children who are abandoned by parents or guardians or are otherwise uncared for. Youths live in inadequate and needy conditions, which are usually not the fault of their parents or other adult guardians. There is usually no intentional neglect. For example, there may be conditions of extreme poverty in which the parents do not have the means to provide adequate food, clothing, or shelter.
- *Neglected children.* Child victims who do not receive proper care from parents or other guardians. Youths live in inadequate and needy conditions, which are intentionally created by their parents or other adult guardians. Substance abuse such as alcoholism and drug addiction are frequently present and contribute to family financial distress, parental health problems, and parental death. Common types of neglect are physical, emotional, and educational neglect.
- *Abused children.* Children who are assaulted physically, sexually, or emotionally by their parents or other adult guardians.

Child Dependency and Neglect

Juvenile justice systems have always had jurisdiction over dependent and neglected children. However, the two categories were often conflated (mixed), so that no differentiation was made between youths who were dependent and those who were neglected. In the modern era, a distinction has been made between the two, in recognition of the underlying causes and characteristics of these conditions. Experts now understand that parents and guardians of children in need can act either proactively or passively to cause hardship for their children. That is, they can either intentionally create dangerous environments (proactive), or be responsible for these environments without an intentional contribution to the outcome (passive). Children in need suffer regardless of whether their conditions are the result of parental action or inaction—the outcome is the same. These children are likely to develop emotional and psychological problems, and they often become status offenders, delinquents, and criminals.

Although child dependency and neglect govern similar conditions, they are distinguishable by parental intentions and the quality of parents' behavior. Child dependency is characterized by parents' complete *inability* to provide for the basic needs of their children, whereas child neglect is characterized by proactive parental *intention* to deprive children of their basic needs. In comparison, abuse is by definition an example of extremely proactive behavior by parents and guardians. It is intentionally carried out and potentially extremely dangerous. In all of these categories—dependency, neglect, and abuse—the juvenile justice system will often intervene very aggressively for the best interests of the child.

Neglected and dependent children frequently grow up in families that have been devastated by death, divorce, or economic distress. In addition to severe family disruption, they may also be victims of extreme poverty. Experts have identified three common types of neglect:[32]

- *Physical neglect.* "Abandonment, expulsion from the home, delay or failure to seek remedial health care, inadequate supervision, disregard for hazards in the home, or inadequate food, clothing, or shelter."
- *Emotional neglect.* "Inadequate nurturance or affection . . . maladaptive behavior and other inattention to emotional/developmental needs."
- *Educational neglect.* "Permitting the child to be chronically truant or other inattention to educational needs."

Signs of neglect and dependency include inadequate clothing (for example, in cold climates), malnutrition, poor medical care, and unhealthy hygiene. Neglected and dependent children may also exhibit behavioral problems such as stealing, substance abuse, listlessness at school and elsewhere, and never being supervised by an adult. Without basic necessities or positive adult role models, neglected and dependent children can become alienated, emotionally dysfunctional, and psychologically damaged. Because neglected children in particular tend to be unsupervised, they are often brought into the juvenile justice system for status offenses such as truancy or curfew offenses. This can lead to career escalation and future criminality.

Child Abuse

Households that practice physical, sexual, or emotional abuse are by definition very damaging environments for children. From the child's perspective, these environments are filled with fear, uncertainty, and danger. Self-esteem is eroded, dysfunctional norms become a way of life, and children reared in abusive homes often grow up to be violent teenagers and adults. One factor that serves to further aggravate the consequences of abuse is that many physical and emotional abusers convince children that they "deserve" to be abused. Abusive parents frequently justify their mistreatment as disciplinary measures that are needed to correct the child victim's unacceptable behavior. Abused children can come to believe this explanation and blame themselves for their parents' conduct.

Two fundamental concepts should be understood about physical and sexual abuse: Physical abuse is tantamount to assault and battery, whereas sexual abuse involves the exploitation of children for sexual pleasure or financial gain. These types of abuse exist within every demographic group and economic class in every region of the country, so that it is clearly a national problem affecting all communities. And yet, research has identified associations between higher rates of abuse and low educational level, unemployment, poverty, and young age of the abuser. Research also indicates that child abusers tend to be mothers, parents, or other family members; relatively few abuse cases involve friends of the family or caregivers. Domestic violence and sexual abuse are hidden crimes because they frequently occur inside homes or within insular (secretive or closed) institutions. Incidents occur among families, which are among the most insular institutions in our culture. Thus, most cases of physical and sexual abuse go unreported for many reasons, often because of embarrassment, fear of retaliation, or a person's dysfunctional conclusion that abuse is somehow a "normal" way of life. It is estimated that one to two million children have been physically assaulted or threatened with deadly weapons.[33]

Compared with emotional abuse, cases of physical or sexual abuse are fairly easily identified because of the physical trauma and abnormal behavior that often occurs. Emotional abuse is very difficult to measure because of the absence of physical scars and presence of subtle psychological scars. In essence, children "hurt on the inside" when abused emotionally. An emotionally abused child is one who is regularly insulted, criticized, blamed, ignored, or given overly intrusive attention. Their emotional needs are not nurtured, and they are frequently the object of rages, parental self-pity, or verbal assaults. The effect on children can be equally as damaging as physical or sexual abuse. Emotional abuse is recognized as a form of abuse in many jurisdictions.

Laws Governing Child Abuse and Neglect. To combat child abuse and neglect, the federal government passed the **Child Abuse Prevention and Treatment Act** in 1974, as amended in 1978. It criminalized child abuse and neglect caused by parents or guardians:

> . . . physical or mental injury, sexual abuse or exploitation, negligent treatment, or maltreatment of a child under the age of eighteen, by a person who is responsible for the child's welfare under circumstances, which indicate the child's health, or welfare is harmed or threatened.

The federal law also mandated reporting of child abuse and neglect. Similarly, every state has enacted child abuse and neglect statutes. The scope of these laws varies from state to state, with some providing expansive definitions of abuse and neglect and others using a more narrow approach. Every state has also enacted **child abuse reporting statutes**, which are laws mandating reporting procedures for certain institutions and professions. Under these laws, state agencies have been designated to investigate allegations of abuse, and in many cases there are statutory reporting requirements for school employees, medical personnel, social service workers, and law enforcement officers. Reporting authorities are often granted civil immunity when they report apparent abuse in good faith. Legal privileges such as the physician–patient and husband–wife privileges are waived in many jurisdictions. Thus, child abuse reporting statutes often give legal protection to authorities who come forward with reports of possible abuse and eliminate legal privileges that might have previously protected abusers.

Child abuse reporting statutes represent significant progress in the national effort to end child abuse and neglect. Although these laws are not perfect—many are unclear about what should be reported and who should make the report—they widen the net of the juvenile justice system and place significant responsibility on parents for their behavior.

Rescuing Youths: Helping Children in Trouble and Children in Need

There exists within the juvenile justice system a broad support network of individuals, agencies, and institutions that are responsible for the welfare of children in trouble and children in need. This support network is quite extensive, and its components can be classified as follows:

- *The immediate community*. Made up of families, neighbors, and friends, the immediate community are those who are closest to troubled and needy children.
- *Intervening institutions*. These institutions include schools and law enforcement agencies. Officials within these institutions are key personnel in the effort to help troubled and needy children.
- *Remedial institutions*. Child protective and health care agencies that essentially try to investigate and remediate the damaging effects of troubled and needy environments.

The Immediate Community

Family, neighbors, and friends are "first-line" interveners in the overall effort to help children in trouble and children in need. These persons are closest to youthful offenders and victims and most likely know the adults responsible for their circumstances. Because of this, several presumptions may be made about members of the immediate community and their relationships to juveniles: First, because of their proximity, they are persons most likely to know the juvenile and have personal knowledge about the young person's behavior and environment. Second, these persons are best positioned to bring about quick and immediate intervention from the appropriate officials and agencies. Third, members of the immediate community may very well be *responsible* for the child's environment as their abusers, neglecters, or participants in their deviant behavior. Fourth, because members of the immediate community probably know those persons who are responsible for the juvenile's behavior and environment, they can also be least likely to report this to the authorities out of a skewed sense of loyalty or simply not wanting to get involved.

Although on the front line, the immediate community's frequency and effectiveness of intervention can be quite erratic. Persons often exhibit reluctance to report child maltreatment. Part of the reason is that the maltreatment may be misinterpreted as discipline, in which neighbors and family may conclude that it is none of their business. There is also a fear of retribution, especially if one is the spouse or relative of an abuser. Another reason can be concern about making an important decision such as intervention on incomplete information; that is, concern about being mistaken about one's interpretation of the behavior that is observed. One final reason for erratic reporting is the simple fact that a great deal of child maltreatment occurs secretly within households, so that neighbors, friends, and family members may be completely unaware of the child's environment.

Intervening Institutions

Schools are the single most prevalent reporting authority on child maltreatment, followed by law enforcement agencies.[34] There is an officially mandated reason for this: Child abuse reporting statutes require schools and law enforcement agencies to report evidence of child maltreatment. Under this mandate, schools and law enforcement agencies have come to play a critical role in identifying troubled and needy children and informing child welfare authorities about their conditions. It is now routine policy for these intervening institutions to employ trained experts who are adept at identifying maltreatment, and who have been empowered to act officially on behalf of these institutions.

It should be understood that schools sit *in loco parentis* and are charged to be *proactive* intervening institutions, whereas law enforcement agencies become involved when there is a problem and are usually *reactive* institutions. Within the context of our discussion, the term *schools* refers to the many professionals working within the education system: administrators, teachers, nurses, coaches, and counselors. These professionals are in close contact with young people for extended periods of time each day, as well as over weeks and months. Therefore, they are arguably the best resource within the juvenile justice system to proactively identify maltreatment and carry out effective intervention expeditiously. In comparison, law enforcement officials do not become aware of, and do not respond to, child maltreatment until someone reports a possible problem—hence, they are reactive in their intervention. Reports may come from members of the immediate community, or from remedial institutions. For example, neighbors or family members might call the police during an abusive incident, or emergency medical personnel could call the police after treating an injured or terrified child.

Remedial Institutions

Health care agencies treat physically and emotionally damaged children, and child protective agencies investigate and process allegations of maltreatment. Both remedial institutions are obligated under law (e.g., in accordance with child abuse reporting statutes) to report identified cases of maltreatment. Thus, they are linked by law to other components of the juvenile justice system.

Health care agencies intervene through hospital emergency rooms, emergency medical services, mental health agencies, doctor's examinations, and public health clinics. As with the cases of schools and law enforcement agencies, personnel are trained to identify child maltreatment and are authorized to act officially on behalf of their agencies. Child protective agencies work closely with all juvenile justice institutions, because large numbers of cases are referred to them by other agencies. Schools, law enforcement agencies, and health care agencies all rely on child protective services to intervene as investigators and protectors of maltreated juveniles. Of the investigations conducted by child protective services, more than 50% of cases result in findings of no maltreatment, roughly 35% to 40% of allegations are substantiated or suspicion of maltreatment is found, and the remaining cases involve either no finding or false reports.[35]

PROFESSIONAL PROFILE CHAPTER 5

Juvenile Division Commander—Major
Urban Police Agency

Major urban police agencies typically establish juvenile bureaus to address the problems of juvenile deviance and victimization. Officers who are assigned to these bureaus are specialists and are specially trained to deal with youth gangs, delinquents, status offenders, and victims. Higher-ranking urban juvenile police officers are experts on a broad range of youth-related problems and issues, and they frequently possess academic bachelor's and master's degrees.

I. Personal Profile

    A. Name:
    Sharyn Buck

    B. Agency:
    Los Angeles Police Department

    C. Rank and/or Title:
    Commanding Officer, Juvenile Division (Captain)

    D. Education (Schools and Degrees):
    AA, Journalism
    BA, Broadcast Journalism
    MA, Conflict Resolution and Negotiation Tactics

E. Professional Training:

Twenty-one years of law enforcement experience, including leadership training, advanced management courses, and extensive everyday application

F. Professional Organizations/Community Group Memberships:

Southern California Juvenile Officer's Association
National Association of Female Executives
National Association of Women Law Enforcement Executives
City of Hope Steering Committee for Women's Professional Golf
International Association of Chiefs of Police
Mayor's Youth Council
Advisory committee for LA's BEST (mayor's after-school program)

II. Professional Profile

A. What personal or other background experiences led to your decision to *choose* this profession?

Wanting a career that offered me opportunities, variety of assignments, challenges, and a good salary, law enforcement was the perfect choice. Growing up I was involved in competitive sports and with LAPD I have had the fortune of representing the Department across the United States in athletic events. Being able to serve the people of the city that I grew up in has been the best part of all! Another plus is that I have two brothers who are law enforcement officers (LAPD), and it was their enthusiasm and excitement that led me to this profession.

B. Please state a few of your personal reasons/motivations for your decision to *continue* in this profession.

Being a Los Angeles police officer is a very rewarding career, as each day brings a different and unique experience. The promotional opportunities, as well as the diversity of job assignments, have certainly been a motivating factor for me to continue in this profession. However, as my leadership responsibilities increased, the opportunity to interact and solve problems with higher levels of the community, such as City Council members, the Police Commissioner, and other law enforcement department heads has also expanded. This experience continues to motivate me to want to contribute as much as I can in the field of law enforcement, as it relates to youth and youth crime.

C. Which job experiences have had an important impact on you?

With a degree in broadcast journalism, I had the very distinct opportunity to be the Officer-in-Charge of the Department's Press Relations Section, where I represented the Department and the Chief of Police in working with the media. In this high-profile assignment, I learned to effectively interact with many different political and community organizations, developing significant long-lasting relationships. In speaking to media representatives from all over the world, I was able to enhance my communication skills, especially in high pressure situations. When you conduct media interviews on events that impact the Police Department, you feel very good about being able to not only deliver the message, but to also represent an agency such as the Los Angeles Police Department.

D.   What has been a particularly *satisfying* job experience?

In my current assignment as the Commanding Officer of the Juvenile Division, I work with a group of dedicated, talented detectives who investigate the most sensitive, yet horrific cases involving children who are victims of physical and/or sexual abuse. It has been a privilege for me to work with such passionate people, striving to protect those that can't protect themselves, the children who are victimized. I feel very satisfied that I can help them do their jobs and enhance morale on a daily basis.

E.   What has been a particularly *challenging* job experience?

All of my assignments have been challenging, as I tend to apply for those type of positions. But, if I had to select one, it would probably be working in the Internal Affairs Division. In that position I investigated and presented cases against officers who were accused of serious misconduct. The assignment was very demanding, but certainly rewarding. I learned so much about our disciplinary system, an experience that provided me significant insight for future promotions and for the management positions I have held throughout my career.

F.   What do you think the future holds for your profession?

The future for law enforcement will continue to be on the cutting edge of keeping communities crime free and safe from terrorism.

As the demands increase for law enforcement officers to be held to the highest standard in their behavior and interaction with the communities they serve, so will the advancement in technology to ensure those standards are adhered to. In the field of child abuse, the needs continue to grow for advancements in Internet safety, specifically in educating children as to the dangers of cyberspace.

G.   What kind of advice/guidance would you give to interested students?

If you are pursuing a career in law enforcement, ensure you prepare yourself both mentally and physically. Obtaining a college degree is certainly a benefit, and being in top physical shape is a plus. The one quality I believe is absolutely essential to a successful career is communication skills. If there is one skill that affords you the opportunity to **succeed** in law enforcement, it is the ability to interact with people, verbally and in writing. Too often people forget that being a police officer requires you to know how to communicate with people, often in critical emergency situations.

Chapter Summary

The expansive juvenile justice network is designed to address modern problems and risk factors of young people. Agencies and individuals are not only charged to redress the behavior of children in trouble but also to provide remediation for children in need. Thus, whereas the adult criminal justice system provides fairly straightforward services within a narrow focus, the juvenile justice system is a complex network with a rather broad mission.

Many modern problems of juveniles are similar to those of the past, but there are newer challenges for juveniles and society. Juveniles are both victims of violence and perpetrators. As victims, they experience criminal violence just as do adults. However, they also experience so-called "hidden" victimization, which occurs secretly in households or institutions. Because of hidden victimization, a significant proportion of physical and sexual assaults are never reported. As perpetrators, juveniles are responsible for committing the same kinds of criminal violence as adults. Although the superpredator phenomenon never arose to any great extent, the fact remains that juvenile-initiated violence makes up a significant proportion of criminal violence in many communities. Another problem is substance abuse, primarily the use of alcohol and marijuana. Other substances, such as hallucinogens and cocaine, are also frequently abused. Poverty and homelessness have potentially devastating consequences for children. Although poverty alone does not create juvenile deviance, it increases family vulnerability. Homelessness is in itself a stressful and dangerous circumstance for young people. Finally, the frequency of missing children is of concern to all sectors of society and the juvenile justice system. Fortunately, programs such as the AMBER Plan serve to coordinate rescue and recovery efforts. Special populations of juveniles also represent new challenges for the juvenile justice system, as do risk factors that may exist within the juvenile's environment.

Children in trouble are juvenile delinquents and status offenders who are designated as such because they have not yet passed the age of majority. They are lawbreakers who receive differential treatment specifically designed for juveniles, so long as they remain within the juvenile justice system. Although the rate of status offenses has remained steady or increased during recent years, juvenile delinquency declined during the 1990s and early millennium after reaching new highs during previous decades. Children in need are dependent, neglected, and abused children. Dependency and neglect are similar, but they are distinguishable because of the role and motivation of the responsible adult. Dependency reflects the inability of parents to provide for the basic needs of their children, whereas neglect is a willful maltreatment. Child abuse is fundamentally damaging for children. Physical, sexual, and emotional abuse are all traumatic for youths and can lead to depression, withdrawal, incorrigibility, and other harmful outcomes. Child abuse prevention laws and child abuse reporting statutes have been enacted to criminalize abuse and to require that specified institutions and professionals report abuse when it occurs.

A broad network of people and institutions has been established to help children in trouble and children in need. Those closest to juveniles are the immediate community, who are often aware of troubled and needy children, but who also are often reticent about reporting these matters to the authorities. Schools and law enforcement agencies are intervening institutions that are required by law to report maltreatment and in fact are the most prevalent reporting institutions. This is because schools are in extended contact with children, while the police are regularly called to respond to reports of maltreatment. Remedial institutions essentially treat and investigate allegations of maltreatment. Health care agencies and child protective agencies are important components of the juvenile justice system because they are able to identify and, in the case of protective agencies, monitor the condition of maltreated juveniles.

Chapter 6 investigates the role of the police in the juvenile justice system. The historical evolution of police interactions during several policing eras is summarized, and an investigation is made of police dispositions, discretion, and procedural formality. Several issues arising from police contacts with juveniles will be discussed, including search and seizure, booking, fingerprinting, interrogations, and the use of force by the police.

Questions for Review

1. What is the difference in definition between children in trouble and children in need?

2. What issues affect juvenile delinquents, status offenders, and victimized youths?

3. In what ways can poverty, underclass status, behavioral issues, and emotional issues be considered to be risk factors?

4. In what ways are children in trouble in conflict with authority?

5. What are the main problems and policy issues associated with children in trouble?

6. In what ways do children in need require intervention?

7. What are the main problems and policy issues associated with children in need?

8. Describe the assistance network that is framed by the community, families, and schools.

Key Terms and Concepts

The following topics were discussed in this chapter and are found in the Glossary:

Age of Majority

AMBER Alerts

AMBER Plan, The

At-Risk Juveniles

Attention Deficit Disorder

Career Escalation

Child Abuse Prevention and Treatment Act

Child Abuse Reporting Statutes

Children in Need

Children in Trouble

Educational Neglect

Emotional Disturbance

Emotional Neglect

Immediate Community, The

Intervening Institutions

Learning Disabilities

Monitoring the Future Study

Physical Neglect

Prenatal Exposure to Disease and Drugs

Remedial Institutions

Risk Factors

Runaways

Supplemental Homicide Report

Thrownaways

DISCUSSION BOX

A National Problem: Children on the Street

This chapter's Discussion Box is intended to stimulate critical discussion about the plight of juveniles who take their chances on the street.

Many children and adolescents have good reason to leave their home environments. Abuse, exploitation, and substance addiction often create intolerable situations for young people. Most runaways return home after a short period of time, but many of them take to the streets for extended periods. In essence, they genuinely move out of their homes to live elsewhere. Living among these victimized youths are other young people who leave home without a real need to escape truly toxic environments—they become runaways for a variety of reasons.

Runaways and thrownaways live in every city in America; some of them are housed in state-run shelters, and others are members of the nation's homeless population. It is very difficult to study them systematically, because neither they nor their parents are keen to discuss the reasons for what is certainly a traumatic circumstance. False and misleading answers to research questions are common among runaways, thrownaways, and their parents or guardians. At the same time that objective interview data are difficult to collect, so too are accurate statistical (quantitative) data on the number of children living on the street or the number of families affected by this problem.

Despite the difficulty of obtaining accurate data on this problem, policy makers and members of the community cannot overlook their obligation to respond to the plight of children on the street.

Discussion Questions

1. Why do children and adolescents become runaways? Why would they prefer life on the street over life at home?

2. From the perspective of parents and guardians, what can be done to mitigate the likelihood that their children leave to live on the street?

3. What kind of research is needed to study the problem of street children? What aspects of this phenomenon should be studied?

4. How should policy makers manage this problem? *Can* they manage it?

5. What type of relief agencies should be established to rescue youths who genuinely take up residence outside of their homes?

Recommended Web Sites

The following Web sites investigate issues concerning children in trouble and children in need, and illustrate the types of agencies and programs available to address these constituencies:

Children's Bureau: http://www.acf.hhs.gov/programs/cb/
National Center for Children in Poverty: http://www.nccp.org/
National Center for Missing & Exploited Children: http://www.missingkids.org/
National Clearinghouse on Child Abuse and Neglect Information: http://nccanch.acf
     .hhs.gov/index.cfm
The Future of Children: http://www.futureofchildren.org/

Note: The Web site URLs and exercises below are also from the book's study site:
     http://www.sagepub.com/martin

Web Exercise

Using this chapter's recommended Internet sites, conduct an online investigation of resources available to children in trouble and children in need.

- How comprehensive are the resources available for children in trouble and children in need?
- How would you compare the scope and quality of resources made available by public agencies vis-à-vis private agencies?
- How effective do you think these programs are?

For an online search of resources available to children in trouble and children in need, students should use a search engine and enter the following keywords:

"Child Abuse and Neglect"

"Juvenile Assistance"

Recommended Readings

The following publications provide discussions on service and remediation policy challenges for children in trouble and children in need.

Bernard, T. J. (1997). *The cycle of juvenile justice.* New York: Oxford University Press.

Best, J. (1993). *Threatened children: Rhetoric and concern about child-victims.* Chicago: University of Chicago Press.

Dorne, C. K. (2001). *Child maltreatment: A primer in history, public policy, and research* (2nd ed.). New York: Harrow & Heston.

Howell, J. C. (2003). *Juvenile justice & youth violence.* Thousand Oaks, CA: Sage.

Howell, J. C. (2003). *Preventing & reducing juvenile delinquency: A comprehensive framework.* Thousand Oaks, CA: Sage.

Notes

1. See Tommy N. Sophapmysay v. City of Sergeant Bluff, Iowa, et al., 218 F. Supp. 2d 1027 (N. Dist. IA, 2002).

2. Snyder, H. N., & Sickmund, M. (1999). *Juvenile offenders and victims: 1999 National report* (p. 41). Washington, DC: U.S. Department of Justice.

3. Ibid.

4. Ringel, C. (1997). *Criminal victimization 1996: Changes 1995–1996 with trends 1993–96* (p. 5). Washington, DC: U.S. Department of Justice.

5. Sickmund, M., Snyder, H. N., & Poe-Yamagata, E. (1997). *Juvenile offenders and victims: 1997 Update on violence.* Washington, DC: U.S. Department of Justice.

6. DiIulio, J. J. (1995, November 27). The coming of the super-predators. *Weekly Standard,* 23.

7. Bennett, W. J., DiIulio, J. J., & Walters, J. P. (1996). *Body count: Moral Poverty . . . and how to win America's war against crime and drugs* (p. 27). New York: Simon & Schuster.

8. Snyder, H. N., & Sickmund, M. (1999). *Juvenile offenders and victims: 1999 National report* (p. 117). Washington, DC: U.S. Department of Justice.

9. For a good analysis of associations between delinquency and other behaviors, see Huizinga, D., Loeber, R., Thornberry, T. P., & Cothern, L. (2000). *Co-occurrence of delinquency and other problem behaviors.* Washington, DC: U.S. Department of Justice.

10. Snyder, H. N., & Sickmund, M. (1999). *Juvenile offenders and victims: 1999 National report* (p. 74). Washington, DC: U.S. Department of Justice.

11. U.S. Department of Health and Human Services. (1998). *Monitoring the future survey*. Washington, DC: Health and Human Services.

12. Sickmund, M., Snyder, H. N., & Poe-Yamagata, E. (1997). *Juvenile offenders and victims: 1997 Update on violence*. Washington, DC: U.S. Department of Justice (p. 115).

13. Lu, H.-H. (2003). *Low income children in the United States*. New York: National Center for Children in Poverty.

14. Ibid.

15. For a good discussion of missing children, see Finkelhor, D., Hotaling, G., & Sedlak, A. (1990). *Missing, abducted, runaway, and thrownaway children in America*. Washington, DC: U.S. Department of Justice.

16. National Coalition for the Homeless. (2002). *Who is homeless?* Washington, DC: National Coalition for the Homeless.

17. Ibid.

18. Adapted from Sickmund, M., Snyder, H. N., & Poe-Yamagata, E. (1997). *Juvenile offenders and victims: 1997 Update on violence* (p. 38). Washington, DC: U.S. Department of Justice.

19. National Center for Missing and Exploited Children. (n.d.). Available online at http://www.missingkids.com

20. Ibid.

21. National Center for Missing & Exploited Children. (n.d.). Available online at http://www.missingkids.org/missingkids/

22. Howell, J. C. (2003). *Preventing & reducing juvenile delinquency: A comprehensive framework* (p. 103). Thousand Oaks, CA: Sage.

23. For a good discussion of these risk factors, see Howell, J. C. (2003). *Juvenile justice & youth violence* (p. 133 et. seq.). Thousand Oaks, CA: Sage.

24. Table adapted from Howell, ibid. (p. 105).

25. See Sickmund, M., Snyder, H. N., & Poe-Yamagata, E. (1997). *Juvenile offenders and victims: 1997 Update on violence* (p. 170). Washington, DC: U.S. Department of Justice.

26. Juvenile Justice and Delinquency Prevention Act. 18 U.S.C. 5031.

27. From Puzzanchera, C., Stahl, A. L., Finnegan, T. A., Tierney, N., & Snyder, H. N. (2003). *Juvenile court statistics 1998*. Washington, DC: Office of Juvenile Justice and Delinquency Prevention.

28. See Terrell, N. E. (1997). Aggravated and sexual assaults among homeless and runaway adolescents. *Youth & Society, 28*. See also Matson, S., & Barnoski, R. (1998). *Assessing risk: Washington State juvenile court early intervention program*. Olympia, WA: Washington State Institute for Public Policy.

29. Adapted from ibid. (p. 37).

30. Data from Snyder, H. N., Sickmund, M., & Poe-Yamagata, E. (1996). *Juvenile offenders and victims: 1996 Update on violence*. Washington, DC: U.S. Department of Justice.

31. See Federal Bureau of Investigation. (2002). *Crime in the United States 2001*. Washington, DC: U.S. Department of Justice.

32. Definitions from Sickmund, M., Snyder, H. N., & Poe-Yamagata, E. (1997). *Juvenile offenders and victims: 1997 Update on violence* (p. 6). Washington, DC: U.S. Department of Justice.

33. See Straus, M. A., & Gelles, R. J. (1986). Societal change and change in family violence from 1975–1985 as revealed by two national surveys. *Journal of Marriage and the Family, 48.*

34. Definitions from Sickmund, M., Snyder, H. N., & Poe-Yamagata, E. (1997). *Juvenile offenders and victims: 1997 Update on violence.* Washington, DC: U.S. Department of Justice.

35. Ibid.

PART II

Process and Systems

Official Components

Part II   Growing up tough in the city. A teenaged couple poses.

6 The Role of the Police

When the police investigate crimes, the trail of evidence is often derived from the statements of witnesses and suspects. Unfortunately, the statements of juveniles are often inaccurate, including seemingly clear confessions of guilt. For example, in January 1998, Stephanie Crowe was found stabbed to death in her house in Escondido, California.[1] During the investigation, the police questioned her brother, Michael Crowe, and two of his friends, Michael Treadway and Aaron Houser. They were all juveniles. During an interrogation of Michael Treadway's brother, Joshua, he gave the police what seemed to be a detailed description of the murder, implicating Crowe, Houser, and his brother Michael. All three were indicted in May 1998 by a grand jury for murdering Stephanie. However, before the trial began, Stephanie's blood was found on the garments of a drifter. Charges against the three boys were dropped, and they were not prosecuted. Joshua Treadway's "description" was a fabrication.

Law enforcement agencies play a key role in the national effort to correct juvenile offenders and protect children in need. Police agencies[2] serve as intervening institutions within the juvenile justice system and are, by their nature, *reactive* institutions that typically intervene only after an emergency has been reported involving juveniles. In comparison to their adult-centered law enforcement duties, the police mission must be modified when dealing with juveniles because they are required to act in the "best interest of the child" to secure the child's safety, and/or to take him or her into custody. As can be imagined, it is not always an easy task for police agencies to keep their personnel and organizational units trained and abreast of new developments in juvenile justice philosophies and policies. Nevertheless, law enforcement organizations continue to be intricately woven into the fabric of the juvenile justice network.

Photo 6.1   Police officers arresting a boy in the late nineteenth century.

When one considers the scope of police involvement in juvenile deviance and victimization, one fact becomes readily apparent: The police are busy. For example, police departments regularly arrest more than 2.5 million persons under the age of 18 years annually.[3] Of these arrests, more than 40% are for larceny-theft, simple assault, drug violations, or disorderly conduct.[4] Police departments were also busy responding to child victimization cases.

According to the Federal Bureau of Investigation's National Incident-Based Reporting System (NIBRS), juveniles make up 12% of victims of serious crimes reported to the police, including more than 70% of victims of sex offenses and 38% of kidnapping incidents.[5] These data point up the societal reality that police intervention is a critical component of the juvenile justice system. Only law enforcement agencies are organized to respond quickly in critical situations.

Law enforcement agencies are expected to de-escalate a broad range of juvenile-related problems. Police officers must come into contact with juvenile lawbreakers whose behavior ranges from status offenses such as drinking and curfew violations to delinquent offenses such as assault, rape, and homicide. Police departments are also called by schools, parents, and community agencies to intervene in victimization cases involving dependent, neglected, and abused children. This multivariate role is unique within the juvenile justice system, and it is the subject of ongoing debate, criticism, and creative adaptation.

There are many subtleties and nuances to the role of law enforcement in the juvenile justice system. For example, juveniles' attitudes toward police officers are often ambiguous and behaviors can vary from cordiality to hostility. Also, police discretion can be affected by factors that are not present when dealing with adult cases. Finally, the organizational profiles and policies of law enforcement agencies must necessarily be periodically modified to reflect contemporary issues and problems of juveniles. In this chapter, our discussion of the role of the police reviews the following:

- Background: Historical Perspectives on Policing
- First Contact With Juveniles: Police Dispositions
- Decision Making: Police Discretion and Procedural Formality
- Issues Arising From Police Contacts With Juveniles
- Accessing the Community: Police Relationship-Building Strategies

CHAPTER PERSPECTIVE 6.1

Police Special Gang Units

Youth gang suppression is a central policy priority for law enforcement agencies, for the simple reason that youth gangs are a seemingly intractable problem in American cities. For example, in a snapshot of the year 2000, researchers identified more than 24,500 youth gangs, an estimated 772,500 gang members, in 3,330 jurisdictions.[6] In order to manage the spread of youth gangs and suppress gang activity, most police departments have created special gang units. Examples of these units include the following:

- **TARGET.** Tri-Agency Resource Gang Enforcement Teams (TARGET) were organized in Orange County in Southern California. The teams used a task force philosophy to focus on entire gangs and individual gang members. Several agencies were represented in each TARGET team, including prosecutors, probation officers, and police/prosecutor gang investigators. Operational emphasis was placed on identifying and arresting individual gang leaders and the most violent hard core members.
- **CRASH.** The Los Angeles Police Department organized an overtly aggressive gang suppression unit called Community Resources Against Street Hoodlums (CRASH). CRASH was formed in 1988 and engaged in suppression campaigns that were intended to intimidate gang members. Unfortunately, CRASH members were implicated in planting evidence on youths, assaulting or killing suspects, and otherwise framing suspected offenders. CRASH members were also accused of acting like gang members, including ganglike initiations.
- **Boston Gun Project/Operation Ceasefire.** The Boston Police established and communicated unambiguous standards of behavior to gang members. When these standards were violated by gang members, equally unambiguous penalties were imposed. The philosophy was to "pull every lever" to suppress gang behavior that violated the established standards.
- **Strategic Response Bureau.** This bureau was established as an office within the Columbus, Ohio, Police Department that operationalized community-oriented policing in their relationship with juveniles. Community Liaison Officers (CLOs) were assigned to police investigators and other officers and were charged to recognize and evaluate problems and then report back to investigators. CLOs became active in assisting in the suppression of violent gang activity.

The foregoing cases reaffirm the creativity and imaginative policy options available to law enforcement agencies in dealing with delinquency and crime. Although these cases deal specifically with gang suppression, they are illustrative of how flexibility and innovation are necessary when deploying law enforcement resources within the juvenile justice system.

Background: Historical Perspectives on Policing

Readers will recall from Chapter 2 that early colonial communities relied on parental authority and severe community sanctions to control unacceptable behavior in youths. The Puritans, for example, considered incorrigibility to be rebellion against God, and both parents and community leaders were empowered to mete out severe punishments to correct youths' behavior. The modern concept of police-juvenile relations did not arise until the advent of the industrial revolution during the early nineteenth century. During this era, workers and their families began to concentrate around factory towns, leading to rapid population growth in new and existing urban areas.

Modern urban police forces were formed to keep order in this new milieu, first in London in 1829, and later in the United States in the 1830s through the 1850s. The first American urban police forces were organized in Boston, New York, and Philadelphia.

Eras of American Policing

By the late 1870s, police forces existed in all large cities in the United States. Operationally, police officers patrolled on foot, walking *beats*, or on horseback, which brought them into regular personal contact with the community. This was a mixed blessing, because the police were frequently used to control the "dangerous classes" of workers, immigrants, ethnic minorities, criminals, gangs, and idle or delinquent juveniles. This era was the first of three policing eras in the United States, which can be summarized as follows:

- *Political Era.* This era lasted from the late nineteenth century to the early twentieth century. During this era, police departments were heavily integrated into urban political machines. Their authority to act and resources came from local politicians, so that the police were adjuncts of local political machines. The police provided a wide range of services, including crime prevention, order maintenance, and finding jobs.

- *Reform Era.* This era extended well into the mid-twentieth century. It promoted a model of impartial, professional police and a narrowed function of crime fighting. This era rejected politics as the basis of police legitimacy, and political influence was seen as a failure of police leadership. The police function was narrowed to crime fighting, and officers were expected to be professionally distanced from civilians, thus heralding the beginning of the "thin blue line" metaphor. Because policing was expected to be done "by the book," police discretion was discouraged.

- *Community-Strategy Era.* This era began in the 1950s and has continued to the present. This era's philosophy emphasized community political support, law, and professionalism. Law became the basic legitimating factor for police conduct. Community support and involvement was also sought and needed to solve problems. Crime control became just one goal of broader community problem solving. This type of policing requires development of intimate relationships between police and residents, so that police discretion is encouraged.

Policing Eras and Juvenile Relations

During the Political Era, police departments had wide latitude in their behavior toward juveniles. This was a particularly corrupt period in American political history, and the police were no exception. Favoritism toward individual citizens and their children was rampant, and the police regularly subjectively categorized children whom they knew as either being "good" or "bad." Police discretion was virtually unlimited, so that children could be selectively arrested, hit, beaten, or verbally abused with impunity.

During the Reform Era, the new emphasis on professionalism and adoption of the concept of crime prevention meant that the police focused on how to prevent juvenile delinquency. Beginning in the 1930s and 1940s, the police regularly patrolled locations where juveniles might congregate and be corrupted (such as pool halls), and many departments set up youth programs such as sports leagues. After the Second World War, policing strategies emphasized specialization, and juvenile units became common in major police departments. Part of the reason for this specialization was a perceived increase in juvenile delinquency and gang activity; this perception lasted well into the post–World War II era.

By the 1950s, at the dawn of the Community-Strategy Era, juvenile relations had become well integrated into most policing strategies, and departments regularly designated officers as juvenile officers within specialized youth divisions. Associations such as the International Juvenile Officers Association were formed,[7] and the concept of helping juvenile offenders and children in need became an integral part of training for juvenile officers. These efforts were continued and expanded up to the present time, with juvenile officers regularly speaking to schools and community groups, and some departments forming cadet programs. However, these efforts are frequently affected by political and economic constraints, with the result being that cutbacks and shifts in operational focus have occurred with some frequency over time.

One interesting historical note is the role of female police officers in juvenile relations. Although very few women were hired as sworn officers by police departments prior to the 1970s, those who were hired as officers were usually assigned to juvenile duty. It was not until the 1970s that women were recruited in significant numbers, or that they were permitted to move beyond juvenile duties and participate in the full scope of police work.

First Contact With Juveniles: Police Dispositions

When the police make contact with juveniles—whether involving simple questioning or taking them into custody—the interaction is termed a **police disposition**. Police dispositions technically refer to *any* contact made by police officers regarding the welfare and safety of juveniles, and they include interactions with both children in trouble and children in need. Dispositions are encounters that can result in no action being taken, or extensive questioning, or referring youths to child welfare agencies, or taking juveniles before juvenile court. Outcomes of police dispositions are affected by many factors, so that each resolution depends on the unique circumstances of each encounter. Two important dispositional factors—police discretion and procedural formality—are discussed in the next section. For now, the point to remember is that police officers exercise professional discretion, which allows them to use a formal or informal resolution to the disposition.

Officers are guided by a variety of limitations on their discretion, not the least of which is whether the disposition involves suspected delinquent or status offenses. Officers generally understand that status offenders can be treated within a broader discretionary framework that is often quite informal, and which frequently ends in a warning or referral to the juvenile's parents. Delinquent offenders—particularly violent offenders—are processed with greater formality under mandated rules of procedure. Unlike status offense dispositions, which involve relatively less serious behaviors, delinquency dispositions necessarily involve established documentary reporting and criminal investigation techniques.

Police dispositions are initiated from several community sources, all of which can be affected by juvenile deviance and victimization. Referrals from these sources very often result in police intervention to address reported delinquency or victimization. The following community centers are involved in initiating police dispositions:

- *Family-initiated dispositions.* Referrals to the police by parents or other family members. Police intervention is requested to either act as a mediator to resolve a dispute or situation, or a request is made for the police to take custody of an incorrigible or delinquent child.
- *Community-initiated dispositions.* Neighborhood or other community residents report deviance or victimization to the police. Business proprietors, property owners, neighbors, and other private citizens often request these referrals.
- *School-initiated dispositions.* Schools act *in loco parentis* to fulfill their obligation to operate on behalf of juveniles. The police are notified when schools discover delinquency or status deviance, or when a child appears to have been abused.

Table 6.1 summarizes the outcome of police dispositions originating from the foregoing sources.

Several dispositional alternatives are central to understanding the nature of interaction by the police with juveniles and the juvenile justice system. These alternatives (all part of the police disposition process) include **initial contact, custody,** and **detention.**

Initial Contact

Initial contact refers to the first occasion of police intervention when youths break the law or are victimized. As discussed previously, most illegal

TABLE 6.1   DISPOSITIONAL SOURCES AND OUTCOMES

Police dispositions originate from several sources, usually from family members, community members, and schools. The police role is usually reactive because these sources notify the police only after an incident has occurred.

   This table summarizes the quality of dispositions and outcomes.

	Disposition Outcome	
Source of Disposition	**Typical Complaint**	**Reactive Police Role**
Family-initiated	Victimization by family member Deviance by family member	Mediation Protection
Community-initiated	Victimization of child in community Deviance by child in community	Law enforcement Protection
School-initiated	Victimization observed in students Deviant behavior by students	Mediation Law enforcement Protection

behaviors and victimizations are never discovered or reported, so it should not be presumed that initial contacts occur for every case. When they do occur, the police may simply counsel and release the juvenile, meaning that the juvenile's brush with the juvenile justice system will end with the initial contact. The following options are available to the police:

- Initial contact without a warning to the youth or parents. No official record is kept.
- Initial contact with a warning to the youth or parents. No official record is kept.
- Initial contact with a formal record made to a juvenile authority. Possible subsequent processing of the youth or family through the juvenile or criminal justice systems.
- Initial contact resulting in taking the juvenile into custody and referring him or her to an agency of the juvenile justice system. This is expected to occur when serious delinquency or victimization has occurred.
- Initial contact by sending the case immediately to a prosecuting attorney or juvenile court.

   Because of this broad range of options available to officers in the field, initial contacts with the police have become the most frequent avenue of referral for juveniles who enter the juvenile justice system. Table 6.2 summarizes the scope of options available to police officers during the initial contact.

TABLE 6.2   INITIAL CONTACT BY THE POLICE

Most juveniles come into contact with the juvenile justice system via initial contacts with the police. Police officers may exercise a broad range of discretionary decisions when they come into contact with juvenile offenders or victimized children. This table summarizes the scope of their discretion.

Type of Initial Contact	Police Disposition	Likely Outcome
No warning to juvenile or parents	No official record	Release
Warning to juvenile or parents	No official record	Release
Formal record	Official record to juvenile justice agency	Possible processing in juvenile justice system
Custody of juvenile	Referral of child and case to juvenile justice agency	Processing in juvenile justice system
Immediate transfer into juvenile justice system	Referral to prosecuting attorney or juvenile court	Prosecution or other processing in juvenile court

Custody

Police dispositions may result in juveniles being taken away by the police and either held at the station house pending notification of a guardian, or referral to a youth service agency. When either type of placement occurs, juveniles are said to have been "taken into custody," which is conceptually distinguishable from an "arrest." An arrest is a procedure whereby the police bring suspected lawbreakers into the criminal justice system for possible prosecution and incarceration. Custody refers to the underlying duty of law enforcement agencies, as members of the juvenile justice system, to further the system's mission of protecting and rehabilitating children in trouble and children in need. Thus, when youths are taken into custody, they are theoretically being protected either from further victimization or from their conflict with adult authority. As with all contacts with youths served by the juvenile justice system, custody must be carried out in the "best interest of the child."

As a practical matter, taking custody of juveniles (or arresting them) is a more involved procedure than the detention of adult suspects. The unique philosophy of the juvenile justice system requires officers to comply with procedural and behavioral standards that differ from those used under the criminal justice system. For example, restraint by officers in their demeanor, language, and overall behavior is expected when police dispositions result in custody. In a sense, an officer's demeanor, language, and behavior is expected to be "softer" when dealing with children in trouble and children in need. At the same time, officers must be mindful to safeguard the constitutional rights of juvenile offenders, just as the rights of adults would be protected.

Detention

One possible outcome of a police disposition is the temporary detention of juveniles. Detention is essentially the period between when a youth is taken into custody, and prior to a hearing before the juvenile court. It is roughly comparable to the adult concept of being "jailed" because in both circumstances a suspect is temporarily housed in a detention facility, pending further processing into the juvenile or criminal justice system. However, unlike the jailing process, detention is fundamentally intended to be protective and rehabilitative. The Juvenile Justice and Delinquency Prevention Act of 1974 (as amended) requires that detained juvenile offenders be effectively separated from adult offenders by "sight and sound." This has necessitated the removal of juveniles from adult jails and other lockups, which is (as discussed in Chapter 2) a significant change from the past practice of incarcerating juveniles in the same facilities and cells as adults.

Most states require that children in custody may be released only to an interested adult, usually a parent or guardian. When an interested adult is unavailable, these youths will be detained and referred to an appropriate agency. At this point, the police disposition ends, and another division of the juvenile justice system (usually the juvenile court) assumes responsibility for the case.

Table 6.3 summarizes the types of dispositions and quality of contacts that fall within the purview of the police.

Decision Making: Police
Discretion and Procedural Formality

The police are often the first responders who encounter children in trouble and children in need. Their discretion at the scene of juvenile encounters usually dictates whether the child will be processed further into the juvenile justice system. In this sense, the police are *gatekeepers* who stand between juveniles and the system. Decisions about release, custody, arrest, and immediate needs are often determined on the street or in station houses. This is a tremendous responsibility that society has devolved to the police, and it necessarily requires the implementation of specialized training and tactics for law enforcement agencies.

As previously noted, juvenile units were one of the first law enforcement specializations in the post–World War II era, and they continue to be one of the most pervasive specialized units in the profession. Virtually all law enforcement agencies have now formed special units that are dedicated to addressing juvenile justice issues. In fact, 97% of police and 95% of sheriffs' departments have adopted written policies for handling juvenile issues.[8] Although most specialized units are dedicated to juvenile delinquency issues, many are also devoted to protecting children in need. Table 6.4 indicates the extent of specialized juvenile units that have been established by law enforcement agencies.[9]

TABLE 6.3   THE QUALITY OF POLICE DISPOSITIONS

Law enforcement officers are empowered and required to exercise professional discretion during police dispositions. The quality of contact and role of the police vary in accordance with the type of disposition.

This table summarizes the quality of police dispositions.

	Dispositional Outcome	
Type of Disposition	**Quality of Contact**	**Role of the Police**
Initial contact	First juvenile contact with juvenile justice system	Exercise of professional discretion
Custody	Physical control over the juvenile	Custodian of the juvenile
Detention	Temporary physical holding of the juvenile	Transporting of the juvenile

TABLE 6.4   SPECIALIZED JUVENILE UNITS IN LAW ENFORCEMENT AGENCIES[a]

Law enforcement agencies are an integral part of the juvenile justice system, and they have responded by creating written directives and specialized units. These measures are quite common across the country and have been developed to address the problems of children in trouble and children in need.

This table summarizes the scope of commitment by law enforcement agencies to addressing juvenile justice issues. It indicates the percentages of agencies that have specialized units to address the indicated problems.

	Type of Law Enforcement Agency	
Specialized Units	**Police Departments (%)**	**Sheriff's Departments (%)**
Drug education in schools	95	79
Juvenile crime	66	49
Gangs	55	50
Child abuse	48	53
Domestic violence	46	37
Missing children	33	28
Youth outreach	32	24

a. Adapted from Snyder, H. N., & Sickmund, M. (1999). *Juvenile offenders and victims: 1999 National report* (p. 139). Washington, DC: U.S. Department of Justice.

Police Discretion

Police discretion refers to an exercise of judgment by individual officers on what type of action to take in a particular situation. When evaluating the facts of a specific case, police officers arrive at decision points about whether to take official action or to resolve the matter unofficially—presumably in consideration of the "best interests of the child." This is a necessary element of police work when dealing with juveniles and adults alike. However, because of the idiosyncratic nature of discretionary decisions, there is an inherent danger of discrimination or unfairness toward particular juveniles.

Although police discretion is encouraged within the overall philosophy of Community Strategy Policing, an individual officer's—and a collective department's—decision-making calculus is affected by many factors, including the following examples:

- *Profile of the juvenile.* Differential treatment can be based on the juvenile's race, gender, family background, or personal demeanor (attitude, style of dress). Socioeconomic status can also be a consideration. An officer may be inclined to be more or less helpful or respectful toward an individual based on these factors. Prior police department contacts with the juvenile will also enter into how he or she is treated in subsequent contacts.
- *Personal idiosyncrasies of the officer.* Life experiences of individual officers enter into their exercise of discretion. Socialization is often based on one's experiences with other ethnic groups, neighborhoods, or economic classes. Favoritism or prejudices can therefore affect one's professional discretion. Collectively, a department or station house can develop an organizational culture based on these idiosyncrasies.
- *Organizational policy.* Discretion can be affected by police department policy declarations or traditions. Organizational policies include both official mandates and unofficial procedures that have been followed as part of a department or station house's culture. For example, priorities may be set to suppress delinquency in specified neighborhoods and blocks, or against gang activity. Or pressure can be brought to bear for using specified methods and guidelines when interacting with juveniles.
- *Nature of specific circumstances.* Officers exercise their judgment about the severity of alleged offenses or possible victimization. They are more likely to act officially if a case is deemed to be serious. However, if in an officer's judgment an offense or possible victimization is relatively minor, the officer may choose to resolve the situation unofficially.
- *Pressure from the community.* Local citizen demands on the police can affect how officers, departments, and station houses approach certain situations. For example, demands might be made to suppress raucous loitering in parks, watch outsiders who have been cruising a neighborhood, or investigate ongoing arguments coming from a particular dwelling.

Juveniles are more likely to come into contact with police agencies than any other component of the juvenile justice system. This fact is important for both juveniles and police departments, because it can bode good or ill for either, depending on the nature and quality of their interaction. Police discretion therefore becomes a central factor in whether the police decide to resolve specific cases officially or unofficially.

Procedural Formality: Official and Unofficial Police Procedures

Police officers have significant procedural latitude during interactions with juveniles. Depending on each situation, and the various factors influencing discretion, officers will decide whether to act officially or unofficially. This *gatekeeping* role is central to police-juvenile relations.

Official police procedures are clearly delineated guidelines that officers must follow when they formally process juveniles. These procedures are written into juvenile court acts, and are reflected in internal procedures adopted by law enforcement agencies. While similar to adult-focused procedures, juvenile procedures typically establish guidelines uniquely tailored for police-youth relations. Because juvenile courts have taken the lead in promoting the philosophy of protecting the "best interests of the child," juvenile officers must necessarily receive specialized training on how to implement official court and department procedures. **Unofficial police procedures** involve the exercise of police discretion at certain decision points. At these decision points, police officers come to a decision on whether to begin formal processing of juveniles, or to resolve the situation outside of officially mandated procedures. Examples of unofficial procedures include the following:

- *Street-corner police decisions.* These decisions occur at the initiation of interaction between police officers and juveniles. They typically involve asking teens to move along, releasing a juvenile after questioning, or issuing a reprimand before release.
- *Station-house police adjustments.* These decisions occur when juveniles are brought into a station house, and parents are called in for consultation. Officers can release the juvenile into the parents' custody, thus ending the case prior to official processing into the juvenile justice system.

Gatekeeping can obviously be a very subjective process. When applied properly, it is often a correct course of action because it alleviates deviance or victimization without the sometimes traumatic referral into the broader juvenile justice system. However, gatekeeping can also cross the line into discriminatory behavior because of idiosyncratic factors on the part of police officers and organizations. This can occur when the following attributes are differentially considered:[10]

- *Gender.* More males receive official processing than do females. This theoretically occurs because of a subjective police sense of *chivalry* toward girls that is not present in their dealings with boys.[11]
- *Race.* Experts and the general public have long debated whether racism is an element in arrests and detentions of racial and ethnic minorities. This is an ongoing debate because research data have consistently shown since the 1960s that African American youths are arrested and detained at greater rates than white youths,[12] and are given more severe sanctions.[13] Various explanations for this discrepancy have included racial prejudice, demands for strong measures from the African American community, and greater incidence of severe offenses perpetrated by African American juveniles.
- *Family.* If known to an officer or station house, one's family background may also be a factor, so that children who come from perceived *good* families may be treated more deferentially than those from perceived *bad* families.
- *Attitude.* Juveniles who are disrespectful or are known to the police as recidivists are more likely to be dealt with officially than are cooperative youths who have had little or no contact with the police.

Issues Arising From Police Contacts With Juveniles

The adoption of laws protecting the rights of juveniles vis-à-vis (in comparison to) the police is a fairly recent phenomenon in the history of juvenile justice process. Prior to several seminal (groundbreaking) U.S. Supreme Court decisions, discussed below and previously in Chapter 2,[14] members of the police component of the juvenile justice system possessed wide latitude in their treatment of youths. Police dispositions operated with few limitations on stops, custody, booking procedures, questioning, witness confrontations, or searches. The police role was simply to promote law and order, often by cajoling or coercing juveniles to comply with acceptable standards of behavior. This has since changed, as several Supreme Court decisions have had a direct impact on police procedures in the areas of search and seizure, booking (including fingerprinting and photographing), interrogation, lineups, and the use of force.

Juvenile Constitutional Rights: Search and Seizure

The Fourth Amendment to the Constitution protects residents against unreasonable searches and seizures. These protections were affirmed in the 1961 U.S. Supreme Court decision in *Mapp v. Ohio,* which held that evidence seized without a search warrant or probable cause is inadmissible in court.[15] Although *Mapp* was decided on facts involving adults rather than juveniles, authorities have held that juveniles are also entitled to protections against unreasonable searches and seizures. There are, however, certain standards that are specifically applicable to cases involving juveniles. For example, on school campuses warrantless official searches are permissible without violating the Fourth Amendment. So long as officials are able to justify the "reasonableness" of their decision to conduct a particular search, warrantless searches can be made of students' lockers, desks, vehicles, purses, and bags. Depending on jurisdictional guidelines, these searches can be carried out by police officers or school officials.

The U.S. Supreme Court case of *New Jersey v. T.L.O.* held that a warrant need not be obtained, nor probable cause established, prior to a search of students' bags by school officials. *T.L.O.* also held that "reasonableness" will be determined by a student's age and gender, the scope of the search, and the student's behavior.[16] Since the *T.L.O.* decision, courts have repeatedly upheld the reasonableness of school searches for weapons, liquor, and drugs and for suspected violations of school regulations.

Procedural Distinctions: Booking, Fingerprinting, and Photographing

The Juvenile Justice and Delinquency Prevention Act of 1974 (as amended) regulates how law enforcement agencies may process ("book") juvenile suspects. The Act required status offenders and delinquent offenders to be separated through deinstitutionalization of status offenders. For example, booking of status offenders requires referral to social service agencies for informal dispositions and cannot result in detention in jails. This example typifies the special parameters that have been established for the booking of juveniles.

Fingerprinting involves the recording of one's fingerprint signature, essentially documenting evidence that is unique to each individual. This can be done using the old "low-tech" inking method or new "high-tech" digital scans of fingerprint signatures. Similarly, photographs can either be recorded using standard photographic imaging or digital technologies. The obvious advantage of digital images is that databases can be readily accessed, shared, and posted almost instantaneously.

When suspects are booked into local jails or lockups, the police routinely make fingerprint and photographic records. Fingerprints and photographs of adult suspects are regularly collected and catalogued by law enforcement agencies. These records are maintained in databases locally and nationally, and a centralized FBI database can be accessed by local law enforcement agencies through its Criminal Justice Investigative Services Division. From the perspective of law enforcement agencies, the purpose of fingerprinting and photographing is to establish an official record for current and future investigations.

Fingerprint and photographic records of juveniles have been historically collected by many police agencies, but it is a controversial practice. The principal criticism is that teenagers may be stigmatized as criminals for life if these records are not sealed and remain accessible to interested parties. Because of this potential problem, many jurisdictions have mandated limitations on the acquisition and use of juvenile fingerprint and photographic records. The following range of practices exists in different jurisdictions:

- No fingerprinting or photographing of juveniles without prior authorization from a judge.
- No access to fingerprints or photographs without a judge's authorization.
- Destruction of fingerprint and photographic records when juveniles pass the age of majority.
- Local police department regulation of fingerprinting and photographing policy. This can include a range of options, from fingerprinting and photographing every juvenile suspect, to strictly following court guidelines.

Organizations such as the American Bar Association have argued that fingerprinting and photographing juveniles should never be routinely implemented and that when it occurs, it should only be done under clear legal or court guidelines. An important case on procedures for juvenile fingerprinting is *Davis v. Mississippi,* in which the U.S. Supreme Court held that fingerprint evidence taken from a juvenile was inadmissible when obtained during an unlawful detention.[17] In *Davis,* a suspected juvenile rapist was detained, interrogated, and fingerprinted without prior authorization from a judicial official.

Interrogating Juveniles

A police interrogation is any behavior exhibited by the police during formal questioning that is likely to elicit information from a suspect. The Supreme Court has long held that physical force cannot be used to elicit confessions,[18] and in *Miranda v. Arizona,* the Court held that suspects must be properly advised of their right to counsel and protections from self-incrimination.[19] These fundamental constitutional rights have not been uniformly applied to cases involving interrogations of juveniles. As discussed in Chapter 2, the seminal case on the devolvement of Fourteenth Amendment rights to juvenile courts was *In re Gault,* which held that juveniles have constitutionally protected rights during juvenile court proceedings.[20] These rights include the right to counsel, the right against self-incrimination, and the right to confront witnesses.

However, *In re Gault* did not address the question of a juvenile's waiver of *Miranda* protections. The fundamental issue in this regard is whether juveniles have the capacity to "knowingly and intelligently" waive their rights

Photo 6.2   A police officer twists a youth's ear. Such practices are impermissible, but occasionally occur.

when read their *Miranda* warning. In other words, when is a confession by a juvenile knowing and intelligent? Analysis of this question has occurred at the state level, so that different analyses have occurred on a case-by-case basis. Although waivers by youths have been upheld in some state courts, it should be noted that states have passed legislation that regulates police and judicial compliance with constitutional protections for juveniles under police interrogation. Among these statutory requirements is the mandatory presence of an "interested adult" such as an attorney or parent during interrogations.

Lineups

A police lineup involves a confidential viewing of suspected offenders by witnesses to an offense. Lineup procedures generally require a number of suspects to stand in a line before concealed witnesses, who attempt to make out the perpetrator. When singled out by a witness, the identified suspect can be booked and sent into the juvenile justice or criminal justice system. There are certain rights that must be afforded to persons in lineups. One right includes the right to counsel, in accordance with the U.S. Supreme Court ruling in **United States v. Wade**, which held that indicted suspects have a right to counsel present at lineups.[21] This right applies to juveniles as well as adults.

Use of Force

Physical force is sometimes required when police officers arrest adults or take juveniles into custody. The police must only use an appropriate degree of physical force as is necessary to gain control over the unique circumstances of each situation. Officers can only apply an amount of force as required to deescalate resistance from a suspect, whether an adult or juvenile.

Procedures for the use of force have been adopted by law enforcement agencies, which reflect similar, but not identical, standards. For example, some agencies require all suspects to be handcuffed, while other agencies delegate the use of restraints to the discretion of individual police officers. Other policies include the use of chemical mace, pepper spray, and electronic stun guns. Procedures also govern incapacitating and painful restraints such as choke holds, arm locks, finger holds, and wrestling grasps. All of these policies and procedures are authorized, and their use depends on the level of resistance by the suspect. The ultimate use of sanctioned force is, of course, lethal force. Deadly force may be used when the police perceive an imminent threat of serious injury or death to themselves or the general public.

All of the foregoing techniques and procedures may be used to subdue or control violent or resistant juveniles.

Table 6.5 summarizes the role of the nature of issues arising from police contacts with juveniles.

Case in Point: Juvenile Records

Police departments and other components of the juvenile justice system keep careful records of official contacts with juveniles. This practice is absolutely necessary for the welfare of society and the best interests of youths, but it has been designed to reflect the unique mission of the system, which has an underlying philosophy of rehabilitation and remediation. Hence, records of juvenile contacts with the system have been historically either destroyed or preserved under rules of strict confidentiality. Two practices were commonly adopted by local jurisdictions:

- *Expungement.* The destruction of files and records that document a particular juvenile's offense history. Expungement decrees generally originate with juvenile courts and are delivered to police departments.
- *Sealing of records.* The preservation of files and records by police departments under strict confidentiality procedures. These files cannot be accessed without a court order, which is theoretically difficult to obtain.

TABLE 6.5   ISSUES ARISING FROM POLICE CONTACTS

Police contacts with juveniles are regulated by state laws and U.S. Supreme Court decisions. Juvenile officers must therefore be trained and advised about appropriate measures to be used during police dispositions.

    This table summarizes several of the issues arising from police contacts.

Type of Contact	Issues Relevant to Juveniles	Role of the Police
Search and seizure	"Reasonableness" of the search and its scope	Searching agency
Fingerprinting and photographing	State-mandated limitations on use and archiving	Booking agency
Interrogations	Capacity for "knowing and intelligent" waivers	Interrogators
Lineups	Right to counsel	Coordinating agency
Use of force	Reasonableness and proportionality	Strict limitations and controls

Records kept by police departments after juveniles pass the age of majority were at one time routinely expunged or sealed. This was considered to be necessary for rehabilitation, so that booking records, fingerprints, photographs, and interrogation notes were all either expunged or sealed. During the 1990s (and continuing into the new millennium) a shift in philosophy occurred. Many states adopted laws and regulations permitting law enforcement and other juvenile justice agencies to keep complete records after juveniles passed the age of majority. Some states permitted records to be kept for several years after the age of majority, and others mandated that records could never be expunged or sealed for serious felonies. Most states also now permit open juvenile proceedings and the release of juvenile records to the public.

Accessing the Community:
Police Relationship-Building Strategies

Law enforcement agencies frequently serve as liaisons between the juvenile justice system, youth service programs and individual juveniles. They often act in partnership with local agencies and assist in the implementation of community-based initiatives. These duties squarely reflect the philosophy of the Community-Strategy Era of policing, because successful liaison requires department policies to be strongly community-oriented. The success of police liaison strategies is dependent on special training for juvenile officers, good relations with community leaders, and cooperation from service workers and the juveniles themselves. Although there are many models and programs, police liaison strategies serve several basic functions:

- Engaging in community-oriented programs with juveniles, parents, and youth service agencies
- Serving as counselors for juveniles and youth service agency personnel
- Providing a personal and public "human" presence for youths
- Investigating allegations of juvenile deviance or victimization

The Role of Specialized Juvenile Units

Most law enforcement agencies have incorporated specialized juvenile units into their organizational structure. In the modern era, this is a virtually universal feature of modern policing strategies, and juvenile specialists are found in both large and small departments. In a sense, all police officers become juvenile specialists when dealing with youthful offenders and victims, but it should be understood that members of special units are full-time juvenile police officers. Juvenile officers have the same law enforcement duties as all police officers, but they are also expected to establish relationships with local youths, either as counselors or as symbols of authority. In this latter role, the police often play a central role in the implementation of delinquency and victimization prevention programs.

Specialized juvenile units operate much as other police units do. For example, in some cities special juvenile units focus their attention on delinquency prevention and youth gangs, so that much of their work involves responding to incidents reported by civilians. In this capacity, these units participate fully in the apprehension of suspects, investigation of cases, and prosecution of offenders. Another, and coequal, duty of juvenile units is to investigate allegations of child abuse, neglect, and dependency. They are responsible for assisting all children in need, including abandoned children, runaways, and thrownaways. Thus, officers assigned to special juvenile units are deployed in a variety of capacities—as law enforcers, counselors, and members of the community. Juvenile specialists are frequently well-educated, with many of these officers possessing college degrees in Public Administration, Administration of Justice, Criminal Justice Administration, and Sociology.

Many large cities have established separate school police departments that operate solely on school campuses. Because schools are often the site of delinquency and status offenses, city and school administrators have considered it necessary as a matter of policy to form school police departments that are independent of urban departments. They may either be employees of the local school district, or retained as contracted private security officers. Most officers are deployed in uniform, but many school districts prohibit the carrying of firearms on campus. School police typically patrol school grounds such as parking lots and restrooms, respond to incidents such as fights, investigate thefts or vandalism, and enforce truancy laws. Ideally, officers are also active in counseling students, getting to know them personally, and generally promoting positive interaction.

Delinquency and Victimization Prevention Programs

One distinguishing aspect of the juvenile justice system in comparison to the criminal justice system is the degree of imagination and flexibility that is permissible for police liaison strategies. In this regard, the police mission departs from its usual reactive role and becomes a proactive obligation. Dozens of local initiatives have been adopted by police agencies in partnership with local institutions to foster delinquency prevention and victimization remediation. The underlying philosophy is to increase youth awareness about dangerous temptations and behaviors, promote collective and individual good citizenship, and educate youths about how to access assistance programs when they encounter harmful environments. Although law enforcement agencies are not always the initiating organizations for these programs, they are usually involved in a central capacity.

The following programs are models that illustrate the diversity and creativity of youth-focused prevention initiatives. The police often act as leaders, liaisons, or advisers for these programs.

- *Alateen/Alanon.* Alcohol abuse is associated with teenage deviance and victimization. Alateen, a nationwide movement that is the teenage equivalent of Alcoholics Anonymous, is specifically organized to help teenage alcoholics. Alanon is also a nationwide movement that has been designed to assist those who are victimized or otherwise affected by the behavior of alcoholics who live in their households.

- *Big Brothers/Big Sisters of America.* A nationwide federation of youth service agencies that promotes mentorship through individual relationships between adults and youths. The federation has existed for almost a century and is intended to promote healthy interpersonal and socialization skills and behaviors in young people as they move through adolescence toward adulthood. Mentorship occurs through regular activities that many persons take for granted, such as taking walks, playing outdoor games, going shopping, and bicycling.

- *Campus Pride.* A national program implemented by school districts to remove gang graffiti from school campuses. This serves as a countermeasure to gang attempts to mark their territory on school grounds.

- *D.A.R.E.* Drug Abuse Resistance Education emphasizes drug awareness education for elementary school students. Police officers from local station houses teach children about the different types of drugs, their effects, and how to recognize them. Officers also explain how to say "no" when drugs are offered. D.A.R.E. began in Los Angeles in 1983 as a partnership between the Los Angeles Police Department and the Los Angeles Unified School District.

- *Explorers Programs.* A number of jurisdictions have established programs that allow youths to learn firsthand about police work. Participants accompany officers on ride-alongs and other duties as a way to give positive experiences to juveniles and promote good relations. Explorers are also encouraged to consider careers in law enforcement.

- *Graffiti Removal Community Service Programs.* Graffiti is often a self-described art form in which *taggers* draw or write messages on private property. It is also a means of communication among street gang members. In some cities, taggers and gang members apprehended by the police are assigned to graffiti removal duty as part of their community service.

- *TIPS.* Teaching Individuals Protective Strategies is typical of federal efforts to sponsor nationwide initiatives. This U.S. Department of Education program emphasized the development of decision-making and reasoning skills for children in kindergarten through 8th grade. These skills included how to reduce victimization vulnerability and the ability to find solutions to potential problems.

The foregoing models are only a few examples of the many national and local prevention initiatives.

PROFESSIONAL PROFILE CHAPTER 6

Chief of Police—Major Urban Police Agency

Police agencies are usually the "first responders" to crime, juvenile delinquency, and juvenile victimization. In major urban areas, police officers are challenged to apply different standards of response to different situations. Urban police agencies are particularly challenged by new technologies, policies, and policy initiatives. They must constantly adapt as these changes occur. This is a difficult task, and urban police chiefs must be constantly aware of these new initiatives, thus adapting their policies and procedures as they occur.

I.   Personal Profile

   A.   Name:
      Robert W. McNeilly, Jr.

B. Agency:

Pittsburgh Bureau of Police

C. Rank and/or Title:

Chief of Police

D. Education (Schools and Degrees):

Duquesne University
BA, Psychology
University of Pittsburgh
Graduate work

E. Professional Training:

FBI Academy (Quantico), National Executive Institute
Senior Management Institute for Police Executives
Command Institute for Police Executives

F. Professional Organizations/Community Group Memberships:

Allegheny County Chiefs of Police
Western PA Chiefs of Police
Pennsylvania Chiefs of Police
International Association of Chiefs of Police
Police Executive Research Forum (treasurer)

II. Professional Profile

A. What personal or other background experiences led to your decision to *choose* this profession?

I was committed to law enforcement throughout high school. My military experience in the U.S. Marine Corps was helpful in regard to understanding rank structure and chain of command. In addition, it was important in understanding discipline and following orders.

B. Please state a few of your personal reasons/motivations for your decision to *continue* in this profession.

I was interested in ensuring people were protected from those who may have been stronger or more powerful than they were and not inclined to demonstrate a respect for others or the law. I was interested in maintaining peace and order within our society.

C. Which job experiences have had an important impact on you?

Being a police officer and working plainclothes allowed me to interact with the victims and community members to understand their problems and to attempt to protect them from those who would victimize individuals and the community overall.

D. What has been a particularly *satisfying* job experience?

Interrupting crimes in progress was rewarding. The realization that police were able to protect our citizens from being victimized and to apprehend criminals to prevent that crime and future crimes was satisfying.

E.   What has been a particularly *challenging* job experience?

Being the Chief of Police opens one to constant criticism for each decision made. Regardless of the matter being decided, there are some who oppose whatever the decision. Hence, each decision made carries with it the challenge of wading through the constant criticism attached to that decision.

F.   What do you think the future holds for your profession?

There will be considerable technological changes and new investigative methods and tools. However, just as those changes occurred in the military but the military still needs to have a well-trained infantry to be successful, policing will continue to require patrol officers who have initiative and intellect in the field.

G.   What kind of advice/guidance would you give to interested students?

Continuing education will continue to be important for successful handling of disputes, solving crimes, and knowing how to interact with various cultures. Having a desire to serve is imperative to be effective and to enjoy the difficulties of that service simultaneously. The simple things such as knowing how to follow instructions/orders, being prompt, and being courteous are a good start in a career. The more important concerns—being accountable, being ethical, and being respectful—are essential in having a successful career.

Chapter Summary

Law enforcement agencies are frontline agencies for linking children in trouble and children in need with the juvenile justice system. This role has evolved through several eras of American policing philosophy. During the Political Era, the police were particularly unrestrained in their interactions with juveniles. This reflected a generalized authoritarian and corrupt approach in policing philosophy. The Reform Era attempted to professionalize police–juvenile relations and saw the rise of specialized police juvenile units that focused on prevention and delinquency suppression. With the advent of the Community-Strategy Era, police dispositions began to emphasize acting in the best interests of the child, so that the police were expected to lend a hand for the betterment of both children in trouble and children in need.

Today, family members, members of the community, and schools can initiate police dispositions. Officers are generally permitted to exercise a great deal of discretion during dispositions, ranging from unofficial verbal warnings to immediately transferring the case for prosecution or appearance before a juvenile court. Intake, custody, and detention usually begin with initial contact with the police and the quality of their discretion and procedural formality. Street-corner decisions and station-house adjustments indicate the scope of police discretion during dispositions.

The U.S. Supreme Court has ruled that juveniles are protected against unreasonable searches and seizures. Youths have also historically received unique treatment when booked, fingerprinted, photographed, interrogated, or brought before police lineups. The use of these records was strictly circumscribed by rules of the juvenile court, and the right to counsel attached early in the booking process. In addition, for much of the modern era juvenile records were either expunged or sealed when juvenile offenders reached the age of majority. The crackdown on crime and delinquency during the latter years of the twentieth century led most jurisdictions to allow law enforcement and juvenile justice agencies to maintain records after the age of majority was passed. Some states require that records should never be sealed or expunged for serious offenses.

Chapter 7 investigates the role of the court in the juvenile justice system. The historical evolution of juvenile courts during several eras will be summarized, and an investigation will be made of juvenile court processes. Special inquiry is made into the widespread and increasing incidence of juveniles being brought before adult criminal courts, tried as adults, and sentenced accordingly. Several issues arising from juvenile contacts with the court system will also be investigated.

Questions for Review

1. What are the historical eras of policing?

2. What was the role of the police during each historical era of policing?

3. What is the modern role of the police in juvenile justice process?

4. Describe initial contact, police discretion, custody, detention, intake, and prosecution.

5. What is a formal police disposition?

6. What is an informal police disposition?

7. Describe some of the constitutional and other controversial outcomes from police contacts with youths.

8. Describe police–community relations.

9. What are the attributes of specialized units, community policing, and police–school relations?

Key Terms and Concepts

The following topics were discussed in this chapter and are found in the Glossary:

Alateen/Alanon

Big Brothers/Big Sisters of America

Campus Pride

Community-Strategy Era of Policing

Custody

D.A.R.E.

Davis v. Mississippi

Detention

Explorers Programs

Expungement

Graffiti Removal
Community Service
Programs

Initial Contact

Mapp v. Ohio

Miranda v. Arizona

New Jersey v. T.L.O.

Official Police Procedures

Police Discretion

Police Dispositions

Political Era of Policing

Reform Era of Policing

Sealing of Records

Station-House Police Adjustments

Street-Corner Police Decisions

TIPS

United States v. Wade

Unofficial Police Procedures

DISCUSSION BOX

The Implications of Police–Juvenile Relations

This chapter's Discussion Box is intended to stimulate critical discussion about the importance of positive relations between the police and juveniles.

Successful community-oriented policing requires positive interactions between the police and their constituent communities. Juvenile police officers in particular must coordinate their efforts with local youth service agencies, parents, and individual juveniles. A critical component of this process is youth attitudes toward the police and the juvenile justice system. Perceptions by youths are often associated with their behavior toward police authority. Thus, it is incumbent on members of specialized police units to act as positive role models and promote good relations during contacts with youths.

The reality of police–juvenile relations is mixed. Not all youths trust or respect the police. Minority youths in particular hold more negative opinions of law enforcement personnel than do white youths. This is because of a perception in minority communities that the police unfairly single them out, often to the point of racially profiling them. The generalized crackdown on crime and delinquency has not lessened tensions in many communities between the police and juveniles.

Of course, the police have a great deal of discretion during the course of police dispositions. Their options include acting aggressively or passively, upholding the "letter of the law" or using informal resolution, and taking youths into custody or releasing them. They also have discretion (and absolute control) over whether they treat juveniles courteously or rudely. All of these factors influence the quality of police–juvenile relations.

Discussion Questions

1. To what extent does the demeanor of the police affect the perceptions of youths toward the police?

2. Are the perceptions of unfair treatment by young members of racial and ethnic groups accurate and a reflection of the reality of their interactions with the police?

3. How can law enforcement officials promote positive police–juvenile relations?

4. Who are the community actors that are (or should be) involved in fostering functional working relationships between juveniles and police officers?

5. Under what circumstances should the police use a "get tough" philosophy with juveniles?

Recommended Web Sites

The following Web sites contain information about the role of the police in the juvenile justice system:

Big Brothers/Big Sisters of America: http://www.bbbsa.org/
Community Policing Consortium: http://www.communitypolicing.org/
Drug Awareness Resistance Education: http://www.dare.com/
Fight Crime: Invest in Kids: http://www.fightcrime.org/
LAPD Juvenile Division: http://www.lapdonline.org/juvenile/

Note: The Web site URLs and exercises below are also from the book's study site: http://www.sagepub.com/martin

Web Exercise

Using this chapter's recommended Internet sites, conduct an online investigation of the role of the police.

- How is the role of the juvenile police presented by agencies?
- In your opinion, are police liaison efforts and programs effective?
- Who should fund police–juvenile liaison programs?

For an online search of the role of the police in the juvenile justice system, students should use a search engine and enter the following keywords:

"Community Policing"

"Juvenile Police"

Recommended Readings

The following publications provide discussions on the role of the police in the juvenile justice system:

Bratton, W. (1998). *Turnaround: How America's top cop reversed the crime epidemic.* New York: Random House.

Kenney, J. P., Fuller, D. E., & Barry, R. J. (1994). *Police work with juveniles and the administration of juvenile justice* (8th ed.). Springfield, IL: Charles C Thomas.

Oliver, W. M. (2000).*Community policing: Classical readings.* Upper Saddle River, NJ: Prentice Hall.

Portune, R. (1971). *Changing adolescent attitudes toward police.* Cincinnati, OH: W. H. Anderson.

Williams, G. H. (1984). *The law and politics of police discretion.* Westport, CT: Greenwood Publishing.

Notes

1. See Michael Crowe, et al., v. County of San Diego, et al., 303 F. Supp. 2d 1050 (S. Dist. CA, 2004).

2. Police agencies refer to local law enforcement agencies, county sheriffs' departments, state agencies, and federal agencies (where noted).

3. See, e.g., Snyder, H. N., & Sickmund, M. (1999). *Juvenile offenders and victims: 1999 National report* (p. 115). Washington, DC: U.S. Department of Justice.

4. Ibid.

5. Finkelhor, D., & Ormrod, R. (2000). *Characteristics of crimes against juveniles.* Washington, DC: U.S. Department of Justice.

6. Egley, A., Jr., & Arjunan, M. (2002). *Highlights of the 2000 national youth gang survey* (p. 1). Washington, DC: U.S. Department of Justice.

7. Juvenile law enforcement officers now typically organize themselves into state-based juvenile officers associations.

8. Snyder, H. N., & Sickmund, M. (1999). *Juvenile offenders and victims: 1999 National report* (p. 139). Washington, DC: U.S. Department of Justice.

9. Ibid.

10. For a good study of arrest decisions and bias, see Sealock, M. D., & Simpson, S. S. (1998, September). Unraveling bias in arrest decisions: The role of juvenile offender type-scripts. *Justice Quarterly, 15*(3).

11. See Visher, C. A. (1983). Gender, police arrest decisions, and notions of chivalry. *Criminology, 21.*

12. See, e.g., Lundman, R., Sykes, R., and Clark, J. (1973). Police control of juveniles. *Journal of Research in Crime & Delinquency, 15,* 74.

13. See, e.g., Heimer, K. (1997). Socioeconomic status, subcultural definitions, and violent delinquency. *Social Forces, 75,* 799.

14. Examples from Chapter 2 include Kent v. United States, 383 U.S. 541, 86 S. Ct. 1045, 16 L. Ed. 2d 84 (1966); In re Gault, 387 U.S. 1, 19–21, 26–28,

87 S. Ct. 1428, 1439–1440, 1442–1444, 18 L. Ed. 2d 527 (1967); and In re Winship, 397 U.S. 358, 90 S. Ct. 1068, 25 L. Ed. 2d 368 (1970).

15. Mapp v. Ohio, 367 U.S. 643, 81 S. Ct. 1684, 6 L. Ed. 2d 1081 (1961).

16. New Jersey v. T.L.O., 469 U.S. 809, 105 S. Ct. 68, 83 L. Ed. 2d 19 (1984). See also Persico, D. A. (1998). *New Jersey v. T.L.O.: Drug searches in schools.* Berkeley Heights, NJ: Enslow Publishers.

17. Davis v. Mississippi, 394 U.S. 721, 89 S. Ct. 1394, 22 L. Ed. 2d 676 (1969).

18. See Brown v. Mississippi, 297 U.S. 278, 56 S. Ct. 461, 80 L. Ed. 682 (1936).

19. See Miranda v. Arizona, 413 U.S. 902, 93 S. Ct. 3065, 37 L. Ed. 2d 1021 (1966).

20. In re Gault, 387 U.S. 1, 19–21, 26–28, 87 S. Ct. 1428, 1439–1440, 1442–1444, 18 L. Ed. 2d 527 (1967).

21. United States v. Wade, 388 U.S. 218, 87 S. Ct. 1926, 18 L. Ed. 2d 1149 (1967).

7

The Role of the Court

In the modern era, juvenile courts are empowered to waive their jurisdiction over certain cases involving juveniles. These juveniles are sent into the criminal justice system and prosecuted as adults. In many jurisdictions, this waiver procedure is automatic for certain serious crimes. Waivers are not often overturned, especially for serious crimes. For example, in 1974 in Muskegon County, Michigan, two 15-year-old teenagers were charged with the murder of a neighbor.[1] The teenagers, Timothy Spytma and Michael Saxton, had become intoxicated on barbiturates and were in the process of burglarizing her home when she happened upon them. The neighbor was beaten, her wrists were slashed, she was sexually assaulted, and she died of her injuries.

Charged with first-degree murder, the probate court (which had jurisdiction over juveniles) transferred the teenagers to adult court for trial. The two were convicted and sentenced to life without parole. For years, Spytma and Saxton appealed their convictions on several grounds, including an allegedly invalid waiver of probate court jurisdiction. The appeals lasted until 2002, when the federal Sixth Circuit Court of Appeals denied their petitions.

The juvenile court is the cornerstone of the modern juvenile justice system. It is the principal agency for determining the official outcome of juveniles taken into custody by the police or placed in detention. This institution protects the community by dealing authoritatively with juvenile offenders, and it protects the well-being of youths who need to be removed from harmful environments. In many respects, the juvenile court system operates as much more than a traditional court system: It is certainly a conventional venue where juvenile offenders are sanctioned and detained, but it is also an innovative institution that has the responsibility to determine the placement of abused, neglected, or dependent children. In addition, judicial discretion is often quite broad—much broader than in adult criminal courts—so that juvenile judges may render innovative decisions at virtually every stage of juvenile judicial process. As a result, many possible variables weigh into the outcome of each case, and these variables have varying degrees of influence on juvenile courts across the country.

In 1999, the United States observed the centennial of the creation of the first modern juvenile court in Chicago. Since its inception, the nation's juvenile court network has served a unique role within the juvenile justice system. For example,

- In comparison to the role of **law enforcement agencies**—which are primarily reactive intervening institutions—juvenile courts necessarily intervene in both a proactive and reactive capacity to serve children in trouble and children in need.
- In comparison to **other court systems,** juvenile courts are expected to protect the best interests of the boys and girls brought before them, seeking the least restrictive alternative in how to minister to these persons.
- In comparison to **child welfare networks,** juvenile courts are empowered to oversee the quality of placements and are authorized to hold placement venues accountable for the quality of treatment received by juvenile clients.

Thus, beginning with the establishment of the first nascent (emerging) court in Chicago during the nineteenth century, the philosophies of treatment, rehabilitation, and remediation have formed the underlying values and goals of these courts. There are now literally thousands of courts having jurisdiction over youthful offenders and victims. These courts are quite busy, handling more than 1.5 million delinquency cases annually.[2] Juvenile courts regularly report more than 150,000 petitioned and disposed status offense (runaway, truancy, ungovernable, and liquor violations) cases.[3] It should be remembered that these officially reviewed cases represent police dispositions and other conflicts with authority (e.g., schools, neighbors, or parents) that were ultimately referred into juvenile court systems; they do not reflect the many cases that were handled informally or unofficially outside of the courts.

As the primary arbiter (one who resolves disputes) of disputes involving young people, the juvenile court arguably plays a very central and critical role in the personal development and experiences of individuals who pass through the system. Consequently, the court has a strong impact on many juveniles for the rest of their lives. In this chapter, our discussion of the role of the juvenile court reviews the following topics:

- Background: The Role of the Juvenile Court
- Implementing Court Authority: Juvenile Court Participants
- Moving Through the System: Juvenile Court Process
- Punishing Criminal Behavior: Juveniles in Adult Court

CHAPTER PERSPECTIVE 7.1

Teenagers on Death Row

The United States stands out among the world's democracies in that it not only permits judges to sentence offenders to death, but also permits persons to be executed who were youths at the time of their crime. The American approach is that persons tried before adult criminal courts will receive the same punishments as adults. In the modern era, the mandatory waiver of juveniles into criminal court has become a common practice throughout the nation. Because of this practice, extended sentences, life terms, and capital sentences are regularly given to juveniles convicted of serious felonies.

A 15-year snapshot is instructive. Between January 1, 1973, and October 31, 1998, 164 persons who were under the age of 18 years when they committed their crime were sentenced to death. Interestingly, "50% of these under-18 death sentences have been reversed, [and] 7% have resulted in executions."[4] The 164 capital sentences were apportioned among the states as follows:[5]

State	Offenders
Texas	42
Florida	23
Alabama	15
Mississippi	10
Louisiana	9
Georgia, South Carolina	7
North Carolina, Ohio, Oklahoma	6
Pennsylvania, Arizona	5
Missouri, Virginia	4
Indiana	3
Arkansas, Kentucky, Maryland, Nevada	2
Nebraska, New Jersey, Washington	1

It remains to be seen whether the rate of incarceration of juveniles on death row will continue apace. It also remains to be seen whether persons sentenced under these guidelines will actually be executed. Regardless of how these questions are answered, it should be understood that there is currently no broad cultural or political sentiment to scale back laws permitting capital sentencing for juveniles. Thus, it is a virtual certainty that teenagers will continue to be sent to death row.

Background: The Role of the Juvenile Court

As discussed in Chapter 2, nineteenth-century juvenile reform movements, such as the Child-Savers Movement, originated the foundational philosophies of the modern juvenile justice system. It will be recalled that these reformers were well-to-do philanthropists (promoters of human welfare) who were patronizingly sincere in their efforts to control the "dangerous classes" and manage the well-being of immigrant children—all in accordance with their own standards of acceptable behavior. The movement toward modern juvenile court systems inevitably grew from this movement.

Reformers and the Origins of the Modern Juvenile Court

By the latter decades of the nineteenth century, court systems in the United States had begun to routinely hear cases involving juveniles. However, these were not true "juvenile" courts in the modern sense of the concept. Rather, they were primarily adult-centered venues that meted out punishments to wayward youths in much the same ways that they dealt with hardened adult criminals. Fortunately, reformers during this era began to appreciate that juvenile offenders were developmentally and emotionally different from adult offenders and therefore required special treatment and services.

Toward the end of the nineteenth century, juvenile reformers active in Illinois concluded that the incarceration of youths with adults in the Chicago House of Corrections and Cook County Jail was an inhumane and unacceptable practice. Conditions in these facilities were dreadfully poor, and experts came to the (now obvious) finding that juveniles confined in this sort of environment with toughened adult offenders would be exposed to severe deviance and abuse and would probably become adult criminals themselves.

This analysis fits squarely within the precepts of the Positivist School of criminology, discussed previously in Chapter 3. It should be remembered that positivism is a deterministic approach to criminality and delinquency, holding that biology, culture, and social experiences can be sources of deviant behavior. Within this analysis, offenders are redeemable if the effects of biological, cultural, and other sources can be mitigated. From the perspective of early juvenile justice reformers, positivist logic mandated the creation of a completely separate judicial institution that would rehabilitate and remediate young offenders and victims.

Breakthrough: The First Juvenile Court

Illinois reformers, using the Positivist School as their foundational philosophy, separated juvenile justice process from the criminal system. Their belief was that juveniles could be more effectively "rescued" within a juvenile judicial and correctional system rather than within the existing adult-centered system. In 1899, the Illinois State Legislature passed the **Juvenile Court Act.** Embracing the underlying philosophy of *parens patriae,* which had been applied by court systems since the inception of the juvenile reform movement, the **Cook County Juvenile Court** was organized in 1899. It was the first truly modern juvenile court because it formulated concepts and procedures that continue to be applied in the present era. The then-innovative principles it adopted included the following:

- *Parens patriae* allows the court to assume full responsibility over children in trouble and children in need.
- Juvenile courts are civil, not criminal, courts. All children brought before the court will receive civil correction and remediation.
- Decisions rendered will be in the best interests of the child. Children in trouble will be rehabilitated, and children in need will be treated.
- Informal procedures and a new terminology are necessary adaptations for the special circumstances of juveniles.
- Referrals of youths to the court can come from schools, the police, community residents, or parents.

In practice, the first juvenile courts had much less formal atmospheres than the adult courts used previously to process juveniles. Courtrooms were not required for cases, and hearings were usually more akin to meetings. Hearings were typically held around tables where all parties (the judge, juvenile officials, parents, and the youth in question) discussed the facts and potential resolutions of cases. Because of the meeting-room atmosphere, the cornerstones of criminal proceedings—rules of evidence, representation by counsel, and standards of proof—were not formally observed. Adversarial (combative) arguments were considered to be inappropriate to the proper functioning of juvenile-focused courts, and hence the presence of attorneys was not required. Records of court proceedings were handled civilly, meaning that they remained confidential and unavailable to scrutiny by persons who did not have an interest in the case. Most important, the language used to describe unacceptable behaviors, court proceedings, and judicial outcomes was "softened" to reflect the civil and rehabilitative quality of the new system. The court also enjoyed great flexibility and discretion in deciding how to decide cases, so that juveniles could be diverted by the court to a wide range of services or correctional programs.

Professionalization: Advancing the Juvenile Court Concept

The Illinois Juvenile Court Act became a template for legislation elsewhere, and the Cook County Juvenile Court served as the model for juvenile court systems in other states. By the late 1920s, most states had adopted juvenile court statutes using similar precepts as those adopted in Illinois. All

Photo 7.1   A 1910 juvenile court proceeding. The first courts often operated with great informality.

were civil court systems that applied the positivist goal of rescuing and rehabilitating juveniles. Broad jurisdictional mandates permitted the new courts to correct children in trouble, treat children in need, assume jurisdiction over families, and exercise significant discretion in their dispositions.

The first courts were not perfect and were criticized by some reformers for being overly secretive, subjective, arbitrary, and informal. Critics also noted that few juvenile rights existed in the new juvenile court systems. Juveniles were undefended by legal advocates before the courts, and judges were accused of abusing their discretion and rendering discriminatory decisions. A new generation of reformers realized that the juvenile court concept, while indispensable to promoting the concept of juvenile justice, was nevertheless in need of greater procedural rigor and professionalism.

Professionalization of the juvenile court system occurred during the decades following the Cook County prototype. Excessive informality was replaced by at least a modicum of formality, often with greater formality being accorded to serious delinquency cases. Significantly, the nineteenth-century tradition of using well-intentioned lay volunteers (often religious activists) as child savers was replaced by a new emphasis on trained professional social workers. Social workers represented a new profession of paid specialists who relied on professional standards of assessment and treatment.

This new concept of a professionalized child welfare system was accessed by judges to advise them on evaluations and recommended treatments for juveniles appearing before the court. Social workers eventually became adept at using theories of causation and treatment, which were developed within the new disciplines of sociology and psychology.

Sources of Court Authority: Juvenile Court Jurisdiction

All juvenile and criminal **justice agencies** have specific duties assigned to them—as delimited by statutes and regulations—which are their defined operational parameters. These operational parameters serve as the **jurisdiction** of these agencies. Broadly defined, jurisdiction refers to

> the territory, subject matter, or persons over which lawful authority may be exercised by a court or other justice agency, as determined by statute or constitution.[6]

Court jurisdiction refers to the lawful power of judicial authorities to hear certain types of cases. In this regard, juvenile courts have limited authority to hear only those cases assigned to them under state law. Juvenile courts usually have jurisdiction over several types of juvenile matters:

- Youths who violate criminal laws, but are classified as delinquents
- Youths who violate status-related laws
- Youths who are abused, neglected, or dependent

Some juvenile courts are also authorized to hear cases on guardianship and adoptions. Many states also grant jurisdiction over adults for specified issues, such as contributing to the delinquency of a minor, child support, or cases involving abuse, neglect, and dependency. The unique **territorial, subject matter,** and **personal** jurisdiction of the juvenile court is what differentiates juvenile court systems from other judicial agencies.

Juvenile Court Territorial Jurisdiction. This type of jurisdiction refers to the geographic scope of a court's authority. Unless otherwise specified by law, a court possesses power to hear cases only within certain territorial limits, defined by political boundaries such as specified municipalities or counties. Juvenile courts must therefore adjudicate offenses and victimizations in the territory where they occurred, and transfer nonresident cases to the proper jurisdiction (unless state law permits otherwise).

Juvenile Court Subject-Matter Jurisdiction. Subject matter refers to issues brought before a court, and subject matter jurisdiction is the authority of a court to decide a particular class of cases. It is in this domain that juvenile courts are most distinguishable from other judicial systems. For example, adult criminal courts may only hear cases that pertain to violations of criminal laws, whether committed by an adult or a juvenile waived into the personal jurisdiction of the criminal court. In comparison, juvenile courts are civil institutions that are empowered to hear only juvenile-related cases as classified by statute. Examples of these classifications include delinquency, status offenses, child abuse and neglect, and dependency. In some states, juvenile courts also have subject matter jurisdiction over matters normally resolved in family court.

Juvenile Court Personal Jurisdiction. This type of jurisdiction refers to the court's power over certain persons. It establishes judicial authority to render judgment on the interests of particular classes of people. In adult criminal and civil court, personal jurisdiction can be (and often is) vigorously argued as a pretrial matter, particularly if one's interests might be more advantageously heard before another court. In juvenile systems, personal jurisdiction is a relatively straightforward and uncomplicated matter, because it is predicated on the determination of one's age. This determination is at the heart of juvenile court personal jurisdiction, which means in practice that jurisdiction is defined by laws that delineate minimum or maximum ages. Minimum age jurisdiction varies among the states, with some states not specifying a minimum age. Maximum age jurisdiction is, of course, governed by statutorily defined ages of majority, as discussed previously in Chapter 5. It should be noted that the personal jurisdiction of juvenile courts was significantly redefined as many states passed laws permitting routine waiver of juveniles into adult criminal court systems.

No Single Model: Types of Juvenile Courts

Although the concept of the juvenile court has become universally accepted in the United States, there are many different approaches for implementing this concept. For example, few states have wholly distinct juvenile courts, and these are found principally in major urban areas. Most states have developed juvenile court "sections" within larger court systems, such as county or municipal courts. Some states have devolved juvenile jurisdiction to several courts, such as family, criminal, or probate court. A helpful means for understanding the variety of juvenile court models is to think of the courts as falling into the following categories:

- *Independent juvenile courts.* Juvenile systems that are completely independent from other courts. Although judges from other courts may be assigned to sit as juvenile judges, the system itself is independent.
- *Designated juvenile courts.* Juvenile systems that are subclassifications of larger county, municipal, or district systems. Juvenile courts function in accordance with their designations as divisions within these systems.
- *Coordinated juvenile courts.* Juvenile courts that are required to coordinate their duties with specialized courts such as family courts.

Implementing Court
Authority: Juvenile Court Participants _____

The juvenile court is arguably the central processing node of the juvenile justice system. Modern juvenile court systems are comprised of specialized judicial institutions that are managed by specialized professionals. Thus, the ability of judges to render sound decisions on cases brought before them is necessarily dependent on competent input and participation from court administrators, attorneys, intake officers, and other personnel.

All juvenile courts rely on specialists to secure efficiency and professionalism in the operation of the overall institution. However, juvenile court systems are idiosyncratic in the sense that many variations exist on the types of specialists employed by local courts. Local adaptations have been made, so that no single profile exists on the various duties of juvenile court participants. Nevertheless, the principal participants most likely to be found in local courts are **juvenile court judges, juvenile court prosecutors, juvenile defense counsel,** and **juvenile intake and probation officers.**

Arbiters of Juvenile Justice: Juvenile Court Judges

The central individual in juvenile court systems is the juvenile judge, who is the final arbiter for disputes and problems brought before the court. She or he is vested with the authority of the state, and tangibly and personally embodies *parens patriae* in a manner that no other individual is capable of fulfilling elsewhere in the juvenile justice system. Duties of juvenile court judges generally include ruling on pretrial motions, detention, evidentiary issues, plea bargains, and waiver to criminal court. However, it should be noted that there is no consensus on the role of the juvenile judge. Some judges preside over courtrooms that are formal and adversarial, while others continue to encourage the traditional philosophy of informality and cooperation. Regardless of which philosophy predominates, juvenile court judges are the most commanding figures in the juvenile justice system.

Foundation of Power: Judicial Discretion. From the early inception of juvenile courts, judges have been expected to adapt their proceedings to accommodate a wide variety of issues and cases brought before them. The first courts were highly informal and nonadversarial, with judges expected to be parental and compassionate. Although this informality has given way to increasing degrees of formality, judges continue to retain a great deal of discretion over courtroom proceedings and dispositions. When appropriate, judges must decide whether to:

- Proceed formally or informally
- Oversee adversarial or nonadversarial hearings

- Protect confidences and privileged information
- Act benevolently or firmly
- Stand *in loco parentis* when there are no responsible guardians

Judicial discretion also includes the authority to render decisions on whether juveniles will be adjudicated delinquent, abused or neglected, or in need of intervention. Juvenile proceedings usually are "bench" proceedings with no jury[7]—the judge's decisions in cases and on juvenile dispositions are final. In many jurisdictions, judges delegate authority to **referees**, who are hearing officers that serve as assistants and advisers to the court. Most delegated cases are routine matters involving simple disputes or factual questions; referees are not assigned to cases requiring decisions on jurisdiction or other serious matters of law and procedure. In jurisdictions that use this approach, juvenile court judges retain the discretion to accept, reject, or modify recommendations of referees.

Qualifications of Judges. State constitutions and statutes govern the selection process and qualifications for juvenile court judges. Each law and process mandates its own prerequisites, so that no single national standard exists. States vary according to court type, method of selection, geographic basis for selection, length of term, and whether a law degree is required as a prerequisite. Although most states require judges to be licensed attorneys, and the National Advisory Committee on Criminal Justice Standards and Goals made this recommendation in 1976,[8] many states do not mandate law degrees. Nevertheless, juvenile court judges must possess juvenile-related legal and practitioner experience, whether or not it is derived from formal legal training. Table 7.1 summarizes the selection and service criteria of several states that have established requirements exclusively for youth-related courts.[9]

Representatives of the State: Juvenile Court Prosecutors

Background. The first juvenile court "prosecutors" were police officers who brought cases before the court. This practice represented a typical application of the nonadversarial informality of the early courts, when there was no recognition of a juvenile's right to counsel, and attorneys were generally absent from the proceedings. Prosecutors were considered to be unnecessary and inappropriate to the theoretically nonadversarial philosophy of juvenile justice. The U.S. Supreme Court ended this informal and arbitrary tradition in decisions such as *In re Gault*[10] and *Kent v. United States*[11] (discussed in Chapter 2), which held that juveniles have a constitutionally protected right to counsel in delinquency proceedings and hearings on waiver to criminal court. As a result, accused juvenile offenders must be permitted to retain professional legal representation to defend themselves against charges brought by the state. Legal representation was also needed by government authorities in order for the state to competently present countervailing

TABLE 7.1   JUDICIAL SELECTION AND SERVICE FOR SELECTED YOUTH-RELATED COURTS[a]

Selection and service criteria for judges serving in youth-related courts are established by state constitutions and statutes. These laws have traditionally varied markedly from state to state, as indicated in this table.

State	Court Type	Method of Selection	Geographic Basis for Selection	Length of Term	Law Degree
Colorado	Denver Juvenile Court	Gubernatorial appointment	District	6 years	Yes
Delaware	Family court	Gubernatorial appointment/ Senate consent	County	12 years	No
Georgia	Juvenile court	Superior court Judge appointment	County/circuit	4 years	Yes
Maryland	Orphan's court	Partisan election	Orphans	4 years	No
Massachusetts	Juvenile court	Gubernatorial appointment	State	Age 70	No
Massachusetts	Probate and family courts	Gubernatorial appointment	State	Age 70	No
Mississippi	Family court	Nonpartisan election	County	4 years	Yes
New York	Family court	Partisan election/ NYC mayoral appointment	County outside NYC	10 years	Yes
Rhode Island	Family court	Gubernatorial appointment/ Senate consent	State	Life	Yes
South Carolina	Family court	Legislative election	Circuit	6 years	Yes
Tennessee	Juvenile court	Partisan election	County	8 years	Yes
Utah	Juvenile court	Gubernatorial appointment/ Senate consent	District	6 years	Yes

a. Adapted from Rottman, D. B., Flango, C. R., Cantrell, M. T., Hansen, R., & LaFountain, N. (2000). *State court organization 1998*. Washington, DC: U.S. Department of Justice.

evidence in juvenile court proceedings. As a result, most jurisdictions now routinely assign juvenile prosecutors to delinquency cases.

Foundation of Power: Prosecutorial Discretion. Prior to the U.S. Supreme Court holdings on juvenile due-process rights, the questions of whether to file petitions on behalf of youths—and the charges against them—were usually the responsibility of intake or probation officers. This function is now the duty of juvenile court prosecutors.[12]

Juvenile court prosecutors are the final arbiters on whether a juvenile will be referred into juvenile court. Prosecutors serve as gatekeepers for bringing juveniles before the court, regardless of whether the case's referral originated from police agencies, schools, or parents. This exercise of **prosecutorial discretion**, which mirrors discretion used in adult criminal cases, places an enormous amount of procedural authority into the hands of prosecutors. Although police officers, teachers, and parents often bring juveniles to the door of the juvenile justice system, prosecutors possess the discretionary authority to turn them away. Prosecutorial discretion has historically been a well-accepted function of prosecuting attorney agencies, and was traditionally wielded without explanation to judges or the public. However, some state legislatures have curtailed prosecutorial discretion on the question of whether to keep cases in juvenile court or waive them into adult criminal court. Lawmakers have included juvenile offenders in their overall crackdown on criminal behavior, so that certification of juveniles as adults, and waiver of their cases into criminal court, have become automatic procedures in many jurisdictions. Because mandatory waiver is now a prevailing philosophy for serious offenses, prosecutors often have no discretion on these matters.

Prosecutorial Conduct. Attorneys who serve as juvenile court prosecutors are employees of prosecuting attorneys' offices, and are usually assigned to juvenile court duty early in their careers. Juvenile prosecutors are typically reassigned to adult criminal court as they become more seasoned. The decision on whether or not to prosecute cases is determined by a number of factors, some of which are more justifiable than others. For example, legitimate factors include the degree of probable cause, the quality of evidence against an accused offender, and due-process issues. Less valid factors include prosecuting high-profile cases at the expense of less sensational cases, personal biases, and political factors. In addition, more "routine" offenses such as property crimes and simple assaults may be selected out as lower priorities in comparison to other offenses.

Prosecutors represent the state in the courtroom, and are trained to represent the interests of the state against accused offenders. Because of the presence of prosecuting and defense attorneys, courtroom proceedings naturally become adversarial. If juvenile court judges do not control prosecutorial conduct, proceedings turn out to be only marginally differentiated from adult criminal prosecutions. For this reason, juvenile judges generally do require prosecutorial restraint in the presentation of evidence and examination of witnesses.

Representing Youths in the Courtroom: The Juvenile Defense Counsel

Background. The first juvenile courts did not incorporate defense advocacy into their proceedings because juveniles were theoretically never in jeopardy. The courts were deemed to be advocates on behalf of the best interests of children, and consequently there was no logical need for juveniles to retain defense counsel. This approach, while theoretically appealing, was unsound in practice. Excessive informality led to due-process abuses, decision inconsistencies, and other mistreatment of youths brought before the court—all of which were eventually curtailed by the U.S. Supreme Court in cases such as *In re Winship*,[13] *In re Gault*, and *Kent v. United States*. These cases effectively require standards of proof and other due-process protections in juvenile proceedings, thus establishing the right (and practical need) for competent legal representation on behalf of juveniles.[14]

Prevalence of Defense Representation. Modern proceedings are adversarial in nature, and juveniles accused of delinquent acts are entitled to legal representation under the same constitutional protections as their adult counterparts in the criminal justice system. Most jurisdictions state as a matter of policy that offenders should receive representation by defense counsel in petitioned cases. Juveniles who have been abused or neglected or who are dependent are often represented by a court-appointed adult advocate known as a *guardian ad litem*. Technically defined as "a guardian appointed by a court of justice to prosecute or defend an infant in any suit to which he may be a party,"[15] modern *guardians ad litem* represent the personal interests of youths who are deemed unable to do so on their own behalf because of their immaturity.

However, the presence of defense counsel is not a universal characteristic of American juvenile court systems, for many reasons. For example, some judges who retain traditional juvenile court values continue to discourage the retention of counsel by either side, with the result that many juveniles continue to be unrepresented by defense counsel. Juveniles and their parents also receive advisement from juvenile intake and probation officers, who often advise them that their cases will be resolved quickly with minimum inconvenience without the intervention of defense counsel.

Quality of Defense Representation. As in the adult criminal system, defense counsels may either be **private attorneys** or **court-appointed counsel**. Private attorneys are those who have private practices and are either personally retained or are appointed as part of a court rotation system. Court appointed counsel are either private attorneys appointed by the court or **public defenders** who are full-time state employees; the latter are essentially the counterparts to prosecuting attorneys. Poor juveniles are represented by court-appointed attorneys, who receive their fees from county-level or other government entities for their labor.

Public defenders are often burdened by heavy caseloads and less-than-adequate resources. In addition, their clients are often admittedly delinquent. These circumstances lend themselves to routine plea bargaining, minimal time for case preparation, and little time spent with clients. Hence, the quality of representation is often inadequate for indigent juveniles. Regarding privately retained attorneys, factors exist that may likewise reduce the quality of representation. Many criminal defense attorneys are sole practitioners or members of small firms who rely on a high volume of adult criminal cases to maintain their practices. Because many of their clients are from relatively low-income backgrounds, and their offenses are frequently minor, criminal defense attorneys typically accept these cases for low fees. Many criminal defense attorneys are reluctant to accept juvenile delinquency cases. As a result, those who do accept juvenile delinquency cases are often relatively new and untested attorneys who do not have the resources or experience to prepare vigorous defenses for their clients. Unfortunately, other members of the legal profession sometimes regard both criminal defense and delinquency defense attorneys with condescension.

In October 2003, the American Bar Association released a fairly grim report on the status of juvenile legal representation. The report presented data collected from six state juvenile justice systems as part of an ongoing nationwide survey of legal representation for juveniles. Findings included the following commonalities found in previous studies and in the six states:[16]

- Juvenile court lawyers have excessive caseloads, preventing many from having meaningful contact with their clients, and receive inordinately low compensation, preventing them from being able to provide effective representation to those clients.
- Many youths do not have counsel at critical stages of juvenile justice process, despite the law's clear mandate and the harmful consequences of not having a lawyer.
- Because most juvenile defense lawyers are not provided training to help identify treatment options that could serve as effective alternatives to detention, lawyers are incapable of effectively protecting their clients' rights and advocating for their treatment needs.
- Because more appropriate alternatives to detention are rarely explored, juvenile justice systems tend to rely too heavily on detention and probation.
- Juvenile detention systems are becoming dumping grounds for mentally ill children and school-related referrals.
- Postdisposition representation of adjudicated youth is virtually non-existent, with lawyers rarely having the time or resources to visit their clients in placement or follow-up to ensure that court-ordered treatment has been delivered and is effective.

- Defense attorneys typically have access to fewer resources, such as investigators and technology, than the prosecutors they face in court.
- Although it is common knowledge that teenage clients pose particular challenges for lawyers, most receive no training in adolescent development.
- The failings of the juvenile justice system have a disproportionate impact on children of color and indigent youth.

Gatekeeping: Juvenile Intake and Probation Officers

Juvenile Intake Officers. The intake process refers to a juvenile offender's first contact with the juvenile court. It is an initial assessment and recommendation on whether to file a petition and whether to send the youth into detention. In some jurisdictions, intake officers are a specific (and separate) professional classification within the juvenile court bureaucracy. In other jurisdictions, juvenile probation officers or other court professionals serve as intake officers. Regardless of which model is used, the intake procedure is a preliminary determination that is made quickly—and, theoretically, fairly—in order to rapidly move cases through the juvenile justice system.

An intake officer's first decision is usually whether or not to recommend detention. Factors weighed include personal safety of the child, risk of flight, and risks to the public. Intake officers technically do not order detention but make recommendations on detention to juvenile court judges, who decide whether detention is warranted. States mandate that detention status be determined within a matter of hours—from as little as 6 hours to 48 hours. Regardless of whether detention is recommended, the fact is that approximately half of cases brought before the court are never processed beyond intake officers into formal adjudication.[17] This is because intake officers exercise significant discretion for deciding or recommending the immediate postintake placement of juveniles. The following decision points are typically available to intake officers:

- Recommend detention for at-risk juveniles
- Recommend case diversion outside of juvenile court and into other sectors of the juvenile justice system
- Postpone consideration of specific charges until after evaluation and treatment occur
- File a petition for adjudication before the juvenile court

Juvenile Probation Officers. Juvenile probation is the most common disposition used in the criminal justice system and is conceptually identical to adult probation. It is a rehabilitative disposition, generally given either to low-risk first-time offenders or as a "least restrictive alternative" for chronic juvenile offenders. Juveniles receiving probation are permitted to remain in the community under supervision by a juvenile probation officer, and community placements can be made with family members and guardians, or under foster care.

Juvenile probation officers are officers of the court who are indispensable participants at critical phases of juvenile justice process. Officers are instrumental in protecting youths from dangerous or corruptive influences, and for promoting rehabilitation. Their role in the juvenile justice system typically includes the following duties:

- Mediating out-of-court settlements between delinquents and victims, or between parents and juvenile authorities in cases of abuse, neglect, and abandonment (typically prior to an adjudication)
- Investigating the social background of juveniles to assist the court in determining practical dispositional alternatives in the best interest of the child (typically after an adjudication)
- Supervising juveniles receiving probation who have been released into the community
- Supervising abusive and neglectful parents

These duties necessarily require probation officers to act as symbols of authority and occasionally discipline juveniles or parents for noncompliance with terms of probation. They are also counselors who advise children in trouble on how to stay away from trouble, and thereby successfully complete probation. This counseling role extends to protecting children in need from abusive or otherwise dysfunctional home environments. As in the adult system, some jurisdictions are less lenient than others with probationers, so that, although many juvenile probation officers act as juvenile advocates, others assume the role of law enforcement officers.

Terms of Probation. Every probationary agreement constitutes an agreement between the court and juveniles or parents. These agreements are effective for specified periods of time, may be lenient or restrictive, and permit probationers to maintain their placement in the community as long as they comply with the requirements of the agreement. Probation is a type of "suspended sentence" in which detention is suspended pending completion of the probationary period.

Terms of probation are conceptually similar to contractual terms, so that breaches of agreed conduct result in penalties—for probation, these penalties involve the revocation of probationary privileges. Juvenile courts frequently impose **general probationary conditions** on all probationers, with additional **specific probationary conditions** that are designed for specific probations. The juvenile court establishes general probationary conditions as *bottom line* requirements for all probationers, and include the following examples:

- Regular school attendance
- Absence of delinquency

- Compliance with status laws
- Visits by juvenile probation officers

Because each juvenile's case is unique, specific probationary conditions are likely to be imposed, and may include the following examples:

- Revocation of driving privileges
- Prohibition from associating with specified individuals
- Prohibition from loitering at specified locations
- Curfew requirements

Since judicial decisions are based on accurate assessments of compliance or noncompliance with the terms of probation, juvenile probation officers are critical participants in this process. Officers are required to maintain accurate records documenting the behavior of their clients, evaluate client behavior, and produce summary reports to the court. Failure to carry out these duties can result in sanctions against probation officers or probation departments.

Moving Through the System: Juvenile Court Process

It is tempting to conclude that juvenile court process is identical to adult criminal court process. This is not an entirely accurate observation because, although processes in juvenile court are quite *analogous* to criminal court procedures, the basic philosophy of the juvenile court is very different. It should be remembered that juvenile courts are expected to apply a philosophy of rehabilitation and remediation within the contexts of ancient paternalistic doctrines such as *parens patriae* and *in loco parentis*. Adult criminal courts do not apply these philosophies. Thus, any procedural similarities between juvenile and adult courts are predicated on distinct doctrines that do not necessarily pertain to both courts.

Table 7.2 summarizes the procedural language of juvenile and adult criminal courts.

Entering the System: Juvenile Custody and Detention

Most juveniles enter the juvenile court system after the police have taken official custody over suspected offenders. Custody is only roughly equivalent to an adult arrest. Like police arrest authority, juvenile lawbreakers may be taken into custody under court order, when observed committing an offense, or after a complaint has been filed with the authorities. Unlike police arrest authority, custody may also occur for the protection of youths, as in the case of police intervention after reported abuse, neglect, or dependency.

After being taken into custody, juveniles must either be released to parents or other guardians, taken before a juvenile court, or sent into a

TABLE 7.2   JUVENILE COURT PROCEDURES: THE LANGUAGE OF REHABILITATION

Juvenile courts have historically practiced a philosophy of rehabilitation. Although procedures can be quite rigorous and formal at times, the underlying principles of the juvenile court are reflected in the terms applied to court processes.

This table illustrates the similarities and fundamental differences in the philosophies of the adult and juvenile systems by comparing the language used for similar procedures.

Juvenile Court Procedure	Procedural Concept	Criminal Court Procedure
Status offense	Laws that regulate the behavior of persons under the age of majority	No equivalent
Delinquent behavior	Serious violent or property offenses	Crime
Delinquent youth	Persons who commit offenses	Criminal
Intake officer	A court official who makes an initial determination about a person's entry into a court system	Magistrate
Juvenile court	A court vested with the jurisdiction to hear cases against suspects	Criminal court
Petition	An order requiring accused offenders to appear before the court	Indictment
Custody	Police officially taking formal control over a suspected offender or other person	Arrest
Detention	The period when a person is temporarily housed in a detention facility, pending further processing	Jail
Adjustment	Agreements between an accused and the authorities on which charges shall be admitted, and which shall be dropped	Plea bargain
Adjudicatory hearing	Proceedings by the court to determine whether a suspect has committed an offense	Trial
Adjudication	Decisions by a court on whether a suspect has committed an offense	Verdict
Dispositional hearing	Proceedings by the court on what to do with suspects found to have committed an offense	Sentencing hearing
Commitment	Decisions by a court on what to do with suspects found to have committed an offense	Sentence
Probation	Supervision by enforcement agencies of suspects found to have committed an offense absent confinement to an institution	Probation
Aftercare	Supervision by enforcement agencies of suspects found to have committed an offense after a term of confinement	Parole
Shelter	Confinement of persons in an institution for their own safety and welfare	Protective custody

detention facility. Parents or other guardians must be notified of the reasons for custody or detention. Detention refers to the period when a juvenile is kept in custody and temporarily housed in a facility, pending further processing. Typical detention accommodations include juvenile delinquent detention centers, group homes, and child welfare agency facilities. Within the context of modern juvenile justice policy, detention is considered to be an extraordinary remedy, intended to be required only for the protection of youths, property, or other persons.[18]

Command Appearances:
Juvenile Petitions and Summons

Juvenile petitions are roughly equivalent to the adult system's filing of complaints or pressing charges. Petitions are documents that request the court's intervention over matters involving juvenile delinquents, status offenders, or children who have been abused, neglected, or are dependent. Unlike adult complaints or pressed charges—which seek some form of restitution or punishment—petitions are issued out of consideration for the best interest of the child. In other words, petitions request court juris- diction as a way to *protect* youthful offenders from their conflict with authority, or victims from their victimizers. Although responsible parties such as police officers, parents, school administrators, or other persons may prepare petitions, petitions will not be formally authorized until a court-designated officer confirms that an official filing is in the best inter- est of the child.

The juvenile court will schedule a hearing date after a petition is filed, usually within 10 days if the juvenile is held in detention. The court will then order appropriate parties to appear on the hearing date by formally issuing a **summons** for the presence of these parties. The summons is issued to the juvenile with the petition (if over the age of 13 years), his or her parents or guardians, and other persons whose presence is deemed relevant by the court. It is delivered five days prior to the hearing date by registered or cer- tified mail to persons with unknown addresses or living outside of the state, or within 24 hours prior to the hearing date for persons with known addresses inside the state. An alternative procedural option available to the court is the delivery of a **notice in lieu of summons** to youths and parents, which is an informal, softer notification to appear before the court. It is an alternative to a formal summons and serves as notice to appear before the court.

It is important to understand that a differentiation has been made in some states between petitions requested on behalf of juvenile offenders and those sought for juvenile victims. Procedurally, these systems issue separate delin- quency petitions for offenders and protective petitions for children in need of protection or services (**CHIPS**). The CHIPS designation is specifically designed to assure that children in need receive appropriate placements and treatment.

Center of the System: Juvenile Court Hearings

Should a juvenile progress through the foregoing procedural phases without diversion outside of the court system, juvenile courts typically proceed by advancing through the following three hearings phases:

- *Preliminary hearing.* Similar to the preliminary hearing in adult court, it is an initial conference on the status of the case.
- *Adjudicatory hearing.* Similar to the trial in adult court, the merits of the case are heard and determined by the court.
- *Dispositional hearing.* Similar to the sentencing hearing in adult court, the court rules on what should become of the juvenile subsequent to the adjudication.

Procedural formality during these phases can range from rather loose applications of rules of evidence or adversarial exactitude, to quite rigorous presentations of evidence by the parties. Different states apply different standards for formality, depending on their local rules of court and the facts of each case.

Preliminary Hearings. As in adult criminal court, the preliminary hearing is an initial *pretrial* conference designed to resolve basic questions prior to permitting the case to proceed to formal resolution of the issues in question. Judges are assisted in these matters by probation officers or other similar officials, who serve as advisers to the court during preliminary hearings. Probation officers and other officials facilitate fairness in these hearings by advising the judge on each child's history and environment, and whether they pose a risk of flight or are a threat to themselves or society. Preliminarily, the juvenile court judge must determine

- Whether parents and juveniles have been informed of, and understand, their rights
- Whether parents and juveniles understand the nature of the charges brought against them
- Whether detention by the juvenile justice system is or is not warranted
- If detention is warranted, the kind of facility where the juvenile should be housed

Reports by probation officers are frequently instrumental in framing the court's decision on detention. The question of where to house youths is contingent on the facts of each case. For example, depending on the nature of the charges brought against them, delinquent children may be detained in quite secure facilities. Similarly, children in need and status offenders are generally housed under foster care. For this latter category of youths, *guardians ad litem* are appointed as advocates—usually assigned from child welfare or other social service agencies. However, in many states *guardians ad litem* are volunteers rather than social workers, who act as community-based advocates on behalf of children in need.

As discussed previously, many states permit juvenile judges to delegate their authority to court-appointed referees, who can be important participants at the preliminary hearing phase. In many jurisdictions, routine cases are automatically referred to referees, while judges hear difficult and serious cases. Thus, referees would not hear questions of jurisdiction, serious cases of violence, or certain family matters. They technically only make *recommendations* to judges as court advisers and do not render final decisions—this is a duty reserved for the judge. In other words, referees are court advisers and should never be viewed as sitting in the place of judges. High caseloads in some jurisdictions often dictate the necessity for referees, who have become instrumental in reducing caseload pressures on many courts.

Adjudicatory Hearings. The adjudication of juvenile-related issues is conceptually similar—though not procedurally identical—to **bench trials** in the adult system. Bench trials involve the resolution of legal and factual issues by a judge (the judicial "bench") without the participation of a jury; in these cases the judge becomes the sole authority on the fate of accused offenders. In the juvenile system, jury-based adjudications are rarely an option, so that all adjudicatory proceedings before the juvenile court are generally bench proceedings by definition.

Adjudicatory hearings are held to ascertain whether the evidence supports allegations in juvenile petitions. In order to determine the appropriate weight of the evidence, juvenile court judges use one of two standards of review:

- *Preponderance of the evidence.* The standard of proof applied for the resolution of status offense cases. It technically refers to the "greater weight of evidence which is more credible and convincing to the mind."[19]
- *Beyond a reasonable doubt.* The standard of proof applied for the resolution of delinquency cases. It technically refers to evidence that is "fully satisfied, entirely convinced, satisfied to a moral certainty . . . the equivalent of the words clear, precise and indubitable."[20]

Hearings are usually recorded, either by court reporters or through written minutes. Traditionally, juvenile records have been sealed or expunged, and juvenile proceedings have been closed to the public. However, some states permit records to be available to prosecutors in subsequent investigations, and other states have permitted open proceedings. The principal criticism of open records and proceedings is that confidentiality will be compromised and will place juveniles in greater jeopardy of reduced rehabilitation and increased stigma. A further trend is an increase in judicial formality and the adversarial nature of juvenile court proceedings.

In the initial phase of the adjudicatory hearing, youths enter a plea to either admit or deny the allegations contained in the juvenile petition. This is procedurally comparable to entering a plea of guilty, not guilty, or no contest in the adult system. During the hearing (assuming the allegations are denied), the juvenile court will consider the **adjudicative facts** of the case, which represent the full scope of facts alleged against youths named in the juvenile petition. If the court renders a decision sustaining allegations raised in the juvenile petition, the judge will make a **finding of fact,** which states the court's determination that the youth has committed a status offense; is delinquent; or has been abused, neglected, and in need of supervision.

After findings of fact are entered, the court will set a date for the dispositional hearing and order that a **predisposition report** be prepared on behalf of the juvenile to aid the judge in preparation for the final disposition. This report is sometimes referred to as a **presentence investigation (PSI)**. Probation officers or similar officials who perform background investigations on the child in question compose predisposition reports. This investigation evaluates the juvenile's overall environment, incorporating assessments of how psychological, cultural, and social dynamics influence the youth's conduct. Predisposition reports typically include the following information:

- Interviews with the juvenile and his or her parents
- Interviews with relatives
- Interviews with the petitioner (victim or other complainant)
- Compilations of police reports, interviews, and witness statements
- Reports on school interviews and records
- Reports on other institutional interviews and records, such as juvenile social service agencies, clergy, or employers
- Reports on psychosocial evaluations of the juvenile and his or her family profile
- Summary of other juvenile justice agency records

The overall information contained in the predisposition report is used as a social history by juvenile court judges to determine which remedy is in the best interest of the child. The report can be—and often is—a deciding factor in the dispositional hearing. A fundamental criterion for the report is that statements and documentation must support the probation officer's findings. Findings may be reported to the court in writing, or on some occasions verbally.

Dispositional Hearings. Sentencing hearings in the adult criminal system are the final phase of proceedings in the trial court. Similarly, dispositional hearings are the final phase of proceedings in juvenile court. However, there is a significant conceptual distinction between the two procedures. Whereas criminal sentences are imposed to punish offenders, dispositions are intended to decree what is to be done in the best interest of the child. The uncomplicated rationale for this approach is the fact that juvenile dispositions must be rendered for both children in trouble (juvenile offenders) and children in need (juvenile victims). Thus, although dispositions for offenders are often quite restrictive—and are imposed for the protection of society—the underlying rationale for dispositional alternatives remains one of rehabilitation or protection from victimization. Dispositions include the following options:

- Dismissal of the case and all charges
- Release to the care of a parent, guardian, or other responsible adult or institution
- Diversion to juvenile programs and service agencies
- Restitution to victims
- Probation
- Detention in a juvenile correctional facility

In practice, the implementation of these alternatives is determined by how a juvenile is classified and the information contained in the predisposition report regarding his or her specific social history. For example, courts will consider whether juvenile delinquents require some combination of treatment, probation, or detention—and craft the disposition accordingly. On the other hand, victimized juveniles are likely to be placed with parents or guardians, subject to court supervision and under established conditions. Regarding status offenders, juvenile courts will often impose coercive intervention remedies as a way to prevent these offenders from overwhelming the court's docket.

A variety of designations have been established to define supervision of juvenile delinquents, victimized juveniles, and status offenders as well as their families, including:

- **JINS**—Juveniles in need of supervision
- **CHINS**—Children in need of supervision
- **FINS**—Families in need of supervision
- **PINS**—Persons in need of supervision

Punishing Criminal Behavior: Juveniles in Adult Court

In the modern era, many juvenile offenders find themselves standing before adult criminal court judges, subject to the same procedures and penalties as any other criminal defendant. This phenomenon has become increasingly common since the inception of the juvenile court. From the beginning, some state juvenile statutes incorporated provisions for hearing some juvenile cases in criminal court. However, prior to 1920 fewer than a dozen states allowed youths to be brought before criminal judges. Now, every state legislature has enacted laws allowing juveniles to be fully tried in criminal proceedings. Because juveniles who enter the adult system are subject to potentially severe penalties—including capital punishment—they are accorded the same constitutional due-process protections as adults.

Juveniles as Legal "Adults": Judicial Waiver and Certification

Judicial Waiver. Juvenile courts may relinquish jurisdiction over cases involving serious offenses and order them removed to the adult criminal court. This process, known as judicial **waiver**, is generally discretionary, allowing prosecutors or other court officials to determine whether waiver shall be invoked. When waiver occurs, the case is removed from the juvenile justice system and juvenile suspects are subjected to the full sanctions of the adult criminal justice system. It will be recalled that the constitutionality of waiver proceedings was decided in *Kent v. United States,*[21] which provided juveniles with the right to a hearing on the question of transfer from juvenile court jurisdiction to adult criminal courts. When waiver occurs, statements made by young suspects prior to removal and transfer are not admissible in the new criminal venue.

Certification. Certification refers to a procedural technicality whereby juveniles are legally certified as adults and processed into the criminal justice system. As with waiver, the consequences of certification are significant because juveniles are no longer protected by the special limitations and protections afforded under the rehabilitative philosophy of the juvenile court. An interesting procedural process known as **reverse certification** has been adopted by some states that normally require automatic criminal court jurisdiction for serious offenses. Reverse certification essentially authorizes criminal courts to transfer over to the juvenile court cases that have been automatically referred into the adult system. Similarly, persons who appear in criminal court and are currently over the age of majority, but who committed an offense when under a specified age, may be referred to juvenile court.

Standards for Waiver and Certification. The frequency of waiver and certification to criminal court has increased in the modern era, with waiver having become the most common method for transferring juveniles into the adult system. Each state has established its own standards for waiver and certification, so that some states emphasize age criteria, while others apply an admixture of the offender's age and the nature of his or her offense. Procedurally, the following four models represent the types of systems adopted by states:

- *Judicial transfer.* Systems that apply judicial waiver. As discussed, juvenile court judges have the authority to waive jurisdiction over juveniles, thus sending them into the adult system. Variations of this model are most commonly found in the states.
- *Prosecutorial waiver.* Systems that permit prosecutors to exercise their discretion in choosing the system (adult or juvenile) before which a case will be brought.

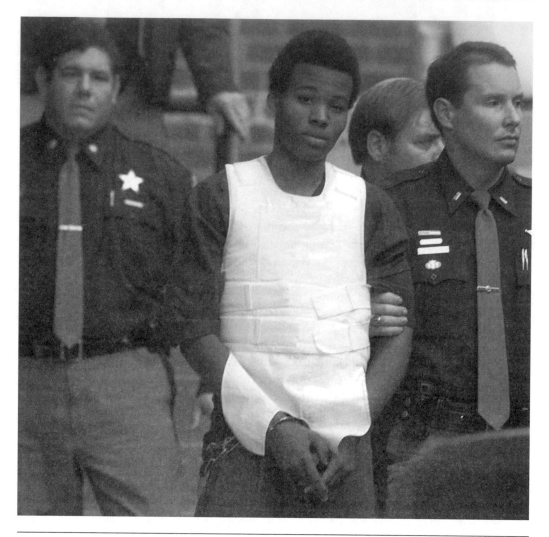

Photo 7.2   Lee Malvo leaves court after being convicted of sniper killings around the
Washington, DC, region.

- *Legislative waiver.* In many states, the concepts of waiver and certification have been modified and codified into legislation mandating the removal of specified offenders from juvenile court. This procedure—commonly known as **statutory exclusion**—requires the assignment of youths suspected of murder or other serious offenses to the adult criminal system.
- *Demand waiver.* Systems that permit juveniles to request waiver to adult court. One factor for this kind of request may be the desire for a jury trial in states that do not permit juries in juvenile court.

Table 7.3 summarizes statutory exclusion provisions involving cases that will automatically originate in criminal court rather than juvenile court.[22]

TABLE 7.3 STATUTORY EXCLUSION PROVISIONS

Many states have passed laws that mandate automatic arraignment of juvenile offenders before adult criminal courts. These laws specify the age of offenders and the type of offense that will be heard in the criminal justice system. This table summarizes statutory exclusion offenses and minimum age criteria for selected states.[a]

State	Minimum Age for Statutory Exclusion	Certain Felonies	Capital Crimes	Murder	Certain Person Offenses	Certain Property Offenses	Certain Drug Offenses	Certain Weapon Offenses
Alabama	16	16	16				16	
Alaska	16				16	16		
Delaware	15	15						
Georgia	15			13	13			
Idaho	14			14	14	14	14	
Indiana	16	16		16	16		16	16
Iowa	16	16					16	16
Louisiana	15			15	15			
Maryland	14		14	16	16			16
Massachusetts	14			14				
Minnesota	16			16				
Mississippi	13	13	13					
Montana	17			17	17	17	17	17
New York	13			13	14	14		
Oklahoma	13			13				
Oregon	15			15	15			
South Carolina	16	16						
South Dakota	16	16						
Vermont	14			14	14	14		
Washington	16			16	16	16		

a. Adapted from Snyder, H. N., & Sickmund, M. (1999). *Juvenile offenders and victims: 1999 National report* (p. 107). Washington, DC: U.S. Department of Justice.

Thus, factors typically include the suspect's maturity, the reported social history, and the degree of danger posed to the community. For example, statutory exclusion laws establish the minimum age for automatic transfer, as well as which offenses will result in the transfer.

Significance of Assignment to Criminal Court

Juveniles who are removed from the juvenile justice system become subject to a very different judicial institution, giving rise to several serious implications for these youths. For example, rather than receiving treatment in accordance with an underlying philosophy of rehabilitation, they will be sent into a system that routinely punishes offenders. In addition, the broad community-based support network found in the juvenile justice system is absent in the criminal justice system. Other implications include the following outcomes, which are not present in juvenile systems:

- Long terms of incarceration
- Imprisonment in large adult correctional institutions
- Capital punishment
- Trial by adult juries as a matter of right

These consequences reflect a broad cultural consensus in the United States that criminal behavior should be punished and that rehabilitation should be secondary to longer terms of incarceration. Offenders—whether adults or juveniles—are subject to the full sanctions of the criminal justice system. Significantly, most states have provisions for sentencing youths to capital punishment. Table 7.4 lists the minimum ages permitted under state law for imposition of the death penalty.[23]

TABLE 7.4   MINIMUM AGES FOR THE DEATH PENALTY

State sentencing codes specify minimum ages for persons to be sentenced to death. Most states permit imposition of the death penalty for juveniles at the ages of 16 to 18 years. This table lists minimum ages for sentencing to capital punishment.[a]

None Specified	Age 16 or Less	Age 17	Age 18
Arizona	Alabama	Georgia	California
Idaho	Arkansas (14)	New Hampshire	Colorado
Louisiana	Delaware	North Carolina	Connecticut
Montana	Florida	Texas	Federal System
Pennsylvania	Indiana		Illinois
South Carolina	Kentucky		Kansas
South Dakota	Mississippi (13)		Maryland
Utah	Missouri		Nebraska
	Nevada		New Jersey
	Oklahoma		New Mexico
	Virginia (14)		New York
	Wyoming		Ohio
			Oregon
			Tennessee
			Washington

a. Adapted from Snyder, H. N., & Sickmund, M. (1999). *Juvenile offenders and victims: 1999 National report* (p. 211). Washington, DC: U.S. Department of Justice.

PROFESSIONAL PROFILE CHAPTER 7

Private Attorney, Former Federal Judge, and Former Prosecutor

The career paths of legal professionals are developed over many years of practice and can be quite interesting. During their careers, many attorneys engage in several areas of practice, often beginning their careers in one type of practice and finally settling into another type. Having said this, it is quite rare for an attorney to have acquired experience and expertise as a prosecutor, judge, and private attorney. In this regard, it is very educational to understand the perspective of one who has served as a law enforcer (state and federal prosecutor), judicial officer (trial and appellate federal judge), and advocate (private attorney).

I. Personal Profile

    A. Name:
        Timothy K. Lewis

    B. Agency:
        Schnader Harrison Segal & Lewis LLP

    C. Rank and/or Title:
        Counsel
        Former Federal Judge, U.S. Court of Appeals, Third Circuit, 1992–1999
        Former Federal Judge, U.S. District Court, Western District of Pennsylvania, 1991–1992
        Former Assistant U.S. Attorney for the Western District of Pennsylvania
        Former Assistant District Attorney in Allegheny County, Pennsylvania

    D. Education (Schools and Degrees):
        Tufts University
        BA, Political Science, 1976
        Duquesne University School of Law
        JD, 1980

    E. Professional Organizations/Community Group Memberships:
        Co-chair of the Appellate Practice Group at the law firm of Schnader Harrison Segal & Lewis
        Member, Board of Directors of the American Arbitration Association
        Member, American Law Institute
        Member, Advisory Committee for the Study of Rules of Practice and Internal Operating Procedures for the U.S. District Court for the Western District of Pennsylvania
        Co-chair, National Committee on the Right to Counsel

II. Professional Profile

    A. What personal or other background experiences led to your decision to *choose* this profession?

        When I was a child, my father, who had overcome segregation to become a dentist, taught me that in America for a black person to be successful he should choose one of the professions, such as medicine, dentistry, or law. I knew from the time I was very young that I wanted to become a lawyer.

B.   Please state a few of your personal reasons/motivations for your decision to *continue* in this profession.

I have always felt that the legal profession offered me the best opportunity to make a difference in the lives of many, particularly in the civil rights and human rights areas. This certainly was true as a judge, and as a former judge it is even more true because I am able to lend my name, my talents, and my experiences to causes that I think help others.

C.   Which job experiences have had an important impact on you?

There are too many to even begin to list, but participating in death penalty appeals in the U.S. Supreme Court; deciding major civil and criminal cases as a federal judge; and representing the United States in federal court as an Assistant U.S. Attorney have all had a major impact on me.

D.   What has been a particularly *satisfying* job experience?

Participating, along with three other former federal judges, in convincing the U.S. Supreme Court to stay the execution of a death row inmate 10 minutes before his scheduled execution in a case in which the Court later overturned his conviction.

E.   What has been a particularly *challenging* job experience?

As a judge, the most challenging experience for me was always imposing sentence, knowing that the words I had just uttered would take away someone's liberty, often for an extended period of time.

F.   What do you think the future holds for your profession?

It's impossible to say, because the profession is so vast and wide ranging.

G.   What kind of advice/guidance would you give to interested students?

Hold on to your ideals, work hard, and use the profession as an instrument to help improve our society as a whole.

Chapter Summary

The juvenile court systems in the United States are in many respects the backbone of the juvenile justice system. The first courts were a logical extension of the juvenile reform movements of the nineteenth century. They reflected the underlying philosophies of rehabilitation and redemption that continue to guide modern courts. Although the informality of the early courts has given way to varying degrees of formality in the modern era, juvenile courts remain more flexible than adult criminal courts.

Juvenile court jurisdiction is conceptually similar to courts in the adult system. Territorial (geographic), subject matter, and personal jurisdiction are guided by the questions of where a case can be brought, what kinds of issues can be heard, and who is subject to judgment. These concepts are applied by the states within several models that have been adopted: independent courts, designated courts, and coordinated courts.

As in adult criminal systems, juvenile court participants include judges, prosecutors, and defense counsel as central officials. However, juvenile intake and probation officers often play central roles as advisers to the court, a situation that is not replicated at the adult level. Proceedings before the juvenile court apply softer rehabilitative terms and standards that are intended to protect and remediate children in trouble and children in need. However, large numbers of juveniles are certified as adults and waived into the adult criminal system for trial and punishment. Many states now forego waiver and certification, and automatically send offenders accused of specified crimes into the criminal system.

Chapter 8 examines the history, philosophy, and structure of juvenile correctional systems. Unique issues peculiar to juvenile corrections are explored, as are the participants in the system.

Questions for Review

1. What is the modern role of the juvenile court?

2. What are the attributes of the modern court's philosophy, jurisdiction, and types of hearings?

3. Who are the principal juvenile court professionals and lay participants?

4. What are the roles of juvenile court professionals and other participants?

5. How are juveniles processed through the juvenile court system?

6. Describe custody, detention, pretrial procedures, the juvenile trial, and juvenile sentencing.

7. Why are juveniles regularly sent to trial before adult criminal courts?

8. Are waiver and certification likely to continue to be applied by the juvenile justice system?

Key Terms and Concepts

The following topics were discussed in this chapter and are found in the Glossary:

Adjudicative Facts

Adjudicatory Hearing

Bench Trial

Beyond a Reasonable Doubt

Certification

CHINS

CHIPS

Cook County Juvenile Court

Court-Appointed Counsel

Demand Waiver

Dispositional Hearing

Finding of Fact

FINS

Guardian ad Litem

JINS

Judicial Transfer

Jurisdiction (Justice Agencies)

Jurisdiction (Personal)

Jurisdiction (Subject Matter)

Jurisdiction (Territorial)

Juvenile Court (Coordinated)

Juvenile Court (Designated)

Juvenile Court (Independent)

Juvenile Court Judge

Juvenile Court Prosecutors

Juvenile Defense Counsel

Juvenile Intake

Juvenile Petitions

Legislative Waiver

Notice in Lieu of Summons

PINS

Predisposition Report

Preliminary Hearing

Preponderance of the Evidence

Presentence Investigation (PSI)

Private Attorney

Probation Officers

Probationary Conditions (General)

Probationary Conditions (Specific)

Prosecutorial Discretion

Prosecutorial Waiver

Public Defender

Referees

Reverse Certification

Statutory Exclusion

Summons

Waiver

DISCUSSION BOX

Who Is Responsible? Parents of Juvenile Offenders

This chapter's Discussion Box is intended to stimulate critical discussion about the roles and responsibilities of juvenile offenders.

Accountability for serious juvenile deviance is not limited to the punishment of individual perpetrators. Parents and guardians of status offenders, juvenile delinquents, and criminals have also been called to account for the harm caused by their children. Judges have required parents to pay restitution to victims, and a sizable number of states have passed laws that directly hold parents responsible for their children's behavior.

Parental accountability laws often permit parents to be arrested or given criminal fines. Some of these laws have been tied to state assistance received by the parents. For example, welfare recipients in some jurisdictions can have their benefits terminated for chronic truancy by their children.

The concept of parental liability is justified by lawmakers as representing sanctions against the parents' failure to properly supervise their children. It is also justified as a practical means to repay society for the harm caused by their lack of supervision. Most of these laws reflect the particular culture and needs of local communities and regions.

Discussion Questions

1. Should parents be called to account for the behavior of their children? Why?

2. What effect do you think parent accountability laws have on the rate of juvenile deviance?

3. Who should bear the responsibility of monitoring parental obligations to society for the behavior of their children?

4. How likely is it that parents will more stringently supervise their children if they know that sanctions are possible?

5. Should governments have the power to engage in this type of enforcement?

Recommended Web Sites

The following Web sites provide information on the role of the juvenile court, court processes, and participants.

Children and Family Justice Center: http://www.law.northwestern.edu/depts/clinic/cfjc/
Children's Defense Fund: http://www.childrensdefense.org/
Juvenile Law Center: http://www.jlc.org
National Council of Juvenile and Family Court Judges: http://www.ncjfcj.org/

Note: The Web site URLs and exercises below are also from the book's study site:
   http://www.sagepub.com/martin

Web Exercise

Using this chapter's recommended Internet sites, conduct an online investigation of the judicial component of the juvenile justice system.

- How are juvenile advocacy agencies similar? How do they differ?
- What is the role of juvenile advocacy and law centers within the broader context of the juvenile justice system?
- In your opinion, how effective are juvenile justice agencies?

For an online search of the role of the juvenile court, students should use a search engine and enter the following keywords:

"Juvenile Court"

"Juvenile Judges"

Recommended Readings

The following publications provide discussions on the juvenile court, court process, and participants in juvenile court proceedings:

del Carmen, R., Parker, M., & Reddington, F. P. (1998). *Briefs of leading cases in juvenile justice.* Cincinnati, OH: Anderson.

Fagan, J., & Zimring, F. E. (Eds.). (2000). *The changing borders of juvenile justice: Transfers of adolescents to the criminal court.* Chicago: University of Chicago Press.

Shepherd, R. E., Jr. (1996). *IJA-ABA juvenile justice standards, annotated.* Chicago: American Bar Association.

Snyder, H., Sickmund, M., & Poe-Yamagata, E. (2000). *Juvenile transfers to criminal court in the 1990s: Lessons learned from four studies.* Washington, DC: U.S. Department of Justice.

Walgrave, L., & Bazemore, G. (Eds.). (2000). *Restorative juvenile justice: An exploration of the restorative juvenile justice paradigm for reforming juvenile justice.* Monsey, NY: Willow Tree Press.

Notes

1. See Timothy Jon Spytma v. Carol Howes, 313 F.3d 363 (6th Cir. 2002).

2. See, e.g., Puzzanchera, C., Stahl, A. L., Finnegan, T. A., Tierney, N., & Snyder, H. N. (2003). *Juvenile court statistics 1998* (p. iii). Washington, DC: U.S. Department of Justice.

3. See, e.g., Puzzanchera, C., Stahl, A. L., Finnegan, T. A., Snyder, H. N., Poole, R. S., & Tierney, N. (2000). *Juvenile court statistics 1997* (p. 37). Washington, DC: U.S. Department of Justice.

4. Ibid.

5. Ibid. (p. 212).

6. Rush, G. E. (2000). *The dictionary of criminal justice* (5th ed., p. 183). New York: Dushkin/McGraw-Hill.

7. In 1997, 12 states permitted jury proceedings in juvenile courts. These hearings were allowed only if the juvenile requested a jury and if the allegations could have resulted in incarceration. See Torbet, P., & Szymanski, L. (1998). *State legislative responses to violent juvenile crime: 1996–1997 Update*. Washington, DC: U.S. Department of Justice.

8. National Advisory Committee on Criminal Justice Standards and Goals. (1976). *Juvenile justice and delinquency prevention*. Washington, DC: U.S. Government Printing Office.

9. Adapted from Rottman, D. B., Flango, C. R., Cantrell, M. T., Hansen, R., & LaFountain, N. (2000). *State court organization 1998*. Washington, DC: U.S. Department of Justice.

10. At 387 U.S. 1, 19–21, 26–28, 87 S. Ct. 1428, 1439–1440, 1442–1444, 18 L. Ed. 2d 527 (1967).

11. At 383 U.S. 541, 86 S. Ct. 1045, 16 L. Ed. 2d 84 (1966).

12. For a good discussion of the role of juvenile prosecutors, see Rubin, H. T. (1980). The emerging prosecutor dominance of the juvenile court intake process. *Crime and Delinquency, 26*.

13. At 397 U.S. 358, 90 S. Ct. 1068, 25 L. Ed. 2d 368 (1970).

14. For a good discussion of the role of defense counsel, see Rubin, H. T. (1996). The role of defense attorneys in juvenile justice proceedings. *Juvenile Justice Update, 2*.

15. Black, H. C. (1968). *Black's law dictionary* (4th ed., rev., p. 834). St. Paul, MN: West Publishing.

16. From LaVera, D. (2003, October 31). ABA president says new reports show "conveyor belt justice" hurting children and undermining public safety. *American Bar Association News Release*.

17. For more information, see Puzzanchera, C., Stahl, A. L., Finnegan, T. A., Tierney, N., & Snyder, H. N. (2003). *Juvenile court statistics 1998*. Washington, DC: Office of Juvenile Justice and Delinquency Prevention.

18. See *OJJDP guide to good juvenile detention practice*. (1997). Washington, DC: U.S. Government Printing Office.

19. Black, H. C. (1968). *Black's law dictionary* (4th ed., rev., p. 1344). St. Paul, MN: West Publishing.

20. Ibid. (p. 204).

21. At 383 U.S. 541, 86 S. Ct. 1045, 16 L. Ed. 2d 84 (1966).

22. Adapted from Snyder, H. N., & Sickmund, M. (1999). *Juvenile offenders and victims: 1999 national report* (p. 107). Washington, DC: U.S. Department of Justice.

23. Ibid. (p. 211).

8 Institutional Corrections for Juveniles

Juvenile correctional facilities are, theoretically, designed to rehabilitate youths rather than punish them in the manner of adult prisons. Many of these facilities are extremely secure, and are designed to hold serious offenders who have been processed through the system as juvenile delinquents. Other facilities serve the same function as jails, holding suspected offenders in secure institutions pending disposition of their cases. This can be problematic. For example, A.M. was arrested in July 1999 on charges of indecent conduct in Lake Township, Pennsylvania.[1] He was taken to the Luzerne County Juvenile Detention Center, a secure facility, pending disposition of his case. While at the detention center, A.M. was physically assaulted repeatedly. Residents hit, beat, and humiliated him on numerous occasions, resulting in cuts and bruises over much of his body.

Although administrators had ordered that he be housed in the girls' wing for his own protection, workers ignored this order several times, resulting in more physical assaults. A lawsuit was brought on behalf of A.M., which was partially successful.

The compulsory (forced) confinement of youths is a drastic, yet commonplace, procedure for dealing with young people who are deemed to pose a danger to themselves and society. Juvenile institutionalization is certainly controversial, but it has long been an acceptable practice, becoming a ubiquitous feature of Anglo-American juvenile justice systems during the nineteenth century. Since that time, institutionalization has evolved into a modern network of detention systems that ostensibly rehabilitate chronically deviant youths. Although the underlying objectives of juvenile institutionalization are rehabilitation and the protection of at-risk youths, there is a significant history of debate on the attributes, organizational models, and management practices of these institutions.

Photo 8.1   A handcuffed teenager in custody awaiting further processing.

At the outset, two important distinctions must be understood regarding juvenile institutions. First, juvenile correctional models generally reflect two types of facilities: **Long-term correctional facilities** and **short-term temporary care facilities**. Long-term correctional facilities include training schools, youth ranches and forestry camps, and boot camps. These facilities usually segregate males and females and incorporate rehabilitative correctional programs for residents. Short-term temporary care facilities include jails, youth shelters, juvenile detention homes, and reception centers. These facilities often accommodate males and females in the same residential site, and do not provide correctional programs. A second distinction is the difference between secure and nonsecure correctional facilities. **Secure correctional facilities** literally lock in juvenile offenders so that residents have no opportunity or discretion to leave the facility, absent an escape plan. Secure facilities include long-term correctional facilities. **Nonsecure correctional facilities** usually require lockups only at specified times during the day, such as at night. They are also less foreboding in design, such as juvenile detention homes and youth shelters.

How many youths live in residential facilities? One comprehensive measurement project is the **Census of Juveniles in Residential Placement** (CJRP), which "collects individual data on each juvenile held in the residential facility, including gender, date of birth, race, placement authority, most serious offense charged, court adjudication status, date of admission, and security status."[2] The CJRP, which is conducted by the Office of Juvenile Justice and Delinquency Prevention, has established criteria for inclusion in its report, including that residents must be

- Under age 21
- Assigned a bed at the time of the survey
- Charged with or adjudicated for an offense
- In residential placement because of the offense

These criteria are termed the *CJRP criteria*. In its first report, the CJRP described the following juvenile residential population:[3]

- There were 125,805 total residents.
- 105,790 residents met CJRP criteria.
- 20,015 did not meet CJRP criteria.
- Of those who met CJRP criteria, 98,913 were incarcerated for delinquency; 35,357 for person offenses; 26,489 for violent offenses; and 6,877 for status offenses.

It is not an exaggeration to comment that juvenile institutionalization has received mixed support since its inception and has often been roundly criticized. Criticisms of juvenile correctional institutions include the following opinions:

- Confinement is too harsh; conversely, confinement is too lenient.
- Few truly rehabilitative programs are available.
- Correctional staff are inadequately or incorrectly trained for the task of working with severely troubled youths.
- Correctional staff do not care about their clients.
- Correctional institutions *prisonize* delinquents so that they become accustomed to being institutionalized, where they do little more than hone their criminal skills.

Discussion of these issues is likely to continue unabated (unending and unresolved) for the foreseeable future. In this chapter, our discussion of the role of institutional corrections for juveniles reviews the following topics:

- Background: Historical Perspectives on Juvenile Corrections
- Understanding the System: Goals of Juvenile Corrections
- Innovation and Ingenuity: Nominal and Intermediate Sanctions
- Detention and Correction: Confinement Options
- Examining Confinement: Controversies and Protections

CHAPTER PERSPECTIVE 8.1

The World Within: Subcultures in Juvenile Correctional Institutions

Juvenile institutions often have elaborate social ubcultures. This is a phenomenon that exists in every type of institution, regardless of whether they are public or private, are mixed gendered, or have high or low levels of security designations. As in the case of adult correctional institutions, youth subcultures are characterized by power centers, hierarchies, and codes of behavior based on reputation and respect. These subcultures also reflect social trends found outside of the institutions, such as gang affiliations and neighborhood reputations.

In male institutions, residents tend to be both aggressive and defensive, so that perceived slights can be met with violence. In fact, boys tend to create subcultures that are similar to those found in adult male prisons.[4] A slight shove, flashing a gang sign, or a wrong look can easily be considered as disrespectful and worthy of retaliation. Codes of respect are paramount and incorporate personal standards for behavior among residents and between residents and staff. Boys in long-term institutions can be highly aggressive, and among the worst labels a male can have is that of being a "punk" within the subculture. The most aggressive—and hence most respected—boys tend to be at the top of the social hierarchy and are left alone. On the other hand, boys with reputations as weak "punks" exist at the bottom of the hierarchy and are often victimized by other boys. This environment frequently leads to the *prisonization* of residents and greatly increases the likelihood of recidivism and career delinquency and crime.

Institutionalized girls tend to replicate subcultures found in adult female prisons.[5] Unlike their male counterparts, who create status arrangements based on strength and power, female subcultures re-create family relationships. Male–female gender roles are adopted by girls, so that surrogate father, mother, sibling, and cousin roles form their institutional status arrangements. These roles tend to be more mutually supportive than male roles, so that violence is not as common as in male facilities—although it certainly occurs. Thus, the prisonization process is less likely to be as strong for girls as it is for boys.

Demographic differences influence the types of subcultures found in correctional institutions. For example, juveniles housed in public long-term institutions represent a proportionately high number of poor, disadvantaged, and nonwhite residents. On the other hand, residents in private institutions tend to be from a more affluent economic background and have a higher proportion of white residents. These differences bring different value systems and personal experiences to bear on an institution's subculture.

Background: Historical Perspectives on Juvenile Corrections

The advancement of juvenile corrections in the United States has always been a manifestation (outgrowth or result) of existing cultural attitudes toward incarceration in general, and youthful offenders in particular. As discussed in previous chapters, the progression of juvenile justice process advanced through several critical eras of American history. All of these eras addressed the remediation of wayward youths within the context of society's prevailing views on child rearing. When social mores changed, so too did accepted practices on dealing with juvenile offenders.

Perspectives on Juvenile Corrections During the Colonial Era

In colonial America, parental authority (always headed by the father) was recognized as the principal arbiter of the fate of rebellious children. Colonial courts regularly acknowledged the absolute authority of parents over their children, and masters over their apprentices. Parents and masters wielded literal power over the lives of children, because colonial laws permitted the death penalty for incorrigible children.[6]

During this era, penal institutions such as prisons and jails often housed men, women, and children together in the same cells. No separation was made between those convicted of felonies and those convicted of misdemeanors, nor was there a differentiation between sane and mentally ill inmates. All received the same treatment in the same institutions. No juvenile correctional system or institutions existed during this era, so that children older than nine years of age were convicted as adults and received the same punishments. Juvenile delinquents and incorrigibles were incarcerated in prisons or other adult facilities, and could also be put in stocks and pillories, flogged, beaten, or publicly humiliated. Some youths were assigned to mandatory apprenticeships, were sent to live with farming families, or were sent away on long voyages aboard fishing and whaling vessels.

Perspectives on Juvenile Corrections During the Refuge and Child-Saving Era

As discussed in Chapter 2, Houses of Refuge and the Child Saving Movement were a response to the growth of a new urban industrial working population. The prevailing attitude of the time was that people were poor because they had chosen to live lives of vice and indolence. Poverty occurred because of criminal behavior, not the reverse.[7] Children born into this population of paupers were—according to philanthropists of the era—particularly vulnerable to urban ills and corrupt influences. If these youths were to be saved from lives of pauperism themselves, they required special treatment. Prisons and jails were considered to be inhumane institutions for juveniles, and reformers established new youth-centered facilities.

Houses of Refuge. Houses of Refuge were established to accommodate both children in trouble and children in need. Initially, confinement was considered to be beneficial for idle, poor, incorrigible, homeless, and delinquent children alike. There was at first no due process in the modern sense, and these youths were sometimes simply taken from the streets and placed in homes. Residents were usually not separated, received identical treatment regardless of their reason for being confined, and were required to participate in the same activities. According to the prevailing theories of the day, these facilities corrected behavior through stern compassion and paternalistic benevolence. Although concerted attempts were made to replicate ordered, disciplined, and compassionate family atmospheres, the buildings themselves were usually modeled after jail and prison architectures, and could be quite ominous in appearance.

Sentences in Houses of Refuge were indeterminate and strictly governed by principles of *parens patriae* and *in loco parentis*—meaning that directors of these institutions decided when juveniles were fit to return to society. Terms of residence could range from several weeks to two or more years. The first Houses were modeled after the congregate system of corrections, in which residents were housed in large cells with many other residents. Work, eating, and other activities were conducted as a regimented group, including marching to institutional functions and standing on parade for inspection. Juveniles wore institutional clothing and were given institutional haircuts (as in adult prisons). Discipline for rule-breaking was severe by modern standards, and included corporal punishment such as whippings, beatings, and uncomfortable physical manipulation. Solitary confinement, bread-and-water diets, and meal deprivation were also typical punishments. However, it was believed that once order, respect, and fear of authority were established, youths would benefit from the paternalism and friendship of House administrators.

Racism was common within this system. Racial disparities in Houses of Refuge existed in both the North and South. Southern youth facilities were invariably segregated by race, and, although some Northern Houses were integrated, African American youths were often sent to jails or prisons.

Child Savers and Reform Schools. Houses of Refuge were ineffective as truly "correctional" institutions. Juvenile crime and pauperism did not appreciably abate in urban areas, and children in need who were housed with delinquents often became victims or were exposed to criminal activity. At the same time, cultural support for the severe methods used in Houses of Refuge began to erode and shift toward new and more enlightened theories of rearing children. Corporal punishment, physical discomfort, and fear of authority as rehabilitative methods were no longer considered to be cure-all alternatives. Thus, although physical punishments continued, and were abusive by modern standards, they were counterbalanced by emotion-based methods to bring about conformity—such as guilt, shame, and persuasion.

As discussed in Chapter 2, the Child-Saving Movement established reformatories (commonly referred to as reform schools) that softened the methods used by Houses of Refuge. Reform programs were emphasized, particularly vocational training, education, and vigorous work. Because of this emphasis on training and education, reform schools also came to be known as industrial schools or training schools. Regardless of their title, reformatories usually continued the old practice of confining dissimilar types of juvenile wards within the same facilities, so that delinquents and nondelinquents were housed together in a congregate manner. Discipline was strictly maintained for all residents, sometimes violently, but it was not as *exclusively* violent as in the Houses of Refuge.

Unlike Houses of Refuge, most reform schools were located in rural districts rather than cities. This represented the implementation of the **cottage system**, or cottage plan, in which reformers designed rural reformatories as compounds with separate structures and dormitories. The belief was that residents who worked in industrial schools in the countryside would absorb wholesome rural values and virtues and thereby grow into responsible and productive adults. Juveniles were housed in dormitory-style cottages with no more than a few dozen residents per cottage. This development—the combination of industrial training and cottage-like dwellings—was an important innovation, because many modern reformatories have replicated and updated this model.

Modern Institutionalization in Perspective

It became clear during the 1960s and 1970s that juvenile correctional facilities—by then largely designed on the industrial school/cottage system model—were, in practice, not serving juveniles as well as envisioned. For example, although institutionalization was intended to be a remedy primarily for the most violent and recidivist offenders, nearly 50% of residents were status offenders.[8] Also, some reformatories continued to administer abusive corporal punishments to rule-breakers and runaways. In response to these reports, reformers in the mid-1970s revamped juvenile correctional systems nationwide.

Two important revisions occurred in the philosophy of managing confined juveniles. First, corporal punishments were officially discouraged, and abusive punishments were prohibited. Second, status offenders were effectively removed from reformatories designed to deal with juvenile delinquents. With the passage of the Juvenile Justice and Delinquency Prevention Act of 1974 (discussed previously in Chapter 2), jurisdictions were prohibited from institutionalizing juveniles solely because they were status offenders. These reforms led to fundamental modifications in juvenile incarceration policies, resulting in fewer status offender residents, an increase of nonresidential programs for nondelinquents, and an end to officially sanctioned physical abuse. In the modern era, most states continue to use the training school model for juvenile correctional institutions, but in conjunction with the deinstitutionalization of status offenders.

TABLE 8.1   HISTORICAL PROFILES OF JUVENILE CORRECTIONS PROGRAMS

Correctional programs have been refined and developed throughout the eras of juvenile justice process in the United States. The programmatic profiles that were adopted during these eras reflected the prevailing degree of enlightenment toward defining and dealing with juvenile offenders. This table summarizes the fundamental features of several eras of juvenile justice process.

Era	Programmatic Profile		
	Treatment Philosophy	Typical Facilities	Desired Outcome
Colonial Period	Fear of authority Corporal discipline	Prisons and jails Public humiliation	Absolute obedience Spiritual salvation
Refuge Period	Paternalism Corporal discipline	Large congregate buildings	Rehabilitation Respect of authority
Child Savers Period	Paternalism Corporal discipline Emotion-based persuasion	Dormitories, cottages	Rehabilitation
Modern Era	Therapeutic intervention	Secure and nonsecure homes and schools	Rehabilitation

Table 8.1 summarizes the philosophies, types of facilities, and desired outcomes of the eras of juvenile corrections.

Understanding the System: Goals of Juvenile Corrections

Modern juvenile correctional systems serve a number of purposes, many of which are similar to those underpinning adult correctional systems. However, it must be remembered that rehabilitation is the underlying philosophy of juvenile corrections—and of the juvenile justice system in general. The adult system is distinguishable in that it emphasizes a strong tendency toward punishment. The following principles and practices are typically cited as rationales for juvenile correctional strategies:

- Protecting society from violent and otherwise antisocial individuals
- Removing offenders from the community for placement in "total institutions" that regulate every aspect of the residents' environment[9]
- Holding offenders accountable for their behavior through mandatory institutionalization
- "Correcting" deviant behavior through the development of interpersonal, social, and vocational skills
- Providing remedial education and training to rehabilitate offenders and prepare them for future reintegration into mainstream society

Political and Popular Culture: Conservatives Versus Liberals

There is no single categorization or descriptor for the goals and objectives of juvenile corrections, largely because several philosophies of corrections have been developed throughout the history of the United States. This has been the case for both juvenile and adult correctional systems. In the modern era, political and popular culture have categorized these philosophies under the headings of "conservative" and "liberal" in an attempt to delineate fundamental differences in policy and methodologies.

The conservative approach to delinquency, crime, and corrections is to promote get-tough law and order policies that punish offenders and remove them from society. Retribution is considered by conservatives to be a perfectly legitimate rationale for institutionalization, and rehabilitation is held to be a secondary goal. Correctional institutions best serve the public interest if they are austere (simple or bare) and severe. Also, the solution to the problem of more offenders receiving longer sentences is simply to build more correctional institutions. The current crackdown on delinquency and crime, which has been the prevailing approach since the early 1980s, is considered to be an application of conservative principles.

In comparison, liberal approaches also recognize the need for institutionalization but tend to emphasize treatment and rehabilitation programs for offenders. Community corrections such as work-release and mandatory community service programs are typical examples of liberal approaches toward the treatment of offenders. Juvenile correctional institutions in particular should be designed to be benevolent re-education centers for youthful offenders.

Classifying Correctional Philosophies

Modern goals for juvenile corrections vary among jurisdictions, but systems generally reflect one or more prevailing correctional philosophies. These philosophies include rehabilitation, deterrence, incapacitation, and retribution.

Rehabilitation. Rehabilitation refers to treatment programs that try to salvage young offenders, and this approach was outlined above under the liberal approach to juvenile corrections. In the current cultural environment in the United States, the influence of rehabilitation has declined contemporaneously with the rising influence of punishment-oriented judgments.[10] Nevertheless, it continues to be a significant philosophy because, as discussed in previous chapters, rehabilitation has historically represented the theoretical foundation for juvenile justice process in the United States.

Most juvenile correctional systems have adopted some degree of rehabilitation as a goal, and they continue to diagnose and treat emotionally and socially dysfunctional youths. One reason for the ongoing viability of rehabilitation programs is the presumption that juveniles are more likely than adults to respond positively to rehabilitative therapies. Many experts believe that youths can be reclaimed from the effects of their limited life experiences, so that juveniles who desire rehabilitation can be rehabilitated. Thus, innovative programs and therapies are designed to help in the recovery of juvenile delinquents while they are still susceptible to positive treatments. Because of these innovations, the juvenile justice system offers a broad range of services for institutionalized youths.

Deterrence. The fear of swift and severe punishment has long been used by governments to control deviant behavior. In theory, harsh punishments will deter individuals who might otherwise be prone to break the law from actually doing so (general deterrence), as well as individuals who have already violated the law (specific deterrence). In previous generations, public hangings and displaying offenders in stocks and pillories served to punish lawbreakers and deter other would-be violators.

Deterrence has become quite popular in the modern juvenile justice system. Confinement, regimentation, and longer sentences are commonly imposed on young offenders. Wilderness camps, boot camps, and juvenile maximum security institutions exist in most states. Whether or not these programs genuinely deter potential delinquents is debatable, because deterrence by its nature relies on one's *knowledge* of existing legal sanctions, and that one will exercise sound reasoning in deciding to forego breaking the law. In fact, juveniles may be completely ignorant of existing laws, or they may calculate that the benefits of delinquency offset its costs, or they may simply act out impulsively with very little calculation involved.

Incapacitation. As a punishment philosophy, the logic of incapacitation is uncomplicated and easily understood: Simply impose a severe penalty that will make an offender incapable of committing further crimes. Incapacitating judgments can include long-term imprisonment or execution. Examples of policies developed in support of incapacitation can include early targeting of career criminals, mandatory life terms for recidivists, and fixed (determinate) sentencing for all offenders.

The application of incapacitation to juvenile offenders has included institutionalization in youth facilities (when processed through the juvenile justice system) and imprisonment (when processed through the criminal justice system). The rationale behind institutionalizing juveniles as an incapacitating remedy is that recidivists will be prevented from breaking the law, and hence a number of crimes will be prevented that otherwise would have occurred. This makes sense in theory, but it is not known if frequent and long-term institutionalization appreciably reduces the delinquency rate.

Retribution. The outright punishment of youthful offenders is a popular and acceptable policy option in the United States. This approach represents the

TABLE 8.2   ESSENTIAL ELEMENTS OF JUVENILE CORRECTIONAL PHILOSOPHIES

The juvenile justice system has historically promoted rehabilitation as the fundamental goal for dealing with young offenders. In comparison, adult correctional theories have always included some measure of punishment. Although rehabilitation is certainly at the center of most juvenile programs, juvenile correctional systems have adopted some of the traditionally adult philosophies of punishment, as is illustrated in this table.

Correctional Philosphy	Programmatic Profile		
	Methods/ Approaches	Effect on Offender	Desired Outcome
Rehabilitation	Innovative programs and therapies	Remediation	Offender as a productive member of society
Deterrence	Publicize examples of severe penalties	General and specific fear of punishment	Reduction in recidivism and criminal behavior
Incapacitation	Removal of offender from society	Unable to commit further crimes	Elimination of offender as a threat to society
Retribution	Retaliation and severe punishment	Suffers consequences of criminal behavior	Punishment of the offender

theoretical separation of rehabilitation options from penalties based on societal anger over the behavior of juvenile delinquents. Treatment becomes secondary to retaliation against youths who break the law. Public support for incarceration and tough conditions inside institutions is a reflection of the popularity of retribution. There exists an underlying acceptance that juveniles who engage in felonious offenses should be treated as adults, because the harm to society committed by youths is identical to harm committed by adults. The policy outcome of this approach is that increasing numbers of delinquents have been diverted into the criminal justice system.

Table 8.2 summarizes the fundamental elements of correctional philosophies used in juvenile and adult systems in the United States.

Innovation and Ingenuity:
Nominal and Intermediate Sanctions

It is important to understand that the process of correcting juvenile deviance does not always begin with institutionalization. In many cases, entry into the juvenile correctional system is considered to be a final remedy, reserved for chronic offenders such as juvenile recidivists and perpetrators of serious felonies. Prior to institutionalization, several middle-ground alternatives are available to youth authorities in state juvenile justice systems.[11] Nominal and intermediate sanctions are generally reserved for first-time offenders who have not committed felonies or engaged in violence. These alternatives—adapted for the requirements of specific jurisdictions—can be roughly categorized as:

- *Nominal sanctions.* Relatively benign admonitions (softened warnings) by the juvenile authorities to young offenders. Judges deliver stern written or verbal warnings to delinquents to instruct them on the significance of their behavior and the types of severe penalties that await them should they break the law again.
- *Intermediate sanctions.* Intensive alternatives to long-term institutionalization. These sanctions include house arrest, "shock" incarceration (for example, boot camps), and electronic monitoring. Supervision of juveniles can be quite intensive.

Nominal sanctions (also referred to as *nominal dispositions*) are usually meted out to first offenders, and are intended to warn them about the ultimate consequences of their antisocial behavior. Nominal sanctions represent an application of rehabilitative corrections for juveniles deemed to be most susceptible to positive intervention and correction. This alternative may originate from a variety of officials within the juvenile justice system. For example, as discussed in Chapter 6, police dispositions can be resolved with nothing more than verbal warnings. This type of disposition is also a nominal sanction, and is an exercise of police discretion after an on-the-scene assessment of the juvenile. Juvenile court judges also possess the discretionary authority during adjudications to deliver nominal sanctions to offenders. In all instances, the decision is based on the individual offender and the nature of the offense.

Intermediate sanctions (also referred to as *intermediate punishments*) usually require some form of intensive supervision either in the community or in an alternative juvenile residential institution. Probation agreements often incorporate intermediate sanctions, and conditions for participation can include highly restrictive correctional options that nevertheless fall short of full incarceration. Sanctions typically include the following restrictions:

- House arrest, involving mandatory home detention except for approved (and sometimes required) activities, such as school attendance
- Electronic monitoring, requiring offenders to wear electronic bracelets and anklets, which are monitored by juvenile justice officials
- Unannounced status visits by probation officers or other officials at the offender's school, home, or other location
- Imposition of curfews
- Drug and alcohol testing
- Limitations placed on associations with certain people, or locations
- Innovative incarceration alternatives, such as boot camps

Although most confinement-oriented alternatives occur in nonsecure institutions, some programs do use secure facilities. However, these programs represent innovative options such as boot camps. All community-based alternatives involve some degree of programmatic supervision and reporting procedures. Careful supervision and evaluation are critical components for successful intermediate alternatives and are conducted by probation officers, social workers, or other officials, who regularly assess their clients' progress and compliance.

An offender who fails to comply with mandated nominal and intermediate sanctions is likely to be assigned to a secure correctional facility for the duration of his or her sentence. There are several advantages for juvenile justice authorities when they implement nominal and intermediate sanctions as preliminary alternatives to final institutionalization:

- Juveniles remain close to their communities and are more easily reintegrated after their sentences expire.
- The recidivism rate is lower for offenders who participate in nominal and intermediate programs in comparison to those who are institutionalized.
- There is an increased likelihood that participants will benefit from community-based vocational and educational remediation.
- The juvenile justice system's "net" is wider for participants, so that a broader range of programs and agencies are available to assist in remediation.
- Nominal and intermediate sanctions are, as a practical matter, cheaper than institutionalization.

_____ Detention and Correction: Confinement Options

Residential juvenile correctional facilities exist in every juvenile justice system. Although approximately 60% of these facilities are privately operated, approximately 70% of juvenile offenders are held in public facilities.[12] The obvious implication of these statistics is that fewer public institutions hold larger populations than do private facilities.

When considering the question of housing juveniles in correctional institutions, a conceptual distinction must be made between preadjudication detention and postadjudication detention. **Preadjudication detention** refers to holding a juvenile in a youth facility prior to the final disposition of his or her case by a juvenile judge. These are short-term confinement facilities, such as nonsecure residential facilities, juvenile detention centers, and jails. **Postadjudication detention** refers to confining juveniles in correctional facilities under court order after their cases have been adjudicated. These include short-term confinement facilities, long-term facilities such as training schools, and alternative detention programs (e.g., wilderness ranches and boot camps).

Photo 8.2   A cafeteria in a secure juvenile facility.

Nonsecure Residential Facilities

Nonsecure residential facilities are institutions that provide a more wholesome atmosphere than locked detention facilities. They are often managed as homes or rescue facilities that provide different kinds of services, ranging from shelter to intensive treatment. Examples of nonsecure residential facilities include shelter care facilities, group homes, and foster homes.

Shelter Care Facilities. These facilities—commonly referred to simply as *shelters*—are nonsecure residential institutions that temporarily house juveniles. They are frequently used as a "middle-ground" alternative, falling between the youth's family home and secure detention facilities. Most shelters do not have locked doors, and are typically used as temporary housing for status offenders and others while they await final placement to another facility or the family home. Residents are housed for periods from overnight to several days. Because of this mission, and the short duration of residency, most shelters are not designed to treat or punish juveniles.

Group Homes. Group homes are designed to treat juveniles, and are widely used in most states. Some group homes are state-run facilities, while others are privately managed. They are by definition nonsecure facilities, managed by professional juvenile corrections workers who serve as administrators, teachers, and counselors. Group homes try to replicate the values and social interactions of families, which in practice means that most homes are not large facilities and usually house approximately a dozen youths. This philosophy has also meant that group homes are integrated into neighborhoods, residents attend community schools, and they are expected to participate in community activities. Within the homes there exists regulated freedom of movement and interaction with the professional staff.

Foster Homes. Foster care programs are very common in the United States. Foster placement is supervised by youth services agencies, managed by visiting caseworkers, and implemented by **foster families**. Foster homes expand the concept of family replication by loosening the institutional restrictions found in group homes, and allowing residents to share a greater degree of freedom of movement and interaction. Homes are nonsecure with a small number of residents. Foster care is generally limited to victims of abuse and neglect rather than lawbreakers. Because residents are victims, foster programs attempt as much as possible to substitute the foster family for a youth's biological family.

Juvenile Detention Centers

Detention centers are roughly comparable to adult jails, and were first established during the late nineteenth century as an alternative to holding juveniles in jails. Unlike shelter care facilities and group homes, detention centers are secure residential facilities with regimented schedules and living conditions. Like jails, detention centers are secure, temporary preadjudication institutions that are used to house accused offenders until the final disposition of their cases.

Most juvenile detention centers are public facilities that are managed by court systems or government agencies. A smaller number of centers are privately owned facilities that are managed by nongovernmental, privately owned agencies. Although juvenile detention centers were considered to be "humane" alternatives to jails, they were anything but humane during much of their history. Until the 1960s and 1970s, conditions at detention centers were usually dysfunctional, and often quite harsh. In the modern era, a concerted effort has been made in many state systems to improve conditions and programs in detention centers.

Jails

The use of jails as a primary institution for holding juveniles ended with the establishment of Houses of Refuge and later juvenile facilities. Conditions in nineteenth-century jails were poor by adult standards and horrendous for children. Youths were frequently abused and preyed on by adults in jails, so that reformers such as the child savers made a concerted effort to remove young people from these institutions.[13] Although they were largely successful in their efforts, and jails have long ceased to be the *principal* holding institution for juveniles, significant numbers of juveniles continue to be processed through jails. Many of these placements are of short duration—often for no more than a few hours—but other placements are made pending adjudication or trial.

In the modern era, there has been a general reduction in the jailing of juveniles. One incentive for the decline in the number of juvenile placements in jails was the passage of the Juvenile Justice and Delinquency Prevention Act of 1974, which tied federal funding to the removal of juveniles from jails and other adult facilities. However, despite the prevailing philosophy of removing youths from adult facilities, and the passage of the Juvenile Justice and Delinquency Prevention Act, several reasons account for the continuing placement of juveniles in adult jails:

- Correctional systems believe that juveniles can be safely housed in jails if they are separated from the adult inmate population. The argument is that the juveniles will be protected, and levels of security are better in jails.
- The modern policy of waiving juvenile offenders into the adult criminal court system for trial has led to the placement of juveniles in the same detention system as anyone else awaiting criminal trial.
- Many jurisdictions argue that they do not have adequate financial or institutional capacity to house youths in facilities set aside exclusively for juvenile offenders. Their argument is that jails are the only acceptable alternative.

The placement of juveniles in jails persists for these and other reasons. As a result, the movement to remove juveniles from adult jails—begun in the nineteenth century—has continued into the present day.

Training Schools

Training schools are secure residential correctional facilities, managed as either public or private institutions.[14] Their numbers have steadily increased in recent years, and they have become commonplace juvenile institutions in most jurisdictions. Although the underlying mission of training schools is to promote rehabilitation by providing intensive training and treatment, many are highly secure institutions—designed in much the same manner as adult jails and prisons. Nationally, there is a great deal of variation in the management of these facilities, whose organizational, administrative, and architectural profiles differ significantly among juvenile justice systems. Differences also exist in programmatic services, numbers of residents, staff qualifications, and the types of residents served. Despite these differences, training schools generally provide a broader range of programs than are found in juvenile detention centers, jails, or alternative detention programs. Academic programs, special education services, vocational training, and medical care are regularly provided.

Most facilities have designated security levels (such as medium and maximum), which are often reflected in the physical architecture of the schools. For example, maximum-security institutions have highly secure fences or walls, cells, locked hallways and doors, and bars. On the other hand, medium-security institutions may resemble dormitories where residents freely intermingle, or they may perhaps use the cottage model. Because serious offenders are often incarcerated in these schools, the culture among residents can be violent and antisocial.

Alternative Detention Programs

Training schools are not the only institutions designed to house juveniles for extended periods of time. Long-term juvenile correctional institutions also include innovative alternative detention programs such as **wilderness programs** and **boot camps**.

Wilderness Programs. The nineteenth-century practice of removing youths from the allegedly corrupting influences of cities and relocating them to the wholesome countryside has been updated in the modern era. Modern-day wilderness programs are minimum-security residential correctional institutions that are located in rural settings. These programs are usually reserved for first-time offenders or other juveniles who have committed minor offenses; serious offenders are sent to training schools or other medium- to maximum-security institutions. Although these facilities are innovative alternatives to training schools, not every state has adopted an updated rural correctional model as a matter of policy. Among the states that have applied this approach, **forestry camps** and **ranches** are typical models for nonurban, minimum-security youth correctional facilities.

Forestry camps are usually established on public lands (such as state parks), where residents perform conservation duties, cleanups of public grounds, land clearing, and other maintenance work. Professional staff members are assigned to the camps to supervise participants and are trained to provide counseling and treatment as needed. Many of these administrators are trained therapists and social workers. Programmatically, treatment includes on-site therapy as well as supervised off-site excursions to neighboring towns.

Ranches are located in only a few states. Similar to forestry camps, professional staff are assigned to manage the camps and provide treatment services. Work assignments for participants are also similar, and residents are required to work the ranch much as any other ranch hand. Unlike forestry camps, which are normally public state-run institutions, ranches are often private institutions.

Boot Camps. Regimentation has long been considered to be a solution to deviant behavior. Military-style discipline, group cohesion, physical training, and strictly enforced obedience to rules can theoretically rebuild an undisciplined offender into a productive member of the community. In the past, youths were subjected to inhumane regimentation and corporal punishment inside the first juvenile correctional facilities. In the modern era, boot camps have come to symbolize an updated approach to regimentation.

Drill instructors replicate training techniques used in boot camps of the armed forces, adapting their methods to the special needs of juvenile offenders. The purpose is to shock residents into socially productive conformity over a period of 30 to 120 days. Boot camps are popular and have become quite common nationally. Experts and many juvenile justice professionals have concluded that juveniles can be rehabilitated by the proper applications of reward, punishment, discipline, responsibility, and self-motivation.

Table 8.3 summarizes the characteristics, duration of confinement, and desired outcomes of juvenile correctional institutions.

TABLE 8.3   JUVENILE CONFINEMENT OPTIONS

Modern-era residential juvenile correctional facilities are a direct outgrowth of nineteenth-century reformist movements. Juvenile correctional systems are designed to allow for short- and long-duration incarceration, as well as a variety of creative alternatives to custody. This table summarizes the programmatic profiles of several confinement options.

Confinement Facility	Programmatic Profile		
	Institutional Descripton	Duration of Custody	Desired Outcome
Nonsecure Residential	Unlocked shelters and homes	Variable, up to age of majority	Resident as a productive member of society
Juvenile Detention Centers	Locked buildings	Temporary pending disposition	Diversion or processing into system
Jails	Locked correctional facilities	Temporary pending disposition	Diversion or processing into system
Training Schools	Locked cottages and dormitories	Variable, up to age of majority	Resident as a productive member of society
Alternative Detention	Restrictive camps and ranches	Variable, short duration	Resident as a productive member of society

Examining Confinement:
Controversies and Protections

Confining youths in juvenile correctional institutions is a very serious dispositional alternative. From the standpoint of greater society, it is also an absolute necessity because communities simply cannot permit certain juveniles to remain at large and must impose institutional constraints upon them. Violent and recidivist juveniles in particular have to be confined for the greater good of the community. Although necessary, confinement and custody without treatment and rehabilitation can become a starting point for careers in delinquency and crime. This is a troubling prospect, because the rate of juvenile institutionalization in correctional facilities has steadily increased.[15]

The Demographics of Confinement

The full picture of residential juvenile correctional systems cannot be understood without a demographic frame of reference. Nationally, minorities are disproportionately confined in juvenile correctional facilities. For example, African Americans are overrepresented in every phase of the juvenile justice system. Also, although minorities represent roughly one third of the juvenile population in the United States, approximately two thirds of the residents of public correctional institutions were from members of minority groups.[16] For violent offenses, members of minority groups account for approximately 70% of juveniles held in custody for violent offenses.[17] Within the overall juvenile population in custody, African Americans represent a much higher rate of institutionalization than do members of other racial and ethnic groups. As a proportion of every 100,000 persons within demographic groups, the following data were found in the CJRP:[18]

- 205 of every 100,000 Asian juveniles were placed in residential correctional facilities.
- 204 of every 100,000 white juveniles were placed in residential correctional facilities.
- 515 of every 100,000 Latino juveniles were placed in residential correctional facilities.
- 525 of every 100,000 Native American juveniles were placed in residential correctional facilities.
- 1,018 of every 100,000 African American juveniles were placed in residential correctional facilities.

Regarding gender statistics, girls account for only approximately 15% of correctional residents.[19]

Fundamental Issues

Confinement in correctional institutions inevitably affects young residents emotionally, psychologically, or socially—and not necessarily in a positive or rehabilitative manner. It is idealistic (and arguably naïve) to presume that the best-laid plans of policy makers succeed in achieving their stated goals exactly. True rehabilitation is quite elusive in many cases, and one important inhibitor against rehabilitation is the reality that juveniles form their own subcultures inside correctional systems. Subcultures are found in all types of facilities, whether they are high-security training schools, minimum-security forestry camps, or short-duration juvenile detention centers. Thus, the overall effect of institutionalization can be profoundly unsettling for many youths.

Within this milieu of mixed programmatic success and unwholesome institutional subcultures are laws and regulations that govern the treatment of juvenile residents. The paternalistic severity and violence common to juvenile institutions in previous eras is no longer permissible. The fundamental reality is that juveniles who are sent to correctional institutions do have legal protection from abuse and neglect and are entitled to receive humane rehabilitative treatment.

Harsh Realities: Quality of Life in Juvenile Institutions

Conditions. Historically, the quality of life for residents of juvenile institutions was indeed grim. Although quality has improved markedly in the modern era, experts continue to find that conditions inside modern youth correctional facilities are often inadequate and frequently in need of improvement. Research indicates that at any given time there are systemic problems of inadequate security, crowded residential space, and improper health care.[20] For example, a study in 2000 reported that 39% of juvenile facilities held more residents than they had standard beds.[21] The behavior of residents inside secure residential juvenile facilities often involves acting out aggressively against other residents and administrators, or self-destructive behavior such as suicidal tendencies.

Facilities with large populations—and especially those that are crowded—generally have higher rates of violence and injury than do smaller, less crowded facilities. Institutional crowding is, in fact conducive to violence because of the administration's inability to closely monitor youths and because subcultural pressures are intensified. Fortunately, not every institution suffers from these problems, and many are quite efficient. In this regard, research has also indicated that, in general, residents are adequately housed, are well fed, receive recreational time, and are properly clothed.[22]

Prisonization. One problem encountered by juvenile authorities, and indeed by all of society, is the impact of long-term confinement on young residents. It is a fact that people become institutionalized when confined to a facility and exposed to certain conditions over a long period of time. For example, adults who are incarcerated for extended periods of time in prison tend to become *prisonized*, meaning that their behavior and social interactions adapt to the prevalent norms of inmate subcultures.[23] These norms are almost always countercultural and fundamentally criminal. However, it is dangerous for inmates to not conform to these prison environments, and prisonization is often a matter of survival within inmate subcultures.

In a similar manner, incarcerated juveniles also adapt by creating institutional subcultures, many of which try to replicate outside gang affiliations or other antisocial affiliations.[24] Residents group themselves according to neighborhood, former peer associations, age, and race. Subcultural norms of behavior can be quite negative for young people, especially if the subculture is one of frequent violence, aggressive dominance, and forced subordination. As in adult prisons, gangs are a prominent feature of juvenile correctional institutions,[25] and rivalries are very common.

Physical harm is certainly a risk in these environments, as are psychological problems, which can arise from extended confinement in dangerous or dysfunctionally restrictive environments. However, there is positive news: Research indicates that the incidence of prisonization decreases in institutions where treatment is emphasized over custody.[26]

Final Thoughts: Correctional Policies and Protections

A Policy Dilemma. How can true rehabilitation be achieved? Which policies and programs best promote individual transformation? Is the search for an effective juvenile corrections policy fundamentally a trial-and-error process? Policy makers have historically applied rehabilitation as the underlying philosophy of the American juvenile justice system. Although past methods were draconian (severe) and abusive by modern standards, most were applied in the best interests of the child; they reflected the most advanced theoretical knowledge of the time. Despite the promising intent of rehabilitative policies, it is now clear that when an institution's conditions are inadequate, and when incarcerated juveniles suffer from physical threats, psychological problems, and anarchic (disordered) social arrangements, their *best interests* are rarely served. Researchers have long concluded that many juvenile justice programs fail to achieve true rehabilitation,[27] and it is questionable whether existing juvenile justice policies can, in fact, rehabilitate young people.

An argument can be made that modern juvenile correctional facilities are poor venues for re-educating and nurturing juvenile delinquents, or for molding them into productive members of society. Programmatic policies can be creative, but they can also produce counterproductive routines. For example, education and vocational schedules typically last for approximately eight hours per day in training schools. After education and vocational training, residents are returned to their facilities (cottages or dormitories), where the juvenile subcultures take hold. Prisonization is likely to occur when youths are exposed to this type of routine over time.

One must remember that institutionalized juveniles will be released into mainstream society when they reach the age of majority or some other official benchmark. Should prisonization occur during institutionalization, there exists a distinct possibility that a child will be "lost" and grow up to become an adult criminal. Thus, if residents have not been reformed prior to release, and instead act out on the effects of prisonization, both the former residents and society will bear the consequences. Indeed, the consequences are readily apparent, as research has shown that recidivism rates are very high among juvenile participants in aftercare (parole) programs.[28]

Protection From Abuse During Incarceration. Regardless of whether existing policies effectively rehabilitate an acceptable proportion of residents, the fact remains that *all* members of correctional populations are vested with certain rights and protections. Due-process concerns such as custody, detention, pretrial procedures, juvenile trials, and juvenile sentencing have been litigated extensively, and are central issues in juvenile court (as discussed in Chapter 7). Federal and state courts have held that fundamental protections also exist for confined juveniles. For example, trial and appellate courts have rendered the following decisions in cases involving the rights of institutionalized youths:

- Administrative applications of excessive isolation, use of tear gas, and beatings are unacceptable practices.[29]
- Measures such as administratively forced tranquilizers, hand restraints, and isolation cannot be punitively applied.[30]
- Denial of access to institutional programs and confinement to unfurnished and windowless padded cells with holes for toilets are unacceptable practices.[31]
- Because the true purpose of juvenile courts is rehabilitation, juveniles have a right to treatment.[32]
- Juveniles cannot be confined to institutions unless they receive rehabilitation.[33]

In many respects, courts have historically set many standards for the treatment and rehabilitation of juveniles. Judicial review is by its nature a reactive process, and becomes effective only after a problem has been identified. In this sense, official protection from abuse often occurs subsequent to the discovery of institutional problems. Although certain practices and conditions were common in the past, many of these practices and conditions were reconsidered (either voluntarily or coercively) after court decisions. Fundamental constitutional protections such as due process have been extended to juveniles through court intervention,[34] and it is arguably true that the courts have also set baseline standards for protection from abuse in correctional institutions.

Chapter Summary

Institutional corrections for juveniles began during the colonial era, when penal institutions were used to house incorrigible children. Parental authority was paramount, and offending children were severely punished. The child savers and other philanthropists established institutions exclusively for juveniles during a time when corporal punishment was considered to be an acceptable correctional option. Houses of Refuge were the first institutions to practice stern paternalism, and were often prison-like in appearance. Reform schools softened this approach, and implemented an industrial cottage system in rural areas. This concept—of training schools housing youths in cottages in the countryside—has continued into the modern era.

Although the fundamental philosophy of juvenile corrections has been to promote rehabilitation, punishing serious offenders has become an acceptable goal. Rehabilitation is now one of several correctional philosophies that include deterrence, incapacitation, and retribution. In many correctional systems, rehabilitation has become secondary to other correctional philosophies. Fortunately for many juvenile offenders, incarceration in correctional institutions is considered to be a final remedy in many jurisdictions, and innovative nominal and intermediate sanctions have been designed to correct behavior without institutionalization.

Confinement is a drastic but necessary instrument for controlling serious juvenile offenders. Confinement options include nonsecure residential facilities such as shelter care facilities, group homes, and foster homes. Secure facilities include juvenile detention centers, jails, and training schools, all of which exist to house serious offenders. Creative residential programs have also been established as alternative forms of detention. These include ranches, forestry camps, and boot camps.

Laws and court decisions have held that juveniles housed in correctional institutions cannot be abused or neglected. However, research has demonstrated that the quality of life in juvenile institutions is often inadequate and in need of improvement. In fact, it is questionable whether correctional facilities effectively promote re-education or other nurturing outcomes and whether rehabilitation genuinely occurs. When prisonization occurs as a result of these environments, both society and the former residents suffer the consequences.

Chapter 9 examines the purposes and effectiveness of juvenile probation, aftercare, and parole. These and similar programs are integral components of all juvenile justice systems.

Questions for Review

1. What has been the historical role of juvenile corrections?

2. Which philosophies have typically been used to correct juvenile deviance?

3. Which policy considerations have been applied to rationalize noncustodial and creative sanctions?

4. What are the confinement options used in the modern era to detain juveniles?

5. How prevalent are institutional subcultures?

6. What are the underlying philosophies of training schools and detention facilities?

7. Which central issues have arisen concerning juvenile corrections?

Key Terms and Concepts

The following topics were discussed in this chapter and are found in the Glossary:

Boot Camps

Census of Juveniles in Residential Placement (CJRP)

Cottage System

Deterrence

Forestry Camps

Foster Families

Foster Homes

Group Homes

Incapacitation

Intermediate Sanctions

Jails

Juvenile Detention Centers

Long-Term Correctional Facilities

Nominal Sanctions

Nonsecure Correctional Facilities

Nonsecure Residential Facilities

Postadjudication Detention

Preadjudication Detention

Ranches

Rehabilitation

Retribution

Secure Correctional Facilities

Shelter Care Facilities

Short-Term Temporary Care Facilities

Training Schools

Wilderness Programs

DISCUSSION BOX

Treating Juvenile Offenders as Adult Criminals

This chapter's Discussion Box is intended to stimulate critical discussion about the placement of juveniles in adult facilities.

Juveniles who are tried and convicted by adult criminal courts are sent into the adult prison system. Prisons are considerably more severe facilities than juvenile training schools. Although both types of institutions are designed to house serious offenders, training schools have some degree of rehabilitation as a core objective. In comparison, prisons are larger, more secure, more crowded, and very dangerous facilities.

Special youth wings or compounds are set aside for juvenile criminals until they reach a designated age (usually 18). After this age, offenders are sent to live among the general prison population. In male institutions especially, inmate subcultures are based on power hierarchies, with the strongest and most aggressive inmates receiving the greatest degree of respect and deference by others. Unfortunately for many young convicts, they begin their sentences at the bottom of the subcultural hierarchy, and are regularly victimized by hardened adult convicts. Violence, rape, and other forms of exploitation against young inmates are common. There is also a greater risk of suicide.[35]

In contrast to training schools, juveniles in prison are afforded fewer youth-oriented therapies, counseling services, or educational opportunities. Despite the obvious hazards of prison environments, juveniles continue to be processed through the adult criminal justice system.

Discussion Questions

1. Why has modern society deemed it appropriate to try and imprison juvenile offenders? Has our culture changed?

2. Is it appropriate to incarcerate juveniles in adult prison facilities?

3. Should special rehabilitative services be provided to imprisoned juveniles?

4. Are the dangers from prison conditions really relevant as a matter of policy?

5. What factors should be considered when formulating policies on which type of correctional facility is appropriate for juvenile offenders?

Recommended Web Sites

The following Web sites contain information about the role of juvenile corrections in the juvenile justice system.

American Bar Association Juvenile Justice Center: http://www.abanet.org/crimjust/juvjus/home.html

Corrections Connection: http://www.corrections.com/links/viewlinks.asp?Cat=30

Juvenile Boot Camps: http://juvenile-boot-camps.com/
Juvenile Information Network: http://www.juvenilenet.org/
Redcliff Ascent Wilderness Treatment Program (Idaho): http://www. redcliffascent.com/
Texas Youth Commission: http://www.tyc.state.tx.us/

Note: The Web site URLs and exercises below are also from the book's study site:
http://www.sagepub.com/martin

Web Exercise

Using this chapter's recommended Internet sites, conduct an online investigation of the role of juvenile corrections.

- What role does rehabilitation play in the stated goals and objectives of juvenile corrections policy makers?
- To what extent are juvenile correctional programs affiliated with adult correctional systems?
- How prevalent are alternative correctional programs?

For an online search of the role of juvenile corrections in the juvenile justice system, students should use a search engine and enter the following keywords:

"Juvenile Corrections"

"Wilderness Programs"

Recommended Readings

The following publications provide discussions on the role of juvenile corrections in the juvenile justice system:

Annie E. Casey Foundation. (2000). *Juvenile detention alternatives initiative*. Baltimore: Annie E. Casey Foundation.

Finckenauer, J. O. (1984). *Juvenile delinquency and corrections: The gap between theory and practice*. Orlando, FL: HBJ Academic Press.

Harden, J., & Hill, M. (Eds.). (1998). *Breaking the rules: Women in prison and feminist therapy*. Binghamton, NY: Haworth Press.

Rosenheim, M. K., Zimring, F. E., Tanenhaus, D. S., & Dohrn, B. (Eds.). (2002). *A century of juvenile justice*. Chicago: University of Chicago Press.

Schwartz, I. M., & Barton, W. H. (Eds.). (1997). *Reforming juvenile detention: No more hidden closets*. Columbus, OH: Ohio State University Press.

Notes

1. See A.M. and J.M.K. v. Luzerne County Juvenile Detention Center, et al., 372 F.3d 572 (3d Cir. 2004).

2. Snyder, H. N., & Sickmund, M. (2000). *Juvenile offenders and victims: 1999 National report* (p. 186). Washington, DC: U.S. Department of Justice.

3. Ibid.

4. See Zingraff, M. T. (1975). Prisonization as an inhibitor of effective resocialization. *Criminology, 13.*

5. See Giallambardo, R. (1974). *The society of imprisoned girls.* New York: Wiley.

6. In practice, the death penalty was rarely imposed on children. See Krisberg, B., & Austin, J. (1993). *Reinventing juvenile justice* (p. 13). Newbury Park, CA: Sage.

7. See Bernard, T. J. (1992). *The cycle of juvenile justice.* New York: Oxford University Press.

8. See Schwartz, I. (1989). *(In)justice for juveniles.* Lexington, MA: Lexington Books.

9. Total institutions exercise complete control over their residents. See Wallace, S. E. (Ed.). (1971). *Total institutions.* New Brunswick, NJ: Transaction Books.

10. See, e.g., Cullen, F. T., Golden, K. M., & Cullen, J. B. (1983). Is child saving dead? Attitudes toward rehabilitation in Illinois. *Journal of Criminal Justice, 11*(1), 1–13.

11. For an assessment of research on custodial alternatives, see Jackson, J. L., deKeijser, J. W., & Michon, J. A. L. (1995). A critical look at research on alternatives to custody. *Federal Probation, 59*(43), 43–52.

12. Sickmund, M. (2002). *Juvenile residential facility census, 2000: Selected findings.* Washington, DC: U.S. Department of Justice.

13. For a discussion of the dangers faced by youths incarcerated in adult facilities, see Ziedenberg, J., & Shiraldi, V. (1998, August). The risks juveniles face: Housing juveniles in adult institutions is self-destructive and self-defeating. *Corrections Today, 60*(5), 22–26.

14. For a classic analysis of training schools, see Street, D., Vinter, R. D., & Perrow, C. (1996). *Organization for treatment: A comparative study of institutions.* New York: Free Press.

15. See Goodstein, L., & Sontheimer, H. (1997). The implementation of an intensive aftercare program for serious juvenile offenders: A case study. *Criminal Justice and Behavior, 14.*

16. Snyder, H. N., & Sickmund, M. (2000). *Juvenile offenders and victims: 1999 National report* (p. 194). Washington, DC: U.S. Department of Justice.

17. Ibid. (p. 195).

18. Ibid. (p. 197).

19. Ibid. (p. 198).

20. For a comprehensive analysis of juvenile residential institutions, see Parent, D. G., Lieter, V., Kennedy, S., Livens, L., Wentworth, D., & Wilcox, S. (1994). *Conditions of confinement: Juvenile detention and corrections facilities.* Washington, DC: U.S. Department of Justice. The report studied all 984 public and private juvenile detention centers, reception centers, training schools, ranches, camps, and farms in the United States.

21. Sickmund, M. (2002). *Juvenile residential facility census, 2000: Selected findings.* Washington, DC: U.S. Department of Justice.

22. Ibid.

23. For an early explanation of prisonization, see Clemmer, D. (1958). *The prison community*. Boston: Christopher.

24. For research on juvenile correctional subcultures, see Feld, B. (1981). A comparative analysis of organizational structure and inmate subcultures in institutions for juvenile offenders. *Crime and Delinquency, 27*.

25. See Mays, G., & Winfree, L. T., Jr. (1998). *Contemporary corrections*. Belmont, CA: West/Wadsworth.

26. Ibid.

27. See Bernard, T. J. (1997). *The cycle of juvenile justice*. New York: Oxford University Press.

28. See Krisberg, B. A., Austin, J. F., & Steele, P. A. (1989). *Unlocking juvenile corrections: Evaluating the Massachusetts Department of Youth Services*. San Francisco: National Council on Crime and Delinquency.

29. Morales v. Turman, 364 F. Supp. 166 (E.D. Tex. 1973).

30. Pena v. New York State Division for Youth, 419 F. Supp. 203 (S.D.N.Y. 1976).

31. Morgan v. Sproat, 432 F. Supp. 1130 (S.D. Miss. 1977).

32. Inmates of the Boys' Training School v. Affleck, 346 F. Supp. 1354 (D.R.I. 1972).

33. White v. Reid, 125 F. Supp. 647 (D.DC 1954).

34. See, e.g., Breed v. Jones, 421 U.S. 519, 533, 95 S. Ct. 1779, 1787, 44 L. Ed. 2d 346 (1975); Davis v. Mississippi, 394 U.S. 721, 89 S. Ct. 1394, 22 L. Ed. 2d 676 (1969); In re Gault, 387 U.S. 1, 19–21, 26–28, 87 S. Ct. 1428, 1439–1440, 1442–1444, 18 L. Ed. 2d 527 (1967); In re Winship, 397 U.S. 358, 90 S. Ct. 1068, 25 L. Ed. 2d 368 (1970); and Kent v. United States, 383 U.S. 541, 86 S. Ct. 1045, 16 L. Ed. 2d 84 (1966).

35. See Redding, R. E. (1999). Juvenile offenders in criminal court and adult prison: Legal, psychological, and behavioral outcomes. *Juvenile and Family Court Journal, 50*.

PART III

Process and Systems

Community-Based Components

Part III Police officers instructing a group of juvenile delinquent boys in 1944 as they prepare to start various games and activities at the Police Athletic League, a police-sponsored recreational organization in Harlem.

9

Juvenile Probation, Parole, and Aftercare

Juvenile probation and parole officers are charged with the important duty of monitoring the rehabilitation and behavior of juveniles who have been assigned to community-based correctional alternatives. In most cases, the probation–parole–community connection works fairly well. Errors do sometimes occur, however, often with serious consequences. For example, in the summer of 1998, Charlie M. was arrested for shoplifting in the Village of Crestwood, Illinois. He was permitted by a juvenile officer to substitute community service in lieu of referral to juvenile court. Service was to be performed at the Blue Island Fire Department, and Charlie was to be supervised by part-time police officer and firefighter Thomas Broukal.

Broukal had been previously convicted of child neglect and acquitted on charges of criminal sexual abuse of a child. He had been rehired by the Village of Crestwood after he had served his court-imposed supervision. Broukal molested Charlie M. on several occasions, and on at least one occasion he molested Charlie's 11-year-old brother, Frank. The boys and their parents filed a lawsuit against numerous officials of the Village of Crestwood, which was partially successful.

This chapter takes a close look at noninstitutional correctional alternatives that are put into practice in the community. In many respects, it is not always appreciated that most juvenile correctional programs are closely linked to the community and that most youths who are adjudicated delinquent or convicted at trial are not institutionalized. They instead serve their sentences in the community under the supervision of juvenile justice agencies. These release-based correctional programs—found in every jurisdiction in the nation—require offenders to comply with stipulated requirements that are established as conditions of release. Juveniles who fail to comply with these contract-like conditions of release can be sent to residential correctional facilities under court order.

Three types of noninstitutional corrections programs are employed by juvenile justice systems:

1. **Probation**. A sentence that is served in the community under supervision by a probation officer. The offender's sentence begins and ends in the community, assuming he or she complies with the requirements of probation.

2. **Parole.** A supervised early release from a residential correctional facility. The offender's sentence begins in confinement and ends in the community under supervision from a parole agency, assuming he or she complies with the requirements of parole. Participants are juvenile delinquents or criminals who have already served time in a correctional institution.

3. **Aftercare**. A term used in approximately half of the U.S. states to describe parole for juveniles.[1] It is essentially the juvenile justice system's equivalent to parole, and it is a supervised early release of youths from a juvenile residential institution after a period of mandated confinement.

Probation, parole, and aftercare are, by definition, *noninstitutional* correctional alternatives.[2] They are intended to give selected offenders an opportunity to integrate themselves into society during the term of their sentence in order to promote rehabilitation. These programs are examples of **community corrections** (also known as *release-based corrections*), which rely on community resources to provide correctional services.[3] The underlying objective is to link offenders to community-centered resources and programs under the authority and guidance of local juvenile justice officials.

Noninstitutional alternatives are intended to serve the needs of both society and offenders: The needs of society are met by requiring offenders to complete some degree of reparations for their behavior, and the needs of offenders are met by permitting them to serve their penance in a more rehabilitative environment. In other words, selected offenders are deemed to require correctional control, but not necessarily inside a correctional institution. In the cases of parole and aftercare, persons who have already served time in regimented institutions are gradually deinstitutionalized through early release from these facilities.

Presidential commissions and other official authorities have long concluded that recidivism and other problems are more likely to occur when young offenders enter the juvenile justice system at a young age and remain inside for extended periods of time. The rationale for probation and early release programs is that incarcerated juveniles can avoid *prisonization* and increase their likelihood of reintegration into society. Under this rationale, probation, parole, and aftercare have several advantages over institutionalization, such as

- An increased likelihood of rehabilitation
- Direct access to community resources
- Immediate reparations (restitution) to the community for the harm done by the offender

- Educational and vocational instruction outside of correctional institutions
- Lower costs associated with community corrections than residential institutionalization

As a counterpoint to these advantages, many critics of community corrections argue that releasing convicted offenders into the community is inherently unsafe, because it increases the risk to society from recidivist delinquents and criminals. The logic behind this reasoning is simple: If they were locked up, there would be no risk. There is another criticism that is also rooted in the modern era's punishment approach to crime: Probation, parole, and aftercare are simply too soft on offenders. From this perspective, delinquents and criminals should receive their just deserts through official retribution, incapacitation, and deterrence.

This chapter discusses the characteristics of juvenile probation, parole, and aftercare and identifies issues and special needs inherent in these correctional alternatives. Our review of these options covers the following:

- Background: The Development of Probation, Parole, and Aftercare
- Noninstitutional Corrections: Juvenile Probation
- Postinstitutional Corrections: Juvenile Parole and Aftercare
- Contending Questions: Ongoing Issues and Special Needs

Photo 9.1 Female gang members drink beer and demonstrate their technique for hiding razor blades inside their mouth. Some policy makers believe that probation and parole should be scaled back for juvenile delinquents.

CHAPTER PERSPECTIVE 9.1

Terms and Conditions for Juvenile Probation, Parole, and Aftercare

Terms and conditions for juvenile probation, parole, and aftercare are essentially the same. All three procedures require participants to comply with general terms mandated for all participants and specific terms mandated for individuals. Failure to comply with mandated terms will provide the basis for transferring juvenile offenders out of community-based corrections and into locked facilities.

The modern trend is to grant release to offenders who have committed "middle ground" offenses; whereas serious offenders are increasingly being sent before adult criminal courts, and minor offenders are being diverted out of the juvenile justice system.

Release-based corrections necessitate an assessment by officials of the characteristics of each case, an evaluation of the candidate's risk to society, and a determination of whether a release-based correction is the best alternative for the juvenile and society. First-time offenders and those who commit relatively minor transgressions such as petty property offenses (theft, school vandalism, etc.) are good candidates for release, whereas recidivists and those who commit offenses against the person (robbery, battery, etc.) are poor candidates.

Structured behavior and close supervision are required conditions of release. Full reintegration into society is, of course, the ultimate goal of release-based corrections, but it is only through fulfilling the terms and conditions of release that offenders will be granted complete freedom of movement and association. In order to enhance the probability of rehabilitation, the quasi-law-enforcement function of probation and parole officers must be supplemented by treatment programs. These include mandatory school attendance, drug and alcohol testing, mental health counseling, and restrictions on peer associations. Distinctive juvenile release programs have been created in most jurisdictions, which bring together specialized treatment programs and agencies, parole and probation officers, and law enforcement agencies.

Background: The Development of Probation, Parole, and Aftercare

Suspended sentences and early release from prison have deep roots in Anglo-American justice. An early procedure known as **judicial reprieve** permitted judges to suspend sentences for offenders, pending appeal to the Crown for clemency. Judges also suspended unfair sentences when deemed necessary. Another concept similar to probation was established in England by the fourteenth century, when courts bound over offenders into the custody of members of the community for good behavior. **Binding** is an ancient English practice for dealing with offenders, intending "to bring or place [them] under definite duties or legal obligations, particularly by a bond or covenant."[4] Parole is also conceptually rooted in binding.

The Origins of Probation

In the United States, a Bostonian boot maker named **John Augustus** is acknowledged to be the first genuine probation officer.[5] His work began in 1841, when he went to court to watch its proceedings. He observed a man who was accused of being a drunkard, and he posted the man's bail after receiving a signed promise from the man never to drink again and to later report back to the court that he had been rehabilitated. This was his first client. Through the 1840s and 1850s, Augustus volunteered before the criminal court to bring qualified offenders to his house in lieu of imprisonment. Although his service began as part-time rehabilitation of drunkards (10 in the first year), Augustus's voluntarism quickly became a full-time practice for the supervision of a variety of offenders. Most of his clients were adults, but Augustus also posted bail for boys and girls with the understanding that he would supervise their rehabilitation. His acceptance of this responsibility is arguably the beginning of juvenile probation. In 1847, Augustus reported the following:

> I bailed nineteen boys, from 7 to 15 years of age, and in bailing them it was understood, and agreed by the court, that their cases should be continued from term to term for several months, as a season of probation; thus each month at the calling of the docket, I would appear in court, make my report, and thus the cases would pass on for 5 or 6 months.[6]

Augustus's work—which eventually assisted 2,000 offenders before his death in 1859—led to the hiring of the first designated professional probation officers in Massachusetts in 1878.

Through the end of the nineteenth century, the concept of probation became quite popular, and the practice had been adopted in many jurisdictions, including Vermont, Missouri, Illinois, Minnesota, Rhode Island, and New Jersey. By the late 1920s, every state had enacted probation laws and hired professional probation officers. In 1925, federal probation began with the enactment of the **National Probation Act**, which granted federal trial judges the authority to impose requirements of probation on offenders and hire professional probation officers. By 1927, 46 states had enacted legislation establishing both juvenile court systems and juvenile-focused probation.[7]

The Origins of Parole and Aftercare

Parole. Sentencing reform policies developed during the mid-1800s in England played an important part in the development of modern parole. A conceptual shift occurred in the English judicial system, in which

indeterminate sentencing was adopted as a modification to the practice of sentencing offenders to a fixed number of years. Instead, some offenders were given minimum and maximum ranges, allowing for the possibility of early release. These practices were codified when the **Penal Servitude Act of 1853** granted early release from prison under supervision by local law enforcement officials.

Parole was first implemented in the United States at the **Elmira Reformatory** in New York in 1876. Elmira was one of the first institutions in the United States to apply indeterminate sentencing with the possibility of early release. A new system of granting "good time" points, or credit, to inmates was designed to encourage proper behavior. The program was the outcome of collaboration between the New York State legislature and progressives to enact laws to promote incentives for early release from prison. From its inception, parole was used to manipulate inmate behavior by holding out the possibility of early release for good behavior. This practice is a good example of indeterminate sentencing, and it encouraged rehabilitation and behavioral conformity. The underlying theory is that inmates will be more likely to conform to institutional rules if their sentences are indeterminate, and officials are granted discretion on early releases for good behavior.

Aftercare. Juvenile-specific early release programs have their origin in the nineteenth century, with the establishment of Houses of Refuge, reform schools, and other specialized facilities. During this period, each resident's progress toward rehabilitation could result in early release from custody, and juvenile officials were authorized to return youths to the community at their discretion. Although some youths were returned to their parents, early release programs also committed many juveniles to terms of apprenticeship. This was an era of widespread child labor, and young offenders were often bound to work in industries, on farms, or for business establishments. In essence, early aftercare-like programs were often simply a process of condemning children to involuntary servitude in conditions that would be unthinkable today.

With the development of juvenile court systems during the turn of the twentieth century, full-time professionals were assigned to monitor early releases. This was the beginning of aftercare in the modern era, although most jurisdictions continued to use parole as the predominant mode of early release. Aftercare developed slowly in the United States, and is still regarded by many jurisdictions as being subordinate to parole systems.

On the Front Line: Juvenile Probation and Parole Officers

Unlike the first nonprofessional philanthropists who served as managers of juvenile placement in the community, modern juvenile probation and parole officers are expected to be professionals. They serve as officers and advisers for both the juvenile court and juvenile correctional systems. They are also liaisons between the juvenile justice system and community services.

These fundamental attributes are implemented in different ways in local jurisdictions. For example, in some jurisdictions probation and parole officers are little more than supervisors (often because of high caseloads); in other jurisdictions they are treatment-oriented caseworkers. In some systems, officers engage directly in counseling; in other systems they are facilitators who steer juveniles into counseling programs. And in some jurisdictions, they perform social work that focuses on rehabilitation; in others, their duties emphasize law enforcement and *control* of young offenders.

Noninstitutional Corrections: Juvenile Probation

As discussed in previous chapters, juvenile correctional authorities oversee a broad range of facilities and programs. Although some facilities and programs are roughly equivalent to those found in adult criminal justice systems, it must be remembered that juvenile corrections are uniquely designed for the remediation of juvenile offenders. In this regard, juvenile probation is similar to criminal probation, and it is legally defined as a procedure allowing a person convicted of some minor offense (particularly juvenile offenders) to go at large, under a suspension of sentence, during good behavior, and generally under the supervision or guardianship of a probation officer.[8]

Juvenile court judges generally uphold the principle that juvenile delinquents are more likely to be rehabilitated when released into the community. For this reason, probation is the most common disposition in cases where youths are adjudicated delinquent. This is not a new trend but has been a consistent phenomenon for an extended period of time. Typically, up to 90% of dispositions result in probation in many jurisdictions. Table 9.1 compares the percentages of youths receiving residential placement with those who are given formal probation.[9]

What Works? Models for Juvenile Probation Systems

There is no consensus among the states on what constitutes an ideal juvenile probation system. Systems tend to be designed to serve the needs of each jurisdiction, and they are uniquely configured using a variety of approaches.[10] Nevertheless, it is safe to say that common programmatic and organizational elements do exist among juvenile probation systems, but they are applied differently within each jurisdiction. For example, states choose to place administrative oversight under either judicial (juvenile court) or executive (mayor or governor) control. Also, funding can be allocated through state-level agencies or local administrative agencies.

Historically, there is a diversity of approaches—and localized quality—for juvenile probation programs in the United States. Many states are quite

TABLE 9.1   COMPARISON OF JUDGMENTS GIVEN TO YOUTHS
ADJUDICATED DELINQUENT

Most youths who have been adjudicated delinquent receive formal probation as
their most severe sanction. Juvenile courts base their decisions in consideration of
the severity of an offender's offense, so that homicide cases have the highest likelihood of residential placement.

This table is instructive because it compares percentages of court-mandated residential placements with the percentages of formal probation given to juveniles who
were adjudicated delinquent.[a]

Offense	Percent of Adjudicated Delinquency Cases	
	Residential Placement (%)	Formal Probation (%)
Total delinquency	28	54
Person offenses	31	53
Criminal homicide	59	30
Forcible rape	43	43
Robbery	46	41
Aggravated assault	31	53
Simple assault	26	57
Property offenses	26	56
Burglary	33	55
Larceny-theft	23	58
Motor vehicle theft	41	48
Arson	27	59
Vandalism	17	60
Trespassing	21	54
Drug law violations	24	54
Public order offenses	32	49
Obstruction of justice	42	45
Disorderly conduct	16	57
Weapons offenses	28	56
Liquor law violations	14	64
Nonviolent sex offenses	39	53

a. Adapted from Snyder, H. N., & Sickmund, M. (1999). *Juvenile offenders and victims: 1999
National report* (p. 159). Washington, DC: U.S. Department of Justice.

innovative in designing their probation systems. For example, to reduce stress
on state-level resources, some states design incentive systems to motivate local

authorities to provide services locally rather than sending offenders into state correctional systems. This type of approach was adopted in 1966 in California, which created the Probation Subsidy Program. The program allowed the state to pay up to $4,000 to counties for offenders (juveniles and adults) who were diverted out of the state system and provided with probation services.

Private-Sector Probation Services. In addition to these public (government-managed) models, many states and localities have retained private contractors to manage aspects of their programs. Aftercare services (discussed below) are also contracted out to private agencies. The rationale for retaining private services is that many private organizations are particularly expert in the provision of certain types of assistance. For example, many private agencies provide exceptional treatment programs for drug abuse and recovery. Agencies also emphasize the removal of youths from dysfunctional environments such as gang activity. High-quality abuse recovery programs are also found in the private sector. Also, specialized services, such as **juvenile intensive probation supervision (JIPS)**, are sometimes delivered under contract by private firms.

Who Should Participate? Assessing Candidacy and Managing Participants

Juvenile probation officers are the principal officials involved in the supervision of juveniles in probationary programs. Although juvenile court judges have ultimate authority over probation as a dispositionary alternative, it is the probation officers who are responsible for case intake, assembling social histories, and managing the evaluation of probation participants.

Case Intake. Candidacy assessment begins during the intake phase of juvenile court proceedings. Intake is a screening process whereby probation officers advise the court on whether the court has jurisdiction. At this phase, officers also begin the task of assembling data on the candidate's personal and family characteristics. During this process, probation officers are likely to interview juvenile offenders and notify parents or guardians of their rights, such as the right to an attorney. Interviews may also include arresting officers, victims, and witnesses. These data are often assembled in cooperation with local prosecutors as a way to determine whether cases should proceed to juvenile court, whether detention is necessary, and whether probation is a viable alternative.

Assembling Social Histories. The creation of social histories is actually begun during the case-intake phase. The purpose of this process is to investigate and construct a complete profile of the juvenile for the court as an advisory duty. This report, often referred to as a *predisposition report* or *presentence investigation,* is presented to the judge at the predisposition phase of court proceedings. Judges use these reports to determine whether to commit juveniles to detention centers or grant probation. Judges consider many factors when determining whether a juvenile should be granted probation or, alternatively, confined for the safety of the community. These factors are generally included in the social history report that is compiled and submitted to the court by juvenile probation officers or social workers. The following attributes and circumstances are elements in a judge's calculation on whether to grant probation:

- Prior offenses as evidence of future behavior
- School records as indicators of attendance and conformity to rules
- Family history to uncover dysfunctional or unstable environments
- Personal history that might mitigate or aggravate an offense
- Victim reports, including the wishes and fears of victims
- Offender's attitude profile, such as showing remorse or ambivalence
- Circumstances of the offense, whether violent or premeditated

Social histories and predisposition reports are integral components in the formulation of probation requirements and conditions (discussed in the next section). They are also important instruments for linking probationers to appropriate agencies for treatment and rehabilitation services.

Managing and Evaluating Probation Participants. Adequate supervision is a key feature of every probation system, and an important duty of juvenile probation officers is to assure that juveniles fulfill the requirements and conditions of their probation. They meet clients regularly at the juvenile's home, the officer's office, or some other designated venue. At these meetings, juvenile probation officers assess the needs of participants, as well as their compliance with stipulated requirements and conditions.

In many jurisdictions, one important duty is to link juveniles with community services and agencies. This is analogous to the duties of social workers, who have a services-driven relationship with their clients. Providing these services often requires juvenile probation officers to complete individual diagnoses of their clients, and identify appropriate treatment programs for them. Although this services-driven approach is by no means universally available, it is an important counterpoint to a strictly administrative and compliance-driven approach to probation.

Restricted Freedom: Requirements and Conditions of Probation

Releases on probationary conditions are *qualified* releases, meaning that an offender's release is a court-mandated privilege and subject to termination. Most probationary requirements last between 6 and 12 months, with the possibility of extensions. Probation officers make the final determination on whether a juvenile has met the requirements of probation. Once probation has been completed, juveniles are released from the jurisdiction of the court.

Probationary sentences are contract-like arrangements, with mandatory requirements and conditions of service that the probationary offender is required to comply with. Some sentences are **unconditional probation** programs, which typically permit some freedom of movement and relatively infrequent intensive communications with probation officers via mail or telephone. Other sentences are **conditional probation** programs, which entail significant restrictions on movement and intensive communications with probation officers, usually involving personal meetings. Regardless of which model is applied, specific provisions of probationary requirements and conditions of service are designed at the discretion of juvenile judges or probation officials. They are crafted for the general welfare of society and the specific welfare of offenders. Typical probationary requirements include the following:

- Prohibitions against associating with certain peers or adults
- Obedience to the law
- Victim compensation
- Community service
- School attendance
- Drug and alcohol testing
- Geographic (movement) limitations

Other probationary alternatives are quite creative, and include JIPS, restitution, and house arrest.

Juvenile Intensive Probation Supervision. In special cases, a juvenile-focused form of **intensive probation supervision (IPS)** is mandated for youths who may pose a risk of flight or noncompliance with the requirements of probation. Adult IPS was originally designed during the 1980s to lower costs and reduce prison overcrowding. JIPS began to be implemented during the late 1980s for the same reasons, and juvenile courts began to assign higher-risk offenders to probation officers for special treatment.[11] It is an intensified version of standard probation that emphasizes increased surveillance, more frequent contacts with probation officers, and enhanced control over participants. Electronic monitoring is commonplace, using electronic transmission bracelets or some similar device. JIPS and JIPS-like programs remain popular because they are much less expensive than residential corrections programs.

Restitution. Some conditions of probation require juvenile offenders to compensate victims and society for the harm they caused. Restitution programs hold juveniles accountable for their behavior and responsible for making recompense. In other words, offenders are required to restore them to wholeness as much as is possible. Restitution is quite common and exists in most jurisdictions. It usually involves participation in community programs for specified hours working for public, private, or nonprofit agencies.[12] Restitution services include working in public parks, day care centers, and neighborhood centers. Specific duties can include assisting the elderly, maintaining public libraries, or assisting youth agencies. Restitution may also include victim compensation and payment of fines.

House Arrest. Confining youths to familiar environments such as their homes is considered to be a progressive intermediate sanction.[13] This type of incarceration is considered by many to be more likely to promote rehabilitation than confinement to detention centers. When youths are confined in their home residences, it is done under conditions that mandate their presence at home during curfews, evening hours, and weekends. Offenders may leave confinement under specified conditions, such as for school attendance, religious worship, and physicians' appointments. Similar to JIPS programs, electronic monitoring is commonplace when youths are placed under house arrest.

Failure to Comply: Revocation of Probation

Failure to comply with stipulated conditions is a violation of probation and constitutes grounds for revocation of privileges. Broadly, three types of behavior are impermissible when serving a probationary term:

1. Being taken into custody or arrested for committing another delinquent act or crime
2. Failure to comply with the original requirements and conditions of probationary service
3. Fleeing from the jurisdiction of the supervising court

Should one or more of these violations occur, probation officers may recommend revocation of probation to a court. The judge will make the final decision on whether to agree to the recommendation and whether to reimpose the original sentence as a penalty. This process is not a discretionary procedure, and it must be done in compliance with standards of due process as established by the U.S. Supreme Court. Revocation hearings must consider the unique circumstances of the violation. Depending on the nature of the case, the court may restore probation, amend the conditions of probation, or accept the recommendation of the probation officer to terminate the privilege.

Postinstitutional Corrections: Juvenile Parole and Aftercare

Juvenile parole and aftercare programs (*aftercare* is the term used in approximately half of the states) are quite common nationally. Both offer the same types of supervisory services as received by adult parolees, but aftercare programs in particular are fundamentally rehabilitative. While juvenile parole systems emphasize supervision and behavioral conformity, aftercare programs also provide connections to community resources. This is not to say that juvenile parole systems are necessarily different from aftercare programs. As with most aspects of the juvenile justice system, correctional programs differ from jurisdiction to jurisdiction, so that many juvenile parole systems are virtually indistinguishable from aftercare programs.

The rationale for implementing parole and aftercare programs is uncomplicated:

- First, to motivate young offenders to pursue rehabilitation
- Second, to provide supervision of participants to enforce the conditions of early release
- Third, to increase the likelihood of rehabilitation
- Fourth (and most pragmatic), to reduce correctional overcrowding

Differentiating Early Release: Parole and Aftercare in Context

Juvenile parole and aftercare are examples of indeterminate sentencing as applied to youthful offenders.[14] Both are designed to afford opportunities for persons who have served time in correctional institutions to fulfill their debt to society. They do this while residing in the community by conforming their behavior to socially accepted standards. Many of the requirements and conditions of parole and aftercare are similar to those developed for probationers. Thus, the basic purposes of parole and aftercare are essentially the same.

Goals of Early Release. Early release programs—regardless of whether they are identified as parole or aftercare—typically promote similar goals. These goals include the following:

- Protection of the community through the monitoring of participants
- Prevention of recidivism by careful prerelease screening of candidates
- The continued holding of offenders accountable for their offenses by clearly defining their early release from incarceration as a continuation of their sentences, to be served in the community
- Rehabilitation of offenders through treatment and participation in community programs

Because these goals are rather broad, parole officials must review each candidate's case to determine whether an early release program would both protect society and benefit the participant. This can be a highly subjective process, and one that can be highly controversial—especially when a participant breaks the requirements and conditions of early release.

Parole. Parole is authorization for early release from a residential correctional facility. It differs from probation in that probation is usually granted by judges, whereas parole is granted by correctional institutions or administrative parole boards. It is managed by parole officers or juvenile hearing officers affiliated with the jurisdiction's correctional system. Parole is defined as a procedure involving:

> A conditional release; condition being that, if prisoner makes good, he will receive an absolute discharge from balance of sentence, but if he does not, he will be returned to serve unexpired term. . . . Release of convict from imprisonment on certain terms to be observed by him, and suspension of sentence during liberty thus engaged.[15]

Aftercare. As discussed previously, aftercare is the corresponding juvenile-specific procedure used for youths who have already served time in a residential correctional facility. It involves the supervision of youths by youth correctional officials for a specified period of time. Aftercare is technically defined as:

> The status or program membership of a juvenile who has been committed to a treatment or confinement facility, conditionally released from the facility, and placed in a supervisory and/or treatment program.[16]

Because aftercare is designed specifically for juveniles, its guiding principles are (at least in theory) treatment and rehabilitation. And because many juvenile offenders come from dysfunctional homes or neighborhoods, aftercare programs must be designed to anticipate problems with reintegrating participants into the community. Aftercare, therefore, has a responsibility to assure that problems are addressed as participants are moved from locked institutions to homes and neighborhoods. Aftercare programs often include the following services:

- Establishing links between the parolee, the parolee's family, and community resources
- A formal agreement that sets forth the objectives of the youth during release
- Prerelease monitored visits to homes and neighborhoods
- Treatment and counseling

What Works? Models for Juvenile Parole and Aftercare Systems

Much like the diversity found in the provision of probation services, there is no uniform model for juvenile parole and aftercare. Instead, state and local systems have been designed to serve the needs of specific regions and populations. Authority to consider parole requests—and to grant or reject these requests—devolved to a variety of supervisory officials and agencies. In this regard, it is possible to identify commonalities, and it may be concluded that parole and aftercare systems reflect variations of three administrative models: Parole boards, court-administered parole and aftercare, and corrections-managed parole and aftercare.

Parole Boards. Parole boards are independent committees whose members are usually appointed by governors and approved by state legislatures. They are unaffiliated with state parole agencies or correctional facilities. Members typically serve alternate (staggered) terms as a safety mechanism to reduce the ability of governors to "stack" parole boards with their appointees. It is important to understand that the principal duty of parole boards is to review one's eligibility for early release; they are not responsible for the provision of treatment or rehabilitation services after parole is granted. This is the duty of other government and community-based agencies.

As with every aspect of juvenile-related services, juvenile justice systems configure their parole boards in different ways, thus reflecting local policies and customs. Two general models exist among state parole systems. The *first type* of board exists in unified parole systems, in which parole boards jointly administer juvenile and adult candidates. Boards in these systems sit to hear cases involving both juvenile delinquents and adult criminals, and theoretically apply appropriate standards designed to serve each group of offenders. In practice, however, similar standards for review are often applied to both juveniles and adults, so that *juvenile* parole and aftercare are subsumed under broader theories of parole. The *second type* of parole board exists in systems that establish discrete juvenile and adult boards. Boards in these systems specialize in juvenile cases and apply standards and theories that are designed to serve the best interests of young offenders. Because of this specialization, juvenile-specific parole and aftercare receive focused attention.

Court-Administered Parole and Aftercare. A judicial-managed model exists, whereby authority has been exclusively granted to the court to grant early release to juvenile offenders. No other body, such as independent parole boards or correctional systems, participates in the consideration of a youth's eligibility for parole or aftercare, and the court has final oversight authority. This authority is implemented in various ways. In some jurisdictions, court administrators oversee the provision of treatment and rehabilitation services, and have the power to mandate adjustments to the requirements of a juvenile's release. In other jurisdictions, the court generally supervises parole and aftercare, while executive agencies manage treatment, rehabilitation, and compliance. Regardless of which specific application is adopted, final authority resides with judges and court administrators.

Corrections-Managed Parole and Aftercare. A third model has developed, whereby correctional administrators are given the authority to approve or deny early release. Senior officials in correctional facilities make recommendations on parole or aftercare for residents, with the advice and counsel of professional social workers who are assigned to the facility. This model often integrates the correctional authority with other areas of the juvenile justice system. In some systems, correctional administrators possess broad discretion on early release, whereas in other systems court permission must be obtained for specified circumstances. It is also not uncommon for the recommendation to go to another level of review such as the court, an executive officer (such as the director of corrections), or a review panel.

Who Should Participate? Assessing Candidacy and Managing Participants

Indeterminate sentencing models require that early release decisions be made during the period of a juvenile's confinement. The decision-making process involves, in part, collecting data on factors that may help predict the likelihood of the juvenile's successful rehabilitation during parole or aftercare.

Factors Affecting Participation. Consideration of each youth's candidacy for parole or aftercare is a process necessitating careful observation of the candidate's behavior while in residency at a correctional facility. During this process, a detailed assessment of his or her behavior will be made by a trained caseworker or other youth specialist and submitted to the appropriate decision-making body. The assessment is weighed in conjunction with the juvenile's social history as a tool to predict the likelihood of success or failure in the community should early release be granted. The following factors are predictors that usually shape the final decision on one's candidacy for parole or aftercare:

- *Family/home environment.* Is the household functional or dysfunctional?
- *Community environment and peer associations.* Will the neighborhood promote rehabilitation?
- *Number of prior offenses.* Does the candidate exhibit recidivist behavior?
- *Severity of prior offenses.* How much of a danger will the candidate pose to society?
- *Prior incarcerations in juvenile correctional facilities.* Has the system been a "revolving door" for the youth?
- *History of drug and alcohol use.* Is there a pattern of substance abuse and delinquent behavior?

Preparing for Early Release. The early release process can either be abrupt or preparatory. Abrupt releases are those in which participants are immediately returned to the community with minimal prior preparation. Preparatory releases refer to releases made after some degree of prerelease preparation. The purpose of prerelease preparation is to inform juveniles about what is expected of them in the community, and what awaits them when they return.

Preparatory releases include home visits, counseling on what to expect after release, how to behave when in the community, and work-release arrangements in local businesses or agencies. These arrangements and other programs—such as halfway houses—are intended to promote a gradual transition from the corrections system to living in the community. In this regard, many juvenile justice systems have designed creative prerelease programs to assist in the transition from locked correctional facilities to home environments. However, few high-security public correctional institutions such as training schools provide extensive preparatory release services. There are also relatively few public placements in halfway houses. It is in private facilities that preparatory releases are more frequently found.

Restricted Freedom, Revisited: Requirements and Conditions of Parole and Aftercare

As with probation, early release on parole or aftercare is a qualified release, and is a conditional privilege. When released into the community, parolees and aftercare participants must fulfill specified obligations. These obligations are requirements and conditions established by local parole authorities, and are similar in purpose and content to probationary requirements. As with probation, requirements can be more or less restrictive, depending on how the granting authority balances the needs of society against the needs of the offender.

General and Specific Conditions. In many jurisdictions, parole and aftercare are contract-like in the sense that standard forms are printed for use among all participants. Thus, many systems establish **general conditions** for parole for all participants (similar to "boilerplate" contract language), and **specific conditions** for the treatment of individual participants. For example, the "boilerplate" parole contract may require educational or vocational training, but specific conditions for treatment will identify designated schools or training programs.

Although the same types of requirements are used for parole and aftercare as are found in probationary programs—such as obeying the law, attending school, and testing for alcohol or drug use—early release requirements can also include other restrictions on everyday behavior, such as the following:

- Prohibitions on debt-generating behavior, such as using a credit card or borrowing money
- Restrictions on when and where a motor vehicle may be used, or complete prohibitions on driving
- Sanctions against enrollment in unapproved school programs, or withdrawal from approved programs

Participants must report in regularly to designated officers, who monitor each offender's compliance with the rules of parole or aftercare. The monitoring process is ongoing and often involves visiting clients in school, at home, or at community service locations. These visits confirm compliance with the parole contract.

Intensive Aftercare Supervision (IAS). The requirements and conditions of early release are sometimes made more rigorous for targeted populations of offenders. It is not uncommon for at-risk juveniles, particularly those released from high-security locked correctional facilities, to be granted aftercare only under strict supervision. These programs are known as Intensive Aftercare Supervision, or IAS. Conceptually similar to JIPS, IAS establishes guidelines for enhanced levels of supervision that are more stringent and invasive than normal supervision. It emphasizes increased surveillance and more frequent contacts with juvenile justice caseworkers, and it often uses electronic monitoring. IAS programs are rather common in the United States and are found in dozens of jurisdictions, probably because they are less expensive than residential corrections programs.

Failure to Comply, Revisited: Revocation of Parole and Aftercare

If juveniles violate the stipulated rules of probation or aftercare, they can be returned to locked residential detention to serve the remainder of their sentence. Many juveniles do return to their old bad habits, such as associating with an old peer group or finding themselves engaging in their previous pattern of delinquent behavior. This sort of recidivist behavior must certainly be suppressed for the good of society. However, there are other behaviors that must be suppressed for the good of the individual. For example, failure to attend school in the community may necessitate the provision of education services while confined in a locked facility. When these behaviors occur, and when authorities investigate them, it must be remembered that cases such as *Morrissey v. Brewer*[17] extended due-process protections to revocation of parole and aftercare. Thus, youths are protected from arbitrary and subjective decisions to reinstitutionalize them.

Why do participants fail to comply with the requirements and conditions of parole and aftercare (or for that matter, probation)? Several factors may explain this problem:

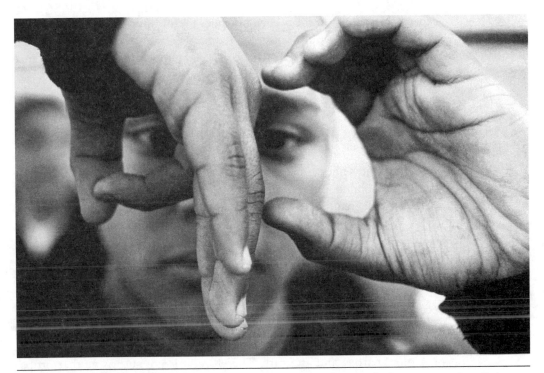

Photo 9.2   Young member of the Cypress Park gang in Los Angeles flashing a gang sign. Relapse is common when released juveniles return to their previous environment.

- Poor supervision
- Inadequate rehabilitation and treatment services
- Idiosyncratic qualities of participants, such as poor attitude or willful and persistent conflict with authority
- Dysfunctional family and neighborhood environments

Many of these factors reflect circumstances that are not under the control of juveniles or their caseworkers. In other words, participants sometimes fail to comply with the requirements of early release through no fault of their own. When this occurs, it is questionable whether a strong argument can be made that returning them to a detention facility is in the best interest of the child.

Contending Questions:
Ongoing Issues and Special Needs

The provision of probation, parole, and aftercare services is rarely an uncomplicated process. Probation and parole officers are often beset by contending pressures from several constituencies who often make contradictory demands on their services. In addition, officers and their agencies must respect the rights of their clients when performing their duties. Many juveniles do not comply with the requirements and conditions of their release, and this is particularly true for special populations such as substance abusers and mentally ill participants.

Who Is Served? Balancing the Duties of Probation and Parole Officers

In theory, juvenile probation and parole officers are officials who provide access to rehabilitation and treatment services—and supervision of compliance with the requirements of these services—on behalf of the juvenile justice system for juvenile offenders. They are not intended to serve exclusively as law enforcement officers but should ideally be caseworkers who are the directors and guides for the reintegration of juvenile offenders into society.[18] Nevertheless (and as discussed previously), the duties of these officers reflect the prevailing policies of their jurisdictions, so that they can become little more than managers of compliance, much as probation and parole officers are in the adult criminal justice system. This balancing process between social control and treatment is a central policy issue for probation, parole, and aftercare. Therefore, it is not surprising that probation and parole officers receive significant pressure from several sources:

• *The community.* Everyday citizens and community-serving agencies rely on juvenile probation and parole officers to provide both rehabilitative treatment and behavioral control. When juvenile offenders are returned to the community or enrolled in agency-based programs, probation and parole officers are viewed as the "managers" for participating youths. When violent or otherwise dangerous offenders are released, pressure increases on these officers to strictly control their clients.

• *The police.* Law enforcement agencies tend to look to probation and parole officers as adjuncts of the criminal justice system, regardless of whether they serve juveniles or adults. To many law enforcers, probation and parole are variants on and underlying policy of social control.

• *The participants.* Juveniles do not always understand or appreciate the role of the officials assigned to oversee their release. These officials are often considered to be nothing more than law enforcers. Compliance with requirements and conditions of release can be quite rigorous and intrusive. For example, mandatory house arrest, school attendance, and other controls on liberty can create a sense of resentment. This is especially true if conditions of release include mandatory drug and alcohol testing.

Given these frequently conflicting demands, how does one measure what is needed to be an effective probation or parole officer? What factors ought to be identified as criteria for effectiveness?

The answer to both of these questions is that truly effective officers require a combination of professional and personal traits—the old adage that only "special persons" are fit to perform well in certain professions. Perhaps the most notable trait is *dedication to their profession,* meaning that they have a fundamental sense of mission that is carried with them on every assignment and over an extended period of time. Effective probation and parole officers also tend to be *empathetic,* having an ability to understand and care about the unique circumstances of individual clients. At the same time, they must develop a degree of *professional instinct* so that they will be able to differentiate genuine progress toward rehabilitation from feigned rehabilitation by juvenile "con artists" who simply want to remain out of locked detention. Officers should use *proportional discipline* so that discipline is used as a corrective measure to *promote* compliance, rather than as a punitive measure to *coerce* compliance. And, in order to fulfill their mission as officers of the juvenile justice system (regardless of the bureaucratic source of their authority), probation and parole officers must exercise *professional discipline* in order to comply with the policies and regulations of their particular jurisdiction.

Which Process Is Due?
The Question of Proper Revocation

Probation and parole officers—and the systems they serve—are required to comply with standards of due process when performing their duties. This is especially true when a juvenile violates his or her probation or parole agreement. Before revoking probation or parole, officers and agencies must be diligent about complying with the offender's rights to notice, opportunity to be heard, and counsel. For example, the U.S. Supreme Court has held that the right to counsel extends to probation revocation hearings.[19] This means that neither probation officers nor probation agencies may summarily deny participants the right to be represented by counsel should they fail to comply with the requirements and conditions of their service. Officials must also show that reasonable efforts have been made to deliver treatment and rehabilitation services, and that the juvenile has failed to comply with the program despite being referred to these services. In other words, officers must prove at revocation hearings that every effort has been made by the system to provide services, that it is the youth's fault that requirements of the program were violated, and that the community will be best served if the client is returned to a locked facility.

What of Special Populations?
Addressing the Needs of Vulnerable Youths

All recipients of probation, parole, and aftercare must receive professional guidance and oversight to assure their full reintegration into society.

There are subsets of juveniles who are particularly vulnerable to recidivist behavior and must receive special treatment. An easily understood example of potentially increased vulnerability is the comparison between probationers and parolees: Young parolees and aftercare participants are particularly vulnerable because they have spent time in locked facilities, and therefore face reintegration problems that are not necessarily experienced by probationers who begin their dispositions in the community.

Mental Health Populations. A particularly vulnerable population is youths who require mental health services. Mentally ill participants require treatment throughout their contact with the juvenile justice system, both when in locked facilities and when participating in release-based corrections. One fundamental problem for program officers is arriving at an accurate diagnosis, and the danger is that they can misdiagnose a condition, or incorrectly determine that it is more or less severe than it really is. Another problem is the question of resources. Simply put, small communities do not provide many needed resources, and participants may therefore find it difficult to adjust to the requirements of their release. Large urban areas do have facilities and programs that can treat mentally ill youths, but even in this scenario the question is whether one has *access* to these resources. Depending on one's diagnosis, treatment can be delivered at varying degrees of intensity.

Dysfunctional Peer Associations. Many, if not most, offenders were members of marginalized peer groups prior to their referral into juvenile correctional systems. Gang affiliations and chronically antisocial peer associations are difficult to break without professional treatment and guidance. This is particularly true for youths who are released on parole or aftercare, because most of the residents continue to exhibit the same behavior and values as they exhibited when among their gang or otherwise marginalized peers. In essence, locked facilities replicate these same values. Treatment programs must address the high likelihood that released offenders will naturally gravitate toward these peer groups. One's initial return to old neighborhoods is a particularly vulnerable moment, and officers must observe and restrict the behavior of participants from the beginning. Schools, the police, and communities have established partnerships to combat dysfunctional peer associations. An example of this type of partnership is Gang Resistance Education and Training (GREAT), which is discussed further in Chapter 11.

Substance Abusers. Another vulnerable population are those who are addicts or substance abusers. Alcohol and drugs are both prohibited substances, with possession of the former constituting a status offense, and possession of the latter constituting a crime. Treatment includes testing for illicit use (an intrusive process), participation in recovery programs (such as Alateen and Narcotics Anonymous), and sensitivity on the part of officers and participating agencies to the special problems of juvenile alcoholics and addicts. As in the case of young people in need of mental health services, those in small communities do not always have access to adequate resources, whereas those in urban areas have a higher likelihood of receiving treatment.

How to Manage the System? An Evolving Philosophy

Probation, parole, and aftercare have become ubiquitous concepts in juvenile justice systems and are applied in accordance with the policies and standards of local jurisdictions. The long development of release programs has required a consistent evaluation of how to define "effectiveness," as well as adaptations of the roles of participants to the needs and standards of juvenile systems. This process of evaluation and adaptation will continue to take place, thus promoting a dynamic and evolving philosophy of release-based corrections.

Several policy and cultural trends will require an ongoing process of programmatic adaptation into the near future. Among these are the following:

- *First,* electronic monitoring technologies will remain an integral part of juvenile and adult release programs. These technologies allow probation, parole, and law enforcement officials to monitor compliance from remote locations. Thus, the need for personal contact on some compliance issues (such as house arrest) is reduced.

- *Second,* the nationwide crackdown on crime and delinquency will continue to remove categories of serious youth offenders from the juvenile justice system, as these offenders continue to be prosecuted before adult criminal courts. At the same time, juveniles at the lower end of the crime spectrum—those who commit minor offenses—are also being diverted out of the juvenile court's jurisdiction and into community programs. As a result, release-based corrections will increasingly be concerned with administering a middle ground of juvenile offenders who are neither serious nor minor offenders.

- *Third,* juvenile courts and other supervising agencies will increasingly hold parents responsible for their children's compliance with the requirements and conditions of release-based corrections. This trend is an outgrowth of policies that impose civil liability on parents for offenses committed by their children.

In a sense, these are not new issues in the history of juvenile justice process. They represent an evolution of fundamental policy and cultural questions that have existed since the beginning of probation and parole programs. The difference is that contemporary technologies, new law enforcement orientations, and evolving conceptions of responsibility are driving modern probation, parole, and aftercare policies.

Chapter Summary

Release-based corrections for juveniles have two theoretical purposes: treatment and rehabilitation. The concept of juvenile-focused community corrections is an old one, dating from old England and nineteenth-century America. Juveniles have been participants in community corrections from the beginning of release-based programs, particularly since the example of John Augustus.

Juvenile probation, parole, and aftercare are now integral features of juvenile justice process. They are conceptually similar in that they use community resources to provide treatment and rehabilitation under the supervision of professional officers. Although each jurisdiction has established its own standards and procedures, there are similarities in requirements and conditions that are imposed on participants. Restrictions on movement, peer association, and curfews are quite common. So too are mandatory school attendance, community service, and testing for illicit substances. Common programs include restitution, intensive supervision, house arrest, and electronic surveillance.

Release-based corrections is an evolving concept, and is consistently adapted and modified as policy and cultural norms transform. Probation and parole officers continue to serve in supervisory roles for youths on release, and they are compelled to manage demands from the community, the police, and their clients. Due-process concerns, the needs of special populations, and programmatic adaptations will continue to challenge professionals and participants in these programs.

Chapter 10 continues the theme of community corrections by investigating noncorrectional alternatives that are based in the community. These community-based alternatives are treatment and rehabilitation oriented, but they are not rooted in the juvenile corrections system. Rather, participating juveniles have been diverted *out* of the juvenile justice system into community-based programs.

Questions for Review

1. What are the purposes and policy considerations underlying probation, aftercare, and parole?

2. How did the underlying purposes and policy considerations develop in the modern era?

3. What is the role of juvenile probation in the juvenile justice system?

4. Describe juvenile probation.

5. What are the roles of juvenile parole and aftercare in the juvenile justice system?

6. Describe juvenile parole and aftercare.

7. What are some of the issues and debates involving probation, aftercare, and parole?

Key Terms and Concepts

The following topics were discussed in this chapter and are found in the Glossary:

Aftercare

Augustus, John

Binding

Community Corrections

Conditional Probation

Corrections-Managed Parole and Aftercare

Court-Administered Parole and Aftercare

Elmira Reformatory

House Arrest

Indeterminate Sentencing

Intensive Aftercare Supervision (IAS)

Intensive Probation Supervision (IPS)

Judicial Reprieve

Juvenile Intensive Probation Supervision (JIPS)

Morrissey v. Brewer

National Probation Act

Parole

Parole Boards

Penal Servitude Act of 1853

Probation

Restitution

Unconditional Probation

DISCUSSION BOX

The Utility of Net Widening

This chapter's Discussion Box is intended to stimulate critical discussion about the implications of expanding the "net" of the juvenile justice system.

Net widening refers to bringing more juveniles into the juvenile justice system who normally might not have been absorbed. One criticism of increasing the number of programs available for the treatment and rehabilitation of juveniles is that more and more juveniles will be referred to those programs. In this way, the "net" of the juvenile justice system has become widened. Net widening is discussed further in Chapter 10, but it is instructive to discuss it within the context of probation, parole, and aftercare.

Within the parameters of this concept, most probation, parole, and aftercare programs can select from a wide range of treatment options. Thus, even though serious and minor offenders may be diverted out of the system, the wider net permits greater numbers of juveniles to be processed into the "middle" range category of offenses. Release-based corrections is therefore a viable alternative to residential corrections because of the wider net.

Discussion Questions

1. Is the juvenile "net" broad enough to accommodate increasing numbers of released offenders?

2. Should more juveniles be released from locked facilities and refereed into parole and aftercare programs?

3. What *disadvantages* come from bringing more youths into the system and referring them out to an ever-expanding release-based corrections net?

4. What *advantages* come from bringing more youths into the system and referring them out to an ever-expanding release-based corrections net?

5. Who should be granted release-based corrections? What types of participants should receive treatment in the net?

Recommended Web Sites

The following Web sites investigate the subject of juvenile probation, parole, and aftercare.

American Probation and Parole Association: http://www.appa-net.org/
Colorado Juvenile Parole Board: http://www.cdhs.state.co.us/OPI/jpboard/
Juvenile Justice Evaluation Center (Aftercare): http://www.jrsa.org/jjec/programs/aftercare/
Pennsylvania Council of Chief Probation Officers: http://www.pachiefprobation officers.org/
Texas Juvenile Probation Commission: http://www.tjpc.state.tx.us/

Note: The Web site URLs and exercises below are also from the book's study site: http://www.sagepub.com/martin

Web Exercise

Using this chapter's recommended Internet sites, conduct an online investigation of juvenile probation, parole, and aftercare.

- How do probation, parole, and aftercare programs differ nationally? In what ways are they similar?
- What are some of the common roles of probation and parole officers?
- Which jurisdictions do you consider to be the best organized and managed systems?

For an online search of probation, parole, and aftercare, students should use a search engine and enter the following keywords:

"Juvenile Aftercare"

"Juvenile Probation"

Recommended Readings

The following publications provide discussions on juvenile probation, parole, and aftercare:

Allen, H. E., Eskridge, C. W., Latessa, E. J., & Vito, G. F. (1985). *Probation and parole in America*. New York: Free Press.

Armstrong, T. L. (Ed.). (1991). *Intensive interventions with high-risk youths: Promising approaches in juvenile probation and parole*. Monsey, NY: Criminal Justice Press.

Ball, R. A., Huff, R., & Lilly, R. (1988). *House arrest and correctional policy: Doing time at home*. Thousand Oaks, CA: Sage.

Ellsworth, T. (Ed.). (1997). *Contemporary community corrections* (2nd ed.). Long Grove, IL: Waveland Press.

McShane, M. D., & Krause, W. (1992). *Community corrections*. New York: Prentice Hall.

Notes

1. See American Correctional Association. (2003). *2003 Directory of adult and juvenile correctional departments, institutions, agencies, and probation and parole authorities*. Laurel, MD: American Correctional Association. See also American Correctional Association. (2003). *2003–2004 National juvenile detention directory*. Laurel, MD: American Correctional Association.

2. For an analysis of adult probation and parole, see Killinger, G. C., Kerper, H. B., & Cromwell, P. F., Jr. (1976). *Probation and parole in the criminal justice system*. St Paul, MN: West Publishing.

3. See Ellsworth, T. (Ed.). (1997). *Contemporary community corrections* (2nd ed.). Long Grove, IL: Waveland Press.

4. Black, H. C. (1968). *Black's law dictionary: Definitions of the terms and phrases of American and English jurisprudence, ancient and modern* (4th ed., rev., p. 213). St. Paul, MN: West Publishing.

5. See Augustus, J. (1972). *John Augustus, first probation officer: John Augustus' original report on his labors—1852.* Montclair, NJ: Patterson-Smith.

6. Snyder, H. N., & Sickmund, M. (1999). *Juvenile offenders and victims: 1999 National report* (p. 86). Washington, DC: U.S. Department of Justice.

7. See Allen, H. E., Eskridge, C. W., Latessa, E. J., & Vito, G. F. (1985). *Probation and parole in America.* New York: Free Press.

8. Black, H. C. (1968). *Black's law dictionary: Definitions of the terms and phrases of American and English jurisprudence, ancient and modern* (4th ed. rev., p. 1367). St. Paul, MN: West Publishing.

9. Adapted from Snyder, H. N., & Sickmund, M. (1999). *Juvenile offenders and victims: 1999 National report* (p. 159). Washington, DC: U.S. Department of Justice.

10. For a good example of a national report on juvenile probation systems, see Hurst, H., IV, & McFall Torbet, P. (1993). *Organization and administration of juvenile services: Probation, aftercare, and state delinquent institutions.* Pittsburgh, PA: National Center for Juvenile Justice.

11. See Walker, E. (1989). The community intensive treatment for youth program: A specialized community-based program for high-risk youth in Alabama. In *Law and Psychiatry Review, 13.* See also Armstrong, T. L. (1988). National survey of juvenile intensive probation supervision, Part I. *Criminal Justice Abstracts, 20.*

12. See Staples, W. G. (1986). Restitution and recidivism rates of juvenile offenders: Results from four experimental studies. *Criminology, 24.*

13. For an opposing view, see Petersilia, J. (1986). Exploring the option of house arrest. *Federal Probation, 50.*

14. For a discussion of determinate and indeterminate sentencing within the context of juvenile parole, see Ashford, J. B., & Le Croy, C. W. (1993). Juvenile parole policy in the United States: Determinate versus indeterminate models. *Justice Quarterly, 10*(2).

15. Black, H. C. (1968). *Black's law dictionary: Definitions of the terms and phrases of American and English jurisprudence, ancient and modern* (4th ed., rev., p. 1273). St. Paul, MN: West Publishing.

16. Rush, G. E. (2000). *The dictionary of criminal justice* (5th ed., p. 8). New York: Dushkin/McGraw-Hill.

17. Morrissey v. Brewer, 408 U.S. 471 (1972). See also Gannon v. Scarpelli, 411 U.S. 778 (1973).

18. See Colley, L. L., Culbertson, R. C., & Latessa, E. J. (1987). Juvenile probation officers: A job analysis. *Juvenile and Family Court Journal, 38.*

19. Mempa v. Rhay, 339 U.S. 128 (1967).

10 Community-Based Juvenile Programs

Community-based programs and facilities are intended to be alternative resources for the juvenile justice system. Inside many facilities, small groups of offenders are housed in homelike atmospheres that are intended to replicate nurturing environments. Nevertheless, residents who break the rules may be subjected to intensive intervention by administrators. For example, in June 1997 three residents of the Haney Cottage building in the Bellewood juvenile facility of Fayette County, Kentucky, were observed behaving strangely.[1] Cottage administrators suspected that they were intoxicated on drugs and decided to search the rooms of all residents. As they conducted the search, one of the residents hinted that she might have drugs hidden in her clothing. Male guards did not wish to conduct a strip search, so a female administrator was located.

The female administrator searched each of the residents individually in the presence of another female witness. Each resident was ordered to disrobe and was subjected to a visual (rather than physical) inspection. No drugs were found. In a lawsuit filed against the facility, one of the girls argued that without a search warrant, the strip searches were unconstitutional. It was held that they were properly conducted under the circumstances.

In previous chapters, the juvenile justice system was defined as an interwoven network of agencies and programs, including government agencies, public and private youth facilities, professional caseworkers, law enforcement personnel, and juvenile courts. Parallel to this official and highly structured network is an affiliated system of schools, parents, youth agencies, and other institutions that serve as guardians of young people. This second category—constituting the basic components of *the community*—is charged with informing, instructing, and nurturing the development of youths into responsible adults.

Photo 10.1   Innovative programming. A youth band plays at Children's Village in New York in 1955.

The community is an integral participant in juvenile justice process. Its role is just as important as any other component of the system, such as the police and the courts. And yet, its configuration is specially designed to meet the needs of each jurisdiction and is usually less structured than other components of the system. Significantly, the community is uniquely capable of providing many more treatment and rehabilitative services than the other components. Youths who are fortunate enough to be diverted out of juvenile court and into community-based programs are likely to have access to more beneficial interventions than are received by court-controlled offenders.

Community-based programs are not the same as community corrections (discussed in Chapter 9); they are conceptually distinguishable. Although both may access the same or similar programs, and apply similar treatment philosophies, they are intended to serve different constituencies. An important difference is that, whereas community corrections programs manage youths who have been processed through the juvenile justice system and fully adjudicated in juvenile court, community-based programs manage youths who have been *diverted out* of the system. Another fundamental difference is that youths diverted out of the system and into the community are placed on a track that minimizes their contact with juvenile justice officials; on the other hand, participants in release-based correctional programs frequently experience highly intrusive contact with officials.

The discussion in this chapter will review the following topics:

- Origins: Background to Community-Based Juvenile Programs
- Juvenile Diversion: A Noninstitutional Alternative
- Widening the Net: Partner Institutions and Placement Alternatives
- Anticipating and Managing Juvenile Problems: Prevention and Treatment Models

CHAPTER PERSPECTIVE 10.1

Broken Windows Theory

If community-based programs are to be advanced, what of the communities that juvenile offenders grow up in? If these communities are dysfunctional, does it make sense to repair and improve them? If so, which features should receive primary attention from policy makers?

Since the 1920s and 1930s, sociologists, criminologists, and urban theorists have studied the relationship between one's personal environment and criminal or delinquent behavior. This field of study—rooted in the influential Chicago School of Sociology—was originally called Social Ecology Theory. It hypothesized that urban physical arrangements such as housing, lighting, and open spaces are conducive to the exhibition of certain behavioral characteristics of neighborhood residents. These *structural* conditions, if deficient, can be fundamentally detrimental. During the 1960s and 1970s, experts built upon the Chicago School's theoretical foundations and identified a number of factors that associate physical environment, social composition, and cultural norms to delinquency and crime.

The Broken Windows Theory refers to a modern conceptualization of the association between structural environment, delinquency, and crime. It regards physical decline in the urban core to be a principal factor in the high crime rates found in many neighborhoods. Communities with poor physical environments are often characterized by indicators of neighborhood blight such as broken windows, rundown buildings, trashed empty lots, graffiti, and poor lighting. In theory, these conditions cause residents to fear for their personal space (safety), and residents essentially give up on maintaining neighborhood infrastructure or a sense of community. According to Broken Windows Theory, this precipitates a generalized social and cultural decline that can last for years. With this decline, delinquency and crime are likely to increase, particularly among poorly mentored youths and marginalized adults. Such neighborhoods become known for their poor environments, thus attracting criminal outsiders such as drug dealers, prostitutes, and thieves.

In order to reverse this trend, Broken Windows theorists hold that the multifaceted "broken windows" must be repaired. This necessitates repair or demolition of old buildings, construction of new housing with adequate security (also known as "defensible space"), provision of adequate lighting, security patrols, safe community areas (such as parks and centers), and general cleanup of empty lots and graffiti. Repair of these "broken windows" will theoretically lead to stronger social relationships, increased pride in protecting stable neighborhoods, and the restoration of a positive cultural identity.

Origins: Background to
Community-Based Juvenile Programs

Although community-based programs are now quite common, it is only recently that the broader community has been integrated into the overall profile of juvenile justice process. The reason for this integration was a conclusion by policy makers that community programs are often more effective in dealing with juvenile deviance than are correctional systems (especially locked facilities). Findings such as those reported in 1967 by the President's Commission on Law Enforcement and the Administration of Justice strongly argued that the effects of stigma and labeling associated with formal processing through the juvenile justice system often led to recidivist behavior.[2]

In order to understand the modern role of the community, it is necessary to first appreciate what is meant by the term *community,* and then identify the programmatic origins of juvenile-focused programs in the modern era.

Fundamental Concepts: Understanding "Community"

What is community? What components make up a community? Who are the central members of the community? Most people understand community to refer to both an objective conceptualization and a subjective one.

Objectively, community refers to identifiable neighborhoods, towns, and cities. These are geographic designations that primarily describe political boundaries, although demographic factors such as ethnicity and class are also important features of an objective approach to community. Under this conceptualization, group interaction is a function of understanding political decisions, ethnic concerns, and class interests.

Subjectively, community is a philosophical concept that transcends political and demographic boundaries. Instead, it is an integration of all facets of a particular locale, and the strength of a community is determined by how functional this integration is. For example, a strong community refers to cooperative, consensus-driven interaction among its constituent participants. A sense of unity drives a value system that is conducive to, and encourages, juvenile reintegration into society. On the other hand, a weak community is one that is largely uncooperative and factionalized. In theory, the former (a strong community) is more likely to provide rehabilitative treatment for youths who have been diverted out of the jurisdiction of the juvenile court.

Regardless of which conceptualization is deliberated, it is the reintegration of youths that is of paramount concern. Youths understand who makes up their community and are familiar with the dynamics—and local rules—of interaction among members of the community. For this reason, caseworkers and other officials must be sympathetic and savvy about local resources and the needs of juveniles who are sent into community-based programs.

Programmatic Origins

Community-based programs are a relatively recent innovation in juvenile justice systems, having their origins in the 1950s and 1960s. From the outset, such programs represented the *deinstitutionalization* leg of the Four Ds philosophy of juvenile justice process.[3]

One of the first community-based programs began in 1950, when the **New Jersey Experimental Project for the Treatment of Youthful Offenders,** commonly known as the **Highfields Project,** was established on the former estate of Charles Lindbergh.[4] Highfields was intended to be an alternative to the existing training school model. It was a short-term residency program in which 20 male delinquents received intensive therapy in group interaction units five times per week. The groups were supervised by trained staff, and each group was expected to be responsible for controlling the behavior of its individual members. Participants worked locally in a psychiatric facility and were permitted to participate in supervised excursions into the community for recreation.

The Highfields model was a very influential prototypical program and was adapted to other jurisdictions. In 1959, Provo, Utah, adapted the Highfields model by requiring boys to participate in the program for five days per week but permitting them to live at home rather than in a residential facility. Similarly, Newark, New Jersey, established a Highfields-type nonresidency program during the 1960s. Also during the 1960s, New York established several residential facilities called Short-Term Adolescent Residential Treatment centers, or **START.**

In all of these early programs, participants were expected to fully participate in treatment programs, with the goal of reintegrating them into the community. The programs were intended to treat youths, rehabilitate them, and divert them away from delinquent behavior. This philosophy distinguished them from traditional juvenile justice programs at the time, which focused more on the locked training school model.

Juvenile Diversion:
A Noninstitutional Alternative

Juvenile **diversion** is the conceptual underpinning for community-based programs. It is a process that moves (diverts) juveniles away from the formal and more authoritarian components of the juvenile justice system. It also attempts to reduce the likelihood of stigma associated with adjudication in juvenile court and incarceration in locked correctional facilities.

Diversion programs reflect a relatively new philosophy and were first implemented nationally during the 1960s and 1970s.[5] The early programs were highly localized, and it was not until the passage of the Juvenile Justice and Delinquency Prevention Act of 1974 that federal laws and resources stimulated a national movement toward diversionary alternatives. As discussed previously, the Act tied federal funding to state restrictions on the detention and institutionalization of juvenile delinquents. In addition, discretionary block grants were released to assist in alternative dispositions of juvenile offenders. These initiatives led to the adoption of diversion programs throughout the nation. The result was that status offenders were deinstitutionalized, and many youths were removed from adult facilities.

Basic Concepts: Models and Principles of Diversion

Diversion programs are coordinated by youth agencies, juvenile courts, or the police. One particular feature of the court- and police-administered programs is that the system imposes a direct threat of referral back into the formal justice system for juveniles who fail to comply with stipulated rules of the program. As with most juvenile justice policies and programs, juvenile diversion models are not uniform in how they are designed.

Two models generally represent diversion programs applied by specific jurisdictions:

- *Pure diversion*—preadjudicatory diversion—is a process of immediate diversion, meaning that young offenders are sent directly into community-based programs before they are adjudicated by a juvenile court and processed into the formal juvenile justice system.
- *Secondary diversion*—postadjudicatory diversion—is a category of diversion programs that release juveniles who have already been processed into the formal juvenile justice system. They are released into community-based programs prior to final disposition.

These models are indicative of the varying degrees of intervention by official components of the juvenile justice system. Although all diversion is intended to significantly reduce exposure to juvenile court and the police, in many jurisdictions these official components still play a prominent role in the supervision or processing of participants.

Despite differences in the implementation of various programs, the following principles outline a basic consensus on diversion:

- *Localized therapy.* Treatment and rehabilitation in the community[6]
- *Minimized stigma.* Reduced possibility of stigmatization that is often associated with exposure to the official juvenile justice system[7]
- *Maximized assimilation.* Maximum feasible reintegration into the community with minimal recidivist behavior[8]

These principles have made diversion a desirable alternative model to formal adjudication, and it continues to be expanded in many jurisdictions.

As a result, the "net" of the juvenile justice system has broadened significantly, and this expansion has led to criticisms of existing diversion programs.

From Theory to Practice: Operationalizing Diversion

One critical feature of policy making is the process of applying theory to practice. Theoretical models and principles may be quite noteworthy, but they are meaningless if they cannot be operationalized (implemented) in the real world. An example of operationalized diversion theory occurred during the 1960s and 1970s, when Youth Service Bureaus and other facilities were established as part of a sweeping reassessment of juvenile justice policy. As discussed in previous chapters, the Youth Service Bureaus represented a nationally coordinated policy, and were intended to be a primary center for dealing with delinquents and status offenders. Bureaus coordinated their activities with juvenile courts, the police, and probation agencies, and about 150 were established.

Modern diversion models and principles are operationalized in many ways, depending on the needs of each jurisdiction. For example, diversion programs either directly provide services to participants, or steer them toward these services. However, certain commonalities can be identified across systems, as most diversion programs tend to be centered on—and are delivered out of—similar institutions. The centers of juvenile diversionary programs may be profiled as follows:

- *Juvenile Courts.* Formal diversionary programs and services with extensive oversight, and with the authority to impose sanctions on those who fail to successfully comply with the requirements of the diversionary program
- *The Police.* Informal diversionary programs and services; usually an exercise of police discretion either at the scene of an offense or after taking an offender into custody
- *Youth Service Agencies.* Formal diversionary programs and services with extensive oversight and coordination of a variety of cooperating agencies; often closely linked to the juvenile court

Linked to these centers of juvenile diversion are many creative programs that coordinate the services of a variety of participants for the delivery of community-based juvenile programs. Among the administrators of these programs are child and youth services, schools, and federal initiatives.

Child and Youth Services. State agencies have been established to provide services to at-risk children and families. The mission of these agencies is twofold: First, to protect the welfare of at-risk children and youths by providing counseling, institutional advocacy, and day or foster care. These services include pregnancy counseling, protection of the rights of children, and the provision of "safe places" during the day or evening. The second facet of the mission of service agencies is to provide assistance to at-risk families, such as counseling, prevention of abuse and neglect, and economic assistance. Services include supervision over the family environment, crisis intervention, and referral to employment and financial programs. State child and youth service agencies frequently enter into partnerships with specialized private agencies to provide these services.

Schools. Educational institutions are ideal venues for diversion programs because they are well integrated into the broader community. They are also already staffed with a variety of professional personnel who are specialists in working with young people. Although schools are not always integral components of diversion programs, they often become participants by adapting existing educational services (routinely provided to *all* juveniles) to the needs of at-risk juveniles. Specialized initiatives for youths in need of supervision include police liaison programs, school-based community service requirements, and skills training through partnerships with community agencies. The key to success for school-based diversion is to regard schools as hubs, or centers, for the provision of a full range of interventions that are available from other public and private agencies.

Federal Initiatives. A number of youth-focused programs have been implemented by the federal government as a way to promote nationwide policy initiatives. Implemented at the local level, these programs have received federal funding, and have emphasized vocational and educational services for poor or otherwise at-risk youths. Although these initiatives have not been diversion programs *per se,* they are indicative of a national consensus favoring intensive interventions for at-risk juveniles. For example, federal **Head Start** programs have delivered preschool and early school educational services to youths from poor or culturally marginalized environments.[9] The objective of Head Start is to provide instruction in basic reading and verbal skills for youths who might otherwise grow up with poor skills, and thereby pose an increased possibility of future delinquency or criminality. The **Head Start Bureau** is managed by the U.S. Department of Health and Human Services.

Disagreement on Implementation: Critiquing Diversion

Diversionary programs and philosophies have been the subject of criticism. This criticism has emanated from practitioners, policy makers, members of the community, and participants. Although most parties accept the general goals of diversion—rehabilitation and removal from the correctional system—there is disagreement about the optimal method for implementing diversion. There is also disagreement about whether it can have a negative impact on society despite its positive goals.

One critique of diversion highlights the types of youths who are processed into diversionary programs. The ideal profile of participants is that they exhibit some degree of the following attributes:

- First offenders
- Status or minor offenses
- Receptive to treatment
- High probability of rehabilitation
- Low probability of recidivism

This ideal profile is open to one fundamental criticism: Not all juveniles are alike, and it is difficult to predict how well diversion will succeed—even with those who fit this profile. For example, some status offenders exhibit highly recidivist behavior. Also, many youths diverted out of the juvenile justice system are repeat (rather than first) offenders; they receive diversion because their offenses are minor. Significantly, many juveniles (especially recidivist status offenders) consider diversion to be a "slap on the wrist" or a "cakewalk." The danger of this attitude is that young people are likely to conclude that society does not consider their behavior to be very serious, and that further offenses will likewise be dealt with leniently. They eventually find themselves in serious trouble because they do not fully understand the ramifications of recidivist behavior, even for relatively minor offenses.

Another critique of diversion (and certainly a central one) is that jurisdictions are likely to consign an increasing number of offenders into these programs, thus bringing more youths into the overall juvenile justice net than would normally be admitted. This process was first introduced in Chapter 9, and is referred to as **net widening**. Net widening, in essence, *increases* rather than decreases the likelihood that youths will be brought into some component of the system.[10] For example, youths who would have merely received warnings from juvenile judges, or "street corner" and "station house" dispositions from the police, are more likely to be transferred into diversionary programs. In effect, the juvenile justice system may unintentionally become larger and more intrusive even though diversion is considered to be a more benign and treatment-focused form of rehabilitation than is formal adjudication. Thus, the authoritarian and coercive components of the official juvenile justice system are theoretically replaced by new modes of authoritarianism and coercion that supposedly exist outside of the official system.

Widening the Net: Partner Institutions and Placement Alternatives

The foregoing discussion—and our discussions in previous chapters—point up the fact that the juvenile justice system casts a very wide net. In comparison to the adult criminal justice system, a multiplicity of institutions comprise this net, with the result that comparable programs found in the juvenile justice system are not routinely offered to offenders in the adult criminal system. Many community-based institutions operate under a more broadly defined mission in the juvenile system, and partners within the net include a variety of social service agencies, volunteers, and community institutions such as schools and community-oriented police programs.

Youths who are diverted into community programs are often children in need of supervision (CHINS) rather than status offenders or delinquents, meaning that an intake officer or judge has determined that treatment can best be obtained through community-based agencies. These agencies provide counseling, shelter, and other services that would otherwise be unavailable in the formal system. For this reason, intake officers and judges are keen to use the network of partner institutions found in the community.

As we move into a discussion of community-based placement, an initial observation must be remembered: It is important to emphasize that there are many nonresidential programs that do not mandate that children be removed from their homes. In other words, placement programs (where youths are housed in community-based institutions) are distinguishable from nonplacement programs. Bearing this distinction in mind, it is helpful to conceptualize partner institutions and placement alternatives as encompassing the following concepts:

- *Restrictive Community Placement.* Placements in the community under defined terms of probation or other diversionary agreements. The activities of participants are regulated, often quite intensively. Group homes are typical examples of this type of community placement.
- *Benign Community Placement.* Less restrictive, and often nonrestrictive community placements. Participants are permitted the same or similar freedoms of movement and association as any other youth. Foster homes are examples of this type of community placement.
- *Experiential Community Placement.* Controlled placements in rural communities. Participants are required to participate in a series of esteem- and character-building maneuvers over an established period of time. Wilderness programs comprise this alternative.

Table 10.1 summarizes the attributes of restrictive, benign, and experiential community placement programs.

Restrictive Community Placement: Group Homes

Readers may recall that group homes were defined in Chapter 8 as nonsecure residential facilities managed by professional staff who serve as administrators, teachers, and counselors. They are distinguishable from secure correctional facilities in that they try to replicate the values and social interactions of family units. Group homes also serve larger residential

TABLE 10.1   COMMUNITY PLACEMENT ALTERNATIVES

Community-based juvenile programs make up the ever-widening "net" of the juvenile justice system. The purpose of these programs is to remove youths from the official components of the system, and thereby reduce stigma and increase the likelihood of rehabilitation.

This table summarizes the fundamental characteristics of three models of community-based placement alternatives.

Placement Alternatives	Placement Profile		
	Typical Facility	**Degree of Liberty**	**Length of Placement**
Restrictive Community Placement	Group homes	Regulated, often intensively	Variable time, often lengthy
Benign Community Placement	Foster homes	Supervised, but nonrestrictive	Variable time, often lengthy
Experiential Community Placement	Wilderness programs	Regulated, focused character-building activities	Fixed time of placement

populations than do foster homes—foster families have as few as one foster child, whereas group home populations often number up to a dozen residents. Nevertheless, attempts are made to integrate facilities and residents into surrounding communities as much as possible. The purpose is to make the entire institution a neighborhood-based center for peer interaction and community service. Counseling and education are ideally designed to treat and give positive direction to residents. Because of this underlying concept, the professional staff also serve as parental role models, but not in the same manner as do foster parents.

Because the assignment of youths to group homes is an intermediate sanction rendered by juvenile courts, judges retain ultimate authority over the disposition of residents. Mandatory schedules are assigned to residents for group and community activities that are managed by the professional staff. Curfews are routinely imposed, and there is a greatly reduced degree of freedom to move about the community at will than is found in foster homes. Thus, supervision and administration are more rigorously enforced than in foster homes, and violators may be returned to the court for an adjusted disposition, including transfer to a locked facility.

Halfway houses are a type of group home that houses up to 30 or 40 youths. Residents are usually youths who are transitioning from correctional or substance abuse institutions to full release. Participants are sent to halfway houses as a way to prepare them for eventual reintegration into the community. If the population is fairly large, residents will be divided into two or more groups with assigned professional supervisors.

Benign Community Placement:
Foster Homes and Day Treatment Centers

Foster homes and day treatment centers are typical community placement alternatives. They are intended to be relatively benign (noncoercive) alternatives to formal processing through the juvenile justice system. The purpose of these institutions is to provide needed services in settings that are as closely linked to the community as possible. Foster homes are usually temporary placements for juveniles, and day treatment centers are conceptually similar to outpatient hospital care in that designated hours are set aside during the day for in-house participation.

Foster Homes (revisited). As discussed in Chapter 8, foster homes are nonsecure residential facilities that are less restrictive than group homes, with relatively small numbers of residents. Circumstances leading to foster placement invariably involve the collapse of a child's family unit, meaning that his or her parents are incapable of properly caring for them. The state (via family or juvenile court) is empowered to remove children from these circumstances and find alternative arrangements with foster families. Foster care usually serves victims of abuse and neglect rather than lawbreakers, and the homes themselves are community-based facilities that attempt as much as possible to substitute functional foster families for dysfunctional biological families.

The heads of group homes are **foster parents,** who—unlike their professional group-home counterparts—are not professionally trained managers. Foster parents ideally nurture their residents and provide them with the guidance that was absent from their homes. The selection of foster families should (if possible) involve a rigorous screening process, followed by a regular monitoring schedule by caseworkers. Unfortunately, one reality is that there are recurrent reports of serious problems in some foster homes, including neglectful foster parents, inadequate funding for essential services, and generally rundown conditions. The worst scenarios occur when problems are allowed to linger for long periods of time because of poor supervision by child and youth agencies. Of course, not all homes suffer from these deficiencies, and an obligation exists for public officials to correct discovered problems and punish the managers of these facilities. This can only be accomplished by rigorous supervision and intervention from child and youth service agencies.

Day Treatment Centers. These institutions are nonresidential facilities that are designed to provide daytime treatment services to at-risk youths. Participants sometimes include juvenile offenders who might otherwise be placed in detention centers.[11] Day treatment centers may be public or private facilities, and it is not uncommon for juvenile or family courts to enter into contracts with private service providers.

Assignment to day treatment centers can be done either as a condition of probation or as a mandated diversionary alternative. Youths receiving such assignments live at home but spend their days participating in treatment programs and return home in the evening. These agencies are designed to be centers for treatment, education, and counseling, with vocational training also being available to develop job skills. Daily therapies can include life skills training, anger management, and peer support. Because many participants require special treatment, supervision is potentially quite intensive—akin in many respects to juvenile intensive probation supervision (JIPS)—depending on the circumstances of each case.

Experiential Community Placement: Wilderness Programs

Wilderness programs were described in Chapter 8 as minimum-security residential correctional institutions, usually modeled as camps or ranches. Facilities are nonsecure, and most placements are reserved for first-time offenders or other juveniles who have committed minor offenses. Most facilities are located in forests, deserts, mountains, or near the sea. Programmatically, they are task-oriented and often involve hiking, obstacle courses, rope challenges, and water navigation.

Wilderness programs are inherently creative and experimental, and provide an opportunity for uniquely rehabilitative encounters.[12] One should think of these programs as "experiential" community-based placements, because rehabilitation is achieved through short-term—though intensive—*experiences* involving choreographed group interactions and activities. They ideally deliver treatment, promote self-esteem, strengthen self-reliance, and engender trust in others. Such programs arguably present less foreboding options for judges, because they are not located in urban-centered neighborhoods; they are, instead, located in close proximity to smaller towns in rural settings. These rural communities offer placid alternatives to the rushed lifestyles of many urban centers. As discussed in the historical overviews in previous chapters, this concept of rural-based rehabilitation has been a prevalent concept since the era of the child savers and other nineteenth century reformers.

The Outward Bound Model.[13] The first modern program was established in Great Britain during the Second World War. It emphasized personal growth and development through positive confrontation with "challenge" obstacles. This concept—known as Outward Bound—was adopted in the United States, beginning in Colorado in 1962. This first program was located high in the Rocky Mountains and stressed group cohesion and individual achievement. It did so by creating a series of challenge activities such as hiking, rock climbing, rappelling, and survival training. Other states adapted this model to their particular needs, designing challenge activities around their own geography and topology.

Most Outward Bound programs emphasize school-like environments where participants learn about individual confidence, trust in others, and the meaning of personal character. Youths are generally housed on-site at Outward Bound schools and camps. Professional counselors manage the challenge programs, which usually last for three weeks and consist of the following four phases:

1. **Training.** Orientation to the program and instruction in fundamental skills

2. **Group Challenges.** An expedition in which participants learn the value of teamwork

3. **Individual Challenges.** Obstacles designed to build confidence within individual participants

4. **Testing.** A short period in which participants are tested on values and lessons learned during the program

A variant on the Outward Bound model was established in 1970 in Massachusetts. This program, known as **Homeward Bound,** also developed personal growth through wilderness experiences.[14] It established a six-week program that provided daytime challenges and nighttime education on survival skills and the natural environment. Other variations on the Outward Bound theme include community-based juvenile programs where participants make daytime excursions to the challenge sites and return to the community centers in the evening.

Most programs such as Outward Bound and Homeward Bound are well integrated into the overall juvenile justice and support systems of their jurisdictions. Juvenile courts, probation agencies, and other components of the system usually give strong support to wilderness experiences—largely because they have some input and control over who is admitted as participants and how the programs are managed. However, not all wilderness programs are closely linked to every facet of the official juvenile justice system, and not all are uncontroversial, as illustrated by the case of VisionQuest.

The VisionQuest Model. Founded in 1973 in Tucson, Arizona, and now located in more than a dozen states, VisionQuest is a privately run, for-profit organization. Participants—many of whom would normally be sent to locked facilities—are assigned for long periods of time, lasting for 12 to 18 months. Although juvenile courts assign participants to this program, probation officers and others have complained that a lack of official oversight has allowed juveniles to be exposed to unacceptable risks and that some youths have been abused by staff. These allegations have certainly caused controversy and debate over the VisionQuest model, but the program has also received a great deal of positive attention from the media over the years.[15]

The VisionQuest program is demanding and requires boot-camp–like conditions. For example, participants have been required to live in tepees with a counselor and several other participants. They have had to sleep on the ground, exercise intensively, perform designated chores, and complete their school work. Those who fail to perform any of these activities are required to undergo direct and instant confrontation with a counselor. The wilderness portion of the program can last for months. Interestingly (and uniquely), VisionQuest is known for its innovative use of a wagon train, sea survival instruction, and wilderness instruction. The wagon train travels for months in the western United States toward Canada. During the trip, participants perform chores and learn how to handle horses and mules. After the wagon train trip, participants are sent to the VisionQuest headquarters in Arizona, where program managers decide whether they can be returned to their communities.

Anticipating and Managing Juvenile Problems: Prevention and Treatment Models

It is clear from the foregoing discussions that community-based juvenile programs are fundamentally rehabilitative—at least in theory. They are comprised of models for intervention that have the ultimate goal of returning functional individuals to the greater community. This goal (of return) is certainly desirable, but as a practical matter can only be achieved through community-based intervention services. These services are categorized as follows:

- *Prevention Services.* Community-based intervention services that anticipate potential problems, and are delivered as a means to reduce the probability that a youth will return to the juvenile justice system
- *Treatment Services.* Community-based intervention services that manage existing problems, and are delivered to rehabilitate youths prior to their reintegration with the community

The providers of these services include community-centered resources discussed in previous chapters, such as families, community agencies, and schools. Most prevention and treatment programs are small, serving approximately 50 participants, and roughly 30% are foster homes, group homes, or shelters.[16] Approximately 50% of community-based programs are managed by nonprofit agencies, 39% by government agencies, and 10% are for-profit programs.[17] It is important to bear in mind that no single prevention or treatment model serves every jurisdiction or every client. The following types of intervention have been identified by researchers as the three most common models for prevention and treatment[18]

1. Skill development.

2. Individual, group, and family counseling

3. Mentoring relationships

Interestingly, many programs that operationalize these models are directly linked to official probation, parole, and aftercare programs. Thus, community-based prevention and treatment programs are often enlisted as partners and integral components of the official juvenile justice system. Thus, when necessary, official components of the juvenile justice system such as the police and courts may be called upon to mandate prevention and treatment services.[19]

Anticipating the Problem: Prevention

Prevention is a philosophy of *proaction* rather than *reaction*. It seeks to marshal community resources to stop emerging problems at their inception, rather than responding to them after the fact. As discussed in Chapter 3, many theories of delinquency causation cite societal and individual risk factors that operate as catalysts for delinquency and crime. In theory, if these risk factors can be preemptively prevented, juveniles can be diverted from self-destructive behaviors and confrontation with authority. If this can be accomplished, at-risk juveniles will be less likely to become associated with the juvenile justice system, or, if they do, then hopefully for less serious offenses.

Understanding Prevention. The philosophy of prevention is rooted in the concept of crime prevention. Crime prevention is essentially a community-wide partnership, whereby the criminal justice system and the broader community attempt to identify and alleviate social and economic problems that increase the likelihood of criminal deviance. Likewise, delinquency prevention rallies the juvenile justice system and the community behind the cause of addressing factors that lead to juvenile delinquency. Three degrees of prevention exist:

1. **Primary Prevention.** Intervention with youths who have not begun breaking the law or otherwise engaging in antisocial deviance.

2. **Secondary Prevention.** Intervention with youths who have only recently begun engaging in antisocial deviance, and are in an early phase of committing relatively minor or status offenses. This is usually predelinquency prevention.

3. **Tertiary Prevention.** Intervention with youths who have engaged in serious and chronic deviance, and who have already entered the juvenile justice system. These youths are technically in need of treatment rather than prevention, because previous efforts to prevent the onset of delinquency have failed. Such youths should be evaluated within the context of rehabilitation and restoration in addition to prevention.

Prevention as a National Goal. Prevention has been a national goal since the early 1970s, as evidenced by the formation of the federal **Office of Juvenile Justice and Delinquency Prevention** (OJJDP),[20] which was established by Congress with the passage of the Juvenile Justice and Delinquency Prevention Act of 1974. The Act (and subsequent amendments) sought to deinstitutionalize status offenders, separate delinquents from adult criminals, and generally reduce the more punitive features of the juvenile justice system. The Act further sought to promote the establishment of prevention and diversion programs nationally.

The mission of OJJDP is to coordinate national policy for preventing juvenile delinquency and victimization. Its principal means for accomplishing this mandate is to conduct independent research, to assist experts and agencies in program evaluation, and to recommend initiatives for delinquency prevention and treatment. OJJDP is a resource for technical assistance and program evaluation and has had an important effect on policy. For example, two important documents were published that addressed the question of a *national* (rather than localized) strategy for delinquency prevention: These are the *Comprehensive Strategy for Serious, Violent and Chronic Juvenile Offenders*[21] and the *Guide for Implementing the Comprehensive Strategy for Serious, Violent and Chronic Juvenile Offenders.*[22] Examples of recommended programs promoting a national prevention strategy have included the following two "encounter" programs that promote prevention through personal interaction:

1. **Students Taking on Prevention (STOP).** STOP is a program that encourages youths to "recognize, report, and reduce" juvenile violence. Encounters consist of interpersonal outreach by juvenile peers to other juveniles. The program was developed by Family, Career and Community Leaders of America (FCCLA)[23] and funded by OJJDP.

2. **JUMP.** A mentorship program administered by OJJDP. Encounters consist of interpersonal mentorship between adults and youths. The program is targeted to communities that potentially produce high rates of at-risk youths, such as areas with high incidence of crime, poverty, or school dropouts.

Prevention at the Community Level. Prevention programs exist at all levels of the community, from statewide initiatives to neighborhood initiatives. These programs include police–school liaisons, Drug Awareness Resistance Education (DARE),[24] Big Brothers/Big Sisters,[25] and Gang Resistance Education and Training (GREAT).[26] Successful implementation of local programs is contingent upon the participation of community agencies and leaders.

Community-based prevention programs focus on specific populations of juveniles, sometimes identified by demographic profile and sometimes by the type of offense (such as truancy, substance abuse, or running away).

Very often, community prevention programs practice *secondary* prevention, so that the targeted populations are first-time, status, or otherwise early offenders. The central purpose underlying these programs is to prevent juvenile deviance from escalating into serious, chronic, and violent delinquency. Research has shown that prevention programs emanating from the family, schools, and the community are effective interventions against further progression toward serious, chronic, and violent behavior.[27]

Federal and state governments often create financial incentives for community agencies to coordinate the implementation of prevention initiatives. Such coordination necessarily requires local leaders and agencies to determine how to rank their problems, as well as how to adapt policies to their unique circumstances. For example, rural delinquency prevention initiatives logically project a different policy profile in comparison to urban initiatives. The same holds true for differences in identifying region-level policy priorities. Nevertheless, common ground does exist, and the following intervention models have been identified as effective prevention programs:[28]

- Behavioral consultation for schools
- School-wide mentoring
- Situational crime prevention
- Comprehensive community intervention
- Community policing and targeted policing of "hot spots"
- Mandatory sentencing for the criminal use of guns

Managing the Problem: Treatment

Treatment involves intensive intervention in the lives of juvenile offenders, and its purpose is to remediate youths who have already violated the law or other societal rules. In this regard, treatment is in many respects an "after the fact" response to juvenile deviance: Public and private institutions intervene to restore juvenile offenders to wholeness *after* they have run afoul of the authorities or have otherwise acted out in violation of the community's norms of accepted behavior. Thus, treatment is arguably an example of *tertiary* prevention, because its fundamental purpose is to reduce the likelihood of further deviant behavior in individual offenders.

Treatment as community-based intervention is an attempt to forestall an individual's escalation toward increasingly serious, chronic, or violent behavior. Community-based resources are enlisted to divert one's further progression along the path of delinquency and crime. In order for community experts and agencies to be effective, careful scrutiny must be made of the social histories of individual offenders. Treatment strategies cannot be applied universally in the same manner to every juvenile; they must take into consideration each youth's family, community, and personal circumstances. Additional factors—such as substance abuse or poverty—must also be identified and evaluated by treatment officers. Under ideal conditions, this

Photo 10.2 Informal proceedings in England. Court decisions are ideally based on the unique background of each juvenile.

personal treatment profile will be used to construct a unique treatment program for each participant.

After a treatment profile has been established, counselors and other professionals create an intervention plan from an inventory of program options. In a general sense, these intervention plans are combinations of treatment strategies and the community corrections options discussed in Chapter 8. Counseling can be very creative, and counselors may design treatment programs from the following menu of alternatives, assembled in a variety of combinations designed for each participant:

- Day, evening, or weekend counseling and treatment
- Vocational and skills training
- Educational and personal mentorship intervention
- Community service and restitution to victims
- JIPS, at-home detention, and electronic monitoring

Treatment can be delivered by many institutions and agencies, including those discussed previously. These include foster homes, day treatment centers, wilderness programs, and specialized schools. Within such facilities, many types of treatment interventions are applied, including peer group therapy, substance abuse counseling, social skills development, and lifestyle education. Underlying all of these programmatic and institutional options is a fundamental motivation to eliminate behaviors that would otherwise lead to future dysfunction and deviance.

An interesting spin on the theme of treatment is found in the concept of **"shock" programs**. These are programs that temporarily place juveniles under intensive (though guided) pressure with the goal of "shocking" them out of their antisocial behavior. Although these programs are of short duration, they have had some success in rehabilitating young offenders. Typical of these programs are juvenile boot camps, which were discussed in Chapter 8. Another program is the so-called **"scared straight"** model, which was first popularized in the 1978 film *Scared Straight*. The film was a documentary of a group of young offenders who spent a day in Rahway State Prison in Rahway, New Jersey.[29] They toured the facility and were then placed in a graphic and intensive encounter session with hardened adult convicts. This cohort of delinquents and inmates was tracked during subsequent years, and, interestingly, the vast majority of the youths and inmates were rehabilitated. The Rahway program and film popularized shock programs nationally and led to adaptations of scared straight in other jurisdictions.

PROFESSIONAL PROFILE CHAPTER 10

Operational Developer—Gang Intervention Nonprofit Agency

Nonprofit agencies are critical components of the juvenile justice system. Such agencies are integral partners in the system's efforts to prevent juvenile delinquency and victimization, and to rehabilitate and treat youths who are brought under the jurisdiction of juvenile agencies. Nonprofit agencies are often highly specialized and offer much-needed expertise for youths with special needs and problems that require special intervention.

I. Personal Profile

    A. Name:
        Carol Chudy

    B. Agency:
        Gang Alternatives Program, greater Los Angeles area

    C. Rank and/or Title:
        Operational Developer

    D. Education (Schools and Degrees):
        California State University Dominguez Hills
        BA (Subject unknown)

California Teaching Credential
MA, Public Administration
Professional Training:
Grantsmanship Center, Los Angeles

E. **Professional Organizations/Community Group Memberships:**
American Society for Public Administration
Pi Alpha Alpha Honor Society
Service Planning Area 8 Children's Planning Council
UCLA/Rand Center for Adolescent Health Promotion Community Advisory
    Board

II. *Professional Profile*

A. **What personal or other background experiences led to your decision to** *choose* **this profession?**

I have chosen to become a fundraiser for nonprofit agencies because I feel that community agencies can make significant changes in children's lives. As an elementary school teacher, I saw the challenges many of my students faced when they went home from school. They often had parents who were substance abusers, in jail, or neglectful. They had brothers and sisters in gangs and in juvenile hall. These young students had few positive role models in their environment. I wanted to make more of an impact in their lives and affect a greater number of children than just those in my classroom.

B. **Please state a few of your personal reasons/motivations for your decision to** *continue* **in this profession.**

Fundraising for community agencies has given me the freedom to work when and where I want. Sometimes, I even work at home. I have also had the opportunity to travel to conferences in Sacramento and Washington, DC, and to meet very interesting, inspirational people.

C. **Which job experiences have had an important impact on you?**

The most influential experience I have had in my career was meeting the National Drug Czar in 1999. I had written a grant proposal to the Office of National Drug Control Policy in Washington, DC, for the South Bay Coalition. We were granted $400,000 to establish an antidrug program for youth in the community, and I was invited to meet the National Drug Czar, General McCaffrey, and attend a conference of community organizations from around the country.

D. **What has been a particularly** *satisfying* **job experience?**

It is very exciting to see a program that I conceived and procured funding for come to fruition. I have been involved in establishing a health care center, a day care center for teen mothers, a counseling center for at-risk youth, and many other worthwhile projects.

E.   What has been a particularly *challenging* job experience?

In Los Angeles, there were over 600 homicides in 2003, mostly gang related. When I drive through areas of South Central, I become overwhelmed with the great need in that community. The problems of gangs, crime, unemployment, homelessness, and the like can be enormous challenges for government and community agencies. I never feel like I am doing enough.

F.   What do you think the future holds for your profession?

As government money becomes more scarce, fundraisers need to look to the private sector to raise money for community-based organizations. I believe that in the future fundraisers will need to become more creative and look for new sources.

G.   What kind of advice/guidance would you give to interested students?

Students who are interested in this field should get their master's degrees early in their careers and join many professional organizations. The networking opportunities are unlimited. It's all about relationships!

Chapter Summary

Community-based juvenile programs are creative alternatives to the official and more onerous components of the juvenile justice system. Community resources are marshaled to prevent juvenile deviance and treat those who are in conflict with authority. Youths who are assigned to community-based programs are deemed to have been diverted out of the juvenile court and correctional systems.

The community is composed of objective geographic designations and subjective concepts of integration and unity. Programs based in the community have their modern origins in the 1950s and 1960s, when states began to experiment with juvenile diversion. Modern diversionary programs are intended to rehabilitate youths either before they have conflicts with authority, or as soon as possible thereafter. Ideally, a wide net of community-based institutions will become partners in an overall system of prevention and treatment. Net widening is certainly controversial, but virtually all jurisdictions believe that it is necessary.

Community placements may be restrictive, benign, or experiential. The foremost institutions for these placements are group homes, foster homes, day treatment centers, and wilderness programs. Counselors and other professionals are charged with the sometimes complicated task of designing prevention and treatment strategies for each participant in community programs. Prevention and treatment are accepted goals at both the national and local levels of government and society.

Chapter 11 is the first chapter in our discussion of final perspectives and projections. It discusses the problem of youth gangs and antisocial lifestyles. This is a serious problem in American society, and is one that has plagued juvenile justice authorities for many decades.

Questions for Review

1. What are the underlying purposes and policy considerations for community-based programs?

2. What is diversion?

3. Describe the role of diversion programs in the juvenile justice system.

4. What is net widening?

5. Identify the important institutional partners in the juvenile justice network.

6. In what ways do institutional partners interact?

7. Identify are the prominent community-based placement institutions.

8. In what ways do prevention programs anticipate juvenile problems?

9. In what ways do treatment programs manage juvenile problems?

Key Terms and Concepts

The following topics were discussed in this chapter, and are found in the Glossary:

Community Placement (Benign)

Community Placement (Experiential)

Community Placement (Restrictive)

Day Treatment Centers

Diversion

Foster Parents

Halfway House

Head Start

Head Start Bureau

Highfields Project

Homeward Bound

JUMP

Localized Therapy

Maximized Assimilation

Minimized Stigma

New Jersey Experimental Project for the Treatment of Youthful Offenders

Office of Juvenile Justice and
Delinquency Prevention

Outward Bound

Prevention Services

Primary Prevention

Pure Diversion

"Scared Straight" Model

Secondary Diversion

Secondary Prevention

"Shock" Programs

START

Students Taking On Prevention
(STOP)

Tertiary Prevention

Treatment Services

VisionQuest

DISCUSSION BOX

"It Takes a Village to Raise a Child"

This chapter's Discussion Box is intended to stimulate critical discussion about the meaning of community and its role in reclaiming wayward youths and promoting juvenile justice.

An old African proverb holds that "it takes a village to raise a child." The obvious wisdom of this statement is that well-adjusted children are the result of positive rearing by an entire community. From this perspective, communities are just as responsible for the welfare of individual children as are the child's parents. In essence, nothing can be gained—and much lost—by ignoring the positive influences of constructive community resources.

Broadly defined, the community consists of schools, agencies, parents, recreational programs, neighborhood organizations, and other juvenile-focused centers. Juvenile justice experts agree that communities and neighborhood environments deeply influence the behavior of many youths and that the community must be an essential partner with the official juvenile justice system for reclaiming at-risk juveniles. In this regard, community-based juvenile programs and organizations have facilitated prevention and treatment programs throughout the country.

In order to encourage the continued growth of this concept, many community-based agencies receive funding from federal and state sources to run these programs. Critics of this ongoing expansion argue that net widening will result in more and more youths being drawn into the system, many of whom might otherwise have remained outside of it. Nevertheless, links between the juvenile justice system and community-based juvenile programs and organizations continue to be encouraged.

Discussion Questions

1. How persuasive is the argument that net widening is a negative consequence of assigning juveniles to community-based programs?

2. Should official components of the juvenile justice system—such as the police and courts—be the primary decision makers for assignments to community-based programs?

3. Should more resources be devoted to building community-based juvenile programs?

4. Are certain types of youths more likely to benefit from community-based programs? Are certain types less likely to benefit?

5. If "it takes a village to raise a child," what should be done if the village is plagued by crime and a poor physical environment?

Recommended Web Sites

The following Web sites investigate the subject of community-based juvenile programs.

Communities in Schools: http://www.cisnet.org/
Families, Career, and Community Leaders of America: http://www.fcclainc.org/
Head Start Bureau: http://www.acf.hhs.gov/programs/hsb/
National Center for Conflict Resolution Education: http://www.nccre.org/
Outward Bound USA: http://www.outwardbound.org/

Note: The Web site URLs and exercises below are also from the book's study site: http://www.sagepub.com/martin

Web Exercise

Using this chapter's recommended Internet sites, conduct an online investigation of community-based juvenile programs and organizations.

- To what extent are community-based programs and organizations linked to juvenile courts and the juvenile correctional system? How closely should they be linked?
- What are some of the common features of community-based programs and organizations? What are some of the differences?
- Which programs and organizations seem to be the most proactive in their approaches to prevention and treatment?

For an online search of community-based juvenile programs, students should use a search engine and enter the following keywords:

"Delinquency Prevention"

"Delinquency Treatment"

Recommended Readings

The following publications provide discussions on community-based juvenile programs.

American Bar Association. (2001). Justice by gender: The lack of appropriate prevention, diversion, and treatment alternatives for girls in the justice system. Washington, DC: American Bar Association/National Bar Association.

Frank, I. C. (1996). Building self-esteem in at-risk youth: Peer group programs and individual success stories. Westport, CT: Praeger.

Magnus, R., Min, L. H., Mesenas, M. L., & Thean, V. (Eds.). (2003). Rebuilding lives, restoring relationships: Juvenile justice and the community. Portland, OR: International Specialized Book Services.

Polier, J. W. (1989). Juvenile justice in double jeopardy: The distanced community and vengeful retribution. Mahwah, NJ: Erlbaum.

Watts, E. (Ed.). (1990). Guidelines for the development of policies & procedures: Juvenile community residential facilities. Laurel, MD: American Correctional Association.

Notes

1. See Katherine Reynolds v. City of Anchorage, et al., 225 F. Supp. 2d 754 (W. Dist. KY., 2002).

2. See President's Commission on Law Enforcement and the Administration of Justice. (1967). *The challenge of crime in a free society.* Washington, DC: U.S. Government Printing Office. See also Task Force on Juvenile Delinquency. (1967). *Task force report: Juvenile delinquency and youth crime.* Washington, DC: U.S. Government Printing Office.

3. The Four Ds are deinstitutionalization, diversion, due process, and decriminalization.

4. See McKorkle, L. W. (1958). *The Highfields story; An experimental treatment project for youthful offenders.* New York: Henry Holt.

5. See, e.g., Fowkes, J. J. (1978). One county's approach to the diversion of youth from the juvenile justice system. *Federal Probation, 42*(4).

6. Binder, A., Schumacher, M., Kurz, G., & Moulson, L. (1985). A diversionary approach for the 1980s. *Federal Probation, 49*(1).

7. See DeAngelo, A. J. (1988). Diversion programs in the juvenile justice system: An alternative method of treatment for juvenile offenders. *Juvenile and Family Court Journal, 39*(1).

8. See Minor, K. I., Hartmann, D. J., & Terry, S. (1997). Predictors of juvenile court actions and recidivism. *Crime and Delinquency, 43.*

9. Head Start Bureau. (n.d.). Available online at http://www.acf.hhs.gov/programs/hsb/

10. See Polk, K. (1984). Juvenile diversion: A look at the record. *Crime and Delinquency, 30*(4).

11. See Wolford, B. I., Jordan, F., & Murphy, K. (1997). Day treatment: Community-based partnerships for delinquent and at-risk youth. *Juvenile and Family Court Journal, 48.*

12. See Castellano, T. C., & Soderstrom, I. R. (1990). *Wilderness challenges and recidivism: A program evaluation.* Carbondale, IL: University of Southern Illinois, Center for the Study of Crime, Delinquency, and Corrections.

13. For background on Outward Bound programs, see Miner, J. L., & Boldt, J. (1981). *Outward Bound USA: Learning through experience.* New York: Morrow.

14. For a discussion of Homeward Bound, see Willman, H. C., Jr., & Chun, R Y. (1974). Homeward Bound: An alternative to the institutionalization of adjudicated juvenile offenders. In Killinger, G. C., & Cromwell, P. F., Jr., (Eds.). *Alternatives to imprisonment: Corrections and the community.* St. Paul, MN: West Publishing.

15. For an assessment of VisionQuest, see Greenwood, P. W., & Turner, S. (1987). *The VisionQuest program: An evaluation.* Santa Monica, CA: Rand.

16. Montgomery, I., & Landon, M. (1994). *What works: Effective delinquency prevention and treatment programs.* Washington, DC: U.S. Department of Justice.

17. Ibid.

18. Ibid.

19. For a good discussion and compendium of 425 effective community-based juvenile justice intervention programs, see Montgomery, I. M., McFall Torbet, P., Malloy, D. A., Adamcik, L. P., Toner, M. J., & Andrews, J. (1994). *What works: Promising interventions in juvenile justice.* Washington, DC: U.S. Department of Justice.

20. Office of Juvenile Justice and Delinquency Prevention. (n.d.). Available online on the OJJDP Web site at http://ojjdp.ncjrs.org/

21. Office of Juvenile Justice and Delinquency Prevention. (1993). *Comprehensive strategy for serious, violent and chronic juvenile offenders.* Washington, DC: U.S. Department of Justice.

22. Office of Juvenile Justice and Delinquency Prevention. (1995).*Guide for implementing the comprehensive strategy for serious, violent and chronic juvenile offenders.* Washington, DC: U.S. Department of Justice.

23. Family, Career and Community Leaders of America. (n.d.). Available on the FCCLA Web site at http://www.fcclainc.org/

24. Drug Resistance Awareness Education. (n.d.). Available on the DARE Web site at http://www.dare.com/

25. Big Brothers/Big Sisters of America. (n.d.). Available online at http://www.bbbsa.org/

26. Gang Resistance Education and Training, Available online at http://www.atf.gov/great/

27. See Catalano, R. F., Loeber, R., & McKinney, K. C. (1999). *School and community interventions to prevent serious and violent offending.* Washington, DC: U.S. Department of Justice, 1999.

28. Ibid (p. 8).

29. The prison has since been renamed East Jersey State Prison.

PART IV

Final Perspectives and Projections

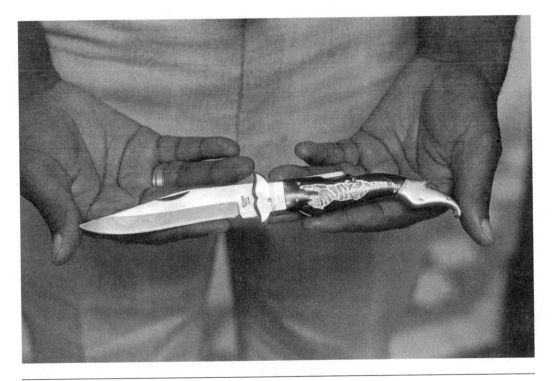

Part IV A Detroit gang squad police officer holds a confiscated knife.

11 Antisocial Youth Cultures and the Case of Youth Gangs

The problem of youth gangs is one that has existed since the early nineteenth century. In the modern era, the gang lifestyle has resulted in hundreds of tragic incidents involving youths. For example, in August 1994, 11-year-old Robert "Yummy" Sandifer shot and killed 14-year-old Shavon Dean in Chicago, Illinois.[1] Sandifer was a member of the Black Disciples street gang, and was acting on behalf of the gang. He quickly became the principle suspect in the murder, and an intensive police manhunt for him ended when his body was found under a viaduct. Yummy Sandifer had been shot twice in the back of the head by another 14-year-old, Derrick Hardaway. Hardaway and his brother Cragg, another member of the Black Disciples, had committed the murder on the orders of a gang leader. Hardaway, who had 19 previous arrests, confessed to the crime and was sentenced to 45 years in prison.

Youths frequently adopt expressions, mannerisms, and other behavioral traits that are intended to demonstrate their individuality. Very often, this is simply a matter of asserting one's independence and personality. It is not an indicator of one's immersion into an antisocial lifestyle or subculture. Having said this, there are certain lifestyles and subcultures that many young people adopt as fundamental expressions of their identity—they *become* what they are expressing. These lifestyles range from harmless social and interest-group behaviors to truly alternative means of expression. For example, youths may self-select themselves into peer associations characterized by attachments to athletics, ethnicity, regional culture, neighborhoods, class, drug use, or lifestyle experimentation. These groupings establish their own norms of behavior and interests, creating peer and behavioral subcultures. Thus, the term **"youth culture"** refers to the development of lifestyles that are peculiar to specific social associations of young people. There is no single youth culture, but rather an assortment of lifestyles and self-selected identifications. Typical features of these lifestyles and identifications include unique group-oriented modes of behavior, including styles of dress, musical expression, "partying," and language. The media and popular culture serve to describe, promote, and define youth culture.

Most expressions of youth culture are manifestations of individuality and social group identity. Unfortunately, some peer associations within the youth culture are antisocial or self-destructive and operate on the fringes of socially acceptable standards of behavior.[2] Examples include gangs, violent groups of youths, drug-related "stoner" lifestyles, and other types of potentially criminal or otherwise self-destructive peer associations. Many youths who become caught up in antisocial associations find themselves in conflict with adult authority figures such as their parents, schools, or the police. The bottom line is that some expressions of youth culture are inherently self-defeating and in conflict with authority. The following behaviors are typically exhibited by youths who immerse themselves in antisocial peer associations:

- *"Outlaw" lifestyles*. Gang membership or an association with groups that regularly engage in delinquency or status offenses
- *Subcultural criminality*. Immersion in lifestyles that promote routine illegal activity such as drug abuse and trafficking
- *Threatening or otherwise violent lifestyles*. Patterns of intimidation and carrying of weapons, perhaps involving firearms violations
- *Educational impediments*. Regular truancy violations and school violence
- *Neighborhood vandalism*. Habitual property destruction and disfigurement, including graffiti "tagging"
- *Youth-specific deviance*. Participation in underage deviance, such as frequent commission of status offenses

Gangs are a particularly troubling manifestation of antisocial behavior within the youth culture, but what is a gang? Gangs are not simply groups of juvenile delinquents who break the law; more is needed before a juvenile group profile can be deemed a gang profile. A **gang** is best described as a self-established, somewhat organized, and antisocial group of youths. Most have an adopted name and a claimed territory, are involved in illegal activity, and exhibit devised symbols.[3] They often have weak family or community connections and frequently represent a significant threat of social disruption to the community. Members of gangs—frequently referred to as **"gangbangers"**—routinely engage in criminal behavior such as drug trafficking, burglary, vehicular theft, and assault. Gang-related violence can be extreme, and some urban neighborhoods have become highly destabilized and crime-ridden as a result of gang activity. Other terms commonly used for this phenomenon are **street gangs**, **youth gangs**, **delinquent gangs**, and **criminal gangs**. Regardless of which term is used, the fact is that there are a large number of gangs and gang members, as indicated in Table 11.1.[4]

TABLE 11.1   ESTIMATED NUMBER OF YOUTH GANGS AND GANG MEMBERS

The modern era has experienced a significant growth in the number of gangs and gang members. This growth has occurred in every region of the country and in every area type.

This table summarizes the estimated number of gangs and gang members in large cities, small cities, the suburbs, and rural areas.[a]

Area Type	Estimated Number	
	Gangs	Gang Members
Large City	12,538	482,380
Small City	8,413	94,875
Suburban County	6,040	176,610
Rural County	1,716	26,368
Total	28,707	780,233

a. Adapted from Office of Juvenile Justice and Delinquency Prevention. (2000). *1998 National youth gang survey* (p. 13). Washington, DC: U.S. Department of Justice.

Photo 11.1   Members of the New York City "Sandman" gang show off their colors in their territory of Coney Island.

Gangs pose many policy challenges to the community, and raise the following questions: What should society do with criminally inclined—and frequently armed—youths who proclaim their opposition to the rules of adult authority? Should the community try to reclaim and rehabilitate gang members? Or, should the community simply crack down on them as harshly as if they were adult criminals? And, what is to be done with the overall problem of extreme expressions of antisocial behavior within the youth culture?

These important policy challenges must be evaluated within the context of the causes of antisocial behavior among youths, as well as the underlying characteristics (profiles) of youth gangs. The discussion in this chapter reviews:

- Background: Causes of Antisocial Behavior Among Juveniles
- History and Implications: Perspectives on Youth Gangs
- Gang Characteristics: Demographics, Organization, and Behavior
- A Policy Dilemma: Responding to the Gang Problem

CHAPTER PERSPECTIVE 11.1

The Influence of Adult Hate Groups on Youth Culture: The Case of the Skinheads

A hate group is an organized association that promotes hatred and intolerance of identified segments of society. They are generally organized around racial and religious hatred, although some hate groups promote fear and intolerance toward government. Many hate groups, such as the neo-Nazi Aryan Nations and National Alliance, were well organized and adept at promoting their beliefs via radio, marches, and rallies. The Internet has become a fertile environment for spreading the message of hate, because it is mostly unregulated, and is an alternative to mainstream mediums of communication and news.

Youths have been an important target for recruitment by hate groups, largely because many young people are seeking a sense of identity, and at-risk youths are especially susceptible to extremist outreach. Aside from individual youths who adopt the ideologies of hate groups, there exists a youth movement and lifestyle that is particularly noted for associating with ideologies of hate, and occasionally with hate groups—the skinheads.

Skinheads are inherently nonconformist and antisocial as a matter of choice. Although some skinheads are not racist—such as **Skinheads Against Racial Prejudice (SHARPS)**—much of the skinhead movement and lifestyle has been woven into the neo-Nazi ideology of white racial supremacy. Skinhead gangs have occasionally been quite violent, and have been implicated in committing a number of hate crimes against nonwhites, immigrants, and Jews. The typical profile of racist skinheads is that they are disaffected white working-class youths who have been unsuccessful in school or at work. They accept ideologies of hate and blame nonwhites and immigrants for their plight, usually viewing themselves as oppressed whites. There exists a music and social "underground" that expresses and promotes the skinhead lifestyle.

Background: Causes of
Antisocial Behavior Among Youths

Chapter 3 presented a detailed discussion of the causes of delinquency and crime. Readers may recall that modern theories of causation are grounded in present-day data on the impact of sociological, psychological, biological, and other factors on the behavior of individuals and groups. These factors should be understood as representing the most credible explanations currently available to experts in the community. They are not absolutely definitive explanations, because they are based on the quality of scientific knowledge and practical experience during this particular point in time. Similar theories have also been developed to explain the existence of youth gangs and other antisocial peer behaviors in juveniles, identifying the following factors as explanatory causes:

- Individual problems (social, psychological, etc.)
- Family dysfunction
- Existence of gangs or other antisocial peer groups already in the community
- Neighborhood characteristics such as high unemployment or poverty
- School quality
- Spatial placement of loitering areas, such as parks, empty buildings, or open lots
- Demography, such as race, ethnicity, and age

Theoretical constructs involving these and other factors will continue to be the subjects of review and revision by experts. This is because explaining group behavior among juveniles is an ongoing process, so that old theories of causation evolve and new ones are developed. In other words, explanatory theories move forward as scientific knowledge in these fields advances.

Explanatory Factors: Focusing
on the Individual's Environment

Young people are influenced by their exposure to the people, culture, and values of their immediate environment. Their understanding of what constitutes acceptable or unacceptable behavior is largely an outcome of the quality of their exposure to good or bad environmental factors. In this regard, **environmental factors** refer to the effects of people, institutions, and other immediate associations on the personal development and behavioral traits of juveniles. As mentioned above, examples of environmental factors that may explain antisocial peer groups and youth gangs include family dysfunction, community and neighborhood problems, and negative school environments. Many youths who grow up within these environments can be socialized to behave in opposition to authority. **Socialization** refers to the process of learning moral and social norms of behavior, as defined within the child's immediate environment.

Family Dysfunction. Dysfunctional families are families that do not interact in a healthy manner. What is considered to be normal behavior in such families is, in fact, abnormal. For example, perhaps personal boundaries are routinely disrespected or ignored. Or, members learn to interact in unwholesome ways, sometimes confrontationally, or often by withdrawing emotionally to inflict the "silent treatment" on others. There may exist neglect or physical, emotional, or sexual abuse. Alcoholism or drug addiction often persist in some dysfunctional families. Single-parent households can exacerbate these problems. One important factor in all of this is the absence of parental responsibility for, or control over, the behavior of their children.

Children from seriously dysfunctional families are often socialized to become juvenile delinquents and adult criminals.[5] Abuse and dysfunction can lead to personality disorders, antisocial behavior, and other problems. Youths who grow up in these environments often gravitate toward similar peers, thus forming antisocial peer associations. These associations and gangs often become surrogate families, so that the development of strong interpersonal relationships becomes based on a kind of "outlaw" lifestyle that is shared by the group.

Community and Neighborhood Problems. Urban poverty and other economic problems have been associated with gang activity.[6] This association is not rooted in the presence of poverty alone, but includes many of the stresses that can result from poverty. Thus, close-knit functional families living in relatively cohesive neighborhoods are less likely to be susceptible to gang activity than are dysfunctional families who live in fragmented neighborhoods.

Readers may recall that the concept of the *underclass* refers to inner-city poor residents who are caught in a chronic generational cycle of poverty, low educational achievement, teenage parenthood, unemployment, and welfare dependence. Underclass theorists argue that antisocial behaviors become norms within many impoverished inner-city environments. In fact, some neighborhoods have reputations for being dangerous, crime-ridden, or the turf of a local gang. They may be dangerous, residents may have poor relations with the police, and family dysfunction may be considered normal. Youths who are reared in these communities are socialized to adopt norms of behavior that are deemed perfectly legitimate within the underclass community, but which are defined as delinquency or crime by mainstream society. Within this environment, gangs and other antisocial associations thrive.

Negative School Environments. As discussed previously, schools operate *in loco parentis*, whereby they take on the role of guardian over students during school hours. As such, they are charged by law to nurture and protect youths. This responsibility, and the quality of development, occur for many hours each day, many weeks each year, and many years until graduation from high school. Thus, schools naturally have a great deal of influence on the socialization of children.

Education in the United States has long included instruction on character and values. The ideal of obtaining a high-quality education includes instruction on how one should behave in accordance with the norms of society. When these qualities are taught well, youths tend to be well-socialized members of society. However, if these qualities are poorly taught, or if dysfunctional or otherwise nonmainstream values are imparted, children can become socially marginalized as they mature. Some schools—both urban and rural—have done a poor job of imparting behavioral values. When school environments are authoritarian, uncaring, run-down, or crime-ridden, it should be no surprise that some students will self-organize into antisocial peer groups. This can be exacerbated when family and community problems concurrently exist, because many children will turn to peer associations from these same milieus. Status offenses, delinquency, and crime often result.

Explanatory Factors: Focusing on the Juvenile Group

Juvenile criminals, delinquents, and status offenders often associate with others during the course of their antisocial behavior. Individuals become members of groups and gangs for many of the reasons discussed previously. For this reason, it is important to understand the nature of antisocial juvenile peer groups.

Individuals Within the Group. One underlying presumption that comes with acceptance of the existence of a youth culture is that young individuals often consider themselves—and conduct themselves—as if they are "part of" a larger social phenomenon. In other words, they self-define themselves as belonging to a social or cultural group, and make it a point to associate with others who have a similar self-identification. Youths who seek approval and acceptance often find them within peer groups, and act in accordance with the group's norms and values. These norms and values can be exhibited not only as harmless social expression, but also as delinquent and criminal behavior.

A great deal of juvenile antisocial behavior is a group phenomenon, in which individuals act out as members of a larger peer group that is engaging in the same proscribed behavior. Certainly, many juvenile delinquents and status offenders act out on their own initiative as individuals. However, there have been many incidents when groups of youths have vandalized property, assaulted people, or fought as "packs" of delinquents. For this reason, gang and antisocial group behavior have become the subjects of group-focused research and policy-making agendas. These research and policy agendas attempt to explain and respond to socially unacceptable *group-level* conduct by juveniles.[7]

Understanding Antisocial Group Behavior. Serious research on urban gangs began during the early decades of the twentieth century. During the 1920s and 1930s, groups of youths were interviewed and observed, and several important theoretical constructs were developed to explain gang-related antisocial behavior.[8] Much of this research was conducted out of the University of Chicago.[9] Early sociologists began to link gang behavior to theories of **social disorganization,** which held that poor urban communities are innately dysfunctional and give rise to criminal behavior. As discussed in previous chapters, this is an old presumption, having been used by the first reformers and child savers during the nineteenth century to justify rescuing slum-dwelling children. However, the advancement of newer theories was rooted in the research agendas of the newly emerging social sciences. For example, during the 1920s pioneering sociologists at the University of Chicago concluded the following about gangs in Chicago:[10]

- Slum dysfunction gives rise to gangs;
- Because of their organization and security, gangs engage in delinquency crime more efficiently than do individuals; therefore,
- Gangs are central causes of delinquency and crime.

Social disorganization theory arguably began the movement toward systematically studying youth gang behavior. During the 1950s and 1960s, researchers began to study antisocial behavior in youths in general rather than gangs *per se,* although the gang phenomenon was often central to research agendas. During this period, newer theories of juvenile (and adult) deviance were developed, including anomie, strain, and differential association theories. These theories were first presented and discussed in Chapter 3.[11]

Critical Theories. Other explanatory theories were more critical, and offered provocative insights into the causes of juvenile deviance, antisocial juvenile peer groups, and gangs.[12] For example, some theorists argued that relative deprivation—the perception that one is deprived in relation to the rest of society—causes some persons to engage in delinquency and crime. This theory was also applied as an explanation for antisocial group behavior among youths.[13] The argument is uncomplicated: Juveniles from lower income neighborhoods and families perceive themselves to be of a lower status. In order to resolve this perceived deficiency in status, some juveniles conclude that they will never be able to attain a higher status through socially accepted avenues (such as quality education and fair employment). Therefore, they resort to socially prohibited avenues (such as crime) and gravitate toward other peers who share the same perception. As a consequence, many of these youths form antisocial peer groups such as gangs. This type of economic and class-oriented explanation will likely continue to be developed.[14]

Multiple Marginality Theory. An important and relatively recent contribution to the theory of antisocial group behavior and the formation of youth gangs is the theory of **multiple marginality**.[15] Multiple marginality refers to the convergence (multiple influence) of many marginalizing factors that result in a group's sense of dislocation, alienation, and isolation. This can be a highly complex process; and these marginalizing factors can include economic, ecological, sociopsychological, and sociocultural components. In theory, when people are marginalized within each of these components—or within complex combinations of the components—antisocial associations of youths will form, including youth gangs. For example, economic marginalization can occur when a group of people is relegated (forced into) to low-wage jobs and poverty. Ecological marginalization can occur when people settle in undesirable sections of cities or other communities that may have poor transportation and infrastructure. According to multiple marginality theorists, these factors will, in combination, lead to breakdowns in order, culture, and group controls. Youths who grow up in this type of environment are more likely to form gangs and other antisocial associations than are those who grow up in functional environments.

History and Implications: Perspectives on Youth Gangs

Groups of antisocial youths have been a feature of American society for nearly two centuries. Urban residents have long experienced cycles of victimization by youth groups specializing in robbery, theft, vandalism, and violence. From the early social problems of idle youths who picked pockets, to the modern gang members who engage in carjackings and drive-by shootings, policy makers have had to deal with self-organized groups of juvenile delinquents.

Whether or not one can accurately classify early groups of antisocial youths as "youth gangs" in the modern sense is rather academic, because adults during every era of juvenile justice have considered these groups to be gravely in need of remediation. As discussed previously in several chapters, each era dealt with antisocial groups in a manner deemed to be appropriate within the context of their culture. Modern designations of antisocial youth groups as gangs (or not as gangs) is important because policy initiatives tend to be crafted based on these designations. Thus, juveniles labeled as hard-core gang members are likely be treated differently—and perhaps more severely—in comparison to other juvenile offenders.

It is important to develop regional and national perspectives of the modern gang problem. Table 11.2 summarizes the percentage of jurisdictions reporting active youth gangs, by region.[16]

TABLE 11.2   JURISDICTIONS REPORTING ACTIVE YOUTH GANGS

Most jurisdictions in the United States report gang activity. Regionally, the West has reported the most gang activity, followed by the Midwest, South, and Northeast. This table summarizes the percentage of jurisdictions that reported active youth gangs during the late 1990s and into the new millennium.[a] It is clear from these data that gang presence has been relatively stable, with slight declines during the period reported.

Region	1996 (%)	1997 (%)	1998 (%)
Midwest Jurisdictions	**54**	**52**	**48**
East North Central	63	61	57
West North Central	42	39	35
Northeast Jurisdictions	**35**	**31**	**29**
New England	44	38	35
Middle Atlantic	29	26	26
South Jurisdictions	**50**	**49**	**48**
South Atlantic	53	49	47
East South Central	43	48	42
West South Central	52	51	48
West Jurisdictions	**75**	**74**	**72**
Mountain	64	64	62
Pacific	82	80	79
Overall Jurisdictions	**53**	**51**	**48**

a. Adapted from Office of Juvenile Justice and Delinquency Prevention. (2000). *1998 national youth gang survey* (pp. 8, 9). Washington, DC: U.S. Department of Justice.

Origins: Historical, Regional, and National Perspectives

From an historical perspective, it is clear that American youths have always joined together to form loose, often antisocial, associations out of a self-defined sense of group identity. The most fundamental sense of youth group identity has been the expression of one's ethnic heritage, so that every immigration wave has brought with it the seeds of antisocial youth groups. In addition to this sense of ethnic commonality, which grew within new immigrant communities, many decades of racial segregation led to youth associations inside the African American community, and with it the rise of African American youth gangs in the urban core. Thus, the origins of the modern-day gang profile are found in historical self-associations of youths based on their ethnic and racial identities.

Regional Perspective: Gang Formation in the East. The first true street gangs originated in New York City during the 1820s, arguably when the first large wave of Irish immigrants settled in the Eastern cities of the United States.[17] The first Irish gangs are an excellent case study in a pattern that repeated itself again and again during the history of immigration to the United States. As was to typify the history of subsequent immigrants, the Irish were treated poorly and discriminated against when they arrived in America. The were relegated to crowded slums which had poor sanitation and minimal health services. Within this milieu, the first Irish street gangs became highly antisocial and often violent. An example of a particularly notorious Irish gang is the case of the Forty Thieves gang.[18]

During the twentieth century, urban areas in the East experienced the rise of Italian, Jewish, African American, and Puerto Rican street gangs. Until the 1950s and 1960s, most street gangs were white. These gangs were usually centered in white ethnic neighborhoods in Eastern and Midwestern cities, where earlier European immigrants had settled. Other gangs certainly existed, but the predominant demographic profile was that of the urban white male youth. Most members of the white ethnic gangs matured out of the gang lifestyle as they become settled, obtained employment, and raised families. Only rarely did gang lifestyles extend into subsequent generations, although it is a historical fact that many individual members progressed into adult criminal lifestyles. Some became famous adult gangsters, and in a few cases were the founders of organized criminal enterprises that have lasted into the modern era.

During the 1950s and 1960s, the profile of white ethnic gangs began to shift toward greater numbers of nonwhite gangs, as African American migrants from the Deep South and Latinos from Puerto Rico and elsewhere settled in relatively poor and segregated urban enclaves.[19] Newcomers often settled in neighborhoods that were more poor and less well serviced than other neighborhoods. In contrast to the original white gangs, gang members residing in the new migrant communities grew up among nonmainstream urban norms—such as the underclass values discussed in previous chapters— which helped to perpetuate the existence of gangs from one generation to the next. Thus, older members regularly recruited younger members, who became part of a cycle of gang rejuvenation.

Regional Perspective: Gang Formation in the West. On the West Coast, nonwhite gangs and other juvenile associations have long defined the character of the antisocial youth culture. For example, during the late nineteenth and early twentieth centuries, Chinese immigrants in San Francisco formed trade associations called **tongs**. Most tongs were legitimate trade associations, but a few engaged in criminal activity, often using juveniles as "auxiliaries" for their enterprises. These auxiliaries eventually formed the first Chinese street gangs. In Southern California during the post-World War II period, Mexican and African American youths established the predominant typologies of gang culture.

The seeds of the modern Western gang era began in Los Angeles during the 1920s with the first wave of Mexican immigration to Southern California. Economic opportunity first drew immigrants to the Los Angeles area, where they settled in towns and encampments. With the hardship of the Great Depression during the 1930s, discrimination against Mexicans by Anglos became common, and many immigrants were deported. Dislocation, isolation, prejudice, and harassment precipitated the so-called Zoot Suit Riots of 1943.[20] Ongoing police harassment of Mexican youths, in combination with the forces of dislocation and isolation, led to the formation of true gangs out of what were previously antisocial peer associations. From these beginnings, Latino gangs were organized in East Los Angeles and elsewhere.

A generation later, the first western African American gangs grew from migrant communities established by people who migrated from the Deep South to seek a better life and escape racial segregation. During the 1960s, new African American gangs were organized among second-generation youths in neighborhoods where the original Southern migrants had been relegated to live because of racial restrictions in the housing market. This process arguably originated in the aftermath of the Watts Riot of 1965, which had a roughly similar effect on African American youths as the Zoot Suit Riots had on Mexican youths. Poverty, discrimination, and isolation were fertile conditions for the formation of gangs by alienated youths.

The formation of Mexican and African American gangs in the West is a very important phenomenon , because they became highly influential models for youth gangs across the country in the modern era. They represent the conceptual foundation for understanding the modern gang experience from a national perspective.

National Perspective: Large Gangs in Large Cities. During the 1940s, youth gangs began to engage in fights over claimed urban territory, known as "**turf wars**." These were neighborhood-level territories, often no more than block-sized, but the violence between these gangs significantly disrupted many communities. These gangs were relatively small, loosely-organized, and roughly similar to outlaw clubs. Most engaged in crimes at the local level, and weapons generally included knives, clubs, small-caliber guns, and homemade "zip" guns. This profile continued into the early 1960s, when they were supplanted in large cities by large gangs.

During the 1960s, the smaller turf-focused gangs of previous years began to coalesce into large gangs that claimed hegemony over ever-growing urban territories. Some became quite disciplined, and many became quite violent. During the 1970s, weapons began to include high-powered rifles and semi-automatic weapons. During the 1980s, cheap "crack" cocaine led to an explosion in violent rivalry over drug markets in poor African American and Latino neighborhoods. This was the beginning of an era in which the numbers of gangs and gangbangers rose precipitously, a phenomenon that lasted through the 1990s and into the new millennium. In comparison to previous eras, modern gangs are larger, more violent, and more deeply entrenched in criminal activities.

An interesting example of modern gang behavior—and an excellent case study for broad alliances among gangs—arose within the Chicago gang culture. Two alliances, or "sets," were formed that were amalgamations of gangs that cut across racial and ethnic identities. Known as the **Folk Nation** sets and **People Nation** sets, these alliances are not quite mega-gangs, but rather groupings that identify fellow members as allies.[21] Members of the Folk Nation include Black P-Stone, Latin Kings, Vice Lords, Spanish Lords, El Rukns, Bishops, Gaylords, Latin Counts, and Kents.[22] Members of the People Nation include Black Gangster Disciples, Black Disciples, Gangster Disciples, La Raza, Cobras, Eagles, Latin Disciples, Maniac Latin Disciples, Simon City Royals, Spanish Gangsters, and Two Sixers.[23] These are interesting affiliations because they demonstrate how alliances are often based more on common purpose than identity.

As large Latino and African American gangs arose in major cities, they expanded to form "franchises" in other cities. These new chapters avowedly originated from the same gangs, so that gangbangers across the country began to recognize members from outside of their home cities and turfs. The following are examples of the home cities of several major gangs:

- Los Angeles: Crips, Bloods, 18th Street Gang
- Chicago: Vice Lords, El Rukns, Black Gangster Disciples, Latin Kings
- Miami: Untouchables, 34th Street Players

Organizationally, modern large gangs have adopted several models of leadership. Some gangs have virtually no leadership structure, so that "leaders of the moment" will arise to coordinate an activity. Other gangs have distinctly recognizable power hierarchies, in which several levels of leadership have been established. A middle model exists that allows for shared leadership among several coequal persons.

Societal Implications: Community Perspectives

Gang victimization is a street-level problem. Communities plagued by gang violence and other criminality live with the realities of crime, violence, and insecurity for their children. Gang-infested neighborhoods struggle to maintain decent schools, stable families, viable community programs, and sound infrastructure. Gangs pose a serious threat to community-level security, and often disrupt the positive influences of schools and community programs. They are also responsible for crime victimization, homicides, and defacement of community property.

Many youth-focused turf gangs have been supplanted by new typologies that have serious implications at the community level. Two cases in point arise from the problem of adult involvement in street gangs, and the problem of criminal gangs.

Case: Adult Gangbangers. Policy makers, members of the community, and other interested experts tend to focus their attention on gangs and antisocial groups whose memberships are made up of juveniles—that is, persons who are below the age of 21 or some other criterion (such as the age of majority). However, one phenomenon must be emphasized and clearly understood as a threat to the community: Modern gangs are not always made up entirely of youths. Many include adult members who have remained in the gang well beyond the age of majority. They are persons who never matured out of anti-social group behavior, and have now adopted such behavior as an adult lifestyle. In fact, some gangs have multigenerational members, wherein older cousins, siblings, or uncles are also members. These gangs often operate across large territories that dwarf the much smaller turfs of earlier gangs. For this reason, they can pose a broad threat to the stability of the community.

Case: Gangs as Criminal Enterprises. Serious community-level implications arise from multigenerational, or otherwise adult-led, gangs. Gangs with adult members are frequently engaged in forms of criminality that are much more sophisticated than those exhibited by truly youth-focused gangs. These gangs are often deeply entrenched in the criminal trades of drug trafficking, vehicular theft, murder, extortion, and other serious felonies. They operate out of geographically larger urban territories, and may cooperate with other local criminal enterprises or with groups centered in other cities. These activities are a significant progression beyond the symbolism of wayward street youths in need of remediation; in fact, this can represent a form of organized crime.

Many gangs, such as the Crips and Bloods in Los Angeles and the El Rukns in Chicago, have maintained their cohesion inside prisons. Leaders from these gangs have been known to give orders and manage their compatriots from prison. In fact, members of street gangs have come to challenge the traditional prison gangs for power within the inmate subculture. Again, this represents a more sophisticated threat to the community than do the traditionally turf-level youth gangs. This is because crimes that occur within neighborhoods may be planned by persons who are away in prison or otherwise geographically removed from the community. This creates an environment whereby communities become victimized by the outlawed agendas of larger gangland criminal enterprises.

Gang Characteristics: Demographics, Organization, and Behavior

Beginning during the 1980s, and continuing through the mid-1990s, gang activity received a great deal of attention from the media, law enforcement officials, community leaders, and popular culture. The media repeatedly reported spikes in gang violence, often via dramatic depictions by investigative reporters. Law enforcement agencies adapted strategies and organizational configurations to counter increased gang firepower and criminality. Community leaders tried to maintain some semblance of stability in gang-infested neighborhoods. These responses continue to have an important influence on media coverage, police policies, and community initiatives.

Popular culture has likewise continued to dramatize and publicize the gang phenomenon in films, television, music, and teenage clothing fashions. From this collection of professional and popular perceptions, one can identify certain common characteristics of modern gangs that have continued to evolve into the new millennium.

Common Characteristics: The Definitional Dialogue

How should one differentiate a gang from a group of antisocial youths? What descriptors best serve as criteria for distinguishing the two? These questions form the center of an ongoing dialogue on the fundamental characteristics of gangs. Researchers, community leaders, law enforcement officials, and the general public do not always agree on the exact aspects of gangs. In point of fact, although many definitions have been proffered on what constitutes a gang, some commonalities do exist. The following indicators and elements have been cited by experts as the defining characteristics of gangs:

- *The formal academic definition.* "Self formed association of peers, bound together by mutual interests, with identifiable leadership, well-developed lines of authority, and other organizational features, who act in concert to achieve a specific purpose or purposes which generally include the conduct of illegal activity and control over a particular territory, facility, or type of enterprise"[24]

- *A classic definition.* Self-organized groups that claim a territory or "turf," threaten violence and force, and have personal interactions among members[25]

- *A criminal justice "bottom line."* "Groups of youths and young adults who have engaged in a sufficient amount of antisocial activity to warrant attention by the criminal justice system"[26]

- *Self-defined criminal organizations.* Groups who participate in criminal activities; commit frequent acts of violence; have traditions of territory, clothing, and symbols; and have self-defined rules of internal and external interaction[27]

- *Unity around an antisocial purpose.* Self-formed groups of youths who have developed an "allegiance for a common purpose," and who participate in criminal or otherwise unlawful activity[28]

It should be clear from these definitional constructs that antisocial peer groups can reasonably be labeled as "gangs" if they possess the common elements of self-organization; allegiance to the group; criminality; threat of violence; traditions; claimed territory; and symbolic dress or signals. Certainly, many antisocial groups of youths possess some of these elements, but it should be understood that they remain defined as nongang self-associations unless they represent themselves as gangs by adopting these common elements.

Demographic Characteristics: Age, Ethnicity, and Gender

The prevailing image of street gang membership is generally that of young, ethnically homogeneous, and male-dominated groups of antisocial juveniles. While this is frequently an accurate depiction, it is not *universally* accurate. Depending on the characteristics of individual gangs, there may be an age range, some members may be from other ethnic groups, and females can be integrated into gangs in different ways. The demographic characteristics of gangs are more complicated than the prevailing image.

Age. In previous decades, experts were primarily concerned with suppressing gangs whose memberships were made up of teenagers and other pre-adults. However, it is a fact that modern "youth gangs" are actually composed of young people ranging in age from children to adults in their late twenties. Some gangs actually count middle-aged men as members, with the implication that the gang is a multigenerational "community" of members. As noted previously, adults provide leadership and criminal mentorship to young members. This mentorship involves criminal exploitation, because adults will often call upon young **"juvies"** (juveniles) to commit violent crimes or perform the menial tasks of a criminal enterprise, such as holding or selling drugs. Juvies are often honored as surrogate little brothers and are given nicknames that begin with "li'l" such as "li'l Mikey." Many of these nicknames—and the nicknames of gang members in general—symbolize personal attributes, such as fierceness, intelligence, or loyalty.

Adult membership represents a significant influence on the behavior of street gangs nationally. With the maturity and criminal lifestyles of adult members, gang-initiated criminal enterprises can become very sophisticated, lucrative, and intimidating. Profitable crimes require intensive devotion to the enterprise, which adults are willing to commit themselves to. Therefore, many gangs have a division of labor based on age, whereby older members manage the gang's criminal trade, while younger members engage in turf-level delinquency and crime.

Ethnicity.[29] As discussed previously, there has always been an ethnic dimension to the composition of American street gangs. Although multiethnic gangs have historically been found in the United States, there is ultimately a predominant or exclusive ethnic identity within almost all gangs. In other words, either a gang's membership is entirely from one ethnicity or race, or a small number of members are from outside the predominant group.[30] Interestingly, a large number of gangs are multiracial/multiethnic in

TABLE 11.3   MULTIRACIAL/MULTIETHNIC YOUTH GANGS

The membership of most gangs is composed of a predominant racial or ethnic group. However, a large number of gangs have at least a few members who are from outside of the predominant group. This table indicates the extent of diversity within gangs.[a]

Region	Total Gangs	Multiracial/Multiethnic Gangs	
		Number	Percentage (%)
Midwest	2,804	1,313	47
Northeast	664	198	30
South	4,781	2,017	42
West	6,327	1,758	28

a. Adapted from Office of Juvenile Justice and Delinquency Prevention. (2000). *1998 National youth gang survey* (p. 20). Washington, DC: U.S. Department of Justice.

the sense that at least a few members are not of the predominant racial or ethnic group. Table 11.3 reports the number and percentages of gangs that are multiracial/multiethnic.[31]

As discussed previously, there has been a shift in the ethnic and racial composition of the national gang profile, beginning in the 1950s and 1960s. Whereas in the past most gangs were composed of ethnic whites, in the modern era most gangs are composed of nonwhites. In particular, most modern gangbangers are inner-city Latinos and African Americans—representing roughly four out of five members.

The following demography estimates typical numbers of gang members by race and ethnicity:[32]

- 255,000 gang members are Latinos.
- 184,000 gang members are African Americans.
- 65,000 gang members are white.
- 34,000 gang members are Asians.
- 10,000 gang members are of other racial and ethnic demographic groups.

This ethnic demographic profile of street gangs has been rather consistent since the 1980s.

Gender. Although girls were members of the first gangs in the nineteenth century, the role of gender has long been an understudied facet of gang culture. Most gang-related research and policy initiatives have focused on the behavior of male gang members. This is a natural tendency, because as a practical consideration most members of gangs are boys and young men. Until recently, few studies or community programs addressed the participation of girls and young women in gangs, but this is changing. Although there

TABLE 11.4   GENDER OF YOUTH GANG MEMBERS

Although gang membership is overwhelmingly dominated by males, the proportion of gangbangers who are girls and young women has steadily increased. This table summarizes the relative proportions of males and females who are gang members.[a]

Area Type	Males	Females
Large City	93%	7%
Small City	88	12
Suburban County	90	10
Rural County	89	11
Overall	92	8

a. Adapted from Office of Juvenile Justice and Delinquency Prevention. (2000). *1998 national youth gang survey* (p. 19). Washington, DC: U.S. Department of Justice.

remains a discrepancy in the amount of effort directed toward understanding the behavior of female gang members vis-à-vis males, gender issues are no longer an ignored policy area. This is another practical consideration, because more female gangs have emerged, and girls and young women have become gang members.[33] Table 11.4 indicates the proportional representation of girls and young women in youth gangs.[34]

There is no single profile of female gang members.[35] They generally come from untenable home environments and find a new "family" within the gang. Some marry male gangbangers and have children, thus turning the gang lifestyle into a family lifestyle, and thereby encouraging multigenerational gang membership. This sort of bonding also encourages the perpetuation of a cultural acceptance of the gang lifestyle among some segments of the urban underclass.

Past research emphasized the exploitation and peripheral involvement of girls and young women, but this emphasis presents an incomplete picture.[36] In fact, girls and young women have historically been affiliated with gangs in several ways, with their roles defined by the traditions of the gang, or whether they are members of male/female gangs or exclusively female gangs.[37] Three broad profiles may be drawn:

- *Female Gangbangers.* Members of all-female gangs that are independent from male gangs, and act on their own volition without reference to, or permission from, male gang members. They often are formed as a reaction to the subordination and exploitation found in male gangs, and are a fairly rare phenomenon, usually found in large cities.
- *Female Associates.* Girls and young women who belong to predominantly male gangs, but who are not overly exploited or subordinated by male members. This is in contradistinction to female auxiliaries. Female gang associates are a "middle ground" between female auxiliaries and female gangbangers. They are relatively small in number compared to males.

- *Female Auxiliaries.* Girls and young women who play a subordinate role to male gang members. They do not share in leadership roles, they perform menial or otherwise secondary tasks, and they act in a support role for the gang. Exploitation and abuse of female members by male members may occur.

Regardless of which profile best fits a particular case, it is indisputable that girls and young women are involved in gang activity, and are not simply victims of exploitation and subordination. Female gang members have engaged in criminal activity, often involving violence and serious felonies. Having made this observation, it is exceptionally rare for females to engage in the same patterns of extreme violence (such as drive-by shootings) as male gangbangers.

Operational Characteristics: Living the Life of a Gangbanger

Members of gangs are recruited from among the local youths in a variety of ways. Once one becomes a member, there are lines of authority set out under the gang's internal culture that must be observed. In addition, the role of gang symbols must be understood and respected by members. And, when called upon, members participate in a range of delinquent and criminal activities.

Recruitment and Initiation. From a gang's perspective, recruitment is necessary for the perpetuation of the gang's identity and strength. Modern gangs either actively seek out "new blood" for the group, or passively wait to be approached by youths who aspire to become full-fledged members of the gang. In many neighborhoods, recruitment is quite easy, because youngsters often emulate older gang members by imitating their dress, speech, and symbols. These young imitators are often referred to as **"wannabes"** because they want to be identified as gang members, and frequently aspire to joining the group.

Gangs identify potential members in middle schools and high schools. They find youths with certain attributes, such as courage and fighting skills, and approach them as recruits. Larger gangs with strong reputations frequently do not have to recruit new members, because many youths will readily approach them for consideration as members. Recruitment and initiation can be a highly ritualized process. Virtually every gang poses ritualistic challenges to potential members that test their courage and commitment. Some of these challenges are dangerous and criminal. For example, it is common practice for new recruits to undergo a **"jumping in"** ritual, in which they must fight a group of gang members. Jumping in is little more than delivering a beating to test one's courage and fortitude. It should be noted that in some neighborhoods, participation in recruitment can be a matter of survival, because being an "outsider" in a gang-infested community can be dangerous.

Gang Hierarchies. Once one has been recruited into a gang, they become part of an identifiable division existing within the membership. This division is a kind of hierarchy, although most street gangs do not have a disciplined, vertically-integrated command structure. Nevertheless, organizational strength and cohesion revolve around the following broad categories:

- *Leadership*. Older gangbangers who have been members of the group for some time. Their status is usually determined by their charisma, machismo, toughness, and leadership skills. They set policy, and command respect from the membership.
- *Hard-cores*. Hard-core gang members are loyal "soldiers" of the organization. They are completely devoted to the gang, and their lives revolve around their association with the group. Hard-cores are the most criminal and violent members.
- *Peripheral Members*. Members who move around within the gang's lifestyle, but are not fully devoted to being gangbangers. Often the youngest or newest members, their lives are not totally immersed in gang membership. As peripheral members desire increased status, they may someday become hard-core members.
- *Wannabes*. Nonmembers who imitate gang behavior.

When one becomes fully immersed into a gang lifestyle, many are said to become **Original Gangsters, or "OGs."** OGs are those who are recognized by their reputation for affiliation with a particular gang. They receive a street-level respect for the things they have done to enhance their own status and the status of the gang. These activities can include drive-by shootings, imprisonment, killings, or some other gang-related behavior. OGs are hard-core members who have never "sold out" their gang identification.

Symbols of Self-Identification. "**Representing**" refers to how gang members present themselves as such. For generations, street gangs have traditionally adopted symbolic self-identifiers to set themselves apart and distinguish themselves from other gangs. These identifiers historically created a sense of self-importance and "specialness" for members.

Although many gang members have become wise enough to not use overt symbols—because of the obviously increased likelihood that the police will identify them as gangbangers—examples of symbols of self-identification have included the following attributes:

- *Clothing*. Jackets with an emblazoned gang logo; sports shoes, caps, and other clothing; t-shirts or blue jeans; and often something as simple as a rolled-up pants leg.
- *Colors*. Emblazoned jackets; clothing of a specific color, such as red (for Bloods) or blue (for Crips); colored bandanas, shoes, or other articles of clothing.

- *Hand Signals.* Shaping the hands, fingers, and arms into the letters or numbers of the gang. Hand signals are used as identifiers and as aggressive gestures that are intended to intimidate others.
- *Jewelry.* Necklaces and bracelets, usually gold and shaped into numbers, symbols, or automobile logos.
- *Tattoos.* "Burning" a gang's symbolic logo onto the body. This can be a process that takes place over several phases, with new symbols being "burned" as one progresses further into the gang and proves their allegiance through deeds. This type of identification is very common among Latino and skinhead gangs.

It should also be pointed out that symbolic graffiti has been used as a method for marking gang territory, identifying gang members, or proclaiming the strength of the gang. Graffiti has also been used to send messages to other gangs, and to honor fallen gang members. Its symbolism can be either crudely drawn combinations of letters, numbers, and symbols, or quite intricate murals. Some symbols may be artistically drawn, as may portraits of deceased members. As in the case of symbolic clothing, signals, jewelry, and tattoos, graffiti "tagging" is quite visible to the police, and so many gangs scale back on the use of flamboyant graffiti.

Photo 11.2   Gang members brandish a handgun.

Delinquency and Criminality. Gangs are a type of antisocial peer association. As such, they are inherently prone to accepting "outlaw" lifestyles of nonconformity and are often involved in the commission of delinquent and criminal acts. Unfortunately for many communities, gang criminality can be violent and reduce the quality of life for residents in some urban neighborhoods. In too many instances, gangbangers not only prey on members of the community; they effectively terrorize them. In this regard, gangs commonly exploit members of their own communities, so that the victims of their activities are usually of the same ethnicity. Thus, African American gangs generally prey on members of the African American community, and Latino gangs likewise victimize Latino communities.

Although most street gangs do not participate in criminal enterprises, it is a fact that a sizable proportion of street gangs engage in criminality. Gangs have been implicated in every type of crime and criminal enterprise:

- Gang-initiated crimes include rape, murder, burglary, vandalism, and armed robbery.
- Gang-related criminal enterprises include drug trafficking, extortion, and prostitution.

In point of fact, gangs can pose a serious challenge to the peace of many urban areas because of the frequency of their crimes. Thousands of violent gang-related crimes occur each year, including thousands of gang-related homicides.[38] Several types of violent crime became associated with gang criminality in the public's collective mind, largely because of sensational cases and intensive media scrutiny. These have included the following "signature" crimes:

- *Home invasions.* Violent trespass into homes by groups of youths, who terrorize the residents. Crimes committed by invaders include assault, murder, rape, and robbery.
- *Drive-by shootings.* Shootings by carloads of gun-wielding gang members. Occupants of the vehicles spray gunfire at members of rival gangs, firing wildly and often hitting innocent bystanders or residents inside their homes.
- *Wilding.* Rampages by youths in public areas such as parks or shopping malls. Perpetrators randomly beat or sexually assault people, sometimes seriously injuring them.

Gangs With Common Purposes and Allegiances. Clearly, most groups of youths require certain "bottom line" characteristics in order to be labeled a gang. They all certainly violate society's laws and norms, but these violations do not necessarily occur in the same way. A number of differences can arise from a variety of factors, such as ethnicity, region, city, and neighborhood. Interestingly, there are also differences that arise from a gang's adoption of a predominant common purpose or allegiance. The following are examples of gangs that exhibit a unique and identifiably distinct sense of purpose or allegiance:

- *Drug gangs.* Street gangs that are organized around drugs as a criminal enterprise. They are fundamentally criminal organizations, and are motivated by profit. Usually comprised of youths and young adults, the latter are the leaders and "brains" of the operation.
- *Skinhead gangs.* Lifestyle gangs that are usually associated with white supremacist ideologies. A few are associated with neo-Nazi or other racial supremacist movements. As a counterpoint, some skinheads are antiracist associations of youths that may actually exhibit a multiethnic membership. All cut their hair very short, and adopt distinctive dress such as boots, suspenders, and leather (or "bomber") jackets.
- *Stoner gangs.* Lifestyle gangs that are organized around drug use and hard rock music. They represent a countercultural alternative to mainstream society, and may express themselves with piercings, tattoos, black clothing, and Gothic appearance. Membership is usually made up of white youths.
- *Tagger crews and posses.* Graffiti gangs who vandalize property by marking their territory with graffiti messages. They do little more than travel through neighborhoods painting walls with their messages, and may be described as vandalism gangs. Some tagger crews can be quite artistic, albeit by defacing someone else's property.

A Policy Dilemma: Responding to the Gang Problem

What is to be done about youth gangs? How should policy makers deal with antisocial groups of young men and women? As a matter of policy, it would be folly to presume that the street gang phenomenon is simply a fad, or generational cycle, that will run its course and disappear. Thus, society cannot ignore the problem, and hope that it will go away; this would be simplistic and naïve.

There are three broad policy alternatives for addressing the problem of youth gangs, all of them requiring proactive and intensive initiatives by communities and juvenile justice professionals. These alternatives are **gang suppression, gang prevention,** and **gang intervention.**[39]

Gang Suppression

Crime suppression is a hard-line approach toward law enforcement. When applied as a policy alternative to the gang problem, suppression involves aggressive confrontation of gangs as organizations, and gang members as individuals. Its purpose is easily understood: To either eliminate gangs, or significantly repress their activity. Depending on the circumstances of each gang environment, suppression may be welcomed or criticized by the community.

Gang suppression is welcomed when communities feel a need to react forcefully to eradicate a gang environment. This occurs when gangs are perceived to have taken over a community, or when gang crime and violence spread fear among residents throughout an urban area. Demands are made for law enforcement officials and politicians to take a strong stance against gangs. The response nationally has been a plethora of antigang programs and antigang police units. Tactics can be quite aggressive. For example, antigang police units have engaged in periodic antigang "sweeps" in a number of cities. These sweeps are a show of force and a demonstration of intolerance for gang activity. There have been a significant number of gang members arrested and prosecuted in the aftermath of antigang sweeps.

One influential model for gang suppression programs was the Los Angeles Police Department's (LAPD's) **Community Resources Against Street Hoodlums (CRASH)** unit. CRASH was created during the 1980s to aggressively confront gangs. Intimidation was expressly permitted as a matter of policy. In the beginning, CRASH was widely popular in the community because its tactics did indeed intimidate many gang members. However, the program was disbanded after revelations about scandals involving illegal activities and other inappropriate behavior that violated the LAPD's organizational and procedural regulations. Nevertheless, many jurisdictions have adopted modified versions of CRASH as a hard-line component within broader antigang policies.

Gang Prevention

The philosophy of gang prevention mirrors that of crime prevention. The idea is to eliminate the conditions that lead to delinquency and criminal deviance. Thus, within the purview of prevention strategies, it is believed that delinquency, criminality, and gang creation can be *nipped in the bud* if certain identified conditions are corrected. The myriad theories of juvenile deviance and gang membership discussed previously provide guidance for experts on the question of preventing antisocial group behavior by juveniles. Two important prevention focal points—or nodes—provide officials and communities with excellent opportunities for successfully preventing gang membership. These are the family and schools.

The Family Focal Point. It is said that prevention begins with the family, and that strong family environments promote good values and character among children. Youths learn from household values, and their behavior is significantly affected by the quality of parental supervision, guidance, and mentorship. Thus, functional families are much less likely to produce gang members than are dysfunctional families. And, if gang values already exist within the family, children are very likely to accept them as normal modes of behavior. It is a central principle of gang prevention that communities and juvenile justice officials promote healthy households, and be prepared to intervene with (and perhaps remove) children who grow up in toxic family environments.

The School Focal Point. Gang prevention also occurs in schools. School quality and active participation in antigang (and anticrime) initiatives are important components in the effort to divert youths away from gang lifestyles. Because schools act *in loco parentis* for a significant amount of children's lives, they are ideal venues for prevention programs. Vulnerable children—those from dysfunctional families or toxic neighborhoods—truly need school guidance, because they are not receiving it in their immediate home or community environments. Initiatives such as the **Gang Resistance Education and Training (GREAT)** program (first mentioned in Chapter 9) are commonly promoted in public schools. GREAT is a good case study of how lines of communication can be established between every party to the gang problem—schools, the police, and students—as a way to promote understanding and respect. The importance of GREAT and other similar programs lies in the need for school teachers, administrators, law enforcement officials, and members of the student body to sit down and honestly interact with each other.

Gang Intervention

Intervention is a middle ground between gang prevention and gang suppression, and becomes the predominant antigang option when gang prevention initiatives such as GREAT prove to be unsuccessful. Intervention policies require juvenile justice officials and the community to intervene in the lives of individuals who have crossed the line and adopted (or are about to adopt) the lifestyle of a gangbanger. An important concept to remember is that intervention specialists do not consider these individuals to be lost to society, but rather in need of being rehabilitated and reclaimed by the community.

The intervention process arguably involves higher degrees of subtlety and complexity than are found in the gang suppression and gang prevention processes. Perhaps the most difficult task is to identify juveniles who have committed themselves to gang participation. Once identified, these youths are treated as at-risk juveniles by appropriate treatment authorities. The identification process can be especially complicated when an individual is simply a wannabe rather than a fully initiated member, because he or she may not exhibit every characteristic of a gangbanger. In addition, some youths may be neither wannabes nor gang members, but have simply adopted gang dress and slang as a matter of fashion—these youths run the risk of being misidentified as gang members and misdiagnosed as needing certain types of treatment.

Both community agencies and government agencies participate in intervention programs. The programs are generally managed by schools, nonprofit agencies, religious organizations, and mentorship programs such as Big Brothers/Big Sisters of America.

Chapter Summary

The modern youth culture has an influence on both group and individual identities of young Americans. This is not necessarily a negative influence, and can, in fact, be quite positive. However, antisocial peer groups form within the youth culture that pose a very detrimental danger to those who participate in these groups. In particular, the case of youth gangs poses a problem not only for those who choose this lifestyle—because of the real possibility that they will be "lost" to society—but an additional threat to the community. Because of this threat to society, policies have been devised to address the problem of gangs.

Individuals become members of antisocial peer groups for a variety of reasons that emanate from a number of sources. Direct influences on an individual's decision to associate with antisocial groups include family dysfunction, community and neighborhood problems, and negative school environments. Reasons for the formation of gangs include social disorganization, poverty-ridden neighborhoods, and the need to achieve status through socially unacceptable means.

Youth gangs have historically existed in the United States since at least the 1820s. They have always been associated with geographic territories and composed of a predominant ethnicity. Modern gangs formed regionally in the East and West, and some have grown to become large gangs with recognizable "franchises" in other neighborhoods and cities. From the perspective of many communities, gang victimization and property defacement are serious issues, because the quality of life of residents can become untenable. This is especially true when gangs are influenced by adult members, who often move the gang's operational profile beyond mere turf protection toward involvement in criminal enterprises such as drug trafficking. Although gangs still tend to be male and young, with females serving in auxiliary roles, many girls and young women have become full-fledged gangbangers. In the modern era, most gangs are organized within the Latino and African American communities, although there are also many gangs from other ethnicities. All gangs "represent" themselves in some manner, usually via distinctive clothing, colors, hand signals, tattoos, or jewelry.

Policy makers have designed several broad response categories for addressing the gang problem. Gang suppression is a hard-line approach that attempts to eradicate gangs. Gang prevention programs attempt to preempt gang affiliation before it begins by focusing on the quality of family and school influences on individual youths. Gang intervention initiatives are middle alternatives that try to rehabilitate and reclaim youths who are either at risk of joining gangs, or who have already done so.

Chapter 12 expands the perspective of juvenile justice beyond the context of the United States. An overview of international approaches is presented, and representative programs are discussed. This global context is important, because the Anglo-American approach is only one of many found among the world's nations and cultures.

Questions for Review

1. How should antisocial behavior be defined within the context of juvenile justice?

2. Which possible sources have been identified that possibly explain juvenile antisocial behavior?

3. Describe the possible effects of family dysfunction, problems in school, peer relationships, and "toxic" neighborhoods.

4. How should youth gangs be defined?

5. What are the historical origins of modern youth gangs?

6. In what ways have gang demographics changed over the years?

7. How should gang organizational structure be described?

8. How should gang behavior be described?

9. Which policy options have been formulated to counter gang activity?

Key Terms and Concepts

The following topics were discussed in this chapter, and are found in the Glossary:

CRASH (Community Resources Against Street Hoodlums)

Criminal Gangs

Delinquent Gang

Drive-By Shootings

Drug Gangs

Environmental Factors

Female Associates

Female Auxiliaries

Female Gangbangers

Folk Nation

Gang Intervention

Gang Prevention

Gang Resistance Education and Training (GREAT)

Gang Suppression

Gangbangers

Gangs

Home Invasions

"Jumping In"

"Juvies"

Multiple Marginality Theory

Original Gangsters (O.G.s)

People Nation

"Representing"

Skinhead Gangs

Skinheads Against Racial
Prejudice (SHARPS)

Social Disorganization Theory

Socialization

Stoner Gangs

Street Gang

Tagger Crews

Tongs

Turf Wars

"Wannabes"

Watts Riot

Wilding

Youth Culture

Youth Gang

Zoot Suit Riots

DISCUSSION BOX

Drug Gangs

This chapter's Discussion Box is intended to stimulate critical discussion about gangs that engage in drug trafficking as a criminal enterprise.

Many gangs have long ceased being characterized as turf-focused groups of anti-social youths. They have crossed the line into participating in high-stakes criminal enterprises. They do not simply hang out or roam their neighborhoods. Instead, they engage in drug trafficking and other activities to make a profit. These criminally entrepreneurial gangs have adult members who are essentially professional gangsters.

Obviously, drug gangs specialize in the drug trade. This type of gang arose during the 1980s in major urban areas, their transformation stimulated by the appearance of cheap crack cocaine on the drug market. Turf wars became exceptionally violent as gangs fought to control the crack trade, often involving the use of sub-machine guns and high-powered assault rifles. Many innocent bystanders were killed or injured during drive-by shootings and attempted assassinations of rivals. New York, Miami, Chicago, and Los Angeles became centers of this violence, although drug-related gang violence occurred in many cities. As gangs "franchised" outside of their home turfs and cities, and established recognized affiliates across the country, the gang-based drug trade became an interstate enterprise.

Discussion Questions

1. In what ways does the concept of drug gangs change the threat to the community from gang activity?

2. Does participation in criminal enterprises fundamentally change the definition of what constitutes a *youth* or a *street* gang?

3. How does the existence of drug gangs change the policy calculation for dealing with the gang problem?

4. What should be done about gangs that cross the line to become involved in criminal enterprises?

5. Should drug gangs be dealt with more harshly than other gangs?

Recommended Web Sites

The following Web sites investigate the subject of youth gangs.

Gangs in Los Angeles County: http://www.streetgangs.com/
National Alliance of Gang Investigators Associations: http://www.nagia.org/
National Gang Crime Research Center: http://www.ngcrc.com/
National Major Gang Task Force: http://www.nmgtf.org/
National Youth Gang Center: http://www.iir.com/nygc/

Note: The Web site URLs and exercises below are also from the book's study site: http://www.sagepub.com/martin

Web Exercise

Using this chapter's recommended Internet sites, conduct an online investigation of youth gangs.

- What kind of resources exist to conduct research for future policy initiatives on youth gangs?
- In what ways have national gang centers helped in our understanding of the gang phenomenon?
- Who should be responsible for monitoring gang-related activity?

For an online search of youth gangs and antisocial lifestyles, students should use a search engine and enter the following keywords:

"Street Gang"

"Youth Gang"

Recommended Readings

The following publications provide discussions on youth gangs and organized juvenile deviance.

Donahue, S. (2002). *Gangs: Stories of life and death from the streets.* New York: Thunder's Mouth Press.

Huff, R. C. (Ed.). (2002). *Gangs in America* (3rd ed.). Thousand Oaks, CA: Sage.

Giroux, H. A. (1996). *Fugitive cultures: Race, violence, & youth*. New York: Routledge.

Skelton, T., & Valentine, G. (Eds.). (1998). *Cool places: Geographies of youth cultures*. New York: Routledge.

Vigil, J. D. (2002). *A rainbow of gangs: Street cultures in the mega-city*. Austin, TX: University of Texas Press.

Notes

1. See Derrick Hardaway v. Donald S. Young, 302 F. 3d 757 (7th Cir. 2002).

2. For a discussion of associations between youth culture and juvenile delinquency, see Blazak, R., & Wooden W. S. (2001). *Renegade kids, suburban outlaws: From youth culture to delinquency* (2nd ed.). Belmont, CA: Wadsworth.

3. See Huff, R. C. (1993). Gangs in the United States. In A. P. Goldstein & C. R. Huff. *The gang intervention handbook*. Champaign, IL: Research Press.

4. Adapted from Office of Juvenile Justice and Delinquency Prevention. (2000). *1998 national youth gang survey* (p. 13). Washington, DC: U.S. Department of Justice.

5. See Straus, M. A. (1991). Discipline and deviance: physical punishment of children and violence and other crime in adulthood. *Social Problems, 38*.

6. See Vigil, J. D. (1988). *Barrio gangs*. Austin, TX: University of Texas Press.

7. See, e.g., Miller, W. B. (2001). *The growth of youth gang problems in the United States: 1970–98*. Washington, DC: U.S. Department of Justice.

8. See Ashbury, H. . (1928). *The gangs of New York*. New York: Knopf.

9. Thrasher, F. M. (1927). *The gang*. Chicago: University of Chicago Press. This is a classic study of juvenile gangs, and had a significant impact on subsequent theory and research.

10. See ibid.

11. Important contributions were made in Cohen, A. K. (1955). *Delinquent boys: The culture of the gang*. New York: Free Press; and Cloward, R., & Ohlin, L. (1960). *Delinquency and opportunity: A theory of delinquent gangs*. New York: Free Press.

12. See Whyte, W. F. (1943). *Street corner society: The social structure of an Italian slum*. Chicago: University of Chicago Press.

13. See Cohen, A. K. (1955). *Delinquent boys: The culture of the gang*. New York: Free Press.

14. For an influential explanation of the class-oriented approach to abnormal group behavior in youths, see Miller, W. B. (1958). The lower class culture as a generating milieu of gang delinquency. *Journal of Social Issues, 14,* 5–19.

15. See Vigil, J. D. (1988). *Barrio gangs: Street life and identity in southern California*. Austin, TX: University of Texas Press. Also, Vigil, J. D. (1997). *Personas Mexicanas: Chicano high schoolers in a changing Los Angeles*. Fort Worth, TX: Harcourt Brace.

16. Adapted from Office of Juvenile Justice and Delinquency Prevention. (2000). *1998 national youth gang survey* (pp. 8, 9). Washington, DC: U.S. Department of Justice.

17. See Asbury, H. (2001). *The Gangs of New York: An informal history of the underworld.* New York: Thunder's Mouth Press.

18. Ibid.

19. For a good discussion of gangs in New York, see Schneider, E. C. (2001). *Vampires, dragons, and Egyptian kings: Youth gangs in postwar New York.* Princeton, NJ: Princeton University Press.

20. See Mazon, M. (1988). *The zoot suit riots: The psychology of symbolic annihilation.* Austin, TX: University of Texas Press. See also Pagan, E. O. (2003). *Murder at the sleepy lagoon: Zoot suits, race, & riot in wartime L.A.* Chapel Hill, NC: University of North Carolina Press.

21. See Florida Department of Corrections (n.d.). Available online at http://www.dc.state.fl.us/pub/gangs/index.html

22. Ibid.

23. Ibid.

24. Miller, W. B. (1975). *Violence by youth gangs and youth groups as a crime problem in major American cities.* Washington, DC: U.S. Department of Justice. This is a classic and oft-quoted definition.

25. Thrasher, F. M. (1927). *The gang.* Chicago: University of Chicago Press.

26. Conly, C. H., Kelly, P., Mahanna, P., & Warner, L. (1993). *Street gangs: Current knowledge and strategies.* Washington, DC: National Institute of Justice.

27. Curry, D. G., & Spergel, I. A. (1988). Gang Homicide, Delinquency, and Community. *Criminology, 26,* 381–406.

28. Jackson, R. K., & McBride W. D. (1992). *Understanding street gangs.* Placerville, CA: Copperhouse.

29. For a good discussion of the ethnic characteristics of gangs, see Christensen, L. (1999). *Gangbangers: Understanding the deadly minds of America's street gangs.* Boulder, CO: Paladin Press.

30. See Conly, C. H., Kelly, P., Mahanna P., & Warner L. (1993). *Street gangs: Current knowledge and strategies.* Washington, DC: National Institute of Justice.

31. Adapted from Office of Juvenile Justice and Delinquency Prevention. (2000). *1998 national youth gang survey* (p. 24). Washington, DC: U.S. Department of Justice.

32. From Office of Juvenile Justice and Delinquency Prevention. (2000). *1998 national youth gang survey* (p. 20). Washington, DC: U.S. Department of Justice.

33. See Campbell, A. (1990). Female participation in gangs. In C. R. Huff (Ed.). *Gangs in America* (pp. 163–182). Newbury Park, CA: Sage.

34. Adapted from Office of Juvenile Justice and Delinquency Prevention. (2000). *1998 national youth gang survey* (p. 19). Washington, DC: U.S. Department of Justice.

35. See Campbell, A. (1991). *The girls in the gang* (2nd ed.). Cambridge, MA: Blackwell.

36. See ibid.

37. See Bjerregaard, B., & Smith C. (1993). Gender differences in gang participation, delinquency, and substance use. *Journal of Quantitative Criminology, 9.*

38. See Office of Juvenile Justice and Delinquency Prevention. (1999). *1997 national youth gang survey.* Washington, DC: U.S. Department of Justice.

39. For a good discussion of youth gang policy alternatives, see Goldstein, A. P., & Huff, C. R. (Eds.). (1993). *The gang intervention handbook.* Champaign, IL: Research Press.

12 Global Perspectives

Juvenile Justice in an International Context

Some cases are so troubling that they begin a process of national soul-searching. In England, one such case left deep impressions on the British national psyche. In February 1993, toddler James Bulger was murdered by Jon Venables and Robert Thompson—both 10-year-old boys—in Liverpool, England. The boys led young Bulger away by hand from a shopping mall as his mother's back was turned. The abduction was caught on the mall's video cameras. They abducted him and walked 2.5 miles to a railroad yard, crossing paths with many adults along the way, who did not intervene despite the fact that James was distraught and apparently injured. The adults who did nothing have come to be called the Liverpool 38. Along the way to the rail yard, James was physically abused, and at the yard he was eventually killed by Venables and Thompson. They left him on train tracks, where a train hit his body.

Venables and Thompson were arrested several days later. They were tried as adults in Crown Court, received a trial by jury, and convicted. They were initially sentenced to a minimum of 8 years in prison, their sentences were raised to 15 years, and in 2000 the terms were reduced again to 8 years.

Until now, our discussion has focused on the American juvenile justice system, with an emphasis on its historical origins in Great Britain and the child welfare movements of the nineteenth century. However, when one considers juvenile justice process from an international perspective, it becomes very clear that the Anglo-American approach to juvenile justice is only one of many approaches. Other nations have developed their own cultural standards for rearing children, and have designed distinct methods for addressing the problems of child welfare and juvenile deviance.[1]

Juvenile justice—and by extension, children's rights—is a global issue. It is a subject that has garnered the attention of world leaders and international organizations for decades. During the latter quarter of the twentieth century, political leaders, governments, practitioners, and nongovernment organizations (NGOs) developed an internationalized concept of juvenile justice. The

Photo 12.1   A juvenile prison in Russia.

new perspective directed a great deal of attention to the special needs of youths around the world. This global context was useful for experts to share their experiences and findings, but it also illustrated a disturbing fact: Many children in the world are severely neglected or abused, and juvenile deviance often occurs within an environment of severe hardship.

To fully appreciate international perspectives on juvenile justice, one must understand why different approaches have evolved around the world. When considering these approaches, it quickly becomes obvious that every nation and culture has its own history, so that there are literally hundreds of unique and distinctive systems and traditions that can be investigated. In order to simplify our understanding of the global perspective, the following framework can be used as a basis for understanding some of the numerous factors associated with the treatment of young people in different cultures:

- *Developed nations*—relatively prosperous nations that have highly developed industrial and technological economies. These countries have abundant resources that can be devoted to managing social problems such as child welfare, delinquency, and crime.
- *Developing nations*—nations that have relatively unsophisticated or poorly developed industrial and technological economies. These countries have limited resources that can be devoted to managing juveniles justice issues.

- *Democratic nations*—open political systems in which the needs of society are communicated to political leaders, who are responsive. Juvenile justice policies are developed from the concerns of local communities. Political power is transferred through elections.
- *Undemocratic nations*—authoritarian political systems in which political leaders dictate policies to local communities, and may or may not be responsive to locally stated needs. Juvenile justice policies are decided by government authorities.
- *Pluralistic societies*—societies that recognize the value of the cultural and political opinions of their diverse constituent cultures, religions, and ethnic groups. In democratic pluralistic societies, juvenile justice policies can be adapted to the needs of different demographic populations. In theory, no group assumes dominance over other groups.
- *Traditional societies*—societies that do not embrace the cultural and political opinions of diverse demographic groups. The values of a predominant culture or group are imposed on all members of society. Juvenile justice policies are designed by the dominant group with the presumption that "what is good for us is good for all."

Table 12.1 summarizes the key elements of this framework.

TABLE 12.1   A GLOBAL FRAMEWORK: UNDERSTANDING SOURCES OF JUVENILE JUSTICE PROCESS

There are arguably as many sources of juvenile justice policy as there are nations and cultures. Nevertheless, there are certain features that can be identified from among the world's political systems and societal norms. This table summarizes common features found within several sociopolitical categories.

Sociopolitical Environment	Quality of Decision-Making Process	
	Domestic Profile	Juvenile Justice Policy Profile
Developed Nations	Strong and developed economies	Abundant resources for managing juvenile issues
Developing Nations	Weak or less developed economies	Limited resources for managing juvenile issues
Democratic Nations	Needs of society communicated to responsive leaders	Community concerns drive juvenile justice policies
Undemocratic Nations	Leaders dictate policy priorities	Leaders dictate juvenile justice policies
Pluralistic Societies	Cultural and political diversity is accepted	Juvenile justice policies are adapted to diversity of needs
Traditional Societies	Cultural and political diversity is rejected	Juvenile justice policies reflect needs of dominant group

It must be remembered that this framework has been broadly designed and should not be considered to embody every conclusive (or exclusive) explanatory variable for every circumstance. Rather, it offers guidelines for understanding common political and cultural influences on juvenile justice process around the world. The discussion in this chapter reviews the roles of the police, courts, and corrections in the juvenile justice systems of several countries. The discussion of the foregoing categories is undertaken within the contexts of developed and developing nations, as follows:

- International Perspectives: Juvenile Justice Process in Developed Nations
- International Perspectives: Juvenile Justice Process in Developing Nations
- Children's Rights: A Global Approach to Juvenile Justice

CHAPTER PERSPECTIVE 12.1

Sweden's Prochild Approach[2]

For most Americans, the frame of reference used to evaluate juvenile justice process is that of the Anglo-American legal tradition. The principles and institutions derived from ancient England have been applied in the United States, Canada, Australia, and elsewhere. However, this tradition is by no means the predominant example of juvenile justice in the world—it is only one of many.

Sweden's approach to juvenile justice process is typical of the Scandinavian systems.[3] Sweden has enacted national legislation that establishes national laws on the treatment of children. By American standards, these laws are very intrusive, because they prohibit behaviors by parents within the household that many in the United States would consider to be no one else's business. For example, Swedish law prohibits corporal (physical) punishment, including spanking. Children's rights are taken very seriously, and the government has assumed responsibility to assure the protection of children.

There is a consensus in Sweden that all citizens have a fundamental right to the basic amenities of a secure life. This includes health care, retirement income, and state-managed protections for at-risk populations such as the poor. Thus, it is not surprising that the concept of juvenile justice strongly emphasizes treatment, protection, and rehabilitation.

Diversion outside of the juvenile justice system is a routine practice in Sweden and is in fact mandatory for offenders younger than 15 years of age. Child welfare agencies have automatic custody over offenders who were younger than 15 when they committed their crime. After that age, many youths continue to be diverted away from the juvenile justice system and into the care of child welfare authorities. Factors such as substance abuse and psychological problems are treated as mitigating factors that lessen the likelihood of punishment. In such cases, offenders are treated more as patients and are referred to Swedish health welfare agencies.

International Perspectives: Juvenile Justice Process in Developed Nations

Developed nations include those that are collectively known as "the West." Conceptually, **Western nations** are those that have highly developed economies, democratic governments, and high literacy rates. Geographically, the West includes Western Europe, North America, Japan, and a few other countries in other regions.

Western societies are functional, and usually quite stable. They also have exceptionally low rates of **absolute deprivation**, but noticeably existing rates of **relative deprivation**. Absolute deprivation refers to members of society who lack or have only the minimal means to survive within a society, such as food and shelter. Relative deprivation refers to being deprived in comparison to the rest of society, such as poverty and poor education. In order to offset social and economic inequalities, most Western countries have designed extensive social welfare systems. These systems—frequently based on democratic socialist models—alleviate the plight of their poor, sick, and elderly citizens through government-funded or -managed programs. This notion of a governmental duty to improve the lives of at-risk populations extends to the provision of juvenile services.

Comparisons can be made between developed nations on the roles of official institutions for managing juvenile justice process. The following discussion summarizes the relative duties of the police, the courts, and corrections systems in several British-influenced Western countries including the United Kingdom,[4] Canada,[5] and Australia.[6] These cases have been selected because of their origins. Quite simply, the United Kingdom is the wellspring for many juvenile justice concepts used in English-speaking-and-influenced countries. From this origin, *parens patriae* and other concepts have come to serve as the foundation for government authority over the rearing of children in many countries.

The Role of the Police in Developed Countries: The Case of British-Influenced Western Nations

As in the United States, the police serve in a "first disposition" role in many developed nations. They often represent the first response of the juvenile justice system when dealing with juvenile deviance, and many juveniles are first brought into the system during the equivalent of an American police disposition. Similarly to police in the United States, the police in developed countries are expected to differentiate their treatment of juveniles from their treatment of adults.

United Kingdom (England and Wales). In England and Wales, the police serve a similar role as American police, in the sense that they are frequently the first official point of contact with children in trouble and children in need. Juveniles may be arrested for the commission of an offense, but police discretion is permissible, and officers may exercise a range of dispositions, from verbal warnings to taking suspects to a police station.

When juveniles are taken into custody, their parents are contacted and told to appear with them. When parents appear, they are confronted by the police, given a warning, and usually given custody of the child. If parents do not appear, a social worker is assigned to the juvenile, and the suspect may be detained by the police. When deemed necessary, the case is referred to the Crown Prosecution Service (discussed in the next section on the role of the court in British-influenced nations).

United Kingdom (Scotland). In many ways, Scotland's juvenile justice system is predicated on a policy that is designed to destigmatize and rehabilitate juveniles who are brought before juvenile authorities. As in England and Wales, the police are authorized to use discretion in the handling of juvenile dispositions. When contact is made with a suspect, an interview is conducted with the juvenile and his or her parents to determine whether the youth should be officially referred to the Children's Panel (discussed in the next section on the role of the court in British-influenced nations). For minor offenses, the police are authorized to keep the child under police supervision. In these circumstances, the case ends with police supervision, and no further referral into the juvenile justice system is made.

Canada. Canada has a law enforcement approach to juvenile deviance, so that serious juvenile offenses are considered to be a crime. When youths are arrested on suspicion of committing a crime, they are informed of their rights, which are similar to the U.S. Miranda warnings, but which also include the right to confer with one's parents. When juveniles choose to cooperate with the authorities, the police must record their waiver of rights in writing, and then proceed with questioning. In some Canadian provinces, statements cannot be taken by the police unless approved by the Crown Counsel. Interestingly, probationary youths are recorded by the police in a computerized national database.

Australia. Police officers are trained to treat juvenile offenders very differently from adult offenders. Juvenile-specific rules and regulations are mandated for the treatment and processing of juvenile suspects. Arrest is used as a last resort, and an emphasis is placed on the use of police discretion to resolve police dispositions. Warnings, both formal and informal, are commonly used for minor offenses, so that maximum flexibility is built into the police role. Formal questioning of youths takes place in the police station before parents or other adult witnesses.

The Role of the Court in Developed Countries: The Case of British-Influenced Western Nations

Courtroom philosophies and procedures vary markedly in different countries. In some systems, juveniles brought before a judicial proceeding will be confronted by a rather onerous, formal, and intimidating institution. In other systems, juveniles will find judicial proceedings that involve panels and laypersons who treat juvenile offenders very differently in comparison to formal court hearings.

United Kingdom (England and Wales). For serious offenses and recidivism, the facts of a case are gathered by a juvenile bureau and passed along to the Crown Prosecution Service. A Chief Inspector evaluates the information and decides whether to release the juvenile, issue a reprimand and warning, or prosecute the individual. The reprimand and warning is referred to as a **caution** and is used extensively in the UK as an alternative to formal processing further into the system. Cautions send a strong message to the juvenile against his or her behavior, and serve as an admonishment that he or she will be taken before the court for any further violations.

If prosecution is deemed necessary, the case is brought before a court. Cases are referred to magistrates, who are lay experts, rather than judges. Most proceedings are overseen by three magistrates and are informal in comparison to adult courtroom trials. They are private "bench" hearings, meaning that they are closed to the public and are conducted without the right to a jury. The actual prosecution is conducted by either the Crown Prosecution Service or the police. The panel of magistrates may impose sentences ranging in severity from discharge to binding over for juvenile custody. Although the underlying philosophy of magistrate panels is to try to divert juveniles out of correctional institutions, they have the authority to impose juvenile sentences for up to six months. For serious offenses, England and Wales permit juveniles to be tried in the same manner as adults before the Crown Court, where they may be sentenced for up to life imprisonment.

United Kingdom (Scotland). Scotland has not had a juvenile court since the **Social Worker Act of 1968** abolished it and created a **Children's Panel** in its stead. The Children's Panel, which has jurisdiction over children 8 to 17 years of age, is comprised of three citizens drawn from the community who are knowledgeable about the needs of juveniles in the community. They are charged to determine whether or not suspects are guilty, and to impose required treatment in the best interest of the child. It is important to observe that members of the Children's Panel are drawn from the citizenry; they are not professional judges, social workers, or other juvenile justice officials.

Children's Panels represent an intentional policy by the Scottish juvenile justice system to recognize the unique quality of juvenile deviance, and to treat young offenders as a distinctive class that requires special intervention. This reflects the philosophy that courts cannot provide genuine treatment for juvenile offenders; only panels comprised of bona fide representatives of the community can render effective rehabilitative decisions. The Scottish system acknowledges all of the causes of juvenile deviance that have been discussed in previous chapters—dysfunctional families, toxic communities, and personal traits—and has concluded that courts are an improper venue for correcting such problems.

Canada. As in the United States, juvenile justice in Canada historically promoted informality and rehabilitation for nearly a century, beginning in the late nineteenth century. Prior to the modern era, juvenile court judges were vested with significant discretion, and court proceedings could be quite informal. It was believed that informality, coupled with strict discipline, was the best way to rehabilitate juvenile offenders. However, this philosophy was curtailed in 1982 with the passage of the **Young Offenders Act,** and Canada now practices official formality, with strict rules and procedures that are similar to the adult criminal court.[7] The Act reflects a juvenile justice consensus that sanctions movement toward a criminal justice model.[8] Thus, juveniles accused of committing serious offenses in the modern era can be sent before the adult criminal court. Juvenile court judges now preside over rather formal proceedings. They have very limited discretion over transferring offenders outside of the jurisdiction of the court into the adult system or into community-based programs. Juveniles may receive long sentences for serious offenses.

Australia. The approach toward juvenile justice in Australia is similar to the United States in that it varies from jurisdiction to jurisdiction. In general, juvenile courts may hear a variety of cases, with specific jurisdictions including some charges but excluding others. Juvenile judges and magistrates are subject to restrictions on their consideration of certain offenses, with some jurisdictions permitting them to hear a greater number of charges than other jurisdictions. Juvenile courts may impose a range of sanctions, including release, community service, and incarceration. Youths may be required to attend school, receive job training, or receive counseling. In some jurisdictions, those found guilty of serious offenses may be sent to adult prisons beginning at the age of 16 years.

Juvenile Corrections in Developed Countries: The Case of British-Influenced Western Nations

The histories of correctional systems paralleled each other in our British-influenced nations under review. Although they did not develop identical systems or philosophies of incarceration, they were quite similar. For example, Australia developed a corrections model that was arguably the first example of awarding points for serving "good time" in prison, leading to early release from incarceration—this is now known as parole.

The approaches of our case studies toward juvenile corrections were also similar, and in each case, for many decades, juveniles were imprisoned with adults and received corporal punishment. These practices gradually ended with the advent of the Child-Saving and Reform Movements of the nineteenth century. Because of these similarities, the programs and philosophies of the British-influenced juvenile corrections systems are familiar to us, and are summarized in the sections that follow.

United Kingdom (England and Wales). As the incarceration of juveniles in adult facilities gradually ended during the nineteenth century, the first nonprison placements were made in private homes for minor offenders. As discussed previously, reformers established the first juvenile facilities for youths. In the modern era, juvenile offenders are regularly housed in detention facilities, where regimentation and discipline are enforced. Several youth facilities have been established:

- *Youth Custody Centers*. Facilities that house juveniles for court-specified periods of time, usually not of long duration.
- *Junior Detention Centers*. Facilities that house juveniles 14 to 17 years of age.
- *Senior Detention Centers*. Facilities that house juveniles 17 to 21 years of age.

United Kingdom (Scotland). Scotland's unique integration of the community into its system of juvenile justice process is also manifested in its approach toward juvenile corrections. Children's Panels render their decisions based on the needs of the child and the functionality of their parents and home environments. When a juvenile is found guilty, or admits guilt, members of the Children's Panel discuss with him or her the reasons for the behavior (often at length), and ask how they can help intervene to prevent repeat behavior. Once a decision is agreed upon, referral is usually made to professional social service agencies for supervision over the child's disposition. Probation agencies do not exist *per se*, but probationary conditions are managed by the social service system.

Canada. As in the United States, juvenile dispositions in Canada include probation (often juvenile intensive probation supervision [JIPS]), community service, community-based corrections, shock incarceration, and detention facilities. Because there is an emphasis on holding youths responsible for their offenses, dispositions can also include fines, victim restitution, and varying degrees of detention. Some juvenile facilities are quite secure, whereas others are campus-like. Hardened juvenile delinquents are usually separated from status offenders as a matter of policy, but status offenders may still be sent into locked facilities. Terms of probation include school attendance, service in the community, counseling, and substance abuse recovery.

Australia. Detention centers in Australia are used to house juvenile offenders, often for several years. Sentences can be determinate, but parole officers are authorized to grant early releases to detained juveniles. Programs within these facilities include job training and educational services. However, Australian facilities have had a historical reputation for hard conditions. Serious juvenile offenders can begin serving their sentences in juvenile facilities, and then are "graduated" to serve time in adult facilities.

Table 12.2 summarizes the roles of the police, courts, and juvenile corrections in the foregoing cases.

TABLE 12.2   JUVENILE JUSTICE PROCESS IN DEVELOPED NATIONS: THE CASE OF
BRITISH-INFLUENCED COUNTRIES

Juvenile justice process in developed nations is usually characterized by a separation of juvenile
process and procedures from adult process and procedures. There tends to be a clear distinction
between the personal and institutional needs of juveniles in comparison to adults. Juvenile justice
concepts in British-influenced countries have adopted similar missions for the components of their
systems. This table summarizes juvenile justice process in several of these countries.

| Juvenile Justice Component | Developed Nations: British-Influenced Cases | | | |
	UK (England and Wales)	UK (Scotland)	Canada	Australia
Police	Similar to U.S. First point of contact Discretionary dispositions	Similar to U.S. Discretionary dispositions	Law enforcement approach Formal dispositions	Specialized treatment of juveniles Discretionary dispositions
Courts	Emphasis on diversion Criminal trials for serious offenses	No juvenile court Children's Panel Treatment focus	Formal proceedings Criminal justice model	Similar to U.S. Decentralized system Criminal trials for serious offenses
Corrections	Use of juvenile facilities Variety of facilities	Usually diverted to social service agency	Similar to U.S. Range of dispositions Secure and unsecured facilities	Youth detention centers Rigorous programs

International Perspectives: Juvenile Justice Process in Developing Nations

Developing nations are those that were known as the "Third World" during the second half of the twentieth century. Conceptually, **Third World
nations** had less developed economies in comparison to the West, frequently had undemocratic governments, and had lower literacy rates than
in Europe or North America. This conceptualization now describes developing countries. In extreme cases, developing nations are in dire economic,
political, and human straights. Geographically, developing nations are
found in virtually every region of the world, and in fact make up the majority of the world; most people live in developing countries. Although many
of these societies are functional, many others are rather fragile and unstable. Some developing nations have significant rates of absolute deprivation,
with large poor populations in cities and the countryside who literally live

at the subsistence level. Although many social and economic problems are managed to some degree, there are a number of problems that can seem insurmountable, such as unemployment and political disenfranchisement. Developing societies constantly struggle to meet the needs of their poor, sick, and elderly citizens.

The following discussion summarizes the relative duties of the police, the courts, and corrections systems in the world's two most populous countries—India[9] and China.[10]

An Overview of Juvenile Justice in Developing Countries: The Cases of India and China

It should be clear by now that the term *juvenile justice* has many different connotations around the world, depending on societal norms, values, and culture. Some juvenile justice systems are highly developed and well-integrated into functional legal systems. Other juvenile justice frameworks barely function, often because the underlying legal system is corrupt or fragmented, or because the notion of juvenile justice has historically resided in local and informal resolution mechanisms. In other words, the very notion of a juvenile justice "system" in many countries is in reality a decentralized patchwork of traditions or arbitrary dispositions.

Indian Juvenile Justice Process. India is an example of fundamental political stability and functionality in the developing world. It is also the world's most populous democracy. Formerly a British colony—the "jewel in the crown" of the British Empire—its government has been able to administer and feed a densely populated society with only occasional outbreaks of instability. India is, in fact, a developing country with an extensive educated professional services sector. The crime rate is relatively low, so that the processing of juvenile offenses is not as pervasive as in the United States.

For youths brought before the authorities, most dispositions are handled informally, often in accordance with local standards and customs. Officially, India's **Children's Act of 1960** was passed to create uniform standards (and an official system) for juvenile justice process. The Act differentiates between boys and girls in its definition of who is a "juvenile"—males under age 16 years and females under age 18 years are considered to be juveniles. "Delinquents" are defined as any juvenile who violates the law. Official standards for juvenile facilities were established under the Children's Act, including professional criteria for staff. However, this official system is greatly circumvented by customary practices based on pre-British traditions and the ancient Indian caste (hierarchical social group) designations. It is also circumvented by extralegal behavior by officials including arbitrariness, corruption, and favoritism. For these reasons, juvenile justice process in India is best described as a decentralized, locally-driven system.

Photo 12.2   A juvenile jail in China.

Chinese Juvenile Justice Process. China is the world's most populous country, and it is governed by an authoritarian regime founded on the ideology of Maoist communism. Politically, urban administration is highly bureaucratic, and rural administration is overseen by Communist Party operatives. Economically, the economy is far smaller than found in developed nations. It is important to understand that China was never conquered by, or became a colony of, another country, so that it has maintained a distinctly Chinese approach to delinquency and crime. This distinctiveness has been implemented as a combination of Maoist principles and traditional practices.

Chinese criminal justice is meted out swiftly, and offenders are punished severely. Incarceration is long, and death sentences are regularly carried out. Political dissent against Maoist principles is not tolerated, so that political "crimes" can be dealt with quite harshly; in fact, it is estimated that hundreds of thousands (or perhaps millions) of Chinese prisoners are political prisoners. Chinese juvenile justice process is informally dispensed within locally driven systems of community participation, with the mandate that they must comply with national standards of law and order. Juvenile justice is mostly based on local traditions and handled informally by communities and parents. Thus, the concept of a completely separate juvenile justice system is weak in China. Instead, there exists a rather unsystematic approach toward dealing with juvenile offenders outside of the formal court system.

The Role of the Police in Developing
Countries: The Cases of India and China

The police in most Western countries are imbued with the principles of crime-fighting and order maintenance. The underlying value is to "serve and protect" the citizenry from criminals. In the developing world, there are many examples of the police being deployed to protect political or social elites. There are also many examples of using the police to maintain the authority of the state against *any* form of dissent or disorder, whether in the form of delinquency and criminal behavior, or as criticism of the government. Thus, the concept of order maintenance can be defined in different ways in various countries, depending on the political and cultural imperatives of domestic circumstances.

India. There is no single model for policing in India, so that each region or city arguably accepts its own standard of police behavior. Officially, the police are charged with enforcing the law. Unofficially, Indian police can be very corrupt, quite arbitrary, and sometimes brutal. The police tend to represent the interests of the wealthy or political elites, and are often used to enforce the authority of dominant politicians or political groups. Because of these practices, it should be no revelation that their treatment of juvenile offenders is frequently informal, arbitrary, and extralegal.

Officially, the police must refer suspected juvenile offenders to juvenile courts or community boards for legal processing. Unofficially, local communities do not want the police to become involved because of extensive mistrust, so that youthful offenders are dealt with outside of the official system from the beginning. The bottom line is that police involvement in juvenile justice process can be unsystematic at best, and haphazard or arbitrary at worst.

China. Chinese police are expected to enforce the law and maintain the authority of the state. They are representatives of the state and promote central authority and order in cities and in the countryside. Criminal deviance is treated by the police as an offense against the state and the people, and the police are permitted a great deal of latitude in obtaining confessions. There is no equivalent to the United States' Miranda protections against self-incrimination. Suspects are expected to cooperate with the police and tell the truth, and the police are authorized to beat a suspect to obtain the facts of a case.

This being said, Chinese police are required to treat juveniles differently from adults. They are not the juvenile justice system's institution of first resort, but instead act in cooperation with, and are advisors to, other sectors that have first contact with young suspects. First contact with troubled juveniles generally comes from Communist Party representatives, teachers, and others. Parents and juveniles are approached by Party members to discuss problems. Party officials are authorized to send offenders to special schools and reformatories. All of this may occur with the knowledge and assistance of the police. When the police are called upon to take a young suspect into custody, they must protect their privacy, and keep them separate from adults.

The Role of the Court in Developing Countries: The Cases of India and China

Many court systems in the developing world are well established and functional. Others are arbitrary or corrupt, and represent the interests of political and social elites. Although many systems were influenced by their former European colonial systems, traditional and cultural notions of justice are frequently integrated into court systems. This means that in practice standards of review on guilt or innocence often reflect local precepts of justice. These traditional principles are frequently applied in juvenile justice proceedings.

India. Recalling that communities try to avoid involving the police in juvenile affairs, the police nevertheless do become involved in many cases. When they do, they are authorized to bring young suspects before formal juvenile courts, which are presided over by professional magistrates. To assist juvenile court magistrates, social workers are assigned to each court to act as mediators and advisors to the court on the requirements of juvenile suspects. However, these social workers are not professionals in the same way that they are in U.S. juvenile justice systems; they are untrained lay persons from the community who are appointed as social workers to the court. In this way, the local community is integrated into official juvenile judicial proceedings.

Aside from the presence of local social workers, witnesses, and family members, juvenile court hearings are not open to the general public. Juvenile magistrates are authorized to render a range of dispositions, including admonishment with release to parents, probation, and detention. Options available to the court in selecting detention facilities include placements in prisons, jails, and youth homes.

China. The Chinese have a well-established and pervasive court system. It is an inquisitorial system, meaning that representatives of the state will investigate the facts of each case, often under a presumption of guilt. When official charges are brought against juveniles, proceedings are presided over by one professional judge and two citizen judges drawn from the community. There is no completely separate juvenile court system, but juveniles brought before Chinese courts are processed under special juvenile-specific laws and procedures.

Eligibility for special consideration as a juvenile is based on one's age. Persons 18 years of age and older who have been accused of serious crimes are tried as adults, and punished accordingly. Likewise, teenagers up to the age of 18 who are accused of serious crimes will also be tried as adults, but with special considerations. If they are ages 14 to 16, they can be punished in the same manner as adults. If they are ages 16 or 17, they may be given the death penalty for especially serious offenses, but will not be executed until they reach age 18. Juvenile-specific penalties include imprisonment, jail, placement in state-run juvenile institutions, and release into the custody of parents or community-based agencies.

Juvenile Corrections in Developing Countries: The Cases of India and China

Imprisonment is rarely anything but the beginning of an unpleasant experience, regardless of whether it occurs in the West or the developing world. In developing countries, imprisonment can be particularly harsh. Overcrowding, poor sanitation, abuse, and corruption are found in many prison systems. Juvenile offenders are often sent into prison systems around the world to be punished, rather than to special youth treatment facilities, and experience these harsh conditions first-hand.

India. As a matter of policy, few juvenile offenders are sent into locked detention facilities in India. Most youths are released into the custody of their parents or the community, meaning that either a home environment or community-run facility will be designated as their placement disposition. When Indian juvenile delinquents are sent to locked custody, there is a great deal of disparity in official and unofficial standards of treatment. There is also much disparity in how children from elite families are treated in comparison to others. In fact, corruption and unequal treatment are the rule rather than the exception.

Officially, juveniles must be placed in facilities that are separated from adult convicts. Unofficially, youths are often placed in the same facilities as adults. This is often a function of social standing, meaning that one's class, caste, and political standing are significant factors in how individual youths are treated. Thus, children from wealthy or high-caste families are more likely to be housed in juvenile facilities than are youths from poor or low-caste families. Conditions in the privileged facilities are fundamentally tolerable—they are safe, guarded, and families may bring food and clothing to residents. Conditions in unprivileged facilities are poor—they are dangerous, unhealthy, and very crowded.

China. The official guiding principle of both the adult and juvenile correctional systems in China is rehabilitation rather than punishment. The official

TABLE 12.3   JUVENILE JUSTICE PROCESS IN DEVELOPING NATIONS: THE CASES OF INDIA
AND CHINA

Developing nations have established official duties for the components of their juvenile justice
process, but these official duties are frequently overshadowed by unofficial rules and procedures.
The unofficial nature of these practices can lead to arbitrariness and abuses. Deference is frequently
given to local customs and traditions, so that the community is an integral part of many systems. This
table summarizes juvenile justice process in several of these countries.

Juvenile Justice Component	Developing Nations: Cases	
	India	China
Police	Official duties outlined. Rampant unofficial dispositions. Corruption and arbitrariness.	Specialized treatment of juveniles. Advisory role to first-contact agencies.
Courts	Formal juvenile magistrate courts. Range of dispositions permitted.	Specialized treatment of juveniles. Juvenile-specific penalties.
Corrections	Few sent into locked detention. Disparity in treatment when detained. Preferential treatment of elites.	Usually diverted to schools, agencies, or families. Re-education is used. Juvenile facilities used for serious offenses.

purpose of imprisonment is to educate and redeem young offenders and
adults through highly structured correctional programs, which may include
laborious work such as farming or textile manufacturing. Such "rehabilitation" duties are mandatory, and poor performance or any type of dissent is
punished. There have been allegations by international human rights monitors that the Chinese have employed convict labor in a slave-like manner.
There have also been rather disturbing allegations of physical and psychological abuse, and even reports on the harvesting of organs from prisoners
for medical uses.

Most juvenile offenders are sent to schools, community-based agencies,
and their families. Those who have been convicted by community-based
agencies, such as schools or the police, may be sentenced to education camps
to undergo "**re-education**" for up to three years. Re-education is also practiced with adults, and involves instruction on the errors of their ways and
how to become better citizens; adults may receive such re-education for
many years. Teenagers convicted of serious offenses are incarcerated in
state-run schools or prisons. When this occurs, the length of incarceration
for most juveniles is up to five years. Interestingly, if parents are deemed to
be unfit to care for their children, these youths will not be released to their
families, and may be sent into detention up to the age of 25 years.

Table 12.3 summarizes the roles of the police, courts, and juvenile
corrections in the foregoing cases.

Children's Rights: A Global Approach to Juvenile Justice

Readers may recall from our previous discussions of juvenile justice process in the United States that the very concept of *juvenile justice* incorporates two broad classes of youths: Children in trouble and children in need. Children in trouble were defined as youths who violate the law, either as juvenile delinquents or as status offenders; children in need were defined as youths who are not properly cared for by an adult, and include abused, neglected, and abandoned children. When these concepts are adapted to incorporate a global concept of juvenile justice, the overall picture becomes one of **children's rights**. Children's rights refers to the entitlement of young people to basic protections from violence and exploitation. Thus, when considered from a global perspective, juvenile justice and children's rights are arguably synonymous.

The question of justice and rights for children is a significant issue worldwide, because millions of youths are victimized by security forces, violence, and exploitation. It is not an exaggeration to conclude that the sheer magnitude of child victimization is staggering. The world community has attempted to respond to this problem. For example, the *Beijing Rules* were the first protocols passed in the United Nations to develop international standards for juvenile justice and the treatment of young people.[11] These rules are admirable, but they are not enforceable domestically unless a government adopts them as part of its own body of law. The following discussion summarizes several juvenile justice/children's rights problems that pose significant challenges to the international community.[12]

Children in Trouble: Conditions of Juveniles in Custody

Juvenile delinquency and crime occur in every country, and are dealt with by the police and other security forces. Because many police and security forces are authorized to use force on behalf of the government or elites as a matter of policy, the treatment of juvenile offenders is often disproportionately harsh by Western standards. In many countries, treatment can be described as brutal and inhumane. In this regard, it must be emphasized that the United States, with all of its democratic traditions and liberties, is broadly criticized for its treatment of juvenile offenders as criminals—in particular the sentencing of juveniles to life terms or execution.

On average, approximately one million youths worldwide are under arrest, awaiting trial, or in locked detention.[13] These forms of custody frequently occur in an extralegal manner, are often arbitrary, and take place without regard for their juvenile status. In countries where the police and military are deployed to maintain political authority and social order, there is no true recourse to judicial review. Both juveniles and adults can be held in custody indefinitely, regardless of guilt or innocence, and without regard to whether the offense was one of juvenile delinquency or a status offense. Conditions in detention can be quite deplorable. Many cases exist in which juveniles are imprisoned with adults, sanitation is minimal, food is poor, and there is little protection from heat and cold. Abuse of children is rampant in many systems. Sources of this abuse come from police or military personnel, and adult convicts within prisons.

At-Risk Populations: Displaced and Victimized Children

Although juvenile victimization in Western countries is documented and disturbing, the types and quality of victimization elsewhere in the world are, in comparison, both extreme and largely unknown. The scale of some of these international problems is quite high.

Displaced Children. War, disease, and abandonment have created large numbers of parentless youths. Some are orphans, while others have been separated from their parents because of political turmoil or some other form of societal catastrophe (such as a famine). They live as refugees or street children, sometimes roaming in gangs and committing crimes in order to survive. Local authorities are often overwhelmed by the plight of displaced children, so that international intervention is sometimes needed. Disturbingly, there are a number of documented cases where the police or other security forces have been deployed to intimidate or even kill street children. Because of their extreme vulnerability, they are frequently exploited by adults.

Victims of Violence. As discussed previously, many children in need are victimized by violence in their homes, schools, and other institutions. In much of the world this violence is culturally permitted as a normal function of rearing children. Thus, what is considered to be abusive in some countries is perfectly acceptable in others. Beatings, being tied up, extended confinement, being struck with objects, and open-hand violence are acceptable and common means of discipline in many societies.

Taking Advantage of the Young: Exploited Children

Exploitation occurs under different circumstances: It is legalized in some countries, it can involve organized crime, and it can be a function of warfare. Victims of exploitation are often placed in dire and life-threatening conditions.

Labor Exploitation. Although child labor laws have been enforced for more than a century in developed countries, many developing countries routinely and legally use child labor. Youths work in dangerous or otherwise harsh conditions as textile workers, farm laborers, and servants. They are exposed to workplace conditions that are illegal in much of the world, such as polluted air, unsafe machinery, and unprotected use of chemicals. It is estimated that 246 million children are used as cheap labor,[14] often producing goods that are sent on to developed countries, such as sports shoes, clothing, and rugs. Most child laborers are found in Asia and Africa.

Trafficking in Children. An illegal underground exists that trades in human beings. Criminal organizations and gangs kidnap and sell women and children. This is a large sector of transnational organized crime, and is comparable to drug and arms trafficking. A large number of children are caught up in this trade, and it is possible that more than one million children are trafficked annually.[15] Many are sold as servants or prostitutes, and are regularly abused sexually—these children are essentially slaves. Others are babies who are sold for adoption in the United States and Europe.

Child Soldiers. Many armed groups routinely "draft" children into their ranks. In many conflicts, rival armies, paramilitaries (militias), and rebel groups round up boys and girls to serve as soldiers, porters, cooks, and sex partners. Child soldiers have been known to be drugged and used to carry out horrific atrocities. With many as young as 10 years old, it is easy for adult commanders to convince them to commit such brutality. It is estimated that there are 300,000 child soldiers fighting in dozens of wars.[16]

Chapter Summary

The international context of juvenile justice requires an appreciation for the great diversity of traditions, laws, and cultures that characterize how societies deal with their children. It is helpful to understand the fundamental framework for the factors associated with the treatment of youths in other cultures. This framework broadly identifies the following systems as representing international juvenile justice processes: Developed nations, developing nations, democratic nations, undemocratic nations, pluralistic societies, and traditional societies.

Our discussion has focused on case studies selected from British-influenced developed nations and from the developing nations of India and China. Among the representative developed nations' cases, the roles of the police, courts, and corrections were similar, but exhibited important differences in some systems. However, the underlying principle of separating juvenile and adult proceedings and standards was commonly applied. Among the developing nations' cases, there was an official recognition that juvenile justice process requires special rules, and that juveniles require special treatment. Unofficially, most cases are handled informally at the local level. In India in particular, differential treatment was meted out to offenders based on their social status.

Within a global context, the concept of juvenile justice merges with that of children's rights. Children in trouble are often kept in harsh confinement, which includes imprisonment and proximity to adult criminals. The plight of children in need is a particularly major issue confronting the world community. Child victimization and exploitation is a global phenomenon affecting millions of young people.

Chapter 13 concludes our investigation of juvenile justice process. Familiar challenges for the immediate future are discussed, as are new issues that are likely to arise.

Questions for Review

1. What are the various national environments within which juvenile justice policies are determined?

2. How has juvenile justice process been implemented in developed countries?

3. Which case studies exemplify juvenile justice process in developed countries?

4. How has juvenile justice process been implemented in developing countries?

5. Which case studies exemplify juvenile justice process in developing countries?

6. Which definitions best describe "children's rights" as a concept?

7. What international responses have been implemented to address the problem of children in need?

Key Terms and Concepts

The following topics were discussed in this chapter, and are found in the Glossary:

Absolute Deprivation	Democratic Nations
Beijing Rules	Developed Nations
Caution	Developing Nations
Children's Act of 1960	Junior Detention Centers
Children's Panel	Pluralistic Societies
Children's Rights	Re-education

Relative Deprivation

Senior Detention Centers

Social Worker Act of 1968

Third World Nations

Traditional Societies

Undemocratic Nations

Western Nations

Young Offenders Act of 1982

Youth Custody Centers

DISCUSSION BOX

Juvenile Justice: The Cultural Dimension

This chapter's Discussion Box is intended to stimulate critical discussion about the importance of the cultural dimension to juvenile justice.

Cultural norms and values are the foundations for how a nation defines the concept of juvenile justice. Based on these norms and values, juvenile justice processes and institutions are created to deal with the problem of juvenile deviance. In many cultures, there is a fundamental cultural intolerance for youths who violate the laws of society. In these societies, juvenile delinquents are defined as criminals, and are punished accordingly. Other cultures are very focused on rehabilitating and redeeming young offenders. In these cultures, delinquents receive as much treatment as possible to give them every opportunity to reintegrate into civil society.

No one can be sure how many young people have been sentenced to prisons or other forms of adult punishment around the globe. Nor is it an easy matter to determine how many juvenile offenders have been dealt with informally outside of official justice institutions. In societies where culturally traditional justice is perfectly acceptable, records of dispositions are uncommon.

Measuring the outcomes of traditional justice vis-à-vis official systems is very difficult. This is also true for measuring the effectiveness of different systems. Inevitably, questions arise about whether one type of system is somehow better than another.

Discussion Questions

1. How effective are the respective systems?
2. Does harsh punishment reduce recidivism, or are treatment models more effective?
3. Is harsh treatment of juveniles a global problem, or just a cultural issue that should be "understood" by outsiders?
4. Should global standards of juvenile justice be established?
5. Does *juvenile justice* truly exist, or is it only a relative term?

Recommended Web Sites

The following Web sites illustrate the different approaches toward juvenile justice found in other countries.

Amnesty International: http://www.amnesty.org
Child Rights Information Network: http://www.crin.org
Human Rights Watch: http://hrw.org
United Nations Children's Fund (UNICEF): http://www.unicef.org
United Nations Educational, Scientific, and Cultural Organization (UNESCO): http://www.unesco.org

Note: The Web Site urls and exercises below are also from the book's study site-http:\\www.

Web Exercise

Using this chapter's recommended Internet sites, conduct an online investigation of international perspectives of juvenile justice process.

- In what way is juvenile justice an international issue?
- From a global context, how is juvenile justice an international human rights issue?
- What impact do you think international children's rights organizations have on the juvenile justice practices of individual countries?

For an online search of international perspectives of juvenile justice process, students should activate the search engine on their Web browser and enter the following keywords:

"International Children's Rights"

"International Juvenile Justice"

Recommended Readings

The following publications provide discussions on international perspectives of juvenile justice process.

Balla, N. B., Hornick, J. P., & Snyder, H. N. (Eds.). (2002). *Juvenile justice systems: An international comparison.* Toronto, Ontario, Canada: Thompson Educational.

Hartjaen, C. A., & Priyadarsini, S. (2004). *Delinquency and juvenile justice: An international bibliography.* Westport, CT: Praeger.

Hayzlehurst, K., & Hayzlehurst, C. (Eds.). (1998). *Gangs and youth subcultures: international explorations.* New Brunswick, NJ: Transaction.

Shoemaker, D. J. (Ed.). (1996). *International handbook on juvenile justice.* Westport, CT: Greenwood.

Winterdyk, J. (Ed.). (2002). *Juvenile justice systems: International perspectives*. Toronto, Ontario, Canada: Canadian Scholars Press.

Notes

1. For a discussion of international perspectives, see Winterdyk, J. (Ed.). (2002). *juvenile justice systems: International perspectives*. Toronto, Ontario, Canada: Canadian Scholars Press.

2. See ibid.

3. For a comparison, see Van Wormer, K. (1990). The hidden juvenile justice system in Norway: A journey back in time. *Federal Probation. 54*, 57–61.

4. For a discussion of the English and Welsh approach, see Gelsthorpe, L., & Fenwick M. (2002). Comparative juvenile justice: England and Wales. In J. Winterdyk (Ed.), *Juvenile justice systems: International perspectives*. Toronto, Ontario, Canada: Canadian Scholars Press.. See also Wakefield, W., & Hirschel, D. (1996). England. In D. J. Shoemaker (Ed.). *International handbook on juvenile justice*. Westport, CT: Greenwood.

5. For an overview of the Canadian system, see Corrado, R., & Markwart, A. (1996). Canada. In ibid.

6. For an overview of the Australian approach, see Seymour, J. (1996). Australia. In ibid. See also Cunneen, C., & White, R. (1995). *Juvenile justice: An Australian perspective*. Melbourne, Australia: Oxford University Press.

7. For a discussion of the Young Offenders Act, see Wass, J., & Marks, R. (1992). Historical overview: Young Offenders Act revamps juvenile justice in Canada. *Corrections Today*.

8. See McGuire, M. (1997). C.19: An act to amend the Young Offenders Act and the criminal code—getting tougher? *Canadian Journal of Criminology, 39*, 185–215.

9. For a discussion of the Indian approach, see Hartjen, C. A., & Kethineni, G. (1996). India. In D. J. Shoemaker (Ed.). *International handbook on juvenile justice*. Westport, CT: Greenwood.

10. For a discussion of the Chinese approach, see Ren, Xin. "People's Republic of China." In ibid.

11. See United Nations. (1986). United Nations standard minimum rules for the administration of juvenile justice: The *Beijing rules*. New York: United Nations.

12. These data are adapted from United Nations Educational, Scientific, and Cultural Organization (UNESCO). (n.d.). Available online at http://www.unicef.org.

13. Ibid.

14. Ibid.

15. Ibid.

16. Ibid.

13

What Is to be Done?

Projections and Conclusion

There are moments in a community's history when residents decide to "do something" about unacceptable behavior. Sometimes the authorities engage in neighborhood sweeps of undesirables such as prostitutes, drug dealers, or gang members. Youths are sometimes caught up in these sweeps. However, one such case indicates how such policies can sometimes be a bit heavy-handed.[1] In October 2000, the Washington, DC transit authority—known as the WMTA—initiated a "zero tolerance" campaign against persons who engage in quality of life offenses. Part of the campaign aimed at enforcing a District of Colombia Code provision that prohibited consuming food or drink while in a rail transit station. Although adult offenders could be fined or jailed for up to 10 days, juvenile offenders would be treated as delinquents.

Ansche H. was a 12-year-old student who purchased French fries and took them into a subway station. As she ate her first French fry, a Metro Transit Police officer arrested her. Ansche M. was searched, her jacket and backpack were confiscated, she was handcuffed, her shoelaces were removed, she was fingerprinted, and held for several hours. She was taken to the DC Juvenile Processing Center, and booked before being released into the custody of her mother three hours later. A lawsuit on behalf of Ansche was unsuccessful.

CHAPTER PERSPECTIVE 13.1

Youth Gangs: An Old Problem in a New Light

Some social problems seem to never have an adequate solution. Regardless of how many methodologies are developed to remedy them, nothing appears to work. The problem of youth gangs is one of these dilemmas, having endured since the first gangs appeared with the advent of large-scale urbanization during the nineteenth century. With every wave of immigration, and every generation of urban poverty, voluntary associations of youths have arisen to form street gangs and other antisocial groups. In many ways, this has always been an unfortunate feature of life in urban America.

Considering the fact that there have always been urban gangs, is it reasonable to presume that there will always be youth gangs? The likely answer is that youth gangs are an enduring problem, and will remain a resilient facet of urban culture. Gangs will likely persist not only into the near future, but also for some time to come. There has never been an easy solution to the conditions that give rise to their formation, nor have juvenile officials and law enforcement authorities consistently suppressed them. Therefore, if one presumes the persistence of conditions that historically gave rise to gang formation, it is quite reasonable to presume that the gang problem will also persist.

The recent history of gang behavior suggests that several trends are likely to continue: First, the weaponry wielded by gangs will be significant. Second, gangs will become involved in criminal enterprises such as drug trafficking that extend beyond traditional turfs. Third, leadership and hard-core gang membership will come from young adults who will provide criminal mentorship for teenage members.

What is to be done about gangs? First, juvenile justice networks must continue to be innovative in their approach to suppressing gang activity. Second, a purely law enforcement approach may be useful for quelling the problem of existing members, but cannot hope to remedy the conditions that lead to the recruitment of new members. Third, only the wider net of the juvenile justice system can provide adequate intervention in the lives of at-risk juveniles.

Thus, future policies will consistently reflect evolving theories and programs that build upon the lessons and mistakes of the past.

Is the past prologue? Are the lessons learned from old policies and practices instructive for the development of future policies and practices? What is the future of juvenile justice process?

In the modern era, juvenile justice has become a pervasive and well-developed concept in the United States and much of the world. Its evolution has progressed quite remarkably from the early colonial Puritanical notions of God-ordained standards of juvenile behavior to the modern culture of national and international youth justice networks. The policy revolution of the nineteenth century—led by well-intentioned (if patronizing) philanthropists—laid the foundations for philosophies about how civil societies should deal with children in trouble and children in need. Since that time, generations of adult experts and lay persons have tried to apply their understanding of the "best interests of the child" to the protection of individual children and the general community.

During the latter half of the twentieth century, policy makers and practitioners were challenged by the problem of violent youths. They responded to this problem by designing policies that reduced process informality and by increasing the likelihood that these offenders would be severely punished. Juvenile protections certainly have not been summarily done away with, but in many ways they have been narrowed to address the remediation of non-violent and nonincorrigible youths. The momentum for this trend acceler-ated during the 1980s and 1990s, and has become fundamental to the American approach to juvenile justice process.

Although the future of juvenile justice process can never be accurately *predicted,* it is possible to design and discuss reasoned *projections* for what lies ahead. It is not unreasonable to conclude that the nature of current chal-lenges, trends, and policies can be used to project the immediate course of juvenile-related process. For example, it is reasonable to make the following projections:

- First, delinquency and crime will be manageable problems in the near future, and there will be no cataclysmic breakdown of law and order. In other words, threatened trends such as the theoretical *superpreda-tor* phenomenon are highly unlikely to arise.[2]
- Second, it is also reasonable to project that the juvenile justice system will continue to be a dynamic network that will evolve and adapt to newly advanced theoretical and cultural trends.
- Finally, it is reasonable to project that the most violent and recidivist juvenile delinquents will receive special attention, the nature of which will depend on the predominating political and cultural consensus of the time. These serious offenders will either continue to be treated in the same manner as adult criminals, or be the recipients of newly devel-oped programs and treatments that are specially designed for the reme-diation of extreme deviance.

One ongoing, and truly unresolved, challenge is the question of how to reconcile the long-standing philosophy of rehabilitation with the present philosophy of order maintenance. Historically, the philosophical balance has usually tipped in favor of rehabilitation, although often by using severe (yet acceptable) methods to accomplish this. In recent decades, widespread concern about maintaining law and order—and the common perception that some delinquents cannot be rehabilitated—have tipped the policy balance in favor of punishing young offenders. This tension between rehabilitation and punishment is now part of the juvenile justice policy-making dynamic, and the influence of both will be significant for some time. For the foreseeable future, juvenile-related policies will reflect the application of these prevailing theories to the manner in which youths are processed through the juvenile justice system.

This chapter concludes our investigation of juvenile justice process. It pre-sents a discussion of contemporary and near-future challenges and problems for experts, practitioners, and the public. Our final topics include:

Photo 13.1   Antisocial behavior by juveniles will continue to be an unfortunate feature of American society.

- What Next? Challenges for the Juvenile Justice System
- Professionals, Process, and Policy: Configuring the Juvenile Justice System
- A Final Thought: Managing the Problem

What Next? Challenges for the Juvenile Justice System

A great deal of progress was made for juvenile justice during the nineteenth and twentieth centuries. There were many important discoveries and conclusions about the special needs of at-risk and antisocial young people. However, as much as the concept of juvenile justice has progressed, the juvenile justice system will continue to be challenged by the same problems and circumstances discussed in previous chapters.

In the projected future, toxic neighborhood environments will persist, youths will continue to be victimized within families, institutions will fail to mentor or protect young people, and new theories will be developed that may or may not be effective. There will also be new generations of antisocial youths, many of whom will become thoroughly marginalized through gang membership or some other self-defeating association. Recalling that each generation has put its stamp on juvenile justice process, there is no guarantee that modern approaches will be abandoned in future generations. Nevertheless, society must, and will, persist in its quest to remedy the problems of children in trouble and children in need.

Factors Shaping the Juvenile's Environment: Enduring Influences on Juvenile Behavior

Projecting the future of juvenile justice process requires an acknowledgement that long-standing and distinctive social and demographic institutions will continue to influence the behavior of juveniles. The primary institutions are

- Families
- Neighborhoods
- Schools

It is not a new revelation that these institutions are centrally associated with juvenile behavior, because experts have frequently focused on them, and much discussion has probed the nature of their influence. What is interesting to note is that they continue to have an enduring influence on youths, and this will continue into the near future. The impact of these features depends on each locale's history, values, culture, and norms.

Families. The concept of "traditional" families was transformed during the twentieth century. In previous generations, the old nostalgic notion was that parents are married at a young age (and forever), the father is the "breadwinner" and "head" of the household, the mother is a "homemaker," and the children must be conformist and deferential. This model has now ceased being the ideal by which all other arrangements are measured. Modern and future families are unlikely to ever again uphold the traditional arrangement as being the chosen norm. New arrangements are based on the following propositions:

- Two-career families are not only common, but necessary.
- Fathers and mothers are coequal partners.
- Children are permitted more latitude for expression.
- Families are smaller in size.

And, importantly, divorce is also a widespread family reality. At the same time, former notions of a correct manner to raise children have changed, so that not all couples are married when they have children, and single-parent households are not uncommon.

The old problems of substance addiction, abuse, neglect, and economic hardship will continue to be problems in many households. As factors in the backgrounds of juvenile delinquents, these old problems are enduring, seemingly intractable, and should not be expected to disappear. Juvenile justice authorities will be pressed—as a matter of necessity—to continue to address these problems within the contexts of new family arrangements. Simpler policies of the past will continue to give way to innovation, with experts conducting tests on an array of innovative theories and programs to redress family-related juvenile issues.

Neighborhoods. Beyond the household, neighborhoods will continue to exert a central influence on youth behavior. In healthy and functional neighborhoods, children are nurtured and "the village" can be a very positive influence on the character and behavior of young people. Unhealthy and dysfunctional neighborhoods put children at risk—neighborhoods can be dangerous or otherwise unwholesome environments. Several enduring inner-city problems have not been resolved, and there are few indications that they will soon be resolved. These include

- Poverty
- Unemployment
- Declining infrastructure
- Underclass values
- Crime

Many youths will continue to act out on the values and circumstances of their environment, whether or not they are accepted by the broader society. Absent significant intervention by government agencies and community-based groups, toxic neighborhoods will persist in producing a relatively high number of socially dysfunctional youths.

Schools. Good schools do not guarantee success, but they provide opportunities to acquire educational skills that enable graduates to pursue desirable jobs and lifestyles. Safe school environments also promote nurturing and meaningful social interactions with peers and teachers. In other words, good schools permit juveniles to focus on education and personal development. Unfortunately, there is good reason to assume that many schools will continue to produce children who have limited educational and social skills. Certain factors, in combination, are likely to produce these detrimental effects in the projected future. They are

- Location in the inner city and impoverished small towns
- Unsafe environments
- Crowding
- Presence of gangs or other antisocial associations

Should these conditions continue to exist in combination, poor schools will facilitate antisocial behaviors and delinquency. In such environments, individual students will continue to be subjected to danger in hallways, bathrooms, and around playgrounds. In these institutions, students are likely to become alienated, greater numbers of teachers will exhibit disinterest or cynicism, and classrooms are unlikely to encourage initiative and inquisitiveness.

In other words, unless school systems markedly improve the conditions of their more marginalized and deprived facilities, young people who attend these schools will continue to be poorly prepared socially and educationally. They also run the risk of either participating in, or being victimized by, antisocial associations of youths.

Factors Shaping Juvenile
Justice Policy: Illustrative Examples

Certain factors will continue to influence the course of juvenile justice policy. They represent social trends and behaviors that have always had an impact on policy in the modern era, and are certainly nothing new. But, they interact with each other to create perceptions and reactions that are not constant across all time periods. The following examples—juvenile violence and community perceptions—have been selected to highlight how near-term trends and behaviors are likely to interact and shape the evolving juvenile justice environment. They are illustrative of ongoing issues that will continue to influence policy choices within this environment.

Juvenile Violence. During the 1980s, the incidence of juvenile violence escalated to unprecedented heights. In comparison to the types of delinquency found in bygone years, modern violence was more widespread and often more vicious. Street gangs in particular engaged in violence that far surpassed previous eras, both in terms of the number of incidents and the quality of violence. The quality of violence changed; it included the use of high-powered rifles, small submachine guns, and expensive automatic pistols. The result was that drive-by shootings and battles over drug turf terrorized many communities.[3] Although these incidents occurred in the inner city, the news from the suburbs was also somewhat grim: Aside from gang-related violence, a number of well-publicized incidents occurred, including school shootings, murders of parents or other adults, and additional violent crimes committed by youths.

The 1980s arguably represented the seminal decade for the modern era of violence by youths and heralded a long-term reconsideration of juvenile justice policy. There was a shift in emphasis away from *treatment* for violent youths and a general acceptance of *punishing* them. In essence, the policy response was to incorporate juvenile delinquency into the overall crackdown on crime. This crackdown has shown no indication of abating, nor has the referral of violent juveniles into the adult criminal justice system lost momentum. The impending implications of this policy shift for the immediate future are several:

- Violent juveniles will be handled in accordance with a philosophy of punishment rather than rehabilitation.
- Many violent youths will lose their status as juvenile delinquents and will be committed to the adult criminal justice system.
- Communities and law enforcement agencies are likely to support the suppression of street gangs and other associations of violent youths as a policy priority.
- Youths who commit nonserious offenses will continue to be diverted into community-based programs and agencies, thus further expanding the juvenile justice net beyond the official system.

Mention must be made of the firepower that is currently available to young people, and which will continue to be available. Weapons now circulating on the street and in the hands of antisocial youths are quite powerful. They can shoot many more bullets at an accelerated rate of fire, with the result that gun-wielding teenagers often outgun responding police officers. Many of these weapons are high-powered, meaning that they hit their targets with enormous impact, thus maiming or killing anyone in the line of fire. Shotguns, civilian military-like weapons, and actual military-grade assault rifles such as AK-47s and M16s have been used in youth violence. Unfortunately, the future does not bode well for this feature of juvenile violence, because gun technologies will improve, access to these technologies will remain possible, and the number of firearms in the hands of antisocial youths will remain high.

Community Perceptions. The general public consistently perceives that delinquency and crime rates are high, even when they are in decline.[4] This is unlikely to change in the immediate future, because reports in the media, personal experiences, and word of mouth all serve to stimulate public passions on the subject of juvenile deviance. When dramatic incidents occur, the media and rumors often have a significant impact on the community's perception of the frequency of these incidents. There is also an impact on their perception of why these incidents occur.[5]

Community perceptions influence political leaders, because their political careers depend on responding to personal appeals from constituents and

Photo 13.2   A group of youths painting a mural on a wall that was once covered with gang graffiti.

adapting to the cultural trends of the jurisdictions they represent. The result is that both the public and political leaders regularly issue calls for greater police protection and stronger measures to manage delinquency and crime. It should also be noted that politicians make claims and allegations about the extent of delinquency and crime for their own political benefit. For example, they often assert, and the public readily believes, the following claims:

- A crime wave exists.
- The criminals are "winning."
- Their opponent is soft on crime.
- Strong leadership is needed to stay the criminal plague.

These political statements serve to manipulate public opinion, so that we have a situation where community concerns and political considerations perpetuate the perceived need for stronger measures against juvenile delinquents. Absent a significant cultural shift, it is reasonable to project that the community's perceptions of delinquency and crime will continue to occur in a similar climate, as will the policy implications of the public mood.

Professionals, Process, and Policy: Configuring the Juvenile Justice System

Juvenile justice professionals obviously represent the principal leadership for designing successful juvenile justice policies. They are the centers of responsibility for running every juvenile system. Will juvenile justice processes change? What are the likely duties and profiles of juvenile justice professionals in the near future? How will the system be configured? In order to answer these questions, it is first necessary to discuss whether a guiding philosophy is needed to respond to juvenile problems, and if so, which one? Next, to further project the prospective nexus between professionals, process, and policy, it is necessary to first discuss several centers of juvenile justice process that will remain vital components for some time to come. These centers are

- An Enduring Institution: Juvenile Court Process and Policy
- Rehabilitation or Punishment? Corrections Process and Policy
- Protecting Due Process: The Legal Advocates (Attorneys)
- Widening the Net: Community-Based Professionals and Policies

Responding to Juvenile Problems: Finding a Guiding Philosophy

Several principles guide the philosophy of the modern American juvenile justice system, including the following:

- Juveniles should be "saved" when they are exploited, or they will run into trouble with the law.
- The adult and juvenile courts and corrections systems must be separated.
- Serious offenders should receive special consideration, possibly involving severe punishment.
- Juveniles who are diverted outside of the official juvenile justice system should be enrolled in community-based programs and organizations.

The difficulty in assessing a guiding philosophy for the near future lies in projecting whether it will emphasize informal or formal procedures, and whether it will stress rehabilitation or punishment. At the heart of these considerations are several important factors:

- The never-ending tension between the adoption of formal, official procedures (as in the adult system), or having a "looser" system of informality and discretion
- A lasting tension between whether juvenile offenders should receive treatment as a precursor to final rehabilitation, or whether formal prosecution and punishment are preferable

- The understanding that there is no such thing as "the" juvenile justice system in the sense that a single system or single model exists across all jurisdictions
- The state-based concept that the implementation of juvenile justice is likely to reflect many local and regional cultural or political values

It should be clear that juvenile justice process is deeply affected by trends in the criminal justice system. When crackdowns on crime occur (as begun during the 1980s), so too do crackdowns on delinquency. Thus, in the modern era juvenile offenders are frequently punished under crimes codes because the criminal justice system has for some time operated under a punishment approach toward sentencing and imprisonment. If the cultural and political pendulum swings against the continuation of this crackdown, then the juvenile justice system will again emphasize rehabilitation programs in juvenile-serving institutions, possibly with increased informality. As it now stands, one can project that the crackdown will continue into the near future, and serious juvenile offenders will be diverted to the criminal justice system.

An Enduring Institution:
Juvenile Court Process and Policy

For more than a century, the juvenile court has been the most prominent institution of the juvenile justice system. It is also the central component for managing juvenile justice process. These features have become so endemic to the American philosophy of dealing with children in trouble and children in need that the court's underlying responsibilities will remain unchanged in the near future. Having said this, there is a probability that the *manner* in which these responsibilities are carried out will be modified from time to time. For example, it is likely that at different times either official or unofficial procedures will be encouraged, depending on the contemporary political and cultural environment. It is also likely that judicial discretion will expand or contract as new theories or political imperatives emerge.

Juvenile court judges will continue to be selected from pools of trained professionals, and the requirement that they be attorneys will continue to be the predominant model. The courts that they preside over will be part of a system that is fully integrated into state judicial branches. It is virtually inconceivable that juvenile judges and court systems will regress to a status that is subordinate to, and dependent upon, adult systems. Their status as independent professionals and systems will remain robust.

Rehabilitation or Punishment?
Corrections Process and Policy

Correctional philosophy in the United States has historically emphasized rehabilitation. Since the advent of truly juvenile correctional institutions during the nineteenth century, many rehabilitative methodologies have been employed to "correct" juvenile deviance. By today's standards, some of these rehabilitative methodologies (such as corporal punishment and silence) probably caused as much harm as good. Personnel who worked in juvenile agencies were originally untrained laypersons, who were usually well-intentioned but not particularly competent as professionals.

In the modern era, punishment is an important option for dealing with serious offenders, and the diversion of juveniles into the adult criminal justice system has become an integral doctrine of juvenile justice process. At the same time, diversion of status and other lesser offenders *out of* the juvenile justice system is also an integral doctrine. The modern juvenile justice profile is likely to persist through the immediate future, and juvenile justice process will continue to encompass the following policies:

- Rehabilitation as an underlying philosophy for juvenile offenders
- Punishment as an acceptable option for serious juvenile offenders
- Diversion into the adult criminal justice system, possibly at increasing rates should the incidence of crime escalate
- Diversion out of the juvenile justice system for status and other minor offenders

New issues and challenges are certain to arise.[6] Current correctional problems and concerns will continue to be debated, and new theories will be developed on how to resolve them. Conditions of confinement is an ongoing issue, so that overcrowding, management problems, and rogue officials will likely be at the heart of periodic scandals in the future. In addition, the problem of designing effective treatment alternatives will be a consistently debated issue, probably well into the distant future; it is an issue that necessarily requires ongoing consideration. Finally, an important question will be how to conceptually and actually separate children in trouble from children in need.

Protecting Due Process:
The Legal Advocates (Attorneys)

Professional advocacy will continue to be a hallmark of juvenile justice process. This is necessitated by the fact that many juvenile court procedures are—and will remain—formal in nature, thus requiring the intervention of trained attorneys. Legal procedures are so entrenched that legal counsel will continue to be necessary for advocating the rights of accused juvenile offenders, as well as advocacy on behalf of the state. Although the staffs of many juvenile advocacy organizations are composed of experts in the field who know the procedures of juvenile courts, it is the attorneys they retain who will bear responsibility for most proceedings. This makes practical sense from the perspective of advocacy organizations, because prosecutor's offices will certainly maintain their juvenile prosecution divisions.

The presence of attorneys was guaranteed by Supreme Court cases such as *In re Gault*,[7] and legal advocacy has become an integral feature of juvenile justice. Other due-process protections were guaranteed by cases such as *In re Winship*,[8] so that judges must demand professional competence from advocates as a matter of constitutional necessity. Thus, the use of attorneys as advocates will continue to be of paramount importance for many proceedings.[9]

Widening the Net: Community-Based Professionals and Policies

On the one hand, juveniles diverted to community organizations will increasingly be serviced by an array of innovative programs. Also, juveniles released into the community under conditions of probation and parole/after-care will find themselves subject to new and innovative obligations and monitoring technologies.[10] As indicated in our previous discussions, there is no single model for community-based programs, and many are quite creative. Assuming that the current trend of deinstitutionalizing minor offenders continues, these community-based initiatives will both grow in number and exhibit increasing creativity.

The professional profile of community-based programs is best described as being multidisciplinary, because every facet of social work is represented at the community level of juvenile justice process. The following profile is likely to characterize community-based initiatives into the near future:

- New programs and theories will be developed.
- The network of organizations will expand.
- The need for greater involvement from a widening array of professionals and experts will increase.
- Attributes of release into the community will increasingly reflect the use of new technologies to monitor and control juvenile participants.
- Community- based diversionary requirements will reflect the innovation and availability of new community-based programs.

Probation and parole/aftercare officers will likely continue to be challenged by high caseloads, especially as more judges grant probation and parole/aftercare to alleviate overcrowding in correctional facilities. However, as significant numbers of serious offenders are sent into the adult criminal system, the need for intensive probation or parole/aftercare supervision may remain steady, or actually decline. But, there is another possibility—intensive probation supervision will be made increasingly easier because of new monitoring technologies, and so it is quite possible that the reverse may occur, meaning that intensive supervision could increase as new technologies are developed.

A Final Thought: Managing the Problem

Just as crime can be managed but never completely eliminated, so too can juvenile problems be managed but not eliminated. Juvenile delinquency, like crime, can be responded to on many fronts. Certainly the use of law enforcement assets will always have an impact on delinquency, and the use of correctional institutions will serve to separate offenders from society. However, within the context of juvenile justice, one must always bear in mind that proper intervention in the lives of young offenders has been shown to increase the likelihood of rehabilitation. Lasting rehabilitation requires effective treatment policies and programs. Thus, the use of law enforcement measures alone is not an adequate response to juvenile deviance. Society must also marshal a broad range of community resources in order to create a true juvenile-focused rehabilitation network. This network, as well as the programs available within the network, casts a much wider net in the lives of young offenders than does the criminal justice system.

The juvenile justice system is also challenged to manage another problem, one that is outside of the purview of the adult criminal justice system in its mission. This is the challenge to manage the plight of children in need. Youths who are victims, or are otherwise at risk, often have no control over their fate. They are quite literally at the mercy of their risky environments. It is the duty of the juvenile justice system, with its wide net, to identify and rescue these youngsters. There is no counterpart to this duty within the adult system. Victimization will certainly occur—it cannot be eliminated—but it can be managed with proper intervention from this network.

Absent a well-established juvenile justice system, many needy youths would be abandoned by society, and many troubled youths would find themselves in untenable conflicts with authority, which they would certainly lose. It is a matter of necessity that local communities and society as a whole assure the viability and fairness of the juvenile justice system so that processes are designed to effectively guide juveniles toward wholeness.

Chapter Summary

Future challenges for the juvenile justice system are likely to originate from the same sources that are now considered central to the juvenile policy environment. Thus, families will continue to be the primary influence on juvenile development. Neighborhoods are likely to yield environmental factors that will shape the values and behavioral traits of youths. Schools have provided, and always will provide, instruction and social interaction that will influence youths for much of their lives. At the same time, the nature of certain factors will shape the fundamental profile of juvenile policy. These factors include the quality and extent of juvenile violence, as well as community perceptions of juvenile problems.

Juvenile justice professionals will continue to be the front-line implementers of juvenile justice policy. At the center of this front line is the juvenile court. It has become an entrenched and enduring guide for the implementation of juvenile justice process. The juvenile correctional system is also a necessary, but constantly evolving, institution. In fact, juvenile correction is as much a concept as it is an institution, with the modern era witnessing a strong debate on whether it should implement a philosophy of rehabilitation or punishment. Legal advocates have become vital participants in the implementation of juvenile justice process, and will continue to act as defenders of the interests of accused juveniles and society. Because of the granting of due-process protections to juveniles, legal advocates are the best qualified professionals to understand and implement the subtleties of official proceedings. Community-based professionals and programs have become cornerstones of the juvenile justice system, and will continue to be central components—in fact, they are likely to increase in importance. Net widening is a unique attribute of the juvenile justice system in comparison to the criminal justice system, and it has proven to be effective in addressing the needs of children in trouble and children in need. Without the possibility of diversion to community resources, the juvenile justice system would be overwhelmed by the volume and responsibilities of juvenile justice process.

Questions for Review

1. How is juvenile justice likely to evolve in the near future?

2. Which challenges and problems will possibly affect juvenile justice process?

3. Which will be the likely juvenile justice processes and personnel in the near future?

4. What kinds of policies are likely to be developed?

DISCUSSION BOX

Juvenile Justice and Law Enforcement in the United States

This chapter's Discussion Box is intended to stimulate critical discussion about the projected continuation of interconnections between juvenile justice process and law enforcement institutions.

It was perhaps inevitable that the crackdown on adult crime that began during the 1980s would result in a concurrent crackdown on juvenile delinquency. With the rise of gang violence, enhanced firepower, and increased involvement in criminal enterprises, law enforcement measures were adopted to suppress juvenile criminality. There began a trend toward treating juvenile offenders as criminal offenders that has continued unabated.

What are the long-term implications of this approach? It would seem that juveniles who are convicted of violent crimes will continue to be incarcerated for significant amounts of time. Thus, young felons will become *prisonized* during extended exposure to adult criminals, and released when they are adults after long periods of institutionalization.

Juvenile justice and law enforcement institutions are deeply intertwined, a fact that may be modified, but which is highly unlikely to end. What is perhaps most probable is that two tracks will be established for juvenile offenders: A criminal track for serious offenses, and a delinquent track for lesser offenses. The criminal track will continue the crackdown policy, and the delinquent track will continue to emphasize juvenile justice process and net widening.

Discussion Questions

1. What are the respective future roles of juvenile justice process and law enforcement in addressing juvenile problems?

2. How will interconnections between the juvenile justice and criminal justice systems evolve?

3. Will the trend toward punishment of serious offenders continue or abate as a matter of policy?

4. Does it make sense to promote two tracks of justice for violent juvenile offenders, vis-à-vis those convicted of less serious offenses?

5. Who has primary responsibility for determining whether juvenile offenders should be primarily processed by juvenile justice or law enforcement authorities?

Recommended Readings

The following publications provide discussions on trends and projections for juvenile justice process.

Bernard, T. J. (1992). *The cycle of juvenile justice.* New York: Oxford University Press.

Howell, J. C. (2003). *Preventing and reducing juvenile delinquency: A comprehensive framework.* Thousand Oaks, CA: Sage.

Katzman, G. S. (Ed.). (2002). *Securing our children's future: New approaches to juvenile justice and youth violence.* Washington, DC: The Brookings Institution.

Kipnis, A. (1999). *Angry young men: How parents, teachers, and counselors can help "bad boys" become good men.* New York: Jossey-Bass.

Krisberg, B., & Austin J. F. (1993). *Reinventing juvenile justice.* Thousand Oaks, CA: Sage.

Notes

1. See Tracy v. H. and Ansche H. v. Washington Metropolitan Area Transit, et al., 284 F. Supp. 2d 145 (DC, 2003).

2. Recall that juvenile superpredators represented a projected new wave of violent young offenders that were expected to arise in the twenty-first century. These youths would theoretically be prone to extreme violence.

3. See Blumstein, A. (1995). Youth violence, guns, and the illicit-drug industry. *Journal of Criminal Law and Criminology, 86*, 10–37.

4. See Fields, C. B., & Jerin, R. A. (1996). "Murder and mayhem" in the media: Public perceptions (and misperceptions) of crime and criminality. In R. Muraskin & A. R. Roberts. *Visions for change: Crime and justice in the twenty-first century.* Upper Saddle River, NJ: Prentice-Hall.

5. See Coalition for Juvenile Justice. (1997). *False images? The news media and juvenile crime.* Washington, DC: Coalition for Juvenile Justice.

6. See Coates, R. B. (1998). The future of corrections in juvenile justice. In A. R. Roberts (Ed.). *Juvenile justice: Policies, programs, and services* (2nd ed.). Chicago: Nelson-Hall.

7. At 387 U.S. 1, S. Ct. 1428, 18 L. Ed. 2d 527 (1967). Gault mandated many due-process protections for state juvenile court proceedings.

8. At 397 U.S. 358, 90 S. Ct. 1068, 25 L. Ed. 2d 368 (1970). Winship held that juveniles accused of delinquent offenses should be accorded the same standard of proof as adults, that is, proof beyond a reasonable doubt. Status offenders may still be adjudicated under the lesser standard of proof by preponderance of the evidence.

9. See Rubin, H. T. (1996). the role of defense attorneys in juvenile justice proceedings. *Juvenile Justice Update, 2*.

10. See Scott, L. (1996). Probation: Heading in new directions. In R. Muraskin & A. R. Roberts (Eds.), *Visions for changes: Crime and justice in the twenty-first century.* Upper Saddle River, NJ: Prentice-Hall.

Glossary

The glossary summarizes terms that were used in this textbook. Readers should refer to the glossary to refresh their knowledge of discussions and case studies explored in chapters, tables, and chapter perspectives.

Absolute Deprivation. Lacking—or having only the minimal—means to survive within a society. (Chapter 12)

Abused Children. Child victims of emotional, sexual, or physical assaults. These are victims of proactive behavior by an abuser. (Chapter 2)

Adjudicative Facts. The facts of a juvenile adjudicatory hearing that represent the full scope of the facts alleged against youths named in the juvenile petition. (Chapter 7)

Adjudicatory Hearing. Similar to the trial in adult court, the merits of the case are heard and determined by the court. (Chapter 7)

Aftercare. A term used in approximately half of the states to describe parole for juveniles. It is essentially the juvenile justice system's equivalent to parole and involves supervised early release of youths from a juvenile residential institution after a period of mandated confinement. (Chapter 9)

Age of Majority. State and federal statutory designations that define one's status as a juvenile by law. After offenders reach the age of majority, they are subject to criminal court jurisdiction. (Chapter 5)

Alateen/Alanon. Alateen is a nationwide movement that is the teenage equivalent of Alcoholics Anonymous and is specifically organized to help teenage alcoholics. Alanon is also a nationwide movement that has been designed to assist those who are victimized or otherwise affected by the behavior of alcoholics who live in their households. (Chapter 6)

AMBER Alerts. Alerts that are broadcast when authorities suspect that a child has been abducted. A feature of the AMBER Plan, these alerts describe the victim, provide a profile of the abductor, and describe any special circumstances of the case. (Chapter 5)

AMBER Plan, The. A voluntary partnership between law enforcement agencies and broadcasters to activate an urgent bulletin in the most serious child-abduction cases. It is coordinated by state and local governments, which ideally cooperate under a nationwide emergency alert umbrella when children are missing. AMBER is an acronym for America's Missing: Broadcast Emergency Response. (Chapter 5)

Anomie and Strain Theories. Sociological theories of criminal causation, which generally refer to a state of "normlessness" in society. Modern strain theory focuses on the availability of goals and means. When the greater society encourages its members to use acceptable means to achieve acceptable goals, and not all members have an equal availability of resources to achieve these goals, they may resort to illegitimate and illicit means. (Chapter 3)

Arrest Data. Data that report the number of cases that were cleared by police agencies. Local law enforcement agencies report cleared cases to the Federal Bureau of Investigation, which publishes this information in its annual Uniform Crime Reports for regions across the nation. (Chapter 4)

At-Risk Juveniles. Youths who live in environments that are conducive to promoting deviant behavior. Also included are juveniles who exhibit anti-social behaviors that can lead to early deviance. In some states, *all* juveniles within defined age ranges are defined as at-risk. (Chapter 5)

Atavism. A biological theory of criminal causation developed during the nineteenth century by Cesare Lombroso. It argued that criminals are anthropological throwbacks to an undeveloped phase in human evolution, and that this atavistic quality is indicated by physical abnormalities. (Chapter 3)

Attention Deficit Disorder. A behavioral disorder typified by deficient attention ability, chronic physical movements, and poor self-control. (Chapter 5)

Augustus, John. The first genuine probation officer in the United States. In the 1850s in Boston, his service began as part-time rehabilitation of drunkards but quickly became a full-time practice for the supervision of a variety of offenders. His work eventually assisted 2,000 offenders before his death in 1859. (Chapter 9)

Bench Trials. The resolution of legal and factual issues by a judge (the judicial "bench") without the participation of a jury. In these cases, the judge becomes the sole authority on the fate of accused offenders. (Chapter 7)

Beyond a Reasonable Doubt. The standard of proof applied for the resolution of delinquency cases. It technically refers to evidence that is "fully satisfied, entirely convinced, satisfied to a moral certainty . . . the equivalent of the words clear, precise and indubitable."[1] (Chapter 7)

Big Brothers/Big Sisters of America. A nationwide federation of youth service agencies that promote mentorship through individual relationships between adults and youths. It promotes healthy interpersonal and socialization skills and behaviors in young people as they move through adolescence toward adulthood. Mentorship occurs through regular activities that many persons take for granted, such as taking walks, playing outdoor games, going shopping, and bicycling. (Chapter 6)

Binding. A concept similar to probation was established in England by the fourteenth century, when courts "bound over" offenders into the custody of members of the community for good behavior. (Chapter 9)

Boot Camps. Residential correctional facilities where drill instructors replicate training techniques used in boot camps of the armed forces, adapting their methods to the special needs of juvenile offenders. The purpose is to "shock" residents into socially productive conformity over a period of 30 to 120 days. (Chapter 8)

Bridewell Workhouse. An institution established in sixteenth century London to put offenders to work under strict discipline. Youthful offenders found begging or loitering were also sent to Bridewell. (Chapter 2)

Campus Pride. A national program implemented by school districts to remove gang graffiti from school campuses. This serves as a countermeasure to gang attempts to mark their territory on school grounds. (Chapter 6)

Career Escalation. The progression from relatively minor status offenses toward more serious criminal or delinquent offenses. (Chapter 5)

Caution. A process of reprimands and warnings used extensively in the United Kingdom as an alternative to formal processing into the juvenile justice system. Cautions involve a strong reprimand to juveniles for their behavior, and serve as a warning that they will be brought before the court for further violations. (Chapter 12)

Census of Juveniles in Residential Placement (CJRP). A national study conducted by the Office of Juvenile Justice and Delinquency Prevention, which "collects individual data on each juvenile held in the residential facility, including gender, date of birth, race, placement authority, most serious offense charged, court adjudication status, date of admission, and security status."[2] (Chapter 8)

Certification. A procedural technicality whereby juveniles are legally certified as adults and processed into the criminal justice system. (Chapter 7)

Child Abuse Reporting Statutes. Laws mandating child abuse and neglect reporting procedures for certain institutions and professions. State agencies are often designated to investigate allegations of abuse. There may also be statutory reporting requirements for school employees, medical personnel, social service workers, and law enforcement officers. (Chapter 5)

Child-Saving Movement. A mid-nineteenth century movement in the United States that sought to rescue children from unwholesome and dangerous environments. A fundamental tenet of the movement was that juveniles should receive treatment rather than punishment. (Chapter 2)

Children in Need.   Juveniles who are not properly cared for by an adult (e.g., abused, neglected, or abandoned children). Children in need are one population of youths served by the juvenile justice system. (Chapter 5)

Children in Trouble.   Juveniles who violate the law, either as juvenile delinquents or as status offenders. Some delinquents are waived into criminal court and tried as adults. Children in trouble are one population of youths served by the juvenile justice system. (Chapter 5)

Children's Panels.   Scottish tribunals that in 1968 replaced juvenile courts. The Panels have jurisdiction over children 8 to 17 years of age and are composed of three lay citizens drawn from the community who are knowledgeable about the needs of juveniles in the community. Panels are charged to determine whether or not suspects are guilty and to impose required treatment in the best interest of the child. (Chapter 12)

Children's Tribunals.   Juvenile hearing tribunals established in Massachusetts in 1874. This tribunal system was a predecessor to modern juvenile courts. (Chapter 2)

CHINS.   Children in need of supervision. (Chapter 7)

CHIPS.   Children in need of protection or services. (Chapter 7)

Chromosome Theory.   Research suggesting that men with an "XYY" chromosomal pattern are more prevalent in prison populations than in society. These "supermales" are theoretically more aggressive than typical "XY" males. (Chapter 3)

Classical School of Causation.   A theoretical school holding that individuals are responsible for their deviant behavior. Punishments for these transgressors should always be proportional, and never excessive. Popular during the late eighteenth and early nineteenth centuries, this theory was revived during the late twentieth century in the United States. (Chapter 3)

Clearances.   Arrests that have been made for reported crimes. (Chapter 4)

Community Corrections.   Nonresidential correctional alternatives that link juvenile offenders to the community and rely on community resources to provide correctional services. Probation, parole, and aftercare are examples of community corrections. Also known as *community-based corrections*. (Chapter 9)

Community Placement (Benign).   Less restrictive, and often nonrestrictive, community placements. Participants are permitted the same or similar freedoms of movement and association as any other youth. Foster homes are examples of this type of community placement. (Chapter 10)

Community Placement (Experiential).   Controlled placements in rural communities. Participants are required to participate in a series of esteem- and character-building exercises over an established period of time. Wilderness programs comprise this alternative. (Chapter 10)

Community Placement (Restrictive). Placements in the community under defined terms of probation or other diversionary agreements. The activities of participants are regulated, often quite intensively. Group homes are typical examples of this type of community placement. (Chapter 10)

Community-Strategy Era of Policing. An era of policing beginning in the 1950s and lasting to the present. This era's philosophy emphasizes community political support, law, and professionalism. Law became the basic legitimization for police conduct. Community support and involvement is also sought and needed to solve problems. Crime control is just one goal of broader community problem-solving. This type of policing requires development of intimate relationships between police and residents. (Chapter 6)

Conditional Probation. Probation programs that entail significant restrictions on movement and intensive communications with probation officers, usually involving personal meetings. (Chapter 9)

Conditioning Theory. A psychological theory of causation that holds that environmental stimuli act as punishers or reinforcers for human behavior. Deviance can arise when criminal or delinquent behavior results in more pleasure than pain. (Chapter 3)

Conflict Theory of Causation. A critical theory of causation that hypothesizes that social tensions and conflicts often pit the *haves* against the *have nots*, with the latter being labeled as criminals or insurgents during these conflicts. Laws and rules are simply instruments of control used by ruling elites to maintain control of key institutions, and thereby shut out others who might challenge the authority of the elites. (Chapter 3)

Cook County Juvenile Court. A court established under Illinois law in 1899. It was the first truly modern juvenile court because it formulated concepts and procedures that continue to be applied in the present era. (Chapter 7)

Corrections-Managed Parole and Aftercare. Systems wherein correctional administrators are given the authority to approve or deny early release. Senior officials in correctional facilities make recommendations on parole or aftercare for residents, with the advice and counsel of professional social workers who are assigned to the facility. (Chapter 9)

Cottage System. A model for juvenile correctional institutions in which nineteenth century reformers designed rural reformatories as compounds with separate structures and dormitories. The belief was that residents who worked in industrial schools in the countryside would absorb wholesome rural values and virtues and thereby grow into responsible and productive adults. (Chapter 8)

Court-Administered Parole and Aftercare.   Parole and aftercare authority that has been exclusively granted to the court. The court has final oversight authority. (Chapter 9)

Court-Appointed Counsel.   Attorneys who are either private attorneys appointed by the court, or public defenders. (Chapter 7)

CRASH (Community Resources Against Street Hoodlums)   A program of the Los Angeles Police Department (LAPD) created during the 1980s to aggressively confront gangs. Intimidation was expressly permitted as a matter of policy. The program was widely popular in the community, but it was disbanded after scandals were identified that involved illegal activities and behavior and that violated the LAPD's internal regulations. (Chapter 11)

Crime Clock, The.   Published annually by the FBI in its Uniform Crime Report, the Crime Clock depicts the frequency of commission of major crimes. (Chapter 4)

Criminal Deviance.   Antisocial behavior by persons who violate laws prohibiting acts defined as criminal by city, county, and state lawmakers or the U.S. Congress. Both adults and juveniles (those waived into criminal courts) can be convicted of crimes. (Chapter 3)

Criminal Gangs.   A term commonly used for gangs that routinely engage in criminal behavior such as drug trafficking, burglary, vehicular theft, and assault. (Chapter 11)

Critical Theory.   Theories of causation that broadly challenge the prevailing "orthodoxy" of criminology. These theories hypothesize that social tensions and conflicts are indelible features of society. Such tensions and conflicts are root causes for criminality and delinquency. Examples of critical theories in the United States are conflict theory and radical criminology. (Chapter 3)

Custody.   The process of asserting physical control over juvenile offenders or victims. Custody is conceptually distinguishable from arrests, and reflects the underlying duty of law enforcement agencies, as part of the juvenile justice system, to further the system's mission of protecting and rehabilitating children in trouble and children in need. (Chapter 6)

D.A.R.E.   Drug Abuse Resistance Education, a program that emphasizes drug awareness education for elementary school students. Police officers from local station houses teach children about the different types of drugs, their effects, and how to recognize them. Officers also explain how to say "no" when drugs are offered. (Chapter 6)

Day Treatment Centers.   Nonresidential institutions designed to provide treatment services to juvenile delinquents and other at-risk youths who might otherwise be placed in detention centers. Assignment to these centers can be done either as a condition of probation, or as a diversionary alternative. (Chapter 10)

Delinquent Gangs. A term commonly used for gangs that routinely engage in criminal behavior such as drug trafficking, burglary, vehicular theft, and assault. (Chapter 11)

Demand Waiver. Systems that permit juveniles to request waiver to adult court. One factor for this kind or request may be the desire for a jury trial in states that do not permit juries in juvenile court. (Chapter 7)

Democratic Nations. Open political systems in which the needs of society are communicated to political leaders, who are responsive. Juvenile justice policies are developed from the concerns of local communities. (Chapter 12)

Demonology. An ancient belief holding that human deviance is the product of evil otherworldly forces, such as demons and devils. Remedies included exorcism of the evil spirits, which often involved ordeals of pain. (Chapter 3)

Dependent Children. Children who are abandoned by parents or guardians, or otherwise uncared for. (Chapter 2)

Detention. The period between when a youth is taken into custody and prior to a hearing before the juvenile court. It is roughly comparable to the adult concept of being *jailed*, because in both circumstances a suspect is temporarily housed in a detention facility, pending further processing. (Chapter 6)

Deterministic Theories of Criminal Causation. Theories that eliminate individual responsibility for criminal behavior. These theories essentially conclude that other factors such as biological or spiritual variables explain an individual's lack of responsible self-control. (Chapter 3)

Deterrence. A punishment alternative based on the fear of swift and severe punishment. In theory, harsh punishments deter individuals who might otherwise be prone to break the law, as well as those who have already violated the law. (Chapter 8)

Developed Nations. Nations that have highly developed industrial and technological economies. Abundant resources exist that can be devoted to managing social problems such as child welfare, delinquency, and crime. (Chapter 12)

Developing Nations. Nations that have relatively unsophisticated or poorly developed industrial and technological economies. Limited resources are available that can be devoted to managing juvenile justice issues. (Chapter 12)

Deviance. "Behavior that is contrary to the standards of conduct or social expectation of a given group or society."[3] (Chapter 3)

Differential Association Theory. A sociological theory of causation that holds that criminals and law-abiding people learn their behavior from associations with others. People imitate or otherwise internalize the quality of these associations, so that criminality and delinquency are learned behaviors that are acquired from interacting with others who participate in criminal lifestyles. (Chapter 3)

Dispositional Hearing. Similar to the sentencing hearing in adult court, the court rules on what should become of the juvenile subsequent to the adjudication. (Chapter 7)

Diversion. The conceptual underpinning for community-based programs. A process that diverts juveniles away from the formal and authoritarian components of the juvenile justice system. Programs may be coordinated by youth agencies, juvenile courts, or the police. (Chapter 10)

Drive-By Shootings. Shootings by gun-wielding gang members from automobiles. Occupants of the vehicles spray gunfire at members of rival gangs, firing wildly and often hitting innocent bystanders or residents inside their homes. (Chapter 11)

Drug Gangs. Street gangs that are organized around drugs as a criminal enterprise. They are fundamentally criminal organizations and are motivated by profit. These gangs are usually composed of youths and young adults, the latter being the leaders and "brains" of the operation. (Chapter 11)

Educational Neglect. Permitting the child to be chronically truant or in some other way inattentive to educational needs. (Chapter 5)

Elmira Reformatory. A facility in New York where parole was first implemented in the United States in 1876. It was one of the first institutions in the United States to apply indeterminate sentencing with the possibility of early release. A new system of granting "good time" points, or credit, to inmates was designed to encourage proper behavior. (Chapter 9)

Emancipated Youths. State systems that permit juveniles to become "emancipated" from the control of their parents or the state under certain circumstances (such as marriage). This is predicated on a threshold age. They become *de jure* (legal) adults, thus allowing them to enter into contracts, own real estate, and accept responsibilities that would normally not be legally binding. (Chapter 1)

Emotional Disturbance. Emotionally disturbed youths exhibit extremes in emotions. These can include impulsiveness, aggression, or polar (extreme) mood swings. (Chapter 5)

Emotional Neglect. Inadequate nurturance or affection given to children. This occurs when basic emotional and developmental needs of juveniles are not met. (Chapter 4)

Environmental Factors. The effect of people, institutions, and other immediate associations on the personal development and behavioral traits of juveniles. (Chapter 11)

Explorers Programs. A number of jurisdictions have established programs that allow youths to learn firsthand about police work. Participants accompany officers on ride-alongs and other duties as a way to give positive experiences to juveniles and promote good relations. (Chapter 6)

Expungement. The destruction of files and records that document a particular juvenile's offense history. Expungement decrees generally originate with juvenile courts and are delivered to police departments. (Chapter 6)

Female Associates (Gangs). Girls and young women who belong to gangs but are not exploited or subordinated by male members, in contradistinction to female auxiliaries. This is a "middle ground" between female auxiliaries and female gangbangers. (Chapter 11)

Female Auxiliaries (Gangs). Girls and young women who play a subordinate role to male gang members. They do not share in leadership roles, and they perform menial or otherwise secondary tasks and behave in a support role for the gang. Extreme exploitation and abuse of female members by male members may occur. (Chapter 11)

Female Gangbangers. Members of all-female gangs. They are completely independent from male gangs and act on their own volition without reference to, or permission from, male gang members. Their gangs are often formed as a reaction to the subordination and exploitation found in male gangs. This is a fairly rare phenomenon, usually found in large cities. (Chapter 11)

Finding of Fact. Findings by juvenile court judges that conclude that the juvenile has committed a status offense; is delinquent; or has been abused or neglected, or is dependent and in need of supervision. (Chapter 7)

FINS. Families in need of supervision. (Chapter 7)

Folk Nation. One of two alliances of gangs, or "sets," formed in Chicago. Along with the People Nation, the Folk Nation is an amalgamation of gangs that cuts across racial and ethnic identities. These alliances are not quite mega-gangs, but rather groupings that identify fellow members as allies. (Chapter 11)

Forestry Camps. An example of wilderness correctional programs. These are minimum security residential corrections facilities, usually located on public lands such as state parks, where residents are required to perform forestry and land maintenance duties. Professional staff manage the ranches and provide treatment and therapy. (Chapter 8)

Foster Families. Families who care for youths assigned to foster homes. (Chapter 8)

Foster Homes.   Nonsecure residential facilities that expand the concept of family replication by loosening the institutional restrictions found in group homes, with a small number of supervisors and residents. Foster care is generally limited to victims of abuse and neglect rather than lawbreakers, and attempts as much as possible to substitute the foster family for a youth's biological family. (Chapter 8)

Foster Parents.   The heads of group homes, who—unlike their professional group home counterparts—are not professionally-trained managers. Foster parents ideally nurture their residents and provide them with the guidance that was absent from their homes. (Chapter 10)

Four Ds, The.   Deinstitutionalization, diversion, due process, and decriminalization. These concepts have been very influential in framing the policy debate in the modern era of juvenile justice process. (Chapter 2)

Free Will Theories of Criminal Causation.   A category of theories that regard deviant behavior as a product of individual rational choice. Such rational choice is grounded in the human desire for pleasure and aversion to pain. (Chapter 3)

Gang Intervention.   Intervention policies require juvenile justice officials and the community to intervene in the lives of individuals who have crossed the line and adopted (or are about to adopt) the lifestyle of a gangbanger. Intervention specialists do not consider these individuals to be lost to society, but rather in need of being rehabilitated and reclaimed by the community. (Chapter 11)

Gang Prevention.   A "middle ground" between gang intervention and gang suppression. The philosophy of gang prevention mirrors that of crime intervention. The idea is to eliminate the conditions that lead to delinquency and criminal deviance. Thus, within the purview of prevention strategies, it is believed that delinquency, criminality, and gang creation can be "nipped in the bud" if certain identified conditions are corrected. (Chapter 11)

Gang Resistance Education and Training (GREAT).   A school-based program that attempts to establish lines of communication between schools, the police, and students to promote understanding and respect. School teachers, administrators, law enforcement officials, and members of the student body to sit down and honestly interact with each other. (Chapter 11)

Gang Suppression.   A policy to aggressively confront gangs as organizations and gang members as individuals. The purpose of suppression is to either eliminate gangs or significantly repress their activity. (Chapter 11)

Gangbangers.   A slang term for members of youth gangs. (Chapter 11)

Gangs.   Self-established, loosely organized, and antisocial groups of youths. Most have adopted a name, claimed a territory, and devised symbols. They often have poor family or community relations and often present a significant threat of social disruption. Other terms for this phenomenon are street gangs, youth gangs, delinquent gangs, and criminal gangs. (Chapter 11)

Graffiti Removal Community Service Programs. Graffiti is often a self-described art form in which "taggers" draw or write messages on private property. It is also a means of communication among street gang members. In some cities, taggers and gang members apprehended by the police are assigned to graffiti removal duty as part of their community service. (Chapter 6)

Group Homes. Nonsecure residential facilities managed by professional juvenile corrections workers who serve as administrators, teachers, and counselors. They try to replicate the values and social interactions of families, which in practice means that most homes are not large facilities. Group homes are integrated into neighborhoods. (Chapter 8)

Guardian ad Litem. A court-appointed representative for juveniles who have been abused or neglected, or who are dependent. They represent the personal interests of youths who are deemed unable to do so on their own behalf because of their immaturity. (Chapter 7)

Halfway House. A type of group home that houses up to 30 or 40 youths. Residents tend to be youths who are transitioning from correctional or substance-abuse institutions to full release. Participants are sent to halfway houses as a way to prepare them for eventual reintegration into the community. (Chapter 10)

Head Start. Federal programs delivering preschool and early school educational services to youths from poor or culturally marginalized environments. Head Start provides instruction in basic reading and verbal skills for youths who might otherwise grow up with poor skills and thereby pose an increased possibility of future delinquency or criminality. (Chapter 10)

Head Start Bureau. An office of the U.S. Department of Health and Human Services that manages the Head Start program. (Chapter 10)

Hidden Victimization. Unreported incidents of child abuse, neglect, exploitation, or other victimization. Often occurring in homes, schools, places of worship, or other insular settings. (Chapter 4)

Highfields Project. The common name used for the New Jersey Experimental Project for the Treatment of Youthful Offenders. An innovative program founded in New Jersey in 1950. (Chapter 10)

Home Invasions. Violent trespass into homes by groups of youths, who terrorize the residents. Crimes committed by invaders include assault, murder, rape, and robbery. (Chapter 11)

Homeward Bound.   A variant on the Outward Bound model, established in 1970 in Massachusetts. The program developed personal growth through wilderness experiences. It also established a six-week program that provided daytime challenges and nighttime education on survival skills and the natural environment. (Chapter 10)

House Arrest.   Confinement of youths to their residences under mandated terms and conditions. Used in juvenile probation, parole, and aftercare programs. (Chapter 9)

Household Data.   Survey data that questions respondents about whether members of their households have been victims of delinquency or crime. (Chapter 4)

Houses of Refuge.   Institutions founded during the 1820s to house vagrant and criminal juveniles, they represent a typical example of Enlightenment-era juvenile justice reforms. (Chapter 2)

Immediate Community, The.   Made up of families, neighbors, and friends, the immediate community is composed of the people who are closest to troubled and needy children. (Chapter 5)

Incapacitation.   A punishment philosophy that imposes severe penalties that make offenders incapable of committing further crimes. Incapacitating judgments can include long-term imprisonment and execution. (Chapter 8)

Incorrigibles.   Youths whose behavior is not controlled, or cannot be controlled, by an authority figure. These are children who are in chronic conflict with authority. (Chapter 2)

Indeterminate Sentencing.   A sentencing philosophy that encourages rehabilitation by offering early release for behavioral conformity. The theory is that inmates will conform if sentences are flexible and indeterminate. (Chapter 9)

Initial Contact.   The first occasion of police intervention when youths break the law or are victimized. (Chapter 6)

Intake.   A process used to determine whether a juvenile should be released or processed through the juvenile justice system. It is roughly comparable to an initial appearance or preliminary hearing in the adult system. (Chapter 1)

Intensive Aftercare Supervision (IAS).   Conceptually similar to Juvenile Intensive Probation Supervision (JIPS), IAS establishes guidelines for enhanced levels of postrelease supervision of juveniles that are more stringent and invasive than normal supervision. (Chapter 9)

Intensive Probation Supervision (IPS).   A probation program mandated for persons who may pose a risk of flight or noncompliance with the terms of probation. Adult IPS was originally designed during the 1980s to lower costs and reduce prison overcrowding. It is an intensified version of standard probation and emphasizes increased surveillance, more frequent contacts with probation officers, and enhanced control over participants. Electronic monitoring is commonplace. (Chapter 9)

Intermediate Sanctions. Intensive alternatives to long-term institutionalization. These sanctions include house arrest, "shock" incarceration, electronic monitoring, and boot camps. Supervision of juveniles can be quite intensive. (Chapter 8)

Intervening Institutions. These institutions include schools and law enforcement agencies. Officials within these institutions are key personnel in the effort to help troubled and needy children. (Chapter 5)

Jails. Formerly the primary institution for holding juveniles, a practice that ended with the establishment of Houses of Refuge and, later, juvenile facilities. Although jails have long ceased to be the *principal* holding institution for juveniles, significant numbers of juveniles continue to be processed through jails. (Chapter 8)

JINS. Juveniles in need of supervision. (Chapter 7)

Judicial Reprieve. An early procedure similar to probation that permitted judges to suspend sentences for offenders, pending appeal to the Crown for clemency. Judges also suspended unfair sentences when deemed necessary. (Chapter 9)

Judicial Transfer. Systems that apply judicial waiver. As discussed, juvenile court judges have the authority to waive jurisdiction over juveniles, thus sending them into the adult system. Variations of this model are most commonly found in the states. (Chapter 7)

JUMP. A mentorship program administered by the Office of Juvenile Justice and Delinquency Prevention. Encounters consist of interpersonal mentorship between adults and youths. The program is targeted to communities that potentially could produce high rates of at-risk youths, such as areas with high incidence of crime, poverty, or school dropouts. (Chapter 10)

"Jumping In." A ritual in which gang recruits must fight a group of gang members. It is little more than a beating. (Chapter 11)

Junior Detention Centers. Juvenile custodial facilities in the United Kingdom (England and Wales) that house juveniles 14 to 17 years of age. (Chapter 12)

Jurisdiction (Justice Agencies). The lawful authority of a court or other justice agency. Jurisdictional power is delimited by territory, subject matter, or persons over which lawful authority is granted by statutes or constitutions. (Chapter 7)

Jurisdiction (Personal).   A court's power over certain persons, as granted by statutes or constitutions. It establishes judicial authority to render judgment on the interests of particular classes of people. (Chapter 7)

Jurisdiction (Subject Matter).   The authority of a court to decide a particular class of cases. (Chapter 7)

Jurisdiction (Territorial).   The geographic scope of a court's authority. Unless otherwise specified by law, a court possesses power to hear cases only within certain territorial limits, defined by political boundaries such as specified municipalities or counties. (Chapter 7)

Just Deserts Model.   A consequence of the crackdown on crime, this model applies the old adage of "an eye for an eye" when determining the fate of an offender. Conceptually, it advocates punishments that fit the crime. As a corresponding approach to the punishment model, juvenile offenders receive the punishments they deserve from juvenile court judges. Obviously, this is appropriate only for offenders; it is not for victims. (Chapter 1)

Juvenile.   A legal classification that is established within the parameters of culture and social custom. It fundamentally refers to those who are below the age of another classification; that is, adulthood. In the modern era, laws determine when a person is an adult, and juveniles are a defined class of nonadult persons who receive special treatment under the law. (Chapter 1)

Juvenile Court (Coordinated).   Juvenile courts that are required to coordinate their duties with specialized courts such as family courts. (Chapter 7)

Juvenile Court (Designated).   Juvenile systems that are subclassifications of larger county, municipal, or district systems. Juvenile courts function in accordance with their designations as divisions within these systems. (Chapter 7)

Juvenile Court (Independent).   Juvenile systems that are completely independent from other courts. Although judges from other courts may be assigned to sit as juvenile judges, the system itself is independent. (Chapter 7)

Juvenile Court Judge.   The central participant in a juvenile court system, who sits as the final arbiter for disputes and problems brought before the court. He or she is vested with the authority of the state, tangibly and personally representing *parens patriae*. (Chapter 7)

Juvenile Court Prosecutors.   Attorneys representing the interests of the state in juvenile delinquency hearings. They retain the traditional exercise of prosecutorial discretion in deciding the question of whether to file petitions on behalf of youths and the charges to be brought against them. (Chapter 7)

Juvenile Court Statistics.   Data on cases processed by juvenile courts. Research reports such as *Juvenile Court Statistics,* published by the Office of Juvenile Justice and Delinquency Prevention and the National Center for Juvenile Justice, contain statistics on juvenile court proceedings. These data include case statistics at the local jurisdiction level. (Chapter 4)

Juvenile Criminals. The modern crackdown on crime has led to the passage of many provisions in state crimes codes that permit the full prosecution of some juveniles in the adult criminal justice system. These youths officially cease to be juvenile delinquents, and become defined as criminals. (Chapter 1)

Juvenile Defense Counsel. Attorneys for juveniles brought before the juvenile court. Juveniles accused of delinquent acts are entitled to legal representation under the same constitutional protections as their adult counterparts in the criminal justice system. (Chapter 7)

Juvenile Delinquents. Persons under the age of majority who commit offenses that would be classified as crimes in the adult criminal justice system. As delinquents, these offenders are processed through the juvenile justice system. (Chapter 2)

Juvenile Detention Centers. Residential correctional facilities for juveniles that are roughly comparable to adult jails. They are secure, temporary preadjudication institutions that are used to house accused offenders until the final disposition of their cases. (Chapter 8)

Juvenile Deviance. Antisocial behavior by youths. It includes status offenses (violations of laws exclusively governing juvenile behavior) and delinquent acts (behavior that would be criminal if juveniles were tried as adults). (Chapter 3)

Juvenile Intensive Probation Supervision (JIPS). Closely monitored probation. Provided to juveniles who may pose a risk of flight or noncompliance with the terms of probation. Electronic monitoring is commonplace, using electronic bracelets or some similar device. (Chapter 9)

Juvenile Justice. The fair handling and treatment of youths under the law. It is a philosophy that recognizes the right of young people to due-process and personal protections. (Chapter 1)

Juvenile Justice Process. Procedures established to assure the fair administration of youths under the law. These procedures are carried out in accordance with institutions designed specifically for the administration of juvenile justice. (Chapter 1)

Juvenile Justice System. Institutions that have been organized to manage established procedures as a way to achieve justice for juveniles. These institutions include the police, juvenile courts, juvenile corrections, and the community. (Chapter 1)

Juvenile Petitions. Documents that request the court's intervention over matters involving juvenile delinquents, status offenders, or children who have been abused, neglected, or are dependent. They are roughly equivalent to complaints or pressing charges in the adult system, but are issued out of consideration for the best interest of the child. (Chapter 7)

Juvenile Victimization.   The ill-treatment young people, including when juvenile delinquents victimize other youths, or when youths suffer abuse or neglect from parents or other family members. Victimization may occur at home, in schools, or on the street. (Chapter 4)

"Juvies."   A nickname for juveniles. Often used by older gang members to denote younger members. (Chapter 11)

Learning Disabilities.   Deficits in learning processes, such as poor reading ability, lack of ability to memorize or follow directions, and incapability to distinguish or otherwise manage letters or numerals. (Chapter 5)

Legal Fictions.   Legal concepts that in general refer to exceptions to an accepted rule, and within the context of juveniles refer to the extraordinary handling of young people outside of usual laws and procedures. (Chapter 1)

Legislative Waiver.   In many states, the concepts of waiver and certification have been modified and codified into legislation mandating the removal of specified offenders from juvenile court. This procedure—commonly known as **statutory exclusion**—requires the assignment of youths suspected of murder or other serious offenses to the adult criminal system. (Chapter 7)

Lex Talionis.   The "law of retaliation." (Chapter 2)

Long-Term Correctional Facilities.   One of two general types of juvenile correctional institutions. These facilities include training schools, youth ranches and forestry camps, and boot camps. The other general type of juvenile correctional institution is short-term temporary care facilities. (Chapter 8)

Monitoring the Future Study.   Research using self-reported data that measure delinquency and drug abuse among a national sample of high school seniors since 1982, with eighth and tenth graders added in 1991. (Chapter 5)

Multiple Marginality Theory.   The convergence (multiple influence) of many marginalizing factors that result in a group's sense of dislocation, alienation, and isolation. Involving a highly complex process, these marginalizing factors can include economic, ecological, sociopsychological, and sociocultural components. When people are marginalized within these components—or within complex combinations of the components—antisocial associations of youths will form, including youth gangs. (Chapter 11)

National Crime Victimization Survey (NCVS).   Data derived from annual household surveys conducted by the U.S. Department of Justice's Bureau of Justice Statistics, in collaboration with the U.S. Census Bureau. The Survey is usually conducted and compiled twice annually, and asks approximately 40,000 to 50,000 respondents whether members of their household have been victims of crimes. (Chapter 4)

National Juvenile Court Data Archive. An extensive archive of automated records of juvenile court cases managed by the U.S. Department of Justice's Office of Juvenile Justice and Delinquency Prevention (OJJDP). The Archive was established to promote research on juvenile justice.

National Youth Survey (NYS). The NYS is an example of self-report data. It is a longitudinal study of a national sample of 1,725 juveniles, involving the distribution of several series of questionnaires to the sample. It has generally reported that the incidence of violent delinquency among youths is significantly higher than reported by official data such as the Uniform Crime Report (UCR) and the National Crime Victimization Survey (NCVS). (Chapter 4)

Naturalism. An ancient belief holding that human deviance is the product of forces in nature, as understood by ancient cultures. (Chapter 3)

Neglected Children. Child victims who do not receive proper care from parents or other guardians. Neglected children include those who are unfed, poorly sheltered, left alone, not cleaned, or otherwise maltreated. (Chapter 2)

Neoclassical Approach to Deviance. A modification of the Classical School that occurred during the early nineteenth century. It recognizes that juveniles and mentally ill adults do not make the same rational choices as mature sane adults. Therefore, special consideration should be given for these classes of offenders. (Chapter 3)

New Jersey Experimental Project for the Treatment of Youthful Offenders. An innovative program founded in New Jersey in 1950. Commonly known as the Highfields Project, it was intended to be an alternative to the existing training school model.

Nominal Sanctions. Relatively benign admonitions by the juvenile court to young offenders. Judges deliver stern written or verbal warnings to delinquents to instruct them on the significance of their behavior and the types of severe penalties that await them should they break the law again. (Chapter 8)

Nonofficial Juvenile Justice Institutions. Community resources and agencies that make up a component of the juvenile justice system. Procedures are usually informal and as welcoming as possible, depending on the circumstances of each case. Community-based agencies are responsible for rehabilitating and rescuing young people. (Chapter 1)

Nonsecure Correctional Facilities. Juvenile correctional facilities that typically require lockups only at specified times during the day or week, such as at night. (Chapter 8)

Nonsecure Residential Facilities. Institutions that provide a more wholesome atmosphere than locked detention facilities. They are often managed as homes or rescue facilities that provide different kinds of services, ranging from shelter to intensive treatment. Examples of nonsecure residential facilities include shelter care facilities, group homes, and foster homes. (Chapter 8)

Notice in Lieu of Summons. An alternative procedural option available to the court that is delivered to youths and parents. It is an informal "softer" alternative to a formal summons, and serves as a notification to appear before the court. (Chapter 7)

Office of Juvenile Justice and Delinquency Prevention (OJJDP). Established under the Juvenile Justice and Delinquency Prevention Act of 1974, the OJJDP coordinates national policy for preventing juvenile delinquency and victimization. It conducts independent research, assists experts and agencies in program evaluation, and recommends initiatives for delinquency prevention and treatment. (Chapter 10)

Official Data. Information compiled by law enforcement agencies, courts, and correctional systems at national, regional, and local levels. These data may be reported in the Uniform Crime Reports, juvenile court data, or the National Crime Victimization Survey. (Chapter 4)

Official Juvenile Justice Institutions. The traditional "triumvirate" of the police, courts, and corrections. Procedures can be quite formal and onerous, just as they are in the criminal justice system. Serious juvenile offenders and those who have committed lesser offenses are processed through official institutions. When juveniles are processed through official institutions, they are under the custody and guardianship of the state. (Chapter 1)

Official Police Procedures. Clearly delineated guidelines that officers must follow when they formally process juveniles. These procedures are written into juvenile court acts, and are reflected in internal procedures adopted by law enforcement agencies. (Chapter 6)

Original Gangsters (OGs). Gangbangers who are recognized by their reputation for affiliation with a particular gang. They receive a street-level respect for the things they have done to enhance their own status and the status of the gang. These activities can include drive-by shootings, imprisonment, killings, or some other gang-related behavior. They are hard-core members who have never "sold out" their gang identification. (Chapter 11)

Outward Bound. Wilderness programs offered in school-like environments where participants learn about individual confidence, trust in others, and the meaning of personal character. Youths are generally housed on-site at schools and camps. Professional counselors manage the challenge programs, which usually last for three weeks and consist of four phases. (Chapter 10)

Parens Patriae. The concept of the monarch as "father of the country." This ancient English doctrine allows the state to intervene as a surrogate parent for the best interests of children whose parents have failed in their duty to protect, care for, and control their children. (Chapter 2)

Parole. A supervised early release from a residential correctional facility. The offender's sentence begins in confinement and ends in the community under supervision from a parole agency, assuming his or her compliance with the terms of parole. Participants are juvenile delinquents or criminals who have already served time in a correctional institution. (Chapter 9)

Parole Boards. Independent parole or aftercare committees whose members are usually appointed by governors and approved by state legislatures. They are unaffiliated with state parole agencies or correctional facilities. (Chapter 9)

Part I Offenses. Eight serious crimes reported in the FBI's annual Uniform Crime Report. These offenses are considered to be inherently serious crimes, or they are those that occur frequently. Part I crimes are punishable by long-term incarceration or capital punishment. (Chapter 4)

Part II offenses. Twenty-one lesser offenses reported in the FBI's annual Uniform Crime Report. These offenses are considered to be less serious than Part I crimes, or they do not occur frequently, or they are considered to be victimless crimes. (Chapter 4)

Paterna Pietas. The concept of "fatherly love" advocated by early Christian philosophers such as Augustine as an alternative to the Roman custom of *patria postestas*, which gave a father absolute control over his household. (Chapter 2)

Patria Postestas. In ancient Roman law, the father had absolute control over his household, including his wife, children, and slaves. Although the father's authority was unquestioned, he was expected to act responsibly. Children were required to give complete obedience to the father. The doctrine became less authoritarian over time. (Chapter 2)

People Nation. One of two alliances of gangs, or "sets," formed in Chicago. Along with the Folk Nation, the People Nation is an amalgamation of gangs that cuts across racial and ethnic identities. These alliances are not quite megagangs, but rather groupings that identify fellow members as allies. (Chapter 11)

Physical Neglect. Abandonment, expulsion from the home, delay or failure to seek remedial health care, inadequate supervision, disregard for hazards in the home, or inadequate food, clothing, or shelter. (Chapter 5)

Physiognomy. The ascribing of moral and behavioral traits to physical appearance. In particular, facial characteristics are deemed to be indicators of moral character. Popular from the Enlightenment through the nineteenth century. (Chapter 3)

PINS.   Persons in need of supervision. (Chapter 7)

Pluralistic Societies.   Societies that recognize the value of the cultural and political opinions of their diverse constituent cultures, religions, and ethnic groups. In democratic pluralistic societies, juvenile justice policies can be adapted to the needs of different demographic populations. (Chapter 12)

Police Discretion.   An exercise of judgment by individual officers on what type of action to take in a particular situation. (Chapter 6)

Police Dispositions.   Any contact made by police officers regarding the welfare and safety of juveniles. Officers may exercise professional discretion to formally or informally resolve the disposition. Many personal and legal factors affect the outcome of police dispositions. (Chapter 6)

Political Era of Policing.   An era of policing extending up to the twentieth century. During this era, police departments were heavily integrated with urban political machines. Their authorization to act and resources came from local politicians, so that the police were adjuncts of local political machines. The police provided a wide range of services, including crime prevention, order maintenance, and finding jobs. (Chapter 6)

Positivist School of Criminology.   A deterministic approach to criminality and delinquency. This approach holds that biology, culture, and social experiences can be sources of deviant behavior. (Chapter 3)

Postadjudication Detention.   The confinement of juveniles in correctional facilities under court order after a case has been adjudicated. These include short-term facilities, as well as long-term confinement facilities such as training schools, alternative detention programs (such as wilderness ranches and boot camps), and diagnostic centers. (Chapter 8)

Preadjudication Detention.   The confinement of juveniles in youth facilities prior to the final disposition of their case by a juvenile judge. These are short-term confinement facilities, such as nonsecure residential facilities, juvenile detention centers, and jails. (Chapter 8)

Predisposition Report.   A report filed by a probation officer to the juvenile judge after findings of fact are entered. It contains a social history of the juvenile and recommends a disposition to the court. This report is sometimes referred to as a **presentence investigation (PSI)** (Chapter 7)

Preliminary Hearing.   Similar to the preliminary hearing in adult court, it is an initial conference on the status of the case. (Chapter 7)

Prenatal Exposure to Diseases and Drugs.   Children born of mothers who either had a venereal disease or abused substances during pregnancy. Babies can contract the mother's disease, or suffer mental retardation or addiction from the mother's prenatal alcohol or drug abuse. (Chapter 5)

Preponderance of the Evidence. The standard of proof applied for the resolution of status offense cases. It technically refers to the "greater weight of evidence that is more credible and convincing to the mind."[4] (Chapter 7)

Presentence Investigation (PSI). See Predisposition Report. (Chapter 7)

Prevention Services. Community-based intervention services that anticipate potential problems and are delivered as a means to reduce the probability that a youth will return to the juvenile justice system. (Chapter 10)

Primary Prevention. Intervention with youths who have not begun breaking the law or otherwise engaging in antisocial deviance. (Chapter 10)

Private Attorneys. Attorneys who have private practices and are either personally retained or are appointed as part of a court rotation system. (Chapter 7)

Probation. A sentence that is served in the community under supervision by a probation officer. The offender's sentence begins and ends in the community, assuming his or her compliance with the terms of probation. (Chapter 9)

Probationary Conditions (General). Conditions of probation that the juvenile court designs as "bottom line" requirements for all probationers. (Chapter 7)

Probationary Conditions (Specific). Conditions of probation that the juvenile court uniquely designs for individual offenders. (Chapter 7)

Prosecutorial Discretion. An exercise of judgment by prosecutors on whether to refer juveniles into the court, and what type of charges should be brought against them. (Chapter 7)

Prosecutorial Waiver. Systems that permit prosecutors to exercise their discretion on which system (adult or juvenile) a case will be brought before. (Chapter 7)

Psychoanalytic Theory. Theory proposed by Sigmund Freud, arguing that humans have three personality components, the ego, id, and superego. Human personalities also progress through several phases of childhood development. Failure to healthily progress through these phases can lead to deviant behavior, as can failure to develop a healthy balance between the ego, id, and superego. (Chapter 3)

Psychopathology Theory. A concept of the psychopathic personality that describes criminals who behave cruelly and seemingly with no empathy for their victims. This apparent inability of some criminals to appreciate the feelings of their victims led to a great deal of research on this behavior. Psychopaths, also known as sociopaths, are considered to be people who have no conscience—in Freudian terms, no superego. Aggressiveness and impulsiveness are typical manifestations of the psychopathic personality, which is why many become lawbreakers. (Chapter 3)

Public Defenders.   Court-appointed defense counsels who are full-time state employees and are essentially counterparts to prosecuting attorneys. (Chapter 7)

Punishment Model.   Also referred to as the *crime control model,* it emphasizes the authority of the state in responding to deviant behavior. Punishment is an end in itself, and the removal of offenders from society is desirable. Under this model, hard confinement, discipline, regimentation, and fear are considered to be effective correctional methods. It parallels the modern crackdown on adult criminality. Obviously, the punishment model is directed toward juvenile offenders rather than victims. (Chapter 1)

Pure Diversion.   Preadjudicatory diversion. A process of immediate diversion, meaning that young offenders are sent directly into community-based programs before they are adjudicated by a juvenile court and processed into the formal juvenile justice system. (Chapter 10)

Radical Criminology.   A critical approach to criminal causation first propounded during the 1960s and 1970s. Proponents argued that because power and wealth have been unequally distributed, those who have been politically and economically shut out understandably resort to criminal antagonism against the prevailing order. (Chapter 3)

Ranches.   An example of wilderness correctional programs. Minimum security residential corrections facilities where residents are required to work on ranches. Professional staff manage the ranches and provide treatment and therapy. (Chapter 8)

Re-education.   A method of rehabilitation used in Chinese correctional facilities for juveniles and adults. It involves instruction on the errors of one's ways and how to become a better citizen. Juveniles are generally re-educated for a few years, but adults may receive such re-education for many years. (Chapter 12)

Referees.   Hearing officers who serve as assistants and advisers to the court. Refereed findings are advisory in nature, and judges have the authority to accept, modify, or reject recommendations. (Chapter 7)

Reform Era of Policing.   An era of policing that extended well into the mid-twentieth century. It promoted a model of impartial, professional police and a narrowed function of crime fighting. This era rejected politics as the basis of police legitimacy, and political influence was seen as a failure of police leadership. The police function was narrowed to crime fighting, and departments contemptuously referred to provision of social services as "social work." Officers were professionally remote from people, heralding the beginning of the "thin blue line" metaphor. (Chapter 6)

Reform Schools. Juvenile facilities established during the Child-Savers Movement in the mid-nineteenth century United States. Reform schools were a programmatic counterpoint to Houses of Refuge in that the schools sought to create a nurturing environment rather than a harsh correctional one. Education and tradecraft were emphasized, as were homelike environments. (Chapter 2)

Rehabilitation. Treatment programs that try to salvage young offenders, often defined as a "liberal" approach to juvenile corrections. (Chapter 8)

Rehabilitation Model. The original approach toward juvenile justice, and still a fundamental concept. Rehabilitation refers to using institutions and programs to reclaim troubled youths. Under this model, methods and agencies are established to mold delinquents into productive adults, and victims into healthy adults. (Chapter 1)

Relative Deprivation. Deprivation that is measured in comparison to the rest of society. (Chapter 12)

Remedial Institutions. Child protective and health care agencies that essentially try to investigate and remediate the damaging effects of troubled and needy environments. (Chapter 5)

"Representing." How gang members present themselves as such, which involves adoption of symbolic identifiers to set themselves apart and distinguish themselves from other gangs. Identifiers create a sense of self-importance and "specialness" for members. (Chapter 11)

Research Accuracy. Data with few errors. Research methodologies are designed to reduce error and increase the likelihood of accurate findings. (Chapter 4)

Research Generalizability. The ability of research findings to be applied to another set of circumstances or question. Most research has limited generalizability. (Chapter 4)

Research Reliability. The ability of the research method to produce the same results each time it is used. In other words, the method is a reliable research tool. (Chapter 4)

Restitution. Conditions of probation, parole, or aftercare that require juvenile offenders to compensate victims and society for the harm they caused. Offenders are required to restore them to wholeness as much as is possible. (Chapter 9)

Retribution. An outright punishment of youthful offenders, which represents the theoretical separation of rehabilitation from penalties based on societal anger over the behavior of juvenile delinquents. Treatment is secondary to retaliation against youths who break the law. (Chapter 8)

Risk Factors.   Indicators of routes juveniles take toward juvenile delinquency. Risk factor environments include families, schools, peer associations, neighborhoods, and individual idiosyncrasies. (Chapter 5)

Runaways.   A subcategory of missing children who voluntarily leave their households, usually under duress, and who are forced to fend for themselves. (Chapter 5)

"Scared Straight" Model.   First popularized in the 1978 film *Scared Straight*. Groups of young offenders spend a day in maximum security prisons. They tour the facility and are placed in a graphic and intensive encounter session with hardened adult convicts. (Chapter 10)

Sealing of Records.   The preservation of files and records under strict confidentiality procedures. These files cannot be accessed without a court order, which is theoretically difficult to obtain. (Chapter 6)

Secondary Diversion.   Postadjudicatory diversion, referring to the release of juveniles who have already been processed into the formal juvenile justice system. They are released into community-based programs prior to final disposition. (Chapter 10)

Secondary Prevention.   Intervention with youths who have only recently begun engaging in antisocial deviance, and are in an early phase of committing relatively minor or status offenses. This is usually predelinquency prevention. (Chapter 10)

Secure Correctional Facilities.   Juvenile correctional institutions that literally lock in juvenile offenders. Residents have no opportunity or discretion to leave the facility. (Chapter 8)

Self-Reported Data.   Surveys of juveniles and adults, asking respondents about their personal criminal behavior within a specified time period. (Chapter 4)

Senior Detention Centers.   Juvenile custodial facilities in the United Kingdom (England and Wales), which are used to house juveniles 17 to 21 years of age. (Chapter 12)

Shelter Care Facilities.   Nonsecure residential facilities that temporarily house juveniles. Shelters are typically used as temporary housing for status offenders and others while they await final placement to another facility or the family home. Most shelters are not designed to treat or punish juveniles. (Chapter 8)

"Shock" Programs.   Programs that temporarily place juveniles under intensive (but guided) pressure with the goal of "shocking" them out of their antisocial behavior. Typical shock programs include boot camps and the scared straight model. (Chapter 10)

Short-Term Temporary Care Facilities. One of two general types of juvenile correctional institutions. These facilities include jails, youth shelters, juvenile detention homes, and reception centers. The other general type of juvenile correctional institution is long-term correctional facilities. (Chapter 8)

Skinhead Gangs. Lifestyle gangs that are usually associated with white supremacist ideologies. Some are associated with neo-Nazi or other racial supremacist movements. As a counterpoint, some skinheads are antiracist groups that may have a multiethnic membership. All cut their hair very short, and adopt distinctive dress such as boots, suspenders, and leather (or "bomber") jackets. (Chapter 11)

Skinheads Against Racial Prejudice (SHARPS) A segment of the skinhead youth movement and lifestyle that rejects white racial supremacy. (Chapter 11)

Social Disorganization Theory. Urban theories that held that poor urban communities are innately dysfunctional and give rise to criminal behavior. (Chapter 11)

Social Ecology (Structural) Theory. A sociological theory of causation that holds that the social structure of inner city areas affect the quality of life for inhabitants. Structural elements include overcrowding, poor sanitation, unemployment, poverty, poor schools, transience, births out of wedlock, and low employment. These factors contribute to high crime and delinquency rates because of the resulting endemic social instability. (Chapter 3)

Socialization. The process of learning moral and social norms of behavior, as defined within the child's immediate environment. (Chapter 11)

Somatotyping. A theory of delinquent and criminal causation that classifies three body types as determinants for deviant behavior: *mesomorphs,* who are muscular, sinewy, narrow in waist and hips, and broad-shouldered; *ectomorphs,* who are fragile, thin, narrow, and delicate; and *endomorphs,* who are pudgy, round, soft, short-limbed, and smooth-skinned. Predominance of mesomorphic traits is theoretically found in delinquents and criminals. (Chapter 3)

START. Residential facilities established during the 1960s in New York. Officially known as Short-Term Adolescent Residential Treatment centers, they were based on the New Jersey Highfields model for community juvenile treatment. (Chapter 10)

"Station House" Police Adjustments. Decisions that occur when juveniles are brought into a police station house, and parents are called in for consultation. Officers can release the juvenile into the parents' custody, thus ending the case prior to official processing into the juvenile justice system. (Chapter 6)

Status Offenders. Offenders who violate laws that regulate the behavior of persons under the age of majority. These laws govern youths who have not reached the age of majority and do not apply to adults. (Chapter 2)

Statutory Exclusion. Codification of the concept of waiver and certification into legislation that mandates the removal of specified offenses from juvenile court. For example, the automatic transferal of youths suspected of murder or other violent offenses. (Chapter 7)

Stigma. The imprinting of disgrace or shame on a person, so that he or she is thereafter judged by adults and peers in accordance with this impression. (Chapter 1)

Stoner Gangs. Lifestyle gangs that are organized around drug use and hard rock music. They represent a countercultural alternative to mainstream society and may express themselves with piercings, tattoos, black clothing, and "Gothic" appearances. (Chapter 11)

Street-Corner Police Decisions. Decisions that occur at the initiation of interaction between police officers and juveniles, typically involving asking teens to move along, releasing a juvenile after questioning, or issuing a reprimand before release. (Chapter 6)

Street Gangs. A term commonly used for gangs that routinely engage in criminal behavior such as drug trafficking, burglary, vehicular theft, and assault. (Chapter 11)

Students Taking On Prevention (STOP). A program that encourages youths to "recognize, report, and reduce" juvenile violence. Encounters consist of interpersonal outreach by juvenile peers to other juveniles. The program is funded by the Office of Juvenile Justice and Delinquency Prevention. (Chapter 10)

Superpredator. A projected a new wave of violent young offenders expected to arise in the twenty-first century. These youths would theoretically be prone to extreme violence. Projections for the superpredator phenomenon were influenced by the growing problem of juvenile violence that continued into the beginning of the 1990s. (Chapter 4)

Supplemental Homicide Report. A report issued by the FBI that provides data and trends for juvenile homicides. (Chapter 5)

Tagger Crews and Posses. Graffiti gangs who vandalize property by marking their territory with graffiti messages. Some tagger crews can be quite artistic, albeit by vandalizing someone else's property. (Chapter 11)

Tertiary Prevention. Intervention with youths who have engaged in serious and chronic deviance and who have already entered the juvenile justice system. These youths are technically in need of treatment rather than prevention, because efforts to prevent the onset of delinquency have failed.

These youths should be approached within the context of rehabilitation rather than prevention. (Chapter 10)

Third-World Nations. A designation developed during the second half of the twentieth century. It refers to countries that have less developed economies in comparison to the West; they are frequently undemocratic governments, and have lower literacy rates than in Europe or North America. (Chapter 12)

Thrownaways. A subcategory of missing children who have been ejected from their households and forced to fend for themselves. (Chapter 5)

TIPS. Teaching Individuals Protective Strategies is typical of federal efforts to sponsor nationwide initiatives. This U.S. Department of Education program emphasized the development of decision-making and reasoning skills for children in kindergarten through eighth grade. These skills included how to reduce victimization vulnerability and the ability to find solutions to potential problems. (Chapter 6)

Tongs. Trade associations formed by Chinese immigrants in San Francisco. Most tongs were legitimate trade associations, but a few engaged in criminal activity, often using juveniles as "auxiliaries" for their enterprises. These auxiliaries eventually formed Chinese street gangs. (Chapter 11)

Traditional Societies. Societies that do not embrace the cultural and political opinions of diverse demographic groups. The values of a predominant culture or group are imposed on all members of society. Juvenile justice policies are designed by the dominant group with the presumption that "what is good for us is good for all." (Chapter 12)

Training Schools. Secure residential correctional facilities, managed as either public or private institutions. The underlying mission of training schools is to promote rehabilitation by providing intensive training and treatment. Many facilities are highly secure institutions—designed in much the same manner as adult jails and prisons. (Chapter 8)

Treatment Model. Also referred to as the *medical model,* this approach applies a therapeutic standard for evaluating the effectiveness of intervention. Psychological counseling, physical (health) regimens, and behavior modification are stressed as foundations for full rehabilitation. Punishment and detention are rejected as being counterproductive to successful treatment and rehabilitation. This approach is applicable for juvenile offenders and victims. (Chapter 1)

Treatment Services. Community-based intervention services that manage existing problems, and are delivered to rehabilitate youths prior to their reintegration with the community. (Chapter 10)

Turf Wars. Fights over claimed urban territory by youth gangs. (Chapter 11)

Unconditional Probation. Probation programs that typically permit some freedom movement and relatively infrequent intensive communications with probation officers via mail or telephone. (Chapter 9)

Undemocratic Nations. Authoritarian political systems in which political leaders dictate policies to local communities, and may or may not be responsive to their stated needs. Juvenile justice policies are decided by government authorities. (Chapter 12)

Underclass, The. A socioeconomic designation in which large numbers of inner-city poor are caught in a chronic generational cycle of poverty, low educational achievement, teenage parenthood, chronic unemployment, and welfare dependence. Underclass theorists argue that antisocial behaviors become norms within chronically impoverished inner-city environments. (Chapter 3)

Uniform Crime Report (UCR). Published annually by the FBI, the UCR is a compilation of arrest data, and lists offenses as Part I offenses and Part II offenses. Police agencies submit information on clearances (arrest data) to the FBI annually. The FBI then constructs a statistical profile of crime in the United States based on these arrest data. (Chapter 4)

Unofficial Police Procedures. The exercise of police discretion at certain decision points. At these decision points, police officers come to a decision on whether to begin formal processing of juveniles, or to resolve the situation outside of officially mandated procedures. (Chapter 6)

Victimization Surveys. These data are derived from surveys of victims of crimes. Most victimization surveys compile household data. The best known victimization survey is the National Crime Victimization Survey, which is an annual household survey conducted by the U.S. Department of Justice's Bureau of Justice Statistics. (Chapter 4)

VisionQuest. A privately run wilderness program founded in 1973 in Tucson, Arizona. It is demanding, and requires boot-camp–like conditions. (Chapter 10)

Waiver. A process whereby juvenile courts may relinquish jurisdiction and remove a case to the adult criminal court. In many states, waiver is mandatory for serious offenses. In other situations the prosecutor determines whether waiver shall be invoked. (Chapter 7)

"Wannabes." Youngsters who emulate older gang members by imitating their dress, speech, and symbols. These young imitators want to be identified as gang members and frequently aspire to joining the group. (Chapter 11)

Ward of the State. A special status accorded to juveniles who have been removed from parental care and placed under the protection of the state. (Chapter 2)

Watts Riot. The first "modern" race riot, which occurred in 1965 in Los Angeles. (Chapter 11)

Western Nations. Countries that have highly developed economies, democratic governments, and high literacy rates. Societies are functional, are usually quite stable, and have exceptionally low rates of absolute deprivation. The West includes Western Europe, North America, and Japan. (Chapter 12)

Wilderness Programs. Juvenile corrections programs centered on minimum-security residential correctional institutions that are located in rural settings. These programs are usually reserved for first-time offenders or other juveniles who have committed minor offenses. Examples include forestry camps, ranches, and well-established programs such as Outward Bound. (Chapter 8)

Wilding. Rampages by youths in public areas such as parks or shopping malls. Perpetrators randomly beat or sexually assault people, sometimes seriously injuring them. (Chapter 11)

Youth Culture. Lifestyles that are peculiar to social associations of young people. There is no single youth culture, but rather an assortment of lifestyles and selected identifications. (Chapter 11)

Youth Custody Centers. Juvenile facilities in the United Kingdom (England and Wales) that are used to house juveniles for court-specified periods of time, usually not of long duration. (Chapter 12)

Youth Gangs. A term commonly used for gangs that routinely engage in criminal behavior such as drug trafficking, burglary, vehicular theft, and assault. (Chapter 11)

Youth Service Bureaus. A program originally recommended in 1967 by a presidential commission report entitled *The Challenge of Crime in a Free Society*. Youth Service Bureaus were intended to be a primary center for dealing with juvenile delinquents and status offenders. The Bureaus coordinated their activities with juvenile courts, the police, and probation agencies. (Chapter 2)

Zoot Suit Riots. Riots in 1943 among the Mexican population in Los Angeles. They were primarily a reaction to racism and harassment of Mexican youths. (Chapter 11)

Notes

1. Black, H. C. (1968). *Black's law dictionary* (4th ed., rev., p. 204). St. Paul, MN: West Publishing.

2. Snyder, H. N., & Sickmund, M. (2000). *Juvenile offenders and victims: 1999 national report* (p. 186). Washington, DC: U.S. Department of Justice.

3. Rush, G. E. (2003). *The dictionary of criminal justice* (6th ed., p. 112). New York: Dushkin/McGraw-Hill.

4. Black, H. C. (1968). *Black's law dictionary* (4th ed., rev., p. 1344). St. Paul, MN: West Publishing.

Appendix A

Important Cases, Laws, and Legislation

This appendix summarizes important cases and legislation that were cited in this textbook. Readers should refer to these summaries to refresh their knowledge of discussions and case studies explored in chapters, tables, and chapter perspectives.

Beijing Rules. The first protocols passed in the United Nations to develop international standards for juvenile justice and the treatment of young people. These rules are not enforceable domestically unless governments adopt them as part of their own body of law (Chapter 12).

Breed v. Jones, **421 U.S. 519, 533, 95 S. Ct. 1779, 1787, 44 L. Ed. 2d 346 (1975).** The U.S. Supreme Court held that jeopardy attaches for juveniles appearing before juvenile courts, and that subsequent prosecution in adult criminal courts for the same offense violates constitutional protections against double jeopardy (Chapter 2).

Child Abuse Prevention and Treatment Act. A federal statute passed in 1974 and amended in 1978. It criminalized child abuse and neglect caused by parents or guardians. The law also mandated the reporting of child abuse and neglect (Chapter 5).

Children's Act of 1960. A law in India that was passed to create uniform standards and an official system for juvenile justice process. However, the country's official policy is largely circumvented by informal and unofficial procedures and practices (Chapter 12).

Code of Hammurabi. A Babylonian system of law written circa 1750 B.C. It is the first known universal code of law imposed by a state. Under the code, fathers had absolute authority over their households, and children could be treated as little more than property (Chapter 2).

Code of Justinian. A code of laws written during the reign of Justinian, Emperor of the Eastern Roman Empire. It was originally promulgated in 529 C.E. and comprised twelve books. It became one of four compilations of Roman law known collectively as the *Corpus Juris Civilis* (Chapter 2).

Common Law. English judge-made law that was based on case precedent. It still represents a significant body of law in Anglo-American legal systems (Chapter 2).

Davis v. Mississippi, **394 U.S. 721, 89 S. Ct. 1394, 22 L. Ed. 2d 676 (1969).** A 1969 decision rendered by the U. S. Supreme Court that held that fingerprint evidence taken from a juvenile was inadmissible when taken during an unlawful detention. A suspected juvenile rapist had been detained, interrogated, and fingerprinted without prior authorization from a judicial official. (Chapter 6)

Ex parte Crouse. **4 Whart. 9 (Pa., 1838).** In this influential Pennsylvania case, an incorrigible girl's mother had the girl committed to a House of Refuge in Philadelphia. The father sued for her release, but an appeals court ruled that under *parens patriae,* the state had a duty and an interest to help and reform deviant children (Chapter 2).

Illinois Juvenile Court Act. A law passed in 1899 that created the first independent juvenile court system in the United States. (Chapter 2).

In re Gault, **387 U.S. 1, 87 S. Ct. 1428, 18 L. Ed. 2d 527 (1967).** A 1967 decision rendered by the U.S. Supreme Court that mandated many due-process protections for state juvenile court proceedings. These rights included: Application of the Fourteenth Amendment due-process clause to state juvenile courts; the right to counsel; the right against self-incrimination, and the right to confront witnesses. (Chapter 2)

In re Winship, **397 U.S. 358, 90 S. Ct. 1068, 25 L. Ed. 2d 368 (1970).** A 1970 decision rendered by the United States Supreme Court that held that juveniles accused of delinquent offenses should be accorded the same standard of proof as adults, that is, proof beyond a reasonable doubt. Status offenders may still be adjudicated under the lesser standard of proof by preponderance of the evidence, although in practice many jurisdictions apply the stricter standard to all juvenile proceedings (Chapter 2).

Juvenile Delinquency Prevention and Control Act of 1968. A bill passed by Congress to create an ongoing, nationally coordinated effort to reduce the incidence of juvenile delinquency. The U.S. Department of Health, Education, and Welfare was required to develop and coordinate a comprehensive strategy for reducing juvenile delinquency. States received federal funds for the implementation of state delinquency prevention, juvenile rehabilitation, research, and training programs. In 1974, it was revised and renamed the Juvenile Justice and Delinquency Prevention Act (JJDP) (Chapter 2).

Juvenile Justice and Delinquency Prevention Act of 1974. Legislation passed by Congress that tied federal funding to state restrictions on the detention and institutionalization of juvenile delinquents. Discretionary block grants were released to assist in alternative dispositions of juvenile offenders. This legislation also created the Office of Juvenile Justice and Delinquency Prevention (OJJDP) within the U.S. Department of Justice (Chapter 2).

Kent v. United States, 383 U.S. 541, 86 S. Ct. 1045, 16 L. Ed. 2d 84 (1966). A 1966 decision rendered by the U.S. Supreme Court that provided juveniles with the right to a hearing on the question of transfer from juvenile court jurisdiction to adult criminal courts. The decision also mandated a right to counsel for these hearings, access to records, and a statement of reasons for transfers (Chapter 2).

Lex Talionis. The "law of retaliation" adopted by many societies since antiquity. It allows the state to impose harsh punishments on criminal offenders. Modern applications of this philosophy include crimes codes that have adopted retribution and just deserts as the legal foundation for sentencing (Chapter 2).

Mapp v. Ohio 367 U.S. 643, 81 S. Ct. 1684, 6 L. Ed. 2d 1081 (1961). A 1961 decision rendered by the U.S. Supreme Court, reaffirming that the Fourth Amendment to the Constitution protects residents against unreasonable searches and seizures, in particular holding that evidence seized without a search warrant or probable cause is inadmissible in court (Chapter 6).

McKeiver v. Pennsylvania, 403 U.S. 528, 547 91 S. Ct. 1976, 1987, 29 L. Ed. 2d 647 (1971). A 1971 decision rendered by the U.S. Supreme Court, holding that trial by jury is not constitutionally mandated in juvenile adjudications (Chapter 2).

Miranda v. Arizona, 413 U.S. 902, 93 S. Ct. 3065, 37 L. Ed. 2d 1021 (1966). A 1966 decision rendered by the U.S. Supreme Court, holding that suspects must be properly advised of their right to counsel and protections from self-incrimination (Chapter 6).

Morrissey v. Brewer, 408 U.S. 471 (1972). A 1972 decision rendered by the U.S. Supreme Court, which extended due-process protections to the revocation of parole and aftercare (Chapter 9).

National Probation Act. Enacted in 1925, this act began federal probation. The law granted federal trial judges the authority to impose terms of probation on offenders and hire professional probation officers (Chapter 9).

New Jersey v. T.L.O., 469 U.S. 809, 105 S. Ct. 68, 83 L. Ed. 2d 19 (1984). A 1984 U.S. Supreme Court decision holding that neither a warrant nor probable cause need be established prior to a search, and that "reasonableness" will be determined by a student's age and gender, the scope of the search, and the student's behavior (Chapter 6).

Penal Servitude Act of 1853. An English law that granted early release from prison under supervision by local law enforcement officials (Chapter 9).

Poor Laws, The. Laws enacted during the reign of Elizabeth I in England. Among other goals involving state regulation of indebtedness and vagrancy, the Poor Laws institutionalized a system of indentured apprenticeship and servitude for idle and neglected youths (Chapter 2).

Schall v. Martin, 467 U.S. 253, 104 S. Ct. 2403, 81 L. Ed. 2d 207 (1984). A 1984 U.S. Supreme Court decision that upheld the practice of preventive detention by juvenile authorities. It held that juveniles can be detained without violating their due-process rights if they pose a high risk of further delinquency (Chapter 2).

Social Worker Act of 1968. A law in Scotland that abolished the juvenile court and established Children's Panels in its stead (Chapter 12).

Stubborn Child Law. A law enacted in 1646 in the Massachusetts Bay Colony. It reflected the Puritan approach toward juvenile justice, namely that incorrigible or otherwise disobedient children should be subjected to severe spiritual corrective measures. These measures included corporal and capital punishment (Chapter 2).

Twelve Tables, The. Developed circa 450 B.C.E., this is the earliest codification of Roman law and the source for later Roman laws (Chapter 2)

United States v. Wade, **388 U.S. 218, 87 S. Ct. 1926, 18 L. Ed. 2d 1149 (1967).** A 1967 U.S. Supreme Court decision that held that indicted suspects have a right to counsel present at lineups (Chapter 6).

Young Offenders Act of 1982. A law in Canada that ended an era when juvenile court judges were vested with significant discretion, and when court proceedings were informal. Canada now practices formality, with strict rules and procedures that are similar to the adult criminal court (Chapter 12).

Appendix B

Juvenile Justice Organizations and Agencies

This appendix provides contact information for juvenile justice organizations and related agencies. Readers should refer to these groups for information about juvenile justice resources, policies, and programs.

Alcohol and Drugs

National Clearinghouse for Alcohol and Drug Information

The U.S. Department of Health and Human Services
200 Independence Avenue, S.W.
Washington, DC 20201
Telephone: 800–729–6686
E-mail: info@samhsa.gov

National Institute on Alcohol Abuse and Alcoholism

5635 Fishers Lane, MSC 9304
Bethesda, Maryland 20892–9304

National Institute on Drug Abuse

National Institutes of Health
6001 Executive Boulevard, Room 5213
Bethesda, MD 20892–9561
Telephone: 301–443–1124
E-mail: Information@lists.nida.nih.gov

Substance Abuse and Mental Health Services Administration

The U.S. Department of Health and Human Services
200 Independence Avenue, SW
Washington, DC 20201
Telephone: 202–619–0257
Toll Free: 877–696–6775
E-mail: info@samhsa.gov

Children in Need

American Professional Society on the Abuse of Children

Tricia Williams, JD
Operations Manager:
APSAC Oklahoma Office
PO Box 26901, CHO 3B3406
Oklahoma City, OK 73190
Telephone: 405–271–8202
E-Mail: tricia-williams@ouhsc.edu

Children's Bureau

Administration for Children and Families
370 L'Enfant Promenade, SW
Washington, DC 20201

Interstate Compact on Adoption and Medical Assistance

The Association of Administrators of the Interstate
Compact on Adoption and Medical Assistance
810 First Street, NE, Suite 500
Washington, DC 20002
Telephone: (202) 682–0100

National Center for Children in Poverty

Mailman School of Public Health
Columbia University
722 West 168th Street
New York, NY 10032–2603
Telephone: 646–284–9600
E-mail: info@nccp.org

National Center for Missing & Exploited Children

Charles B. Wang International Children's Building
699 Prince Street
Alexandria, VA 22314–3175
Telephone: 866–411–5437

Police, Courts, and Corrections

Children and Family Justice Center

357 East Chicago Avenue
Chicago, IL 60611
Telephone: 312-503-0396
E-mail: http://www.law.northwestern.edu/cfjc/

Children's Defense Fund

25 E Street NW
Washington, DC 20001
Telephone: 202–628–8787
E-mail: cdfinfo@childrensdefense.org

Community Policing Consortium

1726 M St. NW, Suite 801
Washington, DC 20036
Telephone: 800–833–3085
E-mail: cpc@communitypolicing.org

Fight Crime: Invest in Kids

2000 P St. NW, Suite 240
Washington, DC 20036
Telephone: 202–776–0027

Juvenile Law Center

The Philadelphia Building
1315 Walnut Street—4th Floor
Philadelphia, PA 19107
Telephone: 215–625–0551
E-mail: info@jlc.org

National Council of Juvenile and Family Court Judges

P.O. Box 8970
Reno, NV 89507
Telephone: 775–784–6012
E-mail: admin@ncjfcj.org

National Major Gang Task Force

Executive Director
338 South Arlington, Suite 112
Indianapolis, IN 46219
Telephone: 317–322–0537 Office
E-mail: nmgtf@earthlink.net

National Youth Gang Center

Post Office Box 12729
Tallahassee, FL 32317
Telephone: 800–446–0912

Family and Community _____

Administration for Children and Families

370 L'Enfant Promenade, SW
Washington, DC 20201

Big Brothers/Big Sisters of America

Big Brothers Big Sisters National Office
230 North 13th St.
Philadelphia, Pa 19107
Telephone: 215–567–7000

Child Welfare League of America

440 First Street, NW, Third Floor
Washington, DC 20001–2085
Telephone: 202–638–2952

Communities in Schools

Communities in Schools National
277 South Washington Street, Suite 210
Alexandria, VA 22314
Telephone: 703–519–8999
Email: cis@cisnet.org

Families, Career, and
Community Leaders of America

Family, Career, and Community Leaders of America, Inc.
National Headquarters
1910 Association Drive
Reston Va. 20191–1584
Telephone: 703–476–4900

National Dissemination Center
for Children with Disabilities

P.O. Box 1492
Washington, DC 20013
Telephone: 800–695–0285
E-mail: nichcy@aed.org

National Center for Conflict Resolution Education

Conflict Resolution Education, Inc.
PO Box 17241
Urbana, IL 61803
Telephone: 217–384–4118 Fax: 217–384–4322
E-mail: info@resolutioneducation.com

Outward Bound USA

National Headquarters
100 Mystery Point Road
Garrison, NY 10524
Telephone: 845–424–4000

Research and Data

Bureau of Justice Statistics

810 Seventh Street, NW
Washington, DC 20531
Telephone: 202–307–0765
E-mail: askbjs@ojp.usdoj.gov

Juvenile Justice Clearinghouse

P.O. Box 6000
Rockville, MD 20849–6000
Telephone: 800–851–3420

National Center for Juvenile Justice

710 Fifth Avenue, Suite 3000
Pittsburgh, PA 15219
Telephone: 412–227–6950

National Gang Crime Research Center

P.O. Box 990
Peotone, IL 60468–0990
Telephone: 708–258–9111
E-mail: gangcrime@aol.com

Office of Juvenile Justice and Delinquency Programs

810 Seventh Street NW.
Washington, DC 20531
Telephone: 202–307–5911

Appendix C

Web-Based Exercises

This appendix summarizes Web-based exercises that were suggested in this textbook.

Chapter 2. Historical Perspectives

Recommended Web Sites

The following Web sites provide general discussions and contextual/ historical overviews of juvenile justice.

American Bar Association Juvenile Justice Center: http://www.abanet.org/ crimjust/juvjus/
Building Blocks for Youth: http://www.buildingblocksforyouth.org/
Children's Advocacy Institute: http://www.caichildlaw.org
Juvenile Justice FYI: http://www.juvenilejusticefyi.com/

Web Exercise

Using this chapter's recommended Internet sites, conduct an online investigation of contextual/historical discussions of juvenile justice.

- What commonalities and differences in perspective do these groups advocate?
- Is there anything that strikes you as being particularly similar to historical approaches to juvenile justice process?
- Are any of the policies advocated by these groups pioneering in their approaches?

For an online search of the history and context of juvenile justice process, students should activate the search engine on their Web browser and enter the following keywords:

"History of Juvenile Justice"

"Juvenile Justice Organizations"

Chapter 3. Juvenile Delinquency: Theories of Causation

Recommended Web Sites

The following Web sites investigate and discuss theoretical causes of juvenile delinquency and violence.

Birth Psychology and Violence (APPPAH):[1] http://www.birthpsychology.com/violence/index.html
Center for Substance Abuse Research: http://www.cesar.umd.edu/
Juvenile Justice Bulletin, October 1998: http://ojjdp.ncjrs.org/jjbulletin/9810_2/contents.html
Partnerships Against Violence Network: http://www.pavnet.org/
Youth Crime Watch of America: http://www.ycwa.org/

Web Exercise

Using this chapter's recommended Internet sites, conduct an online investigation of the causes of juvenile delinquency.

- What are common sources of juvenile deviance and violence?
- What are some of the common approaches used by agencies to explain and address the causes of juvenile delinquency?
- How effective do you think these organizations are?

For an online search of the causes of delinquency, students should use a search engine and enter the following keywords:

"Juvenile Deviance"

"Youth Crime"

Chapter 4. The Delinquency
Picture: Measuring Juvenile Deviance

Recommended Web Sites

The following Web sites report research and data on juvenile delinquency and crime.

Center on Juvenile & Criminal Justice: http://www.cjcj.org/
National Center for Juvenile Justice: http://ncjj.org
National Council on Crime and Delinquency: http://www.nccd-crc.org/
National Juvenile Court Data Archive: http://ojjdp.ncjrs.org/ojstatbb/njcda/
Office of Juvenile Justice and Delinquency Prevention: http://ojjdp.ncjrs.org/

Web Exercise

Using this chapter's recommended Internet sites, conduct an online investigation of research and data on juvenile delinquency and crime.

- In your opinion, which research methodology makes the most sense to you? Why?
- In what ways are the databases similar? How do they differ?
- In your opinion, which database on juvenile delinquency is the most useful for policy makers?

For an online search of delinquency statistics and methodologies, students should use a search engine and enter the following keywords:

"Delinquency Research"

"Delinquency Statistics"

Chapter 5. Children in
Trouble and Children in Need

Recommended Web Sites

The following Web sites investigate issues concerning children in trouble and children in need, and they illustrate the types of agencies and programs available to address these constituencies.

Children's Bureau: http://www.acf.hhs.gov/programs/cb/
The Future of Children: http://www.futureofchildren.org/
National Center for Children in Poverty: http://www.nccp.org/
National Center for Missing & Exploited Children: http://www.missingkids.org/
National Clearinghouse on Child Abuse and Neglect Information: http://nccanch
    .acf.hhs.gov/index.cfm

Web Exercise

Using this chapter's recommended Internet sites, conduct an online investigation of resources available to children in trouble and children in need.

- How comprehensive are the resources available for children in trouble and children in need?
- How would you compare the scope and quality of resources made available by public agencies vis-à-vis private agencies?
- How effective do you think these programs are?

For an online search of resources available to children in trouble and children in need, students should use a search engine and enter the following keywords:

"Child Abuse and Neglect"

"Juvenile Assistance"

Chapter 6. The Role of the Police _____

Recommended Web Sites

The following Web sites contain information about the role of the police in the juvenile justice system.

Big Brothers/Big Sisters of America: http://www.bbbsa.org/
Community Policing Consortium: http://www.communitypolicing.org/
Drug Awareness Resistance Education: http://www.dare.com/
Fight Crime: Invest in Kids: http://www.fightcrime.org/
LAPD Juvenile Division: http://www.lapdonline.org/juvenile/

Web Exercise

Using this chapter's recommended Internet sites, conduct an online investigation of the role of the police.

- How is the role of the juvenile police presented by agencies?
- In your opinion, are police liaison efforts and programs effective?
- Who should fund police-juvenile liaison programs?

For an online search of the role of the police in the juvenile justice system, students use a the search engine and enter the following keywords:

"Community Policing"

"Juvenile Police"

Chapter 7. The Role of the Court

Recommended Web Sites

The following Web sites provide information on the role of the juvenile court, court processes, and participants.

Children and Family Justice Center: http://www.law.northwestern.edu/depts/clinic/cfjc/
Children's Defense Fund: http://www.childrensdefense.org/
Juvenile Law Center: http://www.jlc.org
National Council of Juvenile and Family Court Judges: http://www.ncjfcj.org/

Web Exercise

Using this chapter's recommended Internet sites, conduct an online investigation of the judicial component of the juvenile justice system.

- How are juvenile advocacy agencies similar? How do they differ?
- What is the role of juvenile advocacy and law centers within the broader context of the juvenile justice system?
- In your opinion, how effective are juvenile justice agencies?

For an online search of the role of the juvenile court, students should use a search engine and enter the following keywords:

"Juvenile Court"

"Juvenile Judges"

Chapter 8. Institutional Corrections for Juveniles

Recommended Web Sites

The following Web sites contain information about the role of juvenile corrections in the juvenile justice system.

American Bar Association Juvenile Justice Center: http://www.abanet.org/crimjust/
   juvjus/home.html
Corrections Connection: http://www.corrections.com/links/viewlinks.asp?Cat=30
Juvenile Information Network: http://www.juvenilenet.org/
Redcliff Ascent Wilderness Treatment Program (Idaho): http://www.redcliffascent
   .com/
Juvenile Boot Camps: http://juvenile-boot-camps.com/
Texas Youth Commission: http://www.tyc.state.tx.us/

Web Exercise

Using this chapter's recommended Internet sites, conduct an online investigation of the role of juvenile corrections.

- What role does rehabilitation play in the stated goals and objectives of
  juvenile corrections policy makers?
- To what extent are juvenile correctional programs affiliated with adult
  correctional systems?
- How prevalent are alternative correctional programs?

For an online search of the role of juvenile corrections in the juvenile
justice system, students should use a search engine and enter the following
keywords:

"Juvenile Corrections"

"Wilderness Programs"

Chapter 9. Juvenile
Probation, Parole, and Aftercare

Recommended Web Sites

The following Web sites investigate the subject of juvenile probation,
parole, and aftercare.

American Probation and Parole Association: http://www.appa-net.org/
Colorado Juvenile Parole Board: http://www.cdhs.state.co.us/OPI/jpboard/
Juvenile Justice Evaluation Center (Aftercare): http://www.jrsa.org/jjec/programs/
   aftercare/
Pennsylvania Council of Chief Probation Officers: http://www.pachiefprobationofficers
   .org/
Texas Juvenile Probation Commission: http://www.tjpc.state.tx.us/

Web Exercise

Using this chapter's recommended Internet sites, conduct an online investigation of juvenile probation, parole, and aftercare.

- How do probation, parole, and aftercare programs differ nationally? In what ways are they similar?
- What are some of the common roles of probation and parole officers?
- Which jurisdictions do you consider to be the best organized and managed systems?

For an online search of probation, parole, and aftercare, students should use a search engine and enter the following keywords:

"Juvenile Aftercare"

"Juvenile Probation"

Chapter 10. Community-Based Juvenile Programs

Recommended Web Sites

The following Web sites investigate the subject of community-based juvenile programs.

Communities in Schools: http://www.cisnet.org/
Families, Career, and Community Leaders of America: http://www.fcclainc.org/
Head Start Bureau: http://www.acf.hhs.gov/programs/hsb/
National Center for Conflict Resolution Education: http://www.nccre.org/
Outward Bound USA: http://www.outwardbound.org/

Web Exercise

Using this chapter's recommended Internet sites, conduct an online investigation of community-based juvenile programs and organizations.

- To what extent are community-based programs and organizations linked to juvenile courts and the juvenile correctional system? How closely *should* they be linked?
- What are some of the common features of community-based programs and organizations? What are some of the differences?
- Which programs and organizations seem to be the most proactive in their approaches to prevention and treatment?

For an online search of community-based juvenile programs, students should use a search engine and enter the following keywords:

"Delinquency Prevention"

"Delinquency Treatment"

Chapter 11. Antisocial Youth Culture: The Case of Youth Gangs

Recommended Web Sites

The following Web sites investigate the subject of youth gangs.

Gangs in Los Angeles County: http://www.streetgangs.com/
National Alliance of Gang Investigators Associations: http://www.nagia.org/
National Gang Crime Research Center: http://www.ngcrc.com/
National Major Gang Task Force: http://www.nmgtf.org/
National Youth Gang Center: http://www.iir.com/nygc/

Web Exercise

Using this chapter's recommended Internet sites, conduct an online investigation of youth gangs.

- What kind of resources exist to conduct research for future policy initiatives on youth gangs?
- In what ways have national gang centers helped in our understanding of the gang phenomenon?
- Who should be responsible for monitoring gang-related activity?

For an online search of youth gangs and antisocial lifestyles, students should use a search engine and enter the following keywords:

"Street Gang"

"Youth Gang"

Chapter 12. Global Perspectives: Juvenile Justice in an International Context

Recommended Web Sites

The following Web sites illustrate the different approaches toward juvenile justice found in other countries.

Amnesty International: http://www.amnesty.org

Child Rights Information Network: http://www.crin.org

Human Rights Watch: http://hrw.org

United Nations Children's Fund (UNICEF): http://www.unicef.org

United Nations Educational, Scientific, and Cultural Organization (UNESCO):
     http://www.unesco.org

Web Exercise

Using this chapter's recommended Internet sites, conduct an online investigation of international perspectives of juvenile justice process.

- In what way is juvenile justice an international issue?
- From a global context, how is juvenile justice an international human rights issue?
- What impact do you think international children's rights organizations have on the juvenile justice practices of individual countries?

For an online search of international perspectives of juvenile justice process, students should use a search engine and enter the following keywords:

> "International Children's Rights"

> "International Juvenile Justice"

Note

1. Association for Pre- & Perinatal Psychology and Health.

Index

About the Author

Gus Martin, JD, PhD, is Associate Professor of Public Administration & Public Policy at California State University, Dominguez Hills, where he is chair of the Department of Public Administration & Public Policy and coordinator of the Criminal Justice Administration program. He has also served on the faculty of the Graduate School of Public and International Affairs, University of Pittsburgh, where he was an Administration of Justice professor. His research and professional interests are juvenile justice, terrorism and extremism, administration of justice, and fair housing. He has served as a panelist for university and community symposia and interviews on the subjects of administration of justice, terrorism, and fair housing. He has also been a consultant to government and private agencies. Prior to joining academia, he was a legislative assistant to Congressman Charles B. Rangel of New York and Special Counsel to the Attorney General of the U.S. Virgin Islands. In addition, he served as managing attorney for the Fair Housing Partnership of Greater Pittsburgh, where he was also director of a program created under a federal consent decree to desegregate public and assisted housing.

CENTURY

of

CHANGE

Europe from 1789 to 1918

E. Alyn Mitchner

R. Joanne Tuffs

Reidmore Books

ACKNOWLEDGEMENTS

Reidmore Books wishes to thank the following people for their insights and support in the development of this textbook.

Historical Reviewers

Dr. Bonar A. (Sandy) Gow, Associate Professor,
Department of History, Concordia University College of Alberta

Dr. A.B. Pernal, Professor and Department Chair,
Department of History, Brandon University

Dr. U. Trumpener, Professor Emeritus,
Department of History, University of Alberta

Teacher Reviewers

Bill Bowie
Westwood Community High School
Fort McMurray, AB

Philip LaGrandeur
Ecole Secondaire Beaumont Composite High School
Beaumont, AB

Victor Lehman
Spruce Grove Composite High School
Spruce Grove, AB

Dennis Nosyk
New Sarepta Community High School
New Sarepta, AB

Brian K. Tough
Memorial Composite High School
Stony Plain, AB

M. Craig Wallace
Strathcona Composite High School
Edmonton, AB

Don Zech
Palliser Regional School Division
Lethbridge, AB

ABOUT THE AUTHORS

E. Alyn Mitchner holds a Bachelor of Educatio Bachelor of Arts, and a PhD in History. From 1980 until retirement in 1996, Dr. Mitchner was the Director of t International Baccalaureate Program at Harry Ainl Composite High School in Edmonton. He taught the th ory of knowledge and history for grades 10 through 12.

R. Joanne Tuffs has a Bachelor of Arts, majoring in h tory, and a Bachelor of Education. She became the c riculum coordinator for the International Baccalaurea Program at Harry Ainlay Composite High School in 19 She also teaches the theory of knowledge and history grades 10 through 12.

Canadian Cataloguing in Publication Data
Mitchner, E.A.
          Century of change
ISBN 1-895073-87-1
1. Europe—History—1789-1900. 2. Europe—History—1871-1918
Tuffs, R. Joanne (Renee Joanne), 1944- II. Title.
D299.M57 1997   940.2'8   C96-910875-3

Reidmore Books Inc.
1200, 10109 – 106 Street
Edmonton, AB   T5J 3L7
ph. (403) 424-4420
fax (403) 441-9919
toll-free 1-800-661-2859
http://www.reidmore.com
printed and bound in Canada

Prologue

*H*istory is the record of the human past. It is filled with heroes and villains, changes and conflicts, victories and defeats. Because of our unique ability to store and retrieve knowledge, history is a valuable tool for understanding how we came to be here and where we may be going. Human experience need not be repeated. The wheel does not have to be re-invented every generation. From our understanding of the past we can continue to evolve in every aspect of human endeavour. As such, history is not only interesting and instructive but useful.

History is so vast that few writers ever attempt to relate the broad picture. Most works are surveys of the growth and development of societies along a specific timeline. Most students of history delve into narrower topics such as political, economic, social, military, or religious histories. Before one can do justice to the in-depth study of a specific field, one needs to know the overall pattern of events.

Thus, this book is an introductory survey of the major forces involved in the consolidation of Europe from about 1789 to 1918. Europe was chosen as a focus because, in the nineteenth century, many of the major decisions that affected the world's population were made in Europe. European nations were in the process of changing from agricultural-village societies to industrial-urban societies, giving them a degree of global dominance.

The nineteenth century was one of transformation. All of society's institutions were changed as a result of INDUSTRIALIZATION. The Industrial Revolution that began in the coal fields of England in the mid-eighteenth century mechanized industry and created the first of the industrial-urban nations. Every aspect of life and the relationships between individuals and their nations was altered. By the end of the century, this metamorphosis had spread beyond Europe to Japan, the United States, and Canada.

When machines took over the daily farm labour, surplus workers streamed into cities in search of a better life. London, Paris, Vienna, and Rome became thriving cultural islands where philosophers and artists explored innovative ideas expressed in a variety of forms. New political, economic, and social IDEOLOGIES became hotly debated.

Cities provided the background for political movements that sought to give individuals a role in government and a share in the nation's wealth. The French Revolution introduced the ideas of liberty, equality, and fraternity to rival absolute monarchies. Reformers and intellectuals attempted to rally mass support among the people by awakening them to the advantages of these new concepts. The forces of NATIONALISM born during the French Revolution proved both constructive and destructive.

Industrial growth caused nation-states to have an

insatiable appetite for human and physical resources. When Europe's resources began to run out, the major powers embarked on an era of IMPERIALISM. The imperial age of the late nineteenth century also catered to the pressures of missionary activity, and the need to find new markets for surplus goods and a place to settle unwanted populations. The "scramble for Africa" is a good example of the global power held by Europe. Because none could withstand a determined industrial nation, by the end of the century, few places on earth did not come under the influence of an industrial power.

As spheres of influence expanded, competition and tension grew among industrial powers. Leaders such as Prince Metternich and Chancellor Bismarck managed to keep pressures to go to war at bay for a time. However, they ultimately could not prevent the INTERNATIONAL CONFLICT that developed in the early twentieth century. World War I would bring an end to the century of peace.

To assist in your study of these topics, this book provides a number of learning aids. Each chapter begins

with a Timeline so that you can place important events in proper sequence and draw some conclusions about them. Focus Questions will help you to organize the main concepts of the chapter. Questions, Analysis, and Activities at the ends of chapters will help you to remember what you have read, as well as give you practise in critical and creative thinking.

Sidebars provide more information about historical people, events, and ideas. The Glossary at the back of the book will help you to understand new terms that are used by historians, politicians, philosophers, artists, and scientists. You can use the Index to look up particular subjects found in this book.

In several chapters, you will find Historical Analysis activities. Some present historical documents that you are asked to interpret. Some ask you to analyze differing points of view on a particular event.

The skills you develop by using this book will help you to analyze new historical information and increase your understanding of the nature of humankind and the evolution of society.

UNIT I
Enlightenment Leads to Revolution

Overview

The bloody events of the French Revolution (1789-1799) resounded throughout Europe. Even today we still debate many of the principles upon which the revolution was founded. The French threw off their monarchical system of government and replaced it with a republic dedicated to individual rights and equality. The forces of change were held in check only by the French Army, which took over the government of France during the Napoleonic Period (1799-1815).

The French Revolution was touched off by a financial crisis that forced the king to call the Estates General together to find a solution. Revolutionaries, whose ideas had been worked out and perfected during the Enlightenment, used the meetings to propose sweeping changes in all the institutions of the state. Individual rights and political, social, and legal equality of all became popular slogans. The monarchy was abolished and replaced by the first of France's republics. The new republic, however, turned out to be even more authoritarian than the regime it replaced.

When Napoleon became emperor of France, his French armies set out to conquer Europe. At the same time, they spread the ideas of the French Revolution to other empires and states with far reaching results. The nation soon replaced the monarchy as the primary focus of political loyalty. Attempts to root out these ideas by force all proved to be failures.

The defeat of Napoleon's forces in 1815 provided the opportunity for the other powers to meet in Vienna to restructure the political boundaries of Europe, preserving as much as possible the old borders. The Congress of Vienna also decided to create larger nations by grouping smaller states together so as to limit further French expansion. The powers agreed that they would work together to eliminate any chance of another nation taking control of Europe. Through the Quadruple Alliance, Britain, Russia, Prussia, and Austria pledged to maintain the status quo and to take joint action against any revolutionary movements.

*This painting is called "The Angelus," by Jean François Millet (1814-1875).
During feudal times the life of serfs was extremely hard. Only after the lord of the
manor had received his harvest could the peasants go on the land and glean the
leavings. The peasants put their hope in the Church and its promise of reward in
heaven. Millet captures their character at dusk as the Angelus bell rings from the
cathedral in the background. This bell is the signal to say the Angelus,
a prayer in memory of Christ assuming human form.*

Chapter 1
The Enlightenment

FOCUS ON:

❀

The structure of French society during the 17th and 18th centuries,
and the inequities that resulted from rigid class stratification;

❀

The ideas promoted by French *philosophes* which encouraged societal change;

❀

An analysis of the ideologies that promise to bring society
to a state of utopia.

During the sixteenth and seventeenth centuries, the work of scientists such as Copernicus, Galileo, and Newton resulted in a vision of a structured, orderly, and finite universe that operated independently of divine authority. This **Age of Reason**, as it came to be known, was skeptical of tradition and believed that natural law that had been revealed through science could be applied to the organization of society. European civilization would advance as never before and succeeding generations would enjoy much better living conditions as a result of the political, economic, and social changes that would evolve once society was reorganized according to natural law.

At the beginning of the eighteenth century, a number of signs indicated that Europe was on the threshold of a new era. Towns and cities were growing both in size and number, the power of merchants and lawyers expanded, and trade increased. Improvements in transportation and communication supported these urban developments. In addition there were substantial changes in rural areas. Population growth was considerable, chiefly as a result of improvements in medicine and in agriculture. Two medical advances were the smallpox vaccination and improvements in sanitation. In agriculture, mechanized planting and cultivation, crop rotation, and the use of fertilizer all contributed to increased yields of grain and thus greater food supplies.

~ Feudalism ~
Feudalism was the political-economic organization established during the medieval times. Lords (owners of large estates) offered protection to individuals in exchange for services such as field or road work and a variety of taxes.

Peasant Lifestyle during the Enlightenment

Despite the beginnings of an awareness that "man" shared common political and economic aspirations regardless of class, eighteenth century society exhibited vast differences in life style. Peasants, illiterate and segregated from the upper classes by social conventions, were completely unaware of enlightenment ideas. They still lived in single-room huts with a thatched roof or, in areas of northern Europe, in a wooden cottage designed to give a little more protection against the wind and the cold.

Peasants owned no more than two sets of clothes and a pair of wooden shoes for use in winter, going barefoot in summer. Throughout the year they were clothed in tatters with little to protect them from the elements. Clothing was washed only two or three times a year, a measure that allowed the garments to last longer. Vegetable soup, eggs, cheese, and a heavy bread made from rye or oat flour provided the mainstay of their diet. Occasionally some meat or fish or a bread made from wheat was added as a special treat.

Although a strong bond existed in most families, violence and vulgar, brutal behaviour was common. Drunkenness provided a frequent respite from the harsh reality of every day life. The peasants maintained their religious beliefs primarily out of hope for a better existence in the afterlife.

Lifestyle of the Upper Classes of the Enlightenment

The nobility lived a life of excess in dress, food, entertainment, and housing. Fashion took on an importance comparable to that which it had enjoyed during the Renaissance. Men and women wore powdered wigs. Men wore velvet waistcoats over silk shirts trimmed in lace, knee breeches of leather or finely dyed fabric, and silk stockings. On their feet they wore a high-heeled shoe. Women wore elaborate gowns which fitted tightly at the bodice and voluminous skirts over a large, hooped

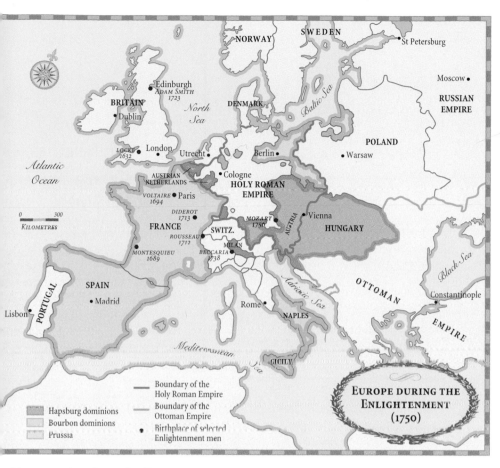

Ideas coming from the Enlightenment set the boundaries for change in Europe. Some of the greatest thinkers of the time came from France and Britain.

By the end of the eighteenth century men's and women's fashions had become ornate and impractical. Women wore hooped dresses and high coiffures. Men wore velvet waistcoats, silk shirts, knee breeches, and silk stockings.

crinoline. In order to fit her dress properly, a whalebone corset was laced onto the lady by her maid. Bathing was infrequent and perfume took the place of soap and water. Often, a beauty mark was painted on a lady's face and she carried a small but elegant fan.

Food for the nobility was plentiful. A dinner consisted of several courses, including meat, and ended with fruit and cheese. Each course was accompanied by wine.

Manners were elegant, demonstrated in dances such as the minuet and in the elaborate rituals at court or in the salons. This superficial behaviour concealed a decline in morality as the nobility felt itself freed from the constraints of traditional religious teachings regarding behaviour. Adultery was common and mistresses were paraded publicly. It was now just as common for a wife to take a lover as in the past it had been acceptable for the husband. Prostitution was acknowledged and in some cases even defended.

Enlightened Philosophy

The intellectual reasoning that prompted the Enlightenment originated in England in the late seventeenth century. Newton's application of mathematics to the material world revealed an orderly and predictable universal structure. If one could discover natural laws by the use of reason, surely reason could also be applied to politics, the organization of society, and perhaps to religion.

The English philosopher John Locke (1632–1704) took the first step in systematically investigating the relationship between the citizen and ruler in *Two Treatises of Civil Government* (1690). In Locke's view human nature was essentially good and possessed natural rights, such as individual liberty, the right to property, and the right to life. Locke then formulated his theory of the organization of society in which individuals entered into a **Social Contract** with the sovereign power in the community. Thus government holds power by permission of its citizens and maintains that power as long as government is conducted in the best interests of the people. If the sovereign power violates the rights of the citizens, its authority to rule is lost—furthermore, it could legitimately be overthrown. Locke's justification of rebellion in the interests of maintaining proper government sanctioned the English rebellion against James II, known as the Glorious Revolution (1688–1689).

Perhaps a more significant contribution to the Enlightenment was Locke's treatise on the nature of knowledge which he outlined in his *Essay Concerning Human Understanding* (1690). Locke theorized that the human mind at birth is a blank slate, or *tabula rasa*. It is only when one perceives the natural world and experiences sensory perceptions that the mind begins to register ideas. The child's simple ideas will then be forged into complex ideas by the application of reason. Since a person's mind is a blank slate at birth, he or she does not possess any innate sense of right or wrong and will simply learn moral values by the experience of pain or pleasure. A good life, according to Locke, is one filled with pleasure, and ethical acts produce the greatest pleasure. Locke believed that the pursuit of happiness was one of humanity's primary goals.

With regard to religion, Locke believed that God established divine laws that could be discovered by reasoning. It was morally wrong to disobey God's laws and, in fact, Christian morality would contribute substantially to humanity's happiness here on earth. Locke's writings were

Eighteenth Century Tourism

Improvements in transportation led to a tremendous increase in travel during the eighteenth century among the upper classes. Tourism began as a form of entertainment for the wealthy. London, Venice, Rome, and, especially, Paris were desirable tourist destinations. Travel books were published and the Venetians introduced the picture postcard. Canaletto painted numerous Venetian scenes which were reproduced for the tourist. They are still sold today as postcards or posters.

widely read during the eighteenth century in France and had considerable influence on the French ***philosophes***, Voltaire, Rousseau, Montesquieu, and Diderot. A fundamental change in human relationships was in the making.

While seventeenth century innovations in science and culture had been dominated by England, the eighteenth century belonged to France. The writings of French *philosophes* challenged accepted views of religion, government, economics, and the very nature of humanity. Writing was now accepted as a profession and the ideas of the *philosophes* were discussed in the clubs and salons of France. The debate included members of the bourgeoisie and "enlightened" aristocrats who saw the need for reform.

The *philosophes* presented a view that fundamentally changed the perception of society. By defining humanity's potential as almost unlimited, and by suggesting the universality of individual rights, they challenged the existing social structure. They were optimistic and felt that progress was inevitable, with each new generation improving its **standard of living** as human nature evolved toward perfection. They suggested that the changes they proposed applied to everyone; their cause was identified with all of humanity. Essentially, the *philosophes* put forward a platform which struck at the heart of the institutions of the Old Regime. Their ideas turned the most dynamic social group in France into hostile critics of the monarchy, the Church, and authority of any sort.

In 1751 the first volume of the *Encyclopédie*, or *Dictionnaire Raisonné des Sciences, des Arts et des Métiers*, was published. It was a major work of the French Enlightenment. By 1775 the encyclopedia had grown to twenty-eight massive volumes in which was compiled, in alphabetical order, writings on all of the important questions of the day by the most famous *philosophes* of the day such as Voltaire, Rousseau, and Montesquieu. It was an advocate of reason, skepticism, and was critical of the Old Regime. The editor, Denis Diderot (1713–1784), suffered continual attacks by both Church and government.

John Locke believed in the underlying goodness of man. His philosophical ideas on human understanding and social organization caused a revolution in thinking in which philosophes began to question the feudal social structure.

uthorities while he laboured to omplete the task. Upon comletion it was a commendable ecord of those champions of eason and liberty who domiated the intellectual communiy of eighteenth century France.

More than 25 000 sets of the *ncyclopédie* were sold. While ne bourgeoisie accounted for nany sales, the books were read videly among the privileged rders of the clergy and the obility. In 1780 a five-volume upplement and two-volume ndex were printed. In addition, bout half of the volumes were old outside of France. One set vas purchased by Catherine the reat of Russia, who prided herelf on intellectual pursuits, as id Frederick the Great of russia, another reader of the olumes.

ultural Capital f Europe

rance, throughout the eighteenth century, was the culural capital of Europe. French became an international nguage and was designated as the language of diplomacy. rench food, clothing, customs, and entertainment were mulated in upper class society throughout Europe. With population of 22 million in 1750, France was by far the ost populous of European countries. In comparison to ther areas of Europe, the standard of living in France was ery good. Social inequities existed but it was easier to urchase a noble title in France than elsewhere and many embers of the bourgeoisie had attained great wealth. The ork of the *philosophes* seems to have been instrumental laying a very sound foundation for the momentous nange that would occur in 1789.

Writing throughout eighteenth century France was domated by Voltaire, Montesquieu, and Rousseau. These three dividuals were literary geniuses who shared the view that ocial organization could be improved, but they differed

widely on the nature of the solution. Charles de Secondat, Baron de la Brède et de Montesquieu (1689–1755), was a noble from Bordeaux who trained as a lawyer. He was president of the **Parlement** of Bordeaux for ten years before selling the office in 1726. Freed from that obligation, he set out on extensive European travels in the interests of studying social and political institutions. He was most influenced by his experiences in England, where he studied the writings of John Locke and examined first hand the workings of the English Parliament.

In 1748 Montesquieu published his monumental work on political systems, *De l'esprit des lois (The Spirit of the Laws)*. Montesquieu's analysis of government derived from his belief that, since humanity is a part of nature, social and political organization must be intricately connected to climate and geography. He identified a direct relationship between the form of government and the size and climate of the area involved. Thus, for example, despotism was the appropriate form of government for a large area with a hot climate. A despotic government was the only form of government that could control distant outlying areas where local rulers aspired to govern.

On the other hand, republics (which might be democratic or aristocratic) would work only in small areas such as city states, preferably those with cold climates. Republican government demanded the assembly of influential members of society in decision making. Hence, Montesquieu felt that only in small areas would this assembly be practical.

In between were the moderate-sized regions which lent themselves to government by a limited monarchy. The monarch must command the respect of his subjects and this was possible through the demonstration of honourable behaviour. This type of government was comparable to that

Deism

of England, and Montesquieu's evaluation of the English parliamentary system was very favourable. He expressed the view that France could improve its government by emulating some of the characteristics of the English system.

The characteristics that Montesquieu most admired in the English system were the establishment of a constitution and the concept of **separation of powers** which, in turn, introduced checks and balances. The constitution provided limits to the power of the monarch. Separation of power, in Montesquieu's view, meant that power would be divided between the monarch and numerous other groups such as the *parlements*, the landed aristocracy, the bourgeois officials, and perhaps even the Church. Thus, absolute power would be abandoned in the interests of tempering the monarch's authority by the will of all those citizens who held power and influence. Common persons were considered unfit for government and their participation would never be allowed.

In addition, Montesquieu suggested the division of the responsibilities of government into

Deism originated in England as a result of the Newtonian explanation of the universe and John Locke's application of Newton's ideas to society. The first clearest expression of Deism was made by John Toland in a work titled *Christianity Not Mysterious* (1696). The book was a direct attack on Christianity and its emphasis on the authority of the Church and the revelation of Christian principles through Church dogma and miracles. Matthew Tindal's *Christianity as Old as the Creation* (1730) is the most complete statement on Deism; frequently it is called "the Deist's Bible." According to Deist thought, God created the world, but once His work was completed, He stepped aside and allowed it to operate according to the natural laws that control the universe. Thus, in a mechanistic world, human reason could discover the essence of Christianity and humanity was responsible for a personal communion with God and the faithful pursuit of Christian morals. As well as believing that God did not intervene in the lives of people, the Deists believed that religious ceremony was useless because God could not be encouraged to interfere with the natural order of the universe at the request of an individual. Deists completely rejected predestination and believed that through the exercise of free will, people would choose good over evil in the interests of attaining salvation.

Catholic Church said it was heretical condemnation of Christianity because it expressed the view of Deist philosophy. This philosophy had become popular among the English intellectuals during the scientific revolution and was, in fact, reflected in Montesquieu's writing. However, the increasingly influential French *philosophes* branded Montesquieu a conservative for his defence of aristocratic superiority and his superficial analysis of government as it related to nature. Despite this criticism, *The Spirit of the Laws* stood as the greatest book of enlightenment France. It was unique in its attempt to analyze comparative governments systematically and to relate the source of government institutions to natural phenomena. It introduced a spirit of inquiry invaluable in extending the philosophical pursuits of enlightenment society.

Voltaire

François Marie Arouet de Voltaire (1694–1778) is considered the best critic of the Enlightenment and the leading exponent in France of reason and its relationship to society. Bourgeois in origin, he was christened François Marie Arouet, but took

executive, legislative, and judicial functions. He believed that this division of power would allow balance in government to be maintained as one branch would provide a check on the others. When the American constitution was being written, this principle was given priority. The American system of government more than any other, illustrates Montesquieu's vision of political organization.

Montesquieu's work was widely criticized. The Roman

the pen name Voltaire. Brilliant and incisive writing flowed from his pen. His published attacks on the aristocracy and government officials resulted in imprisonment in the Bastille, followed by exile in England from 1726 to 1729. During those three years, he studied the works of Isaac Newton and John Locke. He published his analysis of their ideas in a book titled *Letters on the English*.

Voltaire's primary focus was individual liberty. He was

hampion of individual free-
oms, especially those of speech
nd religion. Throughout his life-
me, he fought relentlessly in
upport of liberty which he sug-
ested was only fully possible if
eople would develop and prac-
se tolerance. His most famous
axim is probably that which
elates to intellectual freedom in
hich he says, "I may not agree
ith a word that you say, but I
ill defend to the death your
ght to say it."

Voltaire was an enthusiastic
roponent of Deism. He saw in
us rational approach to spiritu-
ity a way of maintaining belief
God without the tyranny of
aditional church doctrine. His
ritings lashed out at the Church
r the torture and persecution
lministered to those who criti-
zed its dogma.

Voltaire's attention was drawn
a particularly infamous case
at occurred in 1762 when a
rotestant, Jean Calas, was tor-
red to death. Calas had been
ought before court on a false
arge of murdering his eldest
n because he was considering
nversion to Catholicism. Calas

*François Marie Arouet de Voltaire
was one of the principle figures in the
French Enlightenment. Using irony and wit
as a weapon, Voltaire proved the pen more
powerful than the sword in such works as*
Candide, *a play so farcical that it would have
been foolish to prosecute the author. Yet the
ideas of* Candide *undermined the
authority of both church and state.*

published. In this brilliant satire,
Voltaire created an innocent,
optimistic young man whose
adventures bring him into contact with political corruption,
religious abuse, the injustice and
barbarity of war, and all of the
other vices that Voltaire identified in the Old Regime. In exag-
gerated parody, he struck out at
the optimistic attitude of the
Enlightenment period which
claimed that "all was for the
best in the best of all possible
worlds."

Rousseau

Jean-Jacques Rousseau (1712–
1778) proved to be the most radical as well as the most controversial Enlightenment writer. He
was born into poverty in Geneva, ran away from home at sixteen, and achieved little success
in his personal life, unable to
establish stability in family life,
social life, or employment. He
suffered such economic instability that he relinquished all five of
his own children to foundling
homes.

Rousseau did not accept the
rational approach of the Enlight-

as found guilty and executed by being broken on the
heel, an excruciating punishment reserved for the lower
asses. (An aristocrat would have been beheaded.) In his
vestigation, Voltaire discovered that Calas had been con-
cted only on the strength of rumours. For three years
oltaire worked tirelessly to clear the name of Jean Calas
hom he believed to have been the victim of anti-Protes-
ntism in the courts. He was eventually successful. Voltaire
horred this sort of injustice, the direct result of religious
ranny that was in his view one of the gravest forms of
tolerance. "Crush the infamous thing" became his motto
response to the tyranny of the Church.
In 1759, Voltaire's most famous work, *Candide*, was

enment period with the same fervour as the other
philosophes. Instead he introduced the idea of following our
emotions. Impulse and spontaneity, suggested Rousseau,
are more important in discovering truth than critical
thought.

Rousseau believed that "man is born free, and is everywhere in chains." Thus the nature of social organization
inhibits individuals and robs them of the freedom which is
their inherent right. At the root of this bondage, according
to Rousseau, was the ownership of private property.
Rousseau claimed that private ownership of property introduced an element of inequality that resulted in hardship and
misery for those denied property. Greed and oppression

Jean-Jacques Rousseau championed the underclasses. His writings explored the causes of poverty and the plight of the poor. He believed that man's sorry condition was a result of the creation of private property, which divided society between rich and poor.

resulted from those who accumulated property; in turn, they destroyed the rights of others. The most aggressive members of the community would attain the control of property. They would usurp the rights of those weaker members and all of them would then live like prisoners. The stronger members of society would be prisoners of their own greed while the weaker ones would be prisoners of those in control of the property.

Rousseau believed that the solution to this problem came out of the relationship of people with nature. He originated the idea of the **noble savage**, one who lived free and innocent in the wilds of nature but became corrupted and imprisoned by the tyranny of civilization. While it was not practical to return to this idyllic state of nature, it was possible to emulate it by structuring a new community that held property communally and required its members to surrender completely to the power of the community. A new "social contract" would thus be forged which would allow the equality of all members and would encourage moral behaviour from all of its members. Such was the theory put forward by Rousseau in his book, *Du contrat social, (The Social Contract)*, published in 1762. Unlike other Enlightenment writers, Rousseau was lobbying for the rights of the masses. His work suggests that he favoured equality rather than liberty.

Power in Rousseau's revolutionary community would emanate from the common good of society or the characteristic which he dubbed the **General Will**. This general will was the combined will of community members, who were now equal and who subordinated their individual desires to the will of the group. The general will would allow for increased freedom in the sense that an individual would have increased power as a member of the larger group.

While it was possible that no every member would favour pa ticular actions, the commo interest of the group must pre vail.

While Rousseau hoped tha individuals would experience greater sense of belonging in society modelled on this con cept, there was also the potenti for the general will to be used fo dictatorial purposes as the ind vidual was subsumed within th state.

In addition to writings direc ed specifically at political ar social organization, Roussea wrote novels that had significar influence on the thoughts ar behaviour of the upper classe In *Emile*, he described an ed cational program designed lead a young student through variety of experiences in whic he would learn through observ tion and participation all th was important in life. The chi would be in the company of tutor for the duration of his ed cation. Rather than being su jected to a traditional education in which the tutor wou structure a program of instruction based on books and stri discipline, the child would learn first hand by experienci nature. He would not learn to read until he was mature ar he would be exposed to a diverse collection of materials order to develop both the mind and the body. While the co cept was admirable in its pursuit of developing a Rena sance person schooled in all areas of life, it was complet ly impractical. Most students would be unable to hire a tut for their constant companion, or, if they could, years supervision by this tutor would produce a dependence th inhibits academic maturity.

While *Emile* did not produce a revolution in educatic it did raise questions about the nature of education ar encouraged a movement that experimented with altern tive methods of instruction. Rousseau's *Emile* has also be

The Petit Trianon was built at great cost in the gardens of Versailles. This functioning model of an Austrian village was designed to make young Queen Antoinette feel more comfortable away from her Austrian homeland.

Enlightened Economics

In economics, as in politics, the Enlightenment introduced new and revolutionary ideas. France had constructed its economic system on the principles of mercantilism. Louis XIV's finance minister, Jean Colbert, had strengthened the government's hold on the economy by regulating the production of the guilds; providing tax exemptions and subsidies to industries such as silk, tapestries, and glassware; and by preventing the export of foodstuffs in order to keep food prices reasonable.

During the eighteenth century, a group of French economic theorists called *physiocrats* developed the idea that government should let business operate without interference. François Quesnay (1694–1774), the founder of physiocracy, wrote a number of articles for Diderot's *Encyclopédie* describing what he called the **laissez-faire** ("leave alone") laws of economics. This philosophy contended that government regulation interfered with the natural operation of business. Quesnay and the physiocrats believed that the only source of wealth was land, the basis of agricultural production. Thus if government stepped aside and allowed the natural interchange between land and the economy

edited with the romantic adventures undertaken by some the aristocracy in their attempts to experience nature first nd. For example, Marie Antoinette ordered the building a little village on the grounds at Versailles, the Petit Tri- on, where she and her ladies-in-waiting could dress as lk maids and play at imitating a peasant's life.

to occur, the wealth of the nation would increase. Taxes should be imposed on the revenue from land and trade should be freed from government regulation. Taxes imposed on trade simply hindered the natural accumulation of wealth.

Adam Smith, a Scottish academic,
developed a theoretical economic system based on
private enterprise and freedom
from government control.

Changes to the Justice System

nlightenment thought raised questions about the nature of the justice system of the time. The study of natural laws suggested a more humane approach to the administration of justice. Cesare Beccaria (1738–1794) wrote his *Essay on Crimes and Punishments* (1764) in which he identified new directions in the system of criminal law. He argued that the punishment for a crime must be certain but it must also be just. Punishment must have as its goal rehabilitation and the prevention of repeated crimes. He viewed torture as barbaric and, like capital punishment, it should be abandoned for a more appropriate and humane method. His writing was influential. In 1816 Pope Pius VII issued a bull, or decree, banning torture in all Catholic countries. However the practice continues in some areas even today as does the use of capital punishment.

Adam Smith:
Laissez-Faire Economics

Adam Smith (1723–1790), a Scot who was influenced by the economic doctrine formulated by physiocrats, published the definitive work on *laissez-faire* economics in 1776. Titled *An Inquiry into the Nature and Causes of the Wealth of Nations*, it revolutionized economic systems in the western world. Smith disagreed that all wealth derived from the land and argued that labour—whether of tradesmen, agricultural workers, or those engaged in the exchange of services—produced wealth. Business must be free from government interference in order to achieve increased production and contribute to the wealth of the nation as a whole. In Smith's view, private property was the keystone of the system. Only when the owner was allowed the freedom to operate his land as he saw fit could he develop its true potential.

While the old mercantilist theory established government as all powerful, the *laissez-faire* system required individual freedom. Operating out of self-interest, the individual would ultimately contribute to the increase wealth of the community. Thus an artisan would strive produce the best possible product knowing that he or s was in competition with other individuals who were off ing similar items for sale. Prices would be maintained the correct ratio of the number of goods being offered f sale to the demand for those goods. Ultimately, then, t consumer ruled in the marketplace. The willingness lack thereof to buy a good determined the price of th good. The absence of government regulation enhanced competition and self-interest would establish a system th operated in the best interests of both producer and co sumer. The marketplace would operate just as though "invisible hand," in his phrase, guided it to greater weal

Smith had very definite ideas about the role of gove ment in a *laissez-faire* economy. It must provide for t defence of the nation, the protection of citizens and th property, and those essential public services in which p vate business would be unlikely to engage. An example such an essential public service is education which Sm viewed as unprofitable from a business standpoint b essential to the progress of the nation.

Catherine the Great of Russia corresponded with Voltaire and gave financial support to the publication of the Encyclopédic. *Although enlightened monarchs read and may have been swayed by the writings of the* philosophes, *they were generally unsuccessful in making reforms because of opposition from their aristocracies.*

alon Society during ie Enlightenment

iring the eighteenth century, creased literacy among the)per classes led to a desire to scuss the ideas in the books id pamphlets of the day. A new ienomenon was born—the Ion. Wealthy men and, most ten, women held regular and equent social gatherings for e express purpose of intellec- al discussion. Paris was the ntre of salon society. Salons ere usually held in the drawing om or reception area of an dividual who wanted to be volved in the social milieu of e day. Witty conversation pre- iled. The women who domi- ted the salon scene wielded nsiderable political influence d some became famous.

Madame Geoffrin was one of e hostesses who held salons r writers and artists from 1750 about 1775. She was well con- cted to both government offi- ils and influential members of the upper classes and thus ovided opportunities which were otherwise unavailable the bourgeois purveyors of culture. When she discov- ed that artists and philosophers did not associate ami- ly with men of politics, she segregated dinners. The ednesday dinners were the most lively as this was the ening set aside for the *philosophes*. When Diderot was orking on the *Encyclopédie*, Mme Geoffrin donated 0 000 livres to the project. She was a true philanthropist. e purchased numerous works of art and established nsions for some of her favourite writers.

Madame de Staël, a wealthy baroness and writer and a oman of great intelligence and charm, was perhaps the ost famous salon host. Until the French Revolution, her lon was the centre of political discussion in Paris. After e Revolution and exile in England, she returned to ance and reestablished her salon (1802). Napoleon dis- ed her so she lived in Germany for a time. She led a

fascinating life and knew all of the influential people of her day. She published many works and coined the word *Romanticism*.

Enlightened Despotism– Catherine the Great

During the eighteenth century, some of Europe's absolute mon- archs adopted the ideas of the *philosophes*. While this did not mean that they were interested in sharing power with their citizens, it did generally suggest some aca- demic interest in reform. These rulers were called enlightened despots. In Russia, Catherine the Great (1729–1796) corresponded with Voltaire and gave financial support to the publication of the *Encyclopédie*. She read many Enlightenment writings includ- ing Beccaria's *Of Crimes and Punishments* and the works of Locke, Montesquieu, Voltaire, and much of the *Encyclopédie*.

Catherine drew extensively on all of these works in writing up her "Instruction" for the legislative commission of 1767, a body that was charged with reforming Russian institu- tions. While its goals were lofty and could have resulted in progressive change, the commission was composed of inexperienced delegates who could not agree on a course of action on the issue of serfdom or any of the legal or judi- cial issues facing them. As a result they produced only minor reforms and when the commission adjourned in 1768 it simply failed to reconvene.

Catherine maintained close contact with the west throughout her reign and was particularly fond of France. Secular European influences were allowed to penetrate Russian culture during her reign. Although her legislative commission failed, she achieved revolutionary gains in cul- ture by introducing urban influences in place of religious ones. Despite her enlightened interests, she did little to help the mass of Russian people, although she did improve the cultural life of the noble class.

Wolfgang Amadeus Mozart
(1756–1791)

Mozart was a child prodigy who was picking out chords on the clavier at three years and playing pieces by memory by four. His father, Leopold, a composer and violinist, took him on tour of Europe with his older sister, Anna, when he was only five. Mozart also wrote musical compositions prodigiously and he could play harpsichord, violin, and organ. Although he was only 35 when he died, he left the largest body of music of any composer other than Haydn. He mastered every musical genre—symphonies, overtures, concertos, and operas—and perfectly echoed the age of the aristocrat. *The Marriage of Figaro*, *Don Giovanni*, and *The Magic Flute*, are just three of his operas. He married Constanze Webber in 1782. They had six children of whom only two survived. Always broke, he eked out a living by teaching music and obtaining the odd commission. His last work was his *Requiem* which he was unable to finish before his death on 5 December 1791. He died in poverty and after a funeral service in St Stephen's Cathedral in Vienna, he was buried in the churchyard of St Mark's in a pauper's grave.

Wolfgang Amadeus Mozart mastered every musical genre—symphonies, overtures, concertos, and operas— and perfectly echoed the age of the aristocrat.

SUMMARY

The eighteenth century was dominated by intellectuals who challenged the traditional organization of society. If scientists could use reason to understand the orderly workings of nature, was it not possible for *philosophes* to use reason to discover more appropriate ways to organize society? Drawing on the writings of English intellectuals such as John Locke, French thinkers began to challenge the existing political, economic, and social structure of France.

Montesquieu analyzed political systems and determined that the functions of government must be carried out by separate branches. This division of power would allow a system of checks and balances which would prevent autocratic excess and misuse of power.

Voltaire was the most vocal proponent of reason and a strong supporter of individual freedom. Yet he was also critical of the optimism of the age of Enlightenment. In his most famous work, *Candide*, he parodied the vices of the Old Regime in France.

Rousseau focused his writings on the value of equal rather than individual liberty. He was critical of priva ownership of property and determined that society fun tioned best when the interests of the community sup seded the rights of the individual. His views on educati were radical, encouraging alternatives to the traditio methods of teaching.

Denis Diderot organized the writings of the *philosopl* in the *Encyclopédie*, the first compilation of intellect thought in Europe. It was read widely and supported leaders such as Catherine the Great of Russia, who w considered an Enlightened Despot.

Change was also encouraged in economics. The Frer physiocrats influenced the work of Adam Smith who *laissez-faire* system of economics challenged the m cantilist system of the Old Regime.

UESTIONS

Why is the Enlightenment called the Age of Reason?

Identify five signs that indicated the beginning of a new era in eighteenth century Europe.

Compare and contrast the life of a peasant with that of a member of the upper class.

Explain Newton's contribution to the Enlightenment era.

What did John Locke envision as the relationship between government and its citizens?

Explain what Locke meant when he claimed that human beings are born with a mind comparable to a blank slate.

Explain the view of society as presented by the French *philosophes*.

Denis Diderot edited the *Encyclopédie*. Why would this be considered an important accomplishment at this time?

Explain why France was considered the "cultural capital" of Europe during the eighteenth century.

Explain the view of government which Montesquieu put forward in his book, *De l'esprit des lois (The Spirit of the Laws)*.

Explain Voltaire's views on freedom and tolerance.

Explain what Rousseau meant when he said, "Man is born free, and is everywhere in chains." What are the chains?

Why did Rousseau object to the private ownership of property?

Compare and contrast mercantilism with the *laissez-faire* system of economics. Which do you think is the more effective system? Explain.

What role did the salons play in eighteenth-century France?

Explain the term "enlightened despot." Why would Catherine the Great of Russia be considered an enlightened despot?

Describe Mozart's contribution to eighteenth-century culture.

ANALYSIS

1. Explain how twentieth-century western political organization reflects eighteenth-century enlightenment thought. Give three specific examples.

2. What do you think Adam Smith would think about the Canadian economic system? Choose any three economic issues for your comment.

3. Explain how the American government illustrates Montesquieu's ideas on political organization.

4. Compare and contrast the social structure of eighteenth-century France with the social structure of twentieth-century Canada.

5. Make a list of some major ideas put forward by the philosophers. State your own opinions on each idea. Are the ideas practical? What good will they do? How will they change society? State whether you could support them or fight against them.

ACTIVITIES

1. Travel Diary

You are a young noble on a journey around Europe. Write four or five entries in your diary detailing your experiences in Paris, Vienna, and Venice. Include an encounter with peasants in a village along your route. Describe what you saw, how people were dressed, and any entertainment that you enjoyed. Give specific details on your accommodation, food, and mode of transportation. Your journal entries should be neatly written and may be illustrated.

2. Panel Discussion

Establish a panel of enlightenment thinkers to discuss the need for social, political, and economic change. Locke, Rousseau, Voltaire, Montesquieu, Diderot, Adam Smith, and Cesare Beccaria could be included. Audience members should be prepared to ask questions. Choose a moderator to monitor the discussion.

3. Debate

Debate the following resolution: Enlightened despotism is a more effective form of government than **democracy.**

The Palace of Versailles contained hundreds of rooms,
the most spectacular of which is the Hall of Mirrors.
Louis XVI would greet the Estates General in this room on 2 May 1789.

Chapter 2
Causes of the French Revolution

FOCUS ON:

❁

Challenges to the traditional absolute power of the French monarchy;

❁

The role of the economy in creating unrest in France prior to 1789;

❁

The power of populist support for political change
created by the meeting of the Estates General.

In 1788 France was an international leader in military power, wealth, science, and culture. Europeans emulated all that was French. Heads of state built palaces modeled on Versailles; French cuisine was served to the upper classes; and French was the language not only of social gatherings but of diplomacy. It may seem astounding, therefore, that revolution should occur in one of the most advanced countries in the world. An examination of the relationship of political, social, and economic conditions—coupled with a change in the intellectual climate of France, especially among the bourgeoisie—is essential if we are to understand the forces contributing to revolution in 1789.

Liberty, Equality, Fraternity. For the revolutionaries in France this slogan became the battle cry for political, economic, and social change. During the eighteenth century, the abuses of the Old Regime had been targeted by the enlightened ideas of the *philosophes* and discontent over political and social inequality spread among the intellectuals. This discontent led to a desire for change among members of both the bourgeoisie and some of the aristocrats.

Enlightenment ideas had laid an intellectual foundation for change, but throughout the eighteenth century the institutions of the Old Regime remained rooted in past tradition. The political, social, and economic systems had attracted the attention of the *philosophes*, but suggestions for change were discussed in the salons of Paris rather than in government circles. Louis XVI's attempts to introduce economic reforms were largely unsuccessful because he did not have the support of the *parlements*, church, or the aristocracy.

By 1788 economic problems in France had reached crisis proportions. The bankruptcy of the government and harvest failures due to drought proved to be insurmountable problems. The inability of the French government to find solutions led to the calling of the **Estates General**, and ultimately to the French Revolution.

TIMELINE

1774

Louis XVI ascends the throne of France.

1775–1783

War of American Independence

1788

Assembly of Notables convenes.

1788

The Estates General is called.

1789

5 May ❀ The Estates General convenes at Versailles.
17 June ❀ The National Assembly is established.
20 June ❀ The Tennis Court Oath
27 June ❀ The nobles and clergy join the third estate
in the National Assembly.
14 July ❀ Parisians storm the Bastille.

POLITICAL BACKGROUND

Cardinal Richelieu

When Henri IV of Fran (1553–1610) was assassinated a madman, he was succeeded his nine-year-old son, Lou whose mother, Marie de Medi acted as regent. During the rei of Louis XIII (1601–1643) pow was centralized in France p marily by the work of the po erful statesman, Cardinal Rich lieu (1585–1642). Richelieu b came involved in governme through his friendship wi Marie de Medici as her offic advisor and then as chief minister of state to the king, eve tually becoming the real power behind the throne. In t initial years of the regency the diverse factions of the upp classes clamoured for power and in 1614 the Estates Ge eral was called. However, there were so many conflicti interests among them that agreement could not be reach on any issue, and in 1615 the assembly was dismissed Marie de Medici. It would not be called again until the e of revolution. France would be ruled by an absolute mona chy until the revolutionary upheaval of 1789.

Until his death, Cardinal Richelieu worked to centrali and strengthen government and to abolish all oppositi to the Crown. In 1624 Richelieu gained a place in the kin council and very quickly exerted his influence and car to dominate the administration. The young king, Lo XIII, fell under his control. The queen regent was even ally banished in a failed attempt to overthrow the cardin Richelieu sought to centralize government by weakeni the nobles, by strengthening mercantilism, and by destr ing the power of the French Protestants, the Hugueno Thus, *intendants*, or administrative officers, direc responsible to the Crown were installed in the provinc to replace those nobles who had previously had contr over local jurisdictions. Trading companies were su ported by the government—wholesale merchants we even allowed to purchase noble status by making pa ments to the royal exchequer. Richelieu controlled the

It was during the short reign of Henry IV that France began to develop a national identity centred in the capital, Paris.

Marie de Medici acted as regent of France after her husband, Henri IV, was assassinated.

Edict of Nantes—1598

Henri IV (Henri of Navarre) was Protestant when he came to the throne in 1589. Civil wars between Protestants and Catholics still raged across France. Recognizing that the majority of French were still Catholic and that he would never be accepted in Paris as a Protestant, Henri renounced his Protestant beliefs, sought papal absolution, and turned to the Catholic Church. In 1598 he issued the Edict of Nantes granting religious and civil liberties to French Protestants, or Huguenots. Protestant services could now be held openly in towns where Protestantism prevailed and these towns could be defended by Protestant forces. This provision allowed the creation of about 100 Protestant strongholds, most of which were in southwest France. Protestants could run for public office and they could expect equal treatment before the law. Paris remained exclusively Catholic. Those towns that were predominantly Catholic did not have to allow Protestant services. When the Edict of Nantes was revoked by Louis XIV, it led to persecution of the Huguenots.

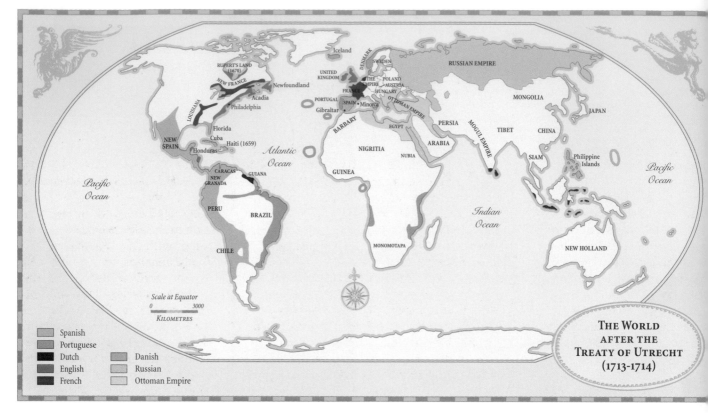

Spanish
Portuguese
Dutch   Danish
English   Russian
French   Ottoman Empire

THE WORLD
AFTER THE
TREATY OF UTRECHT
(1713-1714)

*The Treaty of Utrecht ended the War of the Spanish Succession. Britain emerged from the war
as a major international power, having won Newfoundland and Acadia from France.*

trading companies tightly and supported the development of companies modelled on those of the Dutch and the English. In 1628, the Edict of Nantes was revoked to remove military and territorial rights which the Huguenots had enjoyed. They would retain religious and civil rights until 1685 but their ability to defend their strongholds was destroyed.

Louis XIV

During the reign of Louis XIV (1643–1715) the French state was truly consolidated. ***"L'état, c'est moi"*** ("I am the state") summarizes the centralization of power in the person of Louis XIV, who is often referred to as *Le Roi Soleil*, The Sun King. The monopoly of law and military force defined the system of political absolutism as practised in France in the seventeenth century.

Despite inefficiencies in tax collection, the mercantilist policies of the finance minister Jean Colbert encouraged the development of glass, tapestry, and silk industries. Guilds were regulated to ensure high-quality goods in the hope that foreign buyers would purchase more merchandise. With this tight government control, the French economy did not develop the private enterprise characteristics

that had fueled the English economy, but it did show som improvement in growth during the seventeenth century

Two events late in Louis's reign, however, proved det mental to the French economy. First, in 1685, he revok the Edict of Nantes, making it impossible for Huguenc to live openly in France. They could no longer worsh freely and were persecuted viciously. As a result, many l France for Protestant countries such as Holland England. Since the Huguenots who left were predon nantly involved in commerce, industry, or the professior their loss dealt a severe blow to the French econom Conversely, countries that received them benefitted fro the industry of the Huguenot immigrants.

The second event was the fourth in a series of wars th Louis fought from 1667 onward in his attempt to domina Europe. In 1701 the War of the Spanish Succession beg in an attempt to prevent a French king from succeeding the throne of Spain after the death of Charles II who di childless. Prior to Charles's death the major powers h decided to divide Spain between France and Austria in attempt to maintain the balance of power on the continer But in his will, Charles had determined that the Spani crown should be offered first to France (Louis's grandsc

ilip of Anjou) and if not
cepted by France then to
stria.

When Louis XIV accepted the
rone for his grandson, the
rm bells sounded among
her European countries—
ance was getting too powerful.
eat Britain formed a Grand
iance with Holland and Aus-
a and they declared war on
ance, the War of the Spanish
ccession. They would later be
ned by Portugal and Savoy.
e war was long and costly for
h sides and ended in 1713
h a treaty, the Peace of
echt. The main result of the
aty was the establishment of
alance of power accomplished by dividing the Spanish
pire. The Spanish throne and Spain's American posses-
ns went to Louis XIV's grandson, who was crowned
lip V. Austria received the Spanish Netherlands (the
ure state of Belgium), Milan, Naples, and Sicily. Savoy
eived Sardinia. Great Britain remained in Gibraltar and
nexed the island of Minorca. France gave up Newfound-
d and Acadia in Canada to Great Britain. Great Britain,
ently born from the union of England and Scotland in
07, emerged as a major international power from these
nts. France, despite its losses, shared a balance of power
h Great Britain on the European continent.

Despite its retention of international prestige and status
a major power, France suffered a severe economic blow
a result of the War of Spanish Succession. Additionally,
Sun King died in 1715, soon after his bid for European
mination was thwarted. His great-grandchild, the new
g, Louis XV, was only five years old. His uncle
lippe II, duc d' Orléans, stepped in as regent. He was
ed with enormous war debts and a nobility clamouring
a share of political power.

Divine Right of Kings

Bishop Bossuet, church leader to the court of Louis XIV, wrote a book in 1709 that advanced the theory that all power comes from God and, as such, kings were God's representatives on earth. This "divine right" to govern prevented citizens from defying the king's authority—to do so could be likened to defiance of God. The doctrine of the **Divine Right of Kings** was taught by the clergy and was supposed to result in a just authority that reflected God's will. It supported absolute monarchy, meaning that the Crown was free from interference by the *parlements* (law courts) or citizen groups within the country.

Louis XV

Louis XV reigned from 1715 to 1774. He had neither the will nor the talent of his predecessor although he was still an absolute monarch. His weakness, coupled with the events of the Enlightenment era, contributed to the gradual decline of the French monarchy. The social climate was changing too. During his reign political, economic, and social change was discussed in the salons of Paris and other major French cities. The discussions of ideas that challenged the existing political and social structure became popular enter tainment for the bourgeoisie.

The economic climate was affected by several factors: the crippling losses from the Seven Years' War (1756–1763), which France fought both in Europe against Prussia and in North America against Britain, in the American War of Independence (1775-1783), and the ongoing inability of the French government to raise enough revenue to finance its administration adequately. These created the economic climate that would eventually lead to revolution.

The restoration of the *parlements* by Louis XVI was also a factor that brought France closer to revolution. The centralization of power in the monarchy by Richelieu in the late seventeenth century had eroded the power of the nobility. They were left with only the privileges accorded to citizens of noble birth and some ceremonial functions which were granted to members of the nobility. Before Richelieu's consolidation of royal power, the nobles had been in charge of the local affairs in their own territories. As a result of his reorganization, administrative powers were transferred to administrators, or *intendants*, who were directly responsible to the Crown. As well, a system of royal courts of law called *parlements* had grown in France. The *parlements* were legal and judicial institutions. They registered the king's edicts. The most important of these was the *Parlement du Paris* because it received the king's edicts first and had jurisdiction over one third of France. Failure to

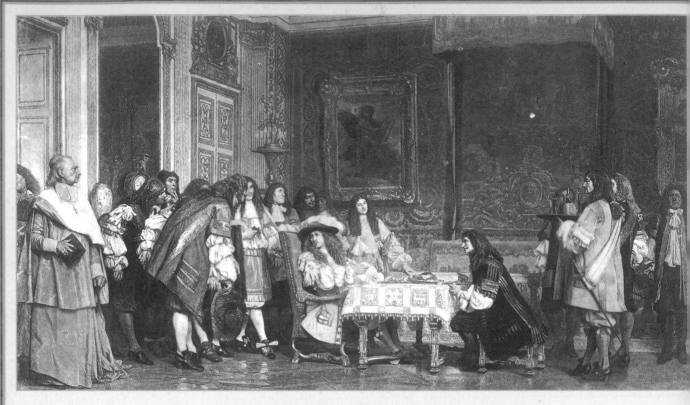

*This engraving shows the French playwright Molière (1622–1673)
breakfasting at Versailles with Louis XIV.*

∼ Versailles ∼

The grandeur and opulence of the reign of Louis XIV is symbolized by the Palace of Versailles. Fearful of living in Paris after witnessing some uprisings while still a young child, Louis built himself an entire city about 20 kilometres out of Paris near the little village of Versailles. Fifty thousand people lived in the city, ten thousand of these right in the palace. The Palace of Versailles was begun in 1661 and was continued by Louis XV and Louis XVI. More than a third of a kilometre long it contains hundreds of rooms, the most spectacular of which is the famous Hall of Mirrors. A formal garden area, including the half-kilometre Grand Canal and numerous walks, fountains, and sculptures were designed by André Le Nôtre, the greatest landscape architect of his time.

About 5 percent of the royal revenue was spent maintaining Versailles. For this investment, Louis paraded France's superiority in worldly splendor. He cajoled the nobility into permanent residence there where they could be entertained with political intrigue and at the same time prevented from interfering in the affairs of the local administrations in their home territory. Nobles who succumbed to Louis's invitation to live at Versailles spent enormous amounts of money on clothing, entertainment, and the upkeep of their living quarters. Only the very wealthy could live at court for an extended period of time, but most nobles craved the prestige of royal favours and sought the privilege of watching the ceremonial acts of royalty rising, eating, and retiring.

Louis XV reigned at a time when the French economy was affected by fighting in the Seven Years' War and the American War of Independence.

gister the king's edicts would ult in confrontation between king and the *parlement* in a *de justice* (a special meeting of *parlement* in which the king sided to dictate his wishes). Magistrates of the *parlements* re nobles who had bought ir offices. This system con- puted to venality and to the ntinuation of tax exemptions the nobility. It was generally cepted that the king's will pre- led but the *parlementaires* ld amend legislation before istering it. They usually did in order to protect the rights privileges of their class, the bility and the clergy. They re often in opposition to the own. In an attempt to reform system in 1771, Louis XV's ncellor, René Nicolas de upeou, sent the magistrates the *Parlement du Paris* into le at Troyes and replaced m with individuals sympa- tic to the Crown. Unfortu- ely, the *parlements* had developed the myth that they re defenders of public justice. Hence they had the sup- rt of a substantial portion of the populace. When Louis I came to the throne in 1774, pressure was exerted on n to restore the *parlements* in their traditional fashion. e attempted judicial reform was short-lived and its fail- had a great deal to do with creating a judicial climate ourable to revolution.

CIAL CONDITIONS
THE OLD REGIME

he population of France grew from 18 million to 26 million people between 1715 and 1789. As France was still an agrarian nation with an underdeveloped ustrial base, this population increase placed tremendous ssures on the peasant class. The burgeoning population was a negative factor whenever harvest failures occurred and bread shortages inevitably re- sulted. Those fortunate enough to buy bread would pay a much higher price than that charged in times of plenty. Landless peas- ants unable to find work in rural areas drifted into Paris. There, at least 10 percent of the popula- tion was always unemployed and in times of crisis this number rose to 50 percent.

French society in the **l'ancien régime** (old regime) was classi- fied into three estates, or groups. The first and highest estate was the clergy, the second estate was the nobility, and the third estate was everyone else. While some of the rights and privileges of the nobility and the clergy derived from medieval times, their privi- leged position had developed during the years when the French economy made the tran- sition from an agricultural econ- omy to a capitalist economy. All levels of society benefitted from some measure of privilege, although the extent of privileges extended to the first and second estates greatly exceeded that accorded the third estate.

First Estate: Clergy

About 100 000 people, or 0.5 percent of France's popula- tion, belonged to the first estate. However, the Roman Catholic Church owned in excess of 10 percent of the land and also collected income and feudal taxes on this prop- erty. In addition to property revenues, the clergy were enti- tled to the tithe, 10 percent of everyone's income. The church also owned much commercial property. In total, the Church's income amounted to roughly one-half of that received by the royal government. Despite such enormous wealth, the Church was not required to pay tax but rather was given the privilege of voting a gift to the king every five years. This "free gift" generally amounted to about 5 percent of its revenue.

This coloured engraving shows four social groups in France in the eighteenth century: clergy, soldier, peasant, and noble. The clergy were in the first estate, the noble in the second estate, and the peasant in the third estate. Soldiers came from either the second or third estate.

The Church, too, was structured like the French society that supported it. Positions of power and influence in the Church hierarchy—bishops, archbishops and abbots—were monopolized by the nobility. Most of the funds raised by Church taxes, fees, and revenues from the land were allocated to these upper levels of Church administration. The middle and lower ranks of the Church hierarchy—monks, nuns, and priests—were filled by the bourgeoisie and the peasantry. The primary responsibilities of church officials were to provide spiritual care to the community, education, relief for the poor, and hospital care. The parish priests conducted the bulk of this work. They were the lowest levels of clergy, underpaid and unacknowledged by either income or title. Between 1768 and 1780 attempts were made to remedy the inequities in the distribution of wealth, the lack of opportunity for promotion to higher offices, and the monopoly held by the upper levels of the ecclesiastical hierarchy on governance of the Church. These attempts failed and, as a result, most of the clergy

was divided on the eve of revolution although some of more liberal-thinking clergy supported change.

Second Estate: Nobility

About 390 000 people, or 1.5 percent of France's popu tion, were nobles. About one-half were nobles-of-t sword, a distinction that meant that the title was won d ing medieval times. Nobles-of-the-sword consider themselves to be the only true nobility in France. The r of the nobility was divided as follows: nobles-of-the-ro to denote those who held royal, judicial, or administrat posts; nobles-of-the-bell to denote those who held mui ipal office; and the *anoblis* who had simply purchas their titles, often with no duties attached. A separate c egory called *hoberaux* ("sparrow hawks") were nob who had lost their wealth and were reduced to seekin commission in the army for their support.

Eighteenth century France was rife with inequity and nobility benefitted handsomely from this condition. T

About 1.5 percent of France's population consisted of nobles.
The nobility was characterized by superior status, social prestige, and
special exemptions from duties or taxes.
This picture shows nobles in the Palais Royal Garden in Paris.

bility was characterized by superior status, social pres-
e, and, most of all, the privileges of special rights or
emptions from duties or taxes. The highest nobles were
owed to live at Versailles and participate in royal occa-
ns. Only the nobility could become officers in the army
attain judicial or administrative posts. Nobles were
owed the exclusive privilege of hunting without any con-
rn for damage they might cause to the peasants' crops.
harged with a civil crime they were usually excused. If
capital offense was committed, they were allowed the
oice of decapitation over the more tortuous death by
nging.

Tax exemptions accorded the nobles were substantial.
ey were not required to pay the *taille*, a property tax, or
e *corvée*, required labour which was assessed for road
nstruction. They escaped much of the *gabelle*, or salt
x, and the *franc-fief*, which was assessed on the trans-
of feudal property. While they were legally obligated to
y the more recent *vingtièmes*, a universal tax on
ome, they were often able to bribe the *intendant* into
usting the amount.

The nobility, like the clergy, was not united in its loyalty
he king or to the traditions of the Old Regime. The most
cal of the liberal element, such as the Marquis de
ayette, the Comte de Mirabeau, and the Duc d'Orléans,

were included as representatives to the Estates General
and would eventually contribute to the demise of their
class.

Third Estate

Ninety-eight percent of the population of the Old Regime
were members of the third estate (about 27 million people). They were from such widely disparate groups as
wealthy bourgeoisie, professionals, artisans, city workers,
wealthy peasant landowners, and landless peasants. For
purposes of organization in attempting to understand the
third estate, we will establish three groups within it: the
bourgeoisie, urban workers, and peasants.

Bourgeoisie

The term bourgeois denotes membership in the oligarchy
of a bourg, or town. To be a member of the bourgeoisie one
might be a very wealthy financier or a shopkeeper, artisan,
lawyer, or bureaucrat. One of the most lucrative ventures
for this group was to become a member of the Farmers
General, an organization of 60 tax directors who collected
taxes for the Crown. By agreeing to turn over a specified
amount to the Crown they were allowed to collect whatever they could and to keep anything in excess of this specified amount. It was not uncommon for these tax farmers

Land Ownership of the Three Estates

	Population (%)	Land Owned (%)
First Estate	0.5	10
Second Estate	1.5	25
Third Estate	98.0	65

to collect double the amount levied by the Crown. The system allowed a guarantee to the Crown but was open to abuse. In their zeal, many tax directors used brutal intimidation to extract the taxes. This privilege of tax collection was the most lucrative privilege accorded the bourgeoisie.

Many among the bourgeoisie aspired to nobility and some bought positions such as membership in the *parlements* that conferred noble status to the family. Enterprising businessmen desirous of joining the nobility invested in land and bought offices that carried a title, using their money to advance their social position rather than to expand their business.

Urban Workers

Paris was France's largest city in the eighteenth century with a population of 650 000. Marseilles and Lyons each had about 100 000 people and no other city exceeded 50 000. France was still predominantly an agricultural country economically; the majority of French industries such as wine, liquor, and luxury goods were tied to agriculture. It lagged behind England in industrial development.

The guild system tightly controlled the number of workers allowed to rise from apprenticeship to journeyman to the masters level. Most guild workers remained at the journeyman level for life but, compared to other workers, they were relatively well paid and reasonably secure.

The most tenuous existence was that of unskilled workers, often peasants who moved into the city when they could no longer eke out a living in the countryside. They were fortunate to find work that paid a subsistence wage. In times of economic crises, thousands of them starved to death in the streets of Paris. This group swelled the angry mobs that rioted and looted during the most volatile days of the revolution.

Peasants

Peasants made up about 86 percent of France's population. This was a widely diverse group, however, with a few wealthy peasant farmers, a great many small landowners, sharecroppers or renters, and a number of landless peasants who worked as day labourers. They were assessed the

taille, or property tax; t *corvée*, or road tax; the *vin* *ièmes*, a tax on income; assortment of feudal du depending on the region which they lived; and the tithe the Church. The total tax t could amount to as much as 70 percent of a peasar income. In spite of the fact that the bulk of the taxation f on the peasantry, they were supportive of the monarchy a were loyal to the Roman Catholic Church. Except for is lated instances such as the Great Fear of 1789 (see Cha ter 3) and their involvement in the army, they lived routi lives while the revolution raged in the cities.

ECONOMIC CONDITIONS LEADING UP TO 1789

The complex and inequitable system of taxati certainly contributed to the economic crisis th precipitated the French Revolution. Since the ti of Louis XIV, France had lived beyond its means. Howev the critical issue in 1789 stemmed from the governmer inability to resolve a financial crisis. The crippling de incurred during France's participation in the Americ War of Independence was compounded by harvest fa ures, famine, and the failure of the Assembly of Notab to sanction tax reform. The result was a bankrupt treasu incapable of financing even the day-to-day operations government.

When Louis XVI ascended the throne in 1774, he claim that what he wanted most was to be loved by his subjec Perhaps this desire is what led him to dismiss Maupe Louis XV's chancellor who had abolished the old *p lements* and taxed the privileged, and to restore the *p lements* to their original status. While this move v immensely popular among members of the first estate the *parlements* jealously guarded the privileges of the a tocracy, this action ensured the failure of any financ reforms. The privileged classes would remain free of n taxation.

The first comptroller-general of finance in Louis X government was the economist and statesman A.R.J. T got (1727–1781), a *philosophe*, a former *intendant*, an

Louis XVI claimed that what he wanted most was to be loved by his subjects.

ysiocrat. He embarked on a ogram of tax reform which minated the worst abuses of e tax farmers, abolished the ilds which were privileged nopolies, freed grain from ernal tariffs in the hope that eater productivity would re-lt, and planned to replace the rvée with a tax on all three ates. He began a review of the ole tax system. It was an ibitious program and initially d the support of the king, but e *Parlement du Paris*, the urch, and the provincial bles, all opposed him. Also, in summer of 1775, the "Flour r" erupted. Harvest failures in preceding year had resulted grain shortages and much her prices for bread. Peasants d urban workers took to the streets, seized bakeries and manded that bread prices be controlled. Turgot was med. Rumours suggested that his reforms had led to the arding of grain and subsequent high prices. In 1776 Tur-t resigned and his attempts at reforms vanished with him.

recalling the *parlements* the king had made reform possible.

he Swiss-born banker, Jacques Necker (1732–1804), laced Turgot. A brilliant financier with excellent bank-g connections, Necker engineered the financing for the ench participation in the American War of Indepen-nce. Rather than raise taxes, Necker borrowed all the ney required for the war effort. By the end of the war, erest on the loans amounted to 50 percent of the year-revenue. In 1781 he published the *compte rendu* ("the al budget") and gave French people their first glimpse the sorry state of the royal finances. The king was out-ed and Necker resigned soon after.

oly de Fleury was comptroller from 1781–1783. He was cessful in putting through the third *vingtième*, a tax on ome, but was otherwise a nonentity. He was replaced by arles Calonne who borrowed heavily, increased taxation, l until 1786 gave the government the appearance of afflu-ce. However, by 1786, France's credit was exhausted and

there appeared to be no solution other than increased taxes. As the crisis grew Calonne put for-ward a plan to the king for reform which included a gener-al tax on all landowners without exception in place of the *taille*; abolition of the *corvée*, and the reform of the *gabelle*, or salt tax, and indirect taxes; the removal of internal customs duties to stimulate economic growth, and the creation of a state bank. He also proposed the establishment of provincial assemblies in which all estates would have equal representation.

To support his reforms, know ing the *Parlement du Paris* would not, Calonne convened a superior body, the Assembly of Notables. The Assembly of Notables was a group of 144 individuals who came from all over France: princes, archbishops, bishops, nobles, *parlementaires*, *intendants*, and representatives of provincial estates and cities. Louis XVI and Calonne were convinced that this aristocratic assembly would support their proposed reforms. The king was alarmed to learn that they refused to consider any tax reforms without a radical revision of the governing system. They wanted conces-sions and a share of government control. There was a deadlock. Led by individuals like the Duc d'Orléans and the Marquis de Lafayette, the Assembly of Notables sug-gested a meeting of the Estates General. The Estates General was a representative body that had not met since 1614. Calonne was dismissed by the king and fled to England where he became known as the "first émigré of the Revolution." The *parlements* won again.

Calling of the Estates General

The office of comptroller-general was then given to Lomenie de Brienne, archbishop of Toulouse, who modi-fied Calonne's proposals prior to presenting them to the assembly. In July 1787 Brienne asked the *Parlement du Paris* to register the tax on property of all three estates. The *Parlement* refused and France entered a year of

The Estates General opened at the Palace of Versailles on 2 May 1789.

intense conflict between the royal government and the *parlements*. On 5 July 1788, with the government at a standstill, and in spite of his misgivings, Louis gave in to the demands of the nobility and issued an edict calling the Estates General to convene the following May, the first time since 1614. With this act, the aristocracy unwittingly signed its own death warrant.

The nobles actually had some liberal ideas but they mistakenly believed that they could control the workings of the Estates General as they had before. After all, the *Parlement du Paris* had ruled that the Estates General would be assembled on the same basis as it had in 1614, with each of the three estates sitting separately and voting as a block.

After Calonne's departure, Louis reappointed Necker as comptroller in an attempt to avert bankruptcy of the royal treasury. Necker was popular with the bourgeoisie. In December, Necker convinced Louis XVI to double the representation in the third estate in an attempt to appease the demands of the bourgeoisie for an equal voice.

In January of 1789, the Abbé Sieyès wrote a pamphlet titled "What is the Third Estate?" In it, the abbé denounced

the nobility and said that the third estate was the most s_nificant estate—in fact, it *was* the nation. His wor_ became the battle cry of the bourgeoisie.

Doubling the representation in the third estate w_ futile, however, without changing the method of voti_ from vote by bloc to vote by head. Male adults over the a_ of 25 could vote. Other qualifications for voting includ_ ownership of property, payment of tax amounting to s_ *livres,* or holding a responsible position. Only wom_ owning feudal lands were allowed to vote and then o_ by proxy.

The king was confident that the first and second esta_ would remain loyal to the Crown. As well, the rural pe_ antry was traditionally loyal to the Crown. The third esta_ however, elected a disproportionate number of lawye_ and no workers or peasants. As a result, the compositi_ of the third estate reflected the liberal *bourgeois* attitud_ of the Enlightenment rather than the traditional conse_ ative view held by the peasants.

Louis XVI asked that the people draw up lists of gri_ ances, or *cahiers,* to indicate their concerns and reque_ for change. A general demand voiced in the *cahiers* w_

American Revolution: 1775–1783

Reflecting on the success of the American Revolution, the eighteenth century British writer Arthur Young wrote, "The American Revolution has laid the foundation of another in France, if government does not take care of itself." He was referring not only to the economic conditions in France that suggested revolution, but to the intellectual impact of liberty on the 9000 Frenchmen who fought alongside the Americans to establish a new and independent nation. As such, the American Revolution had a far-reaching significance in Europe.

The American Revolution, often called the War of American Independence, grew out of the American colonies' refusal to bow to the British demands for taxation without representation in Parliament. From the Revenue Act of 1764, when an attempt was made to impose a tax on sugar, to the Regulating Act of 1773, which cut American tea merchants out of the British tea trade, the Americans and their colonial masters argued bitterly over economic issues.

The American Revolution officially began when the Second Continental Congress adopted the Declaration of Independence on 4 July 1776, although fighting had begun in 1775. Initially, France's involvement was confined to the provision of weaponry. However, after the American victory at Saratoga in 1778, the French government saw the possibility of success and formally joined the Americans by declaring war against Britain. By the time the Treaty of Paris was signed in 1783 to end the war, France had borrowed 1500 million livres to finance its involvement in it. Interest payments on this amount of money totalled 50 percent of the French government's total revenue and became a significant factor in France's inability to resolve its financial difficulties during the reign of Louis XVI.

---

the development of a constitution (a written constitution was not requested). The other major point of agreement was the demand for equality of taxation. Many of the *cahiers* from urban areas wanted individual rights, while rural *cahiers* were concerned with the nobles' hunting rights and the use of pigeon hutches. Examination of the *cahiers* suggested that the representation of the third estate was much more radical than the majority of the French population. A clear distinction between the rural conservative peasantry and their more radical urban counterparts was now quite evident.

The Estates General was greeted by Louis XVI in the Hall of Mirrors at the Palace of Versailles on 2 May 1789. A formal procession was conducted in which Louis greeted each of the representatives. Then on 5 May the meeting convened with an opening speech by the king, followed by a long and tiring analysis on France's financial condition by Necker. Neither speech inspired any confidence in the leadership ability of the Crown. Following the opening, each estate was asked to meet separately to validate the credentials of its representatives.

National Assembly

The first and second estates recognized that the maintenance of privilege rested on the continuation of traditional voting patterns and as such they carried out the king's orders to meet separately. The third estate, however, wished all representatives to meet as a single assembly and vote by head. It refused to give in to the king's demands to accede to the rules for the meeting and instead began to lobby the other two estates to move with them to a single-house assembly which would vote as individuals and work toward the completion of a written constitution. The nobles remained united but a small number of clergy moved to the third estate meeting. By 17 June the third estate felt that it was powerful enough to declare itself the "National Assembly," and it requested that the other two orders join them in this revolutionary move.

On 20 June 1789, the third estate was locked out of its meeting room as preparations were being made for a royal session of all three estates on 22 June. Confused and angry, the delegates met instead at an indoor tennis court on the palace grounds and signed an oath not to disband until

After hearing about Necker's dismissal, Camille Desmoulins (1760–1794) made an impassioned
speech to the crowd outside the Palace of Versailles. Political agitators such as Desmoulins
stirred the city mob to anger. The Paris mob was to play a pivotal role in the French Revolution
until it was brought under control by the army after 1795.

ey had drawn up a constitution for France. The Tennis
ourt Oath signals the beginning of the French people's
fusal to bow to the absolute authority of the king. The
volution had begun.

Meanwhile, the royal session went ahead as planned, on
June 1789. The king granted concessions based on the
mands of the *cahiers*. He further agreed that all three
ders should meet together and vote by head on any issue
cept those which would affect the privileges of the first
d second estates. Louis was acknowledging the people
France and seemed to be moving toward the creation
a constitutional monarchy. However, he was committed
maintaining each of the three orders and assembled
oops in the area of Paris to provide support. On 27 June
89, when the self-styled National Assembly refused to
journ, Louis ordered the nobles and clergy to join the
rd estate in the National Assembly. They began working
a constitution.

As news of the third estates' defiance of the king spread,
gry mobs roamed the countryside. Bread prices had
iched a new high and grain convoys that transported
od to the cities were ransacked by angry peasants.
ages were low and unemployment was high. Labour
uble had broken out in April.)

In an attempt to maintain law and order, 20 000 Swiss
d German mercenaries were brought to Paris from the
ovincial garrisons. Louis gained confidence as the troops
sembled and on 11 July he dismissed the popular
cker. This did not produce the desired effect for the king
both the army presence and the dismissal of Necker
gered the people and encouraged further violence.

ll of the Bastille

14 July 1789, Paris erupted. The crowd, determined to
n itself, first assailed the Invalides fortress from which
y obtained 30 000 muskets. They then moved on to the
stille, an old fortress prison which had long been viewed
a symbol of the king's absolute authority. There, the gov-
or of the Bastille, Count de Launey, met them. The
gry mob demanded arms and freedom for the hordes of
soners believed to be within its walls and attacked the
all garrison of soldiers. De Launey capitulated and the
olution of the people moved forward another step.
ey discovered upon entering the Bastille that there was
large storehouse of weaponry and that it housed only
en prisoners.

Louis XVI responded to the fall of the Bastille by recalling Necker. He also ordered his troops to return to the
provinces. The Paris militia, now called the National
Guard, was put under the command of the Marquis de
Lafayette, a general who would soon be more loyal to the
National Assembly than to the king. To symbolize the juncture of the king and the Paris militia, Lafayette designed a
new insignia for the troops—the tricolour—with the white
of the royal family and the red and blue of the Paris militia.

The Tennis Court Oath signified the inability of the king
to maintain absolute authority. Now, with the fall of the
Bastille and the National Assembly growing in power, the
revolution gained momentum. France would undergo radical change in the course of the next ten years as the revolution dramatically altered the face of the nation.

SUMMARY

*T*he Old Regime in France was characterized by
absolute monarchy, mercantilist economics, and a
rigidly stratified social system. Enlightenment
thought suggested that change in the political, economic,
and social systems in France was essential but the upper
classes supported the king's refusal to consider any of
these ideas.

The Bourbon monarchy ruled without input from the citizens of France. The system of *intendants* which was
implemented by Richelieu in the seventeenth century provided for centralized control of the country. King Louis XVI
believed his responsibility was to rule absolutely.

Only four percent of French society had privileges in the
Old Regime. The nobility and the clergy were allowed tax
exemptions, access to governmental roles, and a variety of
feudal privileges. The agricultural peasants and urban
workers suffered excessive taxation and subsistence living. However, it was the upper level of the third estate , the
bourgeoisie, who agitated most aggressively for change.
The bourgeoisie were professionals, artisans, or business-
people. While many had achieved great wealth, they were
denied a political voice.

Economic issues were a critical factor in the outbreak
of revolution in France. From the time of Louis XIV, France
had spent more money than it received in revenue. During
the eighteenth century, French participation in the Seven
Years' War and the American War of Independence

contributed to a crippling debt. The inequitable tax system, and the government's inability to resolve its financial crisis, contributed to the king's decision to call the Estates General.

Once together, the third estate , supported by a small number of clergy, formed the National Assembly. The king's authority was challenged with the group's decision to remain united until a constitution was drawn up. By 14 July 1789, the revolution had turned violent with the storming of the Bastille. Louis XVI was unable to retain military control and was forced to acknowledge the Paris militia under the leadership of Lafayette. For the next ten years France endured the upheaval of revolution.

QUESTIONS

1. Explain the concept of absolute monarchy. How did absolutism tend to limit attempts at reform?

2. Briefly explain the causes and course of events of the War of Spanish Succession. What was the most significant result of this conflict for France?

3. Explain how foreign wars contributed to the insurmountable French debt.

4. Explain the role of the *intendant* in the French administrative system.

5. What were the *parlements*? How did they contribute to the absolute power of the monarch and the system of privilege which existed in France?

6. Name and describe the three estates which existed in the Old Regime in France.

7. What sources of income did the Roman Catholic Church possess? Explain the "free gift" required of the Church by the king.

8. Make a list of the privileges enjoyed by the nobility France. Assess the impact of these privileges on the peasant.

9. What three groups made up the third estate? Describe each group.

10. List the taxes imposed on the peasant. Evaluate the justice of this tax load in relationship to the second estate.

11. Explain why the practice of purchasing noble statu was considered detrimental to the French economy

12. Make a chart of the economic reforms attempted b Turgot, Necker, de Fleury, Calonne, and de Brienne Which reforms were approved by the king? Which were not? Why did the attempt at economic reform do nothing to solve the problem of France's growin debt?

13. Why did Louis XVI call the Estates General?

14. What were the *cahiers?* Name three demands whic were voiced in the *cahiers.*

15. Explain the difference between the traditional "vot by bloc" and the desired "vote by head" in the Esta General. Why was "vote by head" so important to t third estate ?

16. What was the Tennis Court Oath? What was the significance of this event?

17. Why did the Paris mob attack the Bastille? What w the significance of this attack? Why do you think historians would consider this a critical event in th origin of the French Revolution?

NALYSIS

There is a myth which suggests that the Bastille (the old fortress prison) was filled with political prisoners in 1789. Research the Bastille. Assess its role in the Old Regime. What was its status in 1789. What prisoners were captive when the Bastille was stormed on 14 July 1789? Evaluate the significance of the prison in relationship to the idea of revolution for the average Parisian citizen.

Analyze the revenue and expenditures of the French government in the three decades prior to revolution. How would you have solved the crisis of the French national debt?

Evaluate the role played by the American Revolution in the origins of the French Revolution. Consider the economic impact of French involvement in the American War of Independence, the ideas generated by the American Declaration of Independence as well as personalities like the Marquis de Lafayette and Benjamin Franklin.

ACTIVITIES

1. Estates General
Divide the class into representatives of each of the three estates. There should be twice as many delegates for the third estate as for the first and second. Research the issues of importance for each estate and prepare to meet as this traditional parliamentary body. Louis XVI, Marie Antoinette, and their finance minister (Jacques Necker) should be included in the meeting. Students who role play these three royalist individuals should be prepared to maintain the royalist view on any issues discussed. Louis XVI will act as chairperson.

2. Cahiers
Take the position of any one of the social groups in pre-revolutionary France and prepare a *cahier* outlining a specific grievance. What solution do you propose?

3. Propaganda Speech
Prepare a speech to be delivered to the Jacobins, a club of radicals who endorsed the concept of France as a republic. (You will read more about the Jacobins in the next chapter.) In your speech, extoll the bravery of the citizens of Paris who had stormed the Bastille. Because this is a propaganda speech, you should not be bothered with the facts of the case but rather emphasize its importance as a revolutionary, anti-monarchist action.

Chapter 3
The French Revolution

FOCUS ON:

❀

Legislative changes to the political and social structure of France;

❀

The influence of the Paris mob and the radical Jacobin movement
on the development of the French Revolution;

❀

The conservative reaction to the excesses of radicalism
during the Reign of Terror.

*Paris seethed with discontent throughout the summer of 1792. Hungry,
distrustful of government, and discouraged by failures in the war with Austria,
Parisians grew increasingly restless. On 10 August 1792 they stormed the
Tuileries where the royal family was being held.*

From 1789 to 1799 France experienced a revolutionary upheaval that would change the political, economic, and social structure of the country forever. The fall of the Bastille on 14 July 1789, created a revolutionary fervour far out of proportion to the significance of the attack itself. However, the event did strengthen the resolve of the National Assembly and destroyed any hope that Louis XVI had of intimidating Parisians with foreign troops and regaining control of the city. On 16 July Louis capitulated. He accepted the red cap and tri-colour cockade which combined the white of royalty with the blue and red of Paris, and he appointed Lafayette as head of the National Guard. Henceforth, Louis XVI's power would be tempered by that of the populace and ultimately by the constitution. Absolutism in France was destroyed.

After the capitulation of the king to the Estates General, order collapsed in France. Control was fragmented among the many local authorities which established local councils backed by militias. From 1789 to 1794 the Paris mob played a leading role in the direction of revolutionary activity. It was responsible for much of the violence which became the signature of the **revolution** and that culminated in the Reign of Terror in 1793.

With the collapse of royal authority, committees sprang up in both rural and urban areas. In addition, National Guards were formed as defense against the perceived threats of the aristocrats and in an attempt to provide protection for private property. The *intendants* who had been in charge of local administrations abandoned their posts out

TIMELINE

1789
20 July ❀ The Great Fear spreads across the country.
4-5 August ❀ Feudalism is abolished.
26 August ❀ The Declaration of the Rights of Man is issued.
5 October ❀ Women march on Versailles.
3 November ❀ Church lands are nationalized.

1790
29 May ❀ The National Assembly passes the Civil Constitution of the Clergy. The Assembly also decentralizes power to local councils.

1791
June ❀ The royal family attempts escape to Varennes. Legislative Assembly elected.

1792
The French government declares war against Austria.
10 August ❀ Mob storms Tuileries and captures the royal family.
Monarchy is abolished by the National Convention.
September ❀ France is proclaimed a republic.

1793
21 January ❀ King Louis XVI is executed.
The Committee of Public Safety is established.
Power is ruthlessly centralized under the threat of foreign invasion.
The Law of the Maximum is passed.
Levée en Masse mobilizes the French population for war.

1794
27-28 July ❀ Robespierre is arrested and executed.

1795
September ❀ The Directory is established.

of fear for their own person safety. The *parlements* were d solved and revolutionary fervo spread through the towns a cities. The movement for chan that swept the urban areas France consolidated the revo tion as an urban moveme However, the rural areas eru ed in late July 1789 in wi spread violence against the seigneurial system.

Great Fear

Once the revolutionary spi seized control of Paris, peo in surrounding areas began demand cheaper bread and t suspension of feudal dues. Ru unrest had been present sin the worsening grain shortag of the spring and now the gr supplies were guarded n vously by local militias as bar of vagrants roamed the count side. The peasants began believe rumours that aristocr had hired these vagrants to p tect the new harvest from t peasantry. As civil unrest gr there were attacks on man houses by fearful peasants w armed themselves in s defense against the imagin marauders. Aristocratic pr erty was ransacked and feu records were destroyed. There were isolated incidents violence against the aristocrats, but for the most part, peasants wanted simply to destroy the records in wh the feudal dues were recorded. Grain supplies w attacked and merchants suffered serious losses as pe ants helped themselves to much needed supplies. From July to 5 August 1789, the hysteria spread across the co try but gradually burned itself out as militias imposed and order.

The importance of the written word is underlined by the publication of the aims of the French revolutionaries in their Declaration of the Rights of Man.

...bolition of Feudalism

...he panic of the Great Fear ...owed the peasants' anger with ...e old, outmoded system of feu-...l obligations that still domi-...ted the agrarian life of France. ...uring the first part of August, ...eral members of the landed ...istocracy who were also mem-...rs of the National Assembly ...ized on the idea that the only ...ay to stem the tide of violence ...the countryside was to re-...ounce feudal privileges. On 4 ...gust 1789, the Duc de Noailles ...ade a speech in which he pro-...sed to end feudal dues and ...troduce some equitable means ...taxation. He had participated ...the American Revolution ...der Lafayette and was imbued ...th the spirit of freedom and ...uality. His speech was fol-...wed by the Duc de Anguillon, ...e of the largest landowners in France. Throughout the ...ght the aristocracy rose in the Assembly to strip them-...lves of their feudal rights and privileges.

...When dawn broke on the following day, it appeared that ...udalism had been abolished. However, over the follow-...g week the Assembly noted that feudal obligations that ...iginated out of servitude were different from the ...igneurial dues extracted as rent on property held by the ...stocracy. If property rights were to be respected then ...e rent from that property was due its owner. It appeared ...t the Assembly had acted too hastily in renouncing all ...stocratic privileges. For the week following the 4 ...gust proposal, delegates worked to revise the proposal ...take into account the issue of income from property, ...ich was important to landowners.

...Finally, on 11 August 1789, the Assembly abolished serf-...m and all obligations deriving from it. Taxes would be ...nceforth paid proportionate to income, and the privileges ...exemption which the aristocrats had enjoyed would be ...noved. The Church would cease to claim the tithe, but ...ome from property based on a contractual agreement ...ween Church and renter would be unaffected. The

peasants stopped payment of feudal obligations, order was restored in the countryside, and the revolution would continue without peasant involvement, with the exception of Brittany and the Vendée. In these regions there was opposition to the rev-olution: in Brittany the peasants resented measures taken against the Catholic Church and in 1793 in the Vendée, conscription became a major issue. In both areas, the peasants rose in revolt against the government.

Declaration of the Rights of Man

The resolutions of the Assembly represented a new order for France. A declaration was writ-ten for the people, setting forth the laws and principles of the new state. This historic document, issued on 26 August 1789, was called the Declaration of the Rights of Man. It echoed the sentiments of Enlightenment *philosophes*, the English Bill of Rights, and the American Declaration of Independence. It asserted political and social equality of all men, the sovereignty of the people, and the natural right to liberty, property, security, and resistance to opposition. Taxes could henceforth only be raised by the consent of the people and public servants were held accountable for their actions. Thousands of copies were printed and widely distributed through France and eventually to all of Europe. It became the underlying philosophy of the Revolution.

The Declaration of the Rights of Man ushered in a new era. The Old Regime and the privileges of the aristocracy that it supported were abolished. The change would be characterized by the elevation of the state to new and pre-viously unimagined significance. From a geographical ter-ritory governed by an absolute monarch, the state emerged as the source of all sovereign power. Even the individual citizen, while granted numerous rights, would ultimately be subservient to the state.

The king was soon in conflict with the Assembly. He allowed the document to be printed but objected to its egalitarianism and refused to sign it. Furthermore, Louis XVI wanted an absolute veto while the Assembly favoured a limited veto, one which could suspend legislation for up to six years. Once again Louis began to assemble troops in an attempt to intimidate the Assembly and retain his position as ruler by divine right.

Bread Shortages

While the Assembly debated throughout the spring and summer of 1789, bread shortages had led to civil unrest in both rural and urban areas. Bread was a main source of food then so the supply of it was vitally important. Rumours of aristocratic plots to deprive the peasants of grain sparked violence which usually resulted in the ransacking of a manor or an attack on storehouses of grain. Occasionally, however, the violence escalated to an attack on authority as in the case of the attack on the *intendant* of Paris, Bertier de Sauvigny. He was responsible for food supplies in Paris. On 21 July he was seized by a mob, beheaded, and his severed head displayed on a pike. The abolition of feudalism and the introduction of the Declaration of the Rights of Man stemmed further violence but sporadic attacks occurred as the food shortages continued.

Despite a good harvest in 1789, the grain was not distributed effectively. Urban workers still experienced difficulty in obtaining adequate supplies of bread. On 5 October the women of Paris arrived at the central market of Les Halles to purchase bread but none was available. With crying children clinging to their skirts, they made their way to the Hôtel de Ville (City Hall) where city administrators puzzled over the dilemma of how to deal effectively with a crowd of mothers unable to feed their families. As their numbers increased so did the potential for violence.

Olympe de Gouges

In 1791 Olympe de Gouges published *The Rights of Women and the Citizen*. In this manifesto she claimed that women should be accorded the same rights as men. "Women awake! The tocsin of enlightenment and reason resounds through the universe; recognize your rights." De Gouges supported **constitutional monarchy** and wrote pamphlets throughout the revolutionary period advocating political change and the rights of the individual within a monarchy. During the Reign of Terror she was arrested by the Committee of Public Safety and sent to the guillotine.

One of the officers who ha participated in the seizure of t Bastille suggested that he le the women to Versailles protest the bread shortages Louis XVI. It was about 20 ki metres from Paris and t women would have to walk the rain. It was unlikely that t crowd would be able to traver the mud, he reasoned, but least this plan would have t effect of removing the unru crowd from the vicinity of t Paris councillors.

As the angry women march through Paris, their numbe grew; they were joined by mo women and small numbers men, some of whom were rev lutionary agitators dressed as women. By the time t crowd reached the outskirts of the city it had grown about 6000. They reached Versailles late in the afternoc invaded the palace, and demanded bread from the king. the face of the crowd, Louis XVI ordered that grain su plies be delivered to Paris—and accepted the conditic laid down by the Assembly in the Bill of Rights which st ulated the terms of his veto power. Both the women Paris and the National Assembly had won victories Louis's expense.

The crowd then demanded that the king and his fam return with them to Paris. The following morning wh two of the queen's guards were killed, General Lafaye gave in to the people's demand and persuaded the king return with them to Paris. Louis appeared on a balcc with his family and announced that he would accompa the crowd to Paris. It was a grave mistake on his pa From this time forward the royal family was held capt by the Paris revolutionaries at the Tuileries in Paris. Wh Louis was not in immediate personal danger, it was n clear that the revolutionaries were in control.

On 5 October 1789, angry women (and some men) marched from Paris to Versailles to protest the bread shortage. Do you think the artist of this engraving was a monarchist or republican? How can you tell?

ationalization of Church Lands

e events of the summer of 1789 introduced tremendous
anges to the institutions of France but no solution had
en found for the government's financial problems. The
olition of feudal taxes and the removal of aristocratic
vilege provided for equality in taxation, but no machin-
y was in place for the collection of moneys. As a result,
es were simply not being collected. Expenses mounted
the government paid for the maintenance of the army
d the police. In addition, it provided relief for the unem-
yed and those citizens faced with famine due to food
ortages. By August it was virtually impossible to find a
rce from which the government could borrow money.
he National Assembly was faced with the task of rais-
money to meet the budget. Necker estimated it would
a deficit of 294 million francs, more than double the
icit of 1788. New taxes on property and business were
osed to replace the old, abolished taxes. However, in
attempt to increase revenues, some of these old

indirect taxes, such as the salt tax, were revived. Despite
these measures it was impossible to raise the money
required to pay the interest on the government debt.

The Assembly now began to give serious consideration
to suggestions that had come forward as early as the spring
of 1789 regarding expropriation of Church lands. These
suggestions were based on the following argument: since
medieval times the Church had held lands in exchange for
the services it provided its parishioners. Traditionally, the
Church was responsible for education, orphanages, and
relief for the needy as well as spiritual guidance. Over the
years the Church had acquired control of about 10 percent
of the land in France. Critics of the Church argued that it
had neglected many of the duties considered to be part of
the bargain. It was only just, therefore, that the state now
seize these lands in order to direct the revenue into state
coffers.

Talleyrand, the Bishop of Autun, represented the clergy
at the National Assembly of 1789. He agreed with the argument to expropriate Church lands and proposed that, in

Since medieval times the Church had held lands in exchange for the services it provided its parishioners. Over the years the Church had acquired control of about 10 percent of the land in France. On 3 November 1789, the National Assembly voted to expropriate Church lands.

exchange for receiving Church property, the state would assume those duties which had been the domain of the Church and, in addition, two thirds of the revenue would be directed toward the salaries of church clerics. Honoré Mirabeau, an eloquent spokesperson for the third estate, then moved that all church lands simply be nationalized and the maintenance of the church be part of the government's general expenses. Bitter debate ensued. Conservative clergy anxious to maintain the Church's power pitted themselves against radical anticlerics who wished to secularize Church lands. Finally, on 3 November 1789, the Assembly voted in support of Mirabeau's motion and Church lands were nationalized.

In December, bonds whose value was secured by Church lands, were issued to the government's creditors. The total value of the bonds, called *assignats*, was 400 million francs. The creditors were expected to exchange the bonds for the confiscated properties and as such they would cease to exist as soon as all of the Church lands were dispensed. However, many of these *assignats* were simply exchanged for hard currency and as a result they began to be used as paper money. In addition, some of the *assignats* which were used to obtain property were not burned but rather were returned to circulation. Desperate to increase the flow of cash in the economy, the government printed more *assignats* and by 1792 their value had fallen to 58 percent of the original worth. As the amount of *assignats* in circulation increased and the government debt continued to grow, inflation pervaded the economy. By 1796 the *assignats* were basically worthless. On 4 February 1797, France abandoned its paper currency and returned to hard currency.

Civil Constitution of the Clergy

The **nationalization** of Church lands proved to be only the first step in state control of the Church. On 12 July 1790, the Assembly passed the Civil Constitution of the Clergy to bring the clergy under state control. Church parishes were reorganized and the number of dioceses was reduced. Clergy would now be elected by all citizens and their salaries paid by the state. The pope condemned the move and the Revolution in general. In retaliation, the clergy were required to swear an oath of allegiance to the Civil Constitution of the Clergy, which essentially required the clergy to acknowledge the supremacy of the French government not the pope. Of course, many of the clergy simply could not accept this. By November, it was evident that most of the clergy had refused to take the oath and the government now issued an ultimatum. All clergy had to take the oath within a week or give up their positions. More than half of the clergy and 132 out of the 137 bishops refused the oath.

Fatefully, the Civil Constitution of the Clergy increased the conflict between church and state. The seizure of church lands, and now the secular control of the clergy confirmed the Church's view that the revolution was radically anti-Catholic. Throughout the dispute, Louis XVI was uncomfortable with the ruptured relationship that now existed between France and the pope but he maintained an uneasy silence.

∼ Charles de Talleyrand-Périgord ∼
(1754–1838)

Charles de Talleyrand-Périgord served three French kings and Napoleon. Talleyrand was born into a noble, distinguished family and educated for a career in the Church. In spite of a cynical nature and a notorious reputation, he rose quickly in Church ranks. Named abbot of St Denis in 1775, he later became an *agent-général* to the Church and was named bishop of Autun in 1788 by Louis XVI. The following year the Church elected him to the Estates General. He was among the writers of the Declaration of the Rights of Man. Although a cleric, he proposed the bill to confiscate Church property. His sympathy to the Revolution also led him to be one of the few bishops who swore the oath of allegiance to the revolutionary government. Although he did so while proclaiming his loyalty to the pope, he was excommunicated. Talleyrand spent the years of the Terror in England and was recalled by Napoleon to be minister of foreign affairs, although Napoleon generally ignored Talleyrand's advice.

After Napoleon's overthrow, Talleyrand was instrumental in the restoration of the monarchy in the person of Louis XVIII, younger brother of Louis XVI. He supported this as a peaceful solution to the question of succession after Napoleon. Talleyrand represented France at the Congress of Vienna in 1815 and was ambassador to London until his retirement from public life in 1834.

Throughout the revolutionary period and the reactionary period of post-Napoleonic Europe, Talleyrand was seen as an opportunist—even Louis XVIII was not fond of him—but he was an exceptionally successful statesman.

Restructuring the Administrative Framework

In another direction the National Assembly was faced with a major task—to restructure the administrative framework of France. It began by writing the first French constitution, restructuring the system of representation, and revamping the judicial system.

The centralized system of power that had supported the absolute monarchy had been destroyed in the initial stages of the revolution. In its place local councils were established. These councils became the basic unit of the new decentralized government. France was now divided into 83 *départements* governed by elected officials. Gone were the *intendants* who had been responsible to the central government. Boundaries were redesigned to eliminate the old provincial territories and to create units which were approximately equal in size and wealth.

The *parlements* were abolished and a uniform system of district courts was established. All officials of the courts were elected and all cases were tried in local courts. The Court of Cassation in Paris was the final court of appeal. It did not hear cases but rather ruled on the legality of the findings and then sent the case back to the district court. Juries were selected for criminal cases but civil cases were tried by judges only.

The sweeping reforms enacted by the National Assembly stripped Louis XVI of his power. He was unhappy with his new position. Was he not God's representative on earth? What role was left to him now that he could no longer issue decrees and direct the affairs of state? He was virtually imprisoned in the Tuileries, very much aware of the personal danger in which he and his family lived. Food shortages were a constant concern and could swing the mood of the Paris populace against the royal family in an instant. Mirabeau had been urging the king to leave France ever since the march of the women on Versailles. Although he supported the revolution, Mirabeau remained staunchly loyal to the monarchy and, until his death on 2 April 1791, he produced numerous plans to assist Louis to escape from Paris.

Further unrest in Paris in the spring of 1791 convinced the queen, Marie Antoinette, that the family must flee. With the help of a loyal friend, Count Axel von Fersen, an escape was organized. On 20 June 1791, a carriage carrying the royal family in disguise left Paris bound for Montmedy in Lorraine. They were prepared to continue to Austria if necessary. When they reached Varennes (east of Paris), they were recognized and National Guardsmen escorted them back to Paris through jeering crowds. The king's fate was sealed. The revolutionaries charged the king and queen with treason.

As a result of the king's flight, the constitution was amended. The king was required to uphold the constitution and to **abdicate** if he left the country for longer than two months. He was no longer in control of the army and his veto power was limited to four years. Male citizens over 25 who paid taxes equivalent to three days wages were eligible to vote. The Assembly was to be elected and could not be dissolved by the king. The powers of the three branches of government, the legislative, the executive, and the judicial were clearly divided; and the king's suspensive veto did not extend to judicial or constitutional matters. On 14 September 1791, the constitution was sworn in by Louis XVI in front of the National Assembly. On 30 September 1791, the Constituent Assembly was dissolved for election of a Legislative Assembly which met for the first time on 1 October 1791. In the meantime, the **republican** forces had been building strength and over the next few months radical changes would set the stage for a new phase in the revolution.

Most of the 745 new deputies in the Legislative Assembly were either men of property or lawyers. They had been elected by no more than about 10 percent of the eligible voters. No group claimed a majority although the moderates who sat in the centre had the most seats. Because the Jacobins sat to the left of the speaker, high in the assembly hall, they were called "the Mountain." The Girondins sat near them while the more conservative members sat to the right of the

Queen Marie Antoinette never felt at home in France and longed to return to Vienna. She and the king were charged with treason in 1791 after they tried to escape from France.

speaker. Our modern political definitions of the "left" as ra ical and the "right" as conservative originated in the se ing of the Legislative Assembly.

Georges Jacques Danton (1759-1794)
was the president of the Jacobin club.

Throughout the revolutionary period, political debate was carried on in clubs throughout France. It was there that revolutionary ideas were born before being introduced in government. The numbers and types of clubs quickly increased and by the time the Constituent Assembly was dissolved nearly 1000 clubs existed in France. Women and those men who could not afford the club membership dues gathered together in societies. In addition, women of wealth still wielded

Revolutionary Clubs & Societies

considerable influence in the salons where political discussion and intellectual discourse was pursued.

The Jacobin club was the most important of these groups. Originally called the Club Breton, it originated at Versailles in 1789 when Britanny's deputies to the third estate decided to meet separately before the Estates General in order to consolidate a position on reforms and ensure that Brittany was properly represented. The Club Breton acted as a lobby group and over the summer reacted spontaneously to the events of the revolution. By October the group began to meet in the Jacobin convent in Paris and became known as the Jacobins.

The Jacobins restricted entrance to male patriots of the revolution. Many of the revolution's famous personalities, such as Maximilien Robespierre, perfected their speech-making skills in the club's environment. The Paris Jacobin club was the nerve centre of revolutionary discussion. The Paris branch was affiliated with numerous rural branches.

The flight of the king created a heated debate in the clubs and over the summer a new and more radical brand of Jacobinism emerged. At this point a number of new political groupings emerged. This continued through the next two years. Those members who still supported the monarchy left the Jacobins and formed the Feuillants. Bourgeois libertarians who favoured moderate revolutionary change but objected to centralized power gathered as Girondins. The Jacobins grew steadily more radical and wanted a **republic** with centralized government.

Emigrés

Between 1789 and 1795, from the beginning of the revolution to the installation of the Directory under Napoleon, thousands of people left France. They were called *émigrés*, or emigrants. Prior to 1792 *émigrés* were predominantly aristocrats and those clergy who refused to take the oath of allegiance to the new order. After 1792 when the revolution became more radical, they were from all levels of society. The common bond they shared was a rejection of the radical republican nature of the revolution. The army suffered as a result of this exodus as the officer corps was staffed from the nobility.

France Goes to War against Austria

The Girondins persuaded Louis XVI that France could win a war against Austria. Hence, on 21 April 1792, the French government declared war on Austria. As Prussia was allied with Austria, France found itself fighting a war against both countries. The first foray into the war was in the Austrian Netherlands where the French were not only defeated but routed. The French army had been emasculated by the loss of its officer corps. The only factor that prevented a swift defeat overall was that Russia was busy in eastern Poland. Russia, Austria, and Prussia had begun the partition of Poland in 1772 and neither Austria nor Prussia were willing to allow Russia a free hand in this

*The guillotine was installed in the
Place du Carrousel in front of the Tuileries.
The sharp, heavy blade instantly
severed the head from the body.*

second attempt at partition. As a result, the war with France was a secondary matter and Paris escaped occupation.

Paris seethed with discontent throughout the summer of 1792. Hungry, distrustful of government, and discouraged by failures in the war, Parisians grew increasingly restless. On 10 August 1792 they turned against the king. The mob stormed the Tuileries where the royal family was being held. Killing some of the Swiss guard, they seized the king and royal family. They set up a revolutionary municipal government in Paris. They demanded a new constitution and a convention to replace the Legislative Assembly. They wanted all male citizens to cast a vote for the electors who would choose the new government. These electors would no longer have to meet property qualifications and hence the doors would be opened to the lower levels of the bourgeoisie.

September Massacres

In the fall of 1792, hysteria, uncertainty, and fear gripped the city. Rumours circulated that the 3000 prisoners held in Paris prisons were planning to stage an uprising. Although some of these inmates were criminals, many were political dissidents or priests who had refused to take the oath of allegiance to the new order. French nationalism intensified when other European powers, fearing their own revolutions, became critical of the events in France. News that Verdun was threatened by the Prussian army was the spark that began what are called the "September Massacres." An angry mob stormed the prisons and over the next five days about 1100 prisoners were killed. The mob justified their actions by maintaining that they were preserving the republic.

This action was only a prelu to the Reign of Terror that w unleashed the following ye The guillotine was alrea installed in the Place du C rousel in front of the Tuileries was a new means of executic considered much more huma than other methods. Invented Dr. Antoine Louis, its use w suggested by Dr. Joseph Gu lotin because the sharp, hea blade instantly severed the he from the body. Prior to this, o nobles had been allowed a m cifully quick beheading wh sentenced to death. Lesser in viduals suffered hanging or a number of excruciating and l gering deaths.

National Convention

The Legislative Assembly c solved and was replaced by t National Convention, which n for the first time on 21 Septe ber 1792. One of its first a abolished the monarchy. Frar would now be a republic. T Convention decreed that 17 was Year I of the French Rep lic for purposes of dating pub documents. A committee w struck in order to develop yet another constitution. Jacob such as Brissot, Thomas Paine, and Condorcet provided leadership in this endeavour. By November the Conventi had established an aggressive foreign policy which enco aged international revolution in those areas where peo were attempting to gain liberty and equality.

In the Convention Jacobin leaders soon divided the selves into three very distinct groups. The Girondins g nered their strength from the oratorical skills of men l Brissot and Roland. They favoured a decentralized form government, strict adherence to the constitution, resp for private property and they opposed expanding the w The Jacobins led by Robespierre, Jean Paul Marat, a

Jean Paul Marat (1743-1793)
...as a French revolutionary, journalist, and physician.
...long with Robespierre and Danton, he overthrew the
...irondins. He was assassinated in his bath soon after
by Charlotte Corday.

~
A Revolutionary Song
~

To symbolize the new beginning, the revolutionaries sang a stirring marching song called the "Marseillaise" which became the anthem of the new, First Republic.

Marseillaise
Allons enfants de la Patrie,
Le jour de gloire est arrivé.
Contre nous, de la tyrannie,
L'étendard sanglant est levé,
L'étendard sanglant est levé,
Entendez-vous, dans les campagnes
Mugir ces farouches soldats.
Ils viennent jusque dans nos bras
Egorger vos fils, vos compagnes.
Aux armes citoyens! Formez vos bataillons,
Marchons, marchons!
Qu'un sang impur abreuve nos sillons!

Arise, children of the fatherland,
The day of glory has come.
Against us the blood-stained banner
Of tyranny is raised,
The banner of tyranny is raised,
Hear, in the fields, the roar
Of her fierce soldiers.
They come right into our arms
To slaughter our sons and our consorts.
Patriots, to arms! Form your battalions,
Let's march, let's march!
May the tyrant's foul blood water our furrows!

Translation by T.M. Cartledge. Excerpted from *National Anthems of the World,* edited by W.L. Reed and M.J. Briston, Cassell Press, 1993.

...orges Danton favoured a centralized government, ...ught they could determine the "general will" of the peo- ... They were prepared to abandon the idea of private ...perty in the interests of communal holdings. The ...ondin support came largely from rural areas while the ...obin support was centred in urban areas, particularly ...ris. In between these groups was the "Plain." This was ...rge group in the political centre that remained uncom- ...ted on most issues and was constantly lobbied by both ...remes for support. As the Girondins were the moder- ...s, the Plain usually joined Girondin forces.

...he issue that demanded resolution if the republic was ...be truly secure was what to do with the king. How

should the government dispose of this former absolute monarch? It was determined that he would be brought to trial on charges of conspiracy against the nation. Although he had not committed any of the acts which the constitution of 1791 outlined as conditions under which the king could be brought to trial, the National Convention proceeded. The Jacobins were determined to execute the king; the Girondins wanted clemency. After nearly six weeks of debate and futile appeals in the king's defence, the vote favoured execution by a majority of one. On 21 January 1793, the French government sent its former king to the guillotine. The queen followed a few months later. The Girondins lost all favour with Paris citizens who felt

FRANCE IN 1793

France in 1789
Attacks on Revolutionary France

0   300
KILOMETRES

On 21 April 1792, the French government declared war on Austria and Austria's ally, Prussia. This war began a series of wars that did not end until the defeat of Napoleon in 1815.

Law of the Maximum

In response to the people's demands for cheaper bread, the Committee of Public Safety passed a law in April 1793 setting maximum prices for goods and, later, limiting wages. An army of regulators was sent out to monitor prices and wages. However, the law was unevenly enforced. Goods were sold at the top, or maximum, price. People who had money paid whatever was necessary on the "black market" in order to get food. Those who had no money were still suffering from a shortage of bread. As a result, this attempt at centralized economic control failed and the Law of the Maximum was abandoned in December 1794.

The Sans-Culottes

The term *sans-culottes* referred to a group of working-class men who wore long pants rather than the knee-length pants of the nobility. The long pants were worn with a loose shirt, red cap, and a tricolour cockade. The *sans-culottes* were against all religion and wanted to remove it from French society. They also wanted social equality for everyone. With the beginnings of support for women's rights, they became associated with subsequent movements for the rights of workers. The *sans-culottes* were urban workers led by extreme revolutionaries such as Jacques Hébert. Typically their support could be mustered by crises such as shortages of bread or protestations of political injustice. Between 1792 and 1795 they formed the most substantial portion of the Paris mob, but without effective leadership of their own they were helpless in the face of Jacobin power. The movement fell apart as thousands of the *sans-culottes* drifted out of Paris to the rural areas to join renegade groups.

Levée en Masse

On 23 August 1793, the Committee of Public Safety made a decree that mobilized the entire French population for war. All unmarried men between the ages of 18 and 25 were conscripted. Women worked in hospitals and made clothing and tents for the soldiers, while older men worked in the production of war *matériel* and became part of the propaganda machine marshalling support for the war effort. This was the beginning of national armies that would provide the military with a continual supply of new recruits.

trayed by the Girondin sup-
rt of Louis XVI and the
cobins were now in control of
e Convention. The Revolution
uld now be controlled by the
dical forces, namely the
cobins led by Robespierre.
wer would be ruthlessly cen-
lized in Paris.

ommittee of
ublic Safety

anwhile, the European hos-
ties had expanded so much
at by the summer of 1793
ince was at war with Britain
d all of the European powers
cept Russia. The country con-
ued to be plagued by food
ortages and the Paris popu-
e faced soaring bread prices.
April the government moved
centralize control by appoint-
a Committee of Public
ety. This was, in effect, a
elve-member executive with
eeping powers. It became a
ly revolutionary body, controlling both the domestic
d the foreign policy of France. One of the committee's
in goals was to repress the counter-revolutionaries. By
y, Robespierre had been elected to the group and over
next year it would be through his influence that the
gn of Terror, as it is popularly known, would be
eashed. During that terrible time, any citizen *suspected*
reason against the revolutionary state was sent to the
llotine. Over the next year about 20 000 men, women,
d children perished. These included members of the
al family, aristocrats, clergy, political enemies, and
one suspected of military or political treason.

French Revolutionary Calendar

Calendar of France
14 November 1793—31 December 1805

The calendar had no weekly divisions. Every
month had 30 days. Every tenth day (décodi)
was a day of rest. On leap years, the extra day
was designated Revolution Day.

Vendémiaire	(vintage month)
Brumaire	(fog)
Frimaire	(sleet)
Nivôse	(snow)
Pluviôse	(rain)
Ventôse	(wind)
Germinal	(seed)
Floréal	(blossom)
Prairial	(pasture)
Messidor	(harvest)
Thermidor *or*	
Fervidor	(heat)
Fructidor	(fruit)

Five Feast Days:
Virtue, Genius, Labour, Reason, Rewards

Republic of Virtue

Patriotism inspired by the war
effort was important to the success that the revolutionary government had against supporters
of the Old Regime. The other factors in this success were the
weaknesses of the foreign armies who were also involved in
other matters and in the improvements made in the French
army, now better equipped and
more effectively staffed. For
example, changes to the officer
corps now allowed members of
the third estate to be commissioned on the basis of talent
rather than class.

Social and cultural changes
were implemented by the
Jacobins during the time they
were in control in an attempt to
erase all traces of the Old
Regime and introduce a completely new society. They called
their new society, based on reason, the Republic of Virtue. The
cult of "worship of the Supreme
Being" was introduced in an attempt to destroy Christianity. (However, tradition prevailed. Despite the closure of
churches and a campaign of terror carried out by the government against both the hierarchy and the property of the
Church, the people were not won over to this rather abstract
new movement.) Individuals were now addressed as
citoyen ("citizen"). There was regulated conformity in clothing styles that copied classical dress. Simple cotton garments replaced the heavy, ornate costumes of the Old
Regime. Gone were the powdered wigs and heavy jewellery
of the aristocrats. Simplicity reigned.

In August 1793 a new system of weights and measures
based on the decimal system was introduced. The metric
system was considered to be more compatible with the
emphasis on reason in the new Republic of Virtue. A revolutionary calendar gave new names to days and months
and renumbered the years from 1792, the first year of the
revolutionary republic so that September 22, 1792 was the
first day of Year I.

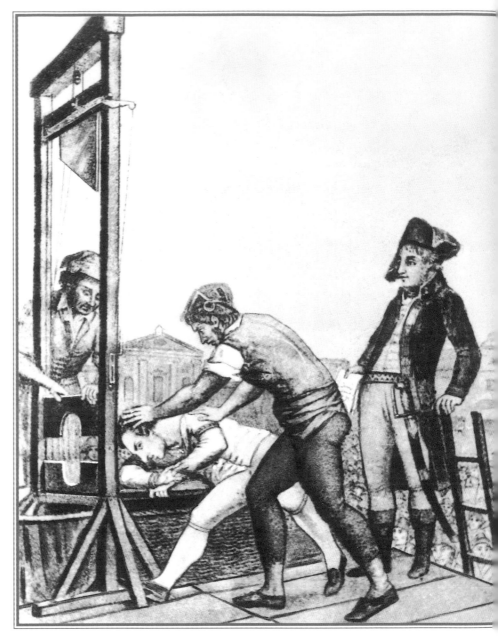

End of Terror

The Committee of Public Safety, sometimes referred to as the Twelve Who Rule, was supported by a Committee of Public Security which was responsible for policing the regime. Enemies of the republic were ferreted out and turned over to Revolutionary Tribunals. Denunciation by three citizens was also used as a means of identifying political enemies. In both cases the accused ended up at the guillotine. About 40 000 people died during the Terror. Some historians have said that the Jacobins were the first to bring in a **totalitarian** system in the name of liberty and **democracy.**

No one was safe. After a year of irrational violence the public rose in opposition to the Jacobin "Terror." Robespierre had demanded an extension of the government's emergency powers to rule by decree. His opponents felt the emergencies were over and wanted a return to normal administration. They feared Robespierre would use his exceptional powers to have them executed, as he had others during the reign of terror. In the

On 27 July 1794, Robespierre was arrested by his opponents. He was sent to the guillotine the next day.

month of Thermidor in the new calendar, Robespierre was deserted by his supporters, accused of being a tyrant, and arrested on 27 July 1794, or 9 Thermidor. The day after his arrest he and some of his followers were sent to the guillotine. He was destroyed by the very system he had created.

The fall of Robespierre led to what historians call the Thermidorean Reaction. Following Robespierre's death the National Convention, solidly bourgeoise, dismantled the machinery of the Terror and reintroduced a climate of moderation to the country. The Revolutionary Tribunal was abolished as were the committees of public safety and

that of public security. The Paris Jacobin club was clos and Girondins were encouraged to rejoin the conventi Churches were reopened and citizens were encouraged resume cultural pursuits.

Despite these changes by the forces of moderation, Pa was filled with civil unrest and the country was unsett for some time. Attacks on remnants of the Jacobin regi and those suspected of supporting the Jacobins w numerous. The end of centralized control led to instabil ty and no system of law and order was immediately int duced to stabilize the country. Over the next year the g ernment worked on a new constitution and, in Septem

95, the passage of this consti-
ion ended the National Con-
ntion.

nstitution of 1795

e Constitution of 1795 re-
ned power to the propertied
ss. The lowest levels of soci-
were denied the vote and no
ntion was made of social
ts such as education or the
ht to work which had been
nsidered so important during
time of the convention. Rather than stressing freedom
d equality, as had the Declaration of Rights of 1789, free-
m and equality were identified but responsibilities were
phasized. For example, citizens were expected to obey
law and respect private property.

he Constitution of 1795 established a two-house legis-
ure which was comprised of the Council of Five
ndred and the Council of Elders. Legislation would be
roduced by the Five Hundred and then approved or dis-
roved by the Elders who numbered 250 members.
ctions for both houses would be held each spring with
e-third of the group seeking reelection each year.
ecutive power would be vested in five Directors chosen
the Elders from a list which the Council of Five
ndred submitted. The regime was called the Directory.
as to last four years (1795–1799).

he Directory struggled to maintain order in the face of
ere economic distress and continuous military and
itical pressure exerted both by foreign and domestic
ces. Harvest failures had once again brought famine;
ic foodstuffs were in such short supply that rationing
to be introduced. To compound the problem, the
ignats completely collapsed after spiralling inflation.
1797 France's experiment with paper money was aban-
ed. The return to metal currency promised some staty. By this time, however, speculators had made for-
es at the expense of the ordinary individual. Tempers
re short and once again class conflict was rife through-
the country. The foundation was being laid for the
p d'état that Napoleon staged in 1799. By that time
nch citizens longed for law and order and a promise of
urity at any price.

~ A Prince's Fate ~

On 8 June 1795 the young son
of Louis XVI and Marie Antoinette died
of tuberculosis after suffering two years of
appalling prison conditions. As heir to the
throne, he would have become
Louis XVII.

SUMMARY

The political, economic,
and social changes which
occurred in France from
1789 to 1799 changed the structure of the country forever. Politically, France changed from an
ab-solute monarchy to a constitutional monarchy, and finally to
a republic. The revolutionary cry
for "Liberty, Equality, Fraternity"
was answered on 11 August 1789
when feudalism was abolished
and the Declaration of the Rights of Man introduced polit
ical and social equality as well as liberty to own property
and have political freedom.

The state took control of the Roman Catholic Church by
nationalizing the church lands. Then the Civil Constitution
of the Clergy made the clergy, effectively, into civil servants.

In June 1791, the king attempted to flee the country. His
capture led to a radical phase in the revolution and ultimately to his execution in January 1793.

The French declaration of war against Austria in 1792
began a series of wars that would not end until the defeat
of Napoleon in 1815.

After the radical Jacobins, led by Robespierre, seized
power, they created a centralized government that controlled all aspects of the country. They monitored wages
and prices in a futile attempt to resolve France's financial
woes.

The Republic of Virtue was introduced to re-order society. The calendar was changed and the metric system was
introduced. In order to control society the regime sent
thousands of people to the guillotine. By July 1794, the
public could no longer tolerate the totalitarian system
which the Jacobins had created, and Robespierre was sent
to the guillotine.

For the last four years of the revolutionary period, the
Directory governed France. Faced with continuing financial and social pressures, the directors were unable to
restore stability. The climate was ripe for a military coup.

QUESTIONS

1. Explain how absolute power of the king was destroyed by the events of July 1789.

2. What was the Great Fear? Describe the conditions which created it.

3. Explain the rationale for the legislation that abolished feudalism.

4. What was the Declaration of the Rights of Man and how was it significant?

5. What was the effect of bread shortages during the initial stages of revolution? Briefly explain the women's march on Versailles on 5 October 1789. What was the result of their meeting with Louis XVI? What was the significance of the royal family's move to Paris?

6. Explain the economic difficulties which existed in France during the first few months of the revolution.

7. What were the *assignats*? How did they contribute to inflation in France?

8. Explain the terms of the Civil Constitution of the Clergy. How did the clergy react to the document?

9. Describe the new administrative structure in France.

10. How was the judicial system reformed?

11. What was Louis XVI's reaction to the reforms instituted by France's new revolutionary government?

12. Describe the royal family's attempted escape on 20 June 1791. What was the significance of this attempted escape both on the royal family and on t future political system in France?

13. Briefly describe the terms of the Constitution of 17

14. Explain the origins and philosophy of the Jacobin Clubs. What role did the clubs play in the evolution of political ideas in France?

15. Explain the origins of our modern understanding o the political "left" and "right."

16. Briefly describe the September Massacres. What w: the significance of this event?

17. Describe the difference of opinion voiced by the Girondins and the Jacobins regarding the fate of th king. What was the result of the debate?

18. Describe the Committee of Public Safety. What wa: its purpose?

19. What was the Reign of Terror? How was it brought an end?

20. What social and cultural changes were implemente by the Jacobins?

21. Explain the terms of the Constitution of 1795. How did it differ from the Declaration of the Rights of Man? Why would this difference be included? Explain the structure of government that this constitution established.

22. What problems did France face during the period of the Directory (1795-1799)?

ANALYSIS

Why was the Declaration of the Rights of Man central to the French Revolution's ideals? Give some thought to the rights you have as an individual in your society. Read the Canadian Charter of Rights and Freedoms. Note the preamble which states that Canadians live under the law in a democratic society. What is the significance of this statement?

The revolutionaries proclaimed political, social, and legal equality for the people of France. How well did the revolutionaries live up to their sloganeering? Speculate on why economic equality was not mentioned. Should all citizens be treated equally? Why or why not?

ACTIVITIES

1. Newspaper
Develop an edition of a newspaper that might have been published by Marat during the French Revolution. Choose a date that allows you to report significant events, and include reports on at least three different issues. Consider including an editorial cartoon, letters to the editor, and an editorial.

2. Trial
Recreate the debate in the Convention regarding the fate of Louis XVI. Present the Girondin and the Jacobin position by having people like Brissot, Thomas Paine, Condorcet, Roland, Robespierre, Marat, and Danton speak.

3. Defence
Prepare a defence for the king against the demands of the revolutionaries for his execution.

4. Meeting of the National Assembly
Recreate the events leading up to the night of 4 August and then role play the meeting that led the nobility to renounce their privileges. Conclude with a discussion among some nobles regarding the serious consequences of their renunciation of privilege.

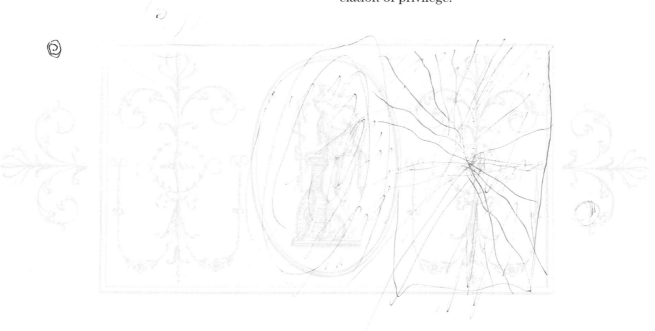

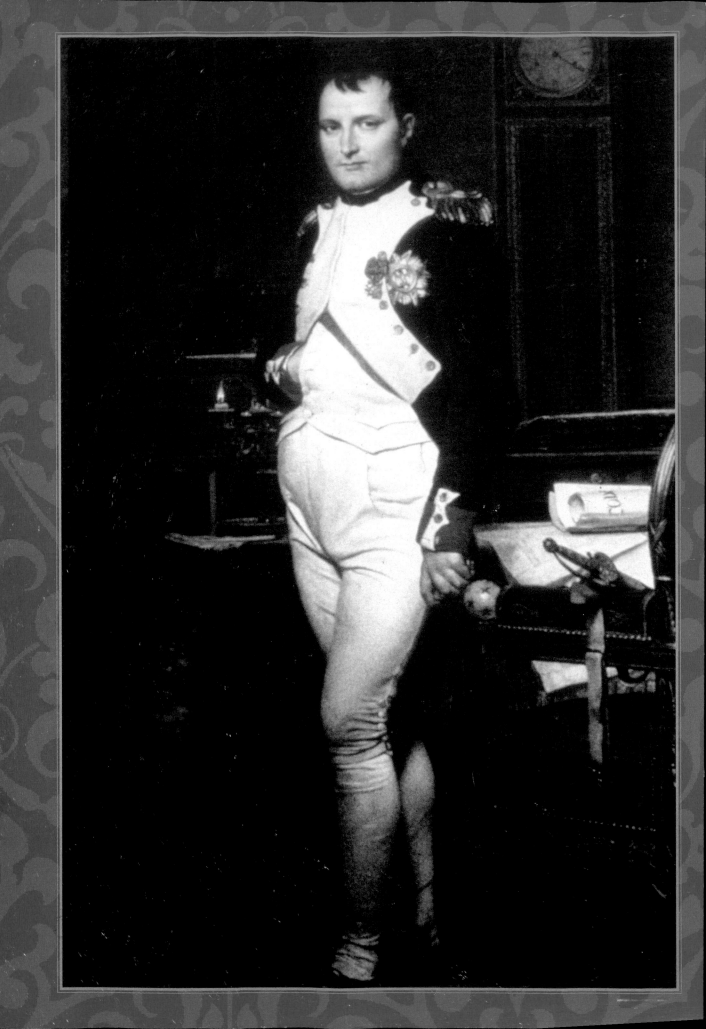

Chapter 4
Napoleon

FOCUS ON:

✿

Napoleon's implementation of domestic reforms in response to
the revolutionary demands of 1789;

✿

Napoleon's strategy to defeat England and dominate the European continent;

✿

Napoleon's rule of France in comparison to the absolute rule
of the Bourbon monarchy.

*Napoleon Bonaparte (1769–1821) established himself as emperor of France and
sought to extend his empire over the entire European continent.*

In 1799 France was still embroiled in social, economic, and political crises. Problems were so serious that people feared the return of the Terror. Abbé Sieyès and Roger Ducos, both directors in the government, plotted to overthrow the Directory. They needed the support of the military and chose General Napoleon Bonaparte, planning to install him later as a figurehead, a leader with largely ceremonial duties, leaving the control of domestic and foreign affairs in their hands. The coup d'état took place 9 November without bloodshed. Neither Sieyès nor Ducos recognized Napoleon's ambition to seize control of government.

Napoleon proclaimed the new republic, which he called the Consulate, and promised new elections. For the next two months, French citizens were bombarded with propaganda in preparation for their vote on a new constitution in February 1800. Weary of the civil unrest and the political intrigue of the revolutionary era, they voted overwhelmingly in favour of the constitution, confirming their confidence in Napoleon, who promised stability after a decade of upheaval.

The government was to be run by three consuls. Napoleon was First Consul and had power to exercise full executive authority including the proclamation of laws. The second and third consuls, Sieyès and Ducos, could only advise. The groundwork was laid for Napoleon's rise to absolute power.

TIMELINE

1798
Egyptian campaign

1799
The Consulate is established.
9 November ❈ Napoleon's coup d'état

1800
French armies advance into central Europe.

1801
15 July ❈ Concordat with Pope Pius VII

1802
March ❈ Treaty of Amiens

1803
Louisiana Purchase

1804
Coronation of Napoleon as emperor of France
Code Napoleon is promulgated.

1805
21 October ❈ Battle of Trafalgar

1806
Confederation of the Rhine as a French protectorate
Berlin Decrees establish the Continental System.

1807
The Peace of Tilsit, between France and Russia, is arrived at.

1808–1813
Spanish campaign

1810
Russia withdraws from the Continental System.

1812
24 June ❈ Grand Armée crosses the Niemen and invades Russia.
7 September ❈ Battle of Borodino, outside Moscow
Retreat of the Grand Armée from Moscow.

1813
16–19 October ❈ Battle of the Nations

1814
6 April ❈ Napoleon abdicates.
Louis XVIII is enthroned.
Congress of Vienna meets.
Napoleon is exiled to Elba.

1815
Napoleon escapes from Elba.
18 June ❈ Battle of Waterloo
Napoleon is exiled to St. Helena.

The new constitution provided for universal male suffrage but the government reserved the right to choose members of the three representative bodies the Senate, the Tribunate, and the *Corps Législatif* from lists provided by the voters. This structure gave people only the illusion of power and allowed Napoleon as First Consul to control the appointments in government. Under the constitution, Napoleon could arrest citizens deemed dangerous to the state. While the Senate had the theoretical power to block Napoleon's actions, the Senate was composed largely of individuals nominated by Napoleon.

CONSOLIDATION OF POWER

Politically, France remained divided between Royalists and Republicans. Napoleon faced the task of attempting to appease yet control both sides, while moving forward to consolidate his own position as head of government. He immediately moved toward the elimination of all opposition, appointing Joseph Fouché as minister of police.

Fouché, an ex-Terrorist, had a reputation as an exceptional policeman and had helped to bring about the fall of Robespierre. His first challenge was to find the perpetrators of a plot on 24 December 1800 to kill Napoleon by bombing his carriage on his way to the opera. The bomb killed several

~ The Bonapartes ~

Josephine was a widow with two children from her first marriage. She married Napoleon in 1789, but they divorced 13 years later because she had not borne him a male heir.

Napoleon Buonaparte (later spelled Bonaparte) was born on 15 August 1769, on the island of Corsica, a colony of France. His family was of the noble class. At the age of ten he entered the military school at Brienne and shortly afterward went on to the royal military school in Paris. He received his first commission in the artillery as second lieutenant when he was only 16. This was the beginning of a military career that altered the course of history.

Napoleon first drew attention to his military talent during the French Revolution when his strategy defeated English forces at Toulon in 1793. In 1795 when the National Convention was threatened by thousands of national guardsmen who wanted the monarchy reinstated, the Vicomte de Barras called upon General Napoleon, then 25, for assistance. Napoleon organized the few troops available so skillfully that he turned back the guardsmen "with a whiff of grapeshot." The Vicomte de Barras then appointed Napoleon to command the Army of the Alps. His successful Italian campaign against the Austrians in 1797 earned him a hero's welcome when he returned to Paris. In 1798 he led an expedition into Egypt. Stranded after the Battle of the Nile, where the British fleet destroyed the French fleet and cut off their supply lines, Napoleon left his army and returned to Paris. The remaining French in Egypt began to exert a major influence there. (See Chapter 10.)

On 9 March 1796, Napoleon married Rose de Beauharnais (he changed her name to Josephine), a widow six years older than he. She had two children, Eugene and Hortense, from her first marriage to Vicomte Alexandre de Beauharnais, a French general executed in the Revolution. In 1809, despite claiming that he still loved her, Napoleon divorced Josephine because she had been unable to bear him the son he desired. On 2 April 1810, he married the Archduchess Marie-Louise of the Austrian Hapsburg royal family. This marriage was contracted in the hope that France would have an ally in Austria and that Napoleon would finally have an heir to the dynasty he was building. On 21 March 1811, Napoleon's son was born. He was named Napoleon II and was given the title King of Rome. When Napoleon was defeated at Waterloo, Marie-Louise took the boy to Austria where he died at 21 of tuberculosis.

Napoleon earned a reputation as a brilliant strategist and is considered to be one of the greatest military geniuses of all time. He was an opportunist who sought power and glory at any cost. He established himself as emperor of the French and sought to extend his empire over the entire European continent.

This is Jacques Louis David's painting of Napoleon's coronation as emperor. Napoleon is shown crowning Josephi
David (1748–1825) was appointed Napoleon's court painter in 1804.

bystanders but missed its target. Before daybreak the plotters were identified as Royalists. Two were shot and many others imprisoned.

Napoleon used the incident to eliminate some people whom he believed were a threat to him. He accused the Jacobins of the conspiracy. With consent of the Senate, he purged his government of many Jacobins by means of a special decree. Seven hundred of these revolutionary radicals were imprisoned and a special tribunal declared that 120 of the traitors would be exiled to the Seychelles Islands. The purge continued, requiring certain deputies to retire. All of those chosen for "retirement" were enemies of Napoleon. They were replaced with acceptable candidates from the national list.

Napoleon's consolidation of power was assisted not only by Fouché but by rigid censorship of the press and political activity. In January 1800 Napoleon censored 60 of the 73 French newspapers in an attempt to silence opposition to the republic. Subsequently, the ministry of the police under Fouché was instructed to censor the press and the ministry of the interior was told to censor the theatre. By

1807 the number of theatres in Paris had been reduce eight and rigid control was imposed on the choice of ductions. Booksellers were also limited to what they c sell and literature was required to support the Napole regime.

By 1802 Napoleon was so popular that the Counc State proclaimed him "Consul for Life." A plebiscit popular vote, overwhelmingly confirmed his posit 3 600 000 to 8600. Napoleon became the chief magis of France for life. It was he who embodied the idea both the Revolution and the Republic.

In May 1804 a new constitution, the Constitution o Year XII, declared that "the government of the repub confided to an emperor." The French Consulate bec the French Empire and Napoleon became Emperc France. He had engineered majority support for his au itarian control by continuing to broaden police auth and by presenting himself to the French as their savi

The new constitution also provided for the inherit of this title by Napoleon's male heirs. His brothers, Jo and Louis, followed in the line of succession behind

. At his coronation on 2 December 1804, in Notre Dame
...hedral, Napoleon took the crown from the hands of
...e Pius VII and placed it on his own head. It was a clear
...ssage that he owed none of his power to the Church but
...her that he had risen with the support of the French cit-
...ry and the army. The coronation regalia used was that
...harlemagne, the legendary king of the Franks, to sym-
...ize that Napoleon was not succeeding the Bourbon
...asty but was continuing the tradition of Frankish
...narchy. The Napoleonic dynasty had begun. During the
...t ten years Napoleon would attempt to extend his
...pire across Europe.

APOLEON'S DOMESTIC POLICY

hile Napoleon's foreign policy pursuits may have
resulted in some of his most dramatic endeav-
ours, his domestic policy was his greatest legacy
...rance. Even today, French institutions reflect the influ-
...e of this Corsican general whose 15 years in power
...le an indelible mark on the life of French citizens. His
... provided the stability in France necessary to consoli-
...e the revolution begun in 1789.

nk of France

...nomic crises had precipitated the French Revolution
..., despite numerous attempts to resolve the economic
...lems during the revolutionary period, the financial sit-
...on in 1800 remained critical. The country's debt
...unted to 474 million francs and the cash reserve held
...167 000 francs.

...apoleon recognized that economic reform was essen
...o increase employment and restore confidence in the
...rnment's ability to foster economic growth. In January
... he created the Bank of France. Funded by a combi-
...on of government and private money and modeled on
...Bank of England, the Bank of France issued govern-
...t securities and conducted private business. The bank
...nded low interest loans to promote industry. In some
...s, new industry was encouraged by the offer of grant
...ey or tax rebates. The franc became the most stable
...ency in Europe. The Bank of France proved to be a
...ficant factor in the stabilization of the French econ-
... and remains as the central financial institution of
...ce today.

Tax Reform

Attempts to reform the system of tax collection during the
revolution had rid the system of its most serious problems.
Napoleon refined the system further by demanding that
tax collectors pay 5 percent of expected revenue up front.
Tax collectors were now professional, government
employees. Direct taxes on land, business licenses, personal property, and servants were maintained at a steady
level as established under the Directory. There were no tax
exemptions based on class. Indirect taxes, such as those
imposed on durable goods were raised as more revenue
was needed. In some cases additional goods were taxed as
in 1805 when tax was imposed on wine, playing cards, and
carriages.

Under the new organization, 840 officials were appointed to levy and collect taxes on income and property. In 1800,
660 million francs were collected. This figure was 185 million francs more than that collected in 1788. The government could now plan its affairs in a more organized way.

The Concordat

During the revolution the French government had created
a serious rift with the Catholic Church by, first, confiscat-
ing its land and, then, by assuming the right to regulate the
Church's affairs as outlined in the Civil Constitution of the
Clergy. As First Consul, Napoleon sought reconciliation
with the Church. On 15 July 1801, he signed an agreement,
or *concordat*, with Pope Pius VII. It was designed specifically to heal the breach between the constitutional priests
(those priests who had taken the oath of allegiance to the
state) and non-juring priests (those priests who refused to
take the oath). It also signalled that the Church recognized
the Republic as the government of France.

The Concordat recognized Roman Catholicism as the
"religion of the majority of Frenchman." Churches were
reopened in April 1802, and the population of France
rejoiced in this rejuvenation of Sunday services. The agreement gave the First Consul the right to appoint bishops
who would then be invested by the pope. The pope had the
right to refuse candidates but the state was responsible for
their salary. The church renounced all right to those lands
that had been confiscated during the revolution thus allowing the new owners, who were primarily peasants, the confidence that they would retain their property. The state
maintained the right to acknowledge civil marriage and
divorce as prescribed by revolutionary law.

On 15 July 1801, Napoleon signed an agreement, or concordat, *with Pope Pius VII. The agreement was a reconciliation between church and state. In this picture, Napoleon is standing behind the table with his arms crossed.*

In addition, religious toleration was extended to Protestants and salaries would also be paid to their ministers. While Jews were not specifically provided for at this time, they were to be protected. Later meetings with Jewish leaders resulted in a decree in 1808 to allow for the toleration of the Jewish religion in France.

The Napoleonic Code

Napoleon wrote to Talleyrand "we are a nation with 300 books of laws yet without laws." Thus he was to embark on one of his most ambitious reforms—the systematic codification of French law. When Napoleon came to power northern France was ruled by customary law which had evolved out

~ Status of Women ~

Women were relegated to the status of second-class citizens under the Napoleonic Code. Even after the defeat of Napoleon, however, French tradition demanded that a woman owe obedience to her husband. Divorce was illegal in France from 1816 to 1884. It was not until 1945 that women were given equal rights and granted voting privileges in France.

~

of medieval tradition, w southern France retained system of law introduced by Romans. In addition, revolut ary governments had passe 400 decrees, further entang the justice system. It became tually impossible to decipher law. Contradiction was ramp Napoleon's law code drew th gional codes and autonom courts together in one syste law.

The code gave male Frenc izens equality before the freedom from arrest without process, equality of taxation right to choose one's work, and religious freedom.

The articles outlining the rights of women, marri divorce, and property were traditional in tone. Napo

Under the Napoleonic Code, women were treated as second class citizens. The woman in this picture is Mlle Duval d'Ognes, as painted by Jacques Louis David.

seriously considered. In summary, they owed obedience to the significant male in their lives and could not act independently.

Divorce was allowed but was difficult to obtain. The traditional justification for this view was that it protected women. Most women had no opportunity to pursue career goals and therefore lacked the ability to support themselves As a result, divorce was economically unfeasible in most instances.

The criminal code was also rewritten. It stressed equality before the law. Arbitrary arrest was prohibited but the deference to authority is evident in the supremacy of the state. The code supported the belief that the state must be protected from the criminal actions of individuals, therefore an individual had to prove his or her innocence. The penal code was brutal. Death by guillotine, labour on a chain gang, or confinement in a workhouse were punishments for those found guilty of crimes.

The Napoleonic Code combined traditional law with laws that were introduced during the revolutionary period. It organized the French legal system and remains the basis of French law to this day.

a conservative background and thus encouraged the ~~ti~~tional provisions of the Code. Women moved from the ~~prot~~ection of their fathers to that of their husbands. ~~Wom~~en were treated like minors and were required to ~~hav~~ a male relative to manage any property which they ~~migh~~t own. Their testimony in a court of law was not

Education

"Equality must be the first element in education," claimed Napoleon. His reforms in that area were extensive, and were designed to produce a skilled bureaucracy to do the work of the state. The education laws of 1802 introduced *lycées*, the equivalent, more or less, of high schools. They

The Arc de Triomphe in Paris was one of Napoleon's
public works projects.

were run on rigid discipline and military training to turn out future civil servants and officers, the new élite of France.

From the *lycées*, male students could proceed to specialized schools of law, medicine, pharmacy, the military, or teaching. Girls were expected to train for household management and child rearing. They could be taught needlework, singing, dancing, and nursing by their mothers.

While the state maintained control of the *lycées* and post-secondary institutions, the Catholic Church was responsible for primary education. Although it no longer controls primary education in France today, the structure of education worked out then still endures. To this day French students attend *lycées* and write baccalaureate examinations to qualify for entrance to university.

The Legion of Honour

In 1802 Napoleon established a means by which he could reward exceptional service to the Republic and, therefore, harness the loyalty of a talented élite. He insisted that the award must be available to citizens who contributed their talents through either civil or military achievement. It would consist of a medal as well as a monetary award ranging from 250 francs to 5000 francs per year. Over his lifetime Napoleon gave the award to 30 000 people. It remains today a symbol of public service and is still awarded to deserving French citizens.

Confederation of the Rhine (1806–1814)

The importance of the Confederation of the Rhine to history is that it signalled the dissolution of the Holy Roman Empire and ultimately led to stirrings of German nationalism, one of the causes of World War I.

The Holy Roman Empire, the successor to Charlemagne's great empire, had been a political entity since 962. The Holy Roman Empire consisted of the German principalities, Austria, Bohemia, Moravia, with Switzerland, the Netherlands, and parts of northern Italy sometimes in the mix.

Napoleon I unified all the German principalities except Prussia and Austria, under French rule. They began to provide him with men and matériel for his increasing war efforts. The ultimate result of the Confederation of the Rhine was to stimulate German desire for unification.

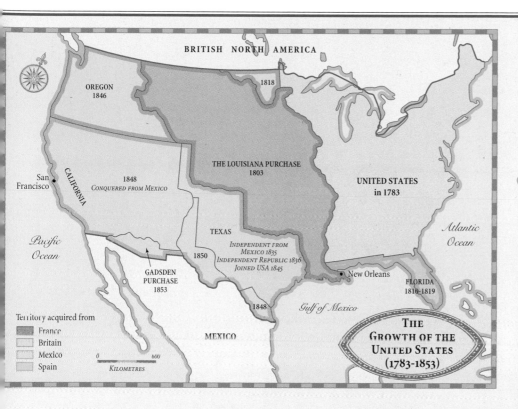

THE
GROWTH OF THE
UNITED STATES
(1783-1853)

The Louisiana Purchase in 1803 played an integral role in the growth of the United States across the southern half of North America.

The Louisiana Purchase

In 1800 the Louisiana territory in the New World was returned to France by Spain. It was a vast tract of land west of the Mississippi River, to the Rocky Mountains and from the Gulf of Mexico to British North America. Napoleon planned to use this land as the headquarters of a colonial empire. He would reimpose slavery in Haiti and export vast quantities of Haiti's major crop, sugar. However, the French army he sent to implement this plan succumbed to yellow fever and was faced with a revolt by black plantation workers. By 1803 Napoleon recognized the futility of the plan. He sold the Louisiana territory to the United States for $15 million. The United States government had been concerned at the thought of the aggressive French emperor as its neighbor and paid the sum proposed by Napoleon's envoys. The purchase doubled the size of the United States.

blic Works

poleon improved transportation and communication by ating the construction of canals, the development of ts at Cherbourg, Brest, and Antwerp, and the con-ction of roads through the Alps to Italy and the Riviera. aris was the beneficiary of many of Napoleon's public ks projects. Roads were paved, new bridges were built oss the Seine, and the sewer system was rebuilt. merous monuments were erected, the most notable g the Arc de Triomphe which still stands as a land-k in Paris.

NAPOLEON'S FOREIGN POLICY

Napoleon's foreign policy was twofold. It was designed to isolate and defeat Great Britain and to subdue Europe by military conquest rather than diplomacy. The Napoleonic period was one of almost continual warfare. Napoleon's armies were composed of conscripts from both France and its dependent territories. Soldiers, fueled by nationalism and directed by Napoleon's military genius, exported the revolutionary ideals of France to neighbouring states of Europe.

Napoleon secured his position in France by his defeat of the Austrians in the northern Italian states. The Treaty of Lunéville in 1801 gave control of the Italian peninsula to France and allowed Napoleon to direct the reorganization of the German states. In effect, the first step in the creation of the future German state under Prussian rather than

This woodcut shows Napoleon resting near the fire just after the battle of Austerlitz in 1805.

Austrian leadership had been taken with this removal of Austrian influence. In 1806 Napoleon's reorganization of many German states into the Confederation of the Rhine gave France control over the region.

From 1792, when the revolutionary government of France first went to war against Austria and Prussia until Napoleon's final defeat in 1815, France was almost continuously at war. After the defeat of Austria at Marengo and the subsequent Treaty of Lunéville, only Great Britain remained at war with France. The Treaty of Amiens signed on 27 March 1802, provided a respite from hostilities until 16 May 1803, when Napoleon arrested British citizens holidaying in France in retaliation for the British seizure of French ships anchored in British ports. Britain and France were at war once more.

Napoleon considered a land invasion of England but ultimately determined to defeat England on the seas. Despite help from Spain, French naval forces suffered a crippling defeat at the hands of British Admiral Lord Nelson at the battles of the Nile, Copenhagen, and Trafalgar. No longer capable of a naval confrontation with England, Napoleon turned his attention to **economic warfare** against the British.

Napoleon's fortunes on land during the autumn of 1 were a counterpoint to his defeat at the hands of British at sea. By the time of the Battle of Trafalgar, Brit Austria, and Russia had joined in a Third Coalition aga France. Napoleon envisioned the Grande Armée sweep victoriously across the continent to the German states. publicized his plans throughout the nation in order to b morale and ensure public support for his campaign. first unqualified success was at Ulm, where on 20 Octo 1805, he drove the Austrians from the field. This was a the prelude to his sensational victory at Austerlitz.

On the first anniversary of his coronation as empero France, 2 December 1805, Napoleon confronted Alexand of Russia and Francis II of Austria in the Battle Austerlitz. Although the French army was outnumbered the Austrians and the Russians (87 000 to 73 0(Napoleon's brilliant strategy resulted in a stunning de of the opposing armies. The battle began at 7 A.M. By 4 the Russians were in full flight and the Austrians w beginning negotiations. With the defeat of Austria, con of the European continent was now within Napole grasp. Peace was established by the Treaty of Pressb (now Bratislava, the capital of Slovakia) on 26 Decem

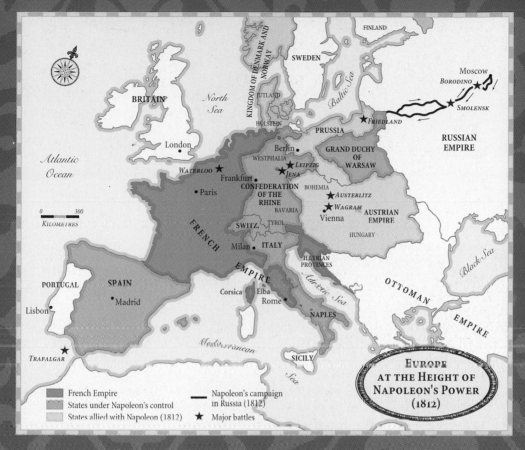

Describe the extent of France's expansion by 1812.
To what do you attribute Napoleon's military successes?

～ Coalitions ～

Coalitions are alliances between countries against another country. In revolutionary France and in Napoleonic times, several coalitions were formed against France and all were eventually dissolved.

Fearing the revolutionary events in France, Austria and Prussia (and later Holland, Spain, and Great Britain), formed a coalition to restore the monarchy in France. The coalition originated in an agreement, the Declaration of Pillnitz, during the summer of 1791, when Austria and Prussia stated that restoration of the French monarchy was important to the stability of Europe. The reports of this agreement in the French press inflamed the revolutionaries of France. In 1795, the French broke up this coalition by making separate peace treaties with each country.

In 1799, Britain, Austria, and Russia joined in a second coalition against the French expansion into the Near East. Again, separate peace treaties with France dissolved the agreement in 1801–1802.

A third coalition, in 1805, united Britain, Austria, and Russia to stop Napoleon's expansion, drive the French out of Belgium, and strengthen Prussia. It fell apart when Napoleon persuaded Tsar Alexander I of Russia to sign the Treaty of Tilsit (1807) making France and Russia allies against Great Britain.

In 1806, when Napoleon reorganized Germany into the Confederation of the Rhine, Russia and Prussia joined forces against France. But Russia was defeated at Austerlitz and Prussia fell at both Jena and Auerstädt.

Later, in 1813, virtually all of Europe came together in a coalition force which defeated Napoleon in the Battle of the Nations. Finally, the combined British and Prussian forces defeated Napoleon in 1815 at the Battle of Waterloo.

The Continental System

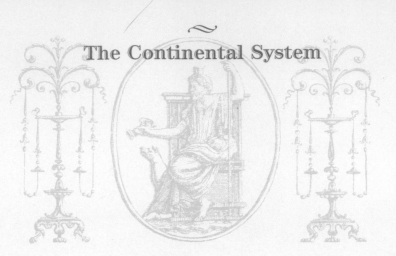

Economic warfare between Britain and France began in May 1806 when Britain placed the entire coast of northwestern Europe from Brest to the Elbe River under blockade. Throughout the summer, ships travelling in the area were subject to inspection by British ships. Those thought to be trading within the restricted area had their goods confiscated.

Napoleon responded in November 1806 with the Berlin Decree . It demanded closure of all European ports to British trade. He called this the Continental System, or Continental Blockade. Its purpose was twofold: to increase the export trade of France and to bring to a standstill the export trade of Britain. Napoleon stated that he was determined "to conquer the sea through the power of the land." He wanted all of Europe to participate in the trade blockade.

From July to November 1807 virtually no British trade was conducted with Europe. Only Sweden continued to trade with the British. The first six months of 1808 were characterized in Britain by a significant decline in the export trade and resultant problems in industrial towns such as Manchester in Lancashire as rising unemployment and rising prices created social disturbances. By August it appeared that the pound would have to be devalued. Napoleon began to sense victory. However, the "Spanish Ulcer," (as Napoleon's ill-fated attempts to defeat Spain between 1808–1813 were called) was about to claim Napoleon's attention, and cracks in the blockade appeared.

After the French invasion of Spain in 1808, European countries began to violate the blockade as their economies were also adversely affected by the ban on trade. As the Continental System subordinated all continental economies to that of France, there was growing resentment of Napoleon's control. This resentment was translated into a willingness to buy smuggled goods when possible. The most serious revolt against the system came in 1810 when Russia refused to continue participation. Napoleon did not have the resources to control the entire port system of Europe. Without the cooperation of all European countries, the system could not be effective. Interestingly, Napoleon violated his own trade restrictions by ordering leather and cloth from England for his army's uniforms.

Overall, the Continental System failed to develop French industry to the extent which was intended. Although sugar beet crops were grown to replace the import of sugar from the West Indies, most local industries suffered from a lack of raw materials. The textile industry which suffered from shortages of cotton and silk was characterized by widespread unemployment and, in some cases, by bankruptcy of factories. From 1805 to 1813 French exports declined by 30 percent.

The Continental System did not destroy the British economy as Napoleon hoped it might. Lost markets were partly offset by smuggling sugar, tobacco, and other goods from the Americas. In addition, new markets were sought in the Americas and Asia.

The 1812 Overture

The Russian composer Peter Ilyich Tchaikovsky (1840–1893) was commissioned to produce a work for the Moscow Exhibition of 1882, and to commemorate the tsar's silver jubilee. The result was the bombastic 1812 Overture, written in the genre of battle music. The *1812 Overture* depicts Napoleon's retreat from Moscow during his disastrous Russian winter campaign 70 years earlier. The work incorporates the French anthem *La Marseillaise* and the tsarist national anthem. It was originally meant to be performed in a Moscow square complete with a large orchestra, military band, cathedral bells, and real cannon fire.

Of this piece Tchaikovsky is recorded as saying, "The *Overture* will be very loud and noisy, but I've written it without affection and enthusiasm, and therefore there will probably be no artistic merit in it." Posterity has proven Tchaikovsky wrong.

---

05. Austria lost territories in th the Italian states and the rman states. Its future enmity th France was assured.

With Austria and Prussia deated, Napoleon's attention ned to Russia. The French rsued the Russians through the winter and, finally, in February, 1807, they fought each er at Eylau. The Russians had ssian reinforcements and did succumb to Napoleon's ces. However, in June 1807 French launched a brutal atk on Friedland that resulted in mplete victory for Napoleon. poleon and Alexander I of ssia met on a raft on the river men near Tilsit and agreed only to establish peace on continent but also to wage nomic war against England. he Peace of Tilsit was signed 7 July 1807, with Prussia suf ng the biggest losses of terri y. The Grand Duchy of Warsaw was created out of the ish area of Prussia and given to the king of Saxony. The man states between the Elbe and the Rhine and part of over formed the Kingdom of Westphalia and were given Napoleon's brother, Jerome. Austria, Prussia, and now sia had all been commandeered by Napoleon to become es." Only Great Britain, Turkey (**Ottoman Empire**), and den remained outside the Napoleonic system and it was Britain that Napoleon now turned his attention. In addi to the recognition of Russian influence in eastern Eu e, Napoleon's agreement with Alexander I at Tilsit re ed the Russians to join in the Continental Blockade nst Britain. Britain's loss of European markets would l a blow to the British economy.

ortugal, a traditional ally of Britain, was reluctant to the Continental Blockade. Napoleon thought that the tinent was vulnerable to British invasion through ugal, and in November 1807 he seized Lisbon. To con date his control over Portugal and to prevent British tary action, Napoleon sent troops to Spain. The French

were initially welcomed but the tide turned when Napoleon replaced the Spanish king, Charles IV of the Bourbon monarchy, with his own brother, Jerome. Further resistance to the French developed as a result of three factors: the new administration attempted to enforce the blockade, noble and clerical privileges were curtailed, and the Inquisition was suppressed. These measures went against Spanish customs and many Spaniards rose in protest. From 1808 to 1813, French armies in Spain and Portugal withstood guerrilla attacks until the British Duke of Wellington finally drove the French army from the Spanish peninsula.

France and Russia at War

French mercantilist policy which was supported by the Continental Blockade resulted in a serious trade imbalance between Russia and France. By 1809 the Russians were allowing "neutral" ships to dock at Riga and by 1810 little commitment to the blockade remained. On 31 December, Alexander I issued a decree officially withdrawing Russia from the Continental System. In addition to problems with trade, the Russians felt the political terms of the Treaty of Tilsit had not worked in their favour. They had hoped to achieve greater control in Turkey and were disturbed by the existence of the Grand Duchy of Warsaw. The Grand Duchy threatened to revive the old Polish state an event which the Russians wished to prevent at all costs.

Napoleon's response to Alexander's actions was to prepare for war. Throughout 1811 and the early months of 1812, he amassed the Grande Armée, 600 000 active soldiers and an additional 130 000 in reserve, the largest army ever assembled. Of these, only about 200 000 were French while the rest were troops from other French-controlled countries. On 24 June 1812, Napoleon's army crossed the

After his empire crumbled, Napoleon abdicated. In this painting,
he bids farewell to his troops.

Niemen River ready to attack the Russians in what was to be a short war. However, the Russians were nowhere in sight. As the French army marched toward Smolensk, its numbers were reduced considerably by heat, disease, and desertion. The Russian army retreated, drawing Napoleon's soldiers farther into the huge landscape of Russia. The Russians destroyed crops and all other food supplies as they retreated so as not to leave the French any provisions. The vast expanse of the Russian landscape proved a formidable opponent even in the summer.

On 17 August, Napoleon reached Smolensk but sparred only briefly with the Russians. It was not until the French reached Borodino outside of Moscow on 7 September 1812, that the Russians under the command of General Kutuzov held their ground and fought. Over an eleven-hour period 77 000 soldiers perished. The Russians had lost 47 000 men to 30 000 French casualties. Both sides claimed victory.

The French were left to scavenge for supplies on their way to Moscow. Instead of standing to defend the city, the Russians again practised a **Scorched Earth Policy** in

their retreat. Much of the city was destroyed by fire during the Russians' retreat. When the French straggled into Moscow on 14 September they found a city with neither soldiers nor supplies. Alexander refused to negotiate. The Russian winter had set in and there was no choice for the French but to go home. What had appeared to be victory at Borodino turned into bitter defeat. Estimates suggest that 380 000 lives were lost. As many as 100 000 may have been taken prisoner. As the ragged column straggled home, the men were harassed by Cossacks and many froze to death or died of starvation along the way. By November only 30 000 men were left; by the end of 1812, the remnant of the main army reached the Prussian border (supposedly 1000 men, 60 horses and 9 cannon). It was one of the greatest disasters in military history.

Napoleon claimed he was defeated by the Russian winter, but other factors must be included. The summer heat took its toll as did the vastness of the areas through which the army had to march. Provisions were difficult and sometimes impossible to obtain. This became more of a problem when the Russians began to burn their crops as they reated. Finally, the composition of the army must be considered. Foreign conscripts lacked the nationalist commitment to Napoleon's cause and morale was difficult to maintain. Desertion became commonplace.

he Final Coalition against France

poleon's star dimmed. On his return to France, poleon managed to raise a new army of 300 000 conipts whom he planned to bring to combat readiness as y marched into the German states. He tasted victory in xony and pushed a combined Prusso-Russian force yond the Elbe. After diplomatic negotiations involving stria failed, Austria and Sweden entered the war against poleon. By now virtually every European state had led in the coalition against France. In October 1813, the mbined force defeated Napoleon at Leipzig in the Battle the Nations. The Napoleonic Empire crumbled. The nfederation of the Rhine collapsed as Napoleon's forr allies turned against him. In April 1814 a coalition ay entered Paris. Napoleon recognized defeat, abdied as emperor, and was exiled to the island of Elba.

poleon's Return from Exile

poleon's exile was short-lived. On 1 March 1815, he aped from Elba, landed in the south of France and, by March, entered Paris. His march from the Mediteran coast inland was cheered by peasants in villages towns along his route. Napoleon made a promise to m to implement a more democratic government. To the es who had defeated him he promised to maintain the ce and govern France within its borders. Louis XVIII, restored Bourbon monarch, fled.

he Allies did not take Napoleon's promises of peace ously and they feared renewed French expansion. The gress of Vienna, which included all the states of ope, declared Napoleon "an Enemy and Disturber of Tranquillity of the World." It is not known whether he intended to keep the peace. However, the international climate convinced him that he had to raise an army and launch an attack on his enemies rather than risk being attacked by another coalition. Four hundred thousand allied troops were scattered around Europe and the Allies had the potential to raise another 300 000. Napoleon faced a truly formidable foe.

Napoleon raised an army and on 15 June 1815, it set off for Brussels to meet a combined British and Prussian force. He defeated the Prussians first at Ligny and the next day turned on the British at Waterloo. Wellington commanded the British force and General Blucher commanded the Prussians. On 18 June 1815, the British met Napoleon in Belgium at Waterloo. The day was sunny but the field was muddy. The French army slightly outnumbered the British. Both Wellington and Napoleon typically sought the advantage of a counterattack. This required standing fast and waiting for the enemy to strike first. However, Napoleon recognized that, in this instance, he must defeat Wellington quickly in order to prevent the possibility of Prussian reinforcements joining the English and outnumbering the French.

Napoleon passed the morning waiting for the field to dry. By about 11 A.M. he decided to attack. The fighting was fierce and losses were heavy. The French fought valiantly and it seemed that the allied line might crumble in the centre. Then in the late afternoon, what remained of Blücher's forces arrived to join Wellington as the battle drew to its bloody close. Two hours of bitter fighting ensued until the Old Guard of the French army began to give way. Rather than surrender, they met death. Napoleon left the field with two battalions of guards. He was sent to the British-held island of St Helena in the south Atlantic, a location so remote that escape was not likely. He died in 1821, probably of stomach cancer.

SUMMARY

Napoleon's promise of stability was welcomed by a French citizenry worn out by revolution. It was a relatively easy task for Napoleon to consolidate his power. The consular form of government named Napoleon First Consul. He eliminated his opposition in government by replacing members who opposed him. He empowered the secret police to censor all publications and theatre performances. By 1802 he had made himself "Consul for Life," and in 1804 proclaimed himself Emperor of France.

Napoleon's domestic policy still affects French institutions today. The Bank of France and tax reform stabilized the economy. The Concordat, signed with Pope Pius VII, healed the relationship between France and the Roman Catholic Church. The Code Napoleon combined traditional and revolutionary laws into one comprehensive system. Education focused on the creation of a system of *lycées* that would train students to be civil servants. A number of public works projects were undertaken to improve transportation and communication. Finally, the Legion of Honor was established to recognize the outstanding contributions of ordinary citizens.

Napoleon's foreign policy was dominated by his attempt to subdue the entire European continent. From 1800 to 1807 he successfully waged war against the European powers. He occupied some of the conquered territories, established a system of satellite states, and arranged alliances with major powers. The Continental Blockade was introduced in 1806 to break Great Britain's power.

Failure to subdue Spain despite war from 1808 to 1813, and the disastrous trek into Russia in 1812, ultimately led to Napoleon's defeat at the Battle of the Nations in 1813. Although he was exiled to the island of Elba, Napoleon returned for a last "Hundred Days" in March 1815. In June 1815 he was soundly defeated at Waterloo, and he was exiled to the island of St Helena.

QUESTIONS

1. Explain how Napoleon came to power in France.

2. Describe the system of government which was established after the coup d'état of 1799.

3. How did Napoleon consolidate his power and eliminate all opposition to his control?

4. Why was the Bank of France created? What was its significance within the French economy?

5. Explain how the tax system was reformed.

6. What was the Concordat? Explain the provisions of this agreement and evaluate its significance.

7. What was the Code Napoleon? Explain how the French legal system was affected by this Code. Give three provisions of the French Criminal Code.

8. What was the rationale for reforming the system of education? Why do you think boys and girls were treated differently?

9. What were the principal features of Napoleon's foreign policy?

10. Explain the terms of the Treaty of Luneville. How would this agreement affect the future political organization of Europe?

11. What was the Confederation of the Rhine? What was its significance?

ANALYSIS

Explain the Continental Blockade. Was it successful? Why or Why not? What was the impact on France?

Why did Napoleon become involved in a war with Spain in 1808? What was the result?

Describe Napoleon's venture into Russia in 1812. What was the result?

What was the Battle of the Nations? What was the result?

Napoleon returned from exile in 1815. How was he finally defeated? Assess the threat which he posed at this time to the security of Europe.

Identify aspects of French influence that Napoleon brought to the rest of Europe. What advantages and disadvantages did these influences bring?

1. The classic model of revolution falls into four stages:
   - Financial crisis is a catalyst to change.
   - Attempts are made to initiate change within the prevailing system.
   - The changes bring about an entirely new system.
   - A period of stability consolidates the revolutionary changes.

   (a) How well does the French Revolution fit the revolutionary model? Explain.

   (b) How did Napoleon's military rule provide the period of stability demanded by the theory?

   (c) Why and until what time did the people of France support Napoleon? How did he lose their support?

   (d) Research a revolution that has happened within the past five years. Does it fit the revolutionary model? Describe similarities and differences between this recent revolution and the French Revolution.

ACTIVITIES

1. Interview
You are a political correspondent. Conduct an interview with Napoleon regarding his goals for France and the rest of Europe. Be sure to ask him how he will implement his goals. You will want to draw out his intent to institute the Continental Blockade and maintain control of the European continent.

2. Cartoon
Create a political cartoon which identifies the response of the satellite states in Europe to Napoleon's policies.

3. Debate
Be it resolved that Napoleon's leadership made France a strong nation.

The Bourbon dynasty was restored to power after Napoleon's abdication.
King Louis XVIII was the younger brother of Louis XVI.

Chapter 5
Reaction to Revolution
The Congress of Vienna: 1814–1815

FOCUS ON:

Security in post-Napoleonic Europe as established
by the Congress of Vienna;

Metternich's influence on the Congress settlement and
the Congress system;

Liberal and nationalist reaction to the Congress settlement.

After Napoleon's exile in 1814, the great powers assumed that a new order would prevail in Europe. Accordingly, in September 1814, all the states of Europe assembled in Vienna for a peace conference. Their task was to remake the map of Europe and establish some means of maintaining peace and security after Napoleon's attempt to extend French influence over the entire continent. Of immediate concern was the establishment of a **balance of power** which would prohibit any of the great powers from threatening the security of its neighbors. In addition, domestic security was to be preserved from the unsettling new ideologies of nationalism and liberalism.

Each of the European states sent representatives to the Congress meeting in Vienna but the decision-making power rested with four—Great Britain, Austria, Russia, and France. Although Prussia was included as one of the great powers, its influence was limited. The inclusion of France in the Congress and the equilibrium established by the territorial settlement ensured a longer period of stability on the continent than might otherwise have ensued. The Vienna meeting was chaired by Prince Metternich (1773–1859), the Austrian foreign minister. Great Britain was represented by Viscount Castlereagh, Prussia by Fürst von Hardenberg, France by Talleyrand, and Russia by Tsar Alexander I.

TIMELINE

1814
Congress of Vienna convenes.
Louis XVIII is restored to the French throne.

1815
Napoleon's 100 days
June ❀ Final document of the Congress of Vienna
September ❀ Holy Alliance
November ❀ Quadruple Alliance

1818
France joins the Quadruple Alliance.
Congress of Aix-la-Chapelle

1819
Carlsbad Decrees

1820
Congress of Troppau

1821
Congress of Laibach

1822
Congress of Verona

1825
Decembrist Revolt

1829
Independence for Greece

1830
July days in France

1832
Mazzini's Young Italy Movement

1848
February ❀ Socialist riots in major capitals.
24 February ❀ Louis-Philippe abdicates.
Lamartine government of the second republic comes into effect.
December ❀ Louis Napoleon Bonaparte is elected president.

Conservatism

Post-Napoleonic Europe w[as] dominated by the traditions f[os]tered by counter-revolution[ary] conservatism. In an attempt [to] establish stable governmen[ts,] the great powers were det[er]mined to reinstate **legitima[te]** heads of state and the rights [of] the aristocracy as much as p[os]sible, and therefore the sett[le]ment was viewed by liberals [as] a return to the old system.

However, the liberal a[nd] **nationalist movements** [un]leashed by the French Revo[lu]tion had terrified the up[per] classes and demonstrated t[he] instability that could result fr[om] mass movements. As such, t[he] great powers were in agr[ee]ment: just as cooperation h[ad] won the war against Napole[on,] cooperation was now vital [in] order to maintain the pea[ce.] They recognized that reinstat[ing] governments that shared th[eir] values would provide the nec[es]sary moral authority to streng[th]en the territorial balance [of] power and thereby lay the fo[un]dation for the peace settleme[nt.]

The main concern of the v[ic]torious allies was to establis[h a] French government and Fren[ch] boundaries to make sure t[hat] France could no longer threa[ten] its neighbours. First, the Bo[ur]bon dynasty headed by Louis XVIII was restored to po[wer] in France after Napoleon's abdication in 1814. Louis rep[re]sented a compromise between Royalists and Republica[ns.] The great powers agreed that he was the best choice [for] stability in France and set out to ensure that the territo[rial] settlement would not be punitive. He issued a constitutio[nal] charter, a document that acknowledged the legal equa[lity] of French (male) citizens, reconciliation with the Chur[ch,]

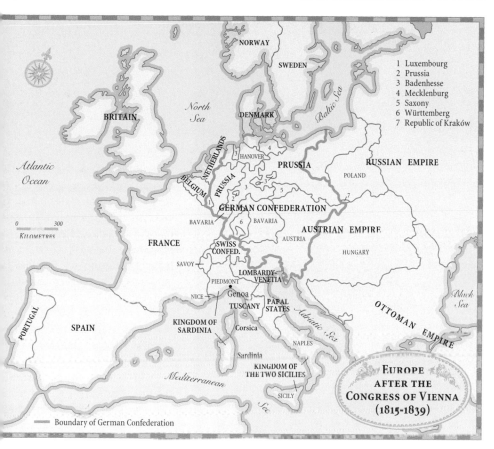

1 Luxembourg
2 Prussia
3 Badenhesse
4 Mecklenburg
5 Saxony
6 Württemberg
7 Republic of Kraków

— Boundary of German Confederation

The Congress of Vienna reestablished territories after the defeat of Napoleon.
French borders were pushed back to where they had been in 1792.

olition of feudalism, and maintenance of the Napoleon-
Code. The charter did, however, assert that the rule of
nis XVIII was theoretically absolute and he was granti-
these powers out of his own beneficence.

he key to containing French power lay in central
rope. The German states, if returned to the fragmented
idition that existed during the days of the Holy Roman
pire, would be too weak to withstand potential en-
achment by stronger neighbours. However, a united
many at this stage was considered a threat to the bal-
e of power. The organization established by Napoleon
he Confederation of the Rhine provided a compromise
he 300 German states had been reduced to 39. Prussia
Austria would now be balanced in power to prevent
nch encroachment from the west or Russian expansion
n the east.

rritorial Settlement

itorial settlement had begun even before the Congress
Vienna convened when the first Treaty of Paris was
ied on 30 May 1814. This agreement established the
nch borders as they had been in 1792. These borders
losed some minor territorial acquisitions from the early

days of the revolutionary wars.
Although there were some cries
for vengeance from areas of
Europe which had endured
Napoleonic occupation, the
great powers were determined
to create a settlement that
would not result in an aggrieved
France. It was imperative to the
stability of Europe that the
French government be allowed
some measure of dignity and
international prestige.

This generous mood changed
after Napoleon's return from
Elba. Now the French borders
were rolled back to those of pre-
revolutionary France. In addition, France was now required
to return all art treasures plun-
dered in the Napoleonic Wars
and to pay an indemnity of 700
million francs. France would
also be required to pay the cost of occupation forces stationed in seventeen frontier garrisons on its eastern border
for up to five years to ensure that France maintained its
commitment to peace.

In order to contain future French expansion, a **buffer
zone** of strong states was established on its borders. The
Netherlands and Belgium were joined under the hereditary monarch of the House of Orange. To the southeast, the
state of Piedmont-Sardinia was strengthened with the
addition of Genoa, Nice, and Savoy. Both Prussia and
Austria were strengthened in order to provide the balance
of power deemed necessary in the German states. Prussia
received territories on the left bank of the Rhine, and
Austria was given control of northern Italy (Lombardy,
Tuscany, and Venetia). The German states were to number
39 including Prussia, Austria, and the kingdoms of Bavaria,
Saxony, and Württemberg.

The first territorial crisis the Congress participants faced
was over the issues of Poland and Saxony when the Grand
Duchy of Warsaw created by Napoleon collapsed. Alexander I wanted to recreate the kingdom of Poland and make
himself its constitutional ruler. Prussia was in agreement
provided that all of Saxony went to Prussia. The proposal,

Charles Maurice de Talleyrand represented France at the Congress of Vienna and became minister of foreign affairs under Louix XVIII.

presented by Russia and Prussia to the Congress of Vienna, alarmed both Metternich and Castlereagh as it suggested Russian westward expansion and a disproportionate Prussian influence in the German states.

The Polish-Saxon question was debated at length and seemed to have no acceptable resolution. Finally, Talleyrand used his diplomatic skill to take advantage of the dissension between the great powers. On 3 January 1815, he convinced Metternich and Castlereagh to sign a secret treaty with France agreeing to use force, if necessary, against Russia and Prussia to prevent their enlargement in central Europe. When news of the secret treaty leaked out, Alexander I agreed to a compromise giving a smaller share of Poland to Russia and creating "Congress Poland" to be governed by a Russian grand duke. Prussia agreed to take only two-fifths of Saxony leaving the remainder to the king of Saxony. Thus the most contentious territorial issue was settled.

Other territorial issues were resolved by the Congress without difficulty. Switzerland was declared independent and was guaranteed neutrality. Denmark's king lost Norway to a new dynasty in Sweden (Norway retained a degree of autonomy in internal affairs). In turn, Finland was confirmed as a state to be ruled by the Russian tsar. Great Britain enlarged its colonial possessions by acquiring the Cape of Good Hope and Ceylon from Holland as well as Malta and Heligoland from France. From this time forward for many years, Britain would have undisputed mastery of the seas. Thus, while a balance of power was in place on the European continent, no other major power could offset the naval power of Britain until the turn of the century when Germany attempted to equal British naval strength by increasing the size of its navy.

The balance of power that the Congress of Vienna established was centred in the strength of the Hapsburg Empire. In addition to the importance of Austria as a counterweight to Prussia in the German Federation, the Hapsburg Empire, with its control of northern Italy, prevented French expansion in the Italian peninsula. Austria's presence in the Balkans also served to thwart Russian designs there. Indeed, many historians credit the maintenance the peace settlement to the preservation of the status quo Germany and Italy by the conservative Metternich system. the mid-nineteenth century the Hapsburg Empire was weaker to the point of being unable control its possessions. The unification of Germany and Italy upset the balance of power which had been established the Congress of Vienna.

The wartime coalition that had defeated Napoleon formed the basis for the Quadruple Alliance, established in November 1815. France was allowed to join in 1818, creating a pentarchy of Britain, Russia, Prussia, Austria, and France. The major powers agreed to act in concert against any state that threatened the stability of the European continent. They agreed to together to suppress any attempts to overthrow legitimate rulers or to change any of the borders that were established in 1815.

In September 1815, Tsar Alexander I proposed a "holy alliance" of the great powers to prevent war and required governments to operate by Christian principles. The Pope and the Ottoman sultan refused to consider the document. Great Britain considered the document a bit of "sublime mysticism" and remained opposed to it. Prussia and Austria agreed to sign the agreement with Russia because Metternich saw in the Holy Alliance support for his conservative policies. The Holy Alliance was used, ultimately as the link between the three conservative empires of the east: Russia, Prussia, and Austria. However, the real power supporting the status quo came from the Quadruple Alliance.

Tsar Alexander I (1777–1825)
proposed a "holy alliance" of the great powers
to prevent war and require governments
to operate by Christian principles.
Prussia and Austria agreed to sign the
agreement with Russia.

[C]oncert of Europe

[Th]e Congress of Vienna was the [fir]st serious attempt by the [ma]jor powers to establish some [sy]stem of **collective security**. [En]gineering the territorial set[tle]ment to provide a balance of [po]wer was the first step in main[tai]ning collective security. The [se]cond part of the process [inv]olved an agreement among [the] great powers to work [tog]ether to thwart revolution [an]d maintain stability. In this [end]eavour, Metternich provided [lea]dership in the establishment [of] a collective will. This collec[tiv]e will would be reinforced by [me]etings called over the years [in] response to events that [thr]eatened to interfere with the [pea]ce and stability of Europe.

[T]he first of these congress [me]etings was held at Aix-la-[Ch]apelle in 1818 to deal with the [iss]ue of occupied France. The [Fre]nch protested the occupation on the grounds that Louis [XV]III would be more widely accepted in France without [the] support of a foreign army. The major powers agreed [an]d withdrew their troops, allowing private bankers to [ad]minister the reparation debt of 700 million francs. [Fra]nce was formally admitted into the **congress system** [at t]his point with entry into the Quadruple Alliance (which [the]n became the Quintuple Alliance).

[S]hortly after this first congress meeting disbanded, the [ma]jor powers were called to meet at Troppau, in 1820 to [dea]l with civil unrest in Spain and Sicily. Bourbon mon[arc]hs had been restored to the thrones of both countries. [Wh]ile constitutions had been adopted by the two areas in [181]2, the Bourbons were ruling as absolute monarchs. [Rev]olutionary opposition to their behaviour arose in [secr]et societies and eventually spread to the military [. W]hen rebellion broke out in 1820 and forced the kings [of b]oth regions to swear allegiance to the constitutions of [181]2, Metternich viewed the events as a threat to the sta[tus] quo. He met first with Alexander I to persuade him to support Austria in condemnation of the revolutionary activity in Spain and Sicily. Metternich then drew up the Troppau Protocol which called upon the international order to band together against the disruptive forces of nationalist or liberal revolts. It proposed intervention by the great powers in the domestic affairs of those countries whose governments were threatened by revolutionary forces.

This protocol proved to be the beginning of a split between the powers. Great Britain and France refused to endorse the protocol and formed a liberal bloc. Russia, Prussia, and Austria emerged as a conservative coalition dedicated to the preservation of the old established order.

After meeting with the great powers once again in congress at Laibach (the modern, Ljubljania in Slovenia) and under the authority of the Troppau Protocol, the Austrians crushed the revolt in Naples in 1821 and restored Ferdinand I as an **autocratic** monarch. The following year the great powers met in Verona to discuss the revolts in Spain and Greece. They authorized French intervention in Spain and 100 000 French troops were sent there. The revolutionaries were completely subdued and hundreds of liberals were either put to death or imprisoned. The Bourbon monarchy was restored in Spain in 1823.

The intervention in domestic affairs sanctioned by the Troppau Protocol and carried out in Italy and Spain did not have the support of the British. In 1823, under the new foreign secretary, George Canning, Britain withdrew from the congress system and from this time forward the three "northern courts" of Russia, Prussia, and Austria would attempt to maintain the stability of the continent alone.

While the Congress settlement established international stability, it was left to each individual nation to attempt to maintain order and provide the framework for effective

*Prince Clemens Lothar Wenzel Metternich
(1773–1859) sought to retain Austrian
domination of the German states by repressing
nationalist movements.*

government in post-Napoleonic Europe. This entailed keeping the forces of liberalism and nationalism in check to prevent the disruption of another major revolution. From 1815 until 1848 the forces of conservatism struggled to maintain the status quo, while the forces of liberalism and nationalism sought to chart a new Europe free from the repressive aristocratic regimes. Until 1848 this liberal movement was primarily the work of the middle classes. It was after the revolutions of 1848 that the masses of working people became involved in a quest for power.

Age of Metternich

The years 1815 to 1848 are often referred to as the Age of Metternich because they were dominated by the conservative policies of Austria's foreign minister. During this period, reactionary domestic policies such as severe censorship were implemented by each of the major powers in the hope of perpetuating the status quo. Meanwhile, the forces of romanticism, liberalism, and nationalism among the middle classes stirred hope that change was possible. Revolutions in Europe and the colonies in the 1820s, in 1830, and in 1848 worked against this last desperate attempt of the aristocracy to maintain its position of power and prestige. While these revolutions were not ultimately successful, they did herald the beginning of a new age that would radically alter the composition of nations and the structure of society.

The Hapsburg Empire had emerged from the Napoleonic wars in a much stronger position than that held prior to the struggle. Dominant in the German federation and possessing control of territory stretching from northern Italy into Galicia, it comprised an area surpassed in size only by Russia. However, while most of the other great powers were somewhat homogeneous in nationality, the Hapsburg Empire remained a conglomerate of peoples. This multiethnic empire was composed of about 8 million Germans,

16 million Slavs (Czechs, S vaks, Ruthenians or Ukrainia Poles, Slovenes, Serbs, a Croats), 5 million Hungaria 5 million Italians, 2 million I manians, and countless Jews

Despite such diversity, and spite of the existence of sec societies aspiring to nationa self determination, the emp held firm. Some of the credit this stability belongs to Meti nich's conservative policies a some is attributed to the loya given to the Hapsburgs fr Germans and those non-G mans who considered the selves in the "service" of the pire.

To preserve order, Metterni imposed rigid control over multinational empire as lined in the Carlsbad Decre Directed specifically at univ sity groups and secret socie that could inflame nationa sentiment, these decrees censored both information the assembly of radical groups. The police ministry, ated in 1789, was given charge of censorship in 180 small staff responsible to Metternich and the police di tor, Sedlnitzky, controlled domestic news.

No criticism of government policy or any of its offic was allowed, nor could one criticize foreign governme especially monarchical rulers. Foreign news was censo by the state chancellery and newspaper editors w required to submit articles a day in advance of publica in order to receive approval. Failure to do so could re in a ban on publication. The censorship of books was ticularly cumbersome as hundreds of rules governed process. The goal was to print only what might build g citizens rather than that which might encourage intel tual development. Similar restrictions on artistic lice were placed on music and the theatre.

In addition to censorship, the state chancellery wa sponsible for employment, transit passes, and regulati regarding the Jewish population. This work fell in with

...eral supervision of spies and ...oversives. The number of staff ...ployed to carry out these po... ...e duties numbered less than ...e thousand and the tactics ...d were designed more to in...idate than injure. Hence, ...oughout the Metternich era ...re is no evidence to suggest ...t the surveillance system in ...ce was more diligent in its ...rk than that of any contem...ary government. Most people ...roved of the government's re...ctions and those academics ...o wished to read prohibited ...terials were usually able to ...cure them without much dif...lty and without fear of ...risals.

...he German federation that ...emerged from the Congress ...lement was a loosely knit or...ization of 39 states dominat...by its two most powerful ...mbers, Austria and Prussia. ...federal diet, or council, was ...posed of diplomatic repre...tatives from each of the 39 ...man states. Although signifi...tly smaller than the Hapsburg ...pire, Prussia had been en...ed by the Congress in order ...eter France from attempting ...establish hegemony once ...re in central Europe. Thus important territory along the ...ne as well as a portion of Saxony was now under Pruss-...control. The Prussian monarchy agreed with Metter-...'s conservative policies and worked with Metternich ...ough the Federal Diet to implement the Carlsbad Decrees ...819.

...lthough the struggle between liberal and conservative ...es was most evident in central and western Europe, ...sia was also affected. Alexander I began his reign as the ...st liberal of tsars but gradually moved to a reactionary ...tion around 1818. Army officers and intellectuals in

The Carlsbad Decrees (1819)

German youth movement called the *Burschenschaft* arose in the German states in 1815. It was made up of university students and was devoted to political discussion on liberal and nationalist ideas. The *Burschenschaft* were viewed with alarm by conservatives, especially by Metternich. At a meeting in 1817 at the Wartburg Castle (famous because Martin Luther had stayed there), rousing speeches spurred the students on to burn reactionary books. In 1819, Kotzebue, a reactionary German writer known to be an informer to Alexander I of Russia was assassinated by a student and the killing was praised by nationalists. Metternich, convinced that a liberal uprising was possible if the *Burschenschaft* was allowed to continue spreading its ideas, determined that the state must act. His only authority came as a result of Austria's membership in the German federation, so he called the most powerful of the German states together for a conference at Carlsbad in Bohemia. The Carlsbad Decrees resulting from this meeting dissolved the student organizations and imposed strict censorship on the press and rights of assembly. Throughout the Metternich years the Carlsbad Decrees provided a check on the spread of nationalist and liberal ideas in the German states.

Russia reacted to his conservative stance by developing an opposition movement founded on liberal ideals. When Alexander died in 1825, an attempt to elevate the Grand Duke Constantine as tsar and thus prevent Nicholas from getting the throne resulted in the Decembrist Revolt. The poorly organized revolt was quickly crushed by supporters of Nicholas. However, it was the first inkling of a revolutionary movement in Russia. The regime of Nicholas I was brutally reactionary, characterized by secret police, censorship, and rigorous control of the population.

Russia had long held interests in the Balkans. When an independence movement broke out in Greece it was feared Russia would seize control of the Bosporus and Dardanelles Straits linking the Mediterranean Sea. The Greek revolt against Ottoman rule flared up in 1821. The rebellion was led by Alexander Ypsilanti, a prominent Greek leader in the Greek War of Independence and a man who had served most of his life in the Russian military. Ypsilanti's little band of renegades hoped to establish a Greek empire in the Balkan region but could not garner enough support for a rebellion there. They were disappointed by the lack of support from Russia and were soundly defeated by the Ottoman Turks.

After Ypsilanti's defeat, a small group of Greek nationals determined to fight for an independent Greek state rather than attempt to control the Balkans. This movement marshalled the support of Britain, France, and Russia who approved of Greek autonomy. Nicholas I was not committed to the Troppau Protocol which condemned revolution against established governments, and he viewed Greek

Liberals in Russia tried to prevent the reactionary Nicholas I (1796–1855) from becoming tsar.

rebellion as a way to remove Ottoman influence from the Balkan region and allow Russian expansion into the area. In 1828 Nicholas declared war against Turkey (Ottoman Empire) in support of the Greeks. In the Treaty of Adrianople of 1829, Turkey was forced to recognize Greek independence, allow Russia to control the area at the mouth of the Danube River, and to declare the Rumanian province a Russian protectorate. As the Ottoman Empire weakened, the **Eastern Question** regarding control of the straits and hegemony in the eastern Mediterranean would plague the great powers of Europe.

The most serious blows to the Metternich system came with a wave of revolutionary activity that began in France in July 1830. Louis XVIII had died in 1824 and was succeeded by the reactionary Charles X. From 1815 to 1826 France had prospered. Industry developed and agriculture flourished. However, by 1827 the international economy was depressed and French goods became more difficult to trade. Harvest failures in the years 1827 to 1829 compounded the problem as did a crisis in the wine industry. A large surplus of wine existed but high tariffs made it difficult to trade. Layoffs in the wine industry contributed to the increasing numbers of unemployed who roamed the countryside in unruly bands.

Political, economic, and social frustration engulfed France as most of the political power was held by a fraction of the population who monopolized votes, money, and power. While there had been some liberal reforms, only 30 percent of the population met the age requirement of 40 years for election as deputy.

Censorship and clerical cont of education were the other t issues which dominated libe attention.

The July Days

The July Days embroiled Fran in a revolutionary crisis, w two opposing sides assault the Bourbon government. Ba ers, industrialists, and m chants formed a bourgeois position demanding a grea share in the existing Bourl government, while Paris workers, students, and radi intellectuals wanted a repul with Lafayette as president.

When conflict erupted, media led the charge. Printwo ers led by newspaper edit such as Adolphe Thiers man the barricades. Charles X flec England. Louis-Philippe, a Bo bon but also a republican soldier in the revolutionary ar of 1792, was chosen to replace Charles X. The age requi ment for deputy was lowered to 30 years and for an elec to 25 years. The July Revolution lasted only three days it struck at the heart of the reactionary Congress settleme initiated reform, and sparked civil disturbances elsewhe

The next uprising occurred in the Netherlands. The C gress settlement had previously united Catholic Belgi with the Protestant Dutch. The union proved be-neficia the economy as Dutch trading terests could promote Belg industry. However, the Belgia who had been used to autonc under Spain and Austria, fo the union politically oppress The Dutch king ruled absolu and was intolerant of French language used in part Belgium.

Disturbances broke out Brussels in September and w the king responded with forc

∼ The Dardanelles ∼

The strategic geographical position of the Dardanelles, also known as the Hellespont, has made control of the narrow strait an important focal point for many historic conflicts. The strait separates Europe from Turkey and is the only outlet from the Black Sea to the Mediterranean Sea and the Indian Ocean.

The Dardanelles separate Europe from Turkey. This view of the strait is seen from Intepe, Turkey.

ns the Belgians declared their independence. They then
med a national assembly and drafted their own consti-
on. The reaction from both the French and the British
s favourable to change, and in 1831 Belgium was recog-
ed by both France and England as an independent con-
utional monarchy. The Dutch did not recognize Belgian
ependence formally until 1839. Because of its strategic
stal location within striking distance of Great Britain,
of the great powers, except Russia, agreed in 1839 to
rantee Belgian neutrality. Russia followed suit in 1852.
s guarantee, while confirming the independence of a
e forged by revolution, acknowledged the territorial
eguards implicit in the Congress settlement.

re Uprisings

other region that spawned serious revolt during this
iod was Poland, still suffering its loss of independence
he hands of the major powers. Three partitions had
urred in the eighteenth century and a fourth partition
urred in 1814–1815 after the Napoleonic Wars. In
ember 1830, the Poles living under Russian adminis-
ion attempted to gain their independence. Violence
ke out in a number of areas and for a very short time it
eared that the Poles might succeed in shaking off their
ign masters—the Russian forces were driven out of
territory and Polish independence was declared. The
ish and the French gave verbal support but it was
lly enough to protect the Poles from the ensuing inva-

sion by the Russian army. Congress Poland now became a
part of Russia under the authoritarian control of Tsar
Nicholas I. Rebels were either shot or deported to Siberia.
A Polish state would not reappear until after World War I.

Uprisings occurred also in some Italian and German
states. In 1831, liberal uprisings occurred in Parma,
Modena, and the Papal States with the goal of uniting
northern Italy. Austrian troops quickly crushed the revolts,
enforcing Metternich's commitment to the status quo.
Liberal forces continued to grow, however, and in 1832 the
revolutionary secret society, Young Italy, was founded by
Giuseppe Mazzini. Young Italy would be instrumental in
stirring Italian nationalism later in the century. The
German states were tightly controlled by conservative governments that adhered to the repressive Carlsbad Decrees.
Hence, the unrest in these areas was limited to street
demonstrations which were quickly disbanded, and revolutionary ferment was suppressed.

The movement toward political change continued to develop, especially among urban youth. By 1848 new unrest
broke out in every major city in Europe. Liberals questioned
the divine rights of royalty and nationalists questioned the
authority of foreign rulers. This pressure for political change
grew throughout the 1840s and was increased by serious
economic problems throughout western Europe.

The agricultural and industrial sectors of the economy
were closely linked—poor harvests meant higher food
prices and serious shortages of bread for urban workers.

In 1845–1847, a potato blight destroyed the crop on which Ireland's peasants depended. Many of those who survived fled to North America.

From 1845 to 1848, agriculture in Europe suffered such hardships that famine swept the countryside and created an urban depression. In Ireland, potato blight destroyed the crop on which the Irish peasant depended, and many thousands who survived the famine fled to North America. In Prussia, peasantry survived on potatoes when the bulk of their agricultural production failed. As food shortages spread to the cities and urban populations felt the effects of crop failures, revolution was in the air.

During 1848 only Great Britain and Russia escaped the throes of revolution and, for a brief time, it appeared that the system established at Vienna was about to be overturned. The countries that had experienced revolution exhibited four distinct phases in the drive for change. In each case the upheaval began with a demand by students, workers, middle class liberals, and nationalists for reform. The established regime was petitioned to grant a constitution or grant national

independence. When reform failed to materialize, spo[n]neous fighting broke out. The demands for change wer[e] similar around the continent that no orchestration of revolt by revolutionaries was necessary.

As revolutionary activity spread through the capital[s] Europe, the established regimes relinquished a measur[e] control. In some cases, the rebels actually gained po[wer] briefly although, more commonly, the established gove[rn]ment granted temporary reforms. Once they had achie[ved] some success, the revolutionaries began to fight am[ong] themselves and revolutionary solidarity was broken. [The] established regime then took advantage of their disunit[y] re-impose power, usually by [mil]itary force. In some areas, br[ief] repression followed. In e[ach] case it demonstrated that w[hile] discontent was widespread, [lib]eral and nationalist moveme[nts] were not yet mature enoug[h to] secure and maintain power.

∼ Liberals ∼

Liberals of nineteenth century Europe desired social and political changes. However, they believed that power should be held only by those people who were educated or who owned property.

volutions of 1848:
ance

revolutions of 1848 began in
nce. Louis-Philippe had been
ble, or unwilling, to solve
nce's growing social and
nomic problems. He had
ted further from any interest
he plight of the lower classes
virtually ignored the mis-
s of the industrial worker.
rt from legislation to limit
d labour and to contribute
ds to primary schools, his
ernment ignored the work-
class. Nor did his govern
t attempt to expand the
t to vote to the workers,
eby contributing to an elec-
te of the social and eco-
ic elite.

e February Revolution, as it
nown, resulted from four

*Alphonse Lamartine (1790–1869) led the short-
lived republican government in France in 1848.*

ses: a demand for a more democratic system of gov-
ment, a protest against the corruption and opulence of
is-Philippe's regime, a resistance by Catholics to the
arent anticlericalism of Louis-Philippe, and an increase
e acceptance of socialist philosophy amongst the pro-
iat. Liberal groups held banquets and demonstrations
odically to publicize the need for reform.

banquet with street demonstrations to follow that was
ned by reformers for 22 Feb-
y 1848, alarmed the govern-
t. François Guizot, the prime
ster, forbade the gathering.
populace reacted by erect-
arricades in the streets and
ng a larger demonstration
the planned banquet. Riot-
occurred the next day and
ral demonstrators were
d by soldiers. The govern-
t's inability to control Paris
soon evident. As casualties
nted, the revolutionary

atmosphere spread and Louis-
Philippe abdicated on 24 February. He fled the city and eventually reached England to live in
exile the rest of his life.

The Provisional Government
headed by Alphonse Lamartine,
a poet and statesman, was
established. It was composed
primarily of republicans, but
included a number of socialists
to appease the workers. Louis
Blanc was one of the socialists.
He was in a position to implement a proposal to establish
state-funded workshops for the
unemployed. A much watered-
down version of his proposal
was established in Paris, primarily to quell the unrest which
was growing among large
hordes of unemployed workers.

Elections were held 23 April
1848, to elect the government of
the Second Republic (the First Republic had existed from
September 1792 to December 1804). Nine million voters
cast their votes as all adult males were now eligible to
select the members of the National Assembly. The rural
voters were conservative and feared the socialist program
which threatened to confiscate the private property so
newly acquired by the peasantry.

As they made up the majority of the voters, the new Constitutional Assembly was made
up of electors who were chiefly
mon-archists or conservative republicans. They closed the national workshops which angered
the thousands of unemployed in
Paris. The urban radicals protested the closures, and the government proclaimed marshal law as
the propertied classes rose up to
prevent a socialist victory. Full-
scale class warfare, called the
June Days, raged throughout
Paris.

～ The ～
National Guard

he government of Louis-Philippe
was confident that it could withstand the civil unrest that grew
out of the demands for reform because the
National Guard was well equipped and
three times as large as it had been during
the uprisings of 1830.

Ея Величество **МАРІЯ АЛЕКСАНДРОВНА.**   Его Величество **АЛЕКСАНДРЪ НИКОЛАЕВИЧЬ.**

Tsar Alexander II (1818–1881)
is known as "the Liberator" because he emancipated the serfs in 1861.
He also reformed the legal and administrative systems in Russia. He was
assassinated in St Petersburg.

~ The Liberator ~

The one positive result of the revolutions of 1848 was the emancipation of the serfs throughout central Europe. Serfdom would remain only in Russia, until Alexander II freed Russia's lowest classes from servitude in 1861. Meanwhile in western Europ the masses gained a new political awareness, and co servative elements faced increased pressure to reco nize demands for liberal reforms.

Louis-Napoleon Bonaparte (1808–1873)

orn to Napoleon I's brother, Louis, King of Holland, Louis-Napoleon was acknowledged as head of the Bonaparte family in 1832. He was influenced by the Italian revolutionary group, the Carbonari and attempted in both 1836 and 1840 to overthrow the government of Louis-Philippe in France.

The June Days (24–26 June 8) resulted in 10 000 dead d wounded and another 10 deported to Algeria. The est continued throughout summer and into the fall and gested that conservative ele-nts still predominated in nce. When the presidential tion was held in December, is-Napoleon Bonaparte (1808–3), a nephew of Napoleon I, eived five and one half mil-n of the six million votes cast. ndidates who ran on a repub-n platform were upstaged by is-Napoleon's promises of order and stability. Louis-poleon would later subvert the constitution of the Sec-d Republic by proclaiming himself Emperor Napoleon Once again, a revolution in France had evolved into an ire.

re Revolutions

ewhere in Europe, spontaneous revolts occurred as lib-s and nationalists attempted to unseat repressive con-ative governments. In Vienna, news of the February olution in France prompted workers and students to against the government. On 13 March 1848, there was n serious rioting that Metternich fled to England. A 15 ch riot in Berlin prompted the king of Prussia to nise a constitution. Also on 15 March, provoked by the cal ideas of the revolutionary hero of Hungary, Louis suth, Hungary declared itself constitutionally separat-rom the Hapsburg Empire. Emperor Ferdinand, believ-hat the Hapsburg Empire was collapsing around him, ted the same status to Bohemia. Indeed, it seemed collapse was imminent. The Austrians were driven of the northern Italian states and Sardinia declared on Austria. Revolutionaries throughout central pe clamoured for liberal governments, national free-, and the abolition of serfdom.

As in France, the initial successes of the revolutionaries in central Europe dissipated by 1849. The movement lost its momentum everywhere as the armies remained loyal to the rulers and the revolutionaries were unable to maintain solidarity.

SUMMARY

fter Napoleon's defeat at the Battle of the Nations, the major powers were required to re-order Europe and establish a means of maintaining peace and security. The Congress of Vienna was convened in 1814. Its task was to remake the map of Europe and arrange for a system of collective security for providing stability. Chaired by Prince Metternich of Austria, the congress was conservative in its approach to peace and reflected the reactionary views of central Europe. The territorial settlement was designed to create a balance of power and prevent the possibility of any one power from upsetting the balance as France had done under Napoleon.

The Quadruple Alliance was created to maintain the peace. In 1818 France was allowed to join, making it a Quintuple Alliance. The major powers agreed to meet whenever peace was threatened. In 1820 the Quintuple Alliance met to discuss civil unrest in Spain and Sicily. The resulting Troppau Protocol condoned the intervention of the major powers in regions where revolutionary forces threatened the stability of the country.

While the Congress settlement maintained peace for most of the nineteenth century, it did not take into account the forces of nationalism and liberalism. In 1830 and 1848 these forces threatened to upset the conservative governments in Europe. However, although the revolutionaries were able to force governments to introduce reforms they were not organized sufficiently to seize power.

QUESTIONS

1. What major tasks faced the Congress of Vienna (1814–1815)?

2. Why was France included in the Congress meeting?

3. Why did liberals view the Congress settlement as reactionary?

4. Explain the conditions of the settlement with regard to the French government and its territory.

5. Explain the importance of central Europe to the peace and stability of Europe. How did the Congress hope to maintain a balance of power in Europe?

6. Why did the Congress participants change their attitude toward France after Napoleon's "Hundred Days"? Explain the final settlement which was imposed on France.

7. Explain the issue which was central to the Polish-Saxon question. Why is this issue significant in the context of peace and stability in Europe? What was the resolution of this issue?

8. Explain the significance of the Hapsburg Empire in the attempts to establish a balance of power in Europe.

9. Compare and contrast the objectives of the Quadruple and Holy Alliances. Which agreement do you think would be the most effective? Why?

10. What were the Carlsbad Decrees and how were they used?

11. Explain how the unrest in Spain and Sicily in 1820 threatened the status quo. What was the Troppau Protocol and how did this agreement affect the relationship of the major powers?

12. Why are the years 1815 to 1848 referred to as the Age of Metternich? Explain what this term meant.

13. Explain the conflict which occurred between Russia, Greece, and Turkey in 1828. Outline the terms of the Treaty of Adrianople and explain their significance to the international community.

14. Briefly describe the economic concerns which plagued France prior to the revolution of 1830.

15. Explain the results of the revolution of 1830 in France. How did this uprising affect the Congress settlement and what effect did it have on the rest of Europe?

16. Explain the issue which caused an uprising in the Netherlands in 1830.

17. Why would the major powers guarantee Belgian neutrality in 1839?

18. Describe the situation in Poland in 1830.

19. Briefly describe the social and economic issues which led to revolutionary upheaval in Europe in 1848? List the four stages which the revolutions of 1848 seemed to follow in their attempts to impose change.

20. Why did the revolutions of 1848 fail to implement lasting change? What were the results of these revolutions?

NALYSIS

Some historians have said that the Congress of Vienna created a balance of power that resulted in a century of peace.

This balance of power depended on a deterrent so powerful that no single state or combination of states would go to war. It also depended on all the major powers being equally armed because weakness in one power could lead to aggression in another. Therefore, the major powers were to arm equally and monitor each other's armaments.

(a) Discuss balance of power as a suitable method for maintaining global peace. What dangers are there to peace should one country become more powerful than all the rest combined? What part do alliances play in keeping balance of power?

(b) Is balance of power still used today? Give examples and defend your answer.

On a map, study the geographic relationships between Russia, Austria-Hungary, and the Ottoman Empire around the Black Sea. The struggle between these three empires to control the Dardanelles and Bosporus Straits is called the eastern question.

(a) Comment on the strategic importance of the straits that connect the waters of the Black Sea to the Mediterranean Sea.

(b) What claim to the straits did each empire put forward?

(c) Why was there outside interference in what was an Ottoman territory?

(d) What were the dangers of the power vacuum created by the inability of the Ottoman Empire to maintain its authority within its own boundaries?

(e) What lessons can be learned from the Eastern Question?

ACTIVITIES

1. Role Play

Recreate the Congress of Vienna. Assign students roles for each major personality who attended the meeting. In the course of the discussion, ensure that the major powers identify the aims of the meeting and how these aims might be accomplished. Each major power should express its own view regarding the settlement. Metternich will chair the meeting.

2. Map Activity

Identify on a map of Europe the territorial settlement which is agreed upon by the participants at the Congress of Vienna.

You have now completed Unit I: Enlightenment Leads to Revolution. *The following activity is based on what you have learned about the French Revolution.*

ISSUE ANALYSIS
Robespierre's Speech on the Moral and Political Principles of Domestic Policy (1794)

On 17 Pluviôse, Robespierre made the following speech on the moral and political principles of domestic policy. In the speech, Robespierre berated the divisive factions in the Assembly and outlined the principles of democratic government, as he saw them. (Skim through Chapter 3 again to review Robespierre's role in the French Revolution.)

Up to the very moment when I am speaking, it must be agreed, we have been guided, in such stormy circumstances, by love of the good and by awareness of our country's needs rather than by a correct theory and precise rules of conduct, which we did not even have time to sketch.

It is time to mark clearly the aim of the revolution and the end we want to reach; it is time to take account of the obstacles which still separate us from it …

What is the end toward which we are aiming? The peaceable enjoyment of liberty and equality; the reign of that eternal justice whose laws have been graven not on marble and stone but in the hearts of all men …

We want to substitute, in our land, morality for egotism; probity for honour; principles for customs; ethics for propriety; the rule of reason for the tyranny of fashion; disdain for vice for disdain for misfortune; self- respect for insolence; spiritual grandeur for vanity; love of glory for love of money; good men for good society; merit for intrigue; genius for wit; truth for brilliance; the charm of happiness for the boredom of sensual pleasure; human greatness for the pettiness of the great; a magnanimous, powerful, happy people for an easy, frivolous, and miserable people: that is, all the virtues and all the miracles of the republic for all the vices and all the absurdities of the monarchy …

What is the nature of the government that can effect these prodigies? Only that government which is democratic or republican …

Democracy is a state in which the sovereign people, guided by laws,which are its own work, does all it can do well, and through delegates all it cannot do itself.

It is, then, in the principles of democratic government that you must look for the rules of your political conduct.

QUESTIONS

1. What power did Robespierre have as a member of the Committee of Public Safety?

2. What factions of the Assembly would support Robespierre's proposals? Which would oppose him?

3. Do you think Roespierre's description of the pre-revolutionary government is accurate? Explain.

4. Evaluate how well Robespierre's own actions in the Committee of Public Safety reflected the ideals expressed in this speech.

5. Did the French Revolution achieve the virtues that Robespierre lists? Explain.

UNIT II
Industrialization and Nationalism

Overview

The Industrial Revolution is the name given to the period in which machines were adapted to the production of goods, and an urban society emerged. Beginning in England in the mid-eighteenth century, industrialization spread to the European continent shortly after the Napoleonic wars of the nineteenth century. Industrialization spread much later to the United States, Russia, and Japan. By using machines in production, nations increased their economic capacity. Cities grew around factories as workers moved into housing close to their work. These wage earners, who were unable to look after themselves when times were difficult, formed a new social class.

Some of the wealth accrued by Europe during the nineteenth century was used to support the arts. The mushrooming wealthy classes became patrons of writers, musicians, sculptors, and painters, leading to the development of the great modern schools of artists. Artists also found a new audience among the mass of urban dwellers. Symphony, opera, and dance halls, art galleries, and theatres were an essential part of urban life.

To be a major industrial power, a nation needed enough human resources to operate factories and to form effective defense forces. Major industrial powers also needed a large enough physical size to attain economic self-sufficiency (autarky). In the 1860s, a number of smaller political units merged into larger federal states. Two of these, Germany and Italy, were to have a major effect on the history of the world. Their creation caused a change in the power structure within Europe that would eventually lead to war in 1914.

The Industrial Revolution changed Europe forever.
People had to adapt to the shift from an agricultural-village society
to an industrial-urban one.

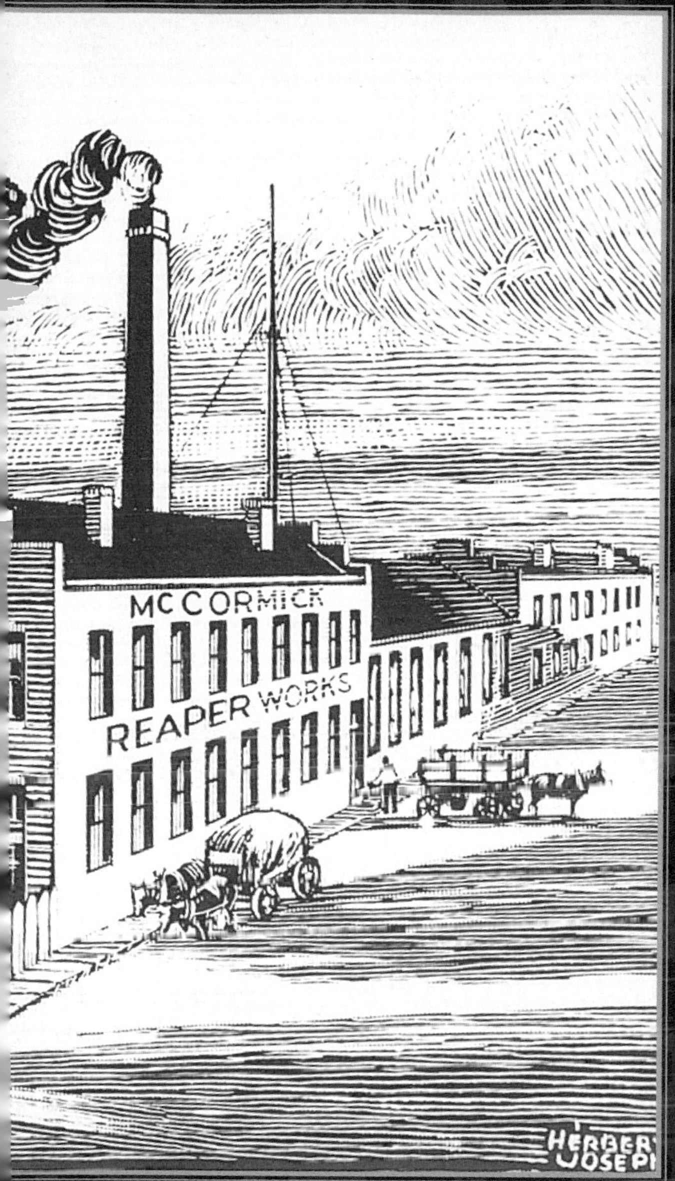

Chapter 6 The Machine Peoples

FOCUS ON:

The impact of industrialization on lifestyle during the 19th century;

The recognition and identification of social injustices by 19th century thinkers;

Ideological solutions proposed to re-order the political and economic systems of 19th century European society.

INDUSTRIALIZATION
1760–1900

*Y*ou have read about the political revolutions that occurred as the result of ideas from the French Revolution. Yet another revolution was occurring. The Industrial Revolution ushered in the Modern Age and the belief that unlimited, material progress was at hand. Unprecedented political, economic, and social changes in the organization of society occurred as a result of adapting machines to increase productivity. In Europe, in the eighteenth and nineteenth centuries, ideas on individual liberty, personal freedom, and political and social equality emerged as a result of the Industrial Revolution. The traditional, aristocratic, class-structured societies were replaced by a new social organization attuned to individual rights and freedoms.

At the centre of the Industrial Revolution was the replacement of animal power by machines. The history of the eighteenth and nineteenth centuries is the story of how people adapted to this change. The traditional village-agricultural societies gave way to the new **urban**-industrial structures.

The Industrial Revolution changed forever the way we live. Relationships within an industrial society are far different from those of an agricultural society. Social institutions within a farming-village society are not suited to a modern industrial state. For industrialization to develop, changes to society have to be made either by peaceful means or through revolution. Societies that came to use machines on a large scale became industrial in nature and developed an urban culture more advanced technologically than those which remained labor intensive. They became known as "machine people."

The Industrial Revolution

The Industrial Revolution began in about 1760 in English textile factories when steam power was first put to use in the woollen and cotton industries. It spread to the European continent during the nineteenth century and into Russia, Japan, and North America by the beginning of the twentieth century. By the early 1900s, the United States had the largest industrial system in the world.

Industrialization made Britain's factory owners and merchants immensely wealthy and gave Britain global economic dominance for nearly a century. Not until industrial

TIMELINE

1760
Industrialization begins in cotton and woolen mills in England.

1799
Steam power is applied to productive processes.

1815
The Romantic Age begins.

1829
Rainhills locomotive trials occur.

1848
Engels and Marx publish *Communist Manifesto.*

1859
J.S. Mill's essay, *On Liberty*, is published.
Darwin's *The Origin of Species* is published.

1868
Meeting of the First International.

1884
The Fabian Society is established.

1889
Meeting of the Second International.

development began in Germany in the 1870s did any s‍ ous challenge arise to the British economy.

The results of the Industrial Revolution were:

1. the substitution of machines for human labour in all methods of production;

2. a dramatic shift in population from villages to urban centres;

3. an unimagined increase in the volume of production

4. an improved standard of living for those who enjoye the benefits of mass production;

5. the concentration of global power and economic wealth within the industrialized nations;

6. the development of new ideologies to deal with the massive changes caused by industrialization.

*Hargreaves' spinning jenny increased output
by having one operator spin
several threads at one time.*

e Industrialization of
British Textile Industry

ngland, demand for cotton goods in place of the more
mon wool garments far outstripped the ability to pro-
e them. The older, cottage-industry system, in which
k was parcelled out among craftspeople in the villages,
ld no longer meet the in
sed orders. The cottage sys-
was slow, inefficient, and
nded almost exclusively on
d labour. Earlier attempts to
ess water power had been
essful but could not gener-
nore than a few horse power.
was not adequate for the
at hand.

Lancashire, textile manu-
urers began to think in
s of centralizing production
factory. They also consid-
using machines in the pro-
ion process. Among the
r innovations of the time

were Hargreaves' "spinning
jenny" (1764) which spun several threads at once; Arkwright's
water frame (1769) which held
up to 100 spindles and was
water powered; and Crompton's
"spinning mule" (1777) which
combined the spinning jenny
and water frame and further
increased production. In 1799
steam power was harnessed to
the whole mechanical process.

The new **factory system**,
based on a division of labour,
mechanization, and the centralization of production, provided
the solution to the overwhelming demands for goods. The
change to a factory system
required workers to leave their
villages and move into larger
urban areas where the factories
were located. This was made possible by radical changes
in agriculture. By using crop rotation and fertilizers more
grain could be harvested from the same amount of land
with less human labour. The excess rural population
streamed into already overcrowded cities seeking work in
the new factories. With seemingly unlimited labour pools,
the mechanization of production, and the development of
the factory system, the prospect
for huge profits loomed large.

In a short period of time, the
transformation of Britain's industrial base to steam power had the
effect of concentrating factories
close to the source of energy, the
iron and coal fields in the north.
The landscape in northern England became dotted with hastily-
constructed factories and row
upon row of workers' flats. Owners employed workers in shifts to
keep production lines going day
and night and smoke stacks continually belched out thick, black
smoke.

Population in Europe (1820–1840)
in millions

Country	1820	1840
Britain	16	27
Spain	11	14
France	27	34
German states	24	31
Italy	18	22
Austria-Hungary	24	30
European Russia	29	38

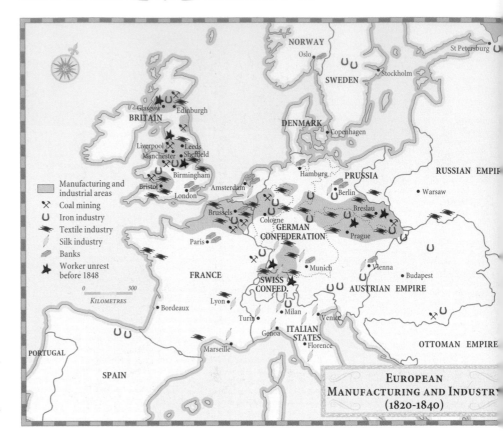

Manufacturing and
industrial areas
✕ Coal mining
U Iron industry
🐟 Textile industry
🪶 Silk industry
🪶 Banks
★ Worker unrest
before 1848

0   300
KILOMETRES

EUROPEAN
MANUFACTURING AND INDUSTRY
(1820-1840)

*Manufacturing and industry began first in England in 1760, then spread throug̶h̶
Europe in the nineteenth century. According to the map, where were the main
industrial and manufacturing centres in Europe from 1820 to 1840?*

Revolution in Transportation

The increase in production touched off a transportation revolution. Greatly increased volumes of goods had to be taken to distribution points far from the mills. At first the solution seemed to be to expand the existing canal system. For hundreds of years Europeans had thought in terms of water transport. However, a new form of transport was on the horizon, the steam engine. It would soon make all previous forms of transport obsolete.

Thomas Newcomen designed steam engines to pump water out of coal mines. Steam engines had been in use since 1712. James Watt increased their power and improved their efficiency. He became partners with Matthew Boulton, a foundry owner, and John Wilkinson, a steel manufacturer. George Stephenson, a collier foreman's son, put the steam boiler on its side and placed it on a carriage thereby inventing locomotion. In 1829 at the Rainhills power trials, his steam engine, The Rocket, reached a speed of 12 km per hour. By 1790, Watt's steam engine was being used in England to power rotary drills for milling machines and railway locomotives. Blast furnaces poured out iron and steel in ever-increasing amounts to fill the demands of railways for more steel for rails and rolling stock. Power-driven machines increased output a thousandfold,

～ Hard Times ～

Charles Dickens was a British novelist who wrote numerous description of life in London during the Industrial Revolution. The following is a passage from his novel called *Hard Times.*

It was a town of red brick, or of brick that would have been red if the smoke and ashes had allowed it; but as matters stood it was a town of unnatural red and black like the painted face of a savage. It was a town of machinery and tall chimneys, out of which interminable serpents of smoke trailed themselves forever and ever, and never got uncoiled. It had a black canal in it, and a river that ran purple with ill-smelling dye, and vast piles of buildings full of windows where there was a rattling and a trembling all day long, and where the piston of the steam engine worked monotonously up and down like the head of an elephant in a state of melancholy madness. It contained several large streets all very like one another, and many small streets still more like one another, inhabited by people equally like one another, who all went in and out at the same hours, with the same sound upon the same pavements, to do the same work, and to whom every day was the same as yesterday and tomorrow, and every year the counterpart the last and the next.

By adding a separate condenser, Watt improved the efficiency of the steam engine by reducing the time to cool and then reheat the main cylinder. By 1790, his steam engine was being used in England to power rotary drills for milling machines and railway locomotives.

the Berlin to Baghdad railways, not all of which were completed.

Railways not only helped to open the interior of the continents, they also compressed time over long distances, thus speeding the pace of development. By 1870 trains had cut the travel time between London and Dover, a distance of 42 km, from four days to twelve hours. Entrepreneurs rushed to develop railways to reach the untouched resources of unexplored regions. The invention of refrigerator cars in the 1890s added to the value of the railways as meat and dairy products could now be shipped safely from agricultural regions such as western Canada, Brazil, and Argentina to urban centres thousands of kilometres away.

Urban Lifestyle

The new, urban lifestyle changed human relationships within society. Urban culture can be fast-

ing British businessmen, bankers, and financiers the
est and most powerful on the globe.

e adaptation of the steam engine for land and water
sport was one of the major developments of the
strial Revolution. Steam-powered ships could sail up
s and against the wind and tides. On land, railways
l cross continents opening them to exploitation and
lopment. Steam power was the miracle of the century.
ilways were crucial to industrial development. They
ced the wagon roads and canals that linked factories
nes and markets. In the 1860s and 1870s railways pen-
ed the interior of the continents, crossing rugged moun-
ranges and plains to link ocean with ocean. In the
d States, several transcontinental lines were built link-
oston, New York, and Baltimore to San Francisco and
ngeles, while in Canada the Canadian Pacific Railway
completed in 1885. Other announced construction
ded the Cape Town to Cairo, the Trans-Siberian, and

paced, lonely, and routine. Still, thousands flocked to the cities seeking jobs. They overwhelmed the labour market and drifted into already crowded slums in pursuit of their dreams. As a result, millions of Europeans chose to emigrate to the New World where prospects of a better future beckoned them to the Canadian-American frontier.

One of the characteristics of industrialization was a dramatic increase in Europe's population, caused in part by agricultural changes providing a better level of diet, by improved sanitation practices, and by discoveries in medicine that had reduced the incidents of disease. Crowded cities became one of the major social issues of the day. In 1750 there were about 157 million Europeans, including Russians. This number had grown to 400 million by 1900. An increasing number of these came to live in urban centres, abandoning self-supporting farms for a life based on weekly wages.

This girl worked in a textile factory in Britain in 1909.

An indication of the size of the problem can be seen in a comparison of urban centres in Europe. In 1779 there were only two large cities in Europe, London at 1 000 000 and Paris at about 650 000. By 1900, there were seven cities in Europe with populations exceeding the million mark, and another twenty-three over 500 000. This major shift in population into the urban centres had far-ranging consequences. The provision of food, clothing, and shelter for such numbers was difficult. Social tensions resulting from the competition for basic necessities sometimes led to violence.

The industrial cities that grew up around the factories had a different social organization from the older villages and towns. The multilayered, traditional class structure gave way to a two-level organization of owners and workers: bourgeoisie and proletariat. Working families crowded into unheated tenements were evidence of the degree of human misery that accompanied industrial growth.

Wage earners were not self-sufficient and in hard times they suffered a miserable existence. Who should look after them in times of need? There were far too many of them for church or volunteer charities to handle. Would the state be forced to intervene in order to guarantee them a decent living? Was there danger to society in their idleness and unemployment?

Prior to government intervention in the 1830s, the w[...] ers' lives were ones of hardship and deprivation. I[...] hours of work were followed by late meals and a s[...] sleep before the day's routine began again. Often, s[...] mattresses and a small stove were a family's only pos[...] sions. A steady diet of bread and potatoes was their m[...] stay.

The average standard of living was barely above[...] subsistence level. Workers accepted whatever work[...] available and suffered fines and punishment for late[...] illness, or for falling behind on the job. The greater the[...] duction, the greater the profits. Many owners explo[...] their workers ruthlessly. With thousands lined u[...] replace the idle, discipline of workers could be exces[...] Workers dared not complain for fear of being fired.[...]

Working days were long and monotonous. Four[...] hours a day in Lancashire or 20 hours a day in Lyon[...] not uncommon. This did not include meal time or the[...] required to get to and from work. In order to save[...] many never left the workplace.

Women and children made up a large part of the[...] force. They seldom rebelled and needed less food, so[...] ally received lower wages than the men. In Lancas[...] 53 000 women and 76 000 children were part of the[...] work force. Those who left their work station for any re[...]

Complaints usually led to dismissal. Only towards the mid-1800s did workers' associations attempt to gain a better living for labourers. This drawing shows the Working Women's Protective Union hearing a complaint against a sewing machine dealer.

lked out of turn could receive 20 lashes if not outright
...issal. They were treated like animals. Yet difficult
...k was better than no work at all. Starvation was often
...only alternative.

...riodically the workers' bitterness spilled over into
...ur unrest and revolution. Although slowdowns and
...es were short-lived, they made their point. In both 1830
...848, workers attempted to better their lot through rev-
...on. Karl Marx, a social critic of the time, based his the-
...of human development on what he observed as a hard-
...g of the class lines between owner and worker. Marx
...icted that unless something were done about working
...itions **class warfare** would occur.

...spite harsh conditions of the initial phases of indus-
...zation, by 1890 the working classes had made real
...omic gains. During the height of the French
...lution and the Napoleonic Age (1789–1815) and the
...rican Civil War (1861–1865) there was plenty of work
...around. In England, wages rose an average of 43 per-
...accompanied by an increasing variety of manufac-
...goods for sale. By the end of the nineteenth century,
...han a third of England's population lived in poverty.

Relief for Workers

At the same time, churches and other voluntary organizations were overwhelmed by a dramatic increase in the
numbers of poor and unemployed. Demand grew for state
intervention to guarantee a basic standard of living for all.
In Britain, factory legislation attempted to protect the
workers. Age limitations, minimum wage laws, labour laws
to protect women and children and the regulation of the
number of hours worked, were among a host of government regulatory measures.

In addition, workers attempted to improve their situation
through the establishment of illegal labour associations and
trade unions. Then, towards the end of the century, having
made only minimal gains, British labour turned to political
action hoping to gain a better standard of living through the
creation of the British Labour Party. In the other industrialized nations of Europe, social democratic parties arose
to pursue the urban demand for a better standard of living.

In another direction, Socialists began to ask if there was
another way to distribute the finished goods. Was there a
method that did not depend on profit as the end result?
Why not a planned, shared economy now that machines

had produced an abundance? Would not the result be economic equality?

Industrialization created many political, economic, and social problems that remain unresolved to this day. The philosophical debate on how to restructure society within the industrial state occupied most of the nineteenth and twentieth centuries. Various ideas or ideologies evolved, each claiming to have the solution to the social questions of the day.

NATIONALISM

Nationalism has been the most powerful political force of the last 200 years. It is the belief that a group of people should have the right to their own nation state along cultural lines. The French Revolution and its aftermath (1789–1815) gave birth to European nationalism, an idea that eventually restructured the boundaries of Europe along ethnic lines. Loyalties are directed within the narrow confines of the individual state, bringing about a powerful dynamism dedicated to each nation's sovereignty.

Nationalism binds people of a common language and culture together. It glorifies the nation and demands unconditional loyalty and patriotism of its citizens. It is a state of mind which unites all classes within a nation. The glory and prestige of the state is its goal.

Nationalism, directed by popular leaders such as Napoleon, Garibaldi, or Bismarck brought national consciousness to their people. These popular leaders mobilized the masses in the

---

Growth ~ of the ~ Public School Systems

As a result of the Industrial Revolution, governments took the initiative to establish state-run, public school systems. No longer the monopoly of the Church, public education was directed towards the practical fields of engineering, mathematics, science, and medicine. The volume of students and the emphasis put on industrial invention resulted in major discoveries in every field of science and engineering. For example, at the turn of the century, German polytechnical schools and Italian laboratories excelled in the new fields of electricity and synthetics.

State-supported technical schools were the forerunners of the mass education systems developed by the industrial nations during the twentieth century.

~

Ideologies of the Nineteenth Century

The Industrial Revolution ushered in the age of ideologies or "isms." Some were systems of thought describing how ideal (utopian) societies can be created.

Many ideologies attempt to describe the organization and purpose of society. They are systems of acceptable social conduct that lead to idealistic goals. Ideologies also reflect the manner of thinking of a given class or elite.

---

name of the right of the peo to be free of the shackles empire. The visions of a n Italy or of a unified Germany examples of nationalism at w in the nineteenth century.

ROMANTICISM 1790–1850

Although there h been romantics in ev age, **romanticism** movement arose as a pop reaction to the cold logic of Enlightenment. Certainly could consider Mozart a ron tic and even the French phil pher, Voltaire, had his roma moments. But the Romantic when romantic ideas pred nated, came about the end of the Napoleonic Wars (18 Only then, after 25 years of warfare, did the Europe unleash a carefree celebration of individual freedom. was to be the age of passion and emotion. In the arts t was an explosion extolling the inner self: intuition and sual feelings were now as important as reason had been ing the Enlightenment.

To the Romantics, imagina was the most powerful of hu forces. Through the imagina as the mind experienced sions and desires, each ind ual could have a separate, sonal reality. At the heart of Romantic Age lay a prof desire to reach beyond the s es in order to discover the pose and meaning of life. T was a need to see the w through spiritual eyes, to mune with the dreamlike tence of the supernatural. T was a new appreciatio

At the age of 18, George Sand (1804–1876) married Baron Dudevant. Nine years later, she left her husband and took her two children to Paris, where she made her living writing novels.

ture. Nature provided an enue by which one could expe- nce the mystic bond between n and God. Nature was God's rk perfected.

he Romantic Age of passion d sensualism reached a peak Paris in the 1830s. There, in brightly lit salons and cafés, ny of the artistic geniuses of period gathered and worked. was in Paris that Frédéric opin (1810–1849) and George d (Aurore Dudevant) met; ere Hector Berlioz created fiery musical works; where gène Delacroix painted his matic and exotic canvases. servation was the spring- rd to imagination and Dela- ix's fascination with North ica came alive in his *Death of danapalus*. There, in graph- colours, Sardanapalus pre- es his household for the ritu- f death.

Paris the popular French ter Victor Hugo (1802–1885), a champion of the people, ed an immense readership with his novels, plays, and try. He stunned the theatrical world in 1830 with his *Hernani* written in the ordinary, everyday French lan- ge rather than the formal language of literature and the rt. Hugo also wrote *The Hunchback of Notre Dame* and *Misérables*.

usic became so popular that composers began to end on repeated performances of their works. Showy sages and abrupt changes in pace wooed a new and nger audience. Orchestras grew larger and the range quality of instruments improved dramatically. In 1820, e 100 piano factories produced over 1000 instruments year to grace middle class homes. There were more o students in Europe than could be taught by all its posers and musicians. The teaching of music became ndustry in itself as did the publication of musical es.

Britain, Romantic poets such as Shelley, Keats, and

Byron evoked the supernatural in their writings. They longed for an idyllic world. They were high- ly devoted to national liberation. Lord Byron and his companions joined a movement for Greek independence from Ottoman rule. The idea was heroic and their participation romantic. It may have seemed an impossible dream, but this did not deter them from landing on Greek soil and proclaiming Greek indepen- dence. Byron was to die tragi- cally at 36 of a fever during this crusade.

Byron (1788–1824) was irre- sistibly romantic—guilt-ridden, sensitive, courageous, passion- ate, cynical, and suicidal. He was born with a club foot, was fatherless from the age of three, and heir to a barony. He swam the Hellespont (a narrow strait of water between Europe and Asia) at the age of 21 in dra- matic imitation of Lysander, the Greek mythological figure, who loved the priestess Hero.

Scandals involving romantic liaisons followed Byron wherever he went. By his mid-twenties, he was the most famous poet of his time. When he sought—and gained—a hero's death in Greece, even the manner of his passing was envied. Lord Byron had all the characteristics, love of nationalism and individual liberty, admired by the Romantics and became the Romantic hero of a generation.

The Romantic period was a time when women made major contributions to the arts. Many women writers, such as George Sand and the Brontë sisters, chose men's names so that their works would be read. Mary Shelley created a literary classic with her tale of Dr. Frankenstein's monster. Her mother, Mary Wollstonecraft (1759–1797) had published *A Vindication of the Rights of Women* in 1792, an appeal for equality for women in education. Society expected women to carry out the daily household duties and women were openly discouraged from writing. Creating their liter- ary masterpieces while seated in a drawing room, open to

Charlotte Brontë (1816–1855) wrote novels under the masculine pseudonym Currer Bell. She and her literary sisters, Anne and Emily, grew up in Haworth, an isolated village on the English moors. Charlotte's novels include Jane Eyre, Shirley, *and* Villette.

every kind of interruption, made these women in themselves heroic.

In 1845, Margaret Fuller published *Woman in the Nineteenth Century*, an expression of her feminist views. She was the first literary critic of the *New York Tribune*. She and her husband and child died in a shipwreck in 1850. They were returning to the United States after participating in the 1848-49 revolution in Italy.

The wild unbridled ecstasy of the romantics began to give way at mid-century as a new generation sought out its own heroes and ideals. In 1846, the poet, Charles Baudelaire (1821–1867) mourned the passing of Romanticism. It was replaced by a renewed realism and, today, the unfettered passions of the Romantic age seem old-fashioned.

CONSERVATISM

Conservatives viewed organization of society a natural hierarchy which some were more capa of political leadership than ers. They believed that lead ship should be provided by upper classes and the chur To Conservatives, ideas of i vidual political, social, or e nomic equality seemed absu How could anyone legisl equality? Change within a c servative society was to be s and evolutionary.

Conservatives believed French Revolution failed w its leaders scrapped the tr tional institutions of *l'anc régime.* To them, the Revolu did not do away with evil rather unleashed a reign of ror. They believed that rev tionaries did not have the answers to the problems of day nor had they plans other than to keep themselve power.

An example of such a Conservative is Edmund Bu the English statesman, who wrote an indictment of

Childe Harold's Pilgrimage

Byron wrote *Childe Harold's Pilgrimage* as a travelogue of poetic verse called Spenserian stanzas. The narrator is a passionate and melancholy tourist who describes his thoughts as he travels through Spain, Portugal, Albania, Greece, Belgium, Switzerland, and Italy. The editors of the *Norton Anthology of English Literature, fifth edition,* describe Byron's work as an expression of "the violent sensibility of that new cultural phenomenon, the Romantic Man of Feeling."

Canto 4, Stanza 179

Roll on, thou deep and dark blue Ocean—roll!
Ten thousand fleets sweep over thee in vain;
Man marks the earth with ruin—his control
Stops with the shore; upon the watery plain
The wrecks are all thy deed, nor doth remain
A shadow of man's ravage, save his own,
When, for a moment, like a drop of rain,
He sinks into thy depths with bubbling groan,
Without a grave, unknelled, uncoffined, and
unknown.

A Vindication
of the
～ Rights of Woman ～

In 1792, Mary Wollstonecraft wrote *A Vindication of the Rights of Woman* in only six weeks. This pioneering work articulately exposes the injustices against women. Women in Wollstonecraft's time did not have political rights, were limited to certain types of jobs, and were required to give their property to their husbands upon marriage. In her work, she also describes how these social conditions affect not only women negatively but men.

Gracious Creator of the whole human race! hast thou created such a being as woman, who can trace thy wisdom in thy works, and feel that thou alone art by thy nature exalted above her,—for no better purpose?—Can she believe that she was only made to submit to man, her equal, a being, who, like her, was sent into the world to acquire virtue? —Can she consent to be occupied merely to please him; merely to adorn the earth , when her soul is capable of rising to thee?—And can she rest supinely dependent on man for reason, when she ought to mount with him the arduous steeps of knowledge?—

Yet, if love be the supreme good, let women be only educated to inspire it, and let every charm be polished to intoxicate the senses; but, if they be moral beings, let them have a chance to become intelligent; and let love to man be only a part of that glowing flame of universal love, which, after encircling humanity, mounts in grateful incense to God.

From A Vindication of the Rights of Women *by Mary Wollstonecraft, A Norton Critical Edition, Edited by Carol H. Poston. Reprinted by permission of W.W. Norton & Company, Inc. Copyright 1975.*

～

In Reflections on the Revolution in France, *Edmund Burke (1729–1797) argued that the problem with the French Revolution was that its leaders ignored the French Constitution and the Rights of Man by acting in self-interest.*

delivered little beyond sloganeering. Were not the French Constitution and the Rights of Man almost immediately ignored by the radicals for their own self-interest? Where were the much-touted individual rights during the Reign of Terror during which thousands of ordinary people were guillotined?

None of the revolutionary leaders could control the Paris mob they had created. None could explain the "general will" or what was meant by the slogan "all men are created equal." In the end, wrote Burke, the French Republic was governed by its own narrow elite and resulted in neither prosperity nor equality.

In Burke's view, the idea put forward by the radicals—that the individual will do social good in his or her own interest—is a myth. This is because the aims of society and the individual seldom coincide. To Burke, political stability and economic security lay in the strength of the upper classes.

ch Revolution in his *Reflections on The Revolution in* ce (1790). In his book, Burke argued that the problem the French Revolution was that its leaders had ised a great deal in the name of the Rights of Man and

This caricature of John Stuart Mill was published in 1873.

LIBERALISM

Liberalism became the dominant force of the nineteenth century. Liberals believed in individual liberty, private property, and freedom from government regulation. Liberalism flourished in Britain and spread to the continent, but had a lesser impact on the nations of Central Europe and none at all in Russia, which was still dominated by an aristocratic elite.

The term *Liberalism* denotes a favourable attitude toward change. Liberals generally believed in parliamentary government, which would enact change through legislation. They supported individual rights (but only for those males who held the franchise or the right to vote), and the gradual expansion of the franchise.

Liberals did not believe in government intervention in society, as did the Socialists, because they believed that any kind of state interference destroyed individual initiative, that idlers did not contribute to society and did not deserve social benefits at the cost of those who worked. The responsibility of caring for the poor was to be left to the church and other volunteer organizations rather than to society as a whole.

Liberals were convinced that the individual would strive to better his or her own standard of living if left to their own devices. Was it not in one's own self-interest to improve oneself? In so doing, the individual was also making society better because the objectives of both coincided. Government, therefore, had no reason to disrupt this natural process through intervention. To the Liberals, society was a collection of individuals who were the best judge of their own needs. Liberals believed that each should count as one except in politics where they would limit the franchise to those males who held property and could read.

In a Liberal system, individu[al] activity could be judged by so[ci]ety. The Utilitarians, such as [the] English philosopher Jeremy B[en]tham (1748–1832), would [rate] each action by how much go[od] it did for the greatest numb[er]. Bentham argued that the b[est] thing government could do [was] to leave the people alone. [He] argued for a much simpler g[ov]ernment, one with few respon[si]bilities and little power.

Although he opposed st[ate] welfare, Bentham did appl[aud] efforts by the government [to] provide universal programs [of] sanitation and education. The[se] he judged were in society's b[est] interests, therefore society co[uld] be responsible for them. [His] support did not extend to the [fine] arts, as he believed they were [not] only non-essential but un[pro]ductive and therefore wastef[ul of] human effort.

The major proponent of Li[ber]alism was John Stuart Mill (1806–1873). His essay *On [Lib]erty*, published in 1859, is the definitive statement on in[di]vidual freedom and liberty. The central thesis is that in[di]viduals should be free to do whatever they want provi[ded] they do not hurt anyone else.

Although in his later years Mill approved of state in[ter]vention to meet the temporary needs of the poor, he [dis]approved of its compulsory nature.

SOCIALISM

Socialists believed that people could rise above "[nat]ural law" and through planning create the per[fect] society. Disillusioned with the results of the Fre[nch] Revolution and discouraged by the individualism of *l[ais]sez-faire*, they proposed state intervention to achieve t[heir] objectives.

Socialists argued that the man ability to plan and to con-l nature through science and hnology could create a soci-ʸ in which all were equal and e from want. Socialists want-to establish a society in which ɔnomic need was abolished ɪ where all were considered litically, socially and econom-lly equal. Their objectives uld require massive state ɪrvention, or statism (when all hts are held by the state).

ɪccording to the Socialists, quality was derived from the ʋate ownership of property. s was not a new belief—ʋsseau had debated this even ore the French Revolution. ɪalists believed that property onged to society as a whole ɪ not to the individual. The nmunists, on the far left wing ʋocialist philosophy, believed t private property should be ɪlished altogether. Their nd of socialism was the most ɪeme use of statism.

was not until 1848 that an ɪmpt was made to fit all the ɪrent socialist ideas into a

Karl Marx (1818–1883) studied at the universities of Bonn and Berlin, where he associated with the followers of Hegel. In 1842, he worked as journalist and editor for the newspaper Rheinische Zeitung. *When the paper was shut down in 1843 for its criticism of the government, Marx moved to Paris and began developing his communist theories.*

KARL MARX: COMMUNISM

arl Marx (1818–1883) was a German philoso-pher and revolutionary. He believed that human society was progressing along a contin-uum toward an unknowable but utopian end. He believed that society was in perpetual change. Marx and his colleague Friedrich Engels created the basis of mod-ern communism. Marx sought to uncover the patterns of human progress and to discover the natural laws that governed them. Engels and Marx wrote some very important books that have influenced history, including the *Communist Manifesto*. Marx also wrote the influential *Das Kapital*, which Engels edited after Marx's death.

Born on 5 May 1818, in Trier, Marx attended a number of uni-versities including the Universi-ty of Berlin. He studied under successors of George Hegel (1770–1831), the great German idealist philosopher, and became a member of the Young Hegel-

cal system. This was done by Karl Marx, one of the ɔr social critics of the nineteenth century. He believed ʸ *laissez-faire* contributed to the worsening condition he workers. The cities were more crowded, the slums ʸe degenerate, and crime and poverty more prevalent ɪ ever before. He disagreed with the liberal view that ʸinterest of the individual operated for the good of soci-ʸ Rather, he believed that a plan for state intervention needed to overcome the evils of **capitalism** such ʸperiodic unemployment and monopoly control of ɪuction.

ians. Marx adopted the idea of progress through a dialec-tic method from Hegel's philosophy.

In the dialectic method, opposing forces compete until one of them is overthrown and a higher synthesis, or com-bination, is reached. Then that synthesis is itself opposed by other forces, and the cycle begins anew. Marx believed that economic classes were the opposing forces in human history, and struggle between classes of society resulted in a progression to higher and more complex systems of civ-ilization. But, he argued, if progress came from economic classes and economies were man-made, then it followed that human injustice could be eliminated through state con-trol of the economy. One of his aims was, therefore, eco-nomic equality.

New Lanark

In England, the industrialist Robert Owen hoped that by providing his workers with a decent environment they would be happier, better workers. For this purpose, he purchased some run-down woollen mills in New Lanark, Scotland, that he transformed into a model factory. New Lanark was to become the working model community of improved housing and social conditions and showed it was possible to increase profits through humane working conditions. Owen boasted that his work crew of 2500 were outproducing what it had taken 600 000 men to do a century before.

Some of Owen's reforms were as follows: his workers were limited to a ten and a half hour work day; they worked in clean, sanitary conditions; they were given medical aid, sick leave, pensions, and proper food. The additional costs of these programs were met from greater productivity. And as he noted, healthy workers were on the job every day. Even when the wool market collapsed, Owen continued to pay his workers at their regular rate of pay.

Owen established the first cooperative store where workers could buy goods at wholesale prices. New Lanark had the first child-care system that cared for children from age two through public schooling.

Robert Owen transformed woollen mills in New Lanark, Scotland into a model factory in which workers were treated more humanely than usual.

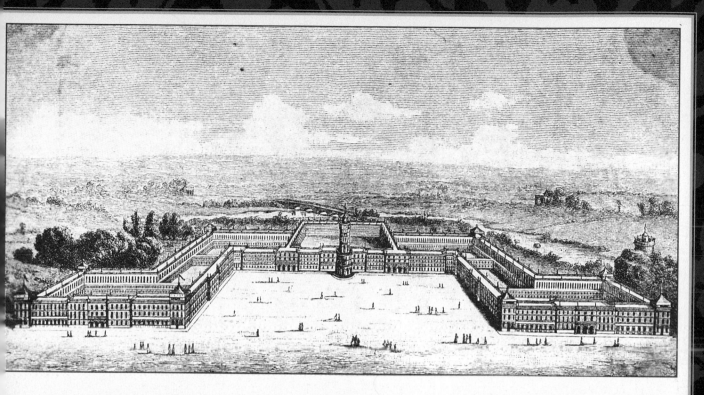

This is a design for Fourier's ideal community. He proposed small, self-contained communities, called phalanxes, that each have 1500 to 1800 members. Notice the similarity of design between the phalanstere and the Palace of Versailles.

Drinking of alcoholic beverages in the community was not permitted.

Owen later fostered the ideas of worker-owned cooperatives. He championed Britain's Factory Acts Legislation, passed over a 45-year period, which limited the working hours and ages of workers (1802), prohibited children under nine from working in textile mills (1833), and limited the work day of women and older children to ten hours (1847). Owen was president of the first Trade Union Congress and supported the first general strike in England. In his last years he gave all his energy to writing and giving lectures on behalf of the labour movement.

Early French socialists saw an answer to the workers' plight in the establishment of smaller communities on the frontiers. There, away from the crowded cities, all social evils could be eliminated in a controlled surrounding. By escaping from the conditions of the urban environment and living in isolation close to nature, humans could perfect their utopia on earth.

Charles Fourier proposed small, self-contained communities that he called phalanxes. Each phalanx, of from 1500 to 1800 members, would be run by military discipline to a rigid time table. Jobs were rotated on a regular basis and all shared equally in the profits of the community. Each member woke, dressed, ate, worked, slept at the same time as all the others, according to the dictates of the manager. However, the managers often became dictators fomenting additional tension within the community.

Etienne Cabet proposed a militaristic communal system in his book *Voyage of the Icaria*. Several of these utopian communities were established in Texas, Illinois, and Iowa, some lasting into the twentieth century. But for the most part, these experiments in social organization seldom outlasted their creators.

Other French Socialists called for a wide variety of types of social regulation. François Babeuf, a revolutionary activist, proposed the absolute sharing of all goods. Louis Blanc, a journalist, proposed state workshops controlled by workers for the unemployed that could undercut private enterprise and drive it out of business. These workshops were set up, and in the June Days of 1848 more than 11 000 rioters were killed in Paris during the insurrection brought on in part by the government's closing of the Paris workshops.

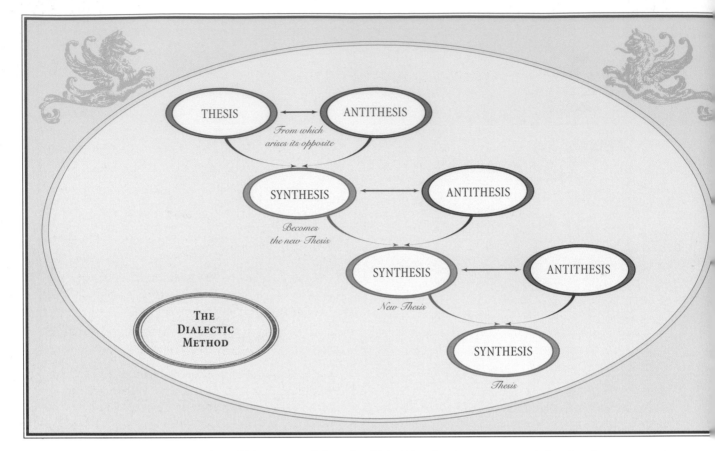

THESIS ⟷ ANTITHESIS

From which arises its opposite

SYNTHESIS ⟷ ANTITHESIS

Becomes the new Thesis

SYNTHESIS ⟷ ANTITHESIS

New Thesis

SYNTHESIS

Thesis

THE DIALECTIC METHOD

In Marx's understanding of history, social and political institutions grow and develop in response to changing economic realities. This growth takes place through the struggle of opposites—the thesis and the antithesis. Each successive resulting stage—the synthesis—is better than the one before and will eventually lead to the emergence of an egalitarian society. For example, feudalism gives way to capitalism, then socialism, until the state withers away and a utopian society emerges.

Marx met Friedrich Engels (1820–1895) in the summer of 1843 in Paris. Engels, the son of a well-to-do German textile manufacturer, was also a philosopher and shared Marx's revolutionary ideas. Engels would support Marx financially, and edit *Das Kapital*, after Marx's death. Earlier, in Manchester, England, Engels had witnessed the horrors of industrialization first-hand. Rows of squalid slums indicated a society completely lacking in social consciousness. Both Marx and Engels became committed to the cause of improving the workers' standard of living. Their collaboration was life long.

In exile in London, Marx attended a meeting of German émigrés who had formed the Young Communist League. They asked him to write a manifesto for their club and the result was, in 1848, the *Commun[...] Manifesto*, a stirring document. Engels co-wrote the d[...] ument. It has become one of the most important writi[...] in political science. Never again would Marx be so c[...] and analytical in describing what he believed would be [...] future outcome of human history.

In the *Manifesto* we find [...] most revolutionary of Ma[...] thoughts. He writes of [...] inevitability of change brou[...] about by the violent c[...] between the workers and [...] owners. The clash would o[...] no matter what steps soc[...] took to avoid it because the [...] of human progress was d[...] mined by unalterable, scien[...] historical laws.

Marx spent the remainde[...] his life in England eking ou[...]

⟿ Marx's Influence ⟿

Marx had little if any influence on the British labour movement but his ideas had far more influence in Germany where industrialization was just beginning. In Germany the plight of the workers was more desperate.

∼ The Communist Manifesto ∼

The *Communist Manifesto* describes Engels and Marx's views on historical determinism and **scientific socialism**: that the path of history is predetermined and cannot be changed, and that the forces governing individual changes are scientific and cannot be altered.

Marx and Engels began the *Manifesto* in romantic terms that all those of the Romantic Age could understand:

> A spectre is haunting Europe—the spectre of communism. All the Powers of old Europe have entered into a holy alliance to exorcize this spectre: Pope and Tsar, Metternich and Guizot, French radicals and German police spies. …

> Two things result from this fact: (1) Communism is already acknowledged by all European Powers to be itself a Power; (2) It is high time the Communists should openly, in the face of the whole world, publish their views. …

> The proletariat will use its power to wrest by degrees, all capital from the bourgeois, to centralize all instruments of production in the hands of the state. In the beginning this cannot be effected except by means of despotic inroads on the rights of property and on the conditions of bourgeois production.

> These measures will of course be different in different countries. Nevertheless in the most advanced countries, the following will be generally applicable:

1. Abolition of property in land and application of all rents to public purposes.

2. A heavy progressive or graduated income tax.

3. Abolition of all rights of inheritance.

4. Confiscation of the property of all emigrants and rebels.

5. Centralization of credit in the hands of the state, by means of a national bank with State capital and exclusive monopoly.

6. Centralization of the means of communication and transport in the hands of the State.

7. Extension of factories and instruments of production owned by the State; cultivation of waste-lands; and improvement of the soil generally in accordance with a common plan.

8. Equal liability of all to labour. Establishment of industrial armies, especially in agriculture.

9. Combination of agriculture with manufacturing industries; and gradual abolition of the distinction between town and country by a more equable distribution of population over the country.

10. Free education for all children in public schools; abolition of children's factory labour in its present form; combination of education with industrial production.

Adapted from Manifesto of the Communist Party, *by Karl Marx and Friedrich Engels, Illinois: Harlan Davidson, 1955.*

existence sustained by journalism and what support Engels could provide. In his writing he expanded his ideas on the inevitable patterns of history. He theorized that history was a series of well-defined stages separated by periods of conflict. These stages he described as primitive communism, slavery, feudalism, capitalism, and a socialist type of utopia.

In the capitalist stage only two economic classes were predominant—the bourgeoisie and the proletariat. Marx predicted that when the final struggle broke out between the proletariat and the bourgeoisie, the proletariat would win, resulting in only one class surviving or, in other words, a classless society.

Marx mistakenly believed that all the workers wanted the same things. He thought they would be satisfied with economic equality, and, with the attainment of economic equality all evil would be destroyed. How or when the final clash would occur he left to the future, but its inevitability remained one of his central principles.

Marx wrote the platform for the First International (1868) where Socialist leaders from around the world met to work on a common ideology and to form a united front against the bourgeoisie. There was little agreement on any of the matters. Some wanted to work for change within existing social structures and others wanted these structures destroyed through revolution. Most believed that the Socialist movement should busy itself with bread and butter issues and seek immediate worker relief while others wanted to strike out at the political structure of the state. Unable to reach agreement, the founding congress floundered.

After the disaster of the Paris Commune in 1870 many Socialists withdrew their support from the idea of an

---

A Voice for Labour

George Bernard Shaw's plays were commentaries on the social conditions of the time. In this excerpt from *Major Barbara*, Shaw voices the sorrow of a man who has lost his job because of his age.

Peter Shirley, just led in through the Salvation Army's yard gate, is half hardened, half worn-out, and weak with hunger.

PETER: I'm not an old man. I'm only 46. I'm as good as ever I was. The grey patch come in my hair before I was thirty. All it wants is three pennorth o hair dye: am I to be turned on the streets to starve for it? Holy God! I've worked ten to twelve hours a day since I was thirteen, and paid my way all through; and now am I to be thrown into the gutter and my job given to a young man that can do it no better than me because I've black hair that goes white at the first change?

Reprinted with permission of The Society of Authors on behalf of the George Bernard Shaw Estate.

International Congress. In 18 the International transferr its headquarters to the Unit States where the organizati eventually ceased to exist.

When Marx died on 14 Mar 1883, few attended his funer He was considered to be t grand old man of Socialist the ry but his writings were cons ered out of date.

In the 1880s most industr nations enacted widespre social legislation providing worker relief. The most a vanced programs were sp sored by German Chancell Otto von Bismarck, who ev proposed state-funded pensio The politicians had taken up t responsibility of looking af the welfare of their workers one fashion or another. T social conscience of weste European society defused call for revolution.

It was during this period t Engels began to edit Mar work, including volumes t and three of *Das Kapital*. Engels restated Marx's basic pr ciples but modified Marx's overall theories more by om sion than amendment. There was little on the violent tra formation from capitalism to socialism, and passages on withering away of the state were purposefully left out.

OTHER SOCIALISTS

In 1884 the Fabian Society was founded in Britain promote Socialism. Its members included playwri George Bernard Shaw. The Fabians saw it as th duty to make available all sorts of information that wo convince parliamentarians to take up the cause of labo The Fabians furnished the decision-makers with facts t they hoped would win the legislators over to their cau

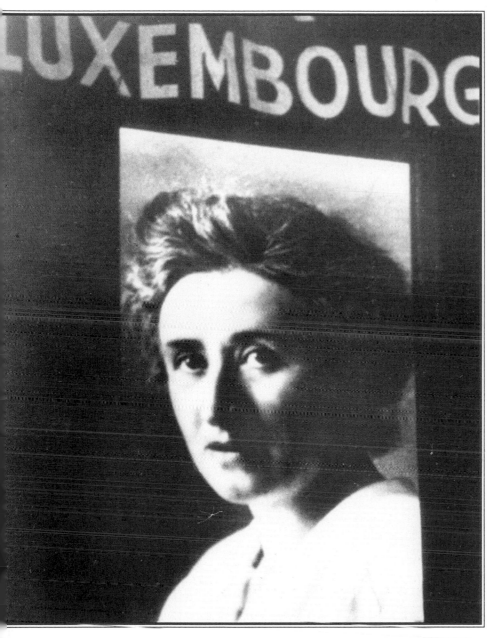

This poster of Rosa Luxembourg (1871–1919) was displayed at a socialist party meeting in Germany. After founding the Polish Social Democratic (Communist) Party, Luxembourg moved to Berlin in 1898, where she became the leader of the left-wing movement. She spent most of World War I in prison, and was murdered shortly after her release.

ideology of dictatorship of the proletariat by revising the theories of Marxism. He believed that change could be brought about peacefully by means of a mass democratic party. Bernstein challenged many of Marx's "scientific theories." In his view there was no need for terror or revolution, as many of the things demanded by the working classes had already been gained within the existing political structure.

At this time class tensions were easing and workers were becoming conservative and nationalistic in outlook. The parliamentary road to change might be the path to follow. Bernstein was expelled from the party for these heretical views. Still he voiced a growing concern that Socialism could be successful in its goals by working within the system.

The Second International was organized by French socialists in 1889 to commemorate the storming of the Bastille a hundred years earlier. The Congress was quickly taken over by the German SPD delegates who largely ignored their French hosts. German revolutionaries Karl Liebknecht and Rosa Luxembourg, refuted Bernstein and tried to keep the ideas of Marx alive. The SPD had risen to a fifth of the vote in Germany

...ey forced official recognition of the need for state inter...tion to end unemployment and to increase workers' ...ges. One result of their work was the establishment in ...0 of the British Labour Party to work within Parliament ... better working conditions.

...n Germany, Eduard Bernstein (1850–1932) tried to ...nge the Socialist Party of Germany (SPD) from an

and appeared ready to become the largest single party in 1890. The conference soon fell to bickering.

The delegates did, however, agree to proclaim a worldwide demonstration of worker solidarity by a global strike set for 1 May 1890. Workers around the world would demonstrate in favour of an eight-hour working day. There was little agreement on anything else.

The Origin of Species

There is grandeur in this view of life, with its several powers, having been originally breathed by the Creator into a few forms or into one; and that, whilst this planet has gone cycling on according to the fixed law of gravity, from so simple a beginning endless forms most beautiful and most wonderful have been, and are being evolved.

From The Origin of Species, *by Charles Darwin.*

Charles Darwin (1809–1882) was not the first to develop the concept of evolution, but he was the first to come up with the idea of natural selection. This idea made evolution a viable theory in the eyes of the scientific community.

Charles Darwin

English philosopher Herbert Spencer (who coined the phrase "survival of the fittest") and William Sumner, an American sociologist, used Darwin's theory of natural selection to support their own ideas of racial superiority. They argued that humans are animals and must live under the same restraints as other species. They supported unlimited, unregulated competition as a natural way to develop the fittest societies. The unfit would be left to their own resources and, if unable to provide for themselves, to die unassisted.

Social Darwinists' views were challenged by English biologist T. H. Huxley (1825–1895), who countered that those who survived were not necessarily the strongest but could be the most intelligent or the luckiest.

Huxley believed that, in many cases, evolution worked against natural forces. People's ability to control and direct nature was to their advantage. He observed that even in the animal kingdom there appeared to be cooperation in matters of survival and social organization. Huxley argued that competition was not the general rule and that cooperation and specialization were more effective than competition at the higher levels.

Natural Selection

In 1859 English naturalist Charles Darwin published his book on biological evolution, *The Origin of Species*, in which he called the process of evolution in the plant and animal kingdoms "natural selection." Natural selection is based on the theories of the survival of those best adapted to the environment and on the need of plants and animals to evolve to the perfect form. Few today believe that natural selection has as predominant a role in evolution as Darwin claimed.

SOCIAL DARWINISM

Social Darwinism is often mixed up with the Socialist movement because of name. This is a mistake, as Social Darwinism is radically different from Socialism. Social Darwinism sanctions a ruthless kind of individual existence and an intolerant treatment of others. The individual not society is all powerful. Social Darwinism supported the racial theories of the day in which it was argued that the white race was superior to all other racial groups. In fact, Victorians believed it was the duty of the white race to carry civilization to the colonies as part of the "white man's burden."

SUMMARY

The transformation of western European society from agricultural-rural to industrial-urban was a long and arduous process. It involved industrializing production on the farm, and establishing factories in the city.

Urban centres grew rapidly because factories needed large numbers of workers living close by. A new type of social animal was born: the wage earner. The growth of urban population created a new list of social problems, including the need to provide adequate housing, sanitation, employment, and standards of living. These problems still exist in industrialized societies today. Unlike the village farmer, the urban worker could not survive when unemployed. During the nineteenth century, various schemes attempted to provide assistance for urban people who could not feed or clothe themselves.

The reorganization of society along industrial lines resulted in ideologies designed to solve the social problems of urban growth. Social Darwinism, Conservatism, Liberalism, and the Socialist philosophies all sought to woo supporters to their particular brand of utopia. None, however, had the complete answer to achieving stability or to sharing the wealth of an industrial state.

Urban wage earners quickly discovered that, in large numbers, they could wield political and economic power. They tried to improve their situation by creating labour associations, trade unions, and political parties.

QUESTIONS

1. What effect did the demand for cotton goods have on the English garment industry?

2. Compare and contrast the cottage system of production with the factory system.

3. Make a chart listing the advantages and disadvantages of the factory system.

4. What was the effect of steam power on the industrial process?

5. Describe the impact of industrialization on the demography of nations that previously were agrarian.

6. Describe the lifestyle of the urban worker. How did England respond to the plight of urban workers who were living and working in very harsh conditions?

7. What is an ideology? How were ideologies changing as a result of the modernization of the world?

8. Define nationalism. Explain how nationalist ideals affected Europe.

9. Briefly describe the romantic movement. Include a definition of romanticism and a brief discussion of the writers and artists of the period.

10. Explain the conservative ideology. What criticism did the conservatives make of the French Revolution?

11. Explain liberal ideology. What were the changes liberals desired?

12. What did John Stuart Mill say about liberty? Mill assumed the needs of the individual were parallel to that of the nation. Give a critical analysis of this assumption.

13. Describe the goals and ideals of the Socialists. What objection did they have to the system of capitalism which governed industry in the eighteenth and nineteenth century?

14. Describe the experiment which Robert Owen implemented at New Lanark. Evaluate its success.

15. Briefly describe the proposals by Charles Fourier and Etienne Cabet for socialist production systems. Why might these proposals meet with approval by workers? What advantages and what problems do you see in these proposals for the worker and for the productive capacity of the plant?

16. What were the opposing forces Marx believed to be in operation in human history? How did Marx propose to end injustice? What stages did Marx identify as the progression of history?

17. What was the purpose of the First Socialist International which was founded in 1868? Evaluate this organization's effectiveness.

18. Describe the role of the Fabian Society in promoting changes in labour legislation.

19. Explain Social Darwinism. What did Thomas Huxley say about this theory?

NALYSIS

Read *Hard Times* by Charles Dickens, examining carefully the way he depicts life in the Industrial Revolution. Is his overall view of the revolution positive or negative? Defend your answer.

Compare and contrast the canal system of transport with the railway. Why are the canals so important to the transfer of goods in Europe and in Canada today?

A capitalist economic system requires market expansion to operate effectively. When the market declines for reasons such as loss of purchase power, change in consumer demand, or overproduction, unemployment occurs.

Socialists believed that society as a whole has a responsibility to care for the unemployed. Eventually all the mainstream political parties came to recognize the need for some kind of social assistance. They differ only in the kind and amount.

(a) Research and write a position paper defending or refuting the concept of social welfare.

(b) Describe the social assistance program you believe a society should provide either on a universal basis or on a basis of individual need.

ACTIVITIES

1. Collage
Create a poster which shows technological changes from 1750 to the present. Focus on industry, consumer goods, or any area of life which has been affected by technological advancement.

2. Debate
Be it resolved that capitalism provides the best environment for economic progress.

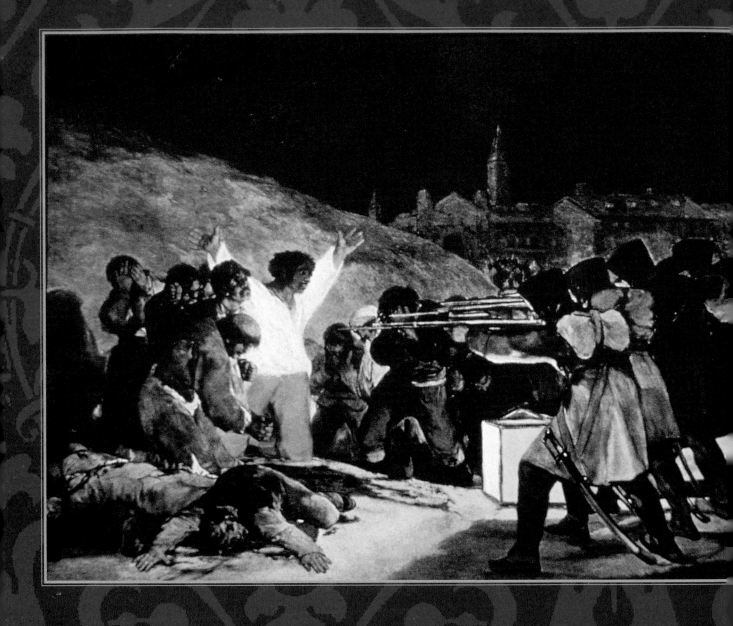

The Third of May, 1808. *(1814-1815) by Francisco Goya.*

Chapter 7
The Arts, Science, and Technology in the Nineteenth Century

FOCUS ON:

❀

Artistic responses to industrialization;

❀

The role of the arts in human development;

❀

Promotion of the arts by the upper-class salon society;

❀

The advances in science and technology within
an industrial society.

The industrialization of Europe created sweeping changes, not only in the political, military, social, and economic systems of the era, but it had a similarly profound effect on art, science, and technology.

FINE ARTS

The Industrial Revolution created a wealthy, new middle class—capitalists and townspeople—who wished to show off their riches and who had the leisure to do so. The middle classes now required family portraits to hang on the walls of their homes and offices. Evening soirées were graced by the latest in musical tastes and scientific demonstrations. These *nouveau riche* purchased books, often left unread, to fill the libraries they were expected to display. Artists, writers, and musicians found unlimited markets for their works.

In addition to the arts market created by the wealthy, the massive public building programs under construction in London, Paris, St Petersburg, Vienna, New York, Washington, Ottawa, and other cities in Europe and North America made equally attractive demands. A nation's prestige was reflected in the calibre of its houses, symphony halls, and art galleries.

TIMELINE
Birth and death dates of significant people

Fine Art
1746–1828 Goya, Fransico José de
1775–1851 Turner, Joseph
1776–1837 Constable, John
1832–1883 Manet, Édouard
1839–1906 Cézanne, Paul
1839–1899 Sisley, Alfred
1840–1917 Rodin, Auguste
1840–1926 Monet, Claude
1841–1919 Renoir, Pierre Auguste
1853–1890 Van Gogh, Vincent
1864–1901 Toulouse-Lautrec, Henri
1866–1944 Kandinsky, Vasily
1869–1954 Matisse, Henri
1881–1973 Picasso, Pablo
1898–1967 René Magritte

Music
1770–1827 Beethoven, Ludwig van
1792–1868 Rossini, Gioacchino Antonio
1810–1849 Chopin, Frédéric
1811–1886 Liszt, Franz
1813–1883 Wagner, Richard
1813–1901 Verdi, Giuseppe
1825–1899 Strauss, Johann, `the younger'
1833–1897 Brahms, Johannes
1840–1893 Tchaikovsky, Peter Ilyich

Literature
1797–1851 Shelley, Mary Wollstonecraft
1802–1885 Hugo, Victor
1816–1855 Brontë, Charlotte
1818–1848 Brontë, Emily

Science
1706–1790 Franklin, Benjamin
1728–1809 Boulton, Matthew
1733–1804 Priestly, Joseph
1809–1882 Darwin, Charles
1813–1898 Bessemer, Henry
1822–1895 Pasteur, Louis
1825–1895 Huxley, Thomas
1847–1931 Edison, Thomas
1858–1947 Planck, Max
1867–1934 Curie, Marie
1871–1937 Rutherford, Ernest
1879–1955 Einstein, Albert

Art of the Nineteenth Century

In their paintings, the midd classes preferred the traditior work of realism developed du ing the Renaissance. Paintin were to represent some aspe of the natural world. Portrai with subjects often posed heroic Roman or Greek gar were worked and reworked the studio. Paintings of one's r atives were preferred to lar scapes. Thousands of artis made a comfortable living cat ing to the demands of patro for traditional art.

Goya

A revolution in painting beg with the Spaniard, Francis Goya (1746–1828). A painter the realist style, he secured place at the Spanish court 1808 when Carlos III expelled foreign artists from Spain. court, Goya continued to work traditional modes. He was p vided with a handsome livi and maintained his reputation a superb realist. However, Go also experimented with new forms that were far from real. sketched fantastic visions ghosts and apparitions, perha inspired by his nightmares of t atrocities committed during war with France from 1808 1813.

When Carlos IV, his wife Ma Louisa, and their son Ferdina quarrelled over the succession the Spanish throne, Napole Bonaparte offered to media Napoleon invited the Span

yal family to meet with him in
uthern France. As the Spanish
yal family left Madrid, for their
eeting with Napoleon on 2 May
08, gathering crowds feared
e French escort were taking
em to their execution. Riots
oke out and French soldiers
ened fire, killing a number of
aniards. Gathering up a num-
r of the rioters, the French sys-
matically had them executed
firing squad. When the royal
nily arrived in France, Na-
leon held them captive and
ced his own brother Joseph
the Spanish throne.
Goya's depictions of the exe-
tions broke every acceptable
ndard of art. He brought his
n emotions onto the canvas
vivid colours. He wanted the
server to react emotionally to
e brutality of the firing squad.
injecting his own deep feel-
s into the painting, he had
ken a major step away from
e simple recording of an
nt. His bold colours evoked a
sual response demonstrating
t colours alone could be used
stir the onlooker.
For the next six years Spain
d Portugal would be the
ne of a vicious guerrilla war between the French forces
occupation and a small English army under the Duke of
ellington. Wellington captured Madrid from Marshall
rat in 1812 and claimed victory over the French armies
Vitoria in 1813. Ferdinand was placed on the Spanish
one the next year. Goya's portrayals of the events of the
rrilla war were the beginning of the break with tradi-
nal realism in art.

glish Patrons of Art

ring the French Revolution and the Napoleonic period,
ndon became the major centre for the arts. Wealthy

Les Misérables

In his novel *Les Misérables*, published in 1862, Victor Hugo wrote about poverty in nineteenth century France. In the following passage a sixteen-year-old girl describes what it is like to be starving and homeless.

Before coming to this place, the other winter, we lived under the arches of the bridges. We hugged close to each other so as not to freeze. My little sister cried. How chilly the water is! When I thought of drowning myself, I said: No; it is too cold. I go all alone when I want to, I sleep in the ditches sometimes. Do you know, at night, when I walk on the boulevards, I see the trees like gibbets, I see all the great black houses like the towers of Notre Dame, I imagine that the white walls are the river, I say to myself: Here, there is water there! The stars are like illumination lamps, one would say that they smoke, and that the wind blows them out, I am confused, as if I had horses breathing in my ear; though it is night, I hear hand-organs and spinning wheels, I don't know what. I think that somebody is throwing stones at me, I run without knowing it, it is all a whirl, all a whirl. When one has not eaten, it is very queer.

patrons financed promising writers, musicians, and painters. In return the artists were expected to be present at soirées and to dedicate their works to their patron. The most famous patron was the third Lord Egremont, perhaps the wealthiest man in England, whose ancestors went back to the Norman Conquest of 1066.

Artists and scientists were invited to stay at Egremont's estate as long as they pleased. They mingled together in good fellowship exchanging ideas and techniques. It was there that Blake and Wordsworth trumpeted the Rights of Man—until the Reign of Terror set in. The ideas of Burke and Payne on the freedom of man or the excesses of the citizenry were heatedly debated.

Another important patron of the arts was the Prince Regent, the Prince of Wales. After the Battle of Waterloo, the heir to the British throne held a dinner at Carlton House where the banquet table was over 60 metres long. The table was divided in two by a fountain. Gutters filled with live fish ran the length of the sides. Over 100 dishes were served with copious amounts of champagne. The poet, Percy Bysshe Shelley, railed at the extravagance. However, he had little effect on dampening the celebrations of the victorious end to war with France.

All this glitter and opulence of the upper classes was in contrast with lives of the working classes. In 1830 and again in 1848 barricades were erected in the streets of Paris by workers protesting hunger and poverty. In London each day added another 1000 persons. Housing and jobs fell desperately far behind the need in every city in Europe. A large part of the population was unemployed and homeless. Most of these unfortunate people spent their nights under bridges or along railway embankments. They lived in gangs and turned to crime to stay alive. Their plight was depicted by some of the novelists of the day—Victor Hugo, Charles Dickens, and Emile Zola. Few, including Queen Victoria, believed their works were anything but fiction. Those who recognized the existence of the poor thought the solution to be in forced emigration to the New World.

Turner and Constable

William Turner (1775–1851) and John Constable (1776–1837) were the major English artists of the day. Turner was immensely successful, leaving some 20 000 works of art including sketches, lithographs, oils, and watercolours. Turner's illustrations of Sir Walter Scott's novels increased their sales by thousands of copies. In his later years Turner began to move away from the realist style into **romanticism.** In his Venice series (1833) of the palaces along the Grand Canal he used delicate colour washes for a dreamlike atmosphere of mystery and imagination. The outlines of the palaces are barely visible through the morning mists.

Turner used the same technique to depict the new steam engines crossing the moors or entering their glass- and steel-canopied stations. Here, the bold, precise forms of the realist gradually gave way to the

~

The Crime of Poverty

~

CUSINS: Do you call poverty a crime?

UNDERSHAFT: The worst of crimes. All the other crimes are virtues beside it: all the other dishonors are chivalry itself by comparison. Poverty blights whole cities; spreads horrible pestilences; strikes dead the very souls of all who come within sight, sound, or smell of it. What you call crime is nothing: a murder here and a theft there, a blow now and a curse then: what do they matter? they are only the accidents and illnesses of life: there are not fifty genuine professional criminals in London. But there are millions of poor people, abject people, dirty people, ill fed, ill clothed people. They poison us morally and physically: they kill the happiness of society: they force us to do away with our own liberties and to organize unnatural cruelties for fear they should rise against us and drag us down into their abyss. Only fools fear crime: we all fear poverty…

From Major Barbara, *a play by George Bernard Shaw. Reprinted with permission of The Society of Authors on behalf of the George Bernard Shaw Estate.*

Research

1. Research the playwright and social critic George Bernard Shaw. What were his political and social affiliations?

2. During what period was *Major Barbara* written? What was poverty like at that time?

3. Do you think Undershaft is expressing the opinion of Shaw? If not, whose opinion is he expressing? Explain.

~

blurred outlines of a roman visionary. In the *Burning of t Houses of Parliament* the e immediately reacts to what obviously a terrible tragedy. T centre of the picture glows w bright swirling colours symbo of a fire storm. We first sense t fire and our emotions react our own experiences with fi The message is one of urgen However, on closer examinati we see that the crowds on t bridge and the boaters in t water are only suggested blurred paint strokes. Turr left it to the viewer's eye to fil the details.

Although one could alwa get to Venice or the Alps, tra to the continent was made di cult during the French Revo tion. Constable chose to tra the length and breadth of t British Isles instead, working landscapes. In these paintir Man was made insignificant his relationship with Natu One of his more famous pai ings, *The Hay Wain*, was feet wide. One has to look clo ly at the scene to discover t animals and people. The subj was nature itself.

Constable's work was do outdoors in natural light, not a studio. The idea of painting the open air where the light pure was radical. How co one fix mistakes by rework the canvas if not in a stud Constable's Winchester Cat dral series contains some of finest works and were pain outdoors.

The Hay Wain *(1821) by John Constable.*

in France

r the Napoleonic wars, Paris supplanted London as ope's artistic centre. Artists who had patrons did not e to sell their wares in public. Those who did not took esidence on the outskirts of the city on the left bank e River Seine near the mills of Montmartre where the ings were cheap. There, they wore wide-brimmed , berets, and colourful attire and came to be known as emian.

nsuccessful in having their works judged good enough ang in the Royal Academy, artists of the left bank were ed to set up their own galleries. The Royal Academy been founded in the 1640s by Louis XIV to improve the dards of French art. A jury determined whether a paint- was good enough to be displayed. Those who were ned talented were fortunate in that they would acquire ying public. Those turned away by the jury did not gain ic approval and found it difficult to sell their paintings. y depended on turning out some hurried portraits to money for the rent.

ose who had their works refused by the academy, *les sées*, adopted an air of indifference towards it. They ut to destroy all the traditional forms and acceptable standards of their profession. They painted original works of art in new styles that freed the world of art from tradi- tion. In doing so, they also produced some of the century's greatest art.

Les refusées shocked the public in many ways but mostly in their choice of subject matter—Paris itself. The dominant characteristic of the city was the people, in crowds and at work. *Les refusées* painted the common, working class people as they went about their lives—the crowd at Longchamps race course, the bustling activity of the boulevard cafés, the dancers of the ballet, customers at the Folies Bergère, and always the ever present crowd. But who wants to hang a picture of a working class crowd? The middle classes could not relate to these subjects and refused to purchase them.

After the 1848 revolutions in Europe, Charles Louis Napoleon Bonaparte was elected president and later emperor of France. A patron of the arts, the emperor encouraged *les refusées* to have their own showing in 1863. At the opening of the Galleries des Refusées he was shocked by the experimental art exhibited. Manet's *Luncheon in the Grass* displaying a nude woman having lunch with three clothed gentlemen was too much for the

Bal du Moulin de la Galette *(1876) by Pierre Auguste Renoir.*

empress who described the work as vulgar. The press was even less kind. "Unfinished," "barbaric," "untrained" were some of the adjectives used to describe the works.

Edouard Manet (1832–1883) and Claude Monet (1840–1926) were the leaders of the new wave. Pierre Auguste Renoir (1841–1919), Alfred Sisley (1839–1899), and Vincent van Gogh (1853–1890) were among the others. All studied the traditional styles of art under acknowledged masters at the beginnings of their careers. And all could work in the various traditional styles of painting. It was at the end of their careers that they chose to experiment in new styles.

Manet did his most important work in the last five years of his life. His objective was to get away from the formal, posed paintings of the studio and to work in the open air so as to capture on canvas that first glimpse of nature before the eye could totally focus. Only the central feature of Manet's paintings are in focus the rest are blurred towards the edges. Faces often appear flat with little detail.

Manet claimed that this was in fact how the eye saw thi at a distance. In this aspect, impressions are more ac rate as the eye does not see shapes in detail. It is the m that arranges the sensory data to fit a predetermined fo An impressionist painting is best viewed from a dista of a few metres.

Impressionists wanted to catch the pure colour of l reflecting off an object before the light changed. T worked rapidly with no time to plan or make prelimir sketches. Monet had a little boat fitted out so that he cc drift down the river sketching glimpses of the real nat The term impressionism was used to ridicule a paintin; Monet, *Impression, Fog (Le Havre)* 1872.

The public did not understand the impressionists. T work appeared rough and unfinished. Much of it loo smudged and blurry when examined at close range. critics judged it unfinished. The impressionists were c pletely ignored by the buying public.

Not everyone ignored it, however. Manet's *Olympia,*

Le Baiser (1886) by Auguste Rodin.

nting of a young, nude woman her couch, was brought back France from Holland through the intercession of Georges menceau, later president of nce. Clémenceau was an nirer of impressionist art, ecially that of Manet. In 1907 menceau bought the painting Holland and returned it to nce. The canvas was rushed ough the streets of Paris to Louvre by early morning taxi. eared the reaction if the pub-learned of his stratagem. At net's funeral, Clémenceau ed the black drapery from coffin and replaced it with urful window curtains. net did not use black and k would not do for Manet's final journey.

1870, after the Franco-Prussian War, the leading ressionists took up residence in Argenteuil northwest Paris. Some of their better work was painted there. net's studies of the railway station at St Lazare or his es on Antibes (1888) are examples. The bare hint of ail in these works bespoke the new reality. Painters ald see the world as an impression of colour.

onet and Renoir often painted together, exploring the e river valley. Monet's technique was to finish a paint-at one sitting. The scene was fixed directly on to the vas before the light changed. He cared less for detail a for the effect of the instant. Monet saw magic in light the impression of a view. Renoir wanted to capture the d of ordinary people, their carefree existence, poor happy. He was drawn to the swirling dance of the Paris vds. *Bal du Moulin de la Galette* (1876) shows only the l of one of the dancers in any detail. The rest is sketchy e other figures dissolve before the eyes into unrefined h strokes. Yet the onlooker immediately reacts to what mind perceives as the details of a crowd.

iguste Rodin, the sculptor (1840–1917), joined the bat-or modernism. Rodin was an acknowledged master of itional sculpting in the Michelangelo mode. However, the impressionists, he preferred to leave something to magination of the observer. Rodin frequently left part

of the stone untouched for the effect it had on others. He alone, not the general public or the critics, would decide when his work was finished.

At the end of the century, painting moved even further away from precisely drawn forms. This was in part a response to the success of the camera and that painters did not want their work to be compared with the stark realism of pho-tography.

Paul Cézanne (1839–1906) quickened the move away from realism. Cézanne believed that underlying nature lay a world of geometric forms—cones, trian-gles, and squares. Cézanne did not hesitate to improve on nature by distorting visual objects or changing their position, even mountains, if it improved the composition. This technique made him one of the founders of modern art where accurate form gave way to colour and design.

In Cézanne's painting of Mont Ste-Victoire in southern France, the landscape is bathed in light yet has the solid feel of order and stability. He has conveyed the rich, unbro-ken tones of nature to the subconscious. Cézanne's indif-ference to form started a landslide in new approaches to painting.

Vincent van Gogh (1853–1890) had only ten years as a painter before his suicide at the age of 37. He, too, was a well trained classicist. Van Gogh went to Paris to be with his younger brother, Theo, who worked in an art shop. Theo introduced him to the impressionists with whom van Gogh studied for a brief time before going out on his own. What he saw were not forms, as Cézanne did, but colours.

Van Gogh worked in bold, brilliant colours slapped onto the canvas with broad, short brush strokes communicat-ing the deep feelings he experienced in nature. To van Gogh the world of nature was only the starting point. An artist had to create his or her own reality. There was no effort to blend in the edges or smooth out the oils. Putting paint directly from the tubes onto canvas, he created his own gleaming world of reality.

Starry Night *(1889) by Vincent van Gogh.*
Oil on canvas, 29 x 36 1/4" (73.7 x 92.1 cm).
The Museum of Modern Art, New York. Acquired through the Lillie P. Bliss Bequest.
Photograph © 1997 The Museum of Modern Art, New York.

In December 1888 van Gogh had a nervous breakdown and was placed in an institution for the insane. He had few lucid moments after that until his death in 1890 although he continued to paint. An unfinished letter to Theo was found in his pocket. It was one of many between the two brothers. Their correspondence in part blamed Theo for not selling Vincent's works but as Theo replied he found it difficult to display such works let alone sell them. Who but Vincent could understand them? In his lifetime, he sold only one of his 1700 paintings and that was for only $80. Today a conservative bid for a small work would begin at $11 million.

Henri de Toulouse-Lautrec (1864–1901) experimen with poster art. Toulouse-Lautrec had broken both hip a childhood accident and walked with a strange, rolling He was also extremely short. He was born into a mid class home, but his physical problems caused him to draw from the life of his family. Instead, he sought out night life of the cafés and dance halls, especially the Fo Bergère where his friend, Jane Avril, performed. This the world he painted for the most part—the world of cab singers, clowns, dancers, the *demimonde* of Paris.

In 1900 **les sauvages** burst on the Paris art scene. *sauvages* ignored form in favour of appropriate shapes

Improvisation 30 (Cannons) *(1913)*
by Vasily Kandinsky.

colours. Pablo Picasso (1881–1973), Henri Matisse (1869–1954), and others experimented with design and colour combinations. A painting was redefined as an arrangement of colours on a flat two-dimensional surface. To some, such as Vasily Kandinsky (1866–1944), paintings should not mirror anything in the real world. Art became totally subjective. Recognizable forms were no longer necessary. If forms were to be used then they were to be juxtaposed, such as in the work of the Belgian artist René Magritte (1898–1967) where large rocks floated in air and train engines grew out of fireplaces.

The Dada school grew out of a chance meeting of war refugees in Zurich in 1916. Gathering in a café they protested against a universe that could permit the carnage of the battles of Verdun and the Somme. Insanity seemed the order of the universe and chance was its master. Was not a painting a canvas that received paint thrown at it or dropped on it from above? Tristan Tarza amazed his audience by reading a poem consisting of the same word 147 times. The group chose the name Dada to describe themselves. The name came from a French-German dictionary and meant "rocking horse." It was appropriate, as they wanted to present art in its purest, primitive, form—as that of the untrained child.

In 1913 a famous exhibition highlighting modernist art was held in New York at the Armoury at 291 Fifth Avenue. The showing hit the North American art world like a bombshell. One of the works, *Nude Descending a Staircase, No. 2*, by Dada artist Marcel Duchamp, created an immediate sensation in the art world. It shows a distorted machine-like female figure in fragments of motion.

MUSIC OF THE NINETEENTH CENTURY

Rising nationalism caused nineteenth century composers to look to the folk dances and songs of their native lands. Romanticism entered when the artist expressed his personal emotions to the public in music. Music evoked emotion; it was no longer abstract. It was about life, death, love, pride, and the political struggles of the day.

Beethoven

Ludwig van Beethoven swept away the music of t Enlightenment replacing it with a newfound freedom orchestral themes. His music stirred the depths of emoti with its broad, commanding melodies.

In 1787, at the age of 17 Beethoven played the piano Mozart, who commented to his friends that the young m was someone to watch for as he could evoke the emotic like no other. By 20 Beethoven was an accomplish pianist and was acknowledged as the best perform artist in Europe.

Beethoven's brilliant piano playing made him a huge s cess with the music-loving aristocracy of the salo Although at first he was never without wealthy patrons, the most part he worked independently. He led a full except for his growing deafness. Beethoven's loss of he ing began in his twenties and was accompanied by depr sions. By the end of his career he was quite deaf yet c tinued to compose. Beethoven said he heard the music his mind.

Beethoven conquered his deafness and continued to c ate masterpieces. Through his experience he came believe that a human being could conquer chaos in world. The struggle from despair to conflict to serenit triumph and, finally, joy became his musical theme. believed that art could make up for the deficiencies of real world.

Beethoven rarely performed in public, reserving hims for the salons and his patrons. He decided to pursue cc posing, and went to Vienna at the request of Pri Linchowsky, his first patron. Compositions were j beginning to be performed in the new music halls Beethoven's latter works display a sensitivity to the r public audiences. Prior to the development of public au ences, musical scores were often discarded after a sir performance. Beethoven was the first composer to be a to make a comfortable living on royalties and conduct fees. Now compositions were kept for repeated use.

The public adored Beethoven's dramatic change: mood and tempo and his lyric melodies. Stormy passa open most of his works. These are followed by fast sc zos and slow moving adagios. He often got inspirati from nature in his walks in the Vienna Woods or in the dens of the Belvedere and Schönbrunn palaces.

By 1818 he had written eight of his nine symphon most of his grand piano concertos, his only opera *Fide*

Beethoven's loss of hearing began in his twenties and was accompanied by
depressions. By the end of his career he was quite deaf yet continued to compose.

musical scores or throw parts of them out as it suited them. The only way a composer could ensure his work would be played the way he composed it was to conduct it himself. Unable to hear the audience response because of his deafness, Beethoven stood with sagging shoulders as the last note of the "Ode to Joy" resounded. Finally, one of the singers turned him around to face an audience wild with ecstasy and he realized what a triumph he had achieved.

In 1826, while returning from his brother's place in an open carriage, Beethoven caught a chill. He never recovered and passed away at 57 on 26 March 1827, in the middle of a thunderstorm. Vienna's conductors were his pallbearers and more than 20 000 attended the funeral ceremonies. Those who knew music bemoaned the fact that no one could better the genius of their departed master.

Rossini

The Italian composer Gioacchino Rossini (1792–1868) met Beethoven in 1822. Rossini was 30 years old and had completed several comic operas by that time. He was one of Italy's national heroes. By 21 he had become the toast of Europe. In one year, 23 of his works were being performed in opera houses around the world. The better known of his comic operas were *Cinderella* and *The Barber of Seville* in which a lowly servant, Figaro, gets the better of his rather dull master. Rossini composed more than 39 operas, many of them *opera buffa* ("comic opera") but his *Moses in Egypt* and *Othello* were serious works.

The world adored Rossini's comedies with their sparkling melodies and farcical, racy situations. He wrote quickly composing as many as five major works in any given year.

a Mass in D, plus a score of other works. So difficult complex were his compositions that few symphonies ed to test them out and fewer concert halls of that iod could contain them. After 1813 Beethoven became re isolated as his deafness approached totality. He consed by using writing pads and sign language. His comtion of the *Ninth Symphony*, also called the Choral nphony (1817–1823) with its majestic chorus, "Ode to ," was a crowning achievement in a glorious career. He sted on personally conducting its premiere.

hen, as now, conductors did not hesitate to rearrange

Mary Shelley's Frankenstein *helped to make gothic novels popular.*

Women in the Nineteenth Century

The Brontë sisters were the first to write about the passions women felt; their novels were filled with romance and love. Jane Austen wrote novels that evaluated ordinary human behaviour; Margaret Fuller, a New Englander, wrote about individual liberty; Mary Shelley, at 19 wrote about Victor Frankenstein; Germaine de Staël, daughter of Jacques Necker, studied German romantic literature and "thought like a man." These women were truly intellectual forces of their day.

However, they were the exceptions. This was a century of differentiation between the sexes in manners, dress, and attitude. Rooms were given masculine and feminine roles as were the furnishings within each room. This was because the male was supposed to be rational, athletic, and courageous; women were thought to be feeble and timid. Women were governed by their emotions. They often fainted in public or gave into bursts of crying. Therefore, it was argued, the male dominated and the role of the woman was to obey.

Women were kept inferior by not only the nature of society but also the nature of their education. As a result, they were at a obvious disadvantage in conversation and were assumed to have no thoughts in their heads.

As wives, women kept the house and managed the servants. Stranded and isolated in their large country houses, they affected all sorts of self-induced neuroses such as loss of hearing or speech in order to gain attention. This reinforced the myth of the frailty of women. It was not until the suffragette movement at the turn of the century that women began to gain their independence.

He wrote *The Barber of Seville* in thirteen days. In one instance, when composing while sitting up in bed he dropped a page on the floor. Rather than take the trouble to retrieve it from under the bed he composed a new score.

Rossini moved to Paris in 1829 where he spent considerable time eluding the female friends who had pursued him from Italy. In Paris he retired at the age of 37 from serious composing and spent his last 40 years in carefree splendour, producing songs, piano pieces, and one large work, *Stabat Mater* (1842). He was an acknowledged gourmet, wrote and published a number of cookbooks, put on considerable weight, and gave his name to that famous dish, Tournedos Rossini. He had his picture taken in Paris in 1868, the year of his death, at the 100th performance the capital of his opera *William Tell.*

Salon Society

In the 1800s, Paris was a brilliant assembly: musicians Berlioz, Rossini; writers Victor Hugo, George Sand, Honoré de Balzac; artists Eugène Delacroix, to name just a few. In café society, Victor Hugo could be found at the Procope with his fellow artists, Alexander Dumas *(The Three Musketeers)*, the poet Alfred Musset, and the composer Hector Berlioz, who finished his *Symphony Fantastique* in 18—.

Women were the hostesses of the brilliant salon society that governed London, Paris, Prague, and Vienna.

This portrait shows several composers and writers in a salon. Franz Liszt is at the piano, staring up at the bust of Beethoven. George Sand (in the chair directly behind Liszt), Victor Hugo, Hector Berlioz, and Gioacchino Rossini look on.

opin and Liszt

ly in the nineteenth century, Paris was graced with the val of two of the world's greatest romantic composers, léric Chopin (1810–1849) and Franz Liszt (1811–1886). s adopted the two into its salon society.

hopin's deep passions over the Russian conquest of his ve Poland, and Liszt's emotions over the loss of friends ng the storming of the barricades in the revolutions of) and 1848, gave their music a haunting quality. Revo-nary in nature, their performances were a response to ability of people to endure great losses.

ey poured out their souls in music, Chopin, "the poet ne piano," and Liszt, the master of majestic themes. r music stirred audiences to tears and women often ed during their performances. Liszt was considered

by many to be the greatest pianist of all time. Meanwhile, Chopin's fast waltzes and polonaises were the rage of the salons. He turned music on end using the full range of the new keyboards that were at least an octave longer than those on which Mozart had played. Brilliant runs up and down the keyboard, delicate and light, brought tingles to the spines of his listeners. Chopin was a hopeless romantic and Paris loved him for it.

In 1835 Liszt introduced Chopin to Aurore Dudevant a tiny, trouser-wearing, cigar-smoking *cause célèbre,* known to history as the novelist George Sand (1804–1876). She was 32 and he was 26. She was already the talk of the capital for her unconventional life style. She wrote over 80 novels expressing her feminism, love of nature, and idealism. Her novel *A Year In Majorca* about her time with Chopin is among her best books. She was brilliant and politically radical; he was reserved and conventional. The two had a stormy liaison.

In 1836 they both left the city for holidays in Majorca. It could not have been a worse time for Chopin as the constant rains worsened his tuberculosis. They separated in 1847 over a quarrel concerning her son and daughter. After they separated, Chopin seemed to lose his creativity. He died in Paris two years later at 39. Sand was not informed about his death and did not attend his funeral, a huge event, with royalty and artists gathered to pay homage to him. A box of Polish soil was sent from Warsaw for the funeral to scatter on his grave and his heart was returned to Poland.

Liszt

Franz Liszt was born in Hungary. He spent his early years in the Esterhazy estates outside Budapest where his father was a steward. He showed talent with a violin and was sent to Paris to study music where he met the French Romantics. He admired the great violin player and composer Niccolò Paganini, and later wrote pieces for him.

Liszt had a magnetic stage personality. He acted the performance and audiences responded by throwing bouquets of roses at his feet. Liszt was the pop idol of his day and looked and dressed the part. He never married, but had numerous love affairs, among them George Sand, Marie Duplessis, and Countess Marie d'Agoult with whom he had three children. The countess wrote novels under the name Daniel Stern.

Although he retired from public performances early in his career he continued to compose until his death. His most famous works apart from the Hungarian dances were his piano compositions including "March Funèbre," and his rhapsodies. He is one of the creators of modern piano technique. In his hands the piano became an orchestra. He was an early supporter of Richard Wagner and, at times, conducted Wagner's grand operas. Liszt's daughter Cosima left her first husband the conductor Hans von Bülow to marry Wagner.

In 1848 Liszt met Caroline Wittgenstein, whose estate

～ Pianos ～

In the early part of the nineteenth century there were more than 60 000 pianos in Paris, one for every five households.

～

included 30 000 personal se They fell in love but never n ried as she was unable to ge divorce from her husband. L later entered the Francisc order and spent his last year the Vatican. He passed away 1866 at 75, while on a trip Bayreuth to attend a festiva Wagner's works.

Verdi

In the midst of a snow storm in 1831 Merelli, manage La Scala, Milan's great opera house, met Giuseppe Ve (1813–1901), the great Italian composer. Verdi's wife two children had recently died. He was despondent had vowed never to write again. Merelli told him tha Scala needed a new opera for the opening of the sea and enthusiastically handed him the libretto for *Nabu* (Nebuchadnezzar, King of Babylon). The line, "Go thought on golden wings," on the first page affected V so much that he agreed to read the rest and decide write the opera. It was triumphantly received, and he w on to write many more operas. Verdi became a natio hero as some Italians saw in *Nabucco* their own plight ing under the chains of Austro-Hungarian rule.

Not only the Italians but the whole world came to kr and love Verdi's musical dramas of which there were There was *Rigoletto*, about the hunchback from Vi Hugo's story *Le Roi s'Amuse*; the unforgettable *A* about a beautiful Ethiopian slave girl written for the o ing of the Suez Canal in 1869; *Il Trovatore*, about a r terious Spanish knight; *La Traviata*, about the beau courtesan who renounces love and whose arias remair most popular in all opera; and *Falstaff*, which Verdi w at the age of 80. He was the Michelangelo of the m world.

Brahms

Johannes Brahms (1833–1897) became a familiar or Vienna music scene. Brahms started out as a piano pl in a brothel in the slums of his childhood at the age o Somehow he managed to obtain free piano lessons. By time he was 20 he was a concert violinist's accompa In 1853, he was introduced to Clara and Robert Schum who were famous musicians. They took him under t

Johannes Brahms was a German pianist and composer who lived in Vienna for most of his career.

Strauss

The Viennese Johann Strauss, the younger, wrote for an audience that had become enamoured with the waltz. This was a new dance in which partners faced each other and at times actually touched. It was considered sinful in those days, and so became popular especially with the young. The tunes were pleasurable and easy to remember. Some of Vienna's dance halls held as many as 6000 dancers.

Strauss came from a family of musicians. Johann, the elder, abandoned the family. His wife was determined her son would eclipse the father. Her wishes came true. At his inaugural concert in the Dommayer's Restaurant, when he was only 19, his waltzes were so well received the patrons would not let him stop. Well past midnight he paid tribute to his father by conducting one of his father's waltzes. This gesture brought the house down and resulted in a reconciliation between father and son.

Strauss often conducted his own works in Vienna's outdoor parks or at the Prater. Strauss waltzes were the rage and soon spread across Europe and into North America. The lively tempos were irresistible and every composer attempted to write one or more of the dance tunes but Strauss was the acknowledged king. He wrote 400 waltzes, among them the familiar "Blue Danube" and "Tales from the Vienna Woods." His more serious works included *Die Fledermaus* ("The Bat") in 1874 which played for 100 straight performances in Berlin, and *The Gypsy Baron* in 1885. Strauss died just before the turn of the century in 1899.

Period of Opulence

In the 1850s on the order of Emperor Napoleon III, Paris was rebuilt under the direction of Baron Georges

gs and into their home. Then Robert Schumann had a ntal breakdown. In one of his moments of lucidity he te a glowing report on the work of his young friend. er Schumann's death, Brahms embarked on his four at symphonies. He built complex, broad themes that k over where Beethoven left off. His orchestras were ble the size that Beethoven had composed for and uded many new instruments. Some would argue that hms's symphonies carried symphonic music to its ulti- e end. He also wrote many well-loved piano pieces, gs, choral pieces, and loved German folk music.

rahms led a comfortable life. He had enough pupils to p him busy, and the royalties from his works and per- nance fees gave him financial security. He travelled ely across Europe in the summers and appears to have yed his latter years, although the death of Clara umann devastated him and he died ten months after.

*Peter Ilyich Tchaikovsky (1840–1893) began his
formal musical training in St Petersburg and
taught for several years at a conservatory in
Moscow. After one month of marriage, he left his
wife, quit his job, and retired in the countryside
to concentrate on composing.*

Haussmann. Paris was an exciting place to be at the start of what is labelled by historians as La Belle Epoque. London, too, would be largely rebuilt starting in the 1880s.

The nineteenth century was a period of opulence and wealth. It was a marvellous time to be alive if one were rich and a member of the upper classes. The Ringstrasse in Vienna boasted its sidewalk coffee houses and Paris had its cafés. London had the Covent Garden, Paris its Opéra, Vienna the Staatsoper, and New York Carnegie Hall. New concert halls, each larger than the last, were built. Few paid any attention to the social critic Karl Marx who predicted that bourgeoisie society would be pulled down by the millions of workers who could not partake of the luxuries of high society.

While social pressures built in the urban-industrial societies, music continued to flourish in ever increasingly complex forms. Richard Wagner and Peter Ilyich Tchaikovsky were the first of "the great moderns."

Wagner

Wagner (1813–1883) is one of the greatest composers of all time. His profound "musical dramas" touch on the very nature of existence. Although he died a wealthy man, his early years were spent eluding his many creditors. He was *Kapellmeister* ("chorus master") to the Austrian emperor where his income never quite matched his expenditures. He was self-taught musically and a revolutionary politically.

In Dresden he completed *Tannhäuser* in 1845 and *Lohengrin*, about the search for the Holy Grail, in 1848. Liszt conducted the first public performance of Lohengrin at Weimar. When the revolutions in Europe reached Dresden, Wagner fled with Liszt's help to Switzerland.

During the difficult period between 1853 and 1874 Wagner settled in Zurich and began to compose a series of four operas depicting t changes forced on humanity industrialization, *The Ring the Nibelungen*, or the Ri Cycle. The series is set in t mythological times of the T tonic gods. It forecasts t demise of the gods as huma take over the work of the go through the institutions of la

King Ludwig II of Bavaria, w came to the throne at 18, was taken by Wagner's music that invited the musician to stay w him at Neuschwanstein Bavaria, a palace in which s eral of the rooms were decor ed to depict Wagner's musi settings. Wagner lived in nea Munich as the king comm sioned him to finish his R Cycle. It was there that he fe love with Liszt's daughter C ma (1837–1930). She was m ried to Hans von Bülow, made no secret of her love for Wagner. Despite this stra arrangement, Bülow became one of Wagner's greatest s porters and conducted many of the composer's works. W ner and Cosima began work on a new festival house in Bavarian town of Bayreuth that would be large enough stage the Ring Cycle. Kaiser Wilhelm I of Germany atte ed the gala opening in 1876. The Bayreuth Festival is sti major musical event, thanks to Cosima's efforts.

Tchaikovsky

The most popular works of Peter Ilyich Tchaikovs (1840–1893) are the ballets *Swan Lake, Romeo and Jul Sleeping Beauty*, *The Nutcracker Suite* and the rous symphonic piece, the *1812 Overture* in which real can are fired at the end. Tchaikovsky's works were cro pleasing with their lyrical melodies.

Tchaikovsky began studying the law before he co convince his father he wanted to be a musician. He wor as a government official until at 23 he quit to study m at the conservatory in Moscow. He studied under An Rubenstein for a number of years before taking up his c reer. Rubenstein coldly rejected having any of haikovsky works dedicated to him. After a persistent rsuit, Tchaikovsky married Antoninia Ivanova liukova. The couple often quarrelled and at one point haikovsky immersed himself in the ice cold waters of e Moscow River in a failed attempt at suicide. He was lled from the icy clutches of the river without even :ching a cold, but he plunged into a nervous breakdown. fled Moscow for St Petersburg where he hoped to find ief from both his condition and personal life.

Ie was saved when, in 1877, a mysterious Madame von ck, created a 6000-ruble annual endowment for him ovided he correspond with her only by letter. They were er to meet. The correspondence grew to 771 letters il all contact with his benefactor was abruptly broken l the endowment ended. No reason for the breach was er discovered.

n 1891 Tchaikovsky travelled to New York to conduct he opening of Carnegie Hall. He was paid $2500 for his vices, a huge sum in those days, but he soon tired of the w World and longed for a return to his beloved St ersburg. There he completed his Sixth Symphony, the *hétique*. Only four days after its completion he came wn with cholera and died at 53 with von Meck's name his lips.

IENCE AND TECHNOLOGY

he development of steam power, the explosive growth of the iron and steel industry, the invention of electricity, the development of the germ theory isease, and the resurrection of the atomic theory, were scientific and technological highlights of the nine- nth century.

he application of steam power to industry and trans- tation resulted in the Industrial Revolution. Just as ic Newton had foreseen, the ability to harness the laws ature created an entirely different life style from that grarian feudalism which had been based on the village. ost of the scientific discoveries that accompanied the lution were centred in a small area around the iron coal fields of England and Scotland that produced fuel the textile industry. The industrialists in the textile le were running out of wood and were already using the lable water powered mills from the region's streams

and rivers to full capacity. They turned to steam power to increase the productivity of their woollen and cotton mills. Little did they realize what a complete change to the human condition would result.

The changes were made by a small group of scientists, engineers, and entrepreneurs connected with the textile trade. They not only worked together but they mixed together in their social life. One example was the Lunar Society which met socially once a week. Counted among its members were John Wilkinson (1728–1808) the iron master whose boring machines could turn a cylinder of iron into a cannon barrel; Josiah Wedgwood (1774–1817) the potter; Joseph Priestley (1733–1804) the discoverer of oxygen; and Matthew Boulton (1728–1809) manufacturer of the first steam engines. For the better part of the nine- teenth century, this combination of science and technol- ogy was found only in Britain.

Steam Power

Steam power was the most significant invention of the age. (see chapter 6.) Thomas Newcomen had already produced a steam engine to pump out the mines. Water heated in a tube turned to steam which forced a piston upwards. When the steam cooled a vacuum was created that drew the water up from below. James Watt modified the design of the Newcomen engine by diverting the steam from the main cylinder. This meant the main cylinder did not have to be cooled but retained its heat making it easier to turn the fresh water into steam. Later, George Richardson placed a carriage under the steam boiler and, in 1829, invented steam-powered locomotion. For the next half century, engineers worked to improve the efficiency of the steam engines.

Firemen had their own solution for increasing efficiency. If one shovelful of coal could heat the fire box, then two or more shovelfuls would be even better. What they did not realize was that by adding more heat to the process they could turn the water into superheated steam. Superheated steam generally blew the boilers apart, accounting for the loss at sea of many steamships and the numerous train wrecks that became part of daily operations on a railway. Unless a stronger container could be developed, steam power would reach a plateau. Cast iron had its limits. Rails, wheels and bridges could be made from it but steam boilers and the working parts of machines could not. The answer lay in steel.

James Watt modified the design of the Newcomen steam engine by diverting the steam from the main cylinder.

Steel

Steel quickly became the wonder metal of the age. Strong, able to take and keep an edge, tough and springy, steel could be made liquid and then cooled into any shape required. So precise was the nature of steel that machine parts could be standardized, making them interchangeable from machine to machine. And steel appeared never to wear out.

Steel is iron containing just the right amount of carbon to make it durable. In the 1850s, Henry Bessemer (1813–1898) found the answer to large scale steel production when he invented a way to manufacture steel from crude iron. Oxygen, forced through a furnace smelting pig or crude iron, burns away excess carbon leaving molten steel. The Bessemer converter was one of the major inventions of the century. Bessemer's process was improved by William Siemens who used exhaust gases from the furnaces to preheat the incoming air adding even greater efficiency to production.

Both processes required high grade iron ore but deposits of high grade ore were running out. Then, in 1879, Gilchrist Thomas created a lining for the furnaces that absorbed impurities. Now the lower grade iron ores from Alsace-Lorraine, the Rühr, and Cleveland, Ohio, could be processed into steel. Within three years, the steel industry had adopted Thomas's discovery. By the end of the century, steel had replaced stone and wood as the prime building material. By then Germans and Americans rivaled Britain's massive steel industry.

Electricity

The first new science and source of energy to be introduced in the century was electricity. Electricity was almost completely the result of scientific study and experimentation. It was a planned development and as such it is the first of the modern sciences.

The generation of electricity by mechanical action was demonstrated in 1831 by Michael Faraday's dynamo, copper disk rotating between the poles of a magnet. T led to the commercial production of generators of elec power. The possibilities of this new science w immense. Thomas Alva Edison (1847–1931) pioneere way to distribute electricity by a network of mains lin to street lights and homes. Electric power could turn ni into day. One can hardly imagine what exciting effe electric lights had on the people.

In the eighteenth century, Stephen Grey had discove that electricity produced by rubbing a glass tube coul transmitted around his garden on silk strings. Unkn ingly he had made the first telegraph. His discovery electricity could flow under certain conditions wa amazing as the fact that it was weightless and invisible 1745, von Kleist, a Pomeranian clergyman, attempte pass electricity into a bottle through a nail. Touching nail he received the first electric shock. Soon every wanted to try the experiment and get shocked. Electri became the fashion of the salons. The king of France e trified a whole brigade of guards making them jum electricity passed through their bodies.

Benjamin Franklin (1706–1790), in Philadelphia, he of the new thing called electricity and sent for s

Thomas Alva Edison was one of the principle founders of the new science of electricity.
Electric power would replace steam power in the twentieth century.

ctrical apparatus. He theorized that electricity was rywhere and had its own level of rest, and if a body ame more positive or negative, a flow of electric rges would be created to restore the balance causing rks and magnetism in the process. His invention of the tning rod was designed to protect buildings from dam- in thunder storms. While he was the American ambas- or to France, his hand-held electric sparking machine ame the rage of Paris.

ther discoveries followed. In Italy, Alessandro Volta 45–1827) professor of physics at the University of ua discovered an electric current when two different als were placed together. Luigi Galvani worked to elop electric storage batteries. This was followed in 2 when Humphry Davy (1775–1817) improved on vani's design using sodium and potassium as the met- which he separated by a damp cloth.

sewhere, Hans Oersted (1757–1851), André Ampère 75–1836), Carl Gauss (1777–1855), and Georg Ohm 37–1854) expanded the knowledge of the properties of new source of power. In 1832, Faraday put it all ther in a dynamo motor that created electric power on

command. Storage batteries and their deficiencies were a thing of the past. James Maxwell (1831–1879) provided the theoretical base for electric power in his work on the elec- tromagnetic field. He theorized that electric energy travels in waves equal to the speed of light; light is therefore a form of electro-magnetic radiation.

The increasing application of scientific invention to the modern lifestyle resulted in a change in the scientific com- munity. Previously most discoveries were made by engi- neers and craftsmen improving upon their trade. In this they were from time to time assisted by gifted amateurs whose curiosity had led them into useful inventions. All this was to change with the establishment of schools of sci- entific studies. In England, Charles Babbage established the British Association for the Advancement of Science in the 1830s and even Napoleon Bonaparte had seen the need to create the Ecole Polytechnique. However, Germany lead the way in institutionalizing science in the establishment of a network of polytechnical institutions. By the 1890s there were as many as 55 000 trained, professional scien- tists that had graduated from a program of formal study. Today, there are more than one million.

Louis Pasteur, a German professor of chemistry, formulated the germ theory that was to revolutionize organic chemistry.

The Germ Theory

The English scientist Joseph Priestley (a failed Protestant preacher) and Antoine Lavoisier (who made the fatal mistake of buying a membership in the French Ferme which cost him his head in the French Revolution) were the founders of modern chemistry. Building on their work, Louis Pasteur 1822–1895), a German professor of chemistry, formulated the germ theory that was to revolutionize organic chemistry. In trying to discover why certain batches of beer went bad he found that the air was filled with living organisms he called microbes. Some of the microbes interfered with the brewing process. The cause of the bad beer was not in the chemical reactions at all but was the result of living germs.

In 1865 Pasteur was asked to investigate a silkworm disease that threatened the silk industry. He had not the faintest idea what silkworms were or where they came from, but his studies once more pointed the way to germs that could destroy the crop. One way of controlling germs was to improve sanitary conditions. The washing of hands, improved sewage and waste facilities and the drinking of pure water would all contribute to the elimination of water borne disease. Medical applications of the germ theory resulted in astounding results that revolutionized medical practice and increased life expectancy in the industrial world. Postnatal death rates for women and babies went down when doctors began to wash their hands.

Engineering

In 1851, England held a large scientific exhibition in the Crystal Palace, a building erected for the event, made from glass and steel. The announced date of the exhibition did not permit time to manufacture the millions of bricks that it would have taken to get the structure up in time. Glass and iron were substituted in a tense engineering experiment. The use of the materials also made it possible take down the building and mo it elsewhere when the exhibiti was over. It greatly influenc architecture. Alexandre Eiff tower erected in Paris for world's exposition of 18 demonstrated again the supe ority of the new metals over older wood and stone build materials. For one thing bu ings could be five or six tim higher.

The tower was consider such a magnificent display of ability to tame nature throu machines that it led many believe the end of science wa hand. Newton's revolution of years before had been worl out with the expansion of coveries to cover all possi fields and subfields of scier Little did scientists realize w was on the horizon.

Darwin

A hint of what was to come were the radical theories Charles Darwin (1809–1882) that shook western soci Darwin had been a member of the British scientific ex dition to the Galapagos Islands off the coast of So America. The islands had differing vegetation and Dar noted that the finches had developed physical charac istics that permitted them to survive in the different co He surmised that the characteristics necessary for th survival in this different vegetation had been the resul natural selection. Traits that were helpful in finding fe and shelter were passed on to subsequent generations. conclusion was that only the fittest survived and this a way that nature controlled its species. What was m this evolution was still going on. Darwin hypothesize process for evolution based on survival of the fittest.

Thomas Huxley (1825–1895) responded with the ob vation that in nature cooperation and the sharing resources among members of a species was often m

The Eiffel Tower in Paris was designed by French engineer Alexandre Gustave Eiffel (1832–1923) for the 1889 Paris Exposition. The tower is 300 metres high and consists of iron framework. Architects began using steel instead of stone and wood in the late nineteenth century.

portant to survival than nat-l selection. Huxley also inted out that education and in power often had more to with survival than Darwin uld admit, and introduced possibility of chance as the ermining factor in survival.

he debate over the process evolution and the place of ural selection in the whole cmc of things has muddied study of biology ever since. ortunately, Darwin's theo-. of the importance of physi-superiority were taken up by Social Darwinists and used a scientific justification for r racial policies.

omic Particles

irt from the scientific debate r evolution the debate demon-ted that science was far from iplete. Then at the turn of the tury Rutherford and Bohr, king at McGill University, covered the presence of an atom with what appeared e a nucleus. This ushered in the world of the atomic subatomic particles that did not adhere to any of the ural laws within the **Newtonian system**.

1895, Konrad von Roentgen (1845–1923) a professor hysics at Warzburg University, was toying with a new iode ray tube when he noticed that there appeared to in invisible force operating outside the tube. The force ged photographic plates and could go through animal ue. For want of a better name he called it an X-ray and, 901, won the Nobel Prize in physics for his discovery.

oentgen's discoveries were followed by those of Pierre Marie Curie working in Paris. Madame Curie 57–1934) was the first great woman scientist and eived two Nobel Prizes in her lifetime. The Curies had, period of six short years, worked out the basic theo-of radioactivity. What was so astounding was that their k proved that some materials, such as uranium, were he process of transforming themselves into inert

matter. Under the Newtonian system, transmutation of one element into another was impossible. Yet here before their eyes nature itself was conducting transmutations. This was certainly not Newtonian. Radioactivity was a world in the process of change not stability.

Then Ernest Rutherford (1871–1937), with a team at McGill University, revolutionized the atomic world view. In 1902 they were measuring the incredible speeds of the alpha, beta, and gamma rays given off in radioactive decay when associates Hans Wilhelm Geiger and Marsden noted that one of the atoms had obviously hit something and was coming back on its track. They had discovered the nucleus of the atom. Atoms were not only real but they had a nucleus. What that nucleus was composed of would be the subject of the subatomic particle experiments of the twentieth century.

Before World War I, the ideas of discontinuity and chaos in the subatomic world had been introduced into scientific theory by German physicists, Max Planck (1858–1947) and Albert Einstein (1879–1955). At the atomic and subatomic levels there is a world filled with empty space and chaos where the Newtonian system did not work. Planck showed how bursts of energy, or quanta, were not continuous but explosive and chaotic. They could not be predicted with any degree of certainty but rather appeared to follow probability curves. Who can tell which atom in an icicle is the first to melt? Scientists debated over whether electrons were matter, force, both, or merely the creation in the scientist's mind to describe something that could neither be seen nor measured.

Einstein further upset the Newtonian world with his theories on special relativity in 1905 and general relativity in 1916. In these he indicated that within the universe there

Marie Curie (1867–1934) received two Nobel Prizes for her work in radiation.

were no absolute standards of measurement or time. All was relative.

SUMMARY

In nineteenth-century Europe, the arts and sciences were released from the narrow confines of the Church, palaces, and salons to become a vibrant element of the developing urban society. The middle classes, made wealthy by industrialization, created an exploding market for the arts and sciences. Public buildings, estates, townhouses, and clubs all required paintings to grace their halls. In the sciences, industrial growth forced the pace of discovery.

In painting, the classical forms of portraiture gave way to Constable's scenic views which in turn gave way to Monet and the Impressionist School. Newer forms of abstract art were seen in the figures of van Gogh and Picasso.

In music, Beethoven carried the work of Mozart to new forms which in turn gave way to the mighty symphonies of Brahms. It was the time of grand opera with Verdi's works to be followed by Wagner's. Larger symphony halls and opera houses were constructed to stage ever larger productions. Conductors selected music that was dramatic and so created a music-sensitive public.

The reading public, which was also expanding by leaps and bounds, took some time away from perusing daily newspapers to enjoy the new novels of popular authors. Classical forms of poetry, writing, and drama gave way to new subject matter that not only described the feelings of the inner self but attributed these feelings to the working classes. Shocking in another way was the delicious romantic genre of horror stories, "gothic novels," made popular by Shelley's *Frankenstein.*

At the beginning of the century, Napoleon formalised the study of science with the establishment of a polytechnical school system. Other nations followed suit. The epitome of technical training was the system developed by Germany after the mid-century. German technical schools soon started to turn out tens of thousands of scientists. New are of scientific study were created. Electricity, the germ t ory of disease, steam engines, and Rutherford's atomic t ories appeared before the congratulatory public.

Above all else, the nineteenth century was the age of i and steel. The perfection of steel manufacturing helpe standardise machine parts to the point that they w interchangeable from one machine to another. Steel u in construction, such as the Eiffel Tower, allowed ta structures to be built. The development of the iron steel industry was crucial in building transcontinental i way systems and boilers that contained steam power.

No longer was the advance of science uneven and dep dent upon talented amateurs. It was state funded deemed essential to the material well being of the nati

QUESTIONS

1. Explain why Goya was considered an innovative art

2. Describe the patronage system in regards to the a Who are the patrons of the arts today?

3. What features of the work of Constable and Turne distinguished them from their peers?

4. Explain what characterized the group of artists ca *"les refusées."*

Albert Einstein challenged the Newtonian system of viewing the universe. In Einstein's system, there is no absolute standard of measurement or time. All is relative to the observer

Describe the characteristics of Impressionist painting. Identify two of the impressionists and describe their work.

Explain how the music of the nineteenth century mirrored the age. Describe the music of two of the century's composers.

Describe three scientific discoveries of the late nineteenth century. Assess the effect these discoveries had on the Industrial Revolution.

How did the use of electricity revolutionize society?

Evaluate the accuracy of the following statement: The nineteenth century was a marvellous time to be alive if one were rich and a member of the upper class.

ANALYSIS

Research the life of one of the following women:
(a) Mary Shelley,
(b) Germaine de Staël, or
(c) George Sand (Aurore Dudevant).

What was the role of women in nineteenth-century society? Assess whether or not the woman you have researched conformed to society's expectations.

2. Research three scientific discoveries made within the last half century. Describe the way in which our standard of living has been altered as a result of these discoveries.

3. Assess the role which government should play in the support of a nation's culture. Consider the pros and cons of public funding of the arts. Should government control advertising and the promotion of cultural functions? For example, should tobacco companies be prohibited from sponsoring cultural events?

4. Evaluate the role of art and music in defining a nation's culture. Choose at least one artist and one musician to illustrate your point.

ACTIVITIES

1. Guest Speaker
Invite a local artist to discuss with students the contribution art makes to a culture. You could focus on the nineteenth century and consider the contribution of artists such as Monet, Goya, or Turner. You could also focus on contemporary artists.

2. Panel Discussion
Assemble a panel of students to role play nineteenth-century authors such as Emile Zola, Charles Dickens, and Leo Tolstoy. Have them discuss the ways in which literature reflects the culture it was created in. The audience should be prepared to ask questions regarding the accuracy, intent, and value of the works in one's attempt to understand a period of history.

3. Timeline
Create an illustrated timeline of technological progress from 1750 to the present. Research the most significant discoveries from steam power to nuclear power, as well as specific items such as the computer. Include these on the timeline.

Chapter 8
Changes in the Balance of Power

FOCUS ON:

❀

Challenges to the balance of power in mid 19th century Europe;

❀

Forces of nationalism at work in Italy and Germany;

❀

The new international power structure created by the birth of
the Italian and German nation-states.

*Napoleon III modeled the political structure of the Second Empire
on Napoleon Bonaparte's First Empire.*

TIMELINE

1853
December ❈ Louis-Napoleon declares himself
Emperor of France.

1853-1856
Crimean War

1866
Austro-Prussian War

1870
Franco-Prussian War
Unification of Italy
Unification of Germany

1871
10 May ❈ Treaty of Frankfurt

Great Britain, France, Prussia, Austria, and Russia agreed at the Congress of Vienna (1815) to work together to maintain peace and security on the European continent. Peace was possible as long as the great powers collectively exercised the will to honour the agreement. Difficulties arose in 1853 in the Crimea, and while that conflict was resolved quickly, it was evident that the great power agreement was fragile.

Following the revolutions 1848, nationalist movements central Europe, coupled wi the ascendancy of Prussia a Piedmont-Sardinia, led to wa with Austria resulting in the fo mation of modern Italy a Germany. The creation of the two new states in centr Europe disrupted the arrang ments made at Vienna and u mately changed the intern tional state system.

∼ Napoleon III: The Second Empire in France ∼

In 1852, one year after French voters elected Louis-Napoleon president for a ten-year term, he declared himself emperor of the French. By calling himself Napoleon III, he acknowledged Napoleon's son who had died in exile in Austria in 1832 at the age of 21.

Napoleon III modeled the political structure of the Second Empire on the First Empire. There was a Council of State, a Senate, and a legislative body, but the system was authoritarian. Elections were directed by the government. Voters were expected to support the official candidates. Political meetings were forbidden and censorship of the press was enforced.

Napoleon III was interested in reforming the social and economic conditions of France. During the 1850s a number of developments illustrated his concern in these areas. Baron Haussmann (1809–91), prefect of the Département of the Seine, was instructed to beautify and modernize the city of Paris. He designed and had built wide boulevards, such as the Bois du Bologne, and public squares which he then adorned with monuments or buildings such as the Place de l'Opéra. Under his direction the sewer and water supply systems were improved

and modernized. Slums were razed. The city was trans formed under his ambitious plan.

Programs under Napoleon III included the investmen of money in an integrated railway system, steamboats to replace sail boats, and the building of the Suez Canal Napoleon III also promoted the growth of internationa trade. A believer in free trade, he concluded a free trad agreement with Great Britain in 1860 despite much opposition from French industrialists and politicians Government funds that were set aside to support Frenc industry in the attempts to compete with the mor advanced industrial development in Great Britai proved to be unnecessary. French industry was able to compete effectively on its own.

While Napoleon's domestic policies seemed to stabi lize France, his foreign policy ultimately led to his down fall. His support of Great Britain against Russia in th Crimean War brought France to the forefront of inter national diplomacy in the Peace of Paris. However, war in the Italian states in 1859, in Mexico from 1862 to 186 and against Prussia in 1870 proved to be fatal for th Second Empire.

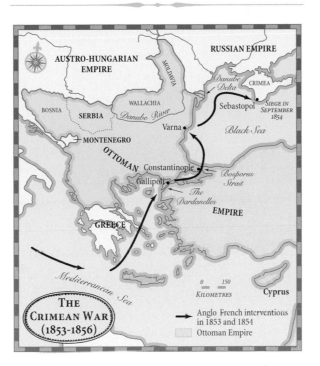

Although the Crimean War of 1853 to 1856 originally began as a religious dispute, it was really a fight for control of the Bosporus and Dardanelles Straits. Russia wanted access to the Mediterranean Sea via the straits.

THE CRIMEAN WAR: 1853–1856

The Crimean War originated over a dispute regarding the safety of Christians in the Ottoman Empire, particularly those located in Jerusalem. There was a conflict over religious ceremonial functions between Orthodox Christians, who were supported by Tsar Nicholas I, and Roman Catholics, who were supported by Napoleon III. The Turkish (Ottoman) sultan ruled in favour of the Roman Catholics and Nicholas I moved troops close to the border, to Moldavia and Wallachia, in protest.

The real issue was control of the waterways, the Bosporus and the Dardanelles, that would allow Russia access to the Mediterranean Sea and trade routes. Russia believed at this point that the British would not object to Russian attempts to dominate Turkey (the Ottoman Empire). This was a miscalculation. Turkey declared war on Russia in October 1853 and by January 1854 Britain and France had joined Turkey. Austria did not want Russia fatally weakened but did not want the Russians to control access to the Danube River.

At risk in this dispute was the European balance of power. Austria was caught in the middle. If Russia won the war, it would be in a strong position to control the Balkans and threaten Austrian hegemony in the region. If Russia was defeated, Napoleon III would emerge as the dominant European power.

When Russian troops pulled out of Wallachia and Moldavia to come to the relief of Sebastopol under seige by a British-French force, Austrian troops moved in to replace them. Britain and France saw Austria as a pawn in the venture. The Prussians remained apart, unwilling to side with either of their powerful neighbours. Russia stood alone against Britain, France, and Turkey.

The conflict ended in 1856 with defeat for Russia and a pretense of Turkish strength, bolstered by the west. On 30 March 1856, the Treaty of Paris was signed. Russia lost control of the Danube delta, the Black Sea became neutral territory (neither Turkey nor Austria could have warships on these waters), and the integrity of the Ottoman Empire was guaranteed.

Russia's defeat allowed the Ottoman Empire to struggle on but its weakness, both militarily and diplomatically, had been exposed. The war affected all the major powers. The Italian leader Cavour, sensing Austria's weakness, gathered support for a unified Italy against Austrian domination of the northern Italian states. This began the isolation of Austria by both east and west and foreshadowed the disintegration of the Hapsburg empire.

During the Crimean War women served as army nurses for the first time. The British disgust over lack of supplies and inhuman conditions faced by their countrymen at war resulted in the minister of defence assigning to Florence Nightingale the task of providing nursing care to the wounded in the Crimean area. She set off with a contingent of 38 nurses to care for the sick and wounded British soldiers.

War and Journalism

The Crimean War was the first war covered by news correspondents. For the first time in history, events of war were relayed to the public by media personnel at the scene. News was relayed by wireless to an eagerly-awaiting public. From now on, the world would know the unfolding of battles as they occurred. Public response to these events was dynamic and began to play a more and more important role in a country's participation in hostilities.

∼ Florence Nightingale ∼
(1820–1910)

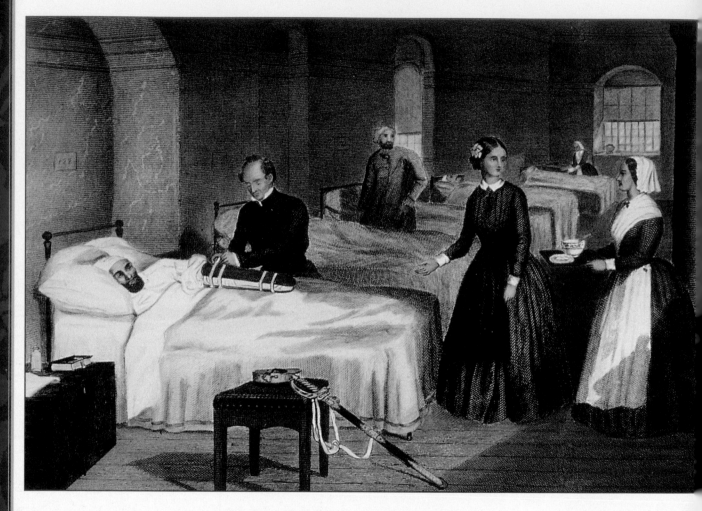

*Florence Nightingale provided nursing care to
the wounded during the Crimean War.*

Nightingale and her nurses landed in Scutari, Albania, late in 1854. They found hundreds of wounded men in an old Turkish barracks which was dirty, unfurnished, and lacking medical supplies. Nightingale set to work with a missionary zeal. She enlisted the help of those men who were well enough to clean the premises. She then petitioned the British government for supplies, established schedules for the orderly care and feeding of the patients and supervised the operation like a general. Her solitary patrol at night was conducted through the corridors with the light of a lamp, earning her the epithet "lady of the lamp."

Nightingale's work revolutionized military medicine. She became renowned throughout the world for her insistence on proper sanitation in medical procedures, which saved countless lives and introduced new standards of nursing. She was consulted by the United States on the establishment of military hospitals during the American Civil War. She was the first woman to be awarded the British Order of Merit.

SWITZERLAND

SAVOY
(TO FRANCE
1860)

AUSTRIA-HUNGARY

LOMBARDY
(1859)
• Milan

VENETIA
(1866)

• Trieste

FRANCE

KINGDOM OF
SARDINIA
PIEDMONT

PARMA
(1860)

Venice

• Fiume

NICE
O FRANCE
1860)

Genoa

MODENA
(1860)

ROMAGNA
(1860)

• Nice

Florence

OTTOMAN
EMPIRE

TUSCANY
(1860)

UMBRIA
(1860)

(1870)

Corsica
(FRENCH)

PAPAL
STATES

(1870)

• Rome

PAPAL STATES
(1870)

KINGDOM OF
SARDINIA
SARDINIA

• Naples

KINGDOM
OF THE
TWO SICILIES
(1860)

UNIFICATION
OF
ITALY
(1859-1870)

Adriatic Sea

Mediterranean Sea

0   150
KILOMETRES

The Crimean War set the stage for the resistance of the Italian states to Austrian rule. The unification of Italy began in 1859 and continued to 1870.

Carbonari was one such society. Giuseppe Mazzini (1805–1872), a great Italian patriot, joined while still a young man. Through his writings, he became a leader of Italian nationalist sentiment and, in 1831, founded a new organization called the Young Italy. Only men under 40 were eligible to join. It became a model for revolutionary groups throughout central Europe.

Mazzini outlined his ideas on nationalism in his book *On The Duties of Man*. He identified a hierarchy of duty that placed duty to God first, duty to the nation second, and duty to family third. Most of Mazzini's life was spent in exile in France— the Hapsburg government imposed strict control on the Italian states and monitored the activities of subversives. He smuggled his literature into the Italian states but his efforts to develop a force strong enough to provoke change failed.

In 1834 he attempted revolution in Sardinia to no avail. Later his brief hope for success during the revolutions of 1848 was dashed when the French army intervened. In 1849, during the revolutionary fervor of this period, Mazzini helped form a republic in Rome. The pope fled to escape the insurrection, but intervention by Napoleon III restored the pope to his position. The republican government that included Mazzini and Giuseppe Garibaldi (1807–1882), a compatriot of his in the Young Italy movement, was driven out by French forces. Italian nationalism had failed to create a united Italian state.

Mazzini's contribution to the nationalist cause had been significant, however. He laid the foundation for the unification of the Italian states. The stage was set for the diplomatic and military manoeuvres of Camillo di Cavour, the prime minister of Sardinia, and Garibaldi to consolidate the union.

NIFICATION OF ITALY

apoleon I can be credited with laying the foundation for a unified Italy. The Napoleonic occupation of the Italian states (1799–1815) contributed to the elopment of Italian nationalist fervor. Deep resentment he tribute of both men-at-arms and money demanded he French festered among the people. The Congress of nna (1815) resulted in the Italian states being governed Austria, the Roman Catholic Church, or France. Sardinia s the only state ruled by a native Italian royal house. A ire to promote Italian culture and to unite Italians under r own sovereign government began to develop. This feel- was called *Risorgimento*, which meant a "resurgence" ationalist sentiment. The people desired the return of grandeur of the Italian Renaissance.

ecret societies sprang up to promote independence. The

Giuseppe Mazzini (1805–1872) organized the Young Italy Association to create a free and united republic of Italy. He was soon banished from Italy in 1831 for trying to urge Charles Albert of Piedmont to lead the struggle for Italian independence.

The Crimean War weakened both Austria and Russia. As these two powers were the most committed to the settlement of 1815 and most opposed to national independence, their weakened condition opened the door to nationalist aspirations in the Italian states. While the Crimean War was ostensibly about the Eastern Question, it became a springboard for Italian unification. Cavour's clever manipulation of a place for Piedmont-Sardinia at the peace table ensured that the Italian cause would be brought to the attention of the international community. The Crimean War set the stage for Italian resistance to Austrian control, but it took the diplomatic skills of Cavour to engineer the events which ultimately allowed unification to occur.

Camillo di Cavour (1810–1861) was a liberal who favoured constitutional monarchy. He edited a newspaper in Turin called *Il Risorgimento*. In 1847 King Victor Emmanuel of Piedmont-Sardinia relaxed censorship and allowed Cavour to publish his program of political and economic reform. By 1850 he was included in the cabinet and in 1852 he was appointed prime minister.

In his position of prime minister, Cavour immediately embarked on a program of reform. He promoted constitutional and judicial reform, encouraged improvements in agriculture, established a policy of free trade, built new railroads, and promoted the separation of church and state. He consolidated Italian nationalist movements under the leadership of the House of Savoy in Piedmont-Sardinia. He had no sympathy with revolutionary republicans. Thus, revolutionary movements such as those led by Mazzini were abolished and, instead, revolutionaries were invited to join in the cause of Italian liberation by rising up against Austria.

Cavour practised **Realpolit** (the use of power in foreign an domestic relations) and, wh there is no evidence to sugge that he intended to unite all t Italian states, that is wh occurred. Initially, Cavour tended to force Austria out of t northern Italian states in order bring Lombardy and Vene under Savoy. The kingdom Sicily and the papal states pos problems which he was n interested in solving at th point.

Cavour was convinced that had to have help from France drive out Austria. Napoleon was no more interested in ur ing all of the Italian states th was Cavour, but he did see t value of enlarging Piedmo Sardinia to include the northe states and perhaps Tuscany Romagna. This would creat larger client state over wh Napoleon III would maint: influence. Traditional Fren interest in maintaining this in ence in Italy and the presence French troops in Rome supported the idea.

Cavour and Napoleon III met at Plombières in 1858 discuss the venture against Austria. It was a meeting m of innuendoes than definitive agreements over territ but it was determined that Cavour would provoke Aust into a declaration of war, allowing France to come to assistance of Piedmont-Sardinia. Cavour's goal was retrieve Lombardy and Venetia from Austria and ther annex neighbouring Tuscany and Romagna. In return its support, France would gain the territories of Nice a Savoy.

In April 1859 Cavour succeeded in provoking Austria i declaring war on Piedmont. Battles were fought at Mag ta and at Solferino. The Austrians were defeated by combined Franco-Piedmontese forces. The defeat of A tria raised fears in Prussia that Napoleon might estab

As prime minister, Camillo di Cavour promoted constitutional and judicial reform, encouraged improvements in agriculture, established a policy of free trade, built new railroads, and promoted the separation of church and state.

o much influence in Italy. Revolutionary fervour in the neighboring Italian states was ignited this initial success and existing governments seemed in jeopardy. Catholics in France feared the pope's safety. With turmoil raging, Napoleon III abandoned his support of Cavour and made a separate peace with the Austrians in July of 1859.

The agreement which Napoleon III worked out with Austria gave Lombardy to Piedmont but allowed Austria to keep Venetia. The revolutionary fervor which continued unabated in the neighboring states of Tuscany, Parma, Modena, and Romagna resulted in plebiscites. The populace voted overwhelmingly in favour of unification with Piedmont and the old rulers were driven out. Piedmont now included all of northern Italy except for the northeastern territory of Venetia. The first parliament of this enlarged state met in Turin in 1860. As agreed, France received the states of Nice and Savoy. Plebiscites in these regions gave unanimous approval for their annexation to France.

The victory against Austria was only the beginning in the Italian drive for unification. Cavour had unleashed the idea of a revolution which could not be contained. The nationalist, Garibaldi now moved to further unification. He assembled an army of loyal followers who numbered just over one thousand. Called "Garibaldi's Thousand," or "Red Shirts," they travelled first to Sicily and then to Naples where they conquered the Kingdom of the Two Sicilies and offered to turn it over to Piedmont.

The Piedmontese army met Garibaldi's troops and gave them a hero's welcome. Plebiscites were held in the Two Sicilies and the Papal States and, without exception, the people voted overwhelmingly in favour of union. As a result of Garibaldi's campaign, all of the Italian states except Venetia and Rome were now united under the House of Savoy in Piedmont. A Kingdom of Italy was proclaimed with Victor Emmanuel II as king.

The final steps in the unification of the Italian states occurred in conjunction with Bismarck's diplomacy which included plans to establish Prussian domination in the German states. The isolation of Austria was a critical factor in Bismarck's scheme. In 1866 Italy was drawn into a war between Prussia and Austria. In exchange for its participation, Italy received Venetia. Now, only Rome remained outside the Italian federation.

In 1870 France and Prussia went to war. In an effort to strengthen the French armies, Napoleon III pulled his troops out of Rome allowing the Italians to seize the area and declare a united Italy. In 1871 Rome became the capital. The pope was allowed to maintain control of the Vatican which occupies 44 hectares within Rome's boundaries. Outraged at this loss of political power, Pope Pius IX withdrew into the Vatican for the rest of his life. The papacy refused to acknowledge the power of the Italian government until 1929 when the Lateran Treaty was signed. Under this agreement the Vatican became a sovereign state.

UNIFICATION OF GERMANY

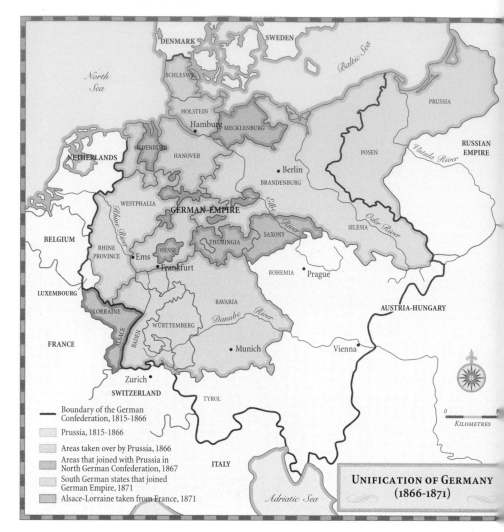

Boundary of the German Confederation, 1815-1866

Prussia, 1815-1866

Areas taken over by Prussia, 1866

Areas that joined with Prussia in North German Confederation, 1867

South German states that joined German Empire, 1871

Alsace-Lorraine taken from France, 1871

UNIFICATION OF GERMANY (1866-1871)

The unification of the German states began in 1806 when Napoleon consolidated Germany's 300 administrative units, (kingdoms, principalities, duchies, free cities, and the states of the imperial knights and counts) into the Confederation of the Rhine. This confederation of states reduced the number of units to 39, with Prussia as one of the largest regions. The Congress of Vienna maintained the basic organization of 39 states, which included Prussia and Austria. For the next five decades, the forces of German nationalism developed within the confederation, while Austria and Prussia sought at the same time to maintain dominance within it.

By 1871, Germany was unified, to the exclusion of Austria and its territories. The capital of the new Germany was the old Prussian capital of Berlin.

The creation of the Frankfurt Assembly was one result of the revolutions of 1848. It attempted to unite the German states through constitutional means, but it lacked power and the support of the masses and, hence, was doomed to failure. When the assembly unravelled, the loose confederation of 1815 was restored.

The Frankfurt Assembly had grappled with the dilemma of German identity. It was a politically impotent body and, driven by nationalism, had been dependent for support on the very states which it hoped to supplant. In attempting to establish the basis of unification, the members of the assembly disagreed on the areas to be included in a united Germany.

The dispute essentially centred on the inclusion of Austria and various outlying German speaking areas. Those who favoured a "Greater Germany" wanted to include Austria, Bohemia, all of Prussia including t[...] which lay outside the old Holy Roman Empire, Schlesv[...] and Holstein. The Austrian Hapsburg monarchy wo[...] provide leadership of such a federation.

Supporters of "Little Germany" wanted to excl[...] Austria, which was peopled by millions of slavs in [...] southern region of the empire. Otto von Bismarck, v[...] was at that time a spokesman for the extreme righ[...] Prussian politics, favoured the "Little Germany" solut[...] as Prussia would take the leadership role.

During the next decade, rivalry between Austria [...] Prussia intensified until Bismarck seized the opportu[...] to establish Prussian **hegemony,** or domination, am[...] the German states in 1870.

Richard Wagner (1813–1883) not only wrote operas, but he also participated in the revolutions of 1848.

German Nationalism

At the turn of the nineteenth century, a national awakening occurred in the German states. Up to then French culture had been admired and copied. Now, a plethora of German writers, musicians, and artists promoted a German national spirit. The Napoleonic occupation helped to crystallize this sense of Germanic pride and to turn Germans away from their acceptance of French culture. German nationalists were particularly supportive of Prussia because it had not cooperated with the French and had attempted to stem the French surge across Europe.

In the nineteenth century the ideas of J. G. Herder (1744–1803) dominated. He had promoted the notion of the *Volksgeist*, or national spirit, years earlier in his book, *Ideas in the Philosophy of the History of Mankind* (1784). In it he wrote that all culture comes from native roots and that all peoples should develop their own culture. *Grimm's Fairy Tales*, a collection of German folk tales published in 1812, gave Germans an identity via a connection with their myths and legends. Beethoven, a master of the Romantic period of music, produced music that gave Germans both enjoyment and pride. Beethoven's *Ninth Symphony* spurred on another great German composer, Richard Wagner, in his musical career. Wagner not only wrote music that stirred the German soul but he also participated in the revolutions of 1848. Overall, the Romantic period was characterized by an awakening and development of German culture charged with nationalism.

The Zollverein

In 1818 Prussia established a *Zollverein*, or customs union, that provided free trade among its scattered territories. In 1834 this trade agreement was expanded to include all the German states except Austria and Bohemia. By 1850 the Industrial Revolution was in progress and the Prussian economy was booming. Prussian cities were linked by an efficient system of transportation and communication with railroads and telegraph lines throughout around the country.

Prussia

After the failure of the revolutions of 1848, Prussia adopted its own constitution. It provided for a parliament composed of two chambers. The lower chamber was elected by universal male suffrage, a feature that even democracies such as Britain had not yet achieved. However, voters were divided into three groups on the basis of the amount of tax which they paid (wealthy, less wealthy, and the common folk). Those who paid one third of the taxes chose one third of the members of parliament. This system resulted in substantial power being allocated to the wealthy *Junkers* (members of the landed aristocracy), who held estates in the East Elbian region, and in a correspondingly conservative tone in the parliament.

Although Prussia was comparatively small, it attained significant strength from a very loyal and well-disciplined army. As the Prussian population had grown significantly since the days of the battles against Napoleon, and no increase in conscription had been implemented, the potential for an expanded armed forces was significant. This military potential, coupled with the emergence of Otto von Bismarck, was a potent force. One could argue that the German states were not *united* but, rather, were *conquered* by Prussia. By 1871 the new German Empire, centred in the old Prussian capital of Berlin, had been forged without Austria and its territories. The industrial might of Prussia had overpowered the older and still agricultural Austria.

In 1862 Otto von Bismarck was appointed prime minister of Prussia. He was a *Junker* from Brandenburg—conservative, Protestant, and intellectually astute. He valued loyalty and discipline and spurned ideas of democracy and liberalism. He was Prussian through and through and rejected German nationalism. His goal was to strengthen Prussia and this he would accomplish through *Realpolitik*.

His control of power was characterized by a pragmatic approach which always maintained an openness to seize opportunities. While it has been widely believed that Bismarck carefully plotted the steps which led to the unification of the German states in 1871, another school of thought suggests that it w[as] never Bismarck's intention [to] unify Germany. Rather, his g[oal] of strengthening Prussia u[lti]mately brought Prussia into c[ol]lision with Austria and, fina[lly] into a union of German sta[tes] with Prussia as leader.

War With Denmark: 1864

In the attempt to maintain [the] balance of power after [the] Napoleonic wars, the two nor[th]ern duchies of Schleswig and Holstein had been plac[ed] under the control of Denmark by the Congress of Vien[na]. This maintained the union which had been in effect si[nce] the fifteenth century. Holstein, populated by Germans, w[as] a member of the German confederation, while Schles[wig] contained both Germans and Danes and remained outs[ide] the German confederation. The relationship of the t[wo] duchies to the Germans and the Danes was controvers[ial]. Should Denmark be allowed to incorporate these t[wo] German areas into a constitutional union or should t[hey] be allowed simply to exist as part of the German conf[ed]eration?

The issue of Schleswig-Holstein erupted during the r[ev]olutions of 1848 when the two duchies rose against the k[ing] of Denmark. Liberals and nationalists could not agree o[n a] solution. Germans rallied in support of the duchies wh[ile] the western powers sided with Denmark. Ultimately, P[rus]sia and Denmark agreed to leave the duchies under the c[on]trol of the Danish monarch, a decision which was confir[med] by the terms of the Treaty of London, signed in 18[52]. Throughout the 1850s repeated attempts were mad[e to] bring the duchies into a constitutional union with Denm[ark]. However, the duchies resisted and German national[ists] protested.

In 1863, Christian IX came to the Danish throne. He i[ndi]cated his intention to include Schleswig as a par[t of] Denmark's national consolidation. The diet, or natio[nal] assembly, of the German Confederation of States issue[d an] appeal to all Germans to come to the aid of their cou[ntry]men living in Schleswig. Bismarck recognized an op[por]tunity. He protested Denmark's action as a contraven[tion] the Treaty of London. When it seemed that a peaceful solution to the problem was unlikely, the door was open for Bismarck to begin his program of Prussian expansion. If Prussia could defeat Denmark, the duchies could be incorporated into German territory and the port of Kiel in Holstein would provide a valuable trade and naval outlet to the Baltic Sea. However, rather than encouraging the participation of all the German states, Bismarck strengthened his position by drawing only Austria into the war against Denmark. Austria favoured the alliance in the interests of protecting its claim to the leadership of the German states and preventing Prussian dominance.

The Danes were quickly defeated by the combined Prussian and Austrian forces and the duchies of Schleswig and Holstein were ceded to Prussia and Austria by the Treaty of Vienna in October. Agreement could not be reached on the administration of the duchies, so, at the convention of Gastein in 1865, it was determined that Prussia would administer Schleswig and Austria would administer Holstein. This denied Prussia the port of Kiel and laid the groundwork for more disputes between the two states. The Treaty of Gastein aggravated rather than solved the problems of Prussian and Austrian control of the duchies of Schleswig and Holstein. Prussia and Austria argued over rights of passage and issues of internal order. Bismarck now set out to isolate Austria and to discredit it in the eyes of the major powers. He was helped by the ill will that remained from the role Austria played in the Crimean War. Neither France nor Russia favoured a powerful Austria.

Austro–Prussian War

The conflict between Prussia and Austria came to a head in 1866 when the German parliament was elected by universal suffrage. The conservative Austrians considered this a direct affront. It was, in fact, a diplomatic position used by Bismarck who certainly did not favour liberalism, but it allowed him to extend a compromise to bridge the gap between the Prussian *Junker* class and revolutionary forces.

However, the quarrel over Schleswig and Holstein continued and Austria took the problem to the diet of the German confederation. Bismarck declared that the diet had no authority in the matter, accused Austria of aggressive action, and moved Prussian troops into Holstein. Austria and Prussia were now at war.

In preparation for a conflict with Austria, Bismarck had previously secured the promise of France's neutrality and Italy's support. In return, Italy was to receive Venetia, still under the control of Austria, after the war.

Despite the cooperation of most of the other German states with Austria, the superior Prussian army, fighting with modern weapons including a rifle which delivered five rounds per minute, defeated the opposition forces. The war lasted only seven weeks. The resounding defeat of Austria at Sadowa in Bohemia decided the outcome. By the time the Great Powers realized what had occurred, the Seven Weeks' War between Prussia and Austria was over.

Prussia's victory eliminated the Austrian presence in a German confederation. Under the Peace of Prague, the duchies of Schleswig and Holstein were annexed by Prussia, as were the duchies of Nassau and Hesse-Cassel. In addition, Hanover and the free city of Frankfurt were taken under Prussian administration. Austria lost no territory except Venetia to Italy but was required to pay a small indemnity. The biggest losses were prestige and having to acknowledge Prussian leadership of the German states.

After the Seven Weeks' War, also called the Austro-Prussian War, the German confederation ceased to exist. In its place Bismarck organized the North German Confederation. Twenty one states joined with Prussia in this new confederation which excluded Austria, Bavaria, Baden, Württemberg, and Hesse-Darmstadt. These five states south of the river Main remained independent units but Bismarck made separate and secret alliances between Prussia and Bavaria, Württemberg, and Baden. The agreements provided that these states would join the Prussians in the event of war and effectively prevented the possibility of an independent union of South German states.

Over the next three years, the South German states seemed isolated in central Europe as they were prevented from joining Austria and yet were not yet open to union with the North German states. Both religious and political differences divided them. The north was Protestant and experimenting with democracy; the south was predominantly Catholic and staunchly conservative. It would take a crisis over the Spanish throne, bringing Germans and the French into conflict, that would allow the final unification of the German states.

Franco-Prussian War

In 1868 revolution drove Queen Isabella into exile and left

Queen Isabella (1830–1904) came to the Spanish throne when she was only three years old. Her mother acted as regent until Isabella was old enough to rule the kingdom.

the Spanish throne vacant. The provisional government offered the crown to a Catholic Hohenzollern prince, Leopold, a cousin of King Wilhelm of Prussia. France could not tolerate the presence of a Hohenzollern on the Spanish throne and made this known to the Prussian government. Leopold refused three offers of the throne—he was not interested in the affairs of state. King Wilhelm was also reluctant to involve his family in the turmoil of Spanish politics. However, when the offer was made a fourth time in May 1870, Leopold relented.

When news of the Hohenzollern acceptance of the Spanish throne reached Paris, the French foreign minister reacted with an aggressive telegram designed to humiliate Prussia and restore French prestige in central Europe. The Hohenzollern dynasty had no desire to provoke an international incident and, on 12 July 1870, Leopold withdrew his candidacy for the Spanish throne. The French demands continued. They now insisted that no Hohenzollern ever occupy the throne of Spain. On July 13 the new threats were delivered to Wilhelm who was visiting a spa at Ems.

Although Wilhelm's reply to the French telegram was conciliatory, Bismarck, in order to provoke the French, edited it to appear that the Prussian king had been insulted. He later claimed responsibility for beginning the war with France through his diplomatic manoeuvring. The "Ems Telegram" is credited with marshalling German nationalism against the French in the final war to be fought in the unification of the German states.

France declared war on Prussia on 19 July 1870. The South German states joined the North German Confederation and France was without any allies. The international community stood inactively by. The British believed Napoleon III had been provocative and in error

in his dealings both in Mexi and with Prussia over t Spanish affair. The Italians we anxious to seize Rome as t final step in the unification Italy; they could accomplish t if the French called their troo home. The Russians wished conduct naval exercises on Black Sea, a measure forbidd by the peace treaty of 1856. (T instability of the internatio power structure would ma this possible in 1870.) T Austrians were still recover from their defeat in 1866 at hands of Prussia and had be forced in 1867 to create the d empire of Austro-Hung allowing some autonomy to Hungarians.

The Franco-Prussian War v over quickly. The French ar was no match for the highly ciplined and well-equip Prussian soldiers. On 2 Septe ber 1870, the French w defeated at Sedan and Napoleon III was taken prisoner. 4 September 1870, Paris was embroiled in an insurrect that resulted in the declaration of the Third Repub Although the French army had been soundly defeated, P. refused to surrender and managed to survive a four-mo siege before finally capitulating.

On 18 January 1871, the new German Empire was claimed in the Hall of Mirrors at Versailles. King Wilh of Prussia was given the title German Emperor. The pe was formally established by the Treaty of Frankfurt sig on 10 May 1871. The terms of the treaty demanded t France pay reparations valued at five billion gold franc Germany and that the territories of Alsace and Lorraine ceded to Germany. Alsace and Lorraine were rich in n erals and contained the bustling commercial centre Strasbourg. The loss to France of such a wealthy reg was a bitter blow and would remain a source of veng feelings up to World War I.

The creation of the new German state drastically alte

This drawing shows Bismarck (on the left) and Napoleon III (on the right) meeting after the battle at Sedan. Napoleon III was taken prisoner at this battle and subsequently lost his title of emperor of France.

the power structure of Europe. Already established as an industrial power, Germany would challenge the settlement established at the Congress of Vienna. Over the next two decades, Bismarck led Germany onto the world stage. It was a political, economic, and military force that seriously challenged the existing international state system.

the southern German states into the union. By 1870 German states were drawn together, and in January 1 the new German Empire was proclaimed. The inter tional power structure was irrevocably altered. The n four decades would see Europe march down the path war.

SUMMARY

The Crimean War of 1853–1856 threatened to upset the balance of power that had been established by the Congress of Vienna. However, the conflict was contained to the region. A serious threat to the European balance of power did not happen until 1870, when the Italian states united to form Italy, and the German states formed Germany.

Napoleonic occupation of the Italian and German states had encouraged a resurgence of nationalism in both regions. In the Italian states, the Young Italy Association, under the leadership of Mazzini, promoted the idea of an independent Italian state. When Cavour became prime minister of Sardinia, he took on the diplomatic and military leadership of the Italian unification. In a series of wars, Cavour drove Austria out of the northern Italian states, accepted control of the Kingdom of the Two Sicilies (conquered by Garibaldi), and gained control of Venetia and Rome during Bismarck's wars to unite the German states.

Prussia and Austria were the dominant German states. In the mid-nineteenth century, Prussia became industrialized while the Austrian Empire remained predominantly agricultural and struggled to survive. Austria was a conservative and reactionary force in the face of liberal and nationalist movements. In 1818, Prussia established a customs union, the *Zollverein*, that excluded Austria. The exclusion was a significant blow to Austria's leadership of the German states.

When Bismarck became prime minister of Prussia, his military prowess led the Prussian drive to control the German states. War with Denmark in 1864 allowed Schleswig and Holstein to be returned to Prussian control. In 1866 Prussia defeated Austria in the Seven Weeks' War and then engineered war against France in 1870 to bring

QUESTIONS

1. What caused the Crimean War? What was the resu of the war? How was Austria affected by the settlement?

2. How did Napoleon I contribute to the unification c the Italian states? What were some of the forces t drew the Italians into a unified federation?

3. Identify the reforms instituted by Cavour in Piedmont-Sardinia. What did Cavour hope to accomplish by practising "Realpolitik"?

4. Explain how Austria lost its control of the norther Italian states. What role did France play?

5. How did the states of Tuscany, Parma, Modena, a Romagna join Piedmont? How did Venetia become part of the new Italian state?

6. Explain the roles Mazzini and Garibaldi played in Italian unification.

7. Why did Napoleon III remove his troops from Ror in 1870? Explain Rome's relationship to the new Italian state. What happened to the Vatican?

8. What role did nationalism play in the unification c Germany?

9. Explain the dilemma faced by the Frankfurt Assembly over the identification of a German uni

Who was Otto von Bismarck? What role did he play in the Prussian government?

Trace the manner in which Bismarck manipulated Austria into a war against Denmark. What was the cause and result of the war?

Why was the Treaty of Gastein considered a problem rather than a solution regarding Schleswig and Holstein?

What caused the war between Prussia and Austria in 1866? What was the result of this Seven Weeks' War?

Analyze Bismarck's insistence on excluding Austria, Austria's multinational empire, and the German states south of the Main River from German unification. What advantages for Germany did Bismarck see in this policy? What disadvantages did he foresee if they were admitted? Speculate where the political and military power would have been centred if all the German states had been allowed to join.

Describe the organization of the North German Confederation. What was the effect of this organization on Austria and the south German states?

What problems can you foresee in the creation of a new federal state such as Germany? What would be the reaction of the rulers of the smaller German states towards unification?

Why did France declare war on Prussia on 19 July 1870? What was the result?

ANALYSIS

1. Read the poem called "Charge of the British Light Brigade" by Alfred Tennyson. This poem immortalizes the attack on the Russian guns at the head of a valley during the Crimean War. Research the effect the poem had on the British public. Speculate as to why the story was told in verse form.

2. What part did artists play in awakening the consciousness of the Germanic peoples towards a nation state? Research the life of Richard Wagner to discover what his role was.

3. List, in order of effectiveness, the national institutions that you are aware of that contribute to placing the Canadian identity above regional (provincial) loyalties.

ACTIVITIES

1. Guest Speaker
Identify an individual who has recently immigrated from an area fraught with nationalist tension. Invite them to speak to the class about the role of nationalism in the conflict.

2. Interview
Prepare questions for an interview with Bismarck in 1870 after the defeat of France in the Franco-Prussian War. Structure your interview to discover the goals and the strategies which governed Bismarck's foreign policy from 1862 to 1870.

3. Debate
Be it resolved that Bismarck used war as a political weapon and not an end in itself.

Chapter 9
The Age of Bismarck
1870–1890

FOCUS ON:

❦

Bismarck's use of ideology and the media to mold public opinion;

❦

Bismarck's foreign policy strategy as an assurance of German security;

❦

Bismarck's use of state socialism in building the new German state.

Otto von Bismarck was the most important factor in every political, military, and diplomatic undertaking by the great powers from 1871 to 1890. This picture shows Bismarck in the uniform of the regiment of Cuirassier.

The Prussian victory over France in 1870 marked the end of French dominance of the European continent. Now the centre of power would shift to the newly created German Empire and, for the next twenty years, Otto von Bismarck (1815–1898), chancellor of Germany, would dominate European affairs. He was the most important factor in every political, military and diplomatic undertaking by the great powers from 1871 to 1890.

Victory in war evoked a widespread outpouring of nationalism in support of Kaiser Wilhelm I as German emperor. The adoration of the military pervaded German society for the next three-quarters of a century. During this time the German officer corps played one of the major roles in determining Germany's destiny.

Although victorious in the war against France, Bismarck had no desire to jeopardize what had been won by going to war against another major power or combination of powers. Germany alone could not win in such a war. Bismarck's plan was to keep German military forces prepared for war but never use them. Only in this way would Germany be given the time necessary to consolidate itself as a nation. Despite warlike moves in public, his underlying policy was to keep Germany out of war and Europe at peace.

FRANCE AFTER THE WAR WITH PRUSSIA

After the disaster of Sedan, the Paris mob stormed the *Corps Législatif* and established a provisional government. Their purpose was to continue the fight against the Prussians. The Prussian siege of Paris began on 23 September 1870.

On 7 October, Leon Gambetta, a leading government figure, escaped from Paris in a hot air balloon. His self-proclaimed task was to raise resistance in the provinces to the Prussian occupation. His efforts failed and Adolphe Thiers, statesman and historian, was elected to negotiate peace with Bismarck.

The French government in Versailles under Thiers agreed to a five billion franc **reparation,** the cessation of Alsace save for Belfort and a third of Lorraine, and the occupation of eastern France until the reparations were

TIMELINE

1870
Prussia defeats France at Sedan.

1873
Three Emperors' League is formed between Germany, Austria, and Russia.

1870s
Anti-Catholic legislation is passed during Kulturkampf.

1871
Unification of Germany begins with the Treaty of Frankfurt.

1875
World-wide depression causes nations to establish protective tariffs.

1878
Congress of Berlin meets to decide the future of the Ottoman Empire and the extent of major power intervention in the Balkans.

1879
Dual Alliance is formed between Germany and Austria-Hungary.

1881
Three Emperors' League is renewed.

1882
French occupation of Tunisia forces Italy into the Triple Alliance.

1884
Germany seeks an overseas empire.

1887
Reinsurance Treaty is signed between Germany and Russia.

1888
Congress of Berlin on African Affairs
Kaiser Wilhelm I dies.
Wilhelm II ascends the throne.

1890
Bismarck resigns as German chancellor.

...d. The surrender touched off a 72-day civil war between ... National Assembly and the Paris Commune, a revolu-...nary city council. After a nine-week siege of Paris by the ...ench army, government forces were let into the city. ...ey blazed a bloody path through the Parisian National ...ards to the hill at Montmartre where 20 000 were exe-...ed. Over 50 000 Parisians were sent to penal colonies ...1 30 000 others sought exile.

...hiers sought to rebuild the nation's morale. Within four ...rs the army was rearmed and became a potent force. ...nchmen oversubscribed to government loans to raise ... five billion franc reparations in order to get the ...ssians off French soil. The monies were raised by 1873, ...months ahead of time.

...1 1873 Marshal MacMahon, a monarchist, became pres-...nt. His goal was to reinstate the monarchy under the ...té de Chambord. When Chambord insisted on flying ...*fleur de lis* of the Old Regime instead of the tricolor it ...s too much even for his supporters. Attempts to bring ...k the monarchy drove the republican forces together. ...1870 even the Senate held a number of republicans.

...uring this period, France experienced steady industrial ...wth. Exports were tripled, iron ore was exported all ...r Europe, and French investors poured money, 45 bil-...1 francs, into the eastern Mediterranean and 25 billion ...ics into Russia. Almost every railway built, except for ...se in Germany, had French backing.

...fter Sedan, French prestige was at its lowest since ...5. It appeared that France had no friends or allies. Yet ...1914 the position was reversed and France was the key-...1e of an **alliance system** that isolated Germany. The ...acle recovery was due to the actions of a handful of ...1. With little public support but lots of bravado they ...rned France to a position of honour. Jules Ferry, ...ophile Delcasse, Georges Clémenceau, and Raymond ...ncaré had a passion for *revanche* (revenge) against ...many. They yearned for the return of Alsace-Lorraine. ...st Frenchmen were indifferent to their cause, but Léon ...mbetta said it best when he ordered patriots "never say ...it always think about it." Coexistence with Germany ... unthinkable to them. They believed there would be ...ther war for which France must be made ready.

...or the next twenty years after Sedan, French foreign ...cy was dormant. An alliance with Russia would place ...1ce in the position of having to support Russia in the

Balkans. France could not join with the British after their occupation of Egypt in 1882. France wanted to be left alone to recover.

Jules Ferry, French statesman and educator, began the process of rebuilding national prestige. Premier for two terms, he urged French colonial officials in Africa and Indo-China to expand the French empire. However, French occupation of Tunisia in 1882 resulted in Italian entry into the Triple Alliance to protect its own north African interests. These small beginnings laid the founda-tion for a more vigorous foreign policy in the 1890s.

THE THREE EMPERORS' LEAGUE

Germany is situated in the middle of Europe. In the nineteenth century it had powerful neighbours on its borders. Bismarck's worst fear was a situation in which Germany would have to fight both Russia and France at the same time. He believed that a war fought on two **battlefronts** could not be won and would result in the destruction of Germany. Germany had nothing to fear from France alone, but France combined with another power would pose a lethal threat to the *Reich* (German Empire). France would have to be isolated and prevented from making any alliance with the other three powers— England, Russia, or Austria-Hungary.

Bismarck believed that the democracies of England and France were the most unstable of the great powers because they had turned their governments over to the whim of their people. Foreign policy within a democracy was impossible to predict as it was subject to public approval and always subject to change. Bismarck believed the democracies could not be trusted. He chose, therefore, not to place German security at risk through alliances with them.

Initially, Bismarck ignored Britain because it was not a continental power. Britain's interests were at sea and with its global empire. France was another matter. With Germany's annexation of Alsace-Lorraine in 1870 and the reparations levied on France at that time, there would always be a faction in France bent on revenge. France would have to be considered a potential enemy.

That left the other two major powers—Russia and Aus-tria-Hungary. Like Germany they were ruled by strong

Power of Emperors

None of the emperors were as powerful as they would liked to have been. Within the cities, the bourgeoisie had become politically active. They demanded a share of national sovereignty through a parliamentary system. The national press were also powerful because they could trigger mob reaction at a moment's notice. Bismarck was keenly aware of the advantages of the press. If handled properly, the will of the people could be manipulated in foreign and domestic matters. However, once the public's usefulness was over how did one shut off the voice of the mob?

In addition to the growing influence of public opinion over policy, ethnic minorities within the Russian and Austro-Hungarian empires were restless. The idea of nationalism sparked discussions of independence, and minority groups within the empires began to seek ways of attaining sovereignty.

The emperors tended to ignore the press unless it suited their purposes. They were isolated in the splendor of their courts and became even more removed from the public mood as the century drew on. They depended on the police and armed forces to keep their subjects under control. They believed that governing was the responsibility of the emperor, not that of the mob.

---

rulers. Bismarck proposed that the *drei Kaiser* ("three emperors") act together to ensure peace in Europe. Kaiser Wilhelm I of Germany, Tsar Alexander II of Russia, and Emperor Franz Joseph of Austria-Hungary would form a *Dreikaiserbund* (Three Emperors' League).

Unlike the Holy Alliance of 1815 which was based on the idea of intervention, the *Dreikaiserbund* was based on the agreement not to interfere in each others' **spheres of influence.** The emperors believed that, as they held absolute power over their people, they could personally maintain peace by simply refusing to go to war against each other.

Friendship with Russia was critical to Bismarck's foreign policy. Russia had the potential of placing an 800 000-man army in the field. Bismarck had no intention of going to war against such a formidable force. Moreover, Germany and Russia had joint interests—keeping a divided Poland quiet, for one. Also, Russia could lend legitimacy to Germany's annexation of Alsace-Lorraine by acknowledging Germany's right to the former French provinces. And, Russia had remained neutral in the Austro-Prussian war of 1866 and the Franco-Prussian war of 1870, neither of which could Prussia have won had Russia attacked from the rear.

Given these factors and the inclination of the absolute monarchs to stick together, Bismarck believed he could establish a lasting Russian alliance. In return, Germany would support Russian attempts to upset the Treaty of Paris (1856) which had denied Russia the right to build a navy on the Black Sea. Germany would also support Russian access, if not control, over the Straits.

Although he was sympathetic to the German proposal,

Prime Minister William Gladstone of Great Britain objected to Germany's unilateral support of Russia's defiance of the Treaty of Paris. He would not tolerate one of the powers tearing up a treaty agreed to by all. Changes could be made only if all the powers agreed. He called the powers to London to deal with the issue, at which time it was agreed that Russia could have a Black Sea fleet and unhindered access to the Straits.

Russia believed it could now count on unqualified German support. This was a dangerous assumption and not entirely correct. Bismarck felt he needed an alliance of at least two other powers, which meant some kind of arrangement with Austria-Hungary. He had been successful in keeping the large multinational Austro-Hungarian empire out of the *Reich* in 1871. Bismarck had no desire to have millions of Hungarians and Slavs within Germany enlarged by a union of German-speaking peoples.

To have such an alliance meant supporting the Emperor Franz Joseph in his expansionist policies in the Balkans. Austria-Hungary might keep the restless Slavs under control but any move against the Balkans was certain to upset Russia. Russia and Austria-Hungary had overlapping spheres of interest in the Balkans—they were the major flaws in Bismarck's strategy.

Both Russia and Austria-Hungary considered the Balkans vital to their own interests. The Austrians would not tolerate Russian dominance in the area. On the other hand, the Russians, who saw the Straits as their economic outlet to the Mediterranean Sea and world markets, would not tolerate an Austro-Hungarian presence in the region.

The three emperors met in Berlin in 1872 to lay

Prime Minister William Gladstone of Great Britain objected to Germany's unilateral support of Russia's defiance of the Treaty of Paris.

as his duty to make certain the two powers never came to blows. France, not party to the agreement, now stood in isolation from the other powers. Bismarck intended to keep it that way.

BISMARCK AND THE REICHSTAG

In 1871 Bismarck drafted a constitution for a Prussian-dominated Germany with the capital in the Prussian city of Berlin. The king of Prussia, Wilhelm I, automatically became the German kaiser. Power lay in his hands and with his appointed chancellor, Bismarck, who managed the federal government. The federal legislative branch consisted of an appointed upper house, the *Bundesrat*, and an elected lower house, the *Reichstag*.

Within the federation, the 25 individual states retained important powers, including the raising of military forces, and control of education, religious matters, police forces, and direct taxation. For example, the Kingdom of Bavaria had its own army and its own war office. There was no federal civil service to speak of as federal programs were administered through state bureaucracies.

The hereditary rulers appointed representatives to the Bundesrat on the basis of population. Prussia's 17 votes out of a total of 58 gave it veto power in the upper house. Because legislation had to be approved by the Bundesrat, Prussia effectively dominated the proceedings. The prime minister of Prussia presided over the Bundesrat. He alone

ndation of the Three Emperors' League signed the folling year. Under the terms of the agreement, the emperagreed to support each other in order to maintain staty in Europe. They agreed not to interfere in each rs' spheres of interest. No solution was found to the sian-Austro-Hungarian rivalry in the Balkans. Both sia and Austria-Hungary believed that if it should come var, Germany would side with them. Bismarck saw it had the authority to set the agenda and bring forward legislation.

Deputies to the *Reichstag* were elected in their states by secret ballot. Bismarck was worried that the deputies would be more concerned with looking after the interests of their own states rather than that of the German nation. He counted on a strong foreign policy to instill nationalism among them. Above all was the need to transfer the people's allegiance from their traditional rulers to that of the kaiser.

The *Reichstag* was given control over part of the federal budget and all federal legislation. If the deputies voted against a bill it was defeated. It was mandatory to place the annual budget before the lower house for its approval. Bismarck considered this a necessary nuisance and often regretted giving the deputies this power. Most funding for the federal government came from arrangements with the individual states, but the *Reichstag* had been given the power of taxing goods in widespread use such as tobacco and liquor. This provided a small but significant portion of the money needed to run the federal government. Bismarck would have to manipulate the political parties in the *Reichstag* or risk losing this source of funding.

Wilhelm I (1797–1888)
was the seventh king of Prussia and
the first German emperor.

ismarck's Legislative rogram

smarck brought two major ues before the *Reichstag*. The st concerned funding for the litary. The chief of staff, neral von Moltke, wanted a nding army of one percent of e population, then equal to a rce of 400 000. Moltke did not e having to come to the *ichstag* for funding, and sug- sted the figure so that the size the army would automatically rease as Germany's popula n grew. The general de- nded the *Reichstag* fund the rman army in perpetuity. cause tax laws remained in ect until changed, he envi- ned never again having to ne begging for funds. His pro- sal would, in other words, nove any interference in ay matters.

Bismarck was cool towards idea of a perpetual army d. As much as he disliked the *Reichstag*, at least he had ntrol over it. Should the army funding be granted in per- uity, it would remove one of Bismarck's means to influ- e the direction of military airs. He arranged to have the essary military funds voted with the provision that the ned forces budget be re- wed every seven years.

he second issue had to do h the rights of the Catholic ority within the state. The *turkampf*, or cultural strug- , occupied the *Reichstag* ughout the 1870s. At the rt of the *Kulturkampf* lay marck's need to manufacture working majority in the

---

~ Decision-Makers ~

Decisions within the German Empire were made by a small, elite group of men and their associates. They were generally from the Junker class and seldom numbered over 200. They came from similar backgrounds and experience and represent- ed the conservative views of the landed aris- tocracy. At the centre of this group was the Kaiser Wilhelm I and Chancellor Bismarck.

Military matters were directly under the kaiser and his military staff. One of the con- tentious issues was the relationship between the chancellor and the army chief of staff. Bismarck would skillfully use the Reichstag's power of approving military funding to main- tain some influence over Germany's war machine.

The imperial armed forces were composed of the armies of the member states. In wartime these were united under Prussian command. The kaiser considered the military his personal responsibility. His leanings toward the military were applauded by the German people. After all, it was the German military that had forged the nation.

Reichstag. To do this he first sought to ally the Liberals and Conservatives against the Catholic Centre Party by attack- ing the rights of the Catholic minority.

In the face of declining moral values in the industrial age, Pope Pius IX wished to reestablish the position of the Roman Catholic Church over the dogma and morals of all Roman Catholics. Industrialization emphasized materialism and had resulted in the abandonment of traditional Christian morals and ethics. In 1870 Pope Pius published an encyclical, a letter to Catholics, that proclaimed papal infallibili- ty. That is, the pope claimed that when speaking *ex cathedra*, on matters of doctrine, his words were binding on all the faithful. This had been preceded by the encyclical *Quantam Cura* in which the pope listed all the modern doctrines that were to be banned because they went against Roman Catholic beliefs and teachings. Many of these ideas were from Liberal and Socialist ideologies.

Bismarck saw an opportunity to get rid of the Catholic Centre Party in the papal claim to direct the beliefs of Roman Catholics in Germany. He raised the spectre of papal interference inside Germany. This, he said, he would not permit. Germany was a Protestant nation where the Reformation had begun three and a half centuries earlier with Martin Luther. Germany would remain Protestant.

Kulturkampf, a term coined by the Liberals, was portrayed in the German press as the final battle for civilisation—a battle

---

~ Ultramontanism ~

The concept of ultramontanism lay at the heart of the centuries-old conflict between church and state. The term originated in France. When French church- men sought to strengthen papal influence in political matters, national leaders viewed this as an unwarranted interference in national sovereignty. The word ultramontanism refers to the centre of the papacy which is in Rome—the other side of the mountains.

between good and evil. Public frenzy was orchestrated over the danger to Germany of being surrounded by Catholic France, Austria-Hungary, Poland, and Orthodox Russia. After all these centuries, Bismarck asked, was Germany now to be endangered by a resurgence of papal power? Should the German people not be called to arms to defeat the *ultramontanes?*

The visible objects of attack were the 90 members of the Catholic Centre Party whom Bismarck charged with being in league with the pope. In reality the Catholic Party was independent of any papal interference to the point where even the German Catholic bishops had no control over it. The members of the Catholic Centre Party were intensely loyal to the kaiser and considered themselves nationalists and patriots. They were not part of an international conspiracy aimed at restoring Roman Catholicism to Germany.

Bismarck would not listen to them and branded them all traitors. He claimed they were just like the Socialists, with an international agenda that placed ideology above the state. Neither he nor the kaiser would go to Canossa as had Emperor Henry IV to do penance before Pope Gregory VII in 1077. The humiliation forced on the German emperor at that time would never be repeated.

Despite Bismarck's ravings, the kaiser and the kaiserine (empress) were rather sympathetic to the Catholic position.

This caricature of Pope Pius IX sitting on the papal throne is titled "The Infallib In 1870, Pope Pius IX published a letter proclaiming papal infallibility, meani that the pope's words were binding on all matters of doctrine in the Roman Cath Church.

iserine Augusta was particularly concerned over what
peared to be a battle that raged only in Bismarck's mind.
her, the whole issue seemed distasteful.

n spite of the kaiser's feelings, restrictive legislation
ainst German Catholics began in May 1872 and contin-
d for the next five years. Catholics lost their positions in
e civil service, were denied entrance into gymnasia and
iversities, and the Catholic education system was sys-
matically dismantled. All matters of a religious nature
re removed from the schools. (The latter ruling applied
Protestant religions as well and caused considerable
ction from the Lutherans.) All priests were to acquire
te licenses by taking appropriate courses in history and
ilosophy. Those who did not comply were banished.
is resulted in some 1400 parishes left vacant by priests
o opposed the legislation. The church's monopoly on
rriage ceremonies was broken with the provision for an
ernative civil ceremony. The Jesuit Order and all of its
ldings were to be abolished and the members of the
er exiled. Most other civil rights were denied Catholics
er this period.

Despite their principles of individual rights , the Liber-
had gone along with the Conservatives in passing the
islation as they despised Catholic doctrines. They
ieved Bismarck when he accused their fellow deputies
treason. The anti-Catholic legislation passed in an out-
rst of patriotism.

As expected, Pius IX declared the anti-Catholic laws
alid. Any German Catholics who obeyed them would be
communicated. There the matter stood until Pius's
ath in 1878 when his successor Leo XIII sought a *rap-
chement.

After having gone to such pains to call down the wrath
the German people on the Catholic Centre Party, Bis-
rck was astounded in the 1874 elections when the Cen-
Party doubled its number of seats. This was the first
ication that the *Kulturkampf* was not working. Four
rs later when the Liberals opposed his tariff policy he
uld reverse his stance and ally with the Centre Party to
k an end to Liberal influence. At that time most of the
i-Catholic laws were rescinded except those dealing
h civil marriage and the Jesuits. Bismarck and the new
e, Leo XIII, believed they should bury their differences
unite forces against a growing Socialist movement that
y believed threatened the stability of the continent.

About Face in the Reichstag

In 1875 Bismarck retired to his estates at Varzin where he
began to consider the withdrawal of his support for the
Liberals in favour of the Conservatives. He realized the
Liberals could never give up their principles on free trade
to meet the demands of German industrialists and agrari-
ans for a protective tariff. A world-wide depression had
cut deeply into Germany's foreign trade when British and
North American firms dumped their excess production
into Europe. A protective tariff was required to stop the
dumping.

At the same time, Bismarck calculated the agrarian
Junkers could be won over to a tariff by banning agricultural imports and giving them a monopoly over German
food supplies. The combination of industrialists and
Junkers could create a Conservative majority in the
Reichstag. This would mean an end to Liberal influence
and Liberal demands for increased parliamentary power.
It might also mean the end of the Socialists. Unlike the
Liberals, who would fight the tariff on ideological grounds,
the Socialists would oppose the tariff on the grounds that
it would increase the price of food for the poor.

Opportunism was once again the driving force behind
Bismarck's policies. The world depression had caused
massive unemployment resulting in social unrest. In
Germany more than 790 iron mills had shut down and
industrial growth was at a standstill. A protective tariff
would stop the inward flow of industrial goods from
England and North America.

The change in policy began innocuously over the need
to renew the army budget. This time Bismarck proposed a
large increase in indirect taxes on commodities for military needs. In this way, the army would not have to depend
on the somewhat unreliable levies on the state governments. A growing demand for an increase in federal funding also came from the federal civil service, expanding
now that Germany was well on its way towards centralization of power.

The Liberals were prepared to vote for the increase in
taxes, provided Bismarck would guarantee not to dissolve
the *Reichstag* once the taxes had been approved. They
were afraid Bismarck would never call the *Reichstag* into
session again once the tax increases had been voted.
Bismarck would give no such assurance thus fueling their
fears.

Anti-Socialism

The Liberals then prepared to vote against the army tax bill over the matter of the future of the *Reichstag*. Bismarck reacted by placing a state monopoly on tobacco and pushed forward his tariff legislation. Both matters were popular but both went against Liberal ideology. This placed the Liberals in a dilemma.

At this critical juncture, two attempts were made on the kaiser's life. Bismarck skillfully used the assassination attempts to his advantage. He engineered an outpouring of loyalty from the nation to the kaiser—anyone opposing either the kaiser or Bismarck was characterized as disloyal.

On 11 May 1878, Hodel, a deranged plumber, shot at Wilhelm but missed. Without waiting to hear the facts, Bismarck blamed the attempt on the Socialists and the so-called "red menace" creeping over the civilized world. Then in June, a Dr. Nobling, fired at the kaiser from an apartment on the Unter den Linden, causing the emperor critical injuries. Wilhelm was 81 and for a time it appeared he would not survive. Distraught over the possible death of the kaiser, Bismarck vowed to break the Socialists and Communists whom he blamed for these outrages.

The 1878 election was a masterpiece of manipulation. The attempted assassinations caused such a reaction that only those deputies who swore they would protect the kaiser were reelected. Bismarck was at his most persuasive in appealing to the instinct of the populace to crush the enemies of the state. Emotions ran high in an outburst of loyalty as a massive landslide in favour of rooting out the traitors engulfed the land. Bismarck was able to put together a coalition of Conservative deputies that gave him a large majority and committed the *Reichstag* firmly to his agenda.

Although there was never any linkage between the assassins and the Socialists, Bismarck promoted the myth that the Socialists were responsible for the attacks on the kaiser. The power of the press was once more unleashed against his political enemies. Bismarck sponsored a series of anti-Socialist laws that would destroy them. Socialists would not be permitted to have trade unions, form any kind of associations, or publish their views.

Surprisingly, he did not legislate away their right to run for election. The Liberals supported the legislation, giving up their belief in civil rights for the sake of demonstrating their loyalty to the kaiser. The anti-Socialist legislation required renewal every three or four years. Attempts to renew it in 1890 led, ironically, to Bismarck's downfall.

State Socialism

Bismarck recognized the material needs of the working classes. He believed that they were best met by the benevolence of the state rather than through trade unions or political action. He brought forward a series of welfare initiatives aimed at wooing the support of the workers away from the unions and opposition parties. Bismarck's motive in this was to destroy the Socialist organizations in Germany.

This concept, which came to be known as **State Socialism**, was included in the throne speech of 1881. Altogether, Bismarck would be responsible for three major pieces of legislation—the last enacted in 1889. Their objective was to provide welfare benefits for those who, through no fault of their own, had fallen on hard times. The state would care for them until they could return to the workforce.

This landmark legislation contained a national health insurance scheme created from joint employer-employee contributions (1881). This was followed in 1884 by a national accident on-the-job insurance plan and, in 1889, by a social security plan that provided modest pensions for those over 65. No other country at that time provided such extensive welfare for its people. Despite the enactment of this radical legislation, the workers continued their political support for the left wing, and Bismarck's motives were thwarted.

THE BALKANS
AFTER THE
CONGRESS OF BERLIN
(1878)

The Congress of Berlin was an attempt to settle Balkan territorial disputes without military confrontation. For the location of Cyprus, see the map titled "The Crimean War (1853–1856)" in Chapter 8. For the location of Batum, see the map "The Russian Revolution (1917–1918)" in Chapter 15.

HE CONGRESS OF BERLIN 1878

n the summer of 1875, the Balkans erupted with yet another insurrection against their Ottoman overlords. Austria-Hungary was concerned the rebellion ght spread to the Slavs within its own southern borders. stria-Hungary was also sensitive to Russia's declared entions to support its Serbian allies in the region. The ssibility of a confrontation between Austria-Hungary d Russia in the Balkans threatened the stability of rope.

n 1877 Russia declared war on the Ottoman Turks and rched its armies south towards the Straits. At Plevna y were held at bay by a brilliant defence carried out by man Pasha. That March, a British fleet sailed into the a of Marmara in support of the Turks. At the same time,

Austria-Hungary announced it wanted to annex Bosnia and Herzegovina. When Britain intervened to support the sultan in Constantinople, it appeared that at long last the major powers were prepared to go to war. Bismarck found it difficult not to take sides but he was not inclined to get involved unless the very existence of Austria-Hungary was at risk.

In order to avoid confrontation, Bismarck called the powers to Berlin in 1878. The Berlin Congress of 1878 evoked memories of the old Congress System and the Concert of Europe that had governed Europe after the fall of Napoleon in 1815. The matters before this congress were the future of the Ottoman Empire and the major powers' spheres of influence in the Balkans.

Because the powers could not agree on how to partition the Ottoman Empire, it was given a new lease on life that lasted until 1918. Unable to police itself or control its minorities, it had come to be known as the "Sick Man of Europe."

Specifically, Bulgaria was not permitted to expand and what there was of it was divided into two parts. (The Bulgarians forged their own union in 1885 creating yet another crisis.) Britain was given the island of Cyprus from which its navy could dominate both the Straits and the Suez Canal. Russia was to get Batum on the eastern shores of the Black Sea and the right to build a fleet on the Black Sea, but Russia was not given control of the Danube mouth, nor the Straits which were to remain under the control of the Sultan. Austria was given permission to pacify and administer Bosnia and Herzegovina but not to annex the region.

The Berlin Congress ended in agreement, but all was not well. The tsar, Alexander II, felt a definite cooling in Germany's relations with Russia. The Germans had consistently

---

A Secret Agreement

Under a secret agreement, Germany promised to help defend Austria against an attack by Italy, while the Austrians would come to the defence of Germany if Germany were attacked by France. After the French invasion of Tunisia, Italy, fearful of French expansion in North Africa, would join the pact in 1882 to form the Triple Alliance. This added a new complication as Austria-Hungary and Italy had a long-standing disagreement over the Tyrol and the port city of Trieste on the Adriatic coast.

---

sided with Austria-Hungary. To Russia, this was most dangerous. Miffed by Bismarck's open friendship with Austria-Hungary, Alexander decided to close Russia's western borders and exert his energies in opening Siberia and the Pacific seaports of Vladivostok and Port Arthur.

The relationship between the three empires was strained—none of them had achieved what they had intended. Throughout the negotiations, the powers ignored the growing nationalism of the Slavic minorities in the Balkan region. The problems of ethnic unrest in the Balkans were unresolved. However the decisions reached at the Congress of Berlin preserved peace in Europe for the next 36 years—a noteworthy watershed in foreign relations.

BISMARCK'S ALLIANCE SYSTEM

Wary over the unresolved question of the Straits and the tendency of the other powers to get involved in each others' spheres of influence, Bismarck acted to secure Germany's borders by means of a series of overlapping defensive alliances. His objective was to keep the other powers from going to war either against Germany or against each other. France was to play no part in Bismarck's alliance system other than to remain in isolation from the other powers.

The Dual Alliance (1879) between Germany and Austria-Hungary was the first treaty in Bismarck's defence strategy. The treaty bound both empires to go to each others' assistance if either were attacked by another power.

Tsar Alexander's concern over the direction of Bismarck's foreign policy resulted in a renewal of the Three Emperors' League in 1881 which promised at least neutrality in the event of an attack on any of the three by a fourth power. This was followed in 1887 by the secret Reinsurance Treaty between Russia and Germany in which Bismarck promised support for Russian policies in the Balkans. In return, Russia promised neutrality in any war

between Germany and Fran while Germany promised ne trality in any war betwe Austria and Russia. That sar year Bismarck concluded t Mediterranean Agreements which the powers, includi Great Britain, agreed to ma tain the status quo with t Eastern Mediterranean.

BISMARCK AND COLONIES 1884

Bismarck's brief ve ture into imperialis in 1884, quietly dro ped the next year, caught the diplomatic world by surpri The chancellor had never given any indication th Germany was interested in colonies. Bismarck had oft stated that his map of Africa was in Central Europe a that he was not a colonial advocate. Why then in 1884 he act with such speed in his bid for colonial possession

Bismarck's quest for colonies sprang from domes needs. In later years, his son and confidant, Herbert, st ed that the whole thing was a matter of *Reichstag* electi and the succession to the German throne. One of Bismarc major concerns in 1884 was the kaiser's health or, rath the health of Crown Prince Friedrich, heir to the thro Both the prince and his wife were filled with British ide about popular sovereignty and parliamentary rule. E marck determined to destroy the British influence at co by provoking an incident over British colonial possessio The national press would be used to invoke German hat of the British. By establishing a climate of hostility tow Britain, Bismarck would make it virtually impossible Friedrich to implement his liberal ideas when he came the throne.

Imperialism also seemed to promise solutions to pressing social problems of the day. Germany's overpo lation, industrial overproduction, and mass unemployme could be solved by gaining colonies. Colonies could ta Germany's excess population, absorb excess producti and provide a safe place for investment. They would a

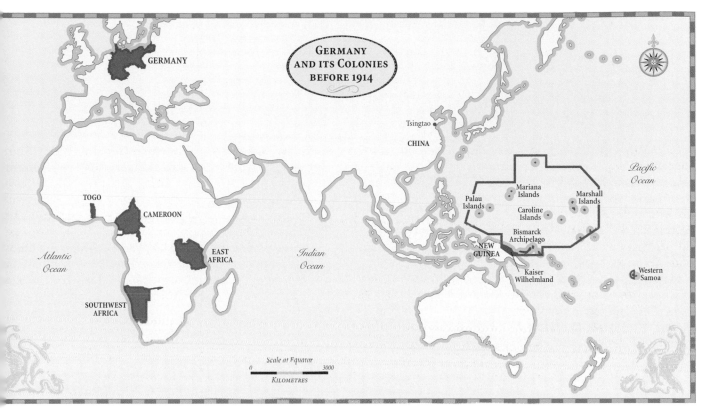

*Bismarck attempted to boost his nation's prestige
by adding overseas colonies to Germany's territorial holdings.*

ovide Germany with its own resources, a factor that
uld be important in a general war.

Bismarck's own goals were to discredit the crown prince
rough a rupture with the British, to make a dramatic ges-
e to gain maximum publicity, to make colonialism a
tional issue, and to blunt the social unrest among the
orking classes.

Bismarck decided on a colonial venture at a time when
ere were only a few regions left on the globe that had
t been brought under foreign control. Among them were
me islands in the South Pacific and part of the African
ntinent. Neither would make Germany a major imperial
wer by their addition to the confederation.

Bismarck forged ahead with German claims to the West
rican coast line between Cape Province and the mouth
the Congo. On the East African coast, as a result of the
plorations of Carl Peters, Zanzibar and the part of East
rica across from it on the mainland came under German
otection. This placed Germany athwart a proposed
tish communications route between Cape Town and
iro. Germany also laid claim to a scattering of Pacific
nds contested by Spain, Australia, and New Zealand.

Bismarck began by writing a diplomatic note to the
tish Foreign Office asking if Britain had any interests in
West African coast line. He also asked Britain to relin-
sh the island of Heligoland in the North Sea. Although

the note was forwarded to the German embassy in London
Bismarck ordered his ambassador in London not to deliver
it. Six months later he challenged Prime Minister
Gladstone over Great Britain's silence to his note. Why had
Britain purposefully insulted Germany by refusing to reply
to a simple request? Was this the way Germany deserved
to be treated? In a number of speeches to the *Reichstag*,
Bismarck railed against British arrogance.

This was the first time the German press was manipulated into an anti-British campaign. It would not be the
last. Until 1884 there had not been much anti-British feeling among German people nor had there been any anti-
German feelings among the British public against the
Germans. However, from this incident onwards, to the outbreak of World War I, hostility against Britain would be
encouraged by the German government and the British
government began to view Germany as an enemy.

Gladstone could not understand Bismarck's aggressive
behaviour over some barren pieces of land that neither
Germany nor England wanted—of course England would
not object to Germany's colonial claims. Germany could
have Heligoland and whatever else it claimed as an empire.

In 1885 Bismarck convened the Congress on African
Affairs in Berlin. The purpose of this conference was to
define claims and lay down rules of occupation in Africa.
During the congress, Bismarck seemed withdrawn and

reluctant to press Germany's colonial claims. In fact by this time he had decided to abandon the whole colonial issue. He had changed his mind on colonies after German merchants and bankers refused to pay for the costs of colonial administration and defence, putting the costs of colonies back upon the state. If it had not been for the loss of prestige, he would have abandoned the quest for colonies at that point.

THE ARMY BILL OF 1887

In 1887 Bismarck brought a new army appropriations bill before the *Reichstag*. New taxes would be required to increase the size of the armed forces. In order to get the bill through, Bismarck created a war scare over a renewed crisis in the Balkans.

Alexander von Battenberg had been made Prince of Bulgaria, with Russian support. Once on the throne Alexander proved a competent and popular ruler. He began, however, to show increasing favouritism towards Austria and even expressed a desire to marry the daughter of Crown Prince Friedrich of Germany. Tsar Alexander III found Battenberg's pro-Austrian leanings dangerous to Russia's position in the Balkans. What really concerned the tsar was the steady advance of Austro-Hungarian and German trade and railway systems toward Constantinople. If completed these could negate Russian influence in the Balkans. The tsar had counted on Battenberg to halt the expansion, not to support it. The tsar insisted Alexander abdicate.

Bismarck reacted with vigour to the tsar's intervention. The public was alerted in the press to the probability of a war between the powers over the Battenberg affair. With war in sight who would deny the armed forces the money to defend the nation? Patriots declared that every penny the army asked for and more would be voted. On Bismarck's urging German banks refused Russian loans on the grounds that the tsar was anti-German and probably pro-French.

But Bismarck's strategy backfired when it drove Russia into the arms of French banking houses. If Germany would not provide economic support for Russian industrialization then France would. French investors lined up to subscribe to the Russian bond issues needed for the Trans-Siberian Railway system and other Russian industrial enterprises.

Finally, when Quartermaster General Waldersee Germany, informed Austria-Hungary that Germany w preparing a preemptive strike on France and urg Austria-Hungary to be aggressive in its support Battenberg, Kaiser Wilhelm brought his advisors to he There would be no war.

But the war scare served its purpose. The army bill w readily passed by the *Reichstag*. Bismarck then dissolv the *Reichstag*. In the subsequent elections, the conser tive parties swept the nation giving Bismarck the larg majority he ever had. He was never as popular again.

DEATH OF THE KAISER

Kaiser Wilhelm I died in March 1888. He was s ceeded by his son Crown Prince Friedrich. T prince was ill with throat cancer and lived to r only 99 days. In June his son Wilhelm became kais Wilhelm II was arrogant and adventuresome. He felt m at home with the Potsdam Guards and found Bismarck 73 to be somewhat befuddled. He could not cont Bismarck, did not like his advice, and was determined ask for the chancellor's resignation at the earliest possi moment. Wilhelm loved the people's adoration and w unwilling to share it with anyone else.

Differences between Wilhelm II and Bismarck aro almost immediately. Bismarck wanted to proceed with n anti-Socialist legislation which would permit the police force suspected Socialists from their houses and into ex The kaiser wanted to be the people's ruler and lighten work load by abolishing Sunday work and by limiting hardships of women and children in the workplace.

Bismarck would not tolerate these ideas and sabota an international conference that the kaiser had called Berlin in 1890 to discuss labour matters. When the kai published his labour decrees Bismarck refused to co tersign them thus they could not become law. The s between them became public.

Bismarck's answer to the social question was to use army to tame the workers. The ongoing Westphalian c miners strike could be ended quickly through milit action. The kaiser refused Bismarck's request to use army. He had no desire to have the blood of his people his hands. Unlike his grandfather, this kaiser was de mined to take an active part in the government.

*Wilhelm II (1859–1941) became kaiser of Germany in 1888.
This painting of the coronation shows Wilhelm surrounded by the princes of the
German states.*

When Bismarck went to the people on the issue of his w anti-Socialist program, the people turned against him. 1890 the government side lost heavily in the elections. Bis-rck then began to plot a military coup that would abolish *Reichstag*. He would appeal to the princes to draft a new nstitution that would consolidate all power in the hands the kaiser and his executive.

he crisis was manipulated over a clause in the anti-cialist legislation that permitted police to seize sus-:ted enemies of the state from their homes and send m into exile without a trial. Bismarck hoped the *ichstag* would vote down the legislation. He would then nmon the army to dissolve the *Reichstag* and restore aristocracy to absolute power.

he Duke of Baden warned the kaiser of Bismarck's ns for a coup. They both considered him quite mad. en Bismarck made a final mistake. When he insisted :, under an 1856 law, all advisors must report to him as ncellor before seeing the kaiser, he went too far. The ser pointed out that he would see whom he pleased. In

1890, when Bismarck refused to adhere to the kaiser's demands, he was asked to resign.

DROPPING THE CHANCELLOR

ismarck will go down in history as one of the powerful individuals who fashioned the events of their times. He was responsible for the creation of the German state when all others considered it a hopeless task. He nursed Germany through its formative period, and maintained a tenuous peace with the other powers. Every year of peace would see Germany increase its military and industrial power. He manipulated the *Reichstag*, forming coalitions that passed his legislative agenda. He was the symbol around which German federalism grew to nationhood.

During this period, when chancellors and foreign ministers were key decision makers, Bismarck managed to avoid a European war. Single-handedly he kept Austria-Hungary and Russia at bay over the Balkans. He deterred France

This political cartoon shows Bismarck's resignation in 1890
over disagreements with Kaiser Wilhelm II. Do you think the cartoonist was
sympathetic to Bismarck or the kaiser? Explain your answer.

from seeking revenge, and he brought England into continental matters through the Mediterranean agreements. His accomplishments were remarkable and Germany benefited from them.

Germany emerged strong and powerful under the Ir Chancellor. He was a man of the princes and his goal to end was Germany's armed might and the authority of kaiser.

Summary of Bismarck's Alliances

Three Emperors' League (1873)
Germany, Austria, and Russia
❋ brought together these three conservative empires to maintain peace in Europe

Dual Alliance (1879)
Germany and Austria
❋ if either were attacked by Russia, they would come to the other's aid
❋ if attacked by a country other than Russia, they agreed to remain neutral
❋ treaty renewed every 5 years until 1918

Renewal of Three Emperors' League (1881)
Germany, Austria, and Russia
❋ significant step towards peace
❋ promised to maintain faithful neutrality in case either of the others was attacked by a fourth power
❋ aimed at a resolution to the conflict in the Balkans between Austria and Russia

Entry of Italy into the Dual Alliance lead to the Triple Alliance (1882)
Germany, Austria, Italy
❋ Bismarck's policy a complete success. He was allied with three of the great powers, friendly with the other – Britain – and France was isolated and posed no threat

Lapse of the Three Emperors' League (1885)
Germany, Austria, and Russia
&
Renewal of the Triple Alliance (1885)
Germany Austria, and Italy
❋ renewed for another five years

Reinsurance Treaty (1887)
Germany and Russia
❋ Bismarck promised support for Russian policy in the Balkans and neutrality in any war between Russia and Austria. In return Russia promised neutrality in any war between Germany and France.

SUMMARY

After the crushing defeat at Sedan in 1869, the centre of European military power shifted away from France to Germany. Chancellor Otto von Bismarck was the German leader who masterminded the creation of the German nation. His policy was to keep Germany's armies strong but never go to war. In this way German nationalism could thrive.

Bismarck strove to maintain stability in Europe through a system of defensive alliances with Russia and Austria-Hungary. The first was the Three Emperors' League in 1873 followed by the Dual Alliance in 1879, the Triple Alliance in 1882, the Three Emperors' League renewed in 1881, and the Reinsurance Treaty in 1887. The alliance system was designed to isolate France. The system worked in that he was able to keep his allies from going to war with each other over competing interests in the Balkans.

In 1878 Bismarck hosted a congress of the major powers in Berlin to reach agreement on the Balkans. During the congress he sided with Austria-Hungary, to Russia's dismay. After the congress Russia began to exert its energies in expansion into the Pacific regions withdrawing for a time from central European affairs.

Bismarck's colonial venture in 1884 was designed to remove the threat of the pro-British attitude of Crown Prince Friedrich. Friedrich would have to adopt the German position and give up his ideas of parliamentary government. The policy proved too costly to maintain and Bismarck withdrew his support in 1885.

The death of the Kaiser Wilhelm I, brought Bismarck's effective administration to an end. Kaiser William II could not tolerate the elder statesman and sought his resignation.

QUESTIONS

1. Explain the significance of the creation of the new German state in 1871.

2. What was the Three Emperors' League? What was its rationale?

3. Why was it critical that Germany remain at peace for a period of time after the wars of unification? What did Bismarck do to maintain peace?

4. Of what significance was the Balkan region to Russia? To Austria-Hungary?

5. Name and describe the policies of the four main political parties in the German *Reichstag*.

6. Describe Bismarck's attempts to restrict the catholic minority in Germany. Evaluate the morality and effectiveness of these attempts.

7. Outline the features of Bismarck's domestic policy in the 1870s.

8. Explain how Bismarck manipulated news of assassination attempts on the kaiser to give him a *Reichstag* firmly committed to his policies.

9. Name and explain three pieces of welfare legislation passed in Germany in the 1880s. Why did Bismarck promote such extensive social policy?

10. Explain the threat of war in 1875. What was the significance of this threat to France? To Germany?

11. Explain how Bismarck's Alliance system with Austria-Hungary and Italy was forged. Why did Bismarck consider this alliance system essential to Germany's security?

12. Why did Bismarck embark on a program of imperialism? Evaluate Germany's attempts to create a colonial empire.

13. Evaluate Bismarck's career as chancellor of Germany.

ANALYSIS

1. Compare the power structure of Germany with that of the federation of Canada.

2. Assess what rights, if any, minorities should have within a nation state. What responsibilities do minorities have?

3. Bismarck's use of the press to encourage a national outpouring of spirit would not seem out of place today when political leaders frequently harangue their peoples. Most have found that once the people are turned on to an issue, it is not as easy to turn them off.

Make a study of a recent terrorist event and try to discern fact from fiction in news reporting. Does the reporter seek to give the facts or to dramatize the situation? Why are suffering women or children more often shown than men? Is the sound of gunfire real from sound clips on file? What advantages or disadvantages do you see in the media becoming too sensational? Can the media stampede governments into war? What effect did the media have on recent interventions in the Balkans, Somalia, or Haiti?

ACTIVITIES

1. Meeting
Reenact the Congress of Berlin in 1878. Select individuals to represent all of the major powers and to present their views regarding the Balkans. Although the Balkans were not represented at this conference, you may wish to present a summary of ethnic conflict in the area.

2. Newspaper Articles
Write a newspaper article depicting the anti-British feeling which was developing in Germany after 1884.

3. Press Release
Write a detailed press release announcing Bismarck's retirement. Include an evaluation of his career from the point of view of a critic who is supportive of Bismarck's dismissal or from the point of view of a supporter of Bismarck who is critical of his dismissal.

You have now completed Unit II: Industrialization and Nationalism. *The following activity is based on what you have learned about the Industrial Revolution.*

ISSUE ANALYSIS
The Role of Human Labour in the Industrial Revolution

During the nineteenth century, European society was transformed by the Industrial Revolution. The response of social critics to the changes in lifestyle which resulted from the implementation of the factory system was diverse. One major issue of the century was the use of child labour. The following readings present a variety of viewpoints. Read each carefully and work through the questions that follow.

1. Excerpt from *An Inquiry into the Nature and Causes of the Wealth of Nations* by Adam Smith (1776)

The real price of everything, what everything really costs to the man who wants to acquire it, is the toil and trouble of acquiring it. What everything is really worth to the man who has acquired it, and who wants to dispose of it or exchange it for something else, is the toil and trouble which it can save to himself, and which it can impose upon other people. What is bought with money or with goods is purchased by labour as much as what we acquire by the toil of our own body. That money or those goods indeed save us this toil. They contain the value of a certain quantity of labour which we exchange for what is supposed at the time to contain the value of an equal quantity. Labour was the first price, the original purchase—money that was paid for all things. It was not by gold or by silver, but by labour, that all the wealth of the world was originally purchased; and its value, to those who possess it, and who want to exchange it for some new productions, is precisely equal to the quantity of labour which it can enable them to purchase or command.

2. Excerpt from *The Philosophy of Manufactures* by Andrew Ure (1835)

It is, in fact, the constant aim and tendency of every improvement in machinery to supersede human labour altogether, or to diminish its cost, by substituting the industry of women and children for that of men; or that of ordinary labourers for trained artisans. In most of the water-twist, or throstle cotton-mills, [however], the spinning is entirely managed by females of sixteen years and upwards. The effect of substituting the self-acting mule for the common mule, is to discharge the greater part of the men spinners, and to retain adolescents and children. The proprietor of a factory in New Stockport states … that, by such substitution, he would save 50 pounds a week in wages, in consequence of dispensing with nearly forty male spinners, at about 25 shillings of wages each. This tendency to employ merely children with watchful eyes and nimble fingers, instead of journeymen of long experience, shows how the scholastic dogma of the division of labour into degrees of skill has been [undermined] by our enlightened manufacturers.

3. Excerpt from *The Sadler Report of the House of Commons* (Friday, 18 May 1832)

In the following excerpt, Michael Thomas Sadler examines Matthew Crabtree.

What age are you? —Twenty-two.
What is your occupation? —A blanket manufacturer.
Have you every been employed in a factory? —Yes.
At what age did you first go to work in one? —Eight.
How long did you continue in that occupation? —Four years.
Will you state the hours of labour at the period when you first went to the factory, in ordinary times? —From 6 in the morning to 8 at night.
Fourteen hours? —Yes.

ISSUE

With what intervals for refreshment and rest?
  —An hour at noon.
*Then you had no resting time allowed in which to
  take your breakfast?* —No.
When trade was brisk what were your hours?
  —From 5 in the morning to 9 in the evening.
Sixteen hours? —Yes.
With what intervals at dinner? —An hour.
How far did you live from the mill?
  —About two miles.
*Was there any time allowed for you to get your
  breakfast in the mill?* —No.
Did you take it before you left your home?
  —Generally.
*During those long hours of labour could you be
  punctual; how did you awake?* —I seldom did
  awake spontaneously; I was most generally
  awoke or lifted out of bed, sometimes asleep,
  by my parents.
Were you always on time? —No.
*What was the consequence if you had been too
  late?* —I was most commonly beaten.

4. Excerpt from *Communist Manifesto* by Karl Marx and
Friedrich Engels (1848)

In the earlier epochs of history, we find almost
everywhere a complicated arrangement of society
into various orders, a manifold gradation of social
rank. In ancient Rome we have patricians, knights,
plebeians, slaves; in the Middle Ages, feudal lords,
vassals, guild-masters, journeymen, apprentices,
serfs; in almost all of these classes, again,
subordinate gradations.

The modern bourgeois society that has sprouted
from the ruins of feudal society, has not done away
with class antagonisms. It has but established new
classes, new conditions of oppression, new forms
of struggle in place of the old ones.

Our epoch, the epoch of the bourgeoisie,
possesses, however, this distinctive feature: It has
simplified the class antagonisms. Society as a
whole is more and more splitting up into the two
great hostile camps, into two great classes directly
facing each other—bourgeoisie and proletariat …

The bourgeoisie has played a most revolutionary
role in history. The bourgeoisie, wherever it has
got the upper hand, has put an end to all feudal,
patriarchal idyllic relations. It has pitilessly torn
asunder the motley feudal ties that bound man to
his "natural superiors" and has left no other bond
between man and man than naked self-interest,
than callous "cash payment."

The bourgeoisie has torn away from the family
its sentimental veil, and has reduced the family
relation to a mere money relation … The
bourgeoisie cannot exist without constantly
revolutionizing the instruments of production, and
thereby the relations of production, and with them
the whole relations of society.

QUESTIONS

1. Explain the issue presented by the Sadler Report.

2. What would Adam Smith, Andrew Ure, Karl Marx,
   and Friedrich Engels say about the conditions
   presented in the Sadler Report?

3. What does Ure really mean when he refers to "our
   enlightened manufacturers"?

4. Consider the political, economic, and social
   conditions of the nineteenth century in Europe.
   Why might parents allow their children to work in
   conditions described in the Sadler Report?

5. Examine the Canada Labour Code. What
   restrictions are placed on child labour in Canada
   today?

6. Compare and contrast the child labour conditions
   in a twentieth century underdeveloped country
   with that of a European country in the nineteenth
   century.

UNIT III
Imperialism

Overview

*M*odern imperialism refers to the period in global history, from 1880 to 1914, when the few remaining independent areas of the globe came under the dominance of one industrial power or another. The renewed interest in empire was caused by the dwindling supplies of resources needed to continue industrial growth. By the 1880s most surface and underground resources in Europe had been exhausted. If standards of living were to improve, then new supplies would have to be attained by expanding empires.

This quest for new resources was global in extent. Railroads were constructed to reach into the heart of continents for the required commodities. Steam-powered ships, which could sail against the wind and the tide, rushed the goods to the waiting factories. Rivalries quickly developed among major powers over control of these new supplies. The **scramble for Africa** is an example of how and why the industrial nations exploited the resources of this untouched continent. By the end of the nineteenth century, all but a few isolated places on the globe had come within the sphere of influence of a major power.

Modern imperialism, however, was not based entirely on economic need. Missionaries brought a religious thrust to the movement in their desire to help less fortunate peoples. They secured a role for themselves in bringing western culture to the outside world through religion, health, and education.

At the end of the eighteenth century, other nations outside Europe, including the United States, Japan, and Russia, began their own long road to industrialization. They too sought spheres of influence and soon competed with the Europeans to control global resources. Tensions developed during this rivalry, sometimes leading to war.

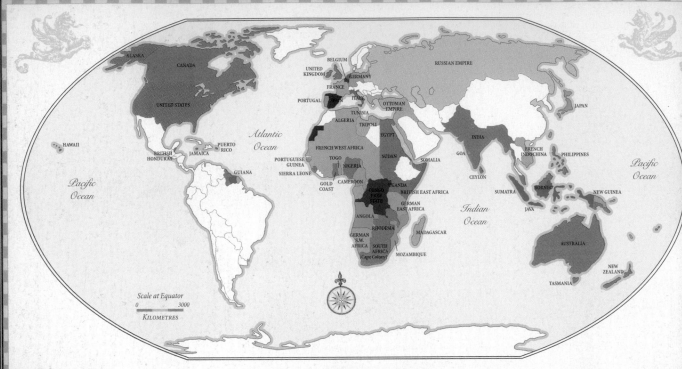

AMERICAN	*BELGIAN*	*BRITISH*		*DUTCH*	*FRENCH*	*GERMAN*	*ITALIAN*	*JAPANESE*
United States	Belgium	United Kingdom (England,	Gold Coast	Netherlands	France	Germany	Italy	Japan
Alaska	Congo Free State	Ireland, Scotland, Wales)	Jamaica	Borneo	Algeria	Cameroon	Eritrea	Formosa
Hawaii		Bahamas	Malta	Celebes	French Guiana	German East Africa	Italian Somalia	
Philippines		Barbados	New Zealand	Dutch Guiana	French Indochina	German New Guinea		*TURKISH*
Puerto Rico		Bermuda	Nigeria	Java	French Somalia	German S.W. Africa		Ottoman Empire
		British East Africa	Rhodesia	New Guinea	French West Africa	New Pomerania		Tripoli
		British Guiana	Sarawak	Sumatra	Guadeloupe	Togo		
		British Honduras	Sierra Leone		Madagascar			
		British Indian Empire	South Africa		Martinique			
PORTUGUESE		British New Guinea	Sudan		New Caledonia			
Portugal		British Somalia	Tasmania		Tunisia			
Angola		Ceylon	Trinidad					
Goa		Commonwealth of Australia	Uganda			*SPANISH*		
Mozambique		Dominion of Canada			*RUSSIAN*	Spain		
Portuguese Guinea		Egypt			Russian Empire	Rio de Oro		

EUROPEAN EMPIRES BY 1900

*By 1900, powerful industrialized nations
had divided up much of the earth's surface.*

Chapter 10
The Imperial Age
1880–1914

FOCUS ON:

The nature of imperialism;

The relationship between imperial powers and their colonies;

The impact of colonial rivalry on European diplomacy.

The Imperial Age refers to the period from 1880 to 1914 when the great powers of Europe sought to dominate the world. It was not the first time that stronger nations have become imperial nor will it be the last. The Industrial Revolution created such a wide difference between the Great Powers of Europe and other nations that the new empire building took a completely different tone. The industrial powers—Great Britain, France, and Germany—seized control of other regions in a race to secure resources needed for continued industrial growth. The subject countries were not strong enough to resist the major powers. The industrial nations had terrifying weapons of war, strong armies and navies that brutally pushed aside all resistance. None could stand in their way as steamships and railways carried imperial forces into the hearts of continents and to the furthest corners of the globe. Thus by the beginning of the twentieth century, almost all the world's peoples had come under the domination of one industrial power or another.

Great Britain had by far the largest empire, bound together by well-protected sea lanes. At its peak it contained a fifth of the world's population and a quarter of its land surface. "The sun never sets upon the British Empire," was a proud British boast. Only after 1880 did France, Germany, and Russia (and at the end of the century the United States and Japan) emerge as rivals.

The competition for empire created tension between the major powers. There was only so much land to be had. The

---

TIMELINE

Egypt and the Nile

1798 ❀ French Army under Napoleon invades Egypt. French influence in Egypt begins.

1869 ❀ Suez Canal completed.

1875 ❀ Egypt sells its shares in the Suez Canal to the British, resulting in a joint Anglo-French administration.

1876 ❀ British-French consortium takes over the Egyptian debt problem.

1880 ❀ Egyptian colonel Arabi (El-Wahid) leads the national resistance against foreign control.

1882 ❀ Britain invades Egypt.

1884 ❀ General Gordon's Nile campaign against the Mahdi leads to the siege of Khartoum.

1898 ❀ British and French forces face each other at Fashoda

Central Africa

1857 ❀ Dr. Livingstone gives his heart of darkness message.

1871 ❀ Stanley meets Livingstone on the Lualaba River.

1876 ❀ International Geographic Congress on Central Africa called by Leopold II of Belgium. King Leopold gains the rights to the Congo for himself.

1880s ❀ Major power thrusts into the Congo region.

1883 ❀ Belgium-French tensions in the Congo region.

1884 ❀ German intrusion in African affairs.

1885 ❀ Berlin Congress on Africa.

South Africa

1877 ❀ Transvaal is declared a British protectorate. Zulu wars

1880 ❀ Boer resistance to British administration brings partial independence to the Transvaal.

1890 ❀ Cecil Rhodes calls for volunteers to make the Pioneer Trek to the Zambesi River so that he can establish Rhodesia.

1895 ❀ The governor of Rhodesia, Dr. Jameson, leads an unauthorized invasion of the Transvaal.

1899–1902 ❀ The Boer War

1910 ❀ The Union of South Africa is created.

---

threat of war was used on ma[ny] occasions over the ownership [of] some barren piece of rock for [no] other reason than the othe[r] must not have it. To be first to [lay] claim to an area was one thi[ng.] To hold it through effective oc[cu]pation was quite another. Th[is] was expensive and requir[ed] strong armies and navies.

The major powers look[ed] upon the older, multination[al] empires of the Spanish, P[or]tuguese, Chinese, and Ottom[an] Turks as easy prey. Howev[er] they could not pursue empire[in] the Americas which had alrea[dy] become established as a Unit[ed] States sphere of influence. Wi[th]in this sphere, the Latin Ame[ri]can countries were able to dev[el]op independently, while the U[nit]ed States and Canada partition[ed] North America. Imperial riva[lry] was strongest in Africa. T[he] scramble to divide the Afric[an] continent among themselv[es] resulted in increasing war[like] competition.

Within the Russian sphere [the] tsarist government forged ahe[ad] with the conquest of Sibe[ria] until coming eventually to Ch[ina] and Japan. The very size [of] China limited western pene[tra]tion to a few small concessi[ons] around Canton and Beijing. T[he] Japanese rushed through th[eir] own industrialization progr[am] and became an imperial po[wer] in their own right thereby preventing imperialist takeo[ver] in their own country. By 1900 they had begun to exert th[eir] influence over Korea.

Imperialism touched off a wave of missionary z[eal] among the Europeans who came to see empire as a me[ans] of transmitting to the conquered the benefits of th[eir]

Queen Victoria (1819–1901) presided over a remarkable period of global expansion that brought wealth and power to Britain. However, there was not a single year during her reign that British forces were not fighting on a frontier on one of the world's continents.

vilization and the Christian ligion. There was a rush of ssions to the heart of the rican continent to minister to e peoples there. Missionaries d colonial administrators ould bring western civiliza- n to what the British poet dyard Kipling called the sser breeds without the law." Kipling believed that empire ovided the means to impose the subject peoples a more mane way of life. Applauding nerican imperialism in the ilippines in 1899, he wrote of e "white man's burden" to civ- e the rest of the world. Impe- lists such as Kipling believed was the moral responsibility the white race to bring the vantages of modern Euro an culture to "inferior" soci- es. The French called it their *ssion civilisatrice*, the Ger- ns diffused *Kultur*, the Amer- ns their "Manifest Destiny." et, in spite of all the high ral tone, the primary motive empire was economic. Need- more resources and wanting re material goods, the major powers looked to colonies imported goods to sustain their standard of living, se population, and industrialization. Colonies would o be useful as protected markets for excess production, ces for investment, and a possible solution to the prob- s of European overpopulation.

hroughout the expanding empires, attempts were made nstill western systems of religion, administration, law taxation, programs of health care and education, net- rks of commerce, transportation and communication, acceptable codes of conduct. This attempt at a mas- transfer of culture on a global scale met with only lim- success. Only within the colonial ruling classes was e of western culture adapted to local needs. For most he colonized people, western culture was to be endured

only as long as the imperial powers were in control.

The industrial nations could not understand why their hu- manitarian crusade was resisted. Yet everywhere resistance arose. During the reign of Queen Victo- ria (from 1837 to 1901), there was not a single year in which British forces were not fighting on a frontier on one of the world's continents. There were so many campaigns that few kept track of them all. To the British public it was a normal way of life.

The first shots were fired shortly after Victoria's corona- tion when William Lyon Macken- zie, sometime mayor of Toronto, tried to turn the Canadas into a republic with American help. At the same time, a rebellion in Lower Canada led by the Rouges was quickly contained with min- imal loss of life. The following year, the first of the Afghan wars broke out, followed by fighting in China, Africa, the Canadian North-West, Australia, New Zea- land, reaching a climax in the Boer War of 1899–1902.

Although some African leaders took the path of open defiance, most decided to bend with the wind and wait out their new masters. They did not completely reject European culture, keeping what was of benefit to them such as transportation networks, educational systems, mil- itary organization, and legal systems. In the end, it was not so much a European culture that survived but rather an urban-industrial culture that today links the business, gov- ernment, and artistic elites on a global scale.

After the Berlin Conference in 1884 the quest for empire became government policy in Europe. The informal arrangements of missionaries and traders gave way to, annexation and occupation. Traders and missionaries sim- ply did not have the means to take on the expense of running empires. Where admin-istration and armed force were required to keep colonies in control, governments would have to get involved.

Political leaders such as Benjamin Disraeli, Bismarck, Theodore Roosevelt, John A. Macdonald, Lord Grey, Lord Salisbury, and a host of others, used the press to manipulate popular support for their expansionist policies. The human, physical, military, and financial costs of empire were often ignored in discussions and writings of the time. The boundaries of empire were to be expanded for no other reason than leaders and populace believed it was a good thing to do.

In the end, empire was per-ceived by the public as a matter of national prestige. Once roused the masses fully supported the use of armed force and conquest. Empire became impor-tant be-cause the press and the public declared it to be so.

Rudyard Kipling

Rudyard Kipling (1835–1936) was a popular English writer, born in India. His works express a romantic view of English imperialism in such poems as "Mandalay," "Gunga Din," and "The White Man's Burden."

Take up the White Man's burden—

Send out the best ye breed—

Go bind your sons to exile,

To serve your captives' need;

To wait in heavy harness,

On fluttered folk and wild—

Your new-caught sullen peoples,

Half devil and half child.

"The White Man's Burden"
from The Five Nations.

he ruled Egypt until 1848. T modernization of Egypt beg during his viceroyship.

An array of palaces and pub buildings was erected, a go system of modern educati was developed. Hundreds Egyptians were sent to stu abroad and bring back n ideas for reshaping Egypti society. New roads and can transformed the Nile Del French officers helped to recr and train an army drawn fr the *fellahin* ("common p ple"). All this and much mo was financed by Europe banks at high interest rates.

Muhammad had visions o revived Egyptian Empire stret ing south along the Nile Ri into Sudan towards the gr lakes that straddle the equa He ordered Egyptian for beyond the mighty cataracts

the place where the White and Blue Nile meet, at Khartou From Khartoum, his armies were poised to invade Sud and destroy the centuries-old slave trade that was the o economic system in the region. He then would send armies to force their way across the barrier of the Gr Sudd, a 160-km-wide papyrus swamp, towards Zanzik This conquest would make the Egyptian empire far grea than ever dreamed of by the ancient pharaohs.

When the Ottoman Empire began showing signs decay, Muhammad became distracted from conquer Sudan and saw his chance to pry Syria from Ottoman c trol. This proved his downfall. The major powers inten the Ottoman Empire to stay in existence. Britain a France agreed to support the sultan against Muhamm to prevent the collapse of the Ottoman Empire and the p sibility that Constantinople would then fall into Russian sphere of influence. (See the Crimean Wa Chapter 8.). Muhammad was forced to withdraw fr Syria and refocus his dreams of empire on Sudan.

EGYPT AND THE NILE

There was rivalry between France and Britain over Egypt when Napoleon I's forces invaded Egypt in 1798. After the British fleet cut the French supply lines and Admiral Nelson destroyed the French Fleet at the Battle of the Nile, Napoleon's expedition to Egypt was over. He abandoned his forces and returned to France. Those French personnel who were left behind began to exert a major influence on Egyptian affairs.

In 1805, Muhammad Ali (ca. 1769–1849), an Albanian adventurer and common soldier who rose through the ranks much as had Napoleon, seized power in Egypt and forced the Ottoman sultan, his overlord, to recognize him as viceroy. Supported by both the British and the French,

This photograph of the Suez Canal was taking during dredging and construction.

...ez Canal

...hammad's son and successor, ...d, signed an agreement with ...rench investment consortium ... dig a canal between the ...diterranean and Red Sea in ...er to cut weeks from the ...gthy sea voyage around ...ica. The Suez Canal was ...gun in 1859 and completed in ...9. It is the largest artificial ...terway in the eastern hemi-...ere, one of the major engi-...ring feats of all time. From ... moment of its opening, it ...ame one of the world's major ... lanes carrying trade between ...ia, Asia, and Europe.

...gypt got little out of the Suez ...nal. It had signed an agree-...nt that gave the Canal Com-...y a 99-year lease on shipping ...s and canal operations. The ...y way an Egyptian could ben-... from the canal was from ...king on it or buying compa-...hares. Said's son, Ismael, borrowed four million pounds ... this purpose.

∾ Suez Canal Facts ∾

1. 160 km long

2. connects the Mediterranean Sea at the north end to the Gulf of Suez and the Red Sea at the south end

3. built between 1859–1869

4. designed by French engineer Ferdinand de Lesseps who supervised its building

5. de Lesseps also worked on the Panama Canal (1878)

6. seized by the British in 1882

7. nationalized by Egypt in 1956

8. closed to all shipping from 1967 to 1975, during the Arab-Israeli War

9. reopened in 1975

10. enlarged to accommodate oil super-tankers, 1976–1980

When Ismael came to power, he wanted to speed up Egypt's industrial development. Larger and larger loans were taken out from European banks at exorbitant interest rates. The loans were guaranteed by the sale of Egyptian cotton. For a brief time, profits poured in but after the end of the American Civil War the market for Egyptian cotton collapsed, leaving Ismael heavily in debt to the amount of 90 million pounds. In 1875 he sold his shares in the canal to the British to avoid bankruptcy.

In 1876 Britain and France took control of Egypt's finances under the Caisse de la Dette Publique and replaced Ismael's advisors with their own. One of the first measures undertaken by the foreign advisors was to stop Egyptian expansion into Sudan.

Ismael had hired British General Charles Gordon (1833–1885) to command the Egyptian forces in the south

EGYPT AND THE EGYPTIAN EMPIRE

In 1882, the British occupied Egypt to protect the Suez Canal. Why is this waterway so difficult to protect?

as they opened up the vast area along the Nile, then under control of slave traders. Both Gordon and Ismael had been warned of the dangers of interference in the slave trade as it would touch off a general uprising. The slave trade was the only commerce being conducted in that part of Central Africa. To destroy it meant total economic collapse and chaos within the region. Orders were to halt all military activity in Sudan.

On 18 February, 1879, a mob kidnapped Nubar Pasha, the Ottoman head of the Egyptian cabinet, and Rivers Wilson, the cabinet's appointed English treasurer. Ismael rushed his soldiers to the scene. They carried out a dramatic rescue. It later became known that Ismael had staged the whole event to show his foreign masters the need for his own return to power.

His plan worked and he was reinstated in control of the cabinet. Ismael promptly replaced his foreign advisers with his own people. He then ordered General Gordon to set out once more to Khartoum, smash the slave trade in Sudan, and conquer Equatoria to the south. The Nile would become a 5000-km Egyptian highway linking the wealth of Central Africa to Cairo. Ismael envisioned a fleet of armed steamers that would ply the waterways above the cataracts and a series of forts built towards the equator and Lake Victoria to hold the subject nations under control.

It was not as easy as it appeared. Gordon's army had to fight its way through inhospitable deserts. Then, reaching the Sudd it had to hack its way through dense brush and reeds in a seemingly never-ending marshland that barred the final approaches to the lakes. As Gordon advanced through the fetid rain forest that stretched westward

across the continent to t[...] Atlantic, he came to realize th[...] there were no riches to be h[...] there. He advised Ismael [...] leave the whole area to the sla[...] traders.

Egypt for the Egyptian[...]

In June of 1879, Khedive Ism[...] was replaced by his son Tewf[...] Shortly after, in 1880, a new ki[...] of nationalism arose in Eg[...] that was to shake the thro[...] Colonel Arabi, El-Wahid ("t[...] only one"), started a moveme[...] of national resistance. He wa[...] ed Egypt for the Egyptians a[...] demanded an end to forei[...] domination—especially to Ot[...] man control from Constanti[...] ple. He drew a large following[...] his cause that called for in[...] pendence from the Briti[...] French, and the Ottoman Tur[...]

Arabi's nationalist movem[...] threatened the security of [...] Suez Canal. Premier Gambe[...] of France urged Prime Minis[...] Gladstone of Britain to join in[...] invasion to get rid of Ara[...] Gladstone agreed that sor[...] thing would have to be do[...] but he and the Liberal pa[...] were sympathetic towards independence movements.

At one point Gladstone suggested using Turkish arm[...] but the French were wary lest this touch off a gene[...] *jihad* ("holy war") that would engulf the Mediterrane[...] The French were already engaged in a costly war[...] annexation against the Berbers in Tunisia. When Gamb[...] was defeated in the elections of January 1882, Fre[...] enthusiasm for the attack disappeared.

In the end, the British acted alone. After the killing o[...] Europeans in Alexandria by Arabi's followers, Adm[...] Seymour ordered the destruction of the city. The mass[...] firepower from the British fleet drove Arabi's men into [...] desert where they were vulnerable.

The goal of the Mahdi (1848–1885)
was to free Sudan from Egyptian control.

Gladstone supported the ...hts of minorities to self-rule. ...t Arabi's actions endangered ...e canal. The Suez Canal had ...come a **lifeline,** linking ...tain to India and East Asia. It ...s' of strategic economic ...portance and had to be pro-...ted. General Wolseley, with ...000 men drawn from Malta ...d Cyprus and a further 10 000 ...m India, was ordered to ...sh the rebellion and restore ...ler. The British invasion of ...ypt in 1882 was a turning ...nt in British imperial history. ...e British were drawn into a ...gthy occupation of Egypt ...t was to last until 1956.

...While all attention was riveted ...Cairo, an even greater threat ...Egypt was rising in Sudan. The ...hdi ("Expected One"), a reli-...us zealot, raised the desert ...ions against the Egyptian invasion forces. Recognized ...some as a descendant of the Prophet Muhammad, he ...w the discontented to his banner. His goal was to free ...dan from Egyptian control. His advance guards came out ...he desert taking fort after fort and routing opposing ...ies. These guards caused difficulties for foreign inter-...s in the Sudan.

...n the face of this new threat, General Gordon was sent ...he Nile in 1884 to evacuate all Egyptian forces and the ...ign missions that remained. Sudan was to be aban-...ed. Before he could bring in the outlying missions and ...isons, Gordon himself was besieged in Khartoum by ...Mahdists. The siege began in March and lasted until the ...owing January.

...took several months before the British government ...ld even debate the need to send a relief expedition to ...don. After all, Gordon was acting for the Egyptian gov-...ment not for Britain. Experience had shown that a ...perly defended city could outlast its besiegers. Surely, ...Mahdists would melt away when their food ran out. ...d not Gordon more than 34 000 soldiers in Khartoum, ...hom 8000 were experienced? Fellow officers believed

he should be able to hold out forever. Thus it was not until September 1884 that a small force was authorized to proceed to his rescue, with General Wolseley at its head.

Instead of the shorter 750-km route from the Red Sea to Khartoum, General Wolsey chose the much longer route of the Nile. He would get his forces over the cataracts just as he had managed to overcome the difficulties of Niagara Falls and the Canadian Shield during the Red River Campaign of 1870. (Many Canadians who had been on the earlier expedition volunteered their services for the Nile campaign. They became the first Canadian troops to serve overseas.)

The march up the Nile was delayed at every turn. There were not enough boats to carry the full force at one time. There was a shortage of food for the camels and not enough of them to carry any sort of relief across the desert. At times the column was strung out for hundreds of kilometres between the cataracts. It was more a progression than a rescue force. At no time was there any evidence of haste. It was not until December that Wolseley reached Dongola, from which the desert column could set out for Khartoum.

Even then, the small British force had to fight its way through to reach Metemma above the sixth cataract, from which armed steamers could carry them the final distance. When they arrived at Khartoum they found they were too late. The city had fallen just 48 hours earlier. Gordon had been killed in fighting on the palace steps.

The fall of Khartoum sent shock waves throughout the Empire. It was just not possible for an untrained poorly-equipped African army to defeat a modern army under British leadership. "Too Late!" screamed the headlines. Why had the government waited so long to send aid? Why had the longer route been taken? What had the British government done in the 11 months Gordon had held out? Queen Victoria made her views known in an open telegram to

Dr. David Livingstone, the famous British missionary and explorer in Africa, wanted to free Africans from the yoke of slavery. How can you tell that this picture was drawn from a European, not African, perspective?

Gladstone. She would have to bear the brunt of the shame. What would the other monarchs think of her? Stung by the outcry Gladstone ordered Wolseley to prepare to crush the Mahdists and wreak havoc on the slave trade. The public wanted revenge and revenge it would have.

However before the Sudan campaign could get under way, a new threat to the empire arose. A minor skirmish between Russian soldiers and Afghans kindled fears that Russia might be trying to take control of the Khyber Pass and invade India. The entire British Army would be needed to defend against this threat. India was the jewel in the British Crown and it would be foolhardy to leave troops in Sudan if India was in peril. The Russian threat turned out to be false but when attention returned to Sudan the British public had lost all interest in it. Wolseley was ordered to return his army to Cairo.

Shortly after capturing Khartoum, the Mahdi died of typhus in 1885 and was entombed at nearby Omdurman. His successor Khalita Abdallahi chose to attack Abyssinia and capture the Red Sea ports rather than march down the Nile against the Egyptians. Along the east coast he encountered and was defeated by the armies of the Ethiopian Emperor Yohannes and a variety of mixed forces including British, Italian, German, and Zanzibar troops.

CENTRAL AFRICA—THE CONGO

In 1857, Dr. David Livingstone, the famous British missionary and explorer in Africa, wrote an emotional plea to the civilized world to bring light to the millions of Africans living in the "**heart of darkness**." After a life-long career exploring and ministering to the nation: Central Africa, he wanted the world to know that the in rior of Africa was not empty as Europeans thought but teeming with millions of people in need of help.

He proposed replacing the slave trade, the only met of commerce in the region, with other forms of indus He called for more medicines to fight malaria and ot insect-borne diseases. He wanted to put an end to the c tinuous tribal warfare and cannibalism among the Afri nations. He was loved and respected by the Africans. called for a Christian crusade to bring civilization to peoples of the rain forest in the name of humanity.

Henry Morton Stanley (1841–1904) was a correspon for the New York *Herald*. His paper sent him in searc Livingstone who was himself in search of the source of

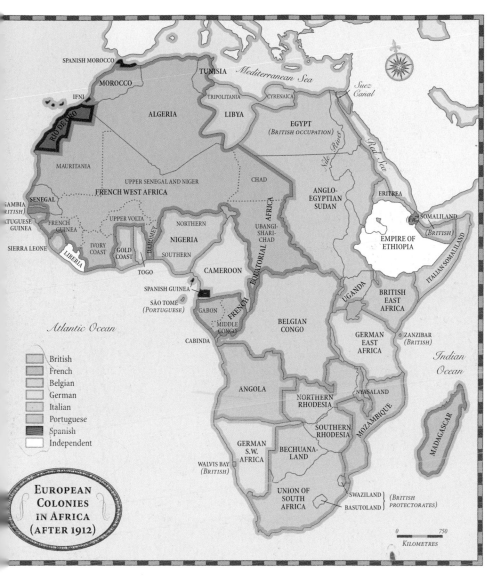

European Colonies in Africa (after 1912)

SPANISH MOROCCO
MOROCCO
IFNI
RIO DE ORO
TUNISIA
Mediterranean Sea
ALGERIA
LIBYA
TRIPOLITANIA
CYRENAICA
Suez Canal
EGYPT
(BRITISH OCCUPATION)
MAURITANIA
Nile River
Red Sea
CHAD
UPPER SENEGAL AND NIGER
FRENCH WEST AFRICA
ANGLO-EGYPTIAN SUDAN
ERITREA
SOMALILAND (BRITISH)
GAMBIA (BRITISH)
SENEGAL
FRENCH GUINEA
UPPER VOLTA
PORTUGUESE GUINEA
SIERRA LEONE
LIBERIA
IVORY COAST
GOLD COAST
DAHOMEY
TOGO
NORTHERN
NIGERIA
SOUTHERN
CAMEROON
SPANISH GUINEA
SÃO TOMÉ (PORTUGUESE)
GABON
MIDDLE CONGO
CABINDA
UBANGI-SHARI-CHAD
FRENCH EQUATORIAL AFRICA
FRENCH
EMPIRE OF ETHIOPIA
ITALIAN SOMALILAND
UGANDA
BRITISH EAST AFRICA
ZANZIBAR (BRITISH)
BELGIAN CONGO
GERMAN EAST AFRICA
Atlantic Ocean
Indian Ocean
ANGOLA
NORTHERN RHODESIA
NYASALAND
MOZAMBIQUE
SOUTHERN RHODESIA
MADAGASCAR
GERMAN S.W. AFRICA
BECHUANALAND
WALVIS BAY (BRITISH)
UNION OF SOUTH AFRICA
SWAZILAND
BASUTOLAND
(BRITISH PROTECTORATES)

British
French
Belgian
German
Italian
Portuguese
Spanish
Independent

EUROPEAN COLONIES IN AFRICA (AFTER 1912)

0   750
Kilometres

By 1912, there were only two African states that had managed to escape European domination.

and Congo rivers that emptied the interior were themselves lost in the thousands of sandbars and deltas that range along the coast. Only a handful of traders lived among the malaria-infected backwaters, eking out an existence from the ivory brought to them by Africans. There were no natural harbours; waterfalls and cataracts blocked attempts to go up river.

Despite these warnings, Leopold volunteered to head a crusade to open Africa in the interests of humanity. The plan was to crusade under the banner of Christianity, commerce, scientific exploration, and ending the slave trade. This crusade would give him claim to the region. An International Association was established with offices in Brussels and Paris. The association was a private enterprise controlled by Leopold who considered Africa to be an empty, uncivilized place, open for the taking. The French were allowed to participate in the crusade because the French explorer Pierre Savorgnan de Brazza had already been active in the Congo. Brazza had claimed huge areas of land for France, trading with the local tribal chiefs for a few trinkets and pieces of cloth.

Leopold needed someone knowledgeable about the region who could go to the Congo and claim it for him. That someone was Stanley. As the International Geographic Congress came to a close, Stanley was leaving on his second attempt to explore the Lualaba from Livingstone Station to wherever it emptied into the sea. He had entered Africa from Zanzibar previously, in 1874, and had spent two years circumnavigating lakes Tanganyika, Victoria, and Albert. He was quite certain now that Lake Victoria was the headwater of the Nile but the Lualaba would have to be descended as final proof.

On 20 October 1876, he set off downstream for the

r Nile. The two met at Livingstone's mission on the aba River in 1871. Both men thought that the Lualaba d be the headwaters of the Nile. The only way to find was to trace its path to the coast. This Stanley mpted in 1871. The river turned out to be the Congo, Stanley's articles about Africa excited the public's rest—and brought him to the attention of King Leopold f Belgium.

eopold had been looking for a colony to seize. He saw tanley's descriptions of Central Africa and in Living- e's plea, the opportunity to carve for himself a huge ony in Africa. To this end, the king assembled the Inter- onal Geographic Congress on Central Africa in 1876. reports on the Congo were not encouraging. Africa's ntic coastline consists of hundreds of kilometres of low- g, mosquito-infested swamps. The mouths of the Niger

Henry Morton Stanley explored the Congo region at the request of King Leopold II of Belgium.

1400-km epic journey through the rain forest. The dry uplands of the east coast that he had become used to quickly gave way to the dank, humid, fetid atmosphere of a watery land canopied by immense jungle trees. The sluggish river entered swamps. Progress was agonizingly slow. The Africans fled at his approach, fearing he was a slave trader; what food there was to be had to be taken forcibly. Day after day his men fought off attacks by the river nations. Staying outside the range of African spears, the Europeans massacred those who stood in their way.

For nine months, Stanley and his men ran the gauntlet of starvation and disease. The seven cataracts of the Stanley Falls were managed, as were the thirty-two of the Livingstone Falls just 130 km beyond. Then on 5 August 1877, from a point above the last cataract, he sent a desperate message to anyone at the coast to bring help as he could no longer go on. Two days later, he and his party were rescued and carried by litter to the trade station at Bomba.

Stanley had proven that the Lualaba was in fact the Congo River and that its whole watershed was really a murky rain forest with little of value for Europeans apart from the slave trade. He had crossed the continent,

travelling 1140 km in 999 days. His diaries chronicled horrors of the final part of the trip beset by hostile nati and short on food and ammunition. But it was the hin palm oil, rubber, and ivory that caught Leopold's attent:

Leopold sent Stanley back to Africa as governor of newly declared Congo Free State. Stanley was to buil road from the coast to above the first cataract to what called the Pool—a long lake that gives access to 8000 of navigable waterway. Belgian steamers would ply upper Congo bringing its resources downstream to tr. Belgian forts and trade stations would dot the riv shores to stop anyone else from trading in the area. objective was effective occupation and monopolizatio trade, not the traditional free trade of the trading con nies.

It would take Stanley the better part of two years to p the road through and when he got to the Pool he dis ered the French were already there. He had been be: by Brazza who had come down from the north to estak himself at a site later known as Brazzaville. The P Branch of the International Association supported Br: and sought to close the Congo to all but French trade

ench in the Congo

emier Gambetta trumpeted the success of France in nging the world to the Congo. The colours of France w proudly over Brazzaville. But the French were grow-; disillusioned of empire as a result of their costly war Tunis against the Berbers and Gambetta's government s toppled. The French withdrawal left the Congo open Stanley who acted quickly to secure the trading region m his base at Leopoldville.

A year later French interests in Central Africa were ived with a plan to strike overland across the Sahara wards the Niger River and Timbuctu African troops ald be poured into the region from Algeria and Tunis hout affecting the strength of the home armies. The nara would act as a land bridge to Central Africa.

The French had been outmanoeuvred by the British in ypt over the Suez Canal but they were resolved not to 'fer that loss of prestige again. France would not be >wed to sink to the level of a third-rate power like Italy. African empire would restore French honour.

n 1883 Colonel Desbordes reached Timbuctu. There s not much for the taking. The capital city was a large hering of mud huts. Disappointed but not discouraged, French decided to venture downstream to the mouth he Niger and contest the palm oil trade with the British. 'rime Minister Gladstone was not keen on getting olved with the French in a war over the Niger trade. At t he tried to revive the idea of a private company that uld handle British interests. But when the company used to meet its responsibilities, the government acted nnex the region. France reacted by sending a gunboat he coast annexing Dahomey. French trading posts soon he under the guns of British gunboats that laid waste h banks of the Niger River for hundreds of kilometres. sions between the two powers now spilled over into opean diplomacy.

he French would not retreat. However at that time gland needed an eight-million-pound European loan, nly from French sources, to help restore Alexandria ch they had destroyed. The French were slow to >ond to the request for a loan, threatening not to go for-d with the request unless some agreement could be hed on Africa. France also received unexpected sup-: from Germany.

erman interest in any colonial venture was unex-ted. It shook the diplomatic community. Bismarck had always maintained that colonies were too costly and that Germany's interests lay solely in Europe. Thus the arrival of the German gunboat *Mowe* off the west coast of Africa was a complete surprise. Germany then proceeded to lay claim to Togo, the Cameroons, German South West Africa, and large areas on the east coast opposite Zanzibar.

BISMARCK'S COLONIAL VENTURE

*B*ismarck had sent secret instructions to lay claim to a colonial empire in Africa. His orders were so secret his closest advisors were not told about them. Bismarck had always maintained that Germany was the most vulnerable of all the major powers because it is situated in the middle of Europe. His policies were always European oriented. In his view, war in Europe had to be made impossible. What then was the German chancellor doing dabbling in the colonial matters where rival claims could lead to war?

Bismarck later told the tsar that his plan had been a scam. He had wanted to discredit the heir to the German throne, Crown Prince Friedrich. Friedrich's admiration of Britain and the British parliamentary institutions of democracy was not approved of by Bismarck or the Kaiser. Bismarck knew that the establishment of German colonies could provoke a struggle with Britain. Friedrich would have to choose sides and be forced to give up his British ideas.

By annexing colonies Bismarck could also get rid of the Liberal nuisance in the *Reichstag*. While raising protective tariffs, he would crush the Liberal platform of free trade. Bismarck was certain that the industrialists and the working classes would rally behind protective tariffs and the throne. But he was wrong.

German trading companies refused to bear the expense of exploration and defence. The German taxpayers would have to shoulder the burden after all. To give up the colonies would mean a loss of prestige, but Bismarck could make certain no new colonies were established. He called another conference on Africa.

In 1885, 14 nations gathered in Berlin to reach an agree-ment on territorial claims to Africa. Most European nations and the United States attended. Leopold of Belgium was par-ticularly anxious to have his claims to the Congo recog-nized. In this he had the support of the Americans.

The chief interest of King Leopold II of Belgium (1835–1909) was to expand Belgium's territories. He invested his family fortune in laying claim to the central interior of Africa.

President Chester Arthur insisted that the American Congress recognize the Congo Free State as belonging to King Leopold. He viewed Leopold's antislavery program for Central Africa as a way to help sway the black voters in the upcoming American elections.

At American insistence Leopold did promise to permit free trade along the Congo River in exchange for international recognition. He also promised that should he ever decide to sell the Congo, the government of France would have first rights of purchase.

German claims to colonies were also recognized. In return the Germans agreed to help evacuate the Christian missions in Sudan and Equatoria and to limit the expansion of the Mahdist forces.

In 1886 a commission partitioned the region around Lake Tanganyika between the British and Germans, giving both access to the lake. The region around Mount Kilimanjaro would become a British **protectorate.** This preserved an all-British land route between Cairo and Cape Town. It also blocked attempts by Germany to link its colonies in a band across the continent, interrupting the British corridor.

THE FASHODA CRISIS

By 1890 the major powers had pushed their African spheres of influence to the watersheds separating Africa's major rivers. Friction and rivalry between the powers came very close to warfare in the years between 1885 and 1900.

There were Portuguese in Angola and Mozambique; Italians had huge parts of Somalia and Eritrea. Germany had colonies in East Africa in the Cameroons and Togo. The French controlled Algeria, Tunis, and most of West

Africa and dreamed of territo from Kakar to the Gulf of Ad The British had visions of "British Africa from Cape Cairo."

Fashoda (now called Koko a mud-hut village in a swan was the setting for a showdo between France and Brita already tense over their rivalry Morocco and Egypt.

In 1898 the French sent Ca tain J. B. Marchand with a sm party from North Africa to fi his way up the Niger and acro the watershed into the N Basin. If challenged, he was claim that France was trying assert its claim to a seat at a future conference called Egypt. The British were cert that Marchand's column w large enough to lay claim to head waters of the Nile and th control the entire waterway cutting off the flow of the ri whenever they chose to do so.

The British, under General Kitchener, were head southward, up the Nile. They had decided at long las make a major effort towards Khartoum. Lord Kitche was ordered to capture Khartoum, defeat the Mahc armies and link up with a second British column approa ing from Uganda to the south. The Ugandan column banded after some of the African troops mutinied a killed their officers.

Marchand arrived at Fashoda first and at once v besieged by Mahdist forces. He had no hope of holding and prayed for rescue by Lord Kitchener's column wh he knew to be then marching up the Nile.

Kitchener had a successful campaign, piling vict upon victory. A young Winston Churchill marched with army. At Omdurman Kitchener destroyed the m Mahdist army of 50 000 and then levelled the city as v as the Mahdi's tomb. He then purposefully moved towards Fashoda and the rescue of Marchand.

The meeting between the two was cordial. Despite

ct that national prestige was at
ake they refrained from shoot-
g at each other. Both sides
ferred Fashoda to their respec-
e governments.

The reality was that Kitchener
uld have destroyed the French
ces at any time. Had such an
cident triggered a major war
tween France and England,
e British fleet would have sunk
e French fleets in the Atlantic
d the Mediterranean in an
ernoon's engagement. Faced
th the reality of British sea
wer, the French ordered Marc-
nd to evacuate his position
d return home.

A major crisis was avoided and
tain remained in control of
e Nile.

British prime minister Benjamin Disraeli (1804–1881) believed colonies were too costly and a heavy drain on the British taxpayer. He was particularly indifferent to Africa, believing that Britain had no strategic interests there.

OUTH AFRICA

ritain had seized control of the Dutch settlements around the Cape of Good Hope during the
Napoleonic Wars. In 1834, when Britain abol-
ed slavery within its empire, thousands of slave-owning
ers (Dutch farmers) trekked north to form the
publics of Natal, Orange Free State, and Transvaal out-
e the British sphere of influence. There they continued
heir traditional farming methods with slaves for farm
our.

By the middle of the eighteenth century there was a con-
erable number of whites in the region. The original set-
s were augmented by British and German immigration,
ticularly miners and land speculators.

n 1842 the British annexed Natal and the port city of Dur-
. Then in 1867 diamonds were discovered in the Trans-
l and thousands of British miners flooded the region to
k. The miners wanted British law and order and a British
liamentary style of government. The Boers were
osed to such a measure. In a democracy they would be
voted. Behind the question of the vote and British annex-
n lay the question of the ownership of the diamond and

gold mines. Did they belong to the Boer Republics or to the Cape Colony?

In 1877 a handful of Englishmen arrived in Pretoria, the capital of the Transvaal, and proclaimed its annexation to Britain. The Transvaal had gone bankrupt in a failed railway scheme that would have linked the interior to the coast. In addition, the continuous raids by Boers across the Zulu border to steal cattle and slaves had created an explosive situation. The British decided their forces were needed to restore order.

Although the Boers objected to the British takeover they all agreed to participate in the government administration, for the time being. Boer Vice-President Paul Kruger hastened to England to protest to the British government about the annexation. He received a friendly hearing from Gladstone and the Liberals who promised a review of the annexation should the Liberals come into power. The Conservative colonial secretary who was in power, Lord Carnarvon, gave Kruger an icy reception and conceded nothing.

Carnarvon had just presided over the successful federation of Britain's North American colonies into the Dominion of Canada. This was to become the model for subsequent groupings of colonies. He hoped to repeat this success in Africa. In Africa, his plan was that Britain would dominate Africa in a solid north/south band of British territory from the Cape to Cairo. He had already planned a railway system, the All Red Route (named after the red colour that denoted British territory on the maps), that would bind the region together. The Boer republics and African kingdoms along the route would have to submit to the master plan.

Although Carnarvon and later colonial secretaries hoped to implement the plan for domination peacefully, they were fully prepared to go to war if the need arose. Fired by the dream of a larger federation, local British governors often acted to seize African lands without London's approval and often acted without London's knowledge.

Conservative Prime Minister Benjamin Disraeli described the scheme as utter foolishness. He believed colonies were too costly and a heavy drain on the British taxpayer. He was more concerned with the tense international situation at Constantinople where Russia persisted in its demands to control the Straits. He was particularly indifferent to Africa, believing that Britain had no strategic interests there. As a seagoing trading nation, Britain should be interested in harbours and coastlines and the protection of its sea lanes by mighty battle fleets. These ventures were costly enough to maintain without having more colonies to support.

Invasion of Zululand

In South Africa the British governor of Cape Province wanted a war of expansion. King Cetewayo was given an ultimatum to disband his powerful army and accept British advisors. The governor informed Cetewayo that the white settlers would no longer stand for the threat of his large army along their borders. Besides, the sporadic massacres of Zulus by the whites would only result in the Zulu army invading Natal to seek revenge. This he could not allow to happen. "Civilization" could not exist with the threat of Cetewayo's army alongside.

Without waiting for a reply to the ultimatum, British forces invaded Zululand in 1877 and camped at a place called Isandlwana. It was a name that was to be written in blood. The British were so contemptuous of the African armies they did not bother to prepare any kind of defence against attack. When the Zulus swarmed over their position, few whites escaped the onslaught. Modern firepower was not enough to stem the tide of black soldiers that kept coming until the British were no more.

News of the massacre shocked Europe. How was it possible that a African force could overwhelm a modern European army? In Britain, the Disraeli government fell from power in disgrace. It would be up to Gladstone and the Liberals to retrieve the situation by destroying Zulu might. In subsequent battles, the Zulus were crushed and their nation divided into thirteen occupied districts.

The battle at Isandlwana did not go unnoticed by the Boers. If the Zulu, armed with spears, could defeat a modern British army why could Boers not do likewise?

Gladstone had promised Kruger that should the Liberals come to power he would act to restore independence [to] the Boer republics. Now all that appeared to have be[en] forgotten. Gladstone had completely dismissed the Bo[er] question from his mind as his government was beset [by] serious problems with Ireland. His hold on Parliament w[as] weak and the Irish MPs led by the Irish nationalist lead[er] Charles Parnell, were his biggest concern.

With the Isandlwana massacre, the difficulties wi[th] France over Egypt and the Niger, and Stanley's race for t[he] Pool, it seemed that Britain's African policy was comi[ng] apart. Despite Gladstone's personal beliefs in indepe[n]dence and self-government he saw his duty as prime mi[n]ister to defend the British Empire at all costs.

In 1880 the Boers in the Transvaal raised their flag [of] independence. They planned to attack Natal and captu[re] Durban. Once again the British forces were caught by s[ur]prise. The situation was stabilized only after reinforc[e]ments were rushed in. Gladstone then offered the Boe[rs] sovereignty in all but foreign affairs and the proviso th[at] Britain could intervene in the republics when it deem[ed] necessary. In return Kruger offered to give the British m[in]ers the vote but only after full independence was grant[ed].

Within a decade the Transvaal had become the rich[est] state in South Africa. Each year gold valued at 24 milli[on] pounds sterling was exported to finance an escalating ec[o]nomic boom.

Although Gladstone wanted to have little to do wi[th] South Africa, British governors in the region thought o[th]erwise. They had been caught up in Carnarvon's plans [for] federation. In particular, Cecil Rhodes, head of the [De] Beers Mining Corporation, openly advocated the All R[ed] Route from the Cape to Cairo. All that remained to do w[as] to seize Bechuanaland to the west of the Transvaal a[nd] then continue north through Matabeleland a[nd] Mashonaland to the Zambesi. There he would establi[sh] Rhodesia (now called Zimbabwe) and forge the last link [in] the chain to the British territories in the north.

Rhodes called for volunteers to make the Pioneer Tr[ek] of 1890 through the densely populated African kingdo[ms] to the Zambesi River. Those that made it would be giv[en] 3000 acres of land and 15 gold claims. As conquerors th[ey] would have an equal share of the African cattle and goo[ds] taken.

The first years in Rhodesia were discouraging for [the] British settlers. Heavy rainfalls drowned out all efforts [at] agriculture. Nor was gold found among the ancient diggi[ngs]

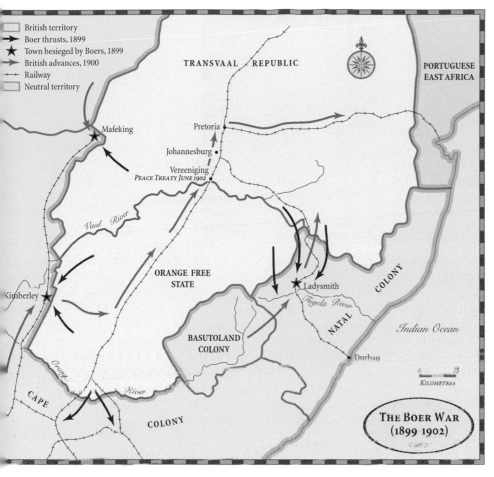

British territory
Boer thrusts, 1899
Town besieged by Boers, 1899
British advances, 1900
Railway
Neutral territory

TRANSVAAL REPUBLIC

PORTUGUESE EAST AFRICA

Mafeking

Pretoria

Johannesburg

Vereeniging
PEACE TREATY JUNE 1902

Vaal River

Kimberley

ORANGE FREE STATE

Ladysmith

Tugela River

NATAL COLONY

Indian Ocean

BASUTOLAND COLONY

Durban

Orange River

CAPE COLONY

0 75
KILOMETRES

THE BOER WAR
(1899–1902)

Although the British defeated the Boers in South Africa, the Boer War raised questions about the stability of Britain's colonial empire.

extent Chamberlain and Rhodes were party to the scheme has never been uncovered—Dr. Jameson later returned to South Africa as prime minister of the Cape Colony.)

In Rhodesia, the Ndebele and Shona nations took the opportunity to rise in a full rebellion. White settlers in the outlying districts were hacked to death by raiders and some servants as the African resistance began to escalate. British forces were rushed to the colony and crushed the uprising, but Rhodes's reputation had been badly tarnished and Chamberlain had to put on hold the plans for federation until the affair had blown over.

Boer War 1899–1902

Not until the Fashoda Crisis in 1898 was Chamberlain able to return safely to his grand strategy for Africa. After Kitchener's successes on the Nile, Chamberlain was determined to provoke a crisis with the wealthy Boer republics to force them into federation with the Cape Colony. On 8 September 1899, he sent an ultimatum to Kruger to accept federation or face the consequences.

Public opinion in Britain backed Chamberlain in his desire to impose British rule on the Boers. Chamberlain vowed he would not flinch from his duty even if it meant war. He firmly believed a show of force from Natal would be enough to cow the Boers into acceptance as he believed their resistance was a bluff. But just to ensure victory he ordered 47 000 reinforcements to South Africa. It was fortunate he did so for Kruger was not bluffing and the Boers were prepared to fight.

The Boers struck first before the reinforcements arrived. They laid siege to Mafeking, Ladysmith, and Kimberley, bottling up the British garrisons. They then dug in along the Tugela River, the border with Natal. British attempts at frontal assaults resulted in disastrous losses. In the first few days 7000 British soldiers were killed or wounded.

Lord Roberts was sent from India to take command with

icved by some to be the biblical King Solomon's mines. ...ancial backers began to panic over their losses.

...he Ndebele and Shona nations were in even worse con-...ion. They had lost their cattle, and the rains followed by ...usts had left them without crops. Then in 1894 rinder-...st infected all the cattle. Out of desperation the Ndebele ...d Shona schemed to rid the land of whites hoping this ...uld restore their greatness.

...n 1895, Joseph Chamberlain was appointed colonial ...retary. Like Salisbury before him and his French coun-...part Delcasse, he was an ardent imperialist. He would ...rsue the idea of federation with all his vigour. His plans ...nt beyond regional federation in that he wanted to ...ablish a fully integrated empire with an imperial parlia-...nt governing the whole. But before he could get settled ...o office, events took place on the Transvaal that almost ...bled him from power.

...n 29 December 1895, the governor of Rhodesia, Dr. ...nder Jameson, led an unauthorized invasion of the ...nsvaal with a small force, including 500 mounted ...icemen, leaving Rhodesia without defence. They were ...tured at Doornkop and thrown into jail. (To what

During the Boer War, troops from Australia, Canada, and other parts of the British Empire fought alongside the British. This painting depicts the British troops crossing the Tugela River under heavy fire from the Boers.

General Kitchener, fresh from his victories at Omdurman and Khartoum, as chief of staff. Forces flooded in from all over the Empire in a planned show of imperial solidarity. British troops were joined by those from Australia, Canada, and other parts of the Empire, more as a visible demonstration to the other European powers of British imperial power than to handle the conflict at hand.

In February 1900 the imperial army overwhelmed the Boer positions. Flying columns raced to relieve the besieged cities and by May the war was over. The Republics were annexed to South Africa and Kitchener was left to bring the fighting to an end.

Although the war was officially over, some of the Boers on the frontier continued to carry on a guerrilla war that grew ugly with acts of terror and reprisal. The Boers established over 100 commando units to carry out surprise attacks, keeping the frontier in flames. They were highly successful and their bravado brought them growing public support. It was feared that the Afrikaners in Cape Colony would join them and the whole federation would be in danger. The commandos would have to be defeated quickly.

To this end Kitchener developed heavy-handed tactics. Many square kilometres of the *veldt* (open country with grass or bushes but few trees) were cordoned off and Boers found within were sent to concentration camps. Farms were stripped of cattle, and crops and buildings were burned to deny the rebels food and shelter. Eventually, 25 000 Boers were held in camps where their large numbers overwhelmed attempts at sanitation and hygiene. Death rates were particularly high among Boer women and children. Belatedly, proper sanitary and medical facilities, nurses, and doctors were brought in to stem disease and starvation.

In the British Parliament, opposition members decried the inhuman conditions of the Boer prisoners. Particular attention was given the dying women and children. The British public reacted with disgust and called for an end to the uncivilized, inhumane camp conditions.

In 1902, the last of the Boer commanders gave himself up. Britain restored a considerable amount of sovereignty to the Boer republics but forc[ed] them into the Union of Sou[th] Africa created in 1910. A thre[e] million-pound payment w[as] made to those who had suffer[ed] from the brutal guerrilla ca[m]paign. The Boers lost 7000 m[en] and 28 000 of their women a[nd] children. It would take years f[or] them to recover.

One thing Britain had learne[d] from the war was how fragile [its] position was. Was Britain alo[ne] with its vast empire not secu[re] within its policy of isolation? Should the policy be chang[ed] to seek an ally among the other major powers to ensure future peace and security? Would Britain's splendid iso[la]tion come to an end?

SUMMARY

A new wave of European imperialism swept t[he] world in the latter part of the nineteenth centu[ry.] The older empires, established in the seventee[nth] century, expanded or disappeared as the globe came und[er] the dominance of one European power or another.

Global conquest was made possible by the adaptation [of] steam power to the various modes of transport. Stea[m] engines never slept and could advance against wind a[nd] tide. They were particularly useful in penetrating the c[on]tinents, opening up their interior for resource exploitati[on] for the first time. Transcontinental railway networks we[re] the symbol of the age.

The most open use of industrial power, backed by arm[ies] with machine weapons, occurred in the scramble to c[on]trol Africa. European dominance over Africa progress[ed] along three geographic axis: the Nile River, the Con[go] River, and the coast of South Africa. At one time [or] another, all major powers were involved in the politi[cal] division of the continent, a division that was not with[out] rivalry and tension.

It was not just the European powers that engaged [in] empire building. The newly industrialized United Stat[es,] Russia, and Japan also exerted their dominance beyo[nd] their own borders when they had reached th[eir]

ontinental limits, or when they found themselves short of
physical resources to fuel their own industrial growth.

QUESTIONS

Why did the major powers establish colonial
empires? Describe the methods they used.

Explain the results of the competition for land which
arose between the major powers. Explain how they
viewed the older empires, the Americas, Asia, and
Africa.

Who benefitted from the Suez Canal when it was first
built?

The Suez Canal was called a "lifeline." What is meant
by the term? How was this lifeline protected?

Describe the role played by the following people:
(a) Muhammad Ali,
(b) Said,
(c) Ismael,
(d) Colonel Arabi (El-Wahid),
(e) The Mahdi.

Compare the Belgian and French ventures in the
Congo. Evaluate their success.

What agreements were reached as a result of the
1885 Conference of Nations on territorial claims in
Africa?

Explain the events leading up to the Fashoda
incident. Assess the severity of the threat to Cairo
and the Nile. How was a major crisis averted?

Briefly outline the events which led to the Boer War.
What were the results of the war?

ANALYSIS

Explain what was meant by "The White Man's
Burden." Research the attempts by missionaries, the
colonial administration, medical, educational or legal
advisers to imprint a European culture on native
populations. Evaluate their successes.

2. Research the life of one African explorer. From what
did this explorer gain his or her notoriety? Suggest
reasons the press and the public treated this explorer
as a superperson.

3. The European powers developed procedures
governing the partition and occupation of Africa.
These agreements were carried over into other parts
of the world such as Asia. Most agreements were
validated by the use of armed force. Using
information you have gained from the text and from
research into the agreements on Antarctica and the
Moon, develop a policy for the exploitation of the
mineral resources of other planets.

4. Research the agreements of the large oil producing
corporations to share the petroleum resources of the
North Sea, the Philippine Sea, and other oil
producing regions peacefully. What makes these
arrangements successful? Can other resources on
earth be shared in the same fashion?

ACTIVITIES

1. Map Assignment
On a map of the world, identify the colonial powers and
their possessions. Provide an accompanying chart which
identifies the types of goods which were obtained from the
colonies, and the worth of goods which the great powers
sold to the colonies.

2. Diary
Write an account of Dr. Livingstone's experience in Africa.
Focus on his contact with African people, identifying their
lifestyle and his concern regarding their well-being.

3. Battle Strategy
You are Prime Minister Neville Chamberlain of Britain.
Write up your strategy for forcing the Boer republics into
a federation with the Cape of South Africa.

In the nineteenth century, Russia was an agricultural country composed of a tiny upper class and millions of serfs. Much of the farm work was done by hand labour.

Chapter 11
Emerging Industrial Powers

FOCUS ON:

The impact of the new industrial powers—
the United States, Russia, and Japan—on the international power structure;

The exploitation of virgin territories by
the United States, Russia, and Japan in order to support industrialization;

Challenges to the old established powers, and the rationale for
the participation of new industrial powers in World War I.

At the end of the nineteenth century, the established industrial powers of Europe found themselves in increasing competition with Russia, the United States of America, and Japan. These new rivals were to play a significant role in international affairs and contributed to growing tensions between the industrial powers.

RUSSIA 1825–1918

After the death in 1825 of Alexander I, Russia was thrown into crisis over who would be the next tsar. The military played an important role in a situation that came to be known as the Decembrist Revolt. Some Russian soldiers who had fought the French during the Napoleonic War had been influenced by the liberal ideas sweeping across Europe. They wanted Alexander's brother, Constantine, to be tsar because they thought he was more open-minded than his brother Nicholas. Although Constantine had declared Nicholas to be the rightful heir and refused the crown, at Nicholas's coronation in December 1825 these rebel soldiers stormed the Senate Square in St Petersburg in protest.

When Nicholas appeared in the square, one of the rebel officers, Yakobovich, raised his hat on his sword to signal the revolt. When none of the rebels moved forward he pleaded a headache, passed back through the rebel ranks and sought out the tsar. Kneeling before Nicholas he assured the tsar of his loyalty. Betraying his fellow conspirators, he then went home and shut hims in his room to await arrest.

Several officers loyal to the tsar then rode across t

TIMELINE

Russia

1825 ❈ Nicholas I becomes tsar of Russia.

1825 ❈ The Decembrist Revolt marks the first significant opposition to the tsar.

1853–1856 ❈ Crimean War results from tension over Russian attempts to control the Balkans.

1855 ❈ Alexander II ascends the throne.

1861 ❈ Serf Emancipation Act

1866 ❈ An era of repression begins as a result of repeated attempts to assassinate the tsar.

1878 ❈ The Congress of Berlin agrees to maintain Ottoman control of the Dardanelles rather than partition the Ottoman Empire among the major powers.

1881 ❈ Alexander III ascends the throne and approves the Exceptional Measures Act providing for military rule of rebellious regions.

1894 ❈ Nicholas II, the last of the Romanov tsars, ascends the throne.

1904–1905 ❈ Russo-Japanese War

1905 ❈ Father Gapon's march of workers to the Winter Palace

1905 ❈ October Manifesto

1914 ❈ Russia enters World War I on the side of the British and French

1917 ❈ Russian Revolution. The tsar abdicates and later is executed.

1918–1920 ❈ Civil War

1918 ❈ Treaty of Brest-Litovsk is signed between Russia and Germany, allowing Russia to leave the war.

United States

1823 ❈ The United States proclaims Monroe Doctrine isolating the western hemisphere from European intrusion.

1861–1865 ❈ American Civil War. Following the civil war a decision was made to expand the boundaries of the United States westward to the Pacific Ocean.

1869 ❈ The Union Pacific Railroad was completed.

1895 ❈ The Venezuela boundary dispute occurs over gold discovered in an undefined border between Venezuela and British Guiana. The United States supports Venezuela against Britain.

1898 ❈ Spanish-American War

1917 ❈ The United States enters World War I against Germany.

1918 ❈ The American Congress refuses to ratify the Treaty of Versailles. Instead it declares hostilities at an end.

Japan

1853 ❈ American Admiral Perry breaks Japanese isolation.

1854 ❈ Treaty of Kanagawa permits limited trade between Japan and the United States.

1868–1912 ❈ The Meiji Era saw the westernization of Japan.

1894 ❈ Japan's war with China over Korea.

1895 ❈ Treaty of Shimenoseki

1902 ❈ Japan and Britain sign a mutual alliance treaty.

1904–1905 ❈ Russo-Japanese war

1914 ❈ Japan enters World War I against Germany.

Nicholas I

In the repressive regime of Nicholas I, his subjects were forbidden to comment on the government either positively or negatively. Those who spoke for him would be as guilty of treason as those who spoke against him. Nicholas ordered that the implementation of a number of Russification programs be imposed on the minorities within the empire. From then on only Russian books and the Russian language were acceptable.

quare to talk with the rebel rces. Each in turn was shot in e back while returning to the yalist ranks. Peter Khovsky, a vilian in the crowd, was doing e killing and for this he came the role model for ture generations of terrorists. growing number of Russians oked on with curiosity. No one emed to know how to handle e situation.

Sometime later a cavalry arge attempted to clear the uare but the horses slipped on e damp cobblestones. This fur-er amused the crowd. Still later, cannon were brought in disperse the protesters. The cannon fire scattered those did not kill or wound and the onlookers fled the square. ose that later returned to the square were arrested. Dead d wounded were shoved under the ice of the Neva River. e ringleaders were rounded up, tortured, and executed. From that day onward, Nicholas distrusted his military ficers. He demanded absolute obedience. Observers mpared his rule to that of an occupying power; his reign as a despotic autocracy. Nicholas I wanted to keep ssia as silent as the grave and for the most part he suc-eded.

n 1825, Russia was an agricultural country composed of iny upper class and millions of serfs. *Serf* was a term at included everyone from craftsmen to field workers. en industrial workers and opera singers were consid-d serfs and, whether they worked at a factory or on ge, they were still tied to their *mir* ("village") or to the ssian Crown. All told there were 48 million serfs and ir families in Russia. Serfs were owned and could be ught or sold. Their lives depended on their owners.

odernization of Russia

cholas could not ignore the modern world forever. The ed to modernize touched off a debate among his advi-s over whether Russia should open its borders to the st or close them and industrialize on its own resources. either case, hundreds of millions of rubles would be ded to pay for the transformation from an agrarian ion to a modern industrial state. Most of the money

could be gained from the sale of cereal crops from the Ukraine on the world market.

The export of grain was critical to Russia's modernization. The grain was shipped across the Black Sea through the Dardanelles to the Mediterranean Sea and global trade routes. Russia could not permit any other power to control the narrow passageway linking the two seas. But Russia had competition in this region—in Austria-Hungary. Both major powers were firmly convinced the Dardanelles were critical to their futures and both wanted the Straits within their own spheres of influence.

The events of the Crimean War, 1853–1856 (see Chapter 8) demonstrated Russia's inability to bring the Straits within its sphere when faced with determined opposition of the other powers. When Russian forces crossed the mouth of the Danube River and advanced on Constantinople, France and Britain reacted by landing 60 000 troops in the Crimea and laying siege to Sebastopol.

Reign of Alexander II

Nicholas I died from influenza in January 1855 before the Crimean War had ended. Alexander II came to the throne and ruled from 1855 to 1881. The Treaty of Paris (1856) which ended the Crimean War neutralized the Black Sea. Neither Russia, Austria-Hungary, or Turkey were permitted to place warships on its waters. Alexander believed he would at least have the support of Austria-Hungary in the peace negotiations. Russian forces had helped Austria-Hungary put down nationalist disturbances in Hungary in 1849. However, when Austro-Hungarian support was not forthcoming, Alexander, with the urging of Otto von Bismarck, then Prussian ambassador to the court at St Petersburg, began to shift Russia's foreign policy in favour of Prussia.

In 1861 Alexander II brought about revolution from above. Although an autocrat, Alexander II was a great reformer. He decreed the serfs free and gave them the right to own land. Under the Act of Emancipation, half the land was to be the collective property of and distributed by the *zemstvos*, local councils in the *mir*. The serfs were to compensate the landlords for their losses. The tsar wanted the landlords to form a new centralized bureaucracy to support the new, modern industrial Russian state.

For the most part the peasants did not pay for the land but merely took it. The *zemstvos* redistributed the farm plots in an unsystematic manner. There was no attempt to consolidate farm plots. Production was low and farming methods were primitive at best. In reality the farming techniques had not changed. The peasants still did not have enough land to maintain a suitable standard of living. There were too many of them on too little land. The uncompensated landlords formed a landless, restless, aristocracy totally dependent on the tsar for their living.

In 1866, after a number of assassination attempts, Alexander gave up his policy of reform and replaced it with one of repression. There would be no change in the political system for the next 40 years. Russia closed its borders to the West and exerted its energies in Asia. Only rarely would the tsar's interest be redirected westward.

One such occasion occurred in 1870 during the Franco-German War. Russia's armed forces remained idle on Prussia's borders during the war. The tsar's position of neutrality was based on Bismarck's promise to support a revision of the Treaty of Paris regarding the Black Sea. When the treaty was revised in 1871, Russia was permitted to deploy warships on the inland waters.

On another occasion, in 1874, after the Ottoman Turks had razed a number of Slavic villages, the tsar sent Russian troops across the Danube towards Constantinople. This was the tenth war that Russia had fought against the Turks since 1676. The possibility of Austria-Hungary becoming alarmed over the advance of Russian forces into the Balkans was strong. Should Austria-Hungary attempt to stop the Russian advance, there was no doubt a war would break out between the two powers.

Bismarck called the powers to Berlin in 1878 in the hope of solving the Balkan question. At the congress Russia felt betrayed when Germany appeared to side with Austria-Hungary. Russia was not given control of the Straits. Instead the Ottoman Empire was supported by the other powers who thought that its existence was necessary to deflect any drift towards war in the Balkans. It was also at this congress that Austria-Hungary was given permission to administer the Balkan regions of Bosnia-Herzegovina.

In Russia Alexander's repressive regime led to the organization of secret terrorist societies. These terroris[ts] believed that terrorism was the only way to fight for ju[s]tice and liberty under an autocracy.

On 5 February 1880, there was a massive explosion [in] the Winter Palace but the tsar had been late coming dow[n] for dinner and escaped the blast. Ten people were kill[ed] and a number wounded from the 200 kilograms of TN[T] smuggled into the dining area. Retribution was swift. [In] addition to the expected executions, thousands of int[el]lectuals and students suspected of opposition to the ts[ar] were sent into exile in Siberia.

This did not stop the terrorists. On 31 March 1881, th[ey] mined the road along one of the Alexander's regul[ar] routes. When they learned he had changed routes th[ey] raced to new positions and hurled hand grenades at t[he] procession, killing a boy in the crowd. The tsar stopp[ed] and went back to give comfort. This was his undoing as [he] encountered one of the assassins and was murdered [on] the spot. Ironically, that same day the tsar had signed a la[w] to liberalize his government by allowing elected comm[is]sioners to sit with the Council of State. Even under t[he] autocracy of tsarism, European liberal ideas, such [as] the abolition of serfdom, had infiltrated this repressi[ve] government.

Alexander III

Alexander II's son, Alexander III, (1881–1894) revert[ed] again to a brutal, repressive regime of police contr[ol]. Power was centralized in St Petersburg and police infor[m]ers were sent out to infiltrate all social and labour orga[ni]zations. Every kind of political action was outlawed. Und[er] the Exceptional Measures Act, entire districts were turn[ed] over to military governors who could guarantee order a[nd] stability. This act remained in effect until 1917 and duri[ng] this time most of Russia was administered under mar[tial] law.

Towards the end of the nineteenth century, Russ[ia's] industrial growth made significant gains. All indust[rial] development was under state control. State-owned fac[to]ries were gigantic and, by design, were established to s[up]port the needs of a growing railway network and [an] expanding military. However, Russia was so far behind [the] West that even the spectacular industrial growth of 8 p[er] cent was submerged in its large population and the va[st]ness of the land.

Tsar Nicholas II, the last of the Romanovs, and Tsarina Alexandra came to the Russian throne at a time of growing terrorism and labour unrest.

honour of the French ambassador.

In February 1904 Japan attacked Russia's Asian possessions. In Russia the tsar's political opponents blamed his administration for the dismal efforts of the Russian armed forces. This grew to public outrage with the loss of Port Arthur and the key transport centre of Mukden. As a result of this humiliating defeat, Russia made considerable concessions in Manchuria and Korea.

The tsar's troubles were just beginning. On Sunday, 9 January 1905, Father Gapon led a demonstration of 200 000 workers to the Winter Palace to ask the tsar for better working conditions. There had been a sharp increase in the number of strikes, causing a loss of production. One of the police officers in Moscow by the name of Zubatov suggested establishing police-sponsored labour unions. In this way the authorities could control what was going on and strikes could be turned into peaceful demonstrations.

Father Gapon led one of these police unions. He believed he

Nicholas II

Nicholas II (1894–1917), the last of the Romanovs, came the throne in 1894 when Alexander III died from nephri-, a kidney disease. Nicholas, a reluctant monarch, faced period marked by growing terrorism and labour unrest. reign began under a dark cloud. At ceremonies on the odyna Fields outside Moscow to celebrate his acces-n, a rumour spread through the 500 000 celebrants that re was a shortage of free beer. A stampede resulted in ich 1000 were trampled to death. Instead of cancelling other events for the day, Nicholas took the advice of his ncillors and callously went to a ball that evening in

had the approval of the city authorities to bring his followers to the palace to present a petition to the tsar. The petition asked for the standard demands of the eight-hour working day, Sunday holidays, and better living conditions. Ironically, the tsar was not in the palace but had left St Petersburg for his palace at Tsarskoe Selo.

The police had cleared the intersections so as not to impede the five columns of marchers converging on the palace. The number of marchers, some 200 000, panicked city officials who hurried troops into the square. Emerging from the streets, the demonstrators surged towards the palace. The thin line of troops believed they were in

*Grigoriy Rasputin (1871–1916) seemed to have
the ability to ease the bleeding of the
hemophiliac crown prince. He became an
advisor to the tsarina. Some historians blame
Rasputin for bringing the monarchy into
disrepute; others uphold him as a
representative of the lower classes
who sought to ease their burdens.*

danger from the oncoming mob and opened fire. About 1500 demonstrators were injured or killed.

Nicholas was horrified when informed of the tragedy. Later, in October, after continuing labour unrest including a crippling strike, the tsar modified his autocratic stance with the creation of a *Duma* ("national assembly"). Despite the liberal terms of the manifesto, the tsar retained full authority over the army and foreign affairs. He also retained the right to veto any *Duma* legislation.

The membership of the first *Duma* was heavily weighted in favour of the aristocracy. It sat for 73 days before being dissolved over a proposal to redistribute all the remaining unclaimed lands, a suggestion to which the aristocracy was unalterably opposed. The second *Duma* was also ineffective. However, the third and fourth *Dumas* accomplished a considerable amount and served their full terms.

During this period, reforms were enacted not by the *Duma* but by the prime minister, Peter Stolypin, by means of royal decree. The imperial lands were placed in a land bank, workers conditions were made more tolerable, peasant debts were waived, and the ownership of farmland was encouraged. So successful were these measures that there was a danger the workers would lose their interest in political revolution, sweeping away any need for political opposition. Opponents of the regime had Stolypin assassinated, resulting in a return to political instability.

World War I slowed further development inside Russia. Four million workers and 11 million peasants were called to arms. After the initial victory in East Prussia disaster followed disaster. In December 1914 the Grand Duke informed the tsar that the Russian armies were incapable

of any further action becau[se] they were badly mauled and o[ut] of supplies. He recommende[d] that Russia stay on the defe[n]sive for the remainder of t[he] war.

In 1915 the tsar went to t[he] front to take command of h[is] armies. He left the governme[nt] under the charge of Tsari[na] Alexandra and her advisor, Gr[ig] oriy Rasputin. Rasputin, a Sib[er] ian, self-appointed "holy ma[n]" had come to court before t[he] war. The tsarina believed th[at] Rasputin alone could save h[er] son—the heir to the throne[—] from bleeding in the event of [an] accident or fall. The boy h[ad] hemophilia and so could bleed [to] death. Rasputin had encourag[ed] this belief and Alexandra b[e] came fully dependent upon hi[m]. He became powerful because [of] his influence on her.

Rasputin lived a life [of] debauchery that brought t[he] Romanovs into disrepute, [al] though his debauchery did n[ot] involve the royal family direc[tly]. Yet the tsarina would not give him up as her advis[or]. Rasputin was assassinated in December 1916 by young members of the royal family but not before he had irre[vo] cably damaged the reputation of the court in the eyes [of] the aristocracy, driving away needed support for [the] throne.

Russian Revolution

The Russian Revolution of 1917 began with a lockout [of] workers in Petrograd (present-day St Petersburg). Fo[od] shortages in the cities in the previous months had touch[ed] off unruly demonstrations that grew in size and intens[ity]. Most of the demonstrations were organized by wom[en] demanding "bread and peace." The angry workers joi[ned] throngs of women standing in line for bread, fuelin[g a] tense situation. Strikes quickly spread to all workplac[es]

On 27 February, a general strike was joined by a third of the Petrograd garrison—what started as a demonstration became a revolution. The army joined the revolution. When the tsar attempted to return from the battlefront, troops stopped his train. Nicholas agreed to abdicate for himself and his son and turn the government over to his brother the Grand Duke Michael. But the grand duke declined the throne and a Provisional Government under Prince Lvov assumed control in March 1917.

The Romanov era ended with hardly a whimper. The tsar and his family were taken to Ekaterinburg and later executed by the Bolshevik regime during the civil war.

A host of local organizations sprang up in an attempt to restore a degree of stability. The most important of these are the *soviets* ("workers and soldiers councils"). There were also attempts to establish an All Russian Congress of Unions, an All Russian Congress of Zemstvos, and an All Russian Congress of Soviets in addition to the Provisional Government. Indeed representatives of the Provisional Government encouraged the formation of these national organizations. The Petrograd Soviet proved to have far more popular support than the Provisional Government. This resulted in two rival political organizations that vied for public support.

The Provisional Government was to govern Russia until national elections in October. The elections would create a Constituent Assembly that would be representative of all the people. The assembly's task was to write a new constitution then to dissolve itself for further elections to a national Assembly in January 1918.

The Provisional Government refused to consider the pressing issues of army desertions, land redistribution, and union demands. These were referred to the Constituent Assembly that would meet in October. In the meantime, the Provisional Government made the decision to keep faith with Britain and France and remain in the war.

The decision to continue the war proved fatal. As inexperienced Russian conscripts poured into the battle lines they were destroyed by the seasoned German forces. Then, in the hot summer months, the Russian army melted away as soldiers turned their backs on their officers and began to walk home. No force on earth could stop the mass desertions.

During World War I Russia had mobilized 15 million men, of which 1.6 million were killed, 3.8 million were wounded, and 2.4 million were taken prisoner or were missing in action.

One of the major figures in the Provisional Government was Alexander Kerensky. He was the only member of the Petrograd Soviet to participate in this government. In May 1917, he was minister of war and, by July, he was the prime minister. He was accused by his enemies of having plotted with General Kornilov to bring his troops into Petrograd to protect the government from the mobs and at the same time to get rid of the Petrograd Soviet. When the railways refused to transport his forces, Kornilov gave up the plan and retreated. Everyone blamed Kerensky for the charade, but recent evidence indicates he was not involved in the affair. Kerensky would shortly leave Russia for refuge in the United States. By September, after eight months of indecision, no one appeared capable of saving the Provisional Government. It had failed in all that it had set out to do.

During the confusion, the Bolshevik (Communist) Party under Vladimir Lenin (1870–1924) plotted to seize power by force. Lenin, along with many other exiles, had been sent back into Russia by the Germans. The Germans hoped the exiles could overthrow the Provisional Government and get Russia to surrender.

Lenin returned to Russia in April 1917 where he made known his political ideas in his "April Theses." The leader of the Bolsheviks called for an end to the war that was destroying Russia, an adequate distribution of bread especially to the cities where workers and their families were starving, and the placement of all government powers in the hands of the *soviets*. His program struck a responsive chord and brought the Bolsheviks considerable support. After a failed Bolshevik uprising in July, the Provisional Government publicly branded Lenin a German spy causing him to flee to Finland until his return in October.

In the meantime, the Bolshevik cause was maintained by Leon Trotsky, the party theorist. He was chair of the Petrograd Soviet and the main supporter of the Bolshevik organization. Many thought that he, not Lenin, should lead the party. Trotsky later was the foreign minister in Lenin's government.

When the Bolsheviks took over the powerful Petrograd and Moscow city *soviets* Lenin called for action. It was time to seize power from the newly elected Constitutional Assembly. He returned to Petrograd to arrange his "dictatorship of the proletariat." The Petrograd garrison and forces from the Kronstadt naval base joined the Bolshevik

Vladimir Lenin was the leader of the Bolsheviks. He called for an end to the war, an adequate distribution of bread, especially to the cities where workers and their families were starving, and the placement of all government powers in the hands of the soviets. This photograph was taken in 1922, two years before his death.

side. With the addition of 6000 volunteer Red Guards, the Bolsheviks seized key buildings in the capital. Although Petrograd appeared to be a city under siege there was little organized opposition to the coup. To Lenin's relief the army had supported the Communists.

After the 25 October coup, Lenin established a Bolshevik government. This single party administration depended on army support to keep it in power.

In the meantime Lenin organized 1000 supply detachments to go out and gather food for the cities. He merged the Red Guards with regular army forces. He needed the army support to bring order out of the anarchy that prevailed. He established a one-party government with himself as the chairman of the Committee of Peoples Commissars. The Cheka, with 30 000 agents, was formed to centralize all police power in the capital.

The following year, when the voting for the national assembly was completed, the Bolsheviks held only 125 deputies out of 707. On its second day of meeting, the assembly was forced to dissolve by the Bolshevik forces,

leaving Lenin in command of a **single party governmen** The forceful dissolution of the assembly began a civil w in Russia that would last from June 1918 to 1920.

In March 1918, the Bolshevik government signed t peace of Brest-Litovsk with Germany. The Russian arr could not fight on and further delay only meant th German forces would occupy more of Russian territo Lenin called it only a scrap of paper but the German tre ment of Russia was harsh. In any case, Lenin had ma good on one of his promises in taking Russia out of t war.

Russia's surrender held dire consequences for the Alli Now Germany could throw its combined might against t Western Front and could just possibly win the war. Alli efforts to keep Russia in the war by overthrowing Leni government ranged from military invasions at Archan and Vladivostok to bribery and assassination. None of t strategies were successful. Russia's future now lay w the Bolsheviks.

*Labourers of European and Asian origin forged through rock
to build transcontinental railway lines in the United States.*

HE UNITED STATES OF AMERICA

365–1918

After the American Civil War (1861–1865) Americans directed their attention westward across the Mississippi River, to the settlement of the Great ins and to seek routes across the Rocky Mountains to Pacific Ocean. In a few years Americans would fill out ir part of the continent, bounded by Canada on the rth and Mexico on the south.

The USA had acquired a vast tract of land from the ench in 1803. The Louisiana Purchase extended from the ssissippi River to the Rocky Mountains and from the lf of Mexico to British North America. In this $15-mil-n transaction, the USA doubled its area. In another nsaction, the USA purchased Alaska from Russia for 3 million in 1867.

The discovery of gold in the Black Hills of South Dakota brought in thousands of miners many of whom went on to stake claims to silver deposits in Nevada. Cattle barons brought six million Texas longhorn cattle onto the high plains of Colorado and Wyoming. Growth was so rapid that by 1890 Americans were lamenting the passing of the frontier from wilderness to settled region.

The 250 000 Native peoples who lived on the plains were to be brutally pushed aside in a series of skirmishes and battles over the next 15 years. By 1876 the Seventh Cavalry had all but subdued the Sioux, Crow, Blackfoot, Cheyenne, Apache, and Arapaho. The victory in 1876 of Sitting Bull and Crazy Horse over General Custer on the banks of the Little Big Horn River was a notable but minor setback to US expansion in the plains.

Railways were the key to western expansion. In 1862 President Lincoln signed a railway bill giving government support of up to $48 000 a mile for transcontinental lines. A group of investors led by Leland Stanford pushed the

In the Spanish-American War, Admiral George Dewey sailed his fleet into Manila Harbour in the Philippines and sank the Spanish fleet at anchor.

line eastward from San Francisco while General Dodge built west from Council Bluffs near Omaha. On 10 May 1869, the two lines were joined by a golden spike at Promontory Point, Utah to form the Union Pacific Railroad. Other transcontinental lines included the Northern Pacific and the Southern Pacific finished in 1883. By 1900 the United States had constructed 360 000 km of railway lines, more than in all Europe combined.

The railways were completed just in time to transport the millions of immigrants arriving from Europe to their new homes in the West. About 16 million immigrants had arrived in North America by the turn of the century and another 18 million would follow by 1930. Immigrants from Northern Europe generally settled in the West. Those from Central Europe, the Mediterranean, or Asia tended to reestablish in the cities.

Ever since its founding, the United States had been reluctant to become entangled in foreign affairs. Protected by vast ocean barriers, the Americans, since 1783, had directed their energies inwards. Their armed forces were

designed to fight and defend American interests in Nor America not in far off places around the globe. The Monr Doctrine (1823) stated the American policy that a European nation attempting to reassert its power in t western hemisphere would automatically find itself at w with the United States. The doctrine applied to mainta ing Latin American countries' newly won independen from Spain and Portugal during the Napoleonic wars. was also a statement of American isolation from the qua rels of the Old World.

American isolation could not be maintained forever when the United States became involved in the Venezue boundary dispute (1895–1897) with Great Britain. Go had been discovered inland in the region of the undefin border between Venezuela and British Guiana. The Unit States threatened to go to war with Great Britain to su port Venezuela until a tribunal decided the boundary qu tion in favour of British Guiana.

This incident was followed in 1898 by war against Spa The conflict began in 1895 when Cubans rebelled agai

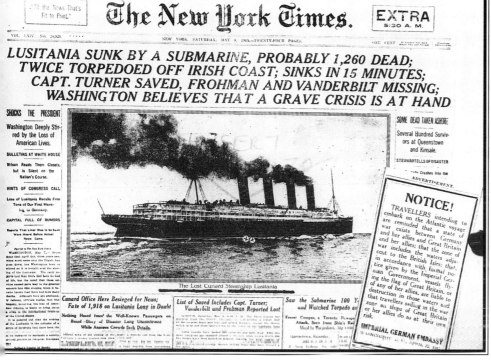

On 7 May 1915 the British passenger liner Lusitania *was torpedoed by Germans off the coast of Ireland. The incident raised American anger and fear because 128 Americans died.*

eir Spanish overlords. Biased, fiery newspaper articles the American press depicted innocent Cuban women d children being brutalized in Spanish concentration mps where disease had taken its toll of the living. In 1898 nen the US battleship *Maine* blew up in Havana harbour e American press raised the call to war. "Remember the aine" was a cry that evoked an emotional response from nericans in all walks of life. From his castle on lifornia's coast, newspaper baron, Randolph Hearst, chestrated his newspapers to demand military interven- n. President William McKinley, seeking reelection, could little but respond. The Americans demanded that Spain thdraw from Cuba and the Spanish responded by declar- ; war on the USA on 24 April 1898.

McKinley was reluctant to take America to war with ain but American forces easily overran the Spanish oops in Cuba. In the Pacific, Admiral George Dewey led his fleet into Manila Harbour in the Philippines and nk the Spanish fleet at anchor. In ten weeks of fighting e war was over. America found itself an imperial power, aining Puerto Rico and the Philippines rather than giv- ; them back to Spain.

When President McKinley was assassinated just six onths into his second administration, Vice-President eodore Roosevelt (1858–1919) assumed office. osevelt mediated the Japanese-Russian War in 1905, ured a 100-year lease on the 16 km-wide Panama Canal

Zone, and established an American naval base at Guantanamo, Cuba. He intervened in the first Moroccan crisis in 1905, where the United States may have exerted some influence over the European powers.

In 1912 the president of Princeton University, Woodrow Wilson (1856–1924), became the twenty-eighth president of the United States. Wilson, a Democrat and noted scholar, hated war but in 1916 found himself sending troops under General Pershing into northern Mexico to stop cross-border raids by rebel leader Pancho Villa and his men. Villa had sought refuge in the northern Mexican states after losing the Mexican presidential elections. Villa was popular among the peasants for his program of land redistribution. Hunted by the Mexican army, he and his followers took refuge in the rugged terrain south of the American border. His men at times strayed across the border onto American soil in search of food, and in 1916 his men killed some Americans in New Mexico. By sending the American army after the rebels, Wilson sought to pacify the frontier.

When World War I broke out, America experienced a genuine feeling of support for the British and French. In an effort to starve the Central Powers, Germany and Austria-Hungary, the British navy established a blockade of major sea ports. The process involved British ships blockading American sea ports and seizing American ships.

In 1915, the Germans declared the waters around Britain to be a war zone and imposed a counterblockade of Great Britain, using submarines to sink all shipping in the zone. The American public reacted with anger. By their very nature submarines cannot take prisoners and at that time submarine commanders could not tell what sort of ship they were attacking. The undersea boats often fired torpedoes without warning, giving no time for passengers and crew to get into lifeboats. This angered the American public who thought it an immoral and uncivilized way to fight a war.

On 29 April 1915, the USS *Cushing* was attacked. On 1 May the *Gullflight*, a tanker, was sunk. On 7 May the

British passenger liner *Lusitania* was torpedoed off the coast of Ireland carrying 128 Americans among the 1200 that were drowned. On 19 August the liner *Arabic* went down off New York. The next day lurid pictures hit the front page of the newspapers showing drowning women and children.

The German strategy of unrestricted submarine warfare caused American outrage and shock. Wilson responded with a strongly-worded statement and the kaiser ordered a halt to the submarine strategy lest it bring America into the war on the side of the Allies.

Americans Enter World War I

President Wilson won reelection in 1916. In spite of his attempts to remain neutral, America embarked on a massive armaments program. Expenditures skyrocketed as news of the battles at Verdun, the Somme, and Galicia became known. Wilson became determined to intervene and put an end to the killing. The United States would enter the war, bringing its overwhelming human and physical resources against the Central Powers.

Although Wilson had decided to enter the war, he had to wait for the moment when he could carry the American people with him. Then in early 1917 a number of events presented Wilson with the right moment. That month the kaiser approved the resumption of unrestricted submarine warfare; five American ships were sunk at sea; the Russian government was overthrown; and Germany's foreign minister, Zimmerman, sent a fateful telegram to Mexico.

The Zimmerman telegram proposed an agreement whereby Mexico would go to war with the United States. This

---

Wilson's Fourteen Points

Wilson's Fourteen Points was a peace plan presented by Woodrow Wilson in January 1918. Wilson wanted to influence the Central European powers to shorten the war and in the subsequent peace discussions. Unfortunately, Wilson's peace plan was lost in the compromises made at the actual peace treaty, the Treaty of Versailles.

Wilson's plan included the following:

an end to secret treaties and secret diplomacy

freedom of the seas in peace and war

removal of trade barriers and inequalities

reduction of armaments world wide

evacuation of occupied territory

self-determination and redrawing of European boundaries along national lines

an international political organization to prevent war

Adapted from A History of the Modern World
by R.Robert Palmer and Joel Colton.
Copyright © 1984 by Alfred A. Knopf Inc.
Reprinted by permission of the publisher

---

would keep the Americans out Europe, permitting Germany win the war. In the meantim Mexico would likely suff defeat. However, after the w was over, Germany would see it that Mexico received its *irr denta*, or old territories, north the border including Texas, Ne Mexico, and Arizona.

Made aware of the contents the telegram, the American pu lic demanded war. On 6 Ap 1917, the United States Congre voted overwhelmingly to decla war on Germany and its allies

Wilson promised to have fo million men under arms with 18 months and 12 million 1920. By December 191 200 000 American infantrym were in Europe facing Germ forces on the western fro American troops also join British and Canadian forces the invasion of Russia Archangel in 1918 and, alo with 14 other nations, in t incursion from Vladivost westward along the Trans-Sib ian railway. The purpose of the invasions was to rescue tonr of arms and other equipme from possible German captu The invasions also held t potential to bring Russia back into the war.

President Wilson sought a peace without victory but British and French publics demanded vengean Germany must pay for its aggression and Germany m be made weak. At the peace conference Wilson did m age to get agreement on the need for a collective secur organization called the League of Nations but gained li else. The American Congress refused to ratify the Tre of Versailles. However, the Congress moved a declarat that the war between the United States and Germany v at an end.

When Admiral Perry returned to Japan in 1854, he demanded that the Japanese sign the Treaty of Kanagawa, which gave the United States certain diplomatic rights and privileges.

APAN 1850–1917

n 1603 the Tokugawa family defeated its rivals the Toyotomi family. The emperor designated Tokugawa the *shogun*, a military head who ruled in the name the emperor, and made Edo (Tokyo) the capital of pan. Tokagawa and 295 *daimyo* (feudal lords) established a feudal system of four classes—peasants, artisans, erchants, and *samurai* (scholars, officials, and warrs). Every other year the *daimyo* nobility were required reside in Edo. However their families were in permanent sidence in the capital, hostages as a guarantee of loyalty. order to prevent further European interference in pan's culture, the *shogun* outlawed Christianity and led off Japan from all outside contact. Few foreigners re allowed to enter and no Japanese were allowed to ve.

n 1853 Japan's self-imposed isolation was broken with arrival of American Admiral Matthew Perry. Perry led into Japanese waters leading his black-hulled warps, with a message from American President Fillmore he *shogun*. Fillmore wanted to open trade and to get a arantee of better treatment for any shipwrecked erican sailors that sought refuge on Japanese coasts. n 1854 Perry returned with eight warships and made

further demands. The Japanese were forced to sign the Treaty of Kanagawa opening Edo and Osaka to trade. The treaty gave the United States the rights of diplomatic legation, foreign resident status with **extraterritorial rights,** and the right to practice the Christian religion.

Surprised over the ease with which the Americans had breached their isolation, partly as a defence against western penetration, and partly out of desire to become a world power, the Japanese decided to copy western culture. Japan would industrialize and become a modern nation equal to the great powers of Europe. By 1885, in a remarkable national transformation, Japan had in all but name become a major industrial power.

It took some time to convince the younger *samurai* of the wisdom of moving from an agrarian society to an industrial one. There was also initial fighting between those Japanese who were traditionalists and those who wanted access to western technology. A number of battles were fought on the main islands until the government prevailed. Japanese were sent abroad to study and bring back whatever information they could on western ways. Foreigners were brought in to modernize Japan's armed forces and reorganize other institutions. An effective transportation system was constructed and factories and arsenals were brought on line. Before long the Yamata steel

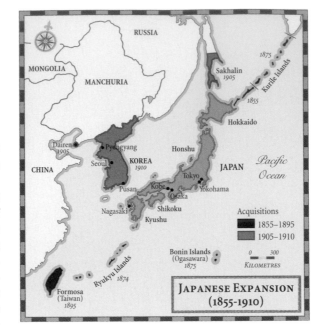

As Japan modernized and expanded its army and navy, it became a rival to European imperialism in Asia.

works was producing 56 000 tonnes of iron and 7500 tonnes of steel on an annual basis.

A small group of courtiers governed Japan in the name of the Emperor Matsuhito. (His reign is called the Meiji era [1868–1912] and saw the westernization of Japan.) Highly educated and far-sighted, they sought wealth and prosperity for the nation. They oversaw the change in culture that affected every facet of Japanese life. Feudalism was abolished, equality before the law was introduced, and an army and navy were established, modelled on European ones.

In Korea the ruling family, Min, attempted, in 1875, to push forward a modernization program in the face of conservative opposition. They first asked the Chinese General Yuan Shih-k'ai to send in troops to quell the rebels. When the Japanese legation was attacked by mobs, Japan landed 1500 men at Inchon. However by that time the rebellion was over and the invasion force was not needed.

Japanese Prime Minister Yamagato then embarked on a 10-year military development program that tripled the size of the army and navy. In 1884 two battalions were sent to Seoul to put down more disturbances and protect Japanese investments. Then, in 1894, Japan went to war with China over Korea and drove the Chinese forces back across the Yalu River. Poised to strike at the imperial capital of Beijing, the Japanese high command thought better of destroying Chinese power. This would only leave a power vacuum that could be filled by westerners. In their view, it was better to end the war and let China exist, and to proceed with the exploitation of Korea's human and natural resources.

The reaction of the Japanese public to this strategy was violent. Riots broke out in Tokyo demanding full-scale conquest. Under the terms of the Treaty of Shimenoseki in 1895, Japan secured Formosa (Taiwan), the Pescadores, and a 360-million yen indemnity. The Japanese were also given the right to navigate the Yangtze River and establish their factories inside China.

maintain the status quo in Asia. Japan promised to lo after British interests in Asia. British warships would withdrawn from Asian waters. Britain agreed to stop oth powers from joining in a war between Russia and Japa Both agreed on the need for Korean and Chinese ind pendence.

Japanese commercial expansion in Korea ran into cc flict with Russian expansion in Manchuria and along t Yalu River where vast timber resources were at har Russia had reached agreement with China for the right build a railway across Manchuria to Vladivostok and a se ond railway from Harbin to Port Arthur. Japan feared th would lead to Russian annexation of a region rich resources that Japan needed to fuel its own industr growth.

The Li-Lobanov agreement, signed at Tsar Nichola accession, pledged Russia to save China from Japane aggression. During the Boxer Rebellion and the siege the foreign legations in Beijing in 1900, Russia sent la forces into Manchuria. These were countered by Japane military expansion on the mainland in Korea and south Manchuria.

Russo–Japanese War

Japanese negotiations with Russia over the timber c cessions along the Yalu River were broken off or February 1904. Two days later a naval skirmish occur off Inchon. This was a forewarning of war. On 9 Febru

Russia felt threatened b Japan's expansion onto th mainland and, with approval the other powers, proceeded modify the treaty. Shantung ar Liaotung were retroceded ar Formosa given its indepe dence. Later Russia would lea Port Arthur. This loss of fac hardened Japan's military lea ers against the west.

In 1902 Japan and Brita signed a mutual alliance trea Britain wanted to concentra its battle fleets in the North S against German naval expa sion. Both nations agreed

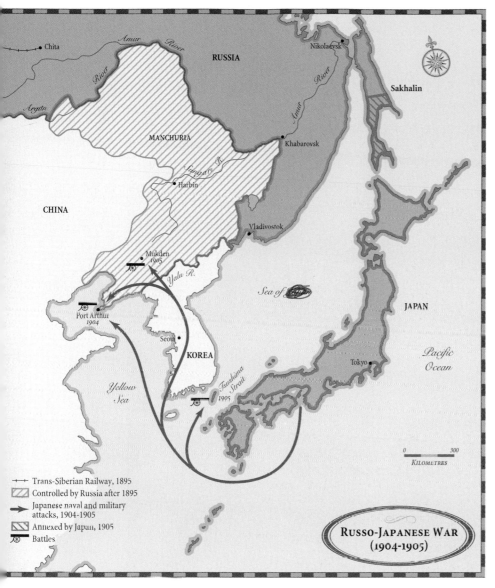

Trans-Siberian Railway, 1895
Controlled by Russia after 1895
Japanese naval and military attacks, 1904-1905
Annexed by Japan, 1905
Battles

RUSSO-JAPANESE WAR
(1904-1905)

Japan's victory over Russia in the Russo-Japanese War signaled its emergence as a military power.

At sea, Admiral Togo maintained Japanese naval superiority. In the only major sea battle of the war, the Japanese smashed the Russian Baltic fleet that had sailed halfway around the world to relieve Port Arthur. In a 24-hour battle in the Straits of Tsushima, all but four of the Russian ships were destroyed.

By 1905 both sides appeared exhausted and welcomed President Roosevelt's offer of mediation. The two warring countries met at Portsmouth, New Hampshire. Under the treaty of Portsmouth, Japan was given a free hand in Korea and control over the southern Manchurian railway system. The southern half of Sakhalin Island was turned over to Japan, and, in a secret agreement made in 1907, Russia agreed to divide Manchuria between the two imperialist powers. After the assassination of a Japanese official in Korea in 1909, Japan annexed the kingdom in 1910.

Japan in World War I

During World War I, Japan seized some of Germany's Pacific possessions and Japanese warships patrolled the eastern Mediterranean in the latter days of the war. With the death of Yuan Shih-k'ai, a power vacuum developed on the mainland that Japan took advantage of. Japan received additional rights in Manchuria and along the Yangtze basin. Japanese settlers were given extraterritorial rights in China, and China agreed to buy at least half its weapons from Japan.

At the peace conference at Versailles, Japan appeared alongside the victors and received recognition for the territorial gains it had made at the expense of Germany.

Japanese struck at Port Arthur in a surprise night attack that destroyed the Russian Pacific Squadron and started the Russo-Japanese War (1904–1905).

Japan had shorter supply lines and enjoyed initial success compared to the Russians, who were supplied over a 5000-km, single track Trans-Siberian railway that was not yet finished. However, the Russians also had a depth of manpower that would count if the war were prolonged. The Japanese siege of Port Arthur lasted 156 days. The following February the Japanese fought a ten-day battle involving 600 000 men outside Mukden. Although the city fell, the Russian army, far from ready to surrender, dug in to the north.

恭 賀 新 年

This postcard shows a column of Japanese soldiers carrying their flag during the Russo-Japanese War.

UMMARY

*A*ttempts by the major powers to limit industrialization to Western Europe, and to keep secrets of industrial production from their rivals, were futile. ...eas and knowledge cannot be confined. The industrial ...d established by Britain, then France and Germany, was ...allenged at the mid-century by the United States, Russia, ...d Japan. Spurred by the objective of transforming their ...rarian societies into modern urban societies, these coun...es sent their students to study abroad and bring back ...stern knowledge to fuel their own development. What ...uld not be produced could be purchased. To fail was to ...ndemn their peoples to a second rate standard of living. ...he United States, Japan, and Russia set out to improve ... Europe's experience and to surpass it in production ...nage as quickly as possible. Transportation systems ...re built across the continents from ocean to ocean to ...ploit the physical wealth in the interiors of the unex...red continents. At the same time, Japan established a ...sthold on the mineral-rich Asian mainland in Korea and ...nchuria. By the turn of the century, political boundaries ...d been filled out by the incorporation of expansive ter...ories.

...he risks were high, the goals were enticing, and the ...ievements stellar. As 1900 came and went the United ...tes, Russia, and Japan had become serious rivals to the ...al powers. These new powers had the potential in ...ources to surpass the older powers in the next few ...ades.

...UESTIONS

Briefly describe Russia at the time of Nicholas I. Outline the policies of Nicholas I.

Explain the results of the end of serfdom in 1861. Why did Alexander II abandon his attempted reforms in 1866?

Describe the Russian government under the leadership of Alexander III.

Nicholas II faced defeat at the hands of Japan in 1904. What was the result of this war?

5. Why did Nicholas II agree to the creation of a national assembly, the *Duma*? What was his role in the *Duma*?

6. Briefly outline the effects of World War I on the Russian economy and its people.

7. Explain the February beginnings of the Russian Revolution. What was the result of the tsar's abdication?

8. What was the condition of Russia's troops in the war? How did the soldiers react to the Provisional Government's decision to remain in the war? Evaluate the effectiveness of the Provisional Government.

9. How did Lenin engineer the October Revolution?

10. What was the significance for Russia of its withdrawal from World War I? What was the significance of Russian withdrawal for the Allies? for Germany?

11. What was the purpose of American expansion westward?

12. What was the Monroe Doctrine? What was its significance in international affairs?

13. The United States had maintained a policy of isolation from international affairs. How did two events at the end of the nineteenth century bring it out of isolation?

14. Why did the United States enter World War I?

15. Briefly outline the role played by Woodrow Wilson in World War I.

16. What event broke Japan's isolation from international affairs? How did the Japanese respond to this contact with the west?

17. Explain the agreement signed by Britain and Japan in 1902.

18. Briefly describe how Japan, by 1918, had become the dominant Asian nation.

ANALYSIS

1. Compare and contrast the Bolshevik Revolution to the French Revolution. Discuss the old and new poltical systems, personalities involved, events, and revolutionary tactics.

    Can political change be carried out without bloodshed and the use of force? Speculate on the need for armed force in a political revolution.

    Evaluate whether the revolutionary governments in France and Russia were an improvement on the old regimes. Defend your position.

2. Can a nation isolate itself from the rest of the world? The United States proclaimed the Monroe Doctrine in an attempt to keep European affairs out of the western hemisphere. Russia tended to shut out the west in favour of development in Siberia after 1878.

    However, both powers became involved in World War I. Explain what brought them out of isolation.

    Can superpowers like the United States remain isolated today? Why or why not? What right have superpowers to interfere with the actions of other nations?

3. Japan was encouraged to be aggressive when Britai withdrew its forces from Asia after 1904. The Unite States held to the western side of the Pacific Ocean leaving no one to balance Japan's growing military power, creating a power vacuum.

    Devise a policy which would deter aggressive natio from taking advantage of a power vacuum. Recommend a role for Canada's armed forces in su a situation.

ACTIVITIES

1. Speech
Write a speech for Lenin to give to the Russian people j prior to the outbreak of revolution in 1917. Be sure to c sider conditions in Russia at this time and the impact the Russian participation in World War I by this point.

2. Newspaper Article
You are the editor-in-chief of the *New York Times*. W an editorial responding to the Zimmermann telegram 1917.

3. Map Activity
On a map of Asia, identify Japanese expansion up to 19 Then identify the territory gained as a result of Japa involvement in World War I.

ISSUE
Analysis

You have now completed Unit III: Imperialism. *The following activity is based on what you have learned about imperialism.*

ISSUE ANALYSIS
The Effects of Imperialism on Culture

Nineteenth century British imperialism resulted in a British empire on which "the sun never set."

This economic expansion provided access to raw materials for the factories at home, markets for finished goods, opportunities for emigration as populations increased, opportunities for missionary work, and the creation of a large network of administrative bureaucracies that demanded an educated workforce.

Imperialism also brought people of different cultures together, resulting in cultural change. Read the following two excerpts and evaluate the effect of imperialism on culture.

1. Excerpt from "An Eastern View of British Imperialism," by K.M. Panikkar (1959)

There is a view generally held by many European writers that the changes brought about in Asia by the contact with Europe are superficial and will, with the disappearance of European political authority, cease to count as time goes on … This point of view would seem to be based on a superficial reading of history …

The first and perhaps the most abiding influence is in the sphere of law. In all Asian countries the legal systems have been fundamentally changed and reorganized according to the post-revolutionary conceptions of nineteenth-century Europe. The first country in which this change was introduced was India where, under the influence of Thomas Babington Macaulay, new legal principles were systematically introduced and applied … The establishment of the great principle of equality of all before law in a country where under the Hindu doctrines a Brahmin could not be punished on the evidence of a Sudra, and even punishments varied according to caste, and where, according to Muslim law, testimony could not be accepted against a Muslim was itself a legal revolution of the first importance …

Another point, one which arises directly out of Europe's long domination over Asia, is the integration of vast territories into great nation states of a kind unknown in the previous history of Asia. India, for instance, all through her long history, had never been welded together into a single state as she is now …

Philosophy and religious thinking, however much they may influence the people in general, are the special interests of the intellectuals. But not so the language, and it is here that the influence of Europe has been most noticeable. From the great literatures of China, India and Japan to the minor languages spoken only by a few million people, everywhere the influence of the West overshadows past traditions."

"An Eastern View of British Imperialism" in Asia and Western Dominance: A Survey of Vasco Da Gama Epoch of Asian History: 1498–1945, *by K.M. Panikkar, London; Allen & Unwin, 1959.*

ISSUE
Analysis

2. Excerpt from *Culture and Imperialism* by Edward W. Said (1993)

Neither imperialism nor colonialism is a simple act of accumulation and acquisition. Both are supported and perhaps even impelled by impressive ideological formations that include notions that certain territories and people require and beseech domination, as well as forms of knowledge affiliated with domination: the vocabulary of classic nineteenth-century imperial culture is plentiful with words and concepts like "inferior" or "subject races," "subordinate peoples," "dependence," "expansion," and "authority." Out of the imperial experiences, notions about culture were clarified, reinforced, criticized, or rejected …

In the expansion of the great Western empires, profit and hope of further profit were obviously tremendously important, as the attractions of spices, sugar, slaves, rubber, cotton, opium, tin, gold, and silver over centuries amply testify. So also was inertia, the investment in already going enterprises, tradition, and the market or institutional forces that kept the enterprises going. But there is more than that to imperialism and colonialism. There was a commitment to them over and above profit, a commitment in constant circulation and recirculation, which, on the one hand allowed decent men and women to accept the notion that distant territories and their native peoples should be subjugated, and on the other replenished metropolitan energies so that these decent people could … rule subordinate, inferior, or less advanced peoples.

From Culture and Imperialism *by Edward W. Said.*
Copyright © 1993 by Edward W. Said.
Reprinted by permission of Alfred A. Knopf Inc.

QUESTIONS

1. Write a brief summary detailing what Panikkar and Said say about the effect of imperialism on subject nations.

2. Why do you think "decent men and women" would, as Edward Said claims, feel an obligation to subjugate the peoples of the empire?

3. Panikkar talks about the impact of the concept of Western law on India. What would you expect to result from this clash of cultures? What do you think should be used as the basis of law in the countries that were British colonies?

4. Research the global culture of the twentieth century. What are the similarities and differences between the culture of the industrialized West and former nineteenth and twentieth century colonies.

UNIT IV
International Conflict

Overview

*R*ivalry among the major European powers resulted in World War I (1914–1918). This "War to End All Wars" was so devastating that even the victors were the losers. The large human losses coupled with the destruction of industrial and economic bases left the nations of Europe bankrupt of power and morality. Unable to arrange their own reconstruction, these nations had to turn to the United States for financial aid. It was the beginning of the end of European global dominance and, as such, the war was a turning point in global history.

Few realized the destructive capabilities of the industrial powers when pitted against each other. Few realized that changing the war into a popular war of good against evil meant that the war aims changed from righting a wrong to total victory over opponents. Only military defeat could bring the fighting to an end. The war had to continue until one side surrendered.

This photograph shows Nicholas II of Russia (left) and Wilhelm II of Germany (right) prior to World War I. Germany's failure to form an alliance with Russia meant that Germany would face war on two fronts instead of one.

Chapter 12
Powers in Conflict

FOCUS ON:

The role of leadership in creating instability in Europe prior to World War I;

The challenge of nationalism to the balance of power and
the international state system;

Foreign policy decisions by the major powers, and the impact of
these decisions on the balance of power.

INDUSTRIAL POWER RIVALRY 1890–1914

New Directions

During the same week in 1890 that Bismarck was dismissed from office, the kaiser gave orders to the new chancellor, Leo von Caprivi, to resurrect the Reinsurance Treaty with Russia. The Reinsurance Treaty had allied Russia and Germany. Throughout the Bismarck era Russia had been kept neutral if not friendly towards Germany.

The large size of the Russian army had made Bismarck careful in his relations with the tsar. In fact, the relationship between Germany and Russia had been at the heart of Bismarck's foreign policy. In particular, it was essential that Russia not form an alliance with any other power, especially France. Although growing in military strength, Germany was not yet strong enough nor united enough to withstand a two battlefront war.

Caprivi, who was not familiar with foreign affairs, sought the advice of the Baron Friedrich von Holstein, a senior official in the foreign ministry. Holstein was aghast at the proposal to reinstate the treaty. As Holstein saw it, the kaiser's proposal would not be in Germany's interest. Bismarck's alliance system was a thing of the past and should not be reestablished. Germany would take new directions in foreign policy, one of which would be to let the Russian alliance go.

He urged Caprivi not to make any hasty decisions until the foreign ministry could change the kaiser's mind. Instead of insisting his commands be obeyed the kaiser was dissuaded from his course. Failure to come to terms

TIMELINE

1891
French naval visit to Russia heralds
a revival of French power.

1894
The Dual Entente between Russia and France
formalizes military agreements made in 1892.

1894
German military planners adopt the Schlieffen plan.

1897
Germany adopts *Weltpolitik*, an aggressive foreign policy
of outward expansion.

1905
The first Moroccan crisis

1906
The naval race between Britain and Germany begins.

1907
Britain, France, and Russia form the Triple Entente.

1908
Austria annexes Bosnia-Herzegovina.

1911
The second Moroccan crisis

1912–1913
Balkan Wars

1914
28 June ❀ Archduke Franz Ferdinand is assassinated.
23 July ❀ Archduke Franz Joseph issues an
ultimatum to Serbia.
28 July ❀ British fleet goes to sea.
30 July ❀ Russia mobilizes.
3 August ❀ Germany invades Belgium.

with Russia would prove fate[...] and start the chain of ever[...] that led to World War I.

Holstein reasoned that a trea[...] with Russia would make G[...] many vulnerable to blackm[...] over the Balkans. He had ne[...] agreed with Bismarck about t[...] need for a Russian alliance. A[...] even under Bismarck, Germa[...] had given assurances to Austr[...] Hungary that Russia would ne[...] be allowed to control the Stra[...]

On the other hand, in a[...] treaty with Germany, Rus[...] would insist on Germany's s[...] port in a war with Austria-H[...] gary over Balkan issues. T[...] same assurances of support[...] the Balkans could not be given[...] rival powers. Bismarck had do[...] so in his complex alliance s[...] tem, but Bismarck had coun[...] on being able to keep Aust[...] Hungary and Russia from atta[...] ing each other. The Iron Ch[...] cellor had never had to choo[...] between the two.

Holstein would not follo[...] policy filled with such duplic[...] If war broke out over [...] Balkans then Germany wo[...] have to choose which ally[...] support. And, in his mind, t[...] support would have to be for Austria-Hungary.

Revising the Balance of Power

From 1890 to 1897 Baron von Holstein's power within [...] foreign ministry was uncontested and Bismarck's proté[...] were quickly removed from all government service. At [...] same time, a wave of militarism influenced by the kais[...] passion for the military arose in Germany.

Bismarck's old alliance system that rested on Russia [...] Austria-Hungary was replaced by a two-directional in[...] tive. This meant that, first, Germany would act to unite [...] nations along the Danube in a confederation thro[...]

*Georges Clémenceau (1841–1929)
was a French physician who became a
politician. He later became premier of France
from 1906 to 1909 and 1917 to 1920.*

:onomic and military means.
owever, the expansion of
:rman economic interests
wards the Balkans was seen as
threat by the tsar and would
ive Russia into an alliance with
:ance—precisely the situation
smarck had avoided.

The second initiative was an
:tempt to force Great Britain
:o joining the Triple Alliance
Germany, Austria, and Italy
lso referred to as the Central
wers). The kaiser believed he
uld create a number of crises
which Great Britain would be
t standing alone. This would
ike Britain aware of the need
r an ally. He calculated that
:eat Britain would not ally
th either Russia because of
nflict over Afghanistan or
th France because of compet-
; interests in Egypt. The only
oice left to the British would
to ally with Germany.

The kaiser wanted Britain on Germany's side as a deter-
it to France and Russia, both of whom were vulnerable
m the sea. Britain was not a continental power and its
all army could be ignored in planning continental strat-
/ but the British fleet was a major factor in international
airs. If Britain were allied to Germany the fears of a
tish naval attack on French and Russian harbours
uld make France and Russia hesitate to start a war
inst Germany.

Vilhelm had some hope from past experience that
tain could be edged away from its isolationist stance.
e British had ventured into the Mediterranean
reements in 1887 in support of the status quo over the
rdanelles. Propping up the crumbling power of the sul-
in Constantinople and leaving the Ottoman Turks in
mmand of the Straits was preferable to a general war.
that time, however, British aims were coincident with
se of the Triple Alliance. This was not true in 1890 and
tain remained aloof from German offers.

s a gesture of friendship, Wilhelm proposed giving

Britain some of Germany's possessions in East Africa. Britain
would have access to its inland
colonies through German territory on the east coast. Germany
would also give the British a
corridor around Africa's Great
Lakes so that the planned Cape
Town to Cairo railway would
not be threatened.

Wilhelm, however, had mis-
read British intentions. The
British refused to give up their
position of isolation from continental affairs. Rebuffed by
Britain, Germany had to fall
back on its ties with Austria-
Hungary and later Italy. For the
moment the kaiser was enraged
over the British refusal. If the
British would not become an
ally then they would be treated
as Germany's enemy.

FRANCE 1890–1914

In the late 1880s anti-German feelings rose to the surface in France. Led by the popular General
Boulanger and politician Georges Clémenceau, public sentiment demanded a tougher stand towards
Bismarck. Until he was brought down over the issue of a
return to the monarchy, Boulanger had a brief period of
fame in which he rekindled thoughts of *revanche* over
Alsace-Lorraine and gathered a following around him that
included Bonapartists, monarchists, and radicals who
wanted war with Germany. Boulanger reinstituted military
parades, fought for rearmament, and became a national
hero. Ironically, Bismarck had been able to rush through
increased military budgets as a result of Boulanger's war-
mongering.

Unfortunately for the patriots, their plans for a revival of
French militarism were drowned in the scandals that rocked
the government towards the turn of the century. The first
concerned the government's financial support for the dig-
ging of the Panama Canal. The Canal Company bribed some

*French counterintelligence accused
Captain Alfred Dreyfus (1859–1935), an army
officer and a Jew, of writing a letter offering to
sell defence secrets to the Germans. They
charged him with treason.*

senators and deputies to pass a proposal for a Panama Canal lottery. When the company folded, millions of francs from the government sponsored lottery were missing. The Panama Canal scandal pushed all other matters into the background. It was charged that two Jewish directors of the Canal Company were behind the swindle. Of those that stood trial in 1893, all were acquitted except for the lone deputy who had confessed. Newspapers cried foul over the obvious government whitewash. In particular, the anti-Semite Edouard Drumont was given a public forum that touched off a wave of anti-Semitism throughout France.

The Dreyfus Affair

Hardly had the Panama Canal scandal subsided when another more damaging scandal rocked the nation—the Dreyfus Affair. In 1894 an unsigned letter was recovered from the wastebasket in the German embassy in Paris in which the writer offered to sell defence secrets to the Germans. French counterintelligence accused Captain Alfred Dreyfus, an army officer and a Jew, with writing the letter and charged him with treason. Drumont raised the public's ire over the possibility that Jewish bankers would see that the charges against Dreyfus were dropped. Under extreme public pressure, the court-martial found Dreyfus guilty and sentenced him to life imprisonment on Devil's Island. The verdict was based on a secret dossier whose contents, it was claimed, were so explosive they might touch of a war with Germany if they were revealed.

Military secrets, however, continued to find their way into German hands. When Colonel Georges Picquart, a counterintelligence officer, read the Dreyfus dossier in 1896 he found the trail led, not to Dreyfus, but to Major Ferdinand Esterhazy. Picquart was immediately dismissed from the army and imprisoned.

Georges Clémenceau the began a press campaign reopen the case. The newsp pers asked: whose welfare wa paramount, the individual's the state's? In the meantim Major Hubert Henry fed dama ing pieces of information to Dr mont who kept the anti-Semit campaign going. The major, was also discovered, had forg additional information to put the original Dreyfus dossier. I later claimed he had been acti under orders.

In 1898, when Esterhazy w brought to trial and acquitt within minutes, the French no elist, Emile Zola, wrote h famous letter, *J'accuse*. In it charged the government of cover up. Zola was arrested a sentenced to a year in prison f spreading antigovernment fe ings. Instead he went into v untary exile in England whe he continued to promote t need to reopen the case.

The Dreyfus Affair caused deep division in French so ety. Duels were fought and families were split over the m ter. The newspaper, *La Croix*, demanded that all Jews stripped of citizenship. The military were incensed th civilians dared to interfere in military matters. In t Assembly all other business was stalled by demands fo new trial. The affair divided French society along cl lines. There were those who championed the needs of state over the individual. Others championed individ rights over the demands of the state.

A new trial was ordered by the minister of war in 18 Major Henry's forgeries were uncovered and he confess his part in the affair. Two days later he committed suic in prison by slitting his throat. Major Esterhazy fled to E land where he gave conflicting evidence about his par the affair. Dreyfus was brought back to stand trial. He w again found guilty but was then pardoned by the presid of France. Later, in 1906, Dreyfus was exonerated i

vilian court, restored to his
nk in the army, and, much later,
ught bravely in World War I. He
as awarded the Legion of Hon-
r for his service in the war.

The treatment of Dreyfus
sulted in a radical sweep of the
ational Assembly. Shamed over
e treatment accorded the cap-
in, a disturbing antimilitaristic,
ticlerical mood grew in the
wer classes of French society.
e minister of war took the
portunity to republicanize the
ficer corps bringing new blood
to the military command.
nceforth all officer promo-
ns would be made from the
nistry of defence and not by
e general staff.

The antimilitaristic mood per-
ded French society until 1911
en tensions within Europe
inted to the inevitable coming
a major war and France began
prepare for the onslaught. At
t time there was a resurgence
national feeling.

al Entente

July 1891 a French naval squadron visited the Russian
al base at Kronstadt to open talks with Russia over pos-
le military cooperation between the two powers. This
s followed by a return visit of Russian warships to
lon. The result of these meetings was the signing of a
itary agreement in 1892. The agreement was formalized
treaty in 1894, and the Franco-Russian military alliance
ame referred to as the Dual Entente.

he entente between France and Russia was master-
ded by Foreign Minister Théophile Delcasse. Taking
antage of Germany's indifference towards Russia, Del-
se had done the impossible and brought France out of
ation. He had to agree to support Russia's claims in the
kans but in return Russia agreed to support the French
sition on Alsace-Lorraine. The Russian alliance became
cornerstone of French defence policy.

≈ Morocco ≈

Attempts in 1905 by France to lay claim to Morocco, the last rich, uncolonized territory on the North African Coast, were thwarted when Germany intervened. The kaiser's state visit to the sultan and his promise of German support against the French stalled the takeover. Delcasse did not believe the kaiser would go to war over Morocco. The next year proved him correct when an international conference forced Germany to back down.

One important result of Germany's intervention in Morocco was the creation of the Triple Entente in 1907 (also referred to as the Allied Powers, or Allies). At that time Great Britain agreed to join France and Russia for mutual interests. In 1911 the kaiser once again interfered in Morocco. The German warship Panther was sent to Agadir to protect German nationals in case of a native uprising against the French. That there were no German nationals in the region did not matter to the kaiser. The presence of a German warship in Moroccan waters was seen as saber-rattling and forced the members of the entente closer together.

≈

In France, President Raymond Poincaré rode an outburst of patriotic fever. The French were becoming convinced that a war with Germany was coming and Poincaré hastened to prepare French defences. The military budget was increased, war plans were rethought, arms and ammunitions were stockpiled close to the German border, and France's support for Russia in the Balkans was restated.

There was some concern in France that Russia might revert to a German alliance. This would doom France to defeat as France and Britain together were no match for Germany. Britain was a sea power and did not have an army large enough to matter in a major land war.

The kaiser attempted to weaken Franco-Russian relations. In 1893 he tried to bring Russia back towards a German alliance when he ordered the tariffs on Russian grain removed, permitting Russian grain to flood into Germany. This change in policy resulted in some political embarrassment when the *Junkers* raised a public outcry against it.

The Russians realized the drop in tariffs was only temporary. In fact, tariffs were reimposed in 1902. However, the kaiser's actions did cause a stormy debate in the *Reichstag* over his seemingly directionless and unproductive foreign policy. It also left the other powers wondering what the kaiser's personal foreign policy would be next.

In 1894 the kaiser decided to embark on new directions in foreign policy overseas. His strategy was to assert Germany's power and see what might come from it. In April there was the Samoan insurrection. Samoa was under the joint administration of Britain, the United States, and Germany. The offer by the kaiser to be the sole administrator was declined. This was followed by German intervention in the war between Japan and Korea, German intervention in the Anglo-Congolese boundary dispute, intervention in the Armenian massacres and, in the fall, there was a challenge to France and Britain over Morocco and the boundaries of Sudan. The kaiser also let it be known he was interested in the sharing out of the Portuguese and Ottoman empires.

It was a busy year and all the activity made the kaiser a hero in the eyes of the German public. The kaiser had brought Germany to a "place in the sun." The fires of ultranationalism were lit among the German peoples and they came to believe they were more powerful than they actually were.

A final break with England came in 1896 as a result of tensions in the Transvaal. On 1 January, the British governor of Rhodesia, Dr. Jameson, led an invasion of the Transvaal. The raiders were captured and thrown into jail. There had been considerable German commercial investment in the region since 1884. Krupp, Siemens, and the Deutsche Bank were among the heavy investors. There were thousands of Germans in the Transvaal and Germans controlled the dynamite and whiskey monopolies in Pretoria and Johannesburg.

The kaiser sent a telegram to Paul Kruger, president of the Transvaal Republic, congratulating the Boers for repelling an invasion by armed bandits and for success in restoring independence and peace against attacks from without. This was too much for the British public who were outraged against the German interference in their sphere of interest.

The depth of anti-German feelings created by the British press was overwhelming. The *Times* claimed the kaiser's telegram to the Boers was deliberately planted to break up the friendly relations between the two nations. The press wanted to know why. Germany was Britain's largest trading partner. Why would anyone want to break their friendly relations? Throughout British territory, mobs descended on the streets smashing windows in German stores, while in Germany the kaiser's popularity reached new heights.

A Place in the Sun

Weltpolitik was an aggressive foreign policy that would give Germany its "place in the sun." It would develop a German global sphere of influence similar to the other powers. It was an outward-looking policy that would bring Germany international prestige and economic power. It involved massive navy and army build up and would be costly. And there was the danger that it could bring Germany into conflict with the other powers, but the German public cheered each step of the way. It also brought Europe another step closer to World War I.

Many years later, in an interview with the *Daily Telegraph* the kaiser claimed he had personally kept Russia from attacking India while the British forces were engaged in South Africa. He also claimed it was he who had devised the plans that enabled Britain to win the Boer War. Such claims astounded the international community and made a mockery of Wilhelm's sincerity. British reaction was one of astonishment and disbelief.

WELTPOLITIK 189

In 1894 Count Alfred von Schlieffen, army chief-of-staff, warned that Germany's rivals had twice as many men under arms and called for an expansion of the German army. The Army Bill to increase manpower was placed before the *Reichstag*. The deputies approved the bill but at the same time reduced the term of military service from three years to two. They also added the provision that a review of the armed forces budget be made every five years instead of every seven.

The kaiser was furious at this attempt to interfere in military matters. Didn't the *Reichstag* realize that the French were getting stronger every day? They would soon be able to defeat Germany and reclaim Alsace and Lorraine. Unable to carry the military position, Caprivi was replaced by Prince Hohenlohe-Schillingsfürst. Hohenlohe would do the kaiser's bidding. Wilhelm planned to counter the *Reichstag* with a brand-new policy that would rouse all Germans regardless of class or profession, to new heights of patriotism. What was required was a worthy international cause.

To this end the government underwent major reorganization. The most important appointments made by the kaiser were Chancellor Bernhard von Bülow and Admiral Alfred Tirpitz. These two aggressive administrators are credited with establishing the policy of *Weltpolitik* that would transform Germany into a dominant world power.

*Admiral Alfred Tirpitz (1849–1930)
initiated a naval program that was aimed
at challenging British naval strength.*

THE NAVAL RACE

Tirpitz's naval strategy was at the heart of *Weltpolitik*. From its inception, the German naval program was aimed at challenging Britain whom he believed to be Germany's principal rival. His attitude destroyed any hope of an Anglo-German alliance.

Tirpitz linked Germany's future economic growth and the nation's standard of living to its access to world markets. He demanded money from the *Reichstag* for battleships to secure a passage across the North Sea into the world's oceans. If Germany did not seize the opportunity it would remain a second-rate power.

In 1898 Tirpitz asked the *Reichstag* to approve funding for 19 battleships, 8 heavy cruisers, 42 cruisers, and a number of smaller craft. In 1900 a supplementary naval bill requested twice that number. The goal was to build a navy two-thirds the size of Britain's, along with a North Sea base to neutralize any British threat. Naval expansion was a popular policy. The building of a great and powerful battle fleet was a project worthy of the nation.

Tirpitz's strategy was to build a battle fleet before Britain could react. Once a fleet was in existence there would be nothing the British could do about it. While attending Queen Victoria's Diamond Jubilee in 1897, the kaiser let it be known what was afoot. At the Spithead naval review, the crowning event of the celebrations, he went so far as to call himself the "Admiral of the Atlantic." His remarks did not go unnoticed.

British reaction was swift. Admiral John Fisher began to concentrate British warships in home waters. He ordered 155 older ships scrapped and replaced by newer and faster vessels. Britain had the capacity to out-build Germany and maintain naval supremacy of at least a two-power standard, that is, enough strength to overwhelm the next two largest battle fleets combined. Germany could not match the British naval program, especially as the German army also made demands on German defence costs. As a land power Germany could never afford to ignore its land forces.

In 1902 Britain came out of its isolation in foreign affairs and signed a mutual defence pact with Japan. The Japanese agreed to look after British interests in Asia while Britain promised to try to moderate Europe's attitude towards Japan. This enabled Britain to recall some of the ships of the Pacific squadron and send them to the Mediterranean and the North Atlantic.

Tirpitz wanted to fight a major naval battle with Britain in the North Sea. Once control of the North Sea had been won, Germany could emerge to lay claim to global power. Even the kaiser thought that this was asking too much, and German army leaders said the cost of building the battle fleet was far too great. The German chief of staff after 1905, General Helmuth von Moltke, wanted the money spent on increasing the size of the land forces.

In 1906 the German navy launched its first submarine. A line of submarines blockading the British Isles had a good chance of starving Britain to death. Tirpitz, however, ignored the idea of a submarine blockade on British ports because he was convinced any war would be over in a matter of a few months. Blockades took time to be effective. Yet, of all the powers, Britain was the most vulnerable to blockade as it stockpiled only a few months' worth of food and other goods. These had to be brought in from the empire over lengthy sea lanes. When the war began Germany had only twenty-two submarines in service.

That same year Britain launched the super-battleship *Dreadnought*. The massive 12-inch (305-mm) guns in movable turrets and the thick armour plating made the ship unsinkable. The *Dreadnought* made conventional fleets obsolete. It was the high-tech weapon of the age. The only

This British Dreadnought *is firing shots during World War I.*
The Dreadnought *was a super-battleship with 302-mm guns and thick armour plating.*
It was a massive, floating fortress.

chance for naval security was for rival fleets to out build each other. The *Dreadnought* was launched just a few months before similarly equipped ships, the USS *Alabama* and the USS *California*. All the sea powers were building these massive, floating fortresses.

Any attempt to slow down the costly **naval race** was met by angry public reaction. In Britain the battle cry was, "We want eight [more] and we won't wait!" Every seagoing nation had to have *Dreadnoughts* in their fleet regardless of the cost.

∼ Naval Strength ∼
(August 1914)

	Britain	Germany	France	Russia	Austria-Hungary	Italy
Dreadnoughts	20	13	13	8	4	4
Battle Cruisers	8	5	–	–	–	–
Old Battleships	40	22	13	3	3	–
Cruisers	102	41	31	6	10	–
Destroyers	103	144	81	106	18	33
Submarines	78	30	67	36	11	14

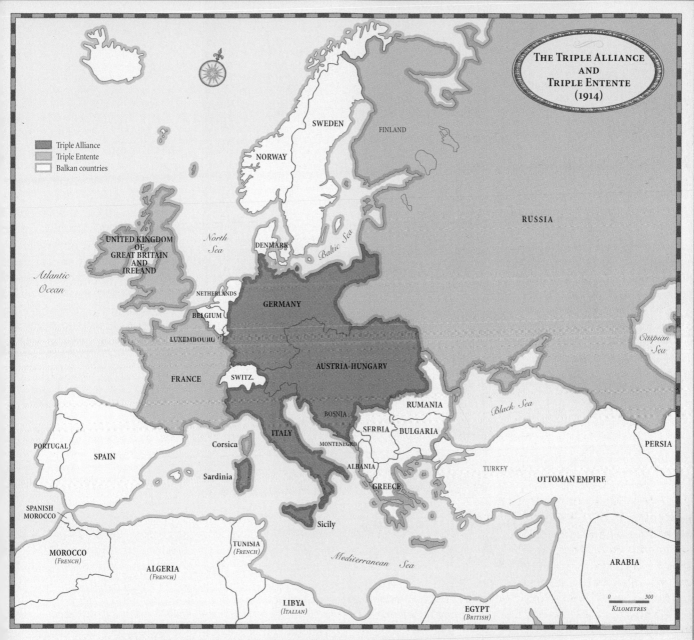

THE TRIPLE ALLIANCE
AND
TRIPLE ENTENTE
(1914)

Triple Alliance
Triple Entente
Balkan countries

What strategic advantage did the Triple Entente have over the Triple Alliance?

～ The Triple Entente ～

Over the period of 1894–1907, France, Russia, and Britain were drawn together in agreements that became known as the Triple Entente. Although not defensive agreements but rather "understandings," these agreements served to bind these powers together against the Triple Alliance of Germany, Austria Hungary, and Italy.

1894

Political and military agreement between France and Russia ends French isolation and provides a defensive arrangement regarding German interference in the Balkans and Alsace-Lorraine.

1904

France and Britain reach an understanding, or "entente cordiale," regarding their presence in North Africa. Britain's occupation of Egypt is recognized by the French, and France's control of Morocco is recognized by the British.

1907

Russia and Britain agree to a more amiable relationship. The British recognize the Russian sphere of influence in the north of Persia while the Russians acknowledge the British sphere of influence in the south of Persia. By 1907, therefore, France, Russia, and Britain are linked in the Triple Entente.

Emperor Franz Joseph of Austria (1830–1916) decided to annex Bosnia and Herzegovina in 1908. His decision to attack Serbia in 1914 would begin World War I.

FOREIGN INTERVENTIONS 1905–1912

When he took office in 1900, Chancellor von Bülow was informed by the kaiser that he was not to worry about foreign policy as he, the kaiser, had it well in hand. In 1905, Wilhelm visited Tangier to protest against French commercial expansion in the region. While in Tangier he told the sultan that Germany would support him against further French intrusions. France and Britain had acted in Morocco without consulting Germany and he would now deliberately intervene hoping to provoke a crisis over Moroccan independence.

The kaiser was posturing but Holstein and Schlieffen took him seriously. They argued that it would be better to go to war against the other powers in 1905 when Germany was better prepared than later when the other powers could be rearmed. In 1905 Russia was weakened from its defeat by Japan and England and France were occupied elsewhere. The German army was ready to fight. Why delay? A preventive war against France would offer many advantages.

To the kaiser's dismay a conference of the powers was called in Algeciras the following year. At the conference Germany lost prestige and found itself isolated. Typically, within a matter of weeks the kaiser had forgotten the whole affair. But the ploy had serious results.

Fear of German aggression led the other powers to begin rearmament programs. In particular, England and France drew closer together. Britain joined Russia and France in the Triple Entente in 1907. Now Germany, not France, appeared isolated by the other powers. The kaiser was left with only Austria-Hungary as a major ally.

In 1908 Austria-Hungary annexed Bosnia and Herzegovina. Austria-Hungary had administered the regions under the terms of the Treaty of Berlin (1878) which gave it the right to annex the provinces at a time of its choosing. Emperor Franz Joseph decided that the time had come to make them part of the Austro-Hungarian Empire.

Opponents advised Franz Joseph against a policy that would bring more Slavs into the empire. The Austro-Hungarian Empire could neither pacify or control the restless Slavs already within its boundaries. Why bring in more? But the emperor was not dissuaded—he had recently been in contact with Moltke, the German chief of staff, who had assured him of German support.

The kaiser reacted in panic at the prospect of a Balkan war. He reminded Franz Joseph that German support depended on Austria-Hungary being the injured party and not the aggressor. Still the impression was left with Franz Joseph that he would have unqualified German support in time of war.

In 1911, the kaiser once more intervened in Morocco. The French had sent troops to occupy Fez and complete the takeover of Morocco. Wilhelm reacted by ordering the warship *Panther* to Agadir in support of the Moroccans. The German press reported that Germany had brought the "rays of the morning sun" to the sultan and unless France withdrew France would find itself at war with Germany.

The kaiser was not serious about starting a war nor did the other powers take the German threat seriously. They all realized that the kaiser was bluffing and would not risk war over a colonial matter. However, French reaction was more serious than the others' and French bankers began to withdraw their loans from German industries.

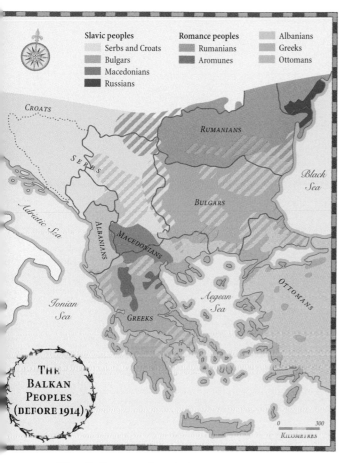

The Balkan region is home to many different ethnic groups.

After centuries of Ottoman domination, the Balkan people fought to win their independence.

The Balkan Wars 1912–1913

In 1911 Italy declared war on the Ottoman Empire by invading Tripoli (in Libya). This move drew the forces of the Ottoman Empire away from the Balkans at a critical time and left a power vacuum west of the Dardanelles. Quick to take advantage of the situation, in 1912 the Balkan peoples in Serbia, Bulgaria, Greece, and Montenegro united against the Ottoman Turks, aiming to push them back out of the region. At the same time, the various ethnic groups within the Balkans wanted to enlarge their own political control.

As the war developed, Russia

An Excuse Needed for War

During the Balkan crisis, on 8 December 1912, Wilhelm II met with his war cabinet. The situation in the Balkans was deteriorating and could lead to a war between the major powers. The German military staff urged the kaiser to go to war as soon as possible. Russia was recovering its armed strength lost in 1905 and France was adding to its defence positions. A German victory over both France and Russia could not be guaranteed after 1916 when these enemies had fully recovered. If war were to be fought the sooner the better. Moltke urged the kaiser to find an excuse then to strike as soon as possible.

came to the support of Serbia and Austria-Hungary backed Bulgaria. Rumania joined the war, too. British and French fleets conducted manoeuvres in the eastern Mediterranean Sea to help safeguard the strategically important Straits. With the Ottoman forces in full retreat, the warring factions were invited to London to arrange a cease fire.

At the London conference the victors fell out among themselves and fighting resumed. The situation grew more serious and the major powers feared they could not keep the fighting localized if Russia and Austria-Hungary decided on military intervention. Fortunately the Balkan War ended in 1913.

∼ La Belle Epoque ∼

In Paris, the idle rich passed away the hours along the boulevards.
This French actress is going for a drive in her private motor car.

There was a foreboding sense of gloom over Europe in the last days of 1913. The period of La Belle Epoque had been one of civilized leisure and splendour for the wealthy classes. Industry and technology had made Europe richer than ever before. Stately homes, wide tree-lined boulevards, and brightly-lit cafés beautified European cities. Amazing new inventions—the radio, motor car, movies, the airplane—all provided whimsical entertainment for the rich.

The arts flourished in an atmosphere of fastidious taste and public manners. But in order to enjoy the fruits of high capitalism, one had to have arrived or been born into the aristocracy. The upper and middle classes enjoyed their palaces and their annual migrations to the spas at Ems or Baden-Baden. Magnificent yachts anchored off Monaco or Biarritz. There were royal hunting expeditions into the forests where beaters flushed out the game. The international set were self-assured. Frivolity and grace predominated. Beautiful ladies in the latest fashions hosted the galleries and salons that were the centre of the artistic and intellectual worlds. For the few it was a good life filled with leisure pursuits.

England had its Ascot races, cricket matches, and polo; Germany had its beer gardens, historic universities, and technical schools. However, the age was centred in Paris—"the city of lights." The idle rich passed away the hours in the clubs or along the boulevards. Men in tails and white gloves escorted their ladies to the latest Stravinsky symphony or to a Nijinsky ballet where they thrilled to his new style.

Below this glittering façade millions laboured to support the life style of the rich. But the workers were restless. Work stoppages were a visible sign of labour unease. The threat of anarchy was in the air. The number of political assassinations in Europe had increased to the point where it was considered a normal risk of the job. The surly world of the masses was stirring to action. They wanted a better standard of living and an end to unemployment. Would the workers pull the whole structure down as Marx had predicted? Would a war put society right and end the grumbling?

The Schlieffen Plan

The German army was not hesitant about war now that General von Schlieffen had found the key to winning a two-front war. Because there would be a difference in the time Russia and France could mobilize for war, Germany would strike at the one that mobilized first. Then, having defeated that power, Germany could regroup its forces to defeat the other. Germany would take on one power at a time. The timing was critical, the strategy precise.

Germany planned to defeat France first. This would take no more than six weeks. Then Germany would transport forces by rail to the eastern front to defeat the Russians, who were calculated not to be able to enter Germany until week eleven. Traditionally the Russian Army was slow to mobilize.

No matter what caused the war, the plan called for an attack on France first, followed by war with Russia. The plan depended on Russia not being mobilized when the war started. To attack France first, German forces would have to go through Belgium to avoid French defences facing the Rhine River. Moving through Belgium would violate Belgian neutrality.

The concept was brilliant but it left Germany in the position of having to start the war and being labelled the aggressor. There would be no attempt to limit the war as it would be an all or nothing affair. In the matter of helping Austria-Hungary to defeat the Serbs, the German army would eventually get there after defeating first France and then Russia. Germany had its priorities and Serbia was not one of them.

The failure of the German army to carry out the **Schlieffen Plan** led to stalemate on the western front and ended all hopes of a quick war. World War I was to last four disastrous years.

RUSSIA

By 1914 the tsar had come to the conclusion that Russia had to reassert itself in the Balkans. Too often in the past century Russia had been forced to back away from military victory over the Ottoman Turks. There had been a long history of wars against the Ottoman Empire and in every one Russia had been denied the occupation of Constantinople and control over the Straits.

What was even more troublesome to the tsar was the appointment in 1913 of a German general, Liman von Sanders, as commander of the First Turkish Army. This, with increased German investment in the Balkans, was evidence of a major German economic thrust that would engulf the Straits. Russia would have to act before either Austria-Hungary or Germany took the region into its sphere of influence.

The tsar's plans for modernization were at stake. The annual profits from some five million tonnes of grain delivered through the Straits to world markets was essential to Russia's economy. Even during the drought and poor harvests at the turn of the century, the grain exports had continued. Villages and peasants starved but the shipments got through. All this suffering would have been for nothing if the Straits were to be closed to Russian shipping. The Russian people would not suffer another setback in the Balkans. The next time Russia would act.

ASSASSINATION

On 28 June 1914, against the strongest advice, Archduke Franz Ferdinand, heir to the Austrian throne, made a state visit to Sarajevo, capital of Bosnia. It was the Serbian national holiday and his visit was viewed by nationalists as an unwelcome reminder of their occupation by Austria. There had been many warnings of an assassination attempt but Franz Ferdinand would not be deterred. In the morning he watched army manoeuvres before going into the city.

The route of the six-car cavalcade had been well publicized. As it approached the centre of the city, a bomb was hurled by one of seven assassins along the route. The bomb exploded, injuring a driver who was sped to hospital. Awakened to the seriousness of his situation, the archduke took precautions. The routes and the times of further

On 28 June 1914, Archduke Franz Ferdinand and his wife Sophie, heirs to the Austrian throne, made a state visit to the capital of Bosnia. Both were assassinated by Gavrilo Princip, a member of a group of Serbian nationalists.

ceremonies were changed. A new driver was found but not told of the change in route. When the escorts sped off all the cars except the one carrying the archduke took the new route. The archduke's driver found himself alone. Reversing the car in order to follow the others, he backed into Gavrilo Princip, one of the other assassins. Princip calmly stepped onto the running board of the motorcar and fired point blank at the archduke and the archduchess. Gavrilo was arrested, sentenced, and died in prison in 1918. His action would cost millions of lives.

The assassination had been planned by the head of Serbian intelligence, Colonel Draguin Dimitrijevic—code name Apis. Russian implication in the plot was also later uncovered. Dimitrijevic had been responsible for the assassination of Serbia's king and queen in 1903. He was leader and founder of the Serbian secret society known as the Black Hand whose objective was the unification of all the southern Slavic peoples. Their principal weapon was terror.

The assassination was the catalyst that brought together all the forces building towards a general war. Yet it took another 33 days for war to begin, as many of the decision makers were away on holidays and were slow to react.

Official reaction to the assassination was delayed until 23 July when Franz Joseph approved an ultimatum to Serbia. Out of courtesy and also to prevent consultation between Paris and St Petersburg, the ultimatum was held back until President Poincaré of France had completed his state visit to Russia.

The ultimatum demanded the Serbs put an end to all anti-Austro-Hungarian activity, stop all smuggling across their common borders, bring the guilty to trial, and permit an Austro-Hungarian investigation of the crime inside Serbia. The Serbs were not expected to accept the ultimatum. Surprisingly, Serbia did accept it except for the last demand

regarding an Austro-Hungaria investigation of the assassin tion. The Serbian governme leaders said it was responsib enough to bring the guilty to tri But Franz Joseph was bent o war and kept the Serbian rep secret until it was too late. T ultimatum had been only a ge ture to gain time for the Austr Hungarian army to prepare assault on Belgrade.

The twenty-fifth of July was black day in Europe as crow gathered in the capitals a major cities awaiting the rep to the ultimatum. The kaiser ha just returned to Berlin fron Baltic cruise and raced throu milling crowds of cheering pe ple all the way from the tra station to the palace. It was rather heady occasion. Nev before had he received su adulation from the crowds.

During the next seven da there was an outpouring of patriotism as massive crow filled the squares waiting for a decision to go to war. Oth monarchs had the same experience. There were hu crowds in their cities demonstrating support for the national leaders.

Although Serbia had accepted most of the terms of t ultimatum, it was too late. Rival governments had alrea sent orders to their armed forces to mobilize. Once set motion, their battle plans could not be reversed.

On 28 July, a month after the assassination, the Brit fleet put to sea. Britain's Lord Grey called for a conferer to defuse the situation but even he did not have the support of the British cabinet. There was a lack of will attempt to harness the military. In any case it would have mattered, for Austria-Hungary declared war Serbia. As the injured party Franz Joseph sought a received German support.

On 30 July Russia mobilized its forces and triggered German response which was to implement the Schlieffen plan. Ultimatums were sent by the Germans

This photograph shows Gavrilo Princip being taken away by police just after he shot and killed the archduke and archduchess of Austria. His actions started a chain of events that led to the First World War.

ussia—to stop mobilization and to France to turn over to erman occupation the border fortresses of Metz and Toul til the crisis passed. The ultimatums were for public nsumption. On 3 August 1914, German forces wheeled wards France as World War I began.

UMMARY

n several occasions, rivalry for resources and territories among European powers led to a threat of war. The major powers looked to the military to cure their own industrial growth and to shield their lonies from outside interference. In Germany, the iser's policy of *Weltpolitik* resulted in the development a German naval fleet to secure access through the North a into the Atlantic Ocean. General Schlieffen's solution a two battlefront war made the kaiser even more bold his relationship with the other heads of state.

Central to the period was the spectacular and costly val race between Britain and Germany, resulting in the velopment of new technology in the form of the super ttleship, the *Dreadnought*. Although Britain launched first ship of this design, the other powers were not far hind in building their own.

At the turn of the century, the kaiser took it upon himself to unilaterally interfere in the foreign affairs of the other powers. This interference upset the balance of power that had been maintained through conferences and agreements since the Congress of Vienna (1814). Uncertainty about Germany's future stance caused a degree of paranoia among powers that feared German dominance in Europe, particularly France.

While the old processes of diplomacy were giving way to unilateral action, a dangerous growth of nationalism took place in all the regions of Europe. Supported by the press and a democratic following, heads of state encouraged a belief of supremacy among their people. Once instigated, the demands of the people could not be ignored.

The assassination of Franz Ferdinand, heir to the Austrian throne on 28 June 1914 in Sarajevo was the flare that touched off World War I. In itself the assassination was no more or less important than the dozens that had already occurred. This time, however, the heads of state were ready to go to war. They all saw a short, general war as a way out of their own domestic problems. Graver crises in the past had been resolved through consultation. But in 1914 peaceful negotiations were not given a chance.

QUESTIONS

1. Why did Bismarck maintain that Russia's relationship with Germany was a critical feature of German foreign policy? Wherein lay Russia's strength?

2. Why did Holstein, Germany's Foreign Minister, fear the resurrection of the Reinsurance Treaty with Russia?

3. Explain how German foreign policy changed during the 1890s from that implemented by Bismarck during his chancellorship.

4. Why did Wilhelm II wish to forge an alliance with Britain? What specifically did Germany propose to Britain? What was the result of these attempts at an agreement?

5. Briefly outline the events which led to the alliance between Russia and France. How did Germany react to this new agreement between Russia and France?

6. Explain the circumstances in the Transvaal which resulted in a rupture of the relationship between Germany and Britain. What was the reaction of the German public?

7. Explain the policy of *Weltpolitik*. What was the significance of this policy for Germany? For the world?

8. What was Germany's reaction to Austria's annexation of Bosnia-Herzegovina?

9. Briefly outline the dispute between France and Germany over Morocco in 1911. How did the French react to the German threats?

10. What was the *Dreadnought?* How did its creation contribute to an arms race?

11. What was the significance of the Balkan crisis in 1912?

12. Evaluate the advantages and disadvantages of the Schlieffen Plan.

13. Briefly describe "La Belle Epoque." How did the bulk of the population live in comparison to the monied class, which could take advantage of artistic and intellectual achievements?

14. Why was the Archduke Franz Ferdinand assassinated? What was the immediate result? Why did diplomatic attempts fail to resolve the international crisis?

15. Outline the chronology of July and early August which took the major powers into World War I. Evaluate whether it is fair to state that the assassination caused the war.

ANALYSIS

1. In France, General Boulanger's popularity increased as a result of his militaristic platform and anti-German stance. Comment on the advantages and disadvantages of directing nationalist feelings against a supposed enemy outside the country. Do you think Boulanger wanted war with Germany or only more political support? Evaluate the effectiveness of bluffing in foreign affairs.

2. *Weltpolitik* was meant to give Germany a "place in the sun." Its implementation created deep tensions among the powers. Yet Germany saw building an empire as a natural extension of its industrial power. Analysts at the time concluded that German economic self-sufficiency required land and resources that were within the spheres of other nations.

a) Analyze the means by which the kaiser implemented his policy of *Weltpolitik?* Could *Weltpolitik* have been achieved without a general war? Speculate on how this could have been brought about? Be careful not to impose your twentieth century views on those of the nineteenth century.

(b) How effective was *Weltpolitik* in fueling German industrial growth?

(c) Research the growth of the German synthetic industry as an alternative supply of resources. Suggest other possible alternatives.

The *Dreadnought* was an entirely new type of weapon. It made other warships obsolete. Every industrial power wanted to have *Dreadnoughts* in their battle fleets and all achieved this goal within a few months of each other. The question was which power could build the most. The winner of the naval race would then have the potential to control all the world's shipping lanes so that economic lifelines would be vulnerable to the new super weapon.

(a) Research the capability of the *Dreadnought*. How powerful was it?

(b) What was the cost to Germany, a land power, of building *Dreadnoughts?* Why did the German people support their naval construction program?

(c) Speculate why publics are enamoured with new, high-tech weapons?

(d) How can the public be persuaded to finance new weaponry in times of peace?

(e) Draw up a program for unveiling the *Dreadnought* to the British public. What kind of press releases would you create? How would the *Dreadnought* appear in movie?

(f) How would the *Dreadnought* contribute to ultra-nationalism?

ACTIVITIES

1. Interview

You are a newspaper reporter. Set up an interview with a prominent member of the Black Hand organization in order to determine its goals for the Balkan peoples. Structure your questions to allow you to discover the type of individual who has been attracted to this organization, the way he or she feels about Austria, and how he or she feels Balkan society should be governed.

2. Cartoon

Develop a cartoon which features one aspect of the decision-making process which occurred among the Great Powers after the assassination of Franz Ferdinand.

3. Chart

Create a chart which outlines the relationships between the major powers at the end of the nineteenth century. Analyze the chart to determine whether any of these powers was likely in themselves to cause a war. Assess which nation was most responsible for the breakdown in diplomatic relations.

4. Debate

Be it resolved that Germany must have the right to establish a global empire. In the course of debate address the reaction of other powers to Germany's international thrust.

THE WAR
ON THE
WESTERN FRONT

BRITAIN

HOLLAND
(NETHERLANDS)

Zeebrugge
Ostend
Dunkirk
Calais
FLANDERS
Boulogne
Ypres
Armentières
Vimy
Passchendaele
Ghent
Antwerp
Brussels
BELGIUM
Mons
Liège
Aix-la-Chapelle
Bonn

English Channel

GERMANY

Meuse River
Rhine River
Moselle River

Frankfurt

Somme
River
St. Quentin
LUXEMBOURG
Luxembourg

Seine River

SAAR

Paris
Château
Thierry
Verdun
Marne
River

LORRAINE

FRANCE

ALSACE

The Allies
The Central Powers
Occupied by the Central Powers
Advances of the Central Powers
Limit of German advance, 1914
Limit of trench warfare, 1914-1917
Hindenburg Line, 1917
Limit of final German advance, 1918
U-boat base
Neutral states

0   60
KILOMETRES

Belfort

SWITZERLAND

On the western front, battles raged along a line of trenches
that stretched across northern France.

Chapter 13
The Beginning of War
to Stalemate
1914–1916

FOCUS ON:

An evaluation of the strategies used by the major powers in World War I;

The impact of technology on World War I;

The failure of the major powers to end the war quickly.

THE WESTERN FRONT 1914

*A*t ten o'clock on a bright, sunny August day in the summer of 1914, a small party of German lancers approached a French sentry post near Belfort. The lieutenant drew his pistol and fired three shots into the sentry's chest. At the same moment the dying sentry fired back at the German knocking him off his horse. These were the opening shots in what was to become one of the bloodiest confrontations in history. The First World War had begun.

On 2 and 3 August a massive German force of over 1 500 000 men, divided into five army groups, rolled into Belgium. It was the largest troop movement in history and it was to plunge an entire generation of young people into the cauldron of war. The war pitted Germany and Austria against Britain, France and Russia. Eventually many other countries joined in. Among them were Japan, Italy, the United States, and China. It was to last four years with the last shots fired 52 months after it had begun. Its human cost was an average rate of 5000 dead each day.

The main thrust of the German attack was a great enveloping movement through Belgium, sweeping south-west across France towards Paris, then swinging back east to take the French armies in the rear. This outflanking movement would surround the French forces and bring the war to a climax in a final clash of arms along the Marne River somewhere in early September. The Germans were so confident of victory that they had made no preparations to continue the battle for France past the first two months. France had to be defeated within the first six weeks in order for their victorious armies to be transported across

---

TIMELINE

1914 on the Western Front

3 August ❈ War begins with Germany's invasion of Belgium.

5–10 September ❈ Battles along the Marne River in France lead to stalemate.

October-November ❈ Attempts by both sides to outflank each other in the Race for the Sea fail. Neither side could prevail. During the winter of 1914–1915, both sides create elaborate networks of trenches.

December ❈ The stockpiles of war supplies run out on both sides. The decision is made to resupply the fighting fronts and continue the war. Efforts to call a peace conference fail.

1914 on the Eastern Front

August-September ❈ Russian forces are defeated at the battles of Tannenburg and the Masurian Lakes.

December ❈ The tsar is advised that his armies can no longer mount an offensive.

1915 on the Western Front

This year is characterized by **trench warfare.**

1915 on the Eastern Front

The German-Austrian armies route the Russian armies in a mid-summer offensive.

Attempts to defeat Germany by creating a third battlefront fail at Gallipoli. Italy enters the war on the side of the Allied forces in return for promised territorial gains after the war. A campaign is launched in the Middle East with the hopes of driving Germany's ally, the Ottoman Empire out of the war.

Germany to meet the Russian on the eastern front. It had bee calculated that the Russia armies, slower to deploy, coul not possibly enter German so until the eleventh week.

The French armies were ma shalled along the Frencl German border from the Alps t Belgium. There had been only few attempts to bring neutra Belgium into the defence ne work but these had proved futil In the hope of escaping invasio the Belgians had insisted o strict neutrality. They would gi the Germans no reason to attac them. Thus 210 kilometres of th French-Belgian border wer undefended. If needed, this ga could be filled by the sma British Expeditionary Force 300 000 plus one of the Frenc armies held in reserve. Th French High Command did n believe this to be a threatene region. Indeed the Belgian bo der was all but ignored in the war plans.

French strategy, contained Plan 17, called for an immedia attack along the German border in Alsace and Lorrain Five armies totalling 1 300 000 men would rise from the positions and deliver an infantry attack that was bound break through the German defences just as Napoleon ha done 100 years before. The fighting spirit of Napoleo troops had counted then and the same spirit would cou again.

Some of the French rejoiced at the prospect of a w that would give them the opportunity to regain Alsace a Lorraine. After 44 years of waiting, French soldiers wou once more tread the soil of the lost provinces. Confide of an early breakthrough, French generals boasted marching their forces straight through the enemy lines Berlin. It should take no more than three weeks.

When the battle started, row after row of Fren

*The main thrust of the German attack was a great enveloping movement
through Belgium, sweeping down towards France. Brussels, the capital of
Belgium, fell to the Germans on 20 August 1914. This is the German
parade of conquerors in the city's main square.*

The Germans had made a rapid deployment of troops, with more than 550 trains each day crossing the Rhine, bringing men and materiel to the battle fronts. The first target was the fortified city of Liège in Belgium. Its 12 outlying forts made Liège one of the most heavily defended cities in Europe, blocking the way into northern France. It could not be bypassed without going into Holland, a strategy forbidden by the kaiser.

Stoutly defended, Liège took longer to capture than anticipated and this delay set back the timetable of the German battle plan. The delay was to prove critical as it permitted the French to begin to redeploy their armies to meet them.

fantrymen, helmetless and in bright uniforms, advanced against an array of German machine guns. The French disdained the use of machine guns as they were considered unreliable, and for the first few hours they were convinced that they were merely facing unusually rapid rifle fire. The breakthrough was bound to occur when the German riflemen ran short of ammunition. Thus wave after wave of infantry were sent into battle only to be slaughtered by an enemy they never saw.

It was not until well into the campaign, when the French had suffered over 500 000 casualties, that they were issued metal helmets and less visible clothing. But the stupid and wasteful strategy of sending men across open ground against well-protected machine gun nests continued for another four years.

At first the French were able to push back the Germans. This fit in with the German plans to lure the French away from the main battle areas. It was not until 20 August that the Bavarian Crown Prince Rupprecht counterattacked forcing the French back inside their own border. In the meantime, the French had discovered to their horror that the main German thrust was not opposite them in Lorraine but was coming through Belgium and was even then rushing headlong towards Paris.

Day after day the German howitzers rained shells on the Liège fortresses reducing them to rubble and, by 16 August, the German juggernaut was once more underway. Brussels was taken on 20 August, with the small Belgian army penned up in Antwerp as the German armies raced into France. It was about this time that the French armies in Lorraine were being pushed back towards the Marne River.

Once through Belgium the German advance swept towards Paris in a swift, crushing blow. Days of heavy fighting brought continuous victory as the French army recoiled before the onslaught. But the rapid advance was not without its costs. Each day new battles had to be fought to clear the French from hastily dug defences.

Alongside the French, the British Expeditionary Force took its toll of the enemy in the slag heaps of the coal fields outside Mons. So rapid was their rifle fire (18 rounds per minute) that von Kluck, commander of the First German Army, thought he was up against machine guns. The battle through France was proving costly to both sides.

It was at this critical juncture that Moltke, the German commander-in-chief, changed the German battle plans to swing his armies east of Paris rather than envelop the city. He thought that the French were beaten and would require

These British soldiers are running across "no man's land," the ravaged land between their trench line and the German's trench line. When soldiers cross no man's land, they are fired at from the enemy trenches. Thousands of soldiers died this way.

only a small push to end the war. He wanted to position the full force of his northern armies on the Marne River before the retreating French armies could get there.

When the German armies, weary from four weeks of fighting, reached the Marne, sporadic fighting broke out followed by a French counterattack all along the front. Thus began what came to be known as the Miracle of the Marne, fought in early September. This tenacious 10-day battle was a series of disjointed thrusts resulting from the collision of over 2 000 000 men. Beginning in the hills north of Meaux it was to extend northwestward along the banks of the Marne River.

The German decision to pass east of Paris exposed the flank of von Kluck's first army. The move away from Paris was reported by a reconnaissance plane and provided the opportunity for the British and French to strike at the vulnerable German flank. Under heavy attack from the side, von Kluck switched the order of his army and brought his spearhead to bear against the attackers. He would advance on Paris after all. In so doing, he opened a 32-kilometre gap between himself and the neighbouring German second army under General von Bülow.

In itself this was not a major problem and did not pose a serious threat to the German advance. However, in the confusion, the Germans ordered a temporary pull back of all their forces to reestablish the battle line. This would also give their men a chance to rest and allow the supply columns to catch up.

The order to pull back was given by a junior officer, I Col. Hentsch, sent to the front from headquarters Luxembourg to report on how the battle was going. He ha full authority from Moltke to make any decisions nece sary to restore the battle line and resume the advanc Unfortunately for the Germans Hentsch's decision was disengage and regroup.

This order cost Germany the battle. It destroyed th momentum and now all hope for a swift victory on th Western front was lost. By 14 September, when th German armies had repositioned themselves, they faced Allied divisions to their own battle-weary 53. The pull bac had been a fatal mistake. Robbed of a swift victor Germany now faced a long war of **attrition**—a war f which it was not prepared.

From mid-September 1914 to the end of November, ea army attempted to get around the others' western flank what has become known as the Race for the Sea. Millio of exhausted men fought to a **stalemate.** It was not mea to have happened and only slowly did the realization s in among the generals that this was going to be a very d ferent war from the one they had planned.

One of the last battles of the year was fought on November at Ypres, over the channel ports of Dunkir Calais, and Boulogne. The Prussian guards moved maje tically in mass formations as if on parade against t British lines. Caught in converging fire, they died compa by company.

A German machine gun company readies a defence line against an attack.
The rapid, indiscriminate fire of the machine gun brought casualty lists to new heights.

In the battle for France each side suffered a staggering million battle casualties. Without victory the opposing ~~mies~~ settled down to wait the coming spring. They bus-~~d~~ themselves with transforming the front line into an ~~e~~laborate network of trenches that reached well to the rear ~~of~~ the battleground. Mine fields and strings of barbed wire ~~w~~ere placed ahead of the defences. Lines of fire were ~~cl~~eared for machine guns, and rows of artillery were ~~si~~ghted into the narrow distance between the lines called ~~no~~ man's land. Each side acted to make its own trench line ~~im~~pregnable to attack—a task in which they succeeded ~~on~~ly too well.

~~T~~he stalemate established in the first weeks of the war ~~w~~as to last almost another four years. In that time the ~~tr~~ench lines of the western front lay relatively unchanged ~~de~~spite repeated attempts by both sides to break through ~~th~~em. Millions more men were to lose their lives trying to ~~r~~each the enemy lines that lay just a few hundred metres ~~aw~~ay. Until 1918 the Allies could not dislodge the Germans ~~no~~r could the Germans break through to Paris.

THE EASTERN FRONT 1914–1915

The key to the Schlieffen Plan lay in knocking France out of the war before Russia could mobilize its forces and attack Germany from the east. In this way Germany would eliminate the dangers of a two-front war by dealing with its enemies one at a time. However, the Russians mobilized ahead of time and threw out the German timetable. In those days mobilization meant the deployment of troops ready for battle. Russia's early mobilization had not been taken into consideration and was one of the reasons Germany had decided to attack France when it did. None of the major powers could afford to have the enemy mobilize first.

The Russian army at mobilization numbered 4.5 million poorly trained men. Still suffering from defeat by the Japanese in 1904, the Russians were not considered an immediate threat. Only 200 000 Germans were left in eastern Germany to contain the Russians until the main armies could arrive. But to the German's surprise the Russians engaged in military operations almost from the outset. The

THE WAR ON THE EASTERN FRONT

Legend:
- The Allies
- The Central Powers
- Occupied by the Central Powers
- Advances of the Allies
- Advances of the Central Powers
- Limit of German advance, 1914
- Eastern Front on the eve of the Russian Revolution, October 1917
- Limit of Allied advances
- Occupied by the Central Powers after Treaty of Brest-Litovsk, 1918
- Neutral states

0   300 *Kilometres*

NORWAY

SWEDEN

FINLAND

• Petrograd

JUTLAND

DENMARK

Baltic Sea

Riga

• Moscow

GERMANY

Masurian Lakes
Tannenberg

Warsaw
• Lódz POLAND • Brest-Litovsk

Pripet Marshes

RUSSIA

Kraków

Danube GALICIA

SWITZERLAND

Vienna *River*

Dnieper River

AUSTRIA-HUNGARY

UKRAINE

Venice *Sava River* • Trieste

Odessa •

Adriatic Sea

ITALY

SERBIA

RUMANIA

Caspian Sea

Black Sea

MONTENEGRO

BULGARIA

ALBANIA

Bosporus Strait

Constantinople •
Gallipoli •

GREECE

The Dardanelles

Aegean Sea

OTTOMAN EMPIRE

PERSIA

Mediterranean Sea

PALESTINE — • Jerusalem

ARABIA

EGYPT

The Central Powers drove the tsar's poorly equipped and untrained army back into Russian territory.

The Russian invasion of East Prussia began well ahead of what the Germans thought possible. Russia dealt a sharp blow to the German forces in the north while pushing the Austrians back to Kraków, Poland in the south.

with each other by transmitting on radio waves.

Unwilling to chance mistakes in decoding, many Russian messages were uncoded. These messages were picked up by the Germans. Fully aware of the Russian battle plans, the Germans were able to lure the Russian forces into battles of annihilation. Whole armies were overwhelmed. Poorly led, ill equipped, and often without training, hundreds of thousands of Russians charged into battle. They were massacred. The Russians lost 250 000 men and all of their weapons and *matériel*. Their commander, General Samsonov, committed suicide.

In the south, the Russians routed the Austrians and drove them deep into Galicia, where the Austrian front collapsed with a loss of 300 000 men. This brought new dangers to the German position. However, the Russian victory was short-lived as Hindenburg was planning a counterattack on Lódz and Warsaw. Thus the stage was set for the savage fighting that lasted until December when the Russian armies began to withdraw.

Four months of fighting left the Russians dreadfully mauled. On 18 December 1914, the Grand Duke Michael reported to Tsar Nicholas that his armies were out of ammunition and that Russia must stand on the defensive for the remainder of the war.

So complete were its victories in the east Germany came to the false conclusion that it would take very little more to get Russia out of the war. With stalemate looming in the west, the Germans decided to place their main effort for 1915 in smashing what was left of the Russian army while staying on the defensive on the western front.

Elsewhere, Austrian forces crossed the Sava River and attacked the mountainous territory held by the Serbs. After all, the whole thing had begun with a Serbian-backed assassination of the heir to the Austrian throne. This seemed forgotten once the major battle fronts developed elsewhere in Europe.

...ussian invasion of East Prussia began on 12 August, well ...head of what the Germans thought possible. Russia dealt ...sharp blow to the German forces in the north while in ...e south the Russians pushed the Austrians 150 kilome- ...es back to Kraków, Poland.

The danger to Germany appeared greater than it was ...ecause the Russians had spent their effort and could not ...ve advanced much farther. Whole army corps advanced ...ithout proper rations, often marching through sandy ...astes to reach the front line. They were not going any- ...here and could have safely been ignored, but the ...ermans decided to counter the Russian invasion by with- ...awing two corps from the western front to bolster their ...astern defences. In the end they did not arrive in time for ...e decisive battles. General Hindenburg was brought out ...' retirement and, with General Ludendorff, sped to the ...ene to eliminate the danger.

Using their efficient railway system, the German com- ...anders were able to deploy what troops they had to deal ...ith each Russian army in turn. The Germans sent 400 ...ains a day to the Russian border compared to 90 trains ...r the Russians. The critical battles were fought in mid- ...ugust to September in the region of Tannenburg and the ...asurian Lakes. There, the advancing Russian forces were ...attered by the terrain and attempted to keep in touch

~ Trench Warfare ~

At night, carrying parties brought forward the supplies and ammunition for the next attack and took out the wounded on their return.

By 1915 the front lines had become transformed into huge networks of trenches and dugouts. Rear trenches incorporated villages, hospitals, artillery parks, and rest and recreation facilities. Yet battle strategy called for unprotected infantry to break through these lines.

In the trenches the lessons of survival were quickly learned. Ears were sharpened to pick up the sound of shells headed one's way. Heads had to be kept down as enemy sniper fire continually ranged across the top of the trenches. Soldiers slept in tunnels and makeshift command posts waiting for the sound that meant the enemy was near.

Night was the worst time. Raiding parties crisscrossed no man's land looking for easy kills or mapping the landscape for the morning's attack. Creeping through the barbed wire, they tossed hand grenades into the trenches or carried off a groggy soldier for interrogation.

Water was boiled on the hot barrels of the machine guns and what wood was available was used as fuel. Often, rains turned the battlefield into a quagmire. When it rained everything became waterlogged for weeks. Trenches and shell holes filled with water adding another barrier to the attack. After the third battle of Ypres in 1917, where 582 000 men were killed, a high-ranking officer from headquarters who came to view the front commented, "Good God, did we really send men to fight in that?" It was as if generals and soldiers were fighting a different war. The high commands and the staff officers seldom visited the front lines, preferring the headquarters areas in the rear.

Before an attack thousands of guns pounded the enemy lines. This was to blow away the barbed wire and destroy the machine gun emplacements. The noise from their muzzles and the exploding shells would crush the enemy and drive the defenders insane. The unremitting bombardment pulverised the ground as high explosive shells churned up the mud and water-filled craters.

In the four-month battle in Flanders, the infantry plodded through no man's land seeking the elusive breakthrough. Timing was all important as hundreds of thousands of men strove to reach the enemy's lines before they could recover from the barrage and ready their machine guns to fire. Sheltered in dugouts as much as 49 metres deep, the enemy safely waited out the storm. Artillery barrages seldom had the required effect and when the shelling was over the defenders raced to the surface to man their gun line.

Huge craters were caused by heavy shelling. These craters are near the Somme River in France.

Whistles gave the command to go over the top. Each man carried his full field pack, a shovel, 200 rounds of ammunition, and three days' rations. They all wondered how many of them would make it through the artillery fire to reach the enemy's barbed wire before the machine guns began to chatter. When the attack was spent those who were alive slipped back towards the safety of their own lines pursued by the enemy.

Big Berthas

arger, longer-range guns were used on fortresses and cities. The German 210-mm guns were so large that they were mounted on railway cars in order to transport them to the front. These railway guns fired 300 shells into Paris from 108 kilometres away. The German 420-mm guns, nicknamed Big Berthas, could fire a shell two metres high weighing a tonne over a distance of 15 kilometres every six minutes. At Verdun these shells penetrated defences composed of two metres of earth, three metres of concrete, and a metre of wall. One had 63 seconds to take cover from the flash of the gun to when the shell arrived.

Anticipating a quick victory ...er the Serbs, the Austrians ...ere set back by the realities of ...ountain warfare. They were ...ot prepared for the ferocious ...ghting over mountain ridges ...d through hidden valleys. They ...ffered horrendous losses as ...ers flooded and mountains ...re covered metres-deep with ...rly snow. Appalling atrocities ...re committed by both sides ...d few prisoners were taken. ...erywhere, the Serbs were vic-...cious. The Austro-Hungarians ...d lost over half their army to ...e Serbs and by December the ...rbs were as firmly entrenched ...ever.

...n May 1915 Germany and ...stria launched a limited attack to protect the Austro-...ungarian forces at Kraków, with unexpected results. The ...ited attack turned into a major Russian defeat. Quick ... take advantage of a breakthrough, the Germans and ...strians launched an all-out attack, slashing great holes ... the Russian lines. By mid-June they had advanced 160 ...ometres and inflicted 500 000 casualties on their enemy. ... the end of the fall, this figure had risen with the destruc-...n of several Russian armies numbering 3.4 million men. ...t the end of 1915, Russian armies existed only by the ...usion of untrained manpower. Youthful cadres of peas-...s and workers were sent into the battle lines in a des-...ate attempt to halt the German onslaught. Exhausted, ...ving marched hundreds of kilometres to get to their ...sitions, they had only their bayonets and hands with ...ich to fight. Regiments cheered when they received 15 ...lls per gun. Many soldiers went into battle without ...apons of any kind. They had to wait until their com-...es were killed so they could pick up their weapons. ...al and obedient, they were no match for the battle-...dened enemy they faced.

...or the Russian army, every new battle meant another ... 000 casualties. Convinced that Russia could not fight ...more, the Germans decided to turn their attention to ... western front in 1916.

WESTERN FRONT 1915

he second year of the war on the western front was characterized by repeated attempts to push the Germans out of northern France. Time after time, large numbers of men were sent into combat hoping to break the enemy hold on the bulge between Ypres and Verdun. Newly-arrived Allied generals contemplated being on the Rhine in a matter of a few more weeks, provided enough manpower could be brought to bear.

However, there seemed to be no end to the ability of the rival armies to bring fresh stocks of men and supplies to the battle areas to replace those already consumed. Fought across the inferno of no man's land the front lines stood witness to some of the bloodiest battles ever known.

The strategists believed the only way to get the Germans out was by frontal attack on their trench lines. Yet only rarely was a front line trench ever captured and there were other trench lines behind the first. Continued infantry attacks against the artillery barrages and barbed wire of the enemy lines resulted in unimagined carnage. Only with the development of the battle tank in 1917 were trench lines effectively overcome.

Until the last months of the war, the western front was characterized by siege warfare between elaborate, interlocking trench networks reaching from the Swiss border to the English Channel. Between the two sides, no man's land stood as a ghostly desert. The men were rotated into the trenches every month, followed by a prolonged period in the rear areas for rest and retraining. If the older veterans were sent to the rear it was a sure sign that an attack was imminent. They were to be saved to train the new recruits and make them ready for battle.

The attackers made their way forward in rushes only to be cut down by machine gun and artillery fire. Only a few would reach the enemy front lines and seldom would a breakthrough occur. The wounded were left dying in the

The Big Bertha could blast holes in armour and concrete. It could hurl a shell up to 15 km and cause heavy destruction of enemy fortifications and cities.

retreat as the counterattack harried the attackers back to their own lines.

Then there were the guns. Tens of thousands of them wheel to wheel. During an attack the only command was to fire and continue firing to saturate the target area. At the third battle for Ypres, 4.3 million shells were used in the opening barrage alone. The carnage was incredible.

After 1914 poison gas shells came into use. Chlorine was the active ingredient in the first attacks against the Canadians at the second battle for Ypres. Urine-moistened rags acted as an effective neutraliser. The surprise use of chlorine caused the French line to collapse abandoning the Canadians who stood their ground despite terrible casualties. A six-kilometre gap temporarily opened that could have given Germany a breakthrough had the Germans been able to exploit it but the clouds of gas and the smoke from the shell fire obscured the opening. The Ypres salient (exposed line of defence) became home to the Canadians who came to know well this most dangerous part of the line where German artillery could fire at them from three sides.

After 1917, phosgene was used and gas masks for both men and animals were the only defence. Then, at the end of the war, when mustard gas was used the problem was to protect all the skin as the gas burned anything it touched. However, gas attacks were used sparingly and usually out of desperation because of the uncertainty of the winds which could shift and blow the gas back on one's own batteries and trenches.

SECONDARY FRONTS 1915–1917

*W*ith stalemate on the western front and the Russians in retreat, the French and British looked to break the deadlock by opening new battlefronts in the Ottoman Empire, the Balkans, Italy, and Arabia. The hope was that victory in the eastern Mediterranean would force the Germans to abandon the western front in order to redeploy their troops in the new theatres of war.

The Ottoman Empire

In November 1914, Enver Pasha took the Ottoman Empi into the war on the side of Germany. This was disastro for the Allies as they needed passage of the Dardanelles get aid to Russia. Not only was a crucial supply route Russia cut off but the Ottoman navy bolstered by t German cruisers *Goeben* and *Breslau* scoured the Bla Sea and bombarded Odessa. At the same time, Ottom land forces became engaged in Palestine and Armenia.

The British planned to capture the Straits a Constantinople by storming the forts that guarded the n rows. With the Straits open Russia could be resupplied a the Allies could mount a campaign up the Danube Riv towards Vienna.

Although the plan was well conceived, the Allied co manders on the spot were not suited to carrying out a co bined forces operation. Commanding officers spent m time bickering with each other than getting on with t war. An attempt to destroy the forts at Kum Kale s ceeded, but when three older British battleships we blown up either by mines or torpedoes and three oth crippled, orders were given to withdraw. The naval bo bardment warned the Ottoman Turks of battles to co and they began to form a defence line across the Gallip Peninsula.

The initial landings on the Gallipoli Peninsula had ev chance of success. The Ottoman Turks were short of s plies and had only 80 000 men to guard 150 kilometres line. On 25 April a five-pronged assault was made on t

Lawrence of Arabia was able to unite several of the desert tribes into an effective fighting force in the desert regions of the Ottoman Empire.

of the peninsula. An Australia-New Zealand (ANZAC) ce was to land farther to the north on the western shore ar Gaba Tepe. They were to rush the heights and push erland to Mal Tepe overlooking the narrows. Of the five idings the three to the west went in unopposed.

The other two landings met with fierce resistance. From heights Ottoman guns rained a curtain of fire on the rrow beaches. The fire was so heavy that the men on the owded beaches could hardly move, let alone attack or reat. Exhausted and shaken they clung to the beaches d hugged the cliffs. Why warships did not come close in ore and blow the enemy off the heights has never been lained. Hundreds of men fell in heaps as they disem-ked from their transports and plunged into the water. n even larger landing took place on Cape Helles in early gust. Once again the local commanders gave the oman Turks time to redeploy instead of dashing for the ghts immediately upon getting ashore.

After the war a senior officer visiting the battlefield ed how easy it would have been had naval gunfire ared the heights or had the Straits been forced. wever, if the invasion had succeeded, could the Allies e held the Straits? When the orders came to evacuate December, some 250 000 Allied casualties had been taken in the nine-month campaign without any visible gains. All that could be reported was that the Ottoman Turks had suffered similar losses.

In other parts of the empire the Ottoman forces were not as fortunate. The Ottoman Turks lost 600 000 men in the desert campaign made colourful by the exploits of Lawrence of Arabia and the Australian cavalry contingent. Lawrence was able to unite several of the desert tribes into an effective fighting force that struck across the desert regions at Ottoman outposts. The one land campaign saw General Allenby capture Jerusalem and push the Ottoman Turks out of Beersheba and Gaza—areas that came into dis-puted ownership with the collapse of the Ottoman Empire in 1918.

Farther to the north the Russians fought against Ottoman forces in Armenia and the Caucasus. At the end of the war, the 800 000-man Ottoman army had been reduced through disease, starvation, battle, and desertions to under 200 000.

The Serbs, who had started the war against the Austro-Hungarian army successfully in 1915, were now to feel the wrath of a combined Austro-Hungarian, German, and Bulgarian invasion. Unable to maintain their mountain strongholds, the Serbs carried out a bitter retreat to the

Adriatic. Scattered Serbian forces continued to wage war in subsequent years in Macedonia.

Italy

In 1915 Italy agreed to join the French and British. The reaction in Vienna was one of disbelief. Were their neighbours to the south actually going to join with France and Britain? Was not Italy signatory to the Triple Alliance? In Vienna mobs poured into the streets demonstrating support for the Austrian emperor and vowing to defeat their former Italian ally.

Italy had struck a deal. Under the terms of the Treaty of London in April 1915, Italy was to be given a $50 million loan and the promise of the Austrian Tyrol, the Trentino, the City of Trieste, and other parts of the Dalmatian coast. That 300 000 Germans and 600 000 Slovenes lived in these areas was of little consequence to the jubilant Italians.

The Balkan wars had left the Italians with a thirst for expansion along the entire Adriatic coast: what had once belonged to the old Venetian empire should now belong to Italy. One of the sought after prizes was Istria which contained the cities of Trieste and Fiume. The area was populated by Italians although some of their suburbs and the surrounding hinterland were Slovenian or Croatian. The Italians coveted these thriving ports, linking the Adriatic to Austria-Hungary. The fiery journalist Benito Mussolini and the nationalist poet Gabriele D'Annunzio called for war to recover the *irredenta,* the border regions where many Italians lived but which had not been brought into unification.

Twelve battles were fought between the Austro-Hungarians and Italians on the Isonzo River to the east of Venice. For the most part the fighting there turned into mountain campaigns where men and guns had to be pulled up the steep alpine cliffs. Command of the ridgelines was essential as a few well-placed men could hold off entire armies climbing upwards from the valleys below. The Italians were not able to drive the Austro-Hungarians from the heights.

Then in 1917 German units appeared on the Italian front. The experienced veterans stormed out of the passes catching the Italians by surprise. In the first day's fighting the Italians were pushed back from Caporetto. They suffered 180 000 casualties and their army began to melt away. British and French forces were rushed up to stem the German advance and the lines held along the Piave River. In the last major battle of the front a combined Allied force routed the disintegrating Austro-Hungarian forces at Vittorio Veneto prior to an armistice with Austria, signed on 4 November 1918.

SUMMARY

World War I began with Germany's implementation of the Schlieffen Plan. However, instead of Germany being able to knock France out of the war in the first weeks, a stalemate evolved on the western front. Unable to achieve victory in the west, the Germans transferred their power to the eastern front to deal with the expected Russian invasion. By December 1914, the major powers were in a deadlock, unable to declare victory. The deadlock was to continue for another four years.

In 1915 the forces along the 644-kilometre western front attempted to achieve their primary objectives of capturing Paris, or of throwing the Germans out of France. The Allied attacks took place along the hinges of the western bulge at Ypres in the north and Verdun in the south. Neither side prevailed.

In the meantime, the Germans had thrust their strength against the Russians on the eastern front with great success, driving the Russians back several hundred kilometres. So startling was their success that the Germans mistakenly believed the Russian army was out of the war and would no longer be a factor. As a result, Germany decided to seek a final victory in the west, at Verdun.

In an attempt to broaden the war and divert Germany's limited resources to other fronts, the Allies opened up secondary battlefronts in Italy and the Ottoman Empire. These battlefronts proved to be more of a drain on Allied resources than German, and were not effective in defeating the Germans on the major battlefronts.

QUESTIONS

Explain the German battle strategy for defeating France and then confronting the Russians.

Compare and contrast the French preparedness for war with that of the Germans.

Describe the "Miracle of the Marne." How did it occur and what was the result?

Describe the state of Russian forces at the beginning of the war. What was the result of their encounters with the Germans?

Compare and contrast the conduct of the war between the western and eastern fronts.

Why did the allied forces decide to deploy their troops in the Mediterranean? Evaluate their success in battles against the Ottoman Empire

Why did Italy enter the war on the side of Britain and France in 1915?

ANALYSIS

Research the effect new machine weapons had upon the conduct of war and battle strategy. Examples include submarines, airplanes, machine-guns, poison gas, flame throwers, and battle tanks.

Research one of the major battles of World War I such as Ypres or Gallipoli. Assess the significance of the battle in the context of the rest of the war.

ACTIVITIES

1. Press Release
World War I has just begun. Write a brief press release for a major newspaper in one of the following countries: Britain, France, Germany, Russia, Italy, or the United States. Be sure to consider the specific point of view which would be taken by the country of your choice.

2. Letter
You are a young Canadian soldier in the trenches on the western front. Write a letter home detailing your experiences. Be specific

3. Radio Broadcast
Select a country involved in the First World War and structure a radio broadcast which either gives an account of a particular battle in the First World War, or uses propaganda to stir up support for the war.

4. Army Supplies
The immense size of modern armies presented problems in itself. Devise a plan to house, feed, and supply an army of 4 million soldiers each day. You must also look after the needs of the millions of horses used for transportation.

When World War I began, Britain established a blockade of all enemy seaports. Germany's access to raw materials outside of Europe was immediately cut off. This photograph shows a small part of the British naval fleet at anchor in the Firth of Forth. A dirigible can be seen in the upper left hand corner.

Chapter 14
Total War
1916–1917

FOCUS ON:

The impact of the front-line stalemate on the major powers;

The home front's contribution to the war effort;

The effects of the submarine and the airplane on the nature of warfare.

The German strategy for 1916 was to seek victory on the western front. The massive victories against Russia the previous year had led them to the conclusion that the Russians were out of the war. All their forces could therefore be concentrated for the final battle that would take place at Verdun.

General von Falkenhayn chose Verdun because it was the strongest point on the French defence line. His opponent, General Joffre, had reduced the garrison at Verdun because he needed men for the upcoming offensive on the Somme and because he did not consider Verdun of great importance. Falkenhayn's strategy was to lure the French into defending the fortress while the Germans stood off at a distance and obliterated the reinforcements with heavy gunfire. Thus he would slaughter the French army without much danger to his own men. The strategy was not to capture Verdun but to use it as bait to bring the French army within the range of the German guns. It was to be a classic battle of attrition with victory going to the one who had more men left. Falkenhayn expected to lose two men to every five Frenchmen.

The opening barrage on 21–24 February tore a huge, gaping hole in the French defences. Some 1200 guns, one for every eight metres, targeted the 60 forts and strong points protecting the citadel. Over 80 000 shells a day hit within a 50-block area. What could possibly be left of the defenders and the defences after such saturated shelling? In the course of the months-long battle 2.5 million shells were dropped on the battle area.

French defenders caught in the open were blown apart, their defences destroyed. Most units lost 98 percent of their men. Many were driven insane by the continuous concussions of exploding shells. Panic set in among the French high command as they realized what they had done in steadily reducing the fighting effectiveness of Verdun by withdrawing many of its guns and troops for other parts of the battle line. The outlying forts contained barely a hundred men. Food was scarce and water even more limited. That they held out for weeks was amazing.

TIMELINE

1916

21 February ⊛ Battle of Verdun
24 June ⊛ Somme Offensive.
31 May 1916 ⊛ Jutland naval battle occurs.
4 June ⊛ Brusilov Offensive
Power is centralized in the hands of the state, in what is termed "total war." Only if every element of society is directed towards the war effort can victory be achieved. Industrial societies resupply the battlefronts on an indefinite basis. Women flood into the work force.

1917

16 January ⊛ The Zimmermann Telegram is sent.
February ⊛ Germany declares a war zone around Britain.
February ⊛ The Russian tsar, Nicholas II, abdicates.
6 April ⊛ The United States enters the war.

Joffre's field general, Philip Pétain, reacted quickly to g men and guns back to Verdu Only one road, the 60-kilomet long Voie Sacrée, was safe fro German gunfire. Pétain org nized a shuttle of 4000 truc down this seven-metre-wi lane to bring in reinforcemer and take out the wounde During the course of the si month battle almost all of t French forces were rotated in the fighting around Verdun one time or the other.

Incredible legends abou about the bravery of the defenders of Verdun. More th 80 percent of the casualties were taken in hand-to-ha fighting in the craters and pillboxes of the outlying defen rings. Flame throwers were used to great effect by bc sides in order to gain a few more meters of ear Miraculously, the outer forts of Le Mort-Homme and Va held out for three months under appalling conditions.

Courage was also demonstrated on the German side, infantrymen crawled up to the forts to drop bundles hand grenades into the galleries. At Douaumont Fort Sergeant Kunze and a handful of men cut their w through the barbed wire, crawled over spiked railings, a crossed a seven-metre-wide moat. They then climbed u four-metre wall into a gun embrasure. They pried ope steel door and wandered along the echoing chambers w guns blazing, barging into the gun rooms and killing gunners. They repeated the manoeuvre in other galler before stopping to feast on wine and eggs in the Frer officers' mess.

Three months after Douaumont's capture, Vaux Fort up an heroic defence. In a ferocious one-hour barra some 2000 shells were hurled at the fortifications. Then Germans stormed up the ridge, swarming over the pa pets and lobbing grenades into the gun slots. The defe ers gave ground grudgingly. Metre by metre the Germ gained ground against sandbagged machine gun nests. the fourth night the French ran out of water and yet t stood fast, among rotting corpses in the corridors. Cra with thirst and badly burned by flame throwers grenades, they surrendered on the seventh day.

*Joseph Jacques Césaire Joffre (1852–1931)
entered the French army in 1870 and became
chief of staff in 1914. Soon after the French
victory at the battle of the Marne, Joffre became
commander-in-chief of the French armies.
Although he resigned after the French defeat at
Verdun in 1916, he was made marshal of
France and became president of
the Allied War Council in 1917.*

ermans suffered 2679 casual-
s. The French toll was 100
ad and wounded.

As the weeks drew on, the Ger-
an attack slowed to a halt.
owever, it was not until other
ttles began that the crown
ince at last called a halt to the
aughter. This was just at the
oment a German patrol reach-
d the heights and looked down
to the citadel. However the
oops were needed elsewhere.
esultory fighting continued for
e rest of the year but the main
ttle was over at a shared cost
978 000 casualties.

The strategy of attrition did
t work as both sides had suf-
red equally. The fighting had
en so dehumanising that the
ench army entered into a pro-
nged period of despair that
t it unfit for battle. In 1917
me mutinies broke out and
rn measures had to be taken
restore order and keep
ench forces in the war.

During the Battle of Verdun the British and Russians
unched their own attacks hoping to draw some of the
rman forces away. The British attacked along the
mme River while the Russians attacked the Austrians in
e east. Their strategy was successful. Von Falkenhayn
s forced to call a halt to the battle of Verdun and trans-
his forces to meet the new threats.

The British had planned a major summer campaign for
16 along the Somme River. For several months men and
tériel had been gathering there for what was hoped to
the decisive victory on the western front. The Allied
d commanders argued against any kind of opening bar-
e because the battle area was low-lying and tended to
n into quagmire at the slightest hint of rain. Shelling the
a would only churn the earth into craters, making an
antry advance impossible. They were ignored by the
h command but those who fought through the mud of

Passchendaele could attest to
the soundness of their advice.

Because of the critical situation at Verdun, Britain's General
Haig began the Somme cam-
paign ahead of schedule in late
June. This time the opening barrage from 1500 guns lasted five
complete days. The British
thought none could live through
such an inferno and when the
barrage lifted there would be
nothing left to do but walk to
the enemies' lines. When the
infantry attack went over the
top, four rows of men walking
only two metres apart, the soldiers were convinced that the
Germans had all been killed.

But the Germans were not in
the frontline trenches. As soon
as the barrage began they withdrew to the rear to wait out the
shelling. Those who remained
were in bunkers deep below
ground level where they played
cards and rested for the trial
that was about to test them.

They knew that within three minutes of the end of the barrage they could be back at their machine gun posts and
ready to open fire.

The British advanced uphill towards the ridges opposite.
Before they could get through no man's land the Germans
had taken their positions and ranged in their artillery and
machine guns. One hundred thousand men took part in the
advance across the plain. At first all bode well for success
but then the machine guns began to stutter. Repeated
attacks drove the death toll to 20 000 on the first day. The
battle was to last another eight weeks to mid-September.
Altogether one million men would contest this narrow,
30-kilometre front.

As the battle of the Somme drew to a close at the end of
1916, both sides counted their dead and wounded. The
British had lost 420 000, the French 200 000, the Germans
450 000. No victory had been achieved and the war would
continue.

Tank Warfare

It was at the Somme that the British unleashed their new secret weapon, the battle tank. Despite their clumsiness, the tanks (modified armour-plated farm tractors) crawled across the trenches impervious to light fire. The onset of the tanks left German outposts dazed and uncertain. They were quickly overrun. As the tanks mounted the trenches, their turrets swivelled and fired down the length of the lines. The Germans cast away their arms and, panic-stricken, ran. There were not enough tanks available to cause a breakthrough. However, after this battle, orders for hundreds of tanks were given priority over all other weapons.

The armoured tank could crawl across defence lines impervious to rifle and machine gun fire. It was the miracle weapon that ended the stalemate on the western front.

EASTERN FRONT 1916

The Brusilov Offensive

The Germans had convinced themselves that the Russians had been so badly beaten in 1915 they could not possibly stay in the war. Yet in 1916 the Russians were back in the fight with new armies. Over the winter, Russia's huge manpower advantage had brought forth thousands of conscripts to defend the homeland.

The tsar would not permit an attack along the eastern front, a line that stretched 880 kilometres from Riga in the Baltic to Rumania. Russian forces were not ready and badly needed training. They did not have enough food or ammunition to mount a major attack along the full line. Shells were so scarce that guns could not be fired in practice or for ranging. The gunners could not even fire their guns at an attacking enemy without permission from headquarters.

Most of the Russian generals agreed with the tsar. To attack the Germans with poorly equipped troops would result in disaster. It was better to stand on the defensive and lure the Germans deeper into Russia where they cou be dealt with.

To the tsar's surprise, General Brusilov went over to t attack, striking south from the Pripet Marshes and drivi a wedge in the Austrian lines. On 4 June his men pour through the Austrian defences into the open, pushing kilometres behind the enemy lines. The attack was so sw and unexpected that the Austrian Archduke Joseph fl his birthday party to join the retreat. But without suppo Brusilov's armies slowed to a halt on 10 August. Howev in this short period of time, he had changed the course the war. Thirty-five German divisions were pulled aw from the western front to come to Austria's aid, resulti in the end of the Verdun massacres.

German retaliation was swift. With only a few sectio of the line under attack they were able to deploy all th strength against Brusilov in battles that ran through t rest of August. A combined force of Germans, Austria and Rumanians reestablished the line, inflicting 500 0 casualties on the enemy. Disillusioned over their lead ship and in despair, the Russian army began to crumb By 1917 it would cease to exist as a fighting force.

Enver Pasha (1881–1922) was the Ottoman minister of war. He agreed to enter World War I on the side of the Central Powers after Germany offered to replace Ottoman ships lost to the British.

HE WAR AT SEA

ie Raiders

e first task of the Allied navies s to hunt down German war- ps at sea. They posed a lethal eat to the merchant sea lanes l would have to be located d destroyed quickly. With 70 cent of the world's surface vered with water and the **com- rce raiders**' ability to be any- ere on the seas, it became an ormous task to track down se elusive warships.

The most dangerous raiders re the battle cruiser *Goeben* d its escort the *Breslau* in the diterranean Sea. When war s declared they shelled the ench North African cities of lippeville and Bône. Hunted a British force, they eluded ir pursuers and sought refuge Constantinople. The flight to nstantinople took everyone surprise as they were expect- to make a run past Gibraltar and escape into the Atlantic. von Moltke said, "There are always three courses open war and the enemy always chooses the fourth."

At the start of the war the British had seized the battle- ps *Sultan Osman* bearing fourteen 12-inch guns, and the aller *Reshadieh*, while both were being built in Britain the Ottoman Empire. The Ottoman Turks were enraged. ick to take advantage, the Germans offered to replace lost ships with the *Goeben* and *Breslau* if the Ottoman pire would enter the war on the side of the Central Powers. The pro-German Enver Pasha complied, thus shutting Straits to Allied shipping. With these additional war- ps the Ottoman navy was free to roam the Black Sea mbarding Odessa and other Russian ports. By mining narrows at Gallipoli, the Ottoman Turks effectively cked any attempt by the British or French fleets to force passage and come to the aid of their eastern ally.

The most famous raider of the war was the *Wolf*. The *Wolf* s specially designed with hatches on its underside so that divers could go outside into the water and make repairs without being seen. The 400-man crew was the cream of German naval volunteers. Leaving home on 30 November 1916, the *Wolf* stayed at sea for 15 months. This weath- er-beaten, former tramp steamer sailed 110 000 kilometres, sink- ing over 120 000 tonnes of Allied shipping before making it safely home.

Apart from the odd, armed passenger liner, the Allied navies had rounded up most of the Ger- man warships and raiders by the end of 1915. Japanese and Aus- tralian navies now patrolled the far eastern waters, taking Ger- many's Pacific colonies under their control. With the sea lanes open, the volume of goods and men required to sustain the bat- tlefronts could flow uninterrupt- ed once more into Britain and France.

Undersea Warfare

The German counterblockade of Britain took the form of undersea warfare. Like its counterpart the airplane, the sub- marine (U-boat) added a third dimension to the battle. The U-boat was a weapon of stealth that struck without warn- ing. Submarines could not take prisoners nor was it wise to give warning of attack. They were a weapon of terror.

German submarine strategy was to ring the coast of Britain with submarines in order to cut off the island's life- lines. The strategy was sound but the German navy never quite had enough U-boats. They started the war with only 25 in service. Most British merchant ships got through this thin line.

At first, Germany was hesitant to adopt unrestricted **sub- marine warfare** lest the United States take offence and enter the war on the Allied side. Inevitably American lives were lost at sea from submarine action. The most spectac- ular incident of this kind was the sinking of the British pas- senger liner *Lusitania* on 7 May 1915, off the Irish coast.

Admiral von Spee

When war was declared Admiral Maximilian von Spee made the decision to bring Germany's Far East Squadron home across the Pacific and around Cape Horn into the Atlantic. He left the cruiser *Emden* behind to see what damage it could do in Asian waters. Before it was caught and destroyed by the Australian cruiser *Sydney*, the *Emden* had sunk 19 ships off Ceylon, bombarded Madras, and entered the harbour at Penang, sinking a Russian cruiser and a French destroyer before proceeding to the wireless station on the Cocos Islands. It was there the *Emden* was found and sunk. In its brief voyage, the *Emden* had accounted for 24 ships in only 95 days.

Another raider, the *Karlsruhe*, having sunk 17 ships, blew up in the West Indies while on the way to shell Barbados. The German raider *Königsberg* roamed the Indian Ocean causing delays in the troop convoys from India, Australia, and New Zealand. It eventually fled to the east coast of Africa where it sought refuge up the Rufiji River. The following year the British brought special floating monitors that could get across the sandbanks to blow it up.

The only fleet actions took place at Coronel off the coast of Chile and the Falkland Islands in the South Atlantic. Admiral von Spee had successfully crossed the Pacific, accounting for 40 ships sunk in the waters around Tahiti. Steaming down the coast of Chile, he ran into and demolished a small British squadron, the *Good Hope* and *Monmouth*, off Coronel. When news reached Britain the public outcry was for vengeance.

A large squadron with two battle cruisers raced south to the Falklands. There the two fleets collided. The British ships were longer ranged and faster. They were able to chase down the German cruisers then stand off and hit the enemy without fear of the German guns. In a single afternoon it was over. Only the *Dresden* escaped to seek sanctuary. Von Spee and two of his sons went down with his flagship.

Blockade

British naval strategy was to establish a long-range blockade of the Central Powers. From bases at Rosyth and Scapa Flow, the Royal Navy made it impossible for Germany to engage in commerce. At first only German ships were seized and taken as prizes. Then neutral countries' ships carrying goods to Germany or that might get to Germany through other countries were captured at sea. As the blockade tightened, all ships were stopped and searched not just for war matériel but anything from food to cloth.

These actions brought angry protests from the United States who insisted on the international agreement on freedom of the seas. American complaints were somewhat dampened when the prize monies were returned to the ships' owners. Many unseaworthy ships filled with unspecified cargo sailed out of American ports hoping to be taken as prizes for the cash rewards.

By 1917 the blockade was beginning to tell. There were shortages of just about everything in Germany. Long lines formed to get bread rations and luxuries were no longer available. Synthetics could cover only a portion of what was needed. Food supplies dwindled to the point of inadequacy, and stockpiles of other goods were used up during what was called the Turnip Winter of 1917.

Public morale began to crack as disease and malnutrition set in. The victories on the eastern front brought hope that Germany could make use of harvests in Poland and the Ukraine. This hope proved to be in vain.

Undersea warfare was conducted with submarines (U-boats). They could strike without warning and did not take prisoners. Let loose in the world's sea lanes, the U-boats threatened to cut off supplies to the Allied forces.

illegally carried ammunition made in the USA for Allied use. The liner sank quickly when it was hit by torpedoes. All told, 1198 of the 1959 passengers and crew drowned including 128 Americans.

On returning to base, the U-boat captain was feted as a hero. After all, the *Lusitania* had been carrying war *matériel* and the ship was in a declared **war zone.** Full warning had been given the passengers and crew in New York about the dangers they faced. But as American protests poured in, the submarine strategy was modified for the next two years, so as not to endanger passenger ships. The sinking of the *Lusitania* contributed to the Americans' growing war fervor and was a critical factor in their joining the war.

Eager to end the war at sea, the Germans reverted to unrestricted submarine warfare. By 1917 the U-boats had sunk

---

Q-Ships & Convoys

Q ships were fitted out to lure surfaced submarines to their death. Disguised as tramp steamers or fishing trawlers, they appeared to be easy prey. Often their crews would seem to be abandoning ship. Crewmen dressed as women added to the subterfuge. But when the submarine came within range, the fake rigging was cast aside to reveal deadly guns. At point-blank range the gunners could hardly miss. But the real deterrent to the submarine threat was the convoy system. Groups of merchants and troopships escorted by warships cut the sinkings dramatically because submarines were not able to penetrate the screen of escorts.

---

millions of tonnes of shipping. On 1 February 1917, a war zone was declared around the British Isles. All ships were now considered targets. As a result another two million tonnes went to the bottom of the sea including seven American merchant ships. On the night of 25 February the *Lanconia* was torpedoed off New York harbour. Lurid pictures of capsized lifeboats and women drowning filled American papers. Still, President Wilson did not think he had enough public opinion behind him to declare war on Germany.

It was not the unrestricted submarine warfare that brought the United States into the war but, rather, the curious incident of the Zimmerman telegram. On 19 January 1917, German Foreign Minister Zimmermann sent a coded cable to the German High Commission in New York for delivery to the president of Mexico.

The telegram offered Mexico the return of New Mexico, Arizona, Texas, and California should Mexico declare war on the United States and keep America out of the European war. The telegram proposed that, in return, since the Mexicans would likely lose and their northern states would be ravaged by the American army, a victorious Germany would insist America turn over these states to Mexico.

Such outright interference in American matters by Germany brought public opinion to a boil. So great was the outrage that many cities and towns changed their German names. President Wilson was able to appear before Congress on 6 April 1917, to deliver a war message against the Central Powers: the United States of America would come to the aid of Britain and France.

Wilson promised to have 12 million American soldiers in Europe fighting side by side with the French, British, and

Thomas Woodrow Wilson (1856–1924) was the twenty-eighth president of the United States. On 6 April 1917, he declared his intention to send American troops to Europe to fight in World War I. Wilson was instrumental in establishing the League of Nations after the war.

Jutland, 31 May 1916

The only pitched battle betwee the rival *Dreadnought* fleet took place off Jutland in th North Sea on 31 May 1916. Th results of the battle were incor clusive but the British retaine control over the North Sea an the German High Seas Flee remained on the defensive fo the rest of the war.

Both fleets were divided int two major armadas. Admiral Beatty and Hipper commande the faster battle cruisers an lighter forces. Their job was t provoke the enemy in such way as to lure the main battl fleets of admirals Jellicoe an Scheer into the open.

The Germans tended to us Zeppelins, or airships, ahead the fleet for scouting purpose On this particular occasion th Germans had stationed a nun ber of submarines outsid British naval bases hoping catch exiting warships. The pla was to have Admiral Hipper

Canadian forces by the end of 1919. The United States would also send large numbers of fighter and bomber aircraft into the fray as well as a powerful fleet.

The promise of such enormous help encouraged the British and French to hold on. It also prompted the Germans to try for a speedy end to the war before the might of the Americans could be brought into battle.

In declaring war President Wilson put forward America's war aims in a series of Fourteen Points (see chapter 11). He had analyzed the causes of war and proposed that the peace should include a League of Nations that would act through collective security to ensure that no future wars occurred.

cruiser force bombard the British seacoast town Sunderland. When the British ships gave chase he woul lead them back towards Scheer's High Seas Fleet lurkir over the horizon. In this way the German fleet would t able to deal with a part of the British fleet at a tim However the British were reading German codes and kne roughly of the plan. Because of a number of factors, the t boats were recalled and in the foggy weather the Zeppeli were of no use. Despite these changes, the Germans saile out to do battle. With his light cruiser forces Hipper w; some 80 kilometres ahead of Scheer in the German His Seas Fleet. Neither one was aware the British had alread put to sea with 95 ships of the Home Fleet.

The first clash, between the cruiser squadrons, start when they both attempted to search a Danish mercha ship off the Norwegian coast. The British were chase back north towards Jellicoe's armada by Hipper's lig

Count Ferdinand von Zeppelin (1838–1917) invented the first rigid airship called a Zeppelin. During World War I, the Germans sent Zeppelins ahead of their troops to find and report the location of enemy fortifications. The Zeppelin in this photograph is flying over Warsaw.

~ Naval Losses ~ in World War I

	Britain	Germany	France	Russia	Austria-Hungary	Italy
Dreadnoughts	2*	1	–	2*	4	1*
Battle Cruisers	3	2	–	–	–	–
Armored Cruisers	13*	6	5	2	3	1
Light Cruisers	12	17	–	–	10	2
Destroyers	67	66	12	20	18	8
Submarines	54	199	14	20	11	8

* indicates one ship in each class sunk by accidental internal explosion

Compare this chart to the one showing Naval Strength in August 1914 in Chapter 12. Which country lost the highest percentage of ships?

rces followed by Scheer. In the ensuing chase two British *eadnoughts*, the *Invincible* and *Queen Mary*, blew up en the flash from their own guns reached their maga-es, turning them into raging infernos. Then at 6:30 P.M. e two main battle fleets came in sight of each other. Scheer found himself in the worst possible position.

There, in an iron line 11 kilometres long, 35 British battleships were passing ahead of him preparing to open fire. In the flash of guns and the smoke and the flying debris, over 100 000 men in 252 ships groped to do battle. In the five minutes of the main battle, scarcely 5 percent of the shells fired hit their targets. As the British shells rained upon his battle line, Scheer realised he had sailed into a deadly trap. With his ships taking heavy hits and with both the fleets converging at 40 knots, he ordered an immediate 180-degree about-turn. Considering the manoeuvre is difficult to carry out in peacetime, it was amazing that none of the German ships collided.

Once out of the trap, Scheer turned his ships about and charged the British position once again, but this time, after only six minutes of further punishment, he slipped away into the darkness. Later that night Scheer decided to make a run for home and smashed through the back of the British line to safety. When dawn broke the German fleet was nowhere to be found.

The British lost three battle cruisers and 11 other ships in the battle. The Germans lost one *Dreadnought* and nine others. There were 6097 British dead compared to 2551 German. Although the German High Seas Fleet did make one or two sorties after Jutland, it never again came out to challenge the guns of the British navy. The kaiser ordered his ships into port rather than risk another battle.

At the end of the war, crews of some of the German ships

Billy Bishop (1894–1956) was a Canadian aviator who became the most successful flying ace on the Allied side. He was the first Canadian to receive a Victoria Cross, the highest award in the Commonwealth given to members of the armed forces for exceptional bravery.

mutinied against an order for a last suicidal dash into the North Sea. Boilers were shut down and anchor cables sabotaged. After the **Armistice** in 1918, the German fleet was ordered to sail to the British fleet base at Scapa Flow for internment. Rather than let their ships be taken over, their captains ordered them scuttled where they rest to this day beneath the waters of the anchorage.

THE WAR IN THE AIR

War in the air added another dimension to the battlefields just as had submarines changed war on the seas. Airships and airplanes could look down on the fighting and bring new strategies into play. Both sides used the awesome gas-filled Zeppelins and dirigibles. The Germans had the larger fleet, used for reconnaissance at sea and also to bomb British and French cities. The British used their airships primarily for fle reconnaissance and U-boat patrols.

Vulnerable to machine gun fire, their end was usually spectacular ball of flame. Fighter pilots thought it wa great sport to track these titanic targets hoping to set the on fire. The 80-kilometre top speed of the airships was ju not good enough to elude pursuing airplanes.

The British had more luck with their dirigibles on co voy escort. Their long range and ability to stay over th merchantmen to spot submarines were of tremendo advantage. They usually carried machine guns for defen against enemy fighters and depth charges to drop o unsuspecting U-boats. As the war drew on, the Briti attached small fighters such as the Sopwith Camel to t underbelly of their airships. Riding beneath the 150-met long body they provided the dirigibles with a modicum fighter defence.

The airplane was another matter. Only 11 years after t

*Airplanes started to come into their own
as independent fighting machines.
Baron von Richthofen (1882–1918) of Germany
was the top flying ace, with 80 kills.*

irst heavier-than-air flight by the Wright brothers at Kitty Hawk, airplanes took part in battle. They were initially used for reconnaissance, to spot enemy troop movements, or for contact patrols to find out where one's own men were. Their role changed to one of bombing and strafing only in the latter stages of the war. At first many ground commanders considered them a nuisance and chose to ignore them completely.

The war in the air was far different from that on the ground. There was knight errantry above the battlefields. The cost of airplanes limited the pilots to the wealthy members of flying clubs and the upper classes. Many airmen had vacationed together or knew each other from school. Thus a gentlemanly attitude developed among the pilots. They sent presents for each others' birthdays. They flew without parachutes hoping to be able to glide to a landing, and no one would think of continuing to fight if the enemy was out of ammunition.

Pilots forced down on enemy aerdromes were treated to a feast in the mess, a refuelling the next day, and sent back to their own base. They visited the wounded in hospital, invited the others to celebrations of national holidays, and attended funeral services for all those comrades in arms unfortunate enough to be killed.

The Italians were the first to carry small bombs aloft, in their laps or in their pockets, to drop on the Ottoman Turks at Ain Zara. The damage was more psychological than physical. The Ottoman Turks claimed that bombs had rained out of the sky hitting a hospital. Nothing was said about the 150 naval shells that had pounded the area the day before. The idea of death from the sky was new and frightening.

A Russian was the first pilot to be killed in the war when he rammed into the tail of Baron von Rosenthal's airplane over the Austrian lines on 26 August 1914. Then on the western front, a British pilot took up a revolver and startled the enemy when he fired at him from close range. Soon every pilot was carrying some sort of weapon. Not much damage was done until the French sheathed their propellers in metal and mounted a forward-firing machine gun. The sheeting stopped the pilots from shooting off their own propellers. The Germans captured one of the planes and took it to Berlin where a Dutchman, Anthony Fokker, examined it. He improved on it by inventing an interrupter gear that synchronised the firing of the guns through the propeller beats. All of a sudden the air war became serious.

Airplanes started to come into their own as independent fighting arms in the last months of the war. No longer did they fly as single scouts but in "wings" of twelve or more. Some of the larger battles pitted more than

Aces in the Air

The French were the first to declare air aces. This commendation went to any pilot that had shot down five planes (the Russian aces had to shoot down ten). Prizes were given by the Michelin Tire Company. Rewards included such things as a dinner in a fine restaurant or additional leave.

Fame and honour went to those who fought bravely in the air. Germany's Baron Manfred von Richthofen was the top ace of the war with 80 kills. Richthofen had started in the cavalry, as had Canada's top ace Billy Bishop who had 72 kills. During the war only twelve pilots downed 50 or more planes.

As more and more men were sent to the front, war industries became short of manpower.
Tradition was broken by permitting women to replace men in the work force.
These women are punch press operators in a General Electric Plant in the United States.

100 airplanes against each other. In the final battles of the Somme, hundreds of airplanes were considered an integral part of the advance. The German wings were called "flying circuses" because of their gaudy and ornamental colouring. Richthofen, Ernst Udet, and Hermann Göring became the commanders of these potent fighting forces.

Larger planes were used to bomb behind enemy lines and create terror among civilians, continuing the work of the Zeppelins that dropped bombs on London and other major centres. A Russian engineer, Ivan Sikorsky, created a four-engine aircraft in 1913 that carried seven machine guns and was considered invincible. Of the 73 constructed only one was shot down.

The airplane was also adapted to work with the fleet. Small airplanes could be stowed on board ships and took flight from the top of gun turrets. These planes served as scouts and were active in spotting and sinking enemy submarines. The first real aircraft carrier was HMS *Furious* with a continuous flight deck that could handle landings as well as take-offs.

Brave just to get into the air, a third of the pilots that flew in World War I lost their lives.

THE HOME FRONT

Total War

The concept of **total war** called for centralization o power in the hands of the state. Only if every element o society was directed towards the war effort could victor be achieved. Industrial societies had the capability c resupplying the battlefronts on an indefinite basis.

Huge bureaucracies were established to control ever facet of life at home. Rationing boards controlled every thing from food supplies to every other type of consume goods. Each month every person was allotted a specifi amount of groceries, clothing, and fuel. Hoarding was di couraged and all purchases had to be accompanied b one's own ration book. Coupons were made available t those that required gasoline for transportation but thes were more difficult to obtain.

The scarcity of food was most keenly felt among th Central Powers where the effects of the British nav blockade were beginning to tell. With the better food all cated to the men at the front, those at home ate meag rations. As in other nations at war, food was bland an monotonous. War bread often contained raw potatoes to give it bulk; coffee and cocoa contained sand or, in some cases, ground-up brick. Flour could only be obtained at the pharmacies and then only with a doctor's prescription. Misery increased and starvation loomed. Luxuries of fresh fruit and desserts were nonexistent.

War departments took over all manufacturing, turning every available machine into war production of some kind or another. Raw materials and outputs were carefully regulated to ensure maximum effort. Victory would not be denied because of shortages in ammunition or weapons. Labour boards issued work permits and allocated workers to the factories. Without a work permit one could not travel or get ration cards. Selective service commissions required all males to register so that those needed at the front could be sent into the armed forces. Conscription did away with the volunteer forces that had not won the war and were now in need of reinforcement. Other government departments took control of transportation and communication until all areas of society had come under the aegis of centralized control.

As more and more men were sent to the front, the danger arose that war industries would be found short of manpower. Tradition was broken only with the gravest of concern by permitting women to replace men in the workforce. German society could not bring itself to take this drastic measure. In the other countries, the women quickly adapted to their new-found roles. Most took up duties in factories but all other areas of work were opened to them. Transport drivers, air raid wardens, women's auxiliaries to the fighting forces, government inspectors—women were there. The women looked upon their new positions as a welcome challenge. They would do their part to win the war and they quickly proved they could do the job.

At the same time the entrance of women into the workplace changed their status within society. Work brought them respect and social acceptance outside the home. It also brought them their own pay cheques. Young women earned extra money by working two or three shifts. They received hefty pay packets from working as much as 95-hour weeks. It was not unusual to find women dining out by themselves or in the company of others. They bought new wardrobes, had their own bank accounts, and patronized a variety of entertainments that had previously been denied them unless in the company of a man. It was a social revolution and after the war there was no turning back.

SUMMARY

German strategy for 1916 was to wear down the French army in battle at Verdun. General von Falkenhayn's plan was to lure French reinforcements to Verdun so that the German troops could stand at a distance and shoot them. Almost all the French army was, at one time or another, drawn into this six-month battle.

The premature British attack along the Somme River in the summer of 1916 was designed to draw the Germans away from Verdun. This battle, too, lasted almost a half a year. At the end of 1916, Verdun had not fallen nor had the Allies broken through the German lines at the Somme. Extremely heavy casualties caused home governments to take total control of all their humanpower, organizing it to reinforce the armies in the field, and directing the remainder toward the production of war matériel. Industrial nations have the capacity to wage war over long periods of time.

In the east, Russia's Brusilov Offensive, from June to August 1916, brought some relief to Verdun. Retaliation by the Germans, Austrians, and Rumanians, however, demoralized the Russian army.

Submarines added another dimension to the war. Blockade and counter blockade strategies prevailed at sea. Unrestricted submarine warfare led to the Germans sinking American ships in the war zone around Britain. American outrage brought the United States closer to entering the war.

War in the air was also new. The ability to wage war from above changed military strategy. At the beginning of World War I, airships and airplanes helped strategists by reporting observations from the air. Only later in the war did airships and airplanes become effective fighting weapons.

QUESTIONS

1. Briefly describe the battles fought at Verdun and the Somme. What was the result of these battles?

2. What role did the allied navies play in World War I? What was the purpose of the German "raiders" such as the *Wolf?*

3. Why did Britain establish a blockade of the central powers? Evaluate the success of this strategy.

4. What was the purpose of the German U-boats? Why was there such an outcry when the *Lusitania* was sunk?

5. What did Germany's Foreign Minister Zimmerman propose to Mexico? What effect did his proposal have on American public opinion?

6. If the results of the Battle of Jutland were inconclusive, why was this a significant sea battle?

7. Airplanes were new technology during the First World War. Explain their role.

8. What changes were made in domestic economies in order to support the war effort?

9. How did the role of women change during the war?

ANALYSIS

1. In the nineteenth century, nations sought to achieve **autarky.** Only when all the essential resources were under direct control could they be safe from a naval blockade that would deny them sustenance. The one nation that could effectively mount a blockade on the world's seaports was Britain. Recall the effects of the British blockade on France in 1812, which included seaports on the American coastline. Remember Napoleon's attempts at counter blockade through the continental system.

   When World War I began, Britain established a blockade of all enemy seaports. Germany's access to raw materials outside of Europe was immediately cut off. Germany then had to turn to resources within Central Europe, or devise substitutes such as synthetic rubber to replace natural rubber.

   By 1917 the British blockade was having visible effects. German resources were low, especially food resources, and the civilian population began to suffer. The Allies hoped the German people would rebel against the war and overturn their government in an effort to end the suffering.

   (a) Describe the strategy behind a naval blockade. On which weaknesses in the enemy does it prey?

   (b) Evaluate the morality of making civilians suffer during a blockade.

   (c) Why did Germany's attempt at a counter blockade against Britain fail? Which nation was the more vulnerable to a blockade strategy, Britain or Germany? Why was the submarine not exploited more fully by Germany?

There is a long standing principle in international law of freedom of the seas. All ships, merchants, and warships have the right to sail in open waters.

Do you consider the declaration of a war zone at sea a violation of international law? Does international law exist in time of war? Do you think nations should have the right to declare part of the ocean a war zone? Why?

What was the reaction of the United States to Germany's declaration of a war zone around Britain? Why did it take Germany so long to make the declaration? What was the American reaction to American ships and American lives lost within the war zone? What effect did the sinking of the passenger ships have on American public opinion?

Research the factors that led to a new role for women in society during the war. Describe the characteristics of the modern woman that arose from total war. How was the position of women in society changed as a result of the war? Why were attempts to remove women from the labour forces unsuccessful after the war? Describe the post-war woman.

ACTIVITIES

1. Role Play
Establish a group to represent the members of the United States Congress of 1917. Discuss the pros and cons of entering the United States into the war. What events eventually propelled the Americans into the war?

2. Research Project
Research the new technology that resulted in the development of aircraft which was used during World War I. Identify the types of aircraft, their capabilities, and the impact they had on the course of the war.

3. Cartoon
Create a historical cartoon which features a significant event during 1916 on the battlefront.

4. Radio Broadcast
Create a radio broadcast which announces the American entry into the war and surveys a number of citizens regarding their views of this action.

In 1917, discontent about Russia's involvement in the war would lead to revolution. These are some of the revolutionary soldiers in Russia's army.

Chapter 15
The Allied Victory
1917–1918

FOCUS ON:

Russian responses to domestic and international instability;

The role of the United States in the Allied victory;

The resolution of the major powers to establish collective security
after World War I;

The political, economic, and social cost of World War I,
and the resulting changes to society.

By 1917 all the armies had suffered horrible losses. The French, Russian, Austro-Hungarian, and Italian forces were close to collapse. Only the British and German armies seemed willing and capable of continuing the battle. It appeared that 1917 would see the triumph of one side or the other. Yet 1917 would bring surprises with the withdrawal of Russia from the war in the midst of revolution and its place being taken by the United States. With the entrance of the United States into the battle, it became critical for the Germans to force the issue before the Americans could move their armies across the Atlantic Ocean to intervene.

TIMELINE

1917
23 February ❀ Revolution in Russia

6 April ❀ The United States enter the war.

24 October ❀ Bolshevik Revolution in Russia

1918
January ❀ Lenin declares a Bolshevik government in Russia. The Russian civil war begins.

8 January ❀ Wilson's Fourteen Points are presented.

3 March ❀ Treaty of Brest-Litovsk
Russia leaves the war.

21 March ❀ Kaiserschlacht
German offensive on the western front.

1 June ❀ Chateau Thierry
Germans come up against the first American troops.

8 August ❀ Last 100 days
continuous advance of the Allied armies.

26 October ❀ Prince Max von Baden is appointed chancellor of Germany.

8 November ❀ Kaiser Wilhelm II abdicates.

9 November ❀ Provisional government in Germany under Chancellor Ebert.

11 November ❀ Armistice takes effect.

1919
18 January ❀ Peace negotiations begin
Treaty of Versailles.

---

join with the demonstrators and shoot their own officers.

While returning to the capital from the front lines where he had taken over the armies, the tsar was stopped by railway workers who demanded his abdication and the transfer of power to the *Duma*. Nicholas agreed to abdicate in favour of a provisional government that could restore order. The imperial family was taken east to Ekaterinburg until a decision could be made on their future.

The provisional government promised to hold elections for a new constituent assembly in the fall but, in the meantime, the representatives in the *Duma* would handle the affairs of state. The *Duma* adopted a number of essential domestic reforms but made a fatal mistake in deciding to continue the war. They argued that, should the Russian front collapse, it would place the entire war in jeopardy. Both France and Britain were terrified of the possibility of Germany being able to concentrate its entire might on the western front. The provisional government chose to keep faith and mounted a summer offensive. The result was another million men lost. This destroyed any credibility the government may have had.

That summer Russian soldiers turned their backs on their officers and deserted their positions. They were going home. They left what little equipment they had behind and the army just seemed to melt away. Germans followed closely behind gobbling up large expanses of territory in Poland and Ukraine. The Germans saw in this disintegration an opportunity to achieve a separate peace on the eastern front followed by a rapid redeployment of their eastern armies to the west.

Timing was critical. Victory had to be reached before American soldiers could arrive in Europe. To hurry Russia's collapse, Germany infiltrated dozens of Russian political exiles into Petrograd and Moscow to promote

EASTERN FRONT 1917

Russia Leaves the War

For three years the Russian armies had obediently marched to war behind their commanders. Ill-trained and poorly equipped, they trudged the 200 km from the railheads across the sandy wastes of East Prussia and the plains of Galicia where their corpses carpeted the land. In 1917, after months of humiliating defeats, the Russian army disintegrated into an uncontrollable mob. Driven out of Galicia and Poland, the Russian armies could not be depended upon to stand and fight. Without adequate food and clothing and without ammunition, Russian soldiers began to desert the front lines and head for home.

The situation inside Russia was no better. Overcome with grief from the dreadful battle death tolls and close to starvation, the people began to rebel. On 23 February, rioters in Petrograd were joined by units of the army who helped distribute what bread and grain they could find. Security forces in the capital could no longer count on their men to obey orders. More likely than not, they would

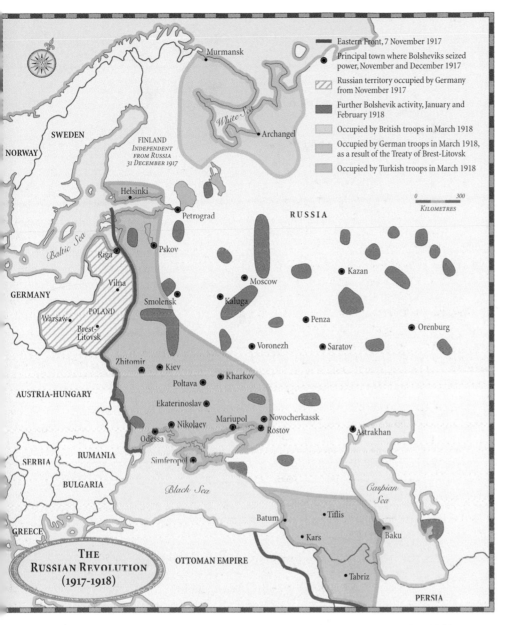

Legend:
- Eastern Front, 7 November 1917
- Principal town where Bolsheviks seized power, November and December 1917
- Russian territory occupied by Germany from November 1917
- Further Bolshevik activity, January and February 1918
- Occupied by British troops in March 1918
- Occupied by German troops in March 1918, as a result of the Treaty of Brest-Litovsk
- Occupied by Turkish troops in March 1918

0   300
KILOMETRES

THE
RUSSIAN REVOLUTION
(1917-1918)

The Bolshevik movement spread rapidly across Russia starting in 1917.

One of Lenin's first acts was to get out of the ruinous war. During negotiations with Germany, whole sections of the Russian front were abandoned. More than 2 million men had deserted their posts since July. An armistice was proposed on 2 December, but Trotsky could not bring himself to agree to the German demands for the annexation of all the occupied territories.

Instead the Bolsheviks reacted by declaring the state of war between Russia and Germany at an end. This strategy did not work. The Germans did not fall for the trick and resumed their advance. Out of desperation, the Bolsheviks were forced to sign a peace treaty at Brest-Litovsk on 3 March 1918. The Central Powers had won the war in the east.

Under the terms of the treaty, Russia gave up 34 percent of its population; 32 percent of its agricultural lands—especially in Ukraine; 54 percent of its industry that had been established at such a great cost; 89 percent of its mines and coal fields; and ceded to Germany its western territories, mainly inhabited by non-Russians. Finland and Ukraine were to become independent states but under German control. German plans to seize the autumn's harvest were unrealistic due to the lengthy negotiations, but the crops for 1918 would be available to end the starvation at home.

The harshness of the treatment accorded Russia was an indication of what the other powers could expect should Germany win the war in the west. Lenin, however, termed the treaty a scrap of paper that could be ripped up at a later date. In the meantime the most pressing matter and his absolute priority was keeping himself in power.

At this time the Bolsheviks made two policy decisions that

anarchy and civil unrest. By the fall of 1917 Russia was ripe for revolution. Vladimir Ilyich Lenin was one of those sent back from exile in Switzerland.

Arriving in Petrograd on 3 April Lenin began organizing the Bolsheviks for revolution. He laboured with Leon Trotsky and a handful of other collaborators to gain control of the *soviets* ("workers councils") in the two major cities. After the disastrous summer offensives, his small group of conspirators seized control of the capital in late October, proclaiming themselves the government of Russia.

Proclaiming their power was one thing; getting the rest of Russia to recognize their right to power was another. It would take Lenin another four years of civil war before the Bolsheviks could consolidate their hold on the nation.

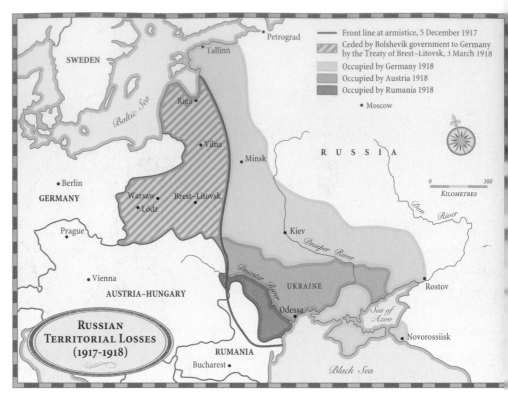

Russia lost considerable amounts of territory and resources
when it withdrew from the war.

were to have a major effect on the western nations. Lenin announced that the new Bolshevik government would renounce the secret promises made by the tsarist government during the war. His government was no longer interested in taking control of the Straits or of Constantinople. The Bolsheviks also denied any responsibility to pay off the loans made to the tsarist regime, especially those from France for railway construction and industrial growth. Failure to recognize these debts as legitimate had disastrous effects on France's postwar recovery.

Frantic over the Russian surrender, the Allies did everything possible to get the Bolsheviks to reopen the eastern front. Promises of large loans were made to both the government and to opposition parties favouring continued fighting. Allied forces invaded Russia on the pretext of safeguarding valuable war supplies at Archangel and Vladivostok.

The armed intervention by the Allies could not move the Russian peasants to re-enlist in the war. In the end the Bolsheviks prevailed and the Allies withdrew from Russian soil.

Lenin and his Bolsheviks seized control of Petrograd
in late October, 1917. Notice the spectators in the background as
Lenin's red guards fire on the winter palace.

This photograph shows American troops in France in 1918, advancing through a mustard gas attack.
All are wearing protective gas masks, except for the man on the left.

THE WESTERN FRONT 1918

Germany Surrenders

War-weary Russia was the first of the major powers to leave the war. The question was whether the other armies were in better condition to continue fighting. Could the British and French forces hold out until the American armies arrived in the spring of 1918?

The final battles of World War I would be fought in the west in 1918. In preparation for the decisive campaigns, 44 German divisions were transferred from the eastern front for the final German offensive on the western front. As early as possible in the spring, Ludendorff planned to hurl 1.5 million men against the allied 1.3 million. The opening attacks would probe for a weak point on the western front between Ypres and Verdun.

On 21 March the Germans stormed out of the early morning fog toward the British lines at St Quentin. High explosives and gas added to the thickness of the heavy fog. The British lines were broken as German soldiers sped towards Albertville with no enemy before them. Then, inexplicably, the German advance came to an abrupt halt. Reports came back of thousands of men looting the countryside of food and wine and sitting down to gorge themselves on their new found bounty. There was an uncontrollable urge to enjoy the comforts denied them over the past three years

and as they feasted the French and British were able to plug the gap.

Other attacks would be mounted against the western bulge until the end of July. All met with the same results. An initial German breakthrough into open areas was followed by a loss of momentum as the troops stopped to enjoy their booty.

On 7 April, near Armentières, mustard gas filled the valleys as a German attack began, bending the Allied lines by as much as 10 kilometres in the first days. But the British yielded ground methodically, exacting an enormous price for every metre gained. In another battle, the Canadians abandoned the ridges at Passchendaele and lured their attackers into coming down the barren slopes into their concentrated fire. Denied success, the Germans probed elsewhere.

On 27 May a barrage of shells broached the lines along the Marne River. German forces gained a dozen kilometres the first day, until Paris lay just 80 kilometres over the horizon. But this was Champagne and, as had happened before, the weary troops soon took to the wine cellars and the advance collapsed of its own accord. A final attack on 1 June at Chateau Thierry saw the Germans come up against the Americans. These were the first of the "doughboys," as US infantrymen were called, to come into action. They were to be followed by 300 000 a month coming into France.

Lloyd George of England, Orlando of Italy, Clémenceau of France, and Wilson of the United States were called the Big Four because they were the leaders who drafted the agreements that ended the First World War.

The results of Germany's last offensive had led to local successes. The western front had been dangerously broken but the gaps were filled and Paris was not captured. The cost of the offensive had been heavy and there were some doubts the German army was capable of further action. Desertion rates were higher than usual and it was noted that the replacement divisions contained an abnormal number of old men and conscripted transportation personnel.

The Allied counterattack went in on 8 August. Spear-headed by Canadians and accompanied by 640 tanks and 800 aircraft, the infantry struck near Amiens and headed toward Mons. The Canadians surprised the Prussian corps at breakfast and six German divisions collapsed by noon. The Germans had not realized the Canadian shock troops were opposite them in the lines. This was the beginning of 100 days of continuous advance for the Allied armies. General Ludendorff declared it the blackest day for the German army. Its morale had been shattered and its will to fight was gone.

By 9 September all the gains of the German offensive had been erased. Now the task was to smash through the Hindenburg defence line and go on to the Rhine. As the German front began to buckle, Ludendorff sought to bring the German forces back to the fatherland intact. The fact that he was able to do so had major consequences for the future of post-war Germany.

As the tide turned against the Germans, members of the *Reichstag* began to discuss the idea of surrender. General Ludendorff, who had dictatorial war powers, told the kaiser to seek a peace settlement. In July 1917 Bethmann-Hollweg had been removed as chancellor when he opposed the reinstitution of unrestricted submarine warfare. He had warned it would only bring the United States into the war but his advice was dismissed. The next chancellor, George Michaelis, was Ludendorff's puppet and a virtual nonentity. When he foolishly suggested evacuating Belgium he was replaced by 73-year-old Count Hertling. In a debate over war financing he permitted the *Reichstag* to pass a motion seeking peace terms along the lines of Wilson's Fourteen Points. The offer was rejected.

Then on 26 October 1918, Germany became a true parliamentary government when Ludendorff ordered the chancellor to be responsible to the *Reichstag* and not to the kaiser. It was hoped that this move towards a democracy might bring better terms from the Americans. As the news from the western front became more grim and as civil unrest exploded throughout Germany, Prince Max von Baden was appointed chancellor. Von Baden was to restore order, preserve the *Reich*, and maintain Germany's social order.

Prince Max announced the kaiser's abdication and his subsequent flight to sanctuary in Holland. The next day, 9 November, he turned the government over to the socialist leader Friedrich Ebert. Ebert immediately began negotiating an armistice to go into effect at eleven o'clock on 11 November 1918.

There had been no other choice. Germany could not have fought on and by surrendering at this time the *Reich* at least would remain intact. Germany's Allies were already out of the war. Bulgaria had surrendered on 29 September, the Ottoman Empire had withdrawn from the war on 30 October, and Emperor Karl of Austria-Hungary had signed an armistice on 4 November.

In Germany the fall months were punctuated by an increasing number of strikes and civil disturbances. As the nation approached anarchy, armed bands attempted to seize power. In Berlin the Spartacists, led by Karl Liebknecht and Rosa Luxembourg, attempted a coup. Ebert called upon the returning soldiers to oust the rabble from the streets.

In Bavaria a communist-socialist government had a brief spell in power before it too was cast out by returning soldiers. Eventually order was restored but the army talked of the members of the *Reichstag* stabbing them in the back by a hasty surrender. As for those who signed the armistice, the German army labelled them the November Criminals.

PEACE

The Paris Treaties of 1919

The signing of the armistice brought jubilation to the victorious powers. As sirens sounded and bells tolled the hour, buildings emptied as hundreds of millions jammed the streets in a release of joy and thanksgiving. For days, crowds milled about in celebration not knowing what to do except be ecstatic. The sudden relief from four years of destruction was overwhelming and soon the men would be coming home.

The victors met in the Hall of Mirrors in Versailles in January 1919 to begin months of peace negotiations. Representatives from the great powers and 28 other nations gathered to assess the costs of the war and set penalties on the defeated.

All the major decisions were made by Britain's Lloyd George, President Wilson of the United States, Premier Clémenceau of France, and, at times, President Orlando of Italy. Known as the Big Four, the Paris Treaties were their creation, although from time to time, as was appropriate,

---

Armistice Terms 11 November 1918

1.
All occupied territory to be evacuated within two weeks

2.
Immediate surrender of 5000 guns, 25 000 machine guns, 1700 aeroplanes.

3.
Immediate surrender of 5000 locomotives, 150 000 trucks, and 5000 lorries.

4.
All allied prisoners of war to be returned immediately

5.
Germans to withdraw immediately to the east bank of the Rhine, creating a demilitarized zone there, six miles wide.

6.
Three bridgeheads east of the Rhine to be granted to the Allies.

7.
All submarines to be surrendered and 70 warships interned.

8.
The treaties of Brest-Litovsk and Bucharest to be repudiated.

---

representatives of the other nations could be heard in committee.

Lloyd George wanted a reasonable treaty that would not leave any issues unresolved. The British wanted their revenge but this was to be tempered by justice. One of the first tasks would be to get German industry working again so that its people could be looked after during the coming months. Foodstuffs should be supplied to ease the starvation so prevalent in Germany's cities.

There was also the fear of a socialist or communist takeover should the traditional structure of society be destroyed. Did not the west need a strong buffer against the machinations of Lenin and the Soviet International (Comintern)? The treaty must not make Germany an enemy of the west.

A large part of the French public demanded vengeance. Premier Clémenceau had little room to manoeuvre. His first thoughts were for French security and to achieve this Germany must be crippled. The worst damage of the war had been done in Belgium and northern France. Four years of trench warfare had taken its toll on the people and the land.

The Germans inflicted additional destruction on allied territory as they laid waste the land on their retreat into Germany. A thousand bridges had been blown up, railway networks destroyed, 300 000 houses blown up, 6000 factories gone, 2000 breweries destroyed, and a million head of livestock taken.

Added to this was the cost of cleaning the battlefields. There were some 300 000 kilometres of barbed wire, mine fields, and trench lines to be made safe. The Germans would not only pay for all this but Germany would be monitored so it could never attack France again.

President Wilson was at a disadvantage at Versailles in that he had to keep returning to the United States to attend to domestic issues in his country. However the Americans had, in a way, won the war. Certainly without them the war could not have been won. Wilson would have to be listened to.

Wilson approached the peace process from a different angle. He had already made several suggestions on how to prevent future war in his Fourteen Points. His concepts of **self determination** and secure boundaries were insightful. If the causes of war were taken away then there would be no war.

He proposed the creation of a collective security as a guarantor of the peace. So certain was he of the ability to prevent the regrowth of German militarism that he would not agree to French annexation of the Rhineland or any other territorial expansion that affected minorities adversely.

The war had shown that a single industrial nation aided by its allies had successfully held the others at bay for four years. Had the United States not entered the war, Germany would have stood a good chance of winning. In order to avoid future wars Wilson suggested a league of all nations bound together in the interests of peace whose members would throw their entire resources against any aggressor. If all the other nations in the world banded together to fight the merest hint of aggression no nation would dare start a war as its own destruction was assured. In theory the idea of collective security was ideal but in reality could all the nations agree who an aggressor was and would all be prepared to take concerted action?

Peace negotiations began on 18 January in the Hall of

War Dead 1914–1918

Country	Number Dead
Britain & Empire	947 000
Belgium	44 000
France	1 400 000
Italy	615 000
Russia	1 700 000
USA	116 000
Portugal	7000
Japan	300
Germany	1 800 000
Austria-Hungary	1 290 000
Montenegro	3000
Serbia	45 000
Greece	5000
Bulgaria	90 000
Rumania	335 000
Ottoman Empire	325 000

Mirrors. The Palace of Versailles was reserved for matters pertaining to Germany. Matters relating to the other enemy nations were discussed in outlying suburbs: St Germaine-en-Laye for Austria, Neuilly for Bulgaria, and the Trianon for Hungary. The war had cost the Allies 5 200 000 dead and 12 800 000 wounded. The Central Powers had suffered 3 500 000 dead and 8 840 000 wounded. At sea over 14 million tonnes of shipping had been destroyed. Damage to buildings and factories had occurred on three continents. The losses were staggering. How would it all be put right and the future guaranteed?

Disarmament

Based on the armistice agreement, the Germans were to withdraw from all occupied territory and surrender their offensive weapons. The Allies would be given three bridgeheads across the Rhine River and were permitted to occupy the Rhineland for a period of five years. The Rhineland was to be evacuated and demilitarized, creating a buffer between French and German forces.

The German fleet was to be interned at Scapa Flow. The Germans were forbidden to have tanks, submarines, and war planes. All means of transport were to be turned over to the Allies for their use. The Germans were to be permitted a 100 000-man army for purposes of internal security in support of the civil power. They were also permitted a small naval force of 15 000 to man six obsolete battleships, six light cruisers, and a handful of smaller craft for coastal patrol. All the powers agreed on the use of German armed force to quell civil unrest within Germany.

Areas lost by
- Germany
- Austria-Hungary
- Bulgaria
- Ottoman Empire
- Russia

**EUROPE AFTER THE WAR
(1919)**

*Many new states were created in Eastern Europe after World War I.
Which boundaries in this new map of Europe were likely to cause problems?*

A New Map of Europe

Territorial changes were designed to reward the Allies and to deal with the problems created by the collapse of the Russian, Ottoman, and Austro-Hungarian empires.

The Treaty of Brest-Litovsk was declared null and void. All of Germany's gains in the east were erased. Germany was to evacuate all non-German regions. The decision was to be communicated to the Bolshevik government which was not represented at the conference. The Germans protested that they had won the war in the east and should be permitted to keep their gains there. Their protests fell on deaf ears.

Against American objections, the British and French insisted on keeping the pledges made to their allies during the war. Italy would be permitted to annex the Trentino and parts of the Dalmatian coastline including Trieste. This did not include Fiume nor Albania; they were given full independence. This left Italy dissatisfied. Japan was excluded from Tsingtao but given other parts of the German-Asian empire. The British insisted on implementing the Balfour

Declaration (1917) which promised the Jews a homeland in Palestine and, by doing so, created a volatile situation yet to be resolved.

Most of the German empire was turned over to the League of Nations under the **mandate** system. Japan, Australia, and New Zealand were the mandate nations in Asia. Britain and France were the mandates in Africa. The non-Turkish parts of the Ottoman Empire were the mandates in the Middle East. In effect, the mandates were a thinly disguised annexation of these territories to the mandate power.

Germany lost 13 percent of its territory. Alsace and Lorraine were returned to France. West Prussia and Posen were given to Poland. Poland was given a corridor through Prussia to the Baltic port of Danzig. This separated East Prussia from the rest of Germany. Poland laid claim to its borders of the partitions of 1772–1795 and soon Polish forces were attacking eastward into Russia.

A number of new nations had been established out of the ashes of the old empires before the war had ended. The ideal had been to replace the multinational empires with independent nation states along ethnic frontiers. This was not to be the case as already powerful groups had made a land grab declaring boundaries as large as could be defended. Once the war was over it was impossible to dislodge them.

All that could be done was to recognize the status quo. All of these new states had large, concentrated, ethnic minorities within their boundaries, a situation that would cause future instability throughout central Europe. The boundaries made no sense. They cut across traditional economic zones in central Europe and along the Danube. For example, Czechoslovakia contained 2 000 000 Germans in the western Sudetenland. More than half the population of some of the new states did not belong to the governing nationality.

The new states were too small to be self-sufficient yet their existence was agreed to because there was no better solution. The Allied armies had been demobilized to the point where even had they wanted to they could not have dislodged them.

Austria was separated from its empire and transformed into a republic with Vienna as its capital. The Ottoman Turks refused to accept their new boundaries until they reached agreement with the Allies at Lausanne in 1923. There Turkey regained western Armenia, the region around Smyrna, and eastern Thrace. About 1 350 000 Greeks and 430 000 Ottoman Turks were resettled as a result.

Principal German Losses

100%	*of*	its pre-war colonies
80%	*of*	its pre-war fleet
48%	*of*	all iron production
16%	*of*	all coal production
13%	*of*	its territory of 1914
12%	*of*	its population

Plebiscites

Many boundary changes resulted from plebiscites in which the inhabitants were asked to vote where they wished to go. The plebiscites held in East Prussia resulted in the province remaining German. The people in the Saar, after 15 years of League supervision, voted to return to Germany. Two border areas of Austria voted to remain Austrian. In Silesia the results were inconclusive and that region was divided between Germany and Poland. Northern Schleswig voted to return to Denmark, while southern Schleswig voted to remain in Germany. In instances of other border changes where the successor states were recognised, large ethnic minorities remained within the boundaries.

Reparations

Reparations were nothing new. Germany had levied heavy reparations on Russia under the Treaty of Brest-Litovsk. At Versailles, the reparations placed against Germany were assigned under Clause 231. The original draft of the clause had stated that Germany was responsible for causing all the losses and damages done by invasion. But this would not permit reparations to be paid to those nations Germany had not invaded such as the United States and Canada. To ensure that the latter were eligible for reparations, the clause was changed to include the phrase "by German aggression." The Germans were quite prepared to admit to the invasions but they were not willing to admit they had carried out aggression. This was quite another thing. In their view, they had fought in self-defence, not as

The League of Nations was created in 1920 to promote peace and international cooperation. This picture was taken when members of the league visited the United States.

aggressors. This single clause was skillfully used by those opposed to the treaty to undermine those who supported it.

The Allies hoped reparations would restore them to prosperity. Stiff penalties were popular and applauded among the populaces. Damage done was immense and most was not as a side effect of battle, as in the case of the German withdrawal from northern France. Germany did not quibble over battle costs or the destruction to northern France but objected to paying war pensions and damage done outside the battle zones.

The amount of reparations was finally established by the Paris Conference at 269 billion German gold marks to be paid in 42 installments. The total was never paid. It was whittled away at a series of international conferences until the process came to an end at Lausanne in 1932. About 53 million gold marks were paid in all. Germany received more in American loans during that time than was paid out in reparations.

The reparations were of many kinds. The German merchant fleet was distributed among the Allies. Livestock, benzol, ocean cables, machinery, gold, jewellery, some 150 000 trucks, 5000 locomotives and railroad rolling stock; coal from the Saar and 48 percent of German iron production (although the French would not accept any reparations that would place French workers out of work).

War Debts

America had funded the latter part of the war and after it was over made demands for repayment. Britain and France wanted the war debts to be tied to reparations.

When they received German reparations they would then pass them on for payment on the American loans. The Americans saw the two issues as separate and demanded payment whether or not reparations were paid. For the first time in its history the United States became a creditor nation.

The result was a major shift in global economic power from Europe to North America.

League of Nations and Collective Security

The covenant of the League of Nations was written into the Treaty of Versailles. The league began its existence in Geneva in November 1920. It provided the international structure for implementing the principle of collective security as opposed to that of balance of power. Its purpose was to promote peace and international cooperation through collective measures. It was responsible for implementing the new European political system that arose out of the Treaty of Versailles. It became involved in administering Danzig, control over the mandates, securing the new borders administration of the Saar, and such other matters as disarmament, economic assistance, and care of displaced persons and fugitives.

The Council of the League consisted of four to six permanent members—Britain, France, Italy, Japan, and, later, Germany. The United States did not join the League. When Germany left in 1933, its seat was taken by the USSR, until its expulsion over the invasion of Poland in 1939. At first six then later nine nonpermanent members of the council were chosen by vote of the general assembly. The

World War I Treaties

Treaty of Versailles

Germany ❀ *signed 16 June 1919;*
effective 10 January 1920.

I ❀ The Covenant of the League of Nations.

II & III ❀ The establishment of the new boundaries.
❀ Germany surrendered Alsace-Lorraine,
Posen and west Prussia and Memel;
❀ Danzig became a free city;
❀ Plebiscites held in Eupen-et-Malmédy,
Schleswig, East Prussia, Silesia , and the Saar.

IV & V 1. Germany gave up all its rights in foreign countries
and its colonies.
2. Disarmament was supervised by allied control
commissions.
3. All war *matériel* were to be handed over.
4. The general staff was to be dissolved.
5. All fortifications to a line 60 kilometres east
of the Rhine River were to be disbanded.
6. An armed force of no more than 100 000 men
was permitted for internal security.

VI ❀ Matters related to prisoners of war and war
cemeteries.

VII ❀ Matters related to war criminals.

VIII ❀ Matters related to reparations in the
amount of 269 billion gold marks.

X & XI ❀ Matters related to international trade and finance,
transportation, civil aviation and railways and all
other matters deemed appropriate

Treaty of St Germain-en-Laye

Austria ❀ *signed 10 September 1919*
❀ would cede the Tyrol to the Brenner Pass to Italy.
❀ would give up Trieste, Istria, and its claims on the
Dalmatian coast.
❀ was to recognize the successor states of
Czechoslovakia, Poland, and Yugoslavia.
❀ could maintain an army of not more than 30 000.
❀ was forbidden Anschluss ("union") with Germany.

Treaty of Neuilly

Bulgaria ❀ *signed 27 November 1919*
❀ would cede the southwest coast to Greece.
❀ could retain access to the sea through
Alexandroúpolis.
❀ could maintain a 20 000 man army.

Treaty of Trianon

Hungary ❀ *signed 4 June 1920*
❀ was to be partly responsible for the war.
❀ was to cede Slovakia and the Carpatho-Ukraine
to Czechoslovakia.
❀ was to cede Croatia-Slovenia to Yugoslavia.
❀ was to cede the Banat to Yugoslavia and Rumania.
❀ was to cede Transylvania to Rumania.
❀ was to cede part of the Burgenland to Austria.
❀ could maintain a 35 000 man force.

Treaty of Sèvres

Ottoman Empire
(Turkey) ❀ *signed 10 August 1920*

(Not ratified by the Turkish government and
superseded in 1923 by the Treaty of Lausanne
which restored parts of Asia Minor to Turkey.)
❀ Internationalization of the Straits under a British
commissioner in Constantinople.
❀ to cede to Greece all of Thrace including the
Gallipoli Peninsula.
❀ to cede to France Syria and Cilicia.
❀ to cede to Britain Iraq and Palestine and a
protectorate over Arabia.
❀ to cede to Italy the Dodecanese and Rhodes.
❀ to maintain a 50 000-man army.

Armenia ❀ to become independent.

Britain ❀ to control Cyprus and Egypt.

Kurdistan ❀ to become autonomous.

assembly consisted of all member states with each nation having one vote.

The council had the more active role, meeting several times a year, but it was somewhat limited by the need to arrive at unanimous decisions. The unanimity factor assumed all nations opposed war and would act collectively to maintain the peace. Difficulties in naming the aggressor or taking into account traditional alliances also weakened the league's efforts. The council had the power to intervene in sovereign states through economic sanctions or military ventures. The question was whether it could intervene in the affairs of non-members.

The unanimity factor made the league, for all intents and purposes, useless. It was remarkable that so much did get done.

The Permanent International Court at The Hague was also affiliated with the League of Nations.

LEGACY

World War I brought a long era of peace in Europe to an end. Britain, France, and Russia, with the help of the United States, defeated the Central Powers at great cost. There was an unprecedented loss of life and destruction of property. A generation of young men was killed. The aristocratic class structure that had prevailed for centuries was toppled. Three multinational empires—Romanov, Hohenzollern, and Hapsburg—dissolved into a plethora of new nation states.

However the war did not answer the question of Germany's place in Europe. Disarmed and beset by heavy reparations, the Germans did not see justice in the Treaty of Versailles. They longed to regain those territories lost at the peace table and they desired an end to reparations. Disillusionment and despair helped fan the flames of ultra-nationalism and lay the groundwork for Adolf Hitler's rise to power in 1933.

The French had sought security but found only an illusion of it. The Americans had forbidden French expansion to the Rhine. Instead the USA would guarantee the French border with Germany. However, the United States did not ratify the treaties and withdrew into political isolation. By 1920 France faced the prospect of a resurgent Germany alone. Only through reparations and a strict adherence to the treaties would Germany be kept under control, but this was not to be.

The new frontiers of the successor states were ill-conceived and would be the cause of later tensions. These new nations, forged out of the collapse of the older empires, were unstable. They contained large concentrations of ethnic minorities that were treated far from equally. None of them had the economic or physical resource base to become independent. The term Balkanisation has come to mean the division of something into parts too small to be effective. The term well describes the successor states.

Society would never be the same again. The Belle Epoque of the turn of the century was gone forever. People demanded a better life after the war. Now a new social structure was being established. Women had made tremendous social gains in the work force and labour had made progress. Wages and working conditions were better than before although there was no work for the returning veterans. Social privileges had melted away but then so had the idea of individual freedom. Governments had had a taste of total control and were loathe to return powers to the individual.

The world would have to face a whole new set of values as it entered the second decade of the twentieth century.

SUMMARY

In 1917, Russia's losses fuelled political turmoil. When Tsar Nicholas II abdicated, he was replaced by a provisional government. The new government, however, was ineffective and failed to extract Russia from the war. The Bolsheviks, under Lenin, staged a coup to replace the government. Once in power, Lenin acted to get Russia out of the war at any cost. The cost was high, but peace with Germany was secured in 1918.

Russia's withdrawal reduced the war to a single battle-front. The Germans attempted to break through to Paris before the American troops arrived in the spring. Despite local successes, their efforts failed

An allied counterattack in August 1918 was followed by 100 days of continuous victories. German morale declined; civil unrest grew in Germany. One by one, Germany's allies surrendered. Then Germany, under the leadership of Friedrich Ebert, began negotiating an armistice on 9 November.

The armistice was agreed to on 11 November 1918. Final peace terms were worked out at Versailles, France. The peace of Versailles was expected to provide stability in Europe. The peacemakers, however, failed to provide a successful formula for European security. A second world war was just over twenty years away.

QUESTIONS

1. Briefly describe the condition of the Russian military in 1917. How did this contribute to the Bolshevik success in the Russian Revolution?

2. Explain the terms of the Treaty of Brest-Litovsk. Why would Lenin agree to such harsh terms?

3. What were the two policy decisions made by the Bolsheviks in 1918 which were particularly important to the western nations?

4. How did the Allies attempt to persuade Russia to remain in the war? Why did the Allies invade Russia in 1918?

5. How was the war eventually concluded? Briefly explain the allied success. How did the German public react to their government's defeat in the war?

6. The victorious powers met at Versailles in January, 1919 to begin the peace settlement. Who were the Big Four? Briefly explain the position which each of these delegates held as representative of their respective countries.

7. Examine the terms on German disarmament. Why were the German permitted any military force at all?

8. What was the effect of plebiscites in central Europe? Explain.

9. What are reparations? Why were reparations assigned to Germany? What was the rationale? What was the amount of reparations expected by the Allies?

10. Explain how the issue of war debts shifted global economic power.

11. Define collective security. Did the League of Nations meet the criterion of collective security?

12. List seven legacies of the First World War. Consider social, political and economic change.

ANALYSIS

1. Evaluate the treatment accorded to Russia by Germany in the Treaty of Brest-Litovsk with that accorded Germany by the Allies in the Treaty of Versailles. Do you feel that the terms of the Treaty of Versailles were harsh or unjust? Assess the reaction of the German army and the German people to the peace terms applied to Germany.

2. Research the German surrender and take a position on the following statement.

   The German army was stabbed in the back by a civilian government that surrendered just as the army was to achieve final victory.

   Justify your position. Did the German negotiators deserve the term November Criminals? Why did the German army make these claims? What was the effect on the future of Germany of these claims?

3. Why did the Treaty of Versailles fail to establish peace and stability in Europe? Evaluate the peace settlement and determine which issues remained unresolved and therefore posed the potential for unrest.

ACTIVITIES

1. Meeting
Write a script for a meeting between Lenin and Trotsky regarding German demands at the end of the war. How could Lenin justify his acceptance of the terms of the Treaty of Brest-Litovsk? What would Trotsky's objections be?

2. Panel Discussion
Recreate the discussion among the major powers regarding the assignment of guilt for the beginning of the war.

3. Map Activity
On a map of Europe, identify the new borders which were created after the First World War. Analyse the effectiveness of the way in which the Austrian Empire and the Ottoman Empire were divided up to create new territories. What potential problems might come forth from these new nations?

ISSUE
Analysis

You have now completed Unit IV: International Conflict. *The following activity is based on what you have learned about World War I.*

ISSUE ANALYSIS
Who Should Take Responsibility for World War I?

The question of responsibility for World War I continues to intrigue historians. The answer varies depending on the nationality of the historian and the age in which he or she writes.

Below are summaries of some historical writings on the question of responsibility. All have a particular bias and objective in mind.

Commission of War Guilt, Paris Peace Conference (1919):

The War Guilt Commission placed the blame for the war solely on Germany and its allies. The commission believed the war was premeditated because of the following circumstances:

- On 5 July 1914, at Potsdam, the kaiser and his military staff decided that the emperor of Austria-Hungary would send an unacceptable ultimatum to the Serbs establishing a cause for war. The only fear was that Austria might not send the ultimatum.

- On 21 July 1914, Germany had begun to call up its reserves.

- On 27 July 1914, Lord Grey of England suggested that a peace conference be called. Germany refused the request pointing out that events were already in motion. On 29 July, Grey asked Germany to suggest a process whereby the powers could avoid a general war over the Balkans. Germany refused.

German representatives to the Commission of War Guilt, initiated revisionist theories (1919):

They claimed that Austria-Hungary only wanted to maintain the status quo. It was France that was anxious to regain Alsace-Lorraine and the Saar Basin, and it was Russia who wanted expansion in the Balkans and control over the Straits. None of these aims could have been achieved without a war. France and Russia were the aggressors. Germany acted in self-defence.

Germany's call up of reserves on 21 July was far smaller than that of France, who declared war first. Germany's 10 to 16 *Dreadnoughts* pale by comparison to those of the British navy.

The war was not decided upon at the 5 July meeting at Potsdam. Those conversations were not policy.

France urged Russia to mobilize when all knew that Russian mobilization would trigger the Schlieffen Plan. Therefore, Russia was to blame for the war.

Germany's declaration of war on Russia was probably a mistake but it was taken out of fear of a two-front attack.

Extreme revisionist theories were developed in the late 1920s:

France wanted the return of Alsace and Lorraine. Russia wanted control of Constantinople and the Balkans. They plotted to trick Germany into a war.

Russia was behind the assassination of the Austrian archduke. Russia wanted to destroy the Austro-Hungarian and Ottoman empires and free the Slavs.

French-Russian diplomatic efforts made negotiation useless. On 31 July, at midnight, the French informed the Russians they were going to war.

Germany did not plot a war with Austria-Hungary. Serbian nationalism was responsible for the sequence of events. Germany's fault was in not keeping tighter control over Austria-Hungary to make certain the Austro-Hungarian emperor was aware of the limitations of the alliance with Germany.

A.J.P. Taylor, the noted British historian, wrote on war guilt during the 1940s:

Taylor said Germany was guilty and should bear the full responsibility for the war. No one in 1914 took the chance of war seriously. Germany gave up a process of negotiation for one of unilateral action. This destabilized foreign relations.

The Schlieffen Plan was the only aggressive plan. After all, Belgium did not ask to be invaded. All other battle plans were defensive in nature.

ISSUE
Analysis

In the 1950s, at a time of rapprochement, French and German historians agreed on what should go into the history books relating to World War I. This was an effort to eliminate hatred and nationalist propaganda within each other's school systems.

1. There was no premeditation by any of the powers for the war.

2. The German military staff wanted war. The German people did not want war.

3. French president Poincaré did not have a war policy.

4. Austria-Hungary and Serbia had a long period of antagonism.

5. The link between Serbia and Panslavism and the assassination of the Austrian archduke is unfounded.

6. The Serbian government's involvement in the assassination is unproven.

7. The Serbian government had foreknowledge of the plot.

8. Russia believed it had to support Panslavism in the Balkans.

9. Russian mobilization was a mistake because it triggered Germany's Schlieffen Plan.

10. French policy determined the need for Russian friendship. France did not advise against Russian mobilization.

11. Germany acted to halt the breakup of the Austro-Hungarian Empire. Germany was guilty of not monitoring Austria-Hungary's actions.

12. Germany believed it could win the war.

13. The division of Europe into two alliances did not cause the war but meant that any war would become general.

14. The Balkans brought about the rupture between the powers but the powers would not have Germany as the dominant power on the continent.

15. There was no guilt, only nation states acting in a normal fashion. What they saw as their own best interests created the conditions for war.

16. Nationalism in the Balkans backed by a great power created tensions in Europe.

Published historical research at Hamburg University, Germany in the 1960s concluded that Germany should take responsibility for the war:
Germany's policies since 1900 were aggressive in nature and designed to create tensions. Germany felt isolated by the other powers and plotted the war. General von Moltke saw the combined forces of France and Russia soar past the 2 200 000 mark in manpower and advised the kaiser to act while Germany could still win a two-front war. Both Chancellor Bethmann and General von Moltke put pressure on Austria to act in the Balkans.

The Hamburg theories touched off a heated debate in Germany. German historians have taken three directions in challenging the thesis of Germany's guilt:

1. to deny it,

2. to accept the thesis and expand the research,

3. to modify the thesis on the grounds that the Hamburg theories overstated the case. The fact that documents are now available in national archives makes total denial of Germany's guilt difficult to prove.

ISSUE
Analysis

Dr. Henry Kissinger, in his recent book called *Diplomacy,* theorizes on a geopolitical level:

Kissinger says it was the balance of power that had kept the peace in Europe for almost a hundred years between 1815–1914 through deterrence. It was the kaiser's indifference to maintaining the balance after 1900 that led to conditions that made war probable. Kissinger notes that historians ask the wrong questions when they attempt to lay blame for the war on one nation or another. The questions should be directed at what underlying forces or conditions made the potential for war possible. It was Germany that upset the relations between the great powers; thus, Germany is responsible for the war.

QUESTIONS

1. What questions should historians be asking about the causes of World War I?

2. Why did the victors demand revenge on Germany and its allies?

3. Do you believe that the conversations that took place at Potsdam were just that and not policy? Explain.

4. Why did the German military staff want war? Why were they convinced they could win?

5. Comment on the statement, "The nation that mobilized first must bear the blame."

6. What were the admitted German mistakes in foreign relations prior to the outbreak of war? the Russian? the French? the English? the Austro-Hungarian?

7. What evidence is there that Russian and French war plans were aggressive?

8. Analyze the claim that France and Russia had aims that could only be achieved through a war.

9. Did Russia wish to destroy the Austro-Hungarian and Ottoman empires?

10. Evaluate the reality of the French-German agreement on reducing nationalist propaganda in textbooks? How valid are the statements they put in the textbooks?

11. Why did the Hamburg theories return to Germany's war guilt touch off such an explosion among Germany historians? How convincing is the argument that the reasearch overstated its case?

12. What would historians look for in order to prove or disprove the Hamburg theories?

13. State the Kissinger thesis on the value of balance of power. Can balance of power maintain stability and peace between nations? How does this work in theory? in practice?

14. Evaluate Kissinger's statement that a balance of power preserves peace among great powers through deterrence. Are there other processes that can maintain peace amongst sovereign states?

15. Write a position paper on the topic: "What nation or nations were responsible for World War I?" Support your arguments by referring to statements made by the historians mentioned in this chapter.

Epilogue

The nineteenth century grew out of the French Revolution and ended with the devastation of World War I. In between the major powers kept the peace. No major war occurred in Europe from 1815 to 1914.

The French Revolution signalled the beginning of the end of absolute monarchy. New forms of political organization were tested against the background of mushrooming industrial and urban growth. These forms included constitutional monarchy and republicanism. The experience of the French Revolution was transported outside France by Napoleon Bonaparte in his attempt to dominate the rest of Europe. As a result, the revolutionary ideas of nationalism, self-determination, individual rights, and the social responsibilities of government were spread widely.

During the nineteenth century, peace was made possible by the determined efforts of the policy makers who believed war was unacceptable. The Metternich system supported the status quo while Bismarck's "balance of power" strategies focused on war prevention. Only at the turn of the century, when nationalist feelings were encouraged by political leaders, did war become a possibility. British attempts to call a congress of powers to ward off World War I were met with indifference by the other powers, who were being urged on by nationalist sentiment. Few predicted the war would last four, long years with tremendous loss of life and property.

Underlying the conflict between the powers was the transformation of western European nations from an agricultural-village society to an industrial-urban one. Increasing demands for social reorganization arose as the urban population grew and labour forces moved

from farm to factory. One solution was to encourage the mass migration of some 20 million people to colonies around the world.

For those who remained in Europe, the rights of the urban wage-earner became a pressing issue. Urban dwellers wielded political power through mass demonstrations and strikes. The mobs in the French and Russian Revolutions were pivotal to change, while a general strike in Britain forced the progress of labour legislation.

The labour movement had the support of the socialists, who supported better working conditions. Karl Marx's *Das Kapital* and *Communist Manifesto* predicted what would happen when the demands of labour were not met. Towards the end of the century, unhappy with the pace of change, labour began establishing its own political parties.

The wealth created by industrialization was a tremendous boon to the arts. Symphony halls, dance halls, and opera houses grew in number and size during La Belle Époque at the end of the century. Artists brought prestige to their patrons and to the nation-state. Arts communities flourished in the major cities of Vienna, Paris, London, and St Petersburg.

The developing material standard of living relied on continued economic growth. As industrial resources dwindled in Europe, the major powers sought to gather new resources through imperial expansion. Resources were found in other continents and brought to the centres of production by railway and steam ship.

By the end of the century a fatal competition had developed between the major powers. Recurring tensions arose over competing spheres of influence, such

as those between Russia and Austria over the Balkans, or Britain and Germany over control of ocean lanes. None would back away. Supported by a vocal press, the hysteria of the public permitted no negotiation.

When war finally came in 1914, it broke out in the Balkans. Germany implemented the Schlieffen Plan when coming to the aid of its ally, Austria-Hungary, against Serbia. During the war, the agrarian-based societies of Russia, Austria-Hungary, and the Ottoman Empire suffered badly. They did not have the capability of maintaining large armies in the field for any length of time. In comparison, the industrial nations of Britain, Germany, and France fought to the end in 1918. They, too, suffered but were able to keep fighting despite the costs.

The entrance into the war of an industrial giant from across the ocean, the United States, brought victory to the allied side. Although American forces played a small part in the waning days of battle, it was their promise of unlimited human and military resources that convinced Germany to end the fighting.

When the peacemakers met in Versailles to draft a peace treaty, they were limited in what they could do by the vengeful spirit of their peoples. The war had gone on too long for victor or vanquished to reach a settlement that satisfied both.

World War I was a turning point for Europe. It signalled the beginning of the end of European global dominance as a new industrial giant, the United States, emerged on the international scene. The European powers had gambled their resources on battle and had lost.

Glossary

To **abdicate** means to agree to give up the throne or a political office.

The **Age of Reason** was a period in history in which philosophers and scientists carried out an exhaustive search into the laws of nature. They resolved to advance humankind through reason and logic as opposed to appeals to the divinity.

The **alliance** system is a grouping of powers with common interests for the purpose of mutual defense or aggression.

L'ancien régime is the old regime, a term denoting the governmental and social structure which existed in Europe before 1789. The social organization of *l'ancien régime* was based on village and agricultural life.

An **armistice** is an agreement for armies to stop fighting pending negotiations for a political peace settlement.

Attrition is a strategy designed to reduce the enemy's ability to wage war to the point where its surrender is inevitable, while at the same time maintaining one's own strength. This strategy avoids engaging the enemy in costly battles.

Autarky is the state of being economically self-sufficient.

An **autocracy** is a political system in which sovereignty lies in the hands of a monarch.

A **balance of power** acts as a deterrent to war because no single power dares to upset the balance to go to war and risk defeat.

A **battlefront** is a geographic location within a war zone.

A **buffer zone** is the territory between major powers that provides a geographic security zone. This zone ensures that each side has a period of time to prepare defenses against their enemy.

Capitalism is an economic theory which asserts that the private ownership of property, division of labour, competition, specialization, and individual self-interest increases production.

Cause célèbre is a notorious, and thus noticeable, individual social event, or a widely debated controversial issue.

Class warfare occurs when the diverse aims of economic classes lead to tension and revolution.

Collective security is a strategy that pits the strength of many countries against an aggressor nation. Because of the overwhelming might of those opposing the aggressor, the destruction of the aggressor is assured. In theory, collective security should provide a strong enough deterrent to aggressor nations that they do not engage in acts of aggression; thus, collective security prevents wars.

Commerce raiders was the name given to long range warships designed to sink unprotected merchant shipping and in this way block enemy lifelines.

The **congress system** was an agreement among the major powers to hold a series of diplomatic conferences in order to maintain the peace established after the Napoleonic Wars.

A **constitutional monarchy** is a political organization in which the monarch's powers are limited by a written constitution or some other arrangement.

The **Continental System** was an attempt by Napoleon from 1806 to 1813 to ruin the British economy by excluding British trade from Europe.

Democracy is a political system in which sovereignty is held by the masses of people.

The **Divine Right of Kings** is the belief that the king is appointed by God to do his bidding on earth. As such, the king cannot be questioned, only endured.

The **Eastern Question** refers to the issue that arose over control of the Balkan region and the Bosporus and Dardanelles Straits. The straits were the vital lifeline linking the Black Sea and the Mediterranean Sea. Although the straits were within the Ottoman Empire, Russia and Austria-Hungary both wanted control over them. Superpower competition over the straits caused tensions among all major powers throughout the century.

Economic warfare is the strategy of blockade and counter-blockade, which is implemented by destroying the enemy's productive capacity and thus its ability to resist.

The **Estates General** was an advisory body to the king of France, comprising of members of the clergy (First Estate), nobles (Second Estate), and the bourgeoisie and professionals (Third Estate).

L'état, c'est moi is a slogan describing the absolute power of the king. It means, "I am the state."

Extraterritorial rights include the right to have one's own laws and social mores applied to one's self when in another country.

The **factory system** was an economic system based on the production of goods in a central place. For the system to work, workers had to leave their villages and relocate in housing close to the factory site. Production in the factory system was based on division of labour, specialization of work, and competition.

Federalism is the division of sovereignty within a nation state between central and regional levels of government. The **federal government** is the central level of government.

The **feudal system** is a social-economic system based on village agriculture and involves the exchange of services between a landowner and a peasant.

The **General Will** is a belief that the view held by the masses is the legitimate view.

"Heart of darkness" is the way missionary Dr. Livingstone described central Africa.

Hegemony is the predominance or control of one nation over other nations, through its spheres of influence.

The **home front** refers to those activities undertaken in times of war by the civilian population to aid the progress of battle.

Imperialism is a movement by major powers to dominate or to take into their spheres of influence all the unattached states in the world.

Impressionism is a school of painting which had as its objective the portrayal of the subject as seen by the eye at first glance.

Industrialization is the replacement, in the production process, of animal and water power by machines.

Irredenta is unredeemed or unrecovered territory. This territory is considered to be the property of the nation state, and as such, every effort will be made to reacquire it.

A *jihad* is a holy war of Muslims against those who do not believe in Islam. In general, a jihad is a war for or against certain positions or doctrines.

Junkers are landowners resident in east Prussia, and members of the German aristocracy.

Laissez-faire is an economic theory which precludes government intervention in business affairs.

Legitimacy was a policy of the reactionary forces towards restructuring Europe after the Napoleonic period. Aware they could not return to the past, the major powers were determined that the government of political units would be returned to the monarchy or the aristocracy as their rightful responsibility. There were to be no more republicans allowed within the traditional governing circles.

Lifeline refers to global trade routes established by major powers to fuel their policies of industrialization and urbanization.

Mandates are territories that were formerly controlled by those empires that were defeated in the First World War. The League of Nations assumed responsibility for their administration and development.

Nationalist movements express the desire of ethnic groupings within multi-ethnic empires for independence and nationhood.

Nationalization is government expropriation of private property.

The **Naval Race** refers to the turn-of-the-century competition between Britain and Germany to build more and better warships.

The **Newtonian system** is a scientific system of natural law in which the activities of nature are seen as predictable when the rules of mathematics and logic are applied to them.

The **noble savage** is a concept used in political science to compare the mythical "humanity in the state of nature" with "humanity in the urban condition."

The **Ottoman Empire** was founded in the thirteenth century by Ottoman Turks. The empire was ruled by the descendants of Osman I, the first sultan. The terms Turkey and Ottoman Empire are used interchangeably. The Ottoman Empire dissolved after World War I. Today, Turkey consists of only part of the original empire.

The **parlement** was a French court of law, not to be confused with the British Parliament, which is a lawmaking body.

The **philosophes** were a group of French academics who sought the answer to the struggle of how to maximize human potential towards the goal of infinite and uninterrupted progress.

A **protectorate** is an established culture over which a more powerful empire has some amount of control. In return for the benefits received by the empire, the protectorate receives the guarantee of protection and security, and is permitted to exercise certain state activities such as policing and taxation.

Realpolitik is the use of power in foreign and domestic relations.

Reparations are economic punishments imposed on a defeated power by the victor. In theory, the amount of reparations levied is to make good the damage done in the battle zones.

A **republic** is a political organization without a monarch. A **republican** is someone who supports such an organization.

A **revolution** is a major change in the underlying organizations within a society, brought about by violent or non-violent means, such as the overthrow of the established government in a state.

Romanticism as a movement arose out of the exuberant celebrations which followed the Napoleonic period. The underlying aim of this movement was to give vent to the emotions and the free expression of personality—to stir the individual's reaction to colour, sound, and craftsmanship.

S

Salons were afternoon, private social gatherings which brought together the social and intellectual giants of the day.

Les sauvages were a group of artists who tended to ignore shape and form in favour of shape and colour.

The **Schlieffen Plan** was a defense strategy, devised in 1905 by General Alfred von Schlieffen, to prevent Germany from having to fight a two-battlefront war—with France in the west and Russia in the east. The plan called for an invasion and quick defeat of France before moving troops to the eastern front to fight Russia. The rationale for this strategy was based on the assumption that Russia would require more time to mobilize than France. Timing was critical, as Germany did not have the people or resources to win a two-front war.

Scientific socialism is a historical theory of Karl Marx in which he predicted that the future would follow inevitable patterns, eventually leading to a classless utopian society.

Scorched Earth Policy is the practice of destroying all food (crops and livestock) and shelter that could possibly aid the approaching enemy.

Scramble for Africa is a reference to the competition among the major powers for control over Africa's land mass.

Self determination is a policy under which national boundaries are established with the consultation and agreement of the people who will be affected by these boundaries.

The **separation of powers** is the division of sovereignty into parts, the legislature, executive, and judiciary, in such a way that each part acts as a check and a balance on the other.

A **single party government** is a political organization in which sovereignty resides within a single political party and in which other political parties and viewpoints are not permitted.

The **Social Contract** is a theory proposed by Rousseau in which the governing and governed each have their own responsibilities and duties within the state.

A **sphere of influence** is a geographic region over which an outside power has influence and control.

A **stalemate** is a condition in warfare in which neither side can prevail in battle. Attempts to break a stalemate are usually costly in terms of people and *matériel.*

Standard of living is a measure of the material goods owned by an individual or society, and the ability to purchase these goods.

State Socialism refers to government-sponsored welfare measures taken to maintain labour support for the governing class.

Submarine warfare added a third dimension to the battlefield. As in the case of air warfare, submarine warfare required that new rules of battle be agreed upon by warring countries.

Successor states was the name given to the new nations that arose out of the defeated Russian, German, Austro-Hungarian, and Ottoman empires after 1919. Poland, an old kingdom, is not usually considered a successor state.

Total war refers to all aspects of a nation being organized towards the war effort. Every aspect of civilian life is controlled by a central government in the interest of attaining victory.

Totalitarianism is the absolute control of the state over the individual.

Treaty ports are ports designated for trade with other nations. Extraterritorial rights and settlements are conceded to the trading nation.

Trench warfare is a condition of war in which the rival front lines consist of armies behind earthen defenses and separated by a no man's land. There is little movement of the forces where this strategy is in place.

Urban means of or having to do with cities or towns. **Urbanization** is the transfer of large numbers of people from the farming countryside to the cities.

A **war zone** is a geographic area in which any military and civilian activities are subject to attack.

Weltpolitik is the name given to Germany's move to global stature after 1894.

Bibliography

Aftalion, Florin. *The French Revolution, An Economic Interpretation.* Cambridge: Cambridge University Press, 1990.

Alioto, Anthony M. *A History of Western Science.* Englewood Cliffs, New Jersey: Prentice-Hall, 1987.

Ashley, Maurice. *The Age of Absolutism: 1648–1775.* Springfield: G&C Merriam, 1974.

Baker, Keith Michael. *Inventing the French Revolution.* Cambridge: Cambridge University Press, 1990.

Baradat, Leon P. *Political Ideologies: Their Origins and Impact.* New Jersey: Prentice-Hall, 1979.

Benier, Olivier. *At the Court of Napoleon.* New York: Doubleday, 1989.

Bernal, J.D. *Science and History.* 4 vols. Cambridge, Massachusetts: MIT Press, 1969.

Brinton, Crane, et al. *A History of Civilization.* New Jersey: Prentice-Hall, 1984.

Burns, Edward McNall. *Western Civilizations: Their History and Their Culture.* New York: Norton, 1973.

Cantor, Norman F. *Inventing the Middle Ages.* New York: Morrow, 1991.

Chirot, Daniel, ed. *The Origins of Backwardness in Eastern Europe: Economics and Politics from the Middle Ages Until the Early Twentieth Century.* Berkeley: University of California Press, 1989.

Cobb, Richard, et al., eds. *Voices of the French Revolution.* Topsfield: Salem House, 1988.

Cobban, Alfred. *A History of Modern France*, Vol. I and II. New York: Penguin, 1984.

Connelly, Owen. *The French Revolution and Napoleonic Era.* Orlando: Holt, Rinehart, Winston, 1991.

Cowie, Leonard W. *Eighteenth-Century Europe.* New York: Frederick Unger, 1964.

Craig, Gordon A. *Germany: 1866–1945.* Oxford: Oxford University Press, 1980.

Cronin, Vincent. *Napoleon.* Glasgow: Fontana, William Collins, 1990.

Dawson, Philip, ed. *The French Revolution.* New Jersey: Prentice-Hall, 1967.

Doyle, William. *The Oxford History of the French Revolution.* Oxford: Oxford University Press, 1989.

Durant, Will and Ariel. *The Age of Voltaire.* New York: Simon and Schuster, 1965.

Durant, Will and Ariel. *Rousseau and Revolution.* New York: Simon and Schuster, 1965.

Dyer, Gwynne. *War.* New York: Crown Publishing, 1985.

Farwell, Byron. *Queen Victoria's Little Wars.* New York: Norton, 1985.

Feher, Ferenc. *The French Revolution and the Birth of Modernity.* Berkeley: University of California Press, 1990.

Furet, Francois and Mona Ozouf, eds. *A Critical Dictionary of the French Revolution.* Cambridge: Harvard University Press, 1989.

Gombrich, E. *The Story of Art.* Oxford: Phaidon Press, 1979.

Herold, Christopher, J. *The Horizon Book of the Age of Napoleon.* New York: American Heritage, 1983.

Holmes, George, ed. *The Oxford History of Medieval Europe.* Oxford: Oxford University Press, 1992.

Howard, Michael. *The Lessons of History.* New Haven: Yale University Press, 1991.

Hsu, Immanuel C.Y. *The Rise of Modern China.* 3rd ed. New York: Oxford University Press, 1983.

Johnson, Paul. *The Birth of the Modern World Society: 1815–1830.* London: Weidenfeld and Nicolson, 1991.

Kelly, Linda. *Women of the French Revolution.* London: Hamish Hamilton, 1987.

Kennedy, Paul. *The Rise and Fall of the Great Powers: Economic Change and Military Conflict from 1500 to 2000.* London: Unwin, Hyman, 1988.

Kennedy, Paul. *The Rise of Anglo-German Antagonism: 1860-1914.* London: Allen and Unwin, 1980.

Kissinger, Henry. *Diplomacy.* New York: Simon and Schuster, 1994.

Macksey, Kenneth, et al. *The Guinness History of Air War-fare.* Enfield, Middlesex: Guinness Superlatives, 1976.

Macksey, Kenneth, et al. *The Guinness History of Land Warfare.* Enfield, Middlesex: Guinness Superlatives, 1973.

Macksey, Kenneth, et al. *The Guinness History of Sea War-fare.* Enfield, Middlesex: Guinness Superlatives, 1975.

Marx, Karl and Friedrich Engels. *Manifesto of the Communist Party,* reprinted in the Croft Classics Series. Arlington Heights, IL: Harlan Davidson, 1955.

Massie, Robert K. *Dreadnaught.* New York: Random House, 1991.

Moulin, Annie. *Peasantry and Society in France Since 1789.* Cambridge: Cambridge University Press, 1991.

Orlow, Dietrich. *A History of Modern Germany.* 2nd ed. Boston University: Prentice-Hall, 1991.

Pakenham, Thomas. *The Scramble for Africa.* New York: Avon Books, 1992.

Palmer, R.R. and Joel Colton. *A History of the Modern World.* New York: Knopf, 1984.

Panikkar, K.M. *Asia and Western Dominance: A Survey of Vasco Da Gama Epoch of Asian History: 1498–1945.* London: Allen and Unwin, 1959.

Reilly, Kevin. *Readings in World Civilizations, Volume 2: The Development of the Modern World.* 2nd ed. New York: St. Martin's Press, 1992.

Riasanovsky, Nicholas V. *A History of Russia.* 4th e Oxford: Oxford University Press, 1984.

Roberts, J.M. *History of the World.* New York: Knopf, 197

Said, Edward W. *Culture and Imperialism.* New Yor Knopf, 1993.

Seaman, L.C.B. *From Vienna to Versailles.* London: Rou ledge, 1988.

Sked, Alan. *The Decline and Fall of the Hapsburg Empir 1815–1918.* New York: Longman, 1990.

Snyder, Louis L. *Fifty Major Documents of the Nineteen Century.* Toronto: Nostrand, 1955.

Spserber, Jonathan. *The European Revolutions, 184 1851.* Cambridge: Cambridge University Press, 1994.

Tarnas, Richard. *The Passion of the Western Mind.* Ne York: Crown Publishers, 1991.

Taylor, A.J.P. *Bismarck: The Man and the Statesman.* Lo don: Hamish Hamilton, 1985.

Taylor, A.J.P. *The Struggle for Mastery in Europ 1848–1918.* Oxford: Oxford University Press, 1984.

Tulard, Jean. *Napoleon: The Myth of the Saviour.* Car bridge: Methuen, 1985.

Winks, Robin W., ed. *British Imperialism: Gold, God, an Glory.* New York: Holt, Rinehart and Winston, 1966.

Wright, Gordon. *France in Modern Times.* 4th e Markham, Ontario: Penguin, 1981.

Index

CREDITS

Editorial:
Leah-Ann Lymer, Eva Radford, Janet Pinno, Marianne Lindvall, David Strand

Index:
Noeline Bridge, Bridgework

Design & Layout:
Leslieanna Blackner Au

Cartography:
Wendy Johnson,
Johnson Cartographics

Photo Credits:
Abbreviations:
Corbis-Bettmann: CB
National Archives of Canada: NAC

Entries
are by page number, coded as follows: T=Top, B=Bottom, L=Left, R=Right

Cover photos:
Top: The Bettmann Archive PG14097
Bottom: The Bettmann Archive BHW386

Page:

We have made every effort to correctly identify and credit the sources of all photographs, illustrations, and information used in this textbook.

Reidmore Books appreciates any further information or corrections; acknowledgment will be given in subsequent editions.